D0068671

# THE PAPERS OF
# WOODROW WILSON

VOLUME 41
JANUARY 24–APRIL 6, 1917

SPONSORED BY THE WOODROW WILSON
FOUNDATION
AND PRINCETON UNIVERSITY

# THE PAPERS OF

# WOODROW
# WILSON

ARTHUR S. LINK, *EDITOR*

DAVID W. HIRST, *SENIOR ASSOCIATE EDITOR*

JOHN E. LITTLE, *ASSOCIATE EDITOR*

FREDRICK AANDAHL, *ASSOCIATE EDITOR*

PHYLLIS MARCHAND AND MARGARET D. LINK,
*EDITORIAL ASSISTANTS*

Volume 41
January 24–April 6, 1917

PRINCETON, NEW JERSEY
PRINCETON UNIVERSITY PRESS
1983

*Note to scholars*: Princeton University Press subscribes to the Resolution on Permissions of the Association of American University Presses, defining what we regard as "fair use" of copyrighted works. This Resolution, intended to encourage scholarly use of university press publications and to avoid unnecessary applications for permission, is obtainable from the Press or from the A.A.U.P. central office. Note, however, that the scholarly apparatus, transcripts of shorthand, and the texts of Wilson documents as they appear in this volume are copyrighted, and the usual rules about the use of copyrighted materials apply.

Publication of this book has been aided by a grant from the National Historical Publications and Records Commission.

Printed in the United States of America
by Princeton University Press
Princeton, New Jersey

# INTRODUCTION

T HE beginning of this volume finds Wilson in the midst of the most ambitious démarche of his career—secret negotiations with the British and German governments for an early peace conference and the end of the war through his own mediation. Only a few days before this volume opens, on January 22, 1917, Wilson has gone before the Senate to announce to the world the kind of peace settlement which the United States would be willing to support through a league of nations: a "peace without victory," a "peace among equals," one based solidly upon mutual understanding and benefit. The French, bent upon revenge and determined to recover Alsace-Lorraine, are appalled and furious. The more subtle British send mixed signals to the White House. But Wilson is unconcerned about the *official* Allied reactions. He is convinced that the British and French peoples desire peace above all things; in any event, he believes the Allied war effort is so dependent upon supplies from the United States that he can force the British and French governments to the peace table. Everything now depends upon the answer from Berlin. As Wilson well knows, he has no such power over Germany as he has over the Allies. Everything, he tells the German leaders, depends upon their desire for a peace of reconciliation and their willingness to grasp his hand of friendship.

Unknown to Wilson, the German leaders have already made their decision at an Imperial conference at Pless on January 9. Naval leaders assure the Emperor that their submarines, if unleashed, will knock Great Britain out of the war within six months; the military commanders agree that unrestricted submarine warfare alone can guarantee victory and that the intervention of the United States, if it comes, will be too late to prevent Germany victory. Brushing aside all warnings by the civilian leaders, the Emperor orders the inauguration, on February 1, 1917, of unrestricted submarine warfare against *all* shipping in European waters.

Ambassador von Bernstorff conveys the announcement to Secretary of State Lansing on January 31; accompanying it is a personal message to Wilson from the German Chancellor which discloses outdated German peace terms and urges Wilson to continue his search for peace. Wilson is dazed, incredulous, and downcast. But he cannot avoid what seems to be the inevitable response; and, on February 3, he tells a joint session of Congress that he has just broken diplomatic relations with the German Empire. But Wilson's heart is still set upon peace, and a precarious peace seems possible during the next month as the Germans refrain from sinking American ships.

Meanwhile, pressures at home for at least armed neutrality mount while American shipowners refuse to send their vessels into the war zone and goods for Europe pile high on wharves in the United States. Then one shocking event pushes Wilson nearer the limit of an undeclared naval war. It is the receipt from the British government of a telegram from the German Foreign Secretary, Zimmermann, to the German Minister to Mexico. It instructs the latter to seek an alliance with Mexico in the event of war between the United States and Germany. In return for Mexican assistance, Germany promises to Mexico "the territory lost by her at a prior period in Texas, New Mexico, and Arizona." His faith in the integrity of the German government destroyed, Wilson goes to Congress on February 26 and requests authority to arm American merchantmen. He releases the text of the Zimmermann telegram on February 28; American newspapers have also just reported the ruthless sinking of the British liner, *Laconia*, with loss of American life.

Amidst cries for war across the United States, the House of Representatives adopts an armed-ship bill by an overwhelming majority on March 1. Republicans in the Senate have already begun a filibuster of important appropriations bills in order to force Wilson to call a special session of Congress. The Republican leaders gladly yield the filibuster to a small group of senators led by La Follette who prevent a vote on the armed-ship bill. The Sixty-fourth Congress expires on March 4, and an angry Wilson denounces the "little group of wilful men" who have rendered "the great Government of the United States helpless and contemptible."

In his second Inaugural, delivered on Monday, March 5, Wilson declares that the United States will adopt armed neutrality since it is the only means of protecting American commerce without resort to full-fledged belligerency. Four days later, on March 9, Wilson announces that he has instructed the navy to put guns and gun crews on liners and merchantmen.

German submarines carry out a devastating campaign but spare the few American ships that venture into the war zone. Then, on March 18, they sink three American merchantmen, two of them without warning and with heavy loss of life. Only a few days before, a liberal group in the Russian parliament have deposed the Czar, established a provisional constitutional government, and promised to fight on for a general democratic peace. Pressed by a growing national demand and the unanimous advice of his cabinet members, Wilson concludes that armed neutrality is not a sufficient or appropriate response to a wholesale German assault on the Atlantic community. He makes what seems to him the inevitable decision for war immediately after a memorable cabinet meeting on March 20.

Then follows the task of writing a war message which, as Wilson says, will be a death warrant for thousands of young men. He goes before a joint session of Congress at 8:32 p.m. on April 2 to perform the awful duty of bidding his fellow countrymen to go to war. Deliberately, methodically, he recounts the crimes and aggressions of the German military autocracy against Americans in their own homeland and on the high seas. He disavows and rebukes any malevolent passions and motives for revenge. The United States, he says with increasing emotion, will fight only for the rights of humanity and to make the world safe for democracy. "God helping her, she can do no other." The Senate approves a war resolution on April 4, the House of Representatives, early in the morning of April 6. Wilson signs it on the same day, Good Friday, at 12:14 p.m., and the United States embarks upon participation in a war on European soil for the first time in its history.

The documents printed herein tell this story in vivid and moving detail. They also tell of many other things: the end of the old imbroglio with Mexico and the failure of the Wilson administration to achieve enactment of its legislation to prevent railroad strikes and to open the natural resources of the nation under restrictions to safeguard the public's interest. Above all, these documents so graphically depict Wilson as he moves for peace and is then forced into the war that we are almost able to live with him through these events which would shape the destiny of the world.

## "VERBATIM ET LITERATIM"

In earlier volumes of this series, we have said something like the following: "All documents are reproduced *verbatim et literatim*, with typographical and spelling errors corrected in square brackets only when necessary for clarity and ease of reading." The following essay explains our textual methods and review procedures.

We have never printed and do not intend to print critical, or corrected, versions of documents. We print them exactly as they are, with a few exceptions which we always note. We never use the word *sic* except to denote the repetition of words in a document; in fact, we think that a succession of *sics* defaces a page.

We usually repair words in square brackets when letters are missing. As we have said, we also repair words in square brackets for clarity and ease of reading. Our general rule is to do this when we, ourselves, cannot read the word without stopping to determine its meaning. Jumbled words and names misspelled beyond recognition of course have to be repaired. We correct the misspelling of a name in the footnote which identifies the person.

However, when an old man writes to Wilson saying that he is glad to hear that Wilson is "comming" to Newark, or a semiliterate farmer from Texas writes phonetically to complain of the low price of cotton, we see no reason to correct spellings in square brackets when the words are perfectly understandable. We do not correct Wilson's misspellings unless they are unreadable, except to supply in square brackets letters missing in words. For example, for some reason he insisted upon spelling "belligerent" as "belligerant." Nothing would be gained by correcting "belligerant" in square brackets.

We think that it is very important for several reasons to follow the rule of *verbatim et literatim*. Most important, a document has its own integrity and power, particularly when it is not written in a perfect literary form. There is something very moving in seeing a Texas dirt farmer struggling to express his feelings in words, or a semiliterate former slave doing the same thing. Second, in Wilson's case it is crucially important to reproduce his errors in letters which he typed himself, since he usually typed badly when he was in an agitated state. Third, since style is the essence of the person, we would never correct grammar or make tenses consistent, as one correspondent has urged us to do. Fourth, we think that it is obligatory to print typed documents *verbatim et literatim*. For example, we think that it is very important that we print exact transcripts of Charles L. Swem's copies of Wilson's letters. Swem made many mistakes (we correct them in footnotes from a reading of his shorthand books), and Wilson let them pass. We thus have to assume that Wilson did not read his letters before signing them, and this, we think, is a significant fact. Finally, printing typed letters and documents *verbatim et literatim* tells us a great deal about the educational level of the stenographic profession in the United States during Wilson's time.

We think that our series would be worthless if we produced unreliable texts, and we go to some effort to make certain that the texts are authentic.

Our typists are highly skilled and proofread their transcripts carefully as soon as they have typed them. The Editor sight proofreads documents once he has assembled a volume and is setting its annotation. The Editors who write the notes read through documents several times and are careful to check any anomalies. Then, once the manuscript volume has been completed and all notes checked, the Editor and Senior Associate Editor orally proofread the documents against the copy. They read every comma, dash, and character. They note every absence of punctuation. They study every nearly illegible word in written documents.

Once this process of "establishing the text" is completed, the manuscript volume goes to our editor at Princeton University Press, who checks the volume carefully and sends it to the printing plant. The volume is set by linotype by a typographer who has been working on the Wilson volumes for years. The galley proofs go to the proofroom, where they are read orally against copy. And we must say that the proofreaders at the Press are extraordinarily skilled. Some years ago, before we found a way to ease their burden, they used to query every misspelled word, absence of punctuation, or other such anomalies. Now we write "O.K." above such words or spaces on the copy.

We read the galley proofs three times. Our copyeditor gives them a sight reading against the manuscript copy to look for remaining typographical errors and to make sure that no line has been dropped. The Editor and Senior Associate Editor sight read them against documents and copy. We then get the page proofs, which have been corrected at the Press. We check all the changes three times. In addition, we get *revised* pages and check them twice.

This is not the end. Our indexer of course reads the pages word by word. Before we return the pages to the Press, she comes in with a list of queries, all of which are answered by reference to the documents.

Our rule in the Wilson Papers is that our tolerance of error is zero. No system and no person can be perfect. We are sure that there are errors in our volumes. However, we believe that we have done everything humanly possible to avoid error; the chance is remote that what looks at first glance like a typographical error is indeed an error.

We take this opportunity to thank Professors John Milton Cooper, Jr., William H. Harbaugh, and Richard W. Leopold for their critical reading of the manuscripts of this volume. Judith May, our editor at Princeton University Press, continues to help us with understanding, skill, and enthusiasm. Finally, we apologize to David Langbart for misspelling his name in the Introduction to Volume 38.

THE EDITORS

*Princeton, N. J.*
*May 12, 1982*

# CONTENTS

# ILLUSTRATIONS

# ABBREVIATIONS

| | |
|---|---|
| ALI | autograph letter initialed |
| ALS | autograph letter signed |
| CC | carbon copy |
| CCL | carbon copy of letter |
| CCLI | carbon copy of letter initialed |
| CLS | Charles Lee Swem |
| CLSsh | Charles Lee Swem shorthand |
| CLST | Charles Lee Swem typed |
| EAW | Ellen Axson Wilson |
| EBW | Edith Bolling Wilson |
| EMH | Edward Mandell House |
| FKL | Franklin Knight Lane |
| FR | *Papers Relating to the Foreign Relations of the United States* |
| FR-1918 Russia | *Papers Relating to the Foreign Relations of the United States, 1918, Russia* |
| FR-WWS 1917 | *Papers Relating to the Foreign Relations of the United States, 1917, Supplement, The World War* |
| Hw, hw | handwritten, handwriting |
| HwS | handwritten signed |
| JD | Joseph Daniels |
| JPT | Joseph Patrick Tumulty |
| JRT | Jack Romagna typed |
| MS | manuscript |
| MSS | manuscripts |
| NDB | Newton Diehl Baker |
| RG | record group |
| RL | Robert Lansing |
| T | typed |
| TC | typed copy |
| TCL | typed copy of letter |
| TCLS | typed copy of letter signed |
| TI | typed initialed |
| TL | typed letter |
| TLI | typed letter initialed |
| TLS | typed letter signed |
| TR | Theodore Roosevelt |
| TS | typed signed |
| WBW | William Bauchop Wilson |
| WHP | Walter Hines Page |
| WW | Woodrow Wilson |
| WWhw | Woodrow Wilson handwriting, handwritten |
| WWsh | Woodrow Wilson shorthand |
| WWT | Woodrow Wilson typed |
| WWTL | Woodrow Wilson typed letter |
| WWTLI | Woodrow Wilson typed letter initialed |
| WWTSL | Woodrow Wilson typed letter signed |

Following the National Union Catalog of the Library of Congress

| | |
|---|---|
| AGO | Adjutant General's Office |
| BIA | Bureau of Insular Affairs |
| CtY | Yale University |
| CtY-D | Yale University Divinity School |
| DLC | Library of Congress |
| DNA | National Archives |
| FFM-Ar | French Foreign Ministry Archives |
| FO | British Foreign Office |
| GBR | General Board Records |
| GFO-Ar | German Foreign Office Archives |
| KyU | University of Kentucky |
| LDR | Labor Department Records |
| MH | Harvard University |
| MH-Ar | Harvard University Archives |
| NDR | Navy Department Records |
| NFM-Ar | Netherlands Foreign Ministry Archives |
| NHpR | Franklin D. Roosevelt Library |
| NjP | Princeton University |
| NN | New York Public Library |
| OClW | Case Western Reserve University |
| PRO | Public Record Office |
| RSB Coll., DLC | Ray Stannard Baker Collection of Wilsoniana, Library of Congress |
| SDR | State Department Records |
| ViU | University of Virginia |
| WC, NjP | Woodrow Wilson Collection, Princeton University |
| WDR | War Department Records |
| WHi | State Historical Society of Wisconsin |
| WP, DLC | Woodrow Wilson Papers, Library of Congress |

SYMBOLS

| | |
|---|---|
| [February 8, 1917] | publication date of published writing; also date of document when date is not part of text |
| [*March 4, 1917*] | composition date when publication date differs |
| [[April 2, 1917]] | delivery date of speech if publication date differs |
| **** *** | text deleted by author of document |

THE PAPERS OF

WOODROW WILSON

VOLUME 41
JANUARY 24–APRIL 6, 1917

# THE PAPERS OF
# WOODROW WILSON

## To Edward Mandell House

My dear House,                    The White House. 24 January, 1917.

I am deeply thankful that the address has been as favourably received as it has and I thank you with all my heart for your letters.

I shall be deeply interested in the opinions reported by Wiseman, but I am even more concerned to find out what Germany is thinking,—I mean what those who have the determination of her course of action in their hands are thinking in their hearts.

I am enclosing messages from Walter Page and Sharp[1] which I know that you will read with interest. What is to be read between the lines of Sharp's message added to things such as you are learning from Hoover convinces me that if Germany really wants peace she can get it, and get it soon, *if she will but confide in me and let me have a chance*. What Bernstorff said to you the other day as trimmed and qualified by what he wrote afterwards amounts to nothing so far as negotiations between the belligerents are concerned. It occurs to me that it would be well for you to see Bernstorff again at once (not where your meeting can be noted, as the last one was, but at some place which is not under observation) and tell him that this is the time to accomplish something, if they really and truly want peace; that the indications that come to us are of a sort to lead us to believe that with something reasonable to suggest, as from them, I can bring things about; and that otherwise, with the preparations they are apparently making with regard to unrestrained attacks on merchantmen on the plea that they are armed for offense, there is a terrible likelihood that the relations between the United States and Germany may come to a breaking point and everything assume a different aspect. Feelings, exasperations are neither here nor there. Do they in fact want me to help? I am entitled to know because I genuinely want to help and have now put myself in a position to help without favour to either side.

He sent a long message to his government the other day, but I do not know what it was about. By the way, if we are to continue to send messages for him, we should know that he is working in this cause and should in each instance receive his official assurance that there is at least nothing in his despatches which it would be unneutral for us to transmit.

Again bless you for the encouragement and support you so constantly give me. I feel very lonely sometimes and sometimes very low in my mind, in spite of myself.

Affectionately Yours,   Woodrow Wilson

WWTLS (E. M. House Papers, CtY).
  [1] WHP to WW, Jan. 20, 1917, and W. G. Sharp to WW, Jan. 21, 1917, Vol. 40.

## Two Letters to Robert Lansing

My dear Mr. Secretary,      The White House. 24 January, 1917.

It is only too probable that Gerard's conjectures in this matter are well founded.[1] I wonder if you have come to any fixed conclusion in your own mind as to whether the recent practices of the British in regard to the arming of their merchantmen force upon us an alteration of our own position in that matter.

Faithfully Yours,   W.W.

WWTLI (SDR, RG 59, 763.72111/4469½, DNA).
  [1] That is, the conjectures stated in J. W. Gerard to RL, Jan. 21, 1917, printed as an Enclosure with RL to WW, Jan. 23, 1917, Vol. 40.

My dear Mr. Secretary,      The White House. 24 January, 1917.

I have no doubt that there is here a real ground of grave complaint;[1] and I think that it is probably our duty to make a very grave protest to the *de facto* government.

May I make this suggestion? Our difficulties in getting the attention of the authorities in Mexico in matters of this kind has been due very often to their feeling that our protests were curt and peremptory. I think it will be entirely worth our while to study in dealing with them the fullest forms of courtesy. I believe it will have a real effect on the results. It is a mere matter of phrases, but it has proved of the essence.

Faithfully Yours,   W.W.

WWTLI (SDR, RG 59, 812.516/157, DNA).
  [1] That is, the letters by J. J. Jusserand cited in RL to WW, Jan. 18, 1917, n. 1 (second letter of that date), Vol. 40.

## To Thomas James Walsh

My dear Senator:          [The White House] 24 January, 1917

I received in due course your letter of January eighteenth[1] about the obstacles in the way of the water power bill and am making arrangements to see the Senators you mention. I hope sincerely that I may be of service.

Faithfully Yours,   Woodrow Wilson

TLS (Letterpress Books, WP, DLC).
[1] T. J. Walsh to WW, Jan. 18, 1917, Vol. 40.

## To Andrew Carnegie

My dear Mr. Carnegie:     The White House 24 January, 1917

Your generous judgment[1] upon my address to the Senate on Monday gives me the deepest pleasure. I know how long and how sincerely you have had the cause of peace at heart, and such words of approval from you I prize most highly and thank you with all my heart.

With the best wishes,

Cordially and faithfully yours,   Woodrow Wilson

TLS (A. Carnegie Papers, DLC).
[1] A. Carnegie to WW, Jan. 23, 1917, Vol. 40.

## From William Bowyer Fleming,[1] with Enclosure

My dear Mr. President:       Washington January 24, 1917.

Now that your great message has been delivered, and should have support from every angle, I venture to enclose herewith a letter I wrote you under date of January 5 and withheld for fear that you might consider me officious.

The statistics furnished in the enclosed letter may be of service.

Let me add that by your recent action you have erected a new Statue of Liberty enlightening the world.

Already the light is beginning to shine. The despatches of yesterday tell us that a great body of men gathered in London who had learned of your utterances cheered your name for five minutes or more.[2]       Very truly yours,   W. B. Fleming

TLS (WP, DLC).
[1] Lawyer and Democratic politician from Kentucky; foreign trade adviser to the Department of State since October 1, 1913; adviser on commercial treaties since January 31, 1916.
[2] A reference to the meeting of the annual conference of the Labour party, which actually met in Manchester on January 23. At that meeting, a passing reference to Wilson's name in a speech led to prolonged cheering. See the *New York Times*, Jan. 24, 1917.

ENCLOSURE

My dear Mr. Wilson:                    Washington January 5, 1917.

I trust the attacks being made for partisan ends upon your noble efforts to bring about conditions which may make for peace in Europe will only strengthen your resolve to persist in the good work.

I need not refer to the terrible destruction of human life that will result from the prolongation of the war with the woe thereby entailed, but it may be some figures bearing on the economic side of the question may be useful to you. Mr. Rudolph Diamant, bond statistician,[1] estimates that the direct cost of the war thus far is 70 billions of dollars. The indirect cost from the maiming and killing of millions of the flower of manhood, and the losses through destruction of property is, of course, incalculable. The overturned conditions of international good will, the oppressive taxation required to carry the burden of interest and amortization of the accumulated debts, the burden of pensions, and the thousand other miseries that follow war, all add to the horror.

These evils are cumulative and growing in intensity with the length of the war.

The increase in war loans during the first five months of the war was at the rate of $1,100,000,000 monthly. During 1915 these loans increased at the rate of $1,650,000,000 monthly and for 1916 at the rate of $2,600,000,000 monthly. At what rate will they increase in 1917 and 1918?

Mr. Diamant estimates the war *debts* up to January 1 at 59 billions of dollars. By January 1918, if the war continues that long, the increase will probably reach 100 billions.

With half the male population of Europe wiped out, how can the impoverished remainder pay even the interest on that debt? Think of a burden like this on the generations to come!

If Providence crowns your efforts to stop the war with success you will have conferred a boon on the world such as never before fell to the lot of mortal man.

                          Sincerely yours,   W. B. Fleming

TLS (WP, DLC).
    [1] Of New York.

## From Cleveland Hoadley Dodge

My dear President                    New York. January 24th, 1917

I have waited 24 hours before writing you, fearing that my first impulse, after reading your address to the Senate, would result in too much gush, but now that I have had time to study it and think over it, I feel that nothing I can say in approval could be too strong.

Your critics say that you are Utopian & a modern Don Quixote, but I cannot help feeling very strongly that not only will the lofty idealism of your program appeal to the hearts and consciences of the peoples of the world, but that also the hard-headed statesmen of the belligerent nations will find in your proposals a practical way out of the ghastly deadlock which now prevails. Oh for a great statesman who might arise in Europe at this critical juncture, but the sad thing is that there doesn't seem to be a great statesman in Europe. The account in the morning paper of the great meeting of laboring men in England, where your name was cheered for five minutes, was very significant. Would that the peoples of Europe might rise in their might and bring about the kind of peace which you have indicated.

I have just spent two interesting hours with Mr. Hoover, & it was gratifying to see how your address had reacted on him.

Probably we ought not to expect too much in the immediate future, but I firmly believe that you have taken a step which will do much to hasten that day which we all hope will soon come when Peace will prevail. How wonderful it all is. The change in sentiment, on the part of many men, I meet, who have been your strong opponents, is surprisingly encouraging.

With warm regard & best wishes

Yours affectionately    Cleveland H. Dodge

ALS (WP, DLC).

## From Lillian D. Wald and Others

[New York] January 24, 1917.

I bring you on behalf of the American Union Against Militarism their profoundest gratitude for your noble speech to the Senate of the United States on January 22, 1917. In their judgment, this day and this utterance will remain memorable in our history and that of the world, and they will be surprised indeed if it does not mark a new epoch in the world's annals.

Ever since the beginning of this war, men and women have been hungering for a new kind of diplomacy which would brush aside chancelleries and all the old forms of intercourse between nations which have so often misrepresented the views of the plain peoples and led them to disaster. You, sir, have answered this longing for direct action and you have done it not merely in the spirit of the America of Abraham Lincoln, you have done it in the spirit of the brotherhood of man. You have spoken outwardly to the Senate but in reality to the people of the entire world. Never, we believe, in the history of this world has any message of a single individual found its way to so many minds and hearts, and in every case the reader has been compelled whether in complete agreement or not to think and to ponder upon a great and statesman-like proposal to rid the globe of its worst curse— war and militarism. It is a service to all humanity which it is impossible to exaggerate and we believe that its profound wisdom and philosophy will become more and more apparent as it recedes into the past. To our minds, it is destined to an immortality as glorious as that of the Gettysburg Address.

For we are certain that whatever may be its reception in the marts of trade and commerce and at the hands of those journalists who are without vision and without the passion to free humanity from "the sum of all villanies," it will find its way straight to "silent mass of mankind everywhere" whom you were fain to reach and now have reached. In every American town and hamlet, the prayers of men and women have gone up for you because you have voiced their hopes and desires, and the vaulted roofs of every church should echo the grateful supplications of worshippers come to give thanks that there is one in mighty office to deny that men's hearts may be chastened only by the scourge of the sword. If there were no other service which you have rendered than your admonition that if peace is to be permanent there must be peace without victory, that alone would make this speech a document of which not only Americans but Liberals of every faith and clime will be proud as long as men write and speak of these times in which we live.

|  |  |
|---|---|
| For the | Lillian D. Wald |
| American Union | Oswald Garrison Villard |
| Against Militarism. | Owen R. Lovejoy |
|  | Paul U. Kellogg |
|  | Amos R. E. Pinchot |

T telegram (L. D. Wald Papers, NN).

## From Julio Betancourt

My dear Mr. President,          Washington, D. C. Jan. 24, 1917.

May I be allowed to voice, on behalf of the Government and people of Colombia, the deep satisfaction which is theirs and in which I feel sure all Latin-America joins that in stating the conditions under which America stands ready to cooperate in guaranteeing peace and justice throughout the world after the present conflict has ceased, you spoke not only for the people of the United States but for the peoples of the New World

Your reference to the political faith and practical conviction which the peoples of America have once for all embraced and undertaken to defend, and the hope you express that the Nations should with one accord adopt the doctrine of President Munroe as the doctrine of the world and protect the rights of small nations, give me the privilege of again pointing with some pride to the fact that, in pursuance of a policy of Pan-Americanism inspired by the same lofty ideals of international harmony you have so eloquently expressed, Colombia has arrived at satisfactory solutions of whatever controversies existed between her and her neighbouring sister-republics of South America.

By a series of arrangements already entered into with Venezuela and Ecuador and negotiations with Peru and Brazil, in some of which Colombia has relinquished territorial claims to which she believed herself entitled, an enduring structure has been raised to safeguard the firm friendships and precious peace now happily existing throughout South-America.

If the Treaty signed on April 6th., 1914, at Bogota between the Republic of Colombia and the United States, now before the Senate of the United States, were ratified, the injustice done by Mr. Roosevelt to Colombia would be repaired and our two countries would once more renew the century-old friendship so cruelly shattered in 1903.

All forward looking statesmen in the New World are alive to the importance of the unification of American interests for the defence of our common ideals of liberty, of democracy and of justice, as well as our material well-being should the situation created by the continuance of the war render the position of neutrals altogether intolerable; but the principles of international harmony upon which Pan-Americanism is founded can be a living force in this world only if we have first abolished injustice from amongst ourselves. The visible sign of the United States being willing to join her sister-republics in so doing will be the ratification of the Treaty of Bogota entered into at its own solicitation and request.

Therefore, my dear Mr. President, I take the liberty on behalf of the Government and people of Colombia of appealing to you personally to take such steps as in your judgment will most rapidly secure the approval of the Treaty.

Permit me, my dear Mr. President, to avail myself of this

opportunity to reiterate to you the assurances of the deep respect and high personal esteem of

Yours very sincerely    Julio Betancourt

TLS (WP, DLC).

## Remarks to the Maryland League for National Defense

25 January, 1917.

Gentlemen: I do not need to prove to you or anybody my deep interest in this subject. I will frankly say to you I would have been more impressed by this memorial[1] if it had been expressed in more restrained language. From some of the unqualified statements in this paper, I must frankly dissent. I think it due to my colleagues on the Hill to say so at this offhand condemnation of the system which they adopted after long debate upon the urgency of many of the leading citizens of the country; it is the least that I can do. You do not commend a cause which deserves the most serious consideration by presenting it as you have presented it.

These things impress me the more after what we have heard from the medical societies. Unquestionably, physical training is needed and will accomplish a great deal, but it can be had without compulsory military service, and compulsory military service does not meet the difficulties which you have alluded to. Any brief service in the Army of the United States withdraws men from civil pursuits, just as much as the recent service on the border does. No service, except a standing army with professional soldiers, prevents that occasional and frequent withdrawal of men from civil pursuits. That may be inevitable, but what you are proposing does not meet the difficulty which you condemn. These things are of the utmost intricacy and difficulty and are not to be settled *ex cathedra*. And yet, notwithstanding the fact that I think you have gone too far, I will say to you that, of course, this will have my most serious consideration. It is receiving serious consideration within the country, and we in Washington, of course, share and feel the great tides of opinion in the United States. I am sure that, speaking, if I may speak for the members of the House of Representatives and the Senate, we are all desirous of doing the wise thing for the defense of the country, and it must and will be done, but we must not close debate by having too dogmatic an opinion as to a method.

I know that you will understand the spirit in which I make that protest and this statement.

T MS (WP, DLC).

1 This memorial, signed by many prominent residents of Baltimore, was read to Wilson at an interview at the White House. The memorial asked Wilson to recommend to Congress the enactment of a law for compulsory universal military training and service and another to draft into the regular army a sufficient number of men to police the Mexican border. It declared that the United States was "in actual present danger of becoming involved in the European war" and cited Lansing as its authority for this remark. It went on to say: "We have practically no army at this time available for our defense in case we are attacked by any of the armed Governments of the world. In case of invasion our people might be subjected to all the horrors which have befallen Belgium, Holland, Serbia, and Northern France."

The memorial continued with the statement: "The voluntary system upon which we are now relying is utterly and absolutely inadequate for the defense of the country." It called the use of militia to police the Mexican border "a disgrace to a civilized people." The full text of the memorial, together with Wilson's reply, is printed in the New York Times, Jan. 26, 1917.

## To Cleveland Hoadley Dodge

My dear Cleve:          The White House 25 January, 1917

Your letter has given me deep pleasure. I must admit that I have been a little low in my mind the last forty-eight hours because of the absolute lack of any power to see what I am driving at which has been exhibited by the men who are looked upon as the leading Republican members of the Senate.[1] After all, it is upon the Senate that I have to depend for the kind of support which will make acts possible, and there are sometimes hours of discouragement connected with trying to lift things into a better air.

But discouragement is weakness and I do not succumb to it long. I firmly believe that I have said the right thing, and I have an invincible confidence in the prevalence of the right if it is fearlessly set forth.

And the best thing that comes to me is the support and loyal friendship of men like yourself in whose character and disinterestedness I know I can have ever true confidence.

Gratefully and affectionately yours,    Woodrow Wilson

TLS (WC, NjP).

1 Republican opposition to the ideas expressed in Wilson's address to the Senate of January 22 had already begun to develop. A few Republican senators, such as La Follette and Clapp, praised the speech immediately after its delivery. Others, such as Lodge and Borah, refused any immediate comment. However, Senator Gallinger was reported to have said that Wilson's program was utterly impracticable. Senator Smoot pronounced it completely useless and of no effect. "We have no right to dictate to either side," he said. Senator Poindexter argued that any attempt to implement Wilson's ideas would bring the United States into the war. Poindexter further objected to the loss of sovereignty involved in membership in a league of nations. New York Times, Jan. 23, 1917.

Senator Cummins, on January 23, introduced a resolution (S. Res. 326) calling for a full-scale Senate debate on Wilson's speech; each senator was to be given up to one hour to speak his mind. Cong. Record, 64th Cong., 2d sess., p. 1807. This resolution was tabled on January 30, but the preliminary discussion about it included such references as that of Senator Sherman on January 24 to "the stump speech from the throne that was delivered in the Senate of the United States by the Chief Executive." *Ibid.*, p. 1884.

On January 25, Senator Borah introduced a resolution (S. Res. 329) reaffirming "the faith and confidence" of the Senate in the Monroe Doctrine and in Washington's and Jefferson's policy of nonparticipation in European politics. *Ibid.*, p. 1950.

The discussion thus begun was to culminate in Senator Lodge's speech to the Senate on February 1 in which he reversed his earlier stand and came out against American membership in a league of nations. *Ibid.*, pp. 2364-70. See also Arthur S. Link, *Wilson: Campaigns for Progressivism and Peace, 1916-1917* (Princeton, N. J., 1965), p. 269, and William C. Widenor, *Henry Cabot Lodge and the Search for an American Foreign Policy* (Berkeley and Los Angeles, 1980), pp. 248-60.

## To Thomas Dixon, Jr.

My dear Dixon:                    [The White House] 25 January, 1917

Thank you for your letter of yesterday about the message to the Senate.[1] I need not tell you how much it gratifies me.

I have kept pretty close to things and I doubt whether you are right in saying that we have no friend among the nations. We may have very few friends in the foreign offices, but they do not express the real feeling of their people any more than some other governments do. Undoubtedly, at present there is a universal excitement of opinion which is unfavorable to calm international understandings, but I think that is merely temporary and that after the war is over many things now distorted will be seen in their right proportions.

In haste          Cordially yours,   Woodrow Wilson

TLS (Letterpress Books, WP, DLC).
[1] T. Dixon, Jr., to WW, Jan. 23, 1917, ALS (WP, DLC).

## To Samuel Seabury

[The White House]
My dear Judge Seabury:                    25 January, 1917

Your letter of January twenty-third has given me the deepest gratification.[1] The country has responded very nobly to what I said, though the Republicans in the Senate have responded very ignobly. I hope that they will some day awake to find out what the true opinion of the country and of the world is.

Cordially and sincerely yours,   Woodrow Wilson

TLS (Letterpress Books, WP, DLC).
[1] It is missing.

## To Herbert David Croly

My dear Mr. Croly:            [The White House] 25 January, 1917

Your letter of January twenty-third[1] has given me the deepest gratification. I was interested and encouraged when preparing my recent address to the Senate to find an editorial in the New Republic which was not only written along the same lines but which served to clarify and strengthen my thought not a little.[2] In that, as in many other matters, I am your debtor.

Your suggestion about the probable advisability of making some speeches through the country after the Congress has adjourned interests me very much and I think has a great deal in it. I agree with you that we cannot afford to leave anything undone which would make us secure in the support of the great popular opinion of the country. I shall watch developments with a very careful scrutiny and shall try to do all that is possible in that direction. Of course, in the meantime events may take a turn which may change the current of our ideas in such matters altogether.

With warmest appreciation,

Cordially and sincerely yours,   Woodrow Wilson

TLS (Letterpress Books, WP, DLC).
  [1] H. D. Croly to WW, Jan. 23, 1917, Vol. 40.
  [2] Wilson referred to "Peace Without Victory," *The New Republic*, IX (Dec. 23, 1916), 201-202.

## To Carrie Clinton Lane Chapman Catt

My dear Mrs. Catt:            [The White House] January 25, 1917

May I not express to you and your organization, as well as to the women of North Dakota, my congratulations upon the passage by the Legislature of that State of a bill granting to the women of the State the right to vote for presidential electors and for municipal officers? As you know, I have a very real interest in the extension of the suffrage to the women, and I feel that every step in this direction should be applauded.

Cordially and sincerely yours,   Woodrow Wilson

TLS (Letterpress Books, WP, DLC).

## To William Charles Adamson

My dear Judge:            [The White House] 25 January, 1917

For fear the gentlemen who prepared the enclosed memorandum did not send you a copy, I send you the enclosed for your consideration.[1] I would like very much to have your opinion regarding it in case the Senate should sustain their Committee on Interstate Commerce in declining to accede to the compulsory feature of the legislation we are proposing with regard to strike investigation.[2]

Cordially and sincerely yours,  Woodrow Wilson

TLS (Letterpress Books, WP, DLC).

[1] W. S. Stone and L. E. Sheppard to WW, Jan. 24, 1917, TLS (WP, DLC). They proposed legislation to create a "commission of mediation and conciliation" to investigate railway labor disputes. The President would appoint this commission made up of equal numbers of railroad managers and of the representatives of railroad labor; the commissioners' terms would run for six years. This group would have plenary powers of investigation and the power to propose a settlement for any particular dispute. If not accepted by both sides, the proposed settlement would then be made public. Stone and Sheppard especially urged that there be an equal number of representatives of management and labor on the commission, with no outside umpire or other party or parties to be appealed to: "Our experience with the past is that there is much more opportunity for an amicable adjustment of a labor difficulty when the parties at interest cannot escape their responsibilities by arbitration or reference to other individuals or tribunals."

[2] By a vote of ten to five, the Senate Interstate Commerce Committee on January 24 had rejected the measure to prevent railway strikes which Wilson had asked for in his Annual Message of December 5, 1916. This action was "generally regarded as marking the defeat of the President's attempt to secure the passage of drastic strike regulation at this session." New York Times, Jan. 25, 1917. Adamson was seeking similar legislation in the House of Representatives. Ibid., Jan. 4, 1917.

## To Francis Griffith Newlands

My dear Senator:          [The White House] 25 January, 1917

I understand that the heads of the brotherhoods have submitted to you a plan for a commission with full powers of investigation which they outlined to me yesterday and concerning which they have now submitted to me a written memorandum.

I would like very much to know what impression the suggestion makes upon yourself and upon your committee.

In haste

Cordially and sincerely yours,  Woodrow Wilson

TLS (Letterpress Books, WP, DLC).

## To Julio Betancourt

My dear Mr. Minister:     [The White House] 25 January, 1917

Your letter of January twenty-fourth has gratified me very much indeed and I want to thank you for the pleasure and encouragement it has given me.

Your feeling that one of the best ways we could prove the sincerity of the doctrines I uttered the other day before the Senate would be to ratify the recently signed treaty between Colombia and the United States I frankly share, and I beg to assure you that I shall do everything in my power to bring about a ratification of that treaty at as early a date as possible.

With much appreciation and sincere good wishes,

Faithfully yours,   Woodrow Wilson

TLS (Letterpress Books, WP, DLC).

## To William Bowyer Fleming

My dear Mr. Fleming:        [The White House] 25 January, 1917

I thank you warmly for your letter of January twenty-fourth and for the accompanying letter of January fifth which you had until now withheld. The figures are indeed terribly impressive.

Cordially and sincerely yours,   Woodrow Wilson

TLS (Letterpress Books, WP, DLC).

## To Ruth Preble Hall, with Enclosure

My dear Ruth:                The White House 25 January, 1917

As soon as I got your letter,[1] I took the matter up with the Secretary of War and am glad to say I received from him yesterday the note which I enclose. I need not tell you how glad I am to be able to contribute in any way to your happiness.

In driving haste, but with affectionate good wishes from us all,

Faithfully yours,   Woodrow Wilson

TLS (received from Lacey Baldwin Smith).
[1] Ruth P. Hall to WW, Jan. 16, 1917, printed as an Enclosure with WW to NDB, Jan. 23, 1917, Vol. 40.

ENCLOSURE

## From Newton Diehl Baker

Dear Mr. President:        Washington. January 24, 1917

I herewith return for your files the note inclosed with your letter of January 23d. I discover that it is entirely consistent with the discipline of the Academy to permit the young lady's brother

to be absent to attend the wedding, and have therefore authorized
it to be done.          Respectfully yours,    Newton D. Baker

TLS (received from Lacey Baldwin Smith).


## From Bernard Nadal Baker

Dear Mr. President:                Washington, January 25, 1917.

Appreciating the honor you have conferred upon me, I deeply
regret that I feel compelled to ask you to withdraw my name as a
member of the Shipping Board. Secretary McAdoo advised me
yesterday of your wish as to the selection of the Chairman of the
Board.[1] Pending the organization of the Board, I cannot agree
to the selection of any one.

With great respect and esteem,
                    Yours sincerely,    B. N. Baker.

TLS (WP, DLC).

[1] McAdoo issued the following statement on January 27: "It is true that Mr.
Bernard N. Baker has resigned from the shipping board and that the President
has accepted his resignation. Mr. Baker resigned because I suggested to him
that I thought it would be wise, in the circumstances, if the board would consider giving the chairmanship to the Pacific Coast. The President was in accord with this suggestion. Mr. Baker said he desired to think the matter over
for the night. The next morning he sent his resignation.

"The selection of suitable men for the shipping board and the proper
organization of the board have been matters of great concern to the Administration ever since the passage of the shipping bill. The suggestion about the chairmanship was made in a spirit of co-operation and with a desire to be helpful.
The board has a right under the law to select its own Chairman, but there is no
reason why a suggestion from the Administration should not receive attention.
I have had a warm regard always for Mr. Baker and I regret his hasty action."
*New York Times*, Jan. 28, 1917.

William Denman of San Francisco was the only member of the board from
the Pacific Coast, and it was reported that Wilson and McAdoo preferred him
in order "to escape the possible pressure of conflicting interests in the shipping
and shipbuilding industries along the Atlantic seaboard." At the first meeting
of the board, on January 30, Denman was unanimously chosen as chairman, but
it was decided not to make the election permanent until Baker's successor was
named. *Ibid.*, Jan. 28 and 31, 1917.


## To William Gibbs McAdoo

My dear Mac.,                The White House. 25 January, 1917.

Here is an extraordinary note from Baker. I do not wish to
answer it before letting you see it. Of course I shall withdraw his
name. Such a note, if interpreted as it seems inevitable to interpret it, shows that he is not a fit man for any board.
                        Affectionately,    W.W.

WWTLI (W. G. McAdoo Papers, DLC).

## From Edward Mandell House

Dear Governor:                    New York. January 25, 1917.

I have made arrangements through Phillips to see Bernstorff tomorrow morning as you suggest in your letter of yesterday.

I think it is better to see him here even if it is known which I do not believe it will be. Any attempt at secrecy would be fatal. The Allied representatives know that he comes here as I make it a point to inform them.

Seeing Bernstorff is the move I intended suggesting to you to-day if you had not made it yourself. In my opinion, the time has arrived when Germany should be pushed to declare her terms. It will make a good impression on the Allies, and if the Germans are sincere, they will now give you material to work on in the furtherance of peace.

Wiseman brought a depressing story from Washington. He said that on the surface and officially your address was accepted with cordiality, but that underneath there was a deep feeling of resentment. The underlying feeling was that you were making a proposal to enforce arbitration in the future while the Allies were giving up both blood and treasure now for the same purpose. If Germany had arbitrated as Grey demanded, this war could not have happened. Germany refused, and the Allies are doing exactly what you suggest should be done in the future. That since they are doing now what you suggest for the future, they should have more sympathy in their present undertaking. They consider it inconsistent for us to want to let Germany go free from punishment for breaking the very rules we wish to lay down for the future.

He says this is the concensus of the Allied view at Washington.

Wiseman's individual view is that in pressing the Allies too hard for peace at this time, you will be doing the cause of democracy harm. He asserts that every belligerent government is now in the hands of the reactionaries and must necessarily be in their hands when the war ends. He believes if we are not careful we will find that these forces in the belligerent governments will all come together when peace is made, and that it is not at all unlikely their concentrated hate for democracy will be centered upon this country.

Peace, he says, must come first and then a plan to enforce arbitration afterwards. He thinks it is possible that after peace is signed, and before the arbitration agreement is made, the reactionary forces might refuse to go into any league for future peace and make some pretext to turn upon us in order to save autocracy.

This seems to me a remote contingency, but nevertheless if I were you, I would speed up the Army and Navy plans as a matter of precaution.

We are in deep and troubled waters but I have an abiding faith in the ultimate good that will come from your noble efforts.

Your affectionate,   E. M. House

TLS (WP, DLC).

## From Robert Lansing, with Enclosure

PERSONAL AND PRIVATE:

My dear Mr. President:          Washington January 25, 1917.

I have just received the enclosed from Colonel House. I spoke to you about the sending forward of Bernstorff's cipher telegram on Tuesday at Cabinet, which called forth this letter.

I would be pleased to have your wishes in the matter or to talk it over when I see you.

Faithfully yours,   Robert Lansing.

TLS (WP, DLC).

E   N   C   L   O   S   U   R   E

## Edward Mandell House to Robert Lansing

Dear Mr. Lansing:          New York City. January 24, 1917.

When Mr. Phillips telephoned yesterday I did not feel like giving a direct reply concerning the advisability of your permitting Bernstorff to send further messages for the reason that we have gotten nothing of much value from his efforts so far.

At first he told me that his government were willing to submit to arbitration; that they were willing to accept such proposals as the President might make for a conference, and they were willing to immediately sign the so called "Bryan Treaty."

This was all said verbally. I concluded it was best to get it in writing and when I did, I found that all he said referred to the future, that is after peace had been made.

Pinned down on the Bryan treaty as to what they would do in regard to their illegal submarine warfare, he again shifted and wanted each case to be decided on its own merits.

If Germany really desires peace she ought now to state her terms. Bernstorff says he is trying to get them and this may or may not be the reason for his further messages. Anyway, I thought it a matter that the President and you should decide between you after knowing the facts.

Sincerely yours,   E. M. House

TLS (WP, DLC).


## From Franklin Knight Lane

Dear Mr. President:                    Washington January 25, 1917.

I saw several people at the Capitol yesterday regarding the general leasing bill. Scott Ferris makes this suggestion, that the leasing bill be passed through the Senate in any form that the Senate desires and then it will necessarily go to conference. He pledges his word that no bill will come out of conference that does not meet with your approval. He would undertake on his own responsibility to block any measure that you think unwise. I do not want the work of four years to go for naught and I fear that if we let this opportunity pass we will never get as far again, for the Republicans are bracing themselves in opposition to any constructive legislation and they will be more masterful in the next Congress than they are in this.

I sent you a memorandum yesterday which I trust you have read showing that Oil Reserve No. 2 cannot be held as a reservoir.[1]                    Faithfully yours,   Franklin K. Lane

TLS (WP, DLC).
[1] FKL to WW, Jan. 23, 1917, Vol. 40.


## From William Joel Stone

Dear Mr. President:                    [Washington] January 25 1917.

In a conversation Senator Bankhead had with me this morning he outlined to me the difficulties in having the so-called Shields Power Bill acted upon by the Conference Committee. He told me he had made the same explanation to you. It seems that when the Shields Bill went to the House Mr. Adamson offered a Bill he had prepared as a substitute. The Adamson Bill was amended in many important particulars, and in a way that Mr. Adamson himself is unwilling to support it, so Bankhead says. Nevertheless, the amended substitute was agreed to by the House. It seems that the House, or Members of the House, exacted a promise or pledge from Mr. Adamson not to consent to any amendment to the House substitute. The Senate Conferees refuse to accept the substitute, which even Adamson himself is opposed to. The Senate Conferees have urged Adamson to report a disagreement to the House and see if the House will not consent to a further conference, *but a free conference*. If that should be done Bankhead says he is sure they would be able to make a bill that would be satisfactory to both Houses.

I am asked to state this case to you and suggest that if in accord with your view that you confer with Mr. Adamson and endeavor to induce him to take the course just suggested. He seems disinclined to report the disagreement because of the pledge he made, amounting to an instruction.

It is important that some water power legislation should be enacted, but the Senate Conferees think that unless you can save the day the chances are that nothing will be done.

Sincerely yours,   Wm J Stone

TLS (WP, DLC).

## From Francis Griffith Newlands

My dear Mr. President:      Washington, D. C. January 25, 1917.

I send you herewith the tentative Bill which I offered in Committee and which has been amended by the Committee.[1] It is practically agreed that I shall be authorized to report this Bill. Meanwhile, however, a suggestion from the Railway Brotherhoods has been presented to you in a letter dated January 24th, of which a copy was handed to me today. I have submitted this letter to a partial attendance of the Interstate Commerce Committee this afternoon, Senators Smith, Cummins, Brandegee, Saulsbury and myself being present. The feeling was that it would be best not to report the Bill in its present form if the Brotherhoods' suggestion is to be accepted. The members of the Committee who were present saw no objection to this suggestion as a substitute for Section 3 of the tentative Bill. I do not know what the views of the Railway Executives regarding this suggestion are.

If you desire to see me upon this subject, I await your convenience.   Very sincerely yours,   Francis G. Newlands.

TLS (WP, DLC).
[1] 64th Cong., 2d sess., printed draft bill (WP, DLC), *To amend certain sections of an Act entitled 'An Act providing for mediation, conciliation, and arbitration in controversies between certain employers and their employees,' approved July fifteenth nineteen hundred and thirteen.* The primary intent of this bill was to prevent interference with or obstruction of trains operating in interstate commerce and to give the President power to take possession of railroads and telegraph and telephone facilities in case of actual or threatened war, insurrection, invasion, or other emergencies which required their use for military purposes. Section 3 of the draft bill provided, however, that the President should

appoint a three-person board of inquiry to ascertain the facts in any case in which a controversy could not be resolved in the manner prescribed by the Railway Mediation Act of 1913, referred to in the title of the draft bill.


## To Francis Griffith Newlands

My dear Senator:          [The White House] 26 January, 1917

I do not think that it would be wise to substitute for Section 3 of the committee's bill the plan proposed by the heads of the brotherhoods, at any rate at this stage. I think it seems quite certain (though I shall know more definitely by this evening) that the House will send you a bill quite different in some respects from that which your committee has voted, and if it does, there will then be an opportunity in dealing with the two bills to bring them into accord with one another by the best process that may offer at the time.

This is a merely provisional judgment. I am hoping to have an opportunity to consult with one or two members of the House before evening.

In the meantime, may I not thank you for your thoughtfulness in sending me the committee bill, and express my very deep regret that the committee was not able to support my proposals in their entirety?

Cordially and sincerely yours,   Woodrow Wilson

TLS (Letterpress Books, WP, DLC).


## To Bernard Nadal Baker

My dear Mr. Baker:          [The White House] 26 January, 1917

I have your letter of yesterday and deeply regret your feeling about the matter, which I confess I cannot quite understand.

I cannot comply exactly with your request, namely, that I withdraw your name as a member of the Shipping Board from the Senate. The Senate has already confirmed my nominations and the commissions have been issued, but I feel obliged to comply with your wishes in substance and, therefore, accept your resignation as a member of the Board.

With renewed expressions of regret that you have felt obliged to take the course you have,

Sincerely yours,   [Woodrow Wilson]

CCL (WP, DLC).

## To Chevalier Willem Louis Frederik Christiaan van Rappard

My dear Mr. Minister:     [The White House] 26 January, 1917

Your note of the twenty-third[1] has given me the deepest gratification. It was certainly an act of thoughtful and generous kindness on your part to write it. I quite understand that you were not speaking for your Government in any sense, but you were speaking, I feel, from your own heart and that is what particularly gratifies and encourages me.

May I not express my real gratitude and warm personal regard?

Cordially and sincerely yours,    Woodrow Wilson

TLS (Letterpress Books, WP, DLC).
[1] It is missing.


## To Edward William Bok

My dear Mr. Bok:          The White House 26 January, 1917

You are very generous in the position you take about reprinting a part of my chapter on the Presidency and your generosity makes me the more loath to disappoint you in any way,[1] but my feeling is that I better not seem to be talking too much just now about the functions of the Presidency. Those functions have their irritating sides, to some of my colleagues in the Senate in particular, and I can do as much without talking about it.

Cordially and sincerely yours,    Woodrow Wilson

TLS (WP, DLC).
[1] Bok had written to Wilson to suggest that a shortened version of Wilson's chapter on the presidency in *Constitutional Government in the United States* be printed in the issue of the *Ladies' Home Journal* directly following his second inaugural. E. W. Bok to WW, Jan. 15, 1917, TLS, with enclosed typescript, WP, DLC. Wilson had replied that it was "literally impossible" for him to examine the abridgment and added: "I must frankly say that I do not feel that any abridgment of the essay would really express my views. Abridgments necessarily leave out the shadings and the qualifications of the thought, and I am very reluctant to authorize the publication of anything which I did not prepare myself." WW to E. W. Bok, Jan. 23, 1917, TLS (WP, DLC). Bok, in his reply, expressed his disappointment and promised not to publish the material without Wilson's knowledge and consent, even though the Columbia University Press, which owned the copyright of *Constitutional Government*, had already consented to the publication of the abridgment. "Abridgment," Bok added, might not have been the best word, for the portions omitted were related to the method of nominating a President in convention, and the portions retained were substantially intact. "However," Bok concluded, "I can imagine how busy you are, and how pressed for time, and I wouldn't for the world add one straw to your burden. Much as I want to print the article, and much as I am sure the public would like to read it, I shall, unless another word comes from you within a week, consider the matter as settled." E. W. Bok to WW, Jan. 25, 1917, ALS (WP, DLC).

## To John Hollis Bankhead

[The White House]
My dear Senator Bankhead:                    26 January, 1917

Senator Stone has repeated to me the suggestion you made to me the other day about the water power bill.

Unfortunately, it is not practicable to carry it out. I have consulted not only with Judge Adamson, but with a number of the members of the House of Representatives about it, and the fact is this: It is useless for Judge Adamson to ask for a disagreement; he has been notified by men of both parties in the House that he cannot get it.

It was in view of that situation that I was so anxious that you and Senator Shields and Judge Adamson and Mr. Sims should have an informal conference with the gentlemen I named to you, namely Mr. Ferris, Mr. Sherley, Mr. Rainey, Mr. Kent, Doctor Foster, and Mr. Lenroot. I really believe that if any legislation is possible at this session, it can be arranged in such a conference as that, and I again very respectfully and urgently press the idea upon you.

Cordially and sincerely yours,    Woodrow Wilson

TLS (Letterpress Books, WP, DLC).


## To Richard Olney

My dear Mr. Olney:          The White House 26 January, 1917

That was a very generous and admirable statement you made the other day in support of my address to the Senate on Monday last,[1] and I thank you for it out of a very full heart.

I heard the other day that you were ill. I sincerely hope that this is not true. If it is, my most hearty good wishes go out to you for a quick and entire recovery.

Cordially and sincerely yours,    Woodrow Wilson

TLS (R. Olney Papers, DLC).
[1] Olney had sent the following message from Boston on January 23 to the New York *World*: "Answering your telegraphic request for a brief word respecting President Wilson's recent address to the Senate. The fundamental idea is nothing less than a stroke of genius.

"If any statesman of any other country has conceived of it, he has lacked the courage to proclaim it—if any statesman of any other country has been endowed with the necessary courage he has lacked the wisdom to realize that only through 'peace without victory' is any peace possible.

"The victory the President has in mind is not merely a defeat from which an organized people may recover and renew the strife, with unimpaired vigor: it is a victory which, judged by purposes expressly avowed, is to utterly crush the beaten combatant and in effect eliminate it from the list of self-governing peoples. Such a result would not merely not be worth the cost to the victor but would be a crime against all mankind.

"It is to the great glory of America not only that its President has kept us out of the present almost world-wide war but has also had the prescience and sagacity to recognize and point out the only road through which a desirable peace can be secured." New York *World*, Jan. 24, 1917.

## To Thomas Davies Jones

My dear Friend:                  The White House 26 January, 1917

I hope that you will not think that I am presuming too much upon your friendship if I ask if you would be willing to consider a place on the Tariff Board.

I am not asking this without first having sounded the Senator who led the opposition to your confirmation when I nominated you for the Federal Reserve Board,[1] and I have his assurance that that opposition would not be repeated.

It was a matter of such genuine grief to me not to get the advantage of your counsel here in Washington on the former occasion that I have continued to cherish the hope that you might be willing to let me propose you for some other post of high responsibility, and I know of none which will require more judgment, more steadiness, and a more sympathetic attitude towards the business development of the country than a position on the Tariff Board. As far as I have gone, I have found men of first-rate quality whom I think it would be a pleasure to be associated with, and I hope with all my heart that you will consent.

If I am asking too much, please ascribe it only to my utter confidence in you and my eager desire to have you in the public service.

Cordially and sincerely yours,    Woodrow Wilson

TLS (Mineral Point, Wisc., Public Library).
[1] James A. Reed.

## Two Letters from Edward Mandell House

Dear Governor:                  New York. January 26, 1917.

Bernstorff has just left. He said the military have complete control in Germany with von Hindenberg and Ludendorff at the head. Ludendorf, as you know, is Hindenberg's chief of staff.

In reply to a direct question as to the Kaiser's influence and power he said he was under the impression that the Kaiser had designedly left things in the hands of Hindenberg. The inference was that whatever mistakes were made and whatever settlement came about, it would be Hindenberg's mistakes and settlement and not the Kaiser's.

Bernstorff believes that none of the belligerent governments can survive such a peace as must necessarily be made. That the final terms will leave the map of Europe pretty much as it was before the war, with the exception of perhaps a new Poland, the [inter]nationalization of the Dardanelles and some minor changes.

I was surprised to hear how easily he took to the general proposition of eliminating Turkey and opening the Dardanelles to the commerce of the world.

I called his attention to the danger that lay in postponing peace, and of the probability of their coming in conflict with us on account of their submarine activities. He admitted this as a real danger, for he said that the submarine warfare would begin with renewed vigor and determination as soon as the spring campaign opened and all signs of immediate peace had disappeared. He thought if the spring campaign began, there could be no peace until the fighting ended in the Autumn. To this I replied that the Allies would not make peace with Germany in the Autumn if the war continued that long, for they would want to carry it over another winter hoping their blockade would be effective. I did this to discourage the idea that peace could come in the Autumn if it did not come now.

I told him that Germany must give you something definite to work on and immediately. I suggested that they state that they would be willing to completely evacuate both Belgium and France and that they would agree to *mutual* "restoration, reparation and indemnity." He rather shied at this last, although in a former conversation he suggested it himself.

I told him you wished something to use with the people of the Allied countries, so that public sentiment might force the governments to discuss peace.

He thought German opinion was pleased with your address, particularly what you said in regard to the freedom of the seas.

After much discussion it was finally decided, at his suggestion, that he send a despatch tomorrow to his government telling them that you had requested a reply from them giving definite terms, and that you thought if their terms were moderate, there was reason to believe something might be done towards bringing about an early peace.

He is to suggest to them that the terms include complete evacuation of Belgium and France. In addition to this he is suggesting that they make an offer to go into a peace conference on the basis of your address to the Senate.

He believes it will be necessary for the Chancellor's own protection to make the terms public even though address[ed] to you. German public opinion would be appeased by a definite statement of terms, and it would be to the Chancellor's advantage to make them in this way rather than to give them to you privately, although the note would be addressed to you and in answer to your request.

The fact that you have made a request of Germany for terms will help with the Allies, and since it meets with Bernstorff's approval, I thought it best to let it go in that way.

If there is anything you want to change in this program please wire tonight in code, for Bernstorff's despatch will not be prepared until tomorrow morning.

Your affectionate,   E. M. House

Dear Governor:          New York City. January 26, 1917.

Wiseman came this afternoon. His whole tone had changed. He said the atmosphere had cleared wonderfully since yesterday.

I told him of Bernstorff's visit and what you had asked him to do. This pleased him and we got down to a discussion of actual peace terms, and the conference which he seemed to now think could be brought about in the event that Germany returns a favorable reply.[1]

He told me in the *gravest confidence*, a thing which I had already suspected and that is that he is in direct communication with the Foreign Office, and that the Ambassador and other members of the Embassy are not aware of it.

I am happy beyond measure over this last conference with him, for I judge he reflects the views of his government.

He went so far as to discuss with me where the conference should be held, and whether or not there should first be a preliminary conference and afterwards a general one. I take it he has heard directly from his government since yesterday for he seemed to speak with authority.

I know you will appreciate the difference between any statement coming from the English as against one coming from the Germans.          Affectionately yours,   E. M. House

TLS (WP, DLC).

[1] Newly discovered documents in the Wiseman Papers clear up the old mystery as to whether Wiseman did in fact talk seriously to House about the possibility of an early peace conference.

Wiseman kept copious notes of his conversation with House and cabled them to Balfour. They follow:

"NOTES OF A CONVERSATION WITH A. [House]—
    FRIDAY, JANUARY 26th.

"*Sequence of events.* C. [Bernstorff] assures A. [House] that Germany is becoming more Liberalized and that the Military Party has lost power; that Hindenburg, Lutendorff, and Bethman Hollweg are in supreme command and their tendencies are all Liberal.

"A. has officially asked C. to get the Germans to state their terms. They agree to evacuation of Belgium and France; to give up some part of Alsace Loraine; and would be willing to accept the term 'mutual compensation, reparation and guarantees.' A. thinks they have, however, given up the idea that there is any chance of peace at present, and that they await the result of the Allies' Spring offensive before trying again. They think the Allies will fail, and that they will then be able to obtain good terms. In the meantime, he does not think that submarine frightfulness will be continued; that they will try and remain on good terms with the States.

"J. [Wilson] has agreed to expulsion of the Turks from Europe, and to practically all the Allies' main terms. J's speech was first suggested in a conversation with * * * * [House].

"A. suggests a conversation to find whether a conference is possible.

"—Drawn War—

"W[ilson]. hopes Kaiser will not make statement personally—our two objects to continue to gain neutral sympathy & foster socialism in Germany. [Handwritten addition by Wiseman]

"FURTHER NOTES ON CONVERSATION WITH A.—
              FRIDAY, JANUARY 26th.

"(1) A. says the information that he gives me is extremely confidential and comes direct from J. He may suspect that I cable to you, but I doubt it. He says that he wishes to get my advice on the Allies' sentiments.

"(2) A. again confirms the following:

(A) G. [Lansing?] and other advisers have convinced A. and J. that the war must be a drawn one. It may be noted that all German propagandists here are now working strongly along the same lines.

(B). C. told A. that Germany had now given up the idea of immediate peace and that she awaits with confidence the result of the Allies' Spring offensive, believing that it will be a failure, and that in any case after the Spring offensive peace must come.

(C). It appears therefore that the chance of the States being drawn into war has become more remote, unless Germany commits some flagrant submarine frightfulness. This A. thinks is now unlikely.

(D). C. has told A. that the Liberal party in Germany is now in control, namely Ludendorff, Bethmann-Hollweg and Hindenburg. The Military Party has lost its prestige, and the Kaiser has lost his personal influence. A. and J. are inclined to believe this.

(E). J. believes that his utterances have and will help the Allies because (1) they strike the anti-Militarist note; (2) the demand for democratic Government; (3) rights of small nations. A. hints that the *idea* is that J. will eventually force Germany into admitting that they are in the wrong. He thinks he will also strengthen the Socialist Party, which is a great factor.

(F). J. is ready to back practically all the Allies' terms, including compensation for invaded factories; expulsion of the Turks from Europe; and a warm seaport, presumably Constantinople, for Russia; also, of course, a really independent Poland.

(G). A. admits that during peace conversations, and while there is any chance of peace, the submarine issues now pending will not be pressed by the United States." T MS (W. Wiseman Papers, CtY).

# From Robert Lansing

PERSONAL AND CONFIDENTIAL:

My dear Mr. President:              [Washington] January 26, 1917.

This letter of David Lawrence's[1] is in substance the same as a conversation which he had with me a few days ago, although he did not go so far as to suggest your addressing Congress on the subject.

Earlier in the session I canvassed, with Senator Stone, the matter of bringing up the Colombian treaty and he told me that he considered it unwise to do so as he did not see any chance of favorable action at this time. The Senator's views confirmed the opinion which I had reached that a rejection of the treaty or a failure to act upon it would result if it was pressed this winter. In addition to the opposition to the treaty which is known to exist the ugly temper of the Republicans aroused by the resentment and disappointment consequent on their defeat in November makes it practically certain that the votes necessary for ratification could not be obtained. I do not think that anything could be done to change this attitude. Senator Stone also holds this opinion.

On the other hand, an attempt to force action which would result in the defeat of ratification would create a very undesirable situation in our relations with Colombia, and make a very bad impression throughout Latin America. Furthermore it would be very difficult to change the votes of Senators who had taken a position against the treaty, so that if it was again brought before the Senate the defeat of ratification would be almost certain.

It seemed to me, therefore, the wiser course to let the matter lie until the passions of partisanship had had time to cool and the Republican Senators were more disposed to consider the subject from the standpoint of right.

Sometime ago I saw the Colombian representative here and went over the possibility of success with him explaining the political situation. He seemed to appreciate the dangers of attempting to force action at this time and to be not unwilling to let the matter go for this session.

I might say that I explained all this to Lawrence, whose only argument was that the next Senate would be less Democratic than the present. This argument did not impress me as very strong.

If your views in this matter do not coincide with mine I hope that you will tell me.    Faithfully yours,    Robert Lansing

TLS (Lansing Letterpress Book, SDR, RG 59, DNA).
1 Printed as an Enclosure with WW to RL, Jan. 23, 1917 (second letter of that date), Vol. 40.

## From William Jennings Bryan

My Dear Mr President:                    En route Jany 26 1917

While I have not reached the same conclusion you have in regard to the wisdom of joining a league to enforce peace, I hope you will allow me to add my voice to the chorus of praise which you have called forth by your brave and timely appeal to the war-mad rulers of Europe. The basis of peace which you propose is a new philosophy—that is, new to governments but as old as the Christian religion, and it is the only foundation upon which a permanent peace can be built. Your message is epoc-making and will place you among the Immortals.

The phrase "Peace without Victory" was "a shot heard round the world"—no one can estimate its power for good. You have given the belligerents the shock they needed—they must settle the account with their people if they refuse to heed.

May your heart be gladdened by an early agreement. My compliments to Mrs Wilson.

With assurances of esteem I am, my dear Mr President,
                    Very truly yours   W. J. Bryan

ALS (WP, DLC).


## From William Charles Adamson

Dear Mr. President:          Washington, D. C. January 26, 1917.

I am in receipt of your note of yesterday transmitting to me the letter of the day before in which Mr. Stone and Mr. Sheppard officially suggest a substitute for your proposed railroad legislation. They state in that letter that Mr. Lee and Mr. Carter concur with them. I know that Mr. Lee does, because I heard him propose the scheme in the hearing before our Committee. I didn't hear Mr. Carter's entire statement and don't know whether he stated it or not, but have no doubt that he does concur with the gentlemen as they say.

The fundamental trouble about the proposition is that, while the gentlemen refer occasionally in their letter to the public, their plan really ignores the public. I have no doubt their plan would secure settlement of controversies, but I can't see any improvement afforded by that plan over the present situation. A commission composed of equal numbers selected from the two classes of employees would not change the situation at all. At present representatives of the Brotherhoods go and confer with the representatives of the Railroad Companies and they negotiate. They would have agreed last year if by their agreement they could have put in force the demands of the Railroad Companies at the same time that the demands of the trainment [trainmen] were recognized.

Four railroad managers and four trainmen on a commission would probably negotiate in the same way. They would be four advocates of each side and, of course, they can trade and agree if they can transfer the burden to the public. The effort to agree last year, if it had been successful, would have given both sides to the controversy what they wanted and passed the burden to the public. The four advocates of either side on a commission would do the same—They would recommend what was considered advantageous to the two parties to the controversy and if it involved increased expenses, of course, the public would suffer.

I think it is hardly fair that they should assume that men of experience and probity are to be found only in the two classes of employees. If they would admit the possibility that the President might find four disinterested men to add to that commission it would nullify the objection insofar as equilibrium is concerned, but it is unnecessary to have so many. One or two from the Brotherhoods and one or two from the Railroad Presidents and an equal number from the public at large would suffice.

The only objection I have to their elimination of political considerations is that there might be a recurrence of what happened last year,—All the parties concerned might belong to one political party and the desire to defeat a party in power might reconcile the parties to the conflict to temporary loss out of political considerations.

The fairest commission that could be appointed would be a commission of three upright men who had never worked in either class, but who from large experience and wide knowledge and good character would be prepared to hear evidence from those who know and pass upon questions and present them to the public. But as they insist on each side being represented, let the public, which is the ultimate loser by their agreements, also be represented in equal degree. They also omit any provision for a restraining order or agreement during the investigation.

I think we have about progressed far enough in the discussion to render it important that I should have another brief conference with you, and I would like to do so Monday afternoon or evening if you could possibly arrange it before we have our meeting of the Committee on Tuesday.

With high regards and best wishes, I remain,

Yours truly,   W. C. Adamson

TLS (WP, DLC).


## From William Kent

Dear Mr. President:          Washington, D. C. January 26, 1917.

I have received a letter from Mr. Tumulty, enclosing a copy of a letter addressed to you by the Chairman of the Federal Trades Commission of the date of January 18, 1917.[1]

I feel sure that under the pressure of your duties and burdens, you did not have time to read this communication or it would not have been forwarded to me.

Permit me to quote the concluding paragraphs, which follow nearly two pages of reasons why some one else ought to act or fail to act:

"The Federal Trade Commission is entrusted with the regulation of trade products with the view to keeping competition free and open, so that competition may regulate prices; and the Department of Justice is the medium for the enforcement of the anti-trust laws."

It is our contention that the Federal Trade Commission was given authority to subpoena witnesses and examine books so that it might learn how to keep competition free and open and to know whether or not it is free and open. If not given these powers for this specific purpose, why should there be a Federal Trade Commission and why should such powers have been granted it?

"My suggestion, therefore, is as follows: If you could see your way clear to appoint a departmental committee, which would invite various interests to appear in a friendly way and make their suggestions, such a committee might be constituted by the assistant secretaries or other representatives of the Department of Agriculture, Department of Commerce and Department of the Interior, with one member of the Federal Trade Commission, and an assistant attorney general.

The moral influence in the presence of the assistant attorney general doubtless would be helpful.

Whatever might be learned in this matter, and I believe a

great deal could be learned by a small departmental committee of this kind, could be applied immediately.

It would not be necessary to ask Congress to give special
powers to the committee. It has been my experience that most
men asked to cooperate with the Government will do so without
force, except in some rare instances."

This toothless, clawless, unarmed and unarmored method of
conducting what is in the nature of a contest between a lot of
disorganized meat producers and consumers on two sides of the
field as against the entrenched packers whom we have no hesitation in declaring to be law breakers, would be laughable if not
tragic. If the Federal Trade Commission is constituted for the
purpose of having the lamb lie down inside of the lion, it would
seem that it is superfluous. There are plenty of means of securing information more or less accurate, such as the packers are
willing to put out but we have been hoping that through the
authority of law we could have the meat business investigated to
the end of obtaining a full, comprehensive knowledge of conditions of production, manufacture, distribution and costs, which
investigation can never be possible except under due authority
of law, with ample powers granted the investigating body.

The alternative to this is Secretary Houston's proposition that
the Market Bureau of the Agricultural Department be granted full
investigating powers. The Secretary frankly stated that he preferred that the Federal Trade Commission should exercise these
powers in that portion of the field of investigation which could
not be penetrated by the ordinary courteous investigations of the
Market Bureau.

You know how averse I am to bothering you with such detail
but I am sure on reading Chairman Hurley's letter that you will
wonder with me what the Federal Trade Commission is for.

                              Yours truly,   William Kent

TLS (WP, DLC).
1 E. N. Hurley to WW, Jan. 18, 1917, Vol. 40.


## From John Palmer Gavit

Dear Mr. President,            Rockledge, Fla. January 26. 1917

I need hardly assure you of the eager interest and delight with
which I read your speech to the Senate. You have done all and
more than all that I had in mind in the conversation we had in
Washington in November, and have indeed rung the bell that the
whole world must hear over the frightful din of slaughter and

destruction. After the chaos has given way to order and sanity, your note to the belligerents and this address in the Senate will be recognized, I believe, as the finest things that have been done in our time. It is of no consequence whatever, or anyway very little consequence, what is thought of them now, especially by those directly interested. The important thing, as I see it, is that someone in a position to say things that cannot be suppressed or distorted, has *spoken out* the things that represent the heart of humanity at its best, regardless of criticism in interested quarters, and regardless of considerations of timid prudence or immediate expediency.

My congratulations and thanks are a bit belated, because I am down here in search of health, trying to shake off an obstinate bronchial cough, and therefore out of touch with news and prompt information; but they are heartfelt, believe me.

Sincerely    John P. Gavit

ALS (WP, DLC).

## From James Hamilton Lewis

Washington, D. C.
My dear Mr. President,          Friday, January 26th 1917

I am able to report to you, that acting within your suggestions, I was able to get the Railroad bill included in the programme of the Steering Committee, for action this session. Also, I am able to report the securing such modification of views of three senators as will now assure an acceptable (to you) measure of a nature to accomplish what you wish as to suspending strikes Etc.

This is merely to report. Dont trouble to acknowledge.

I have the honor to be your obedient Servant

Jas Hamilton Lewis

ALS (WP, DLC).

## Joseph Patrick Tumulty to Robert Lansing, with Enclosure

Personal

Dear Mr. Secretary:          The White House January 26, 1917

In connection with the enclosed telegram from His Holiness, Benedictus P.P. XV, will you not give the President your advice as to an appropriate reply and the form in which it should be sent?                    Sincerely yours,   J. P. Tumulty

TLS (SDR, RG 59, 812.404/132½, DNA).


E N C L O S U R E

## From Benedict XV

Roma. January 26, 1917.

Apprenant avec extreme surprise et hesitant ajouter foi douloureuse nouvelle archeveque orozco et eveque de la mora emprisonnes Mexique sous imputation avoir conspire contre carranza en faveur villa et menaces mort imminente tribunal militaire prions de tout notre ame votre excellence vouloir user haute influence qu'elle exerce au mexique pour eviter contre personnes sacrees condamnation inspiriee peutetre passions politique et proposer le cas echeant que les accusations soient remises judgment impartial saint seige.

Benedictus P.P. XV.

T telegram (SDR, RG 59, 812.404/132½, DNA).


T R A N S L A T I O N

Learning with extreme surprise and hesitating to give credit to the sorrowful news that the Archbishop of Orozco and the Bishop of La Mora imprisoned in Mexico under the imputation of having conspired against Carranza in favor of Villa and menaced with imminent death by a military tribunal, we appeal with great earnestness to Your Excellency please to use the high influence that you exercise in Mexico to avoid this condemnation of these holy persons condemned perhaps on account of political passions and to propose, if such be the case, that the accusations be referred to the impartial judgment of the Holy See.


## Robert Lansing to Garrett Droppers

Washington, January 26, 1917.

Deliver following in manner most agreeable to King:

Quote. Your Majesty: I have been highly gratified to receive through the Chargé d'Affaires of Greece at Washington the communication which Your Majesty did me the honor to dispatch to me by cable on December twenty-ninth[1] and I pray Your Majesty to believe that I am duly appreciative of Your Majesty's valued commendation of my note of December sixteenth to the warring nations. Woodrow Wilson. Unquote.

Lansing

T telegram (SDR, RG 59, 763.72119/366, DNA).
[1] Constantine to WW, Dec. 16/29, 1916, printed as an Enclosure with RL to WW, Jan. 12, 1917 (second letter of that date), Vol. 40.

## Joseph Edward Willard to Robert Lansing

Madrid, Jan. 26, 1917.

318. For the President's personal and immediate information. Called this morning on the Minister of State[1] to pay respects on my return, accompanied by Counsellor of Embassy.[2] Minister introduced subject of President's so-called peace note and address to Senate of January 22nd. He said that tone of Spain's reply to note would have been different if it had been delivered to Spanish Government before delivery to belligerent nations, and especially if Spain had been previously consulted. This reply by no means intended to close door to future cooperation looking towards peace. On the contrary he expressed desire to cooperate with the United States. The Minister said that Spain looks upon herself and United States as leading neutrals, and that Spain occupies distinctly different position from any other European neutral, and that as such feels herself in a position to cooperate with the United States as no other neutral can. He also referred to exceptional position of the King of Spain among European rulers and his great personal influence. Minister stated with some emphasis that address to Senate had made excellent impression in Spain, much better than peace note. As the result of conference today and other information secured since my return, I am convinced, and Counsellor of Embassy concurs, that the cordial cooperation of Spain looking to peace can be secured if the United States Government sees fit to confer with the Spanish Government through such channels as it may select, and in advance of any further public communication with belligerents or other neutrals. I am specially convinced that the Spanish Government feels that its position and position of its King justify a consideration on the part of the United States distinct from that accorded to any other neutral, and that working on this basis its cordial cooperation can be relied upon.          Willard.

T telegram (SDR, RG 59, 763.72119/405½, DNA).
[1] Amalio Gimeno y Cabañas.
[2] Charles Stetson Wilson.

## To Robert Lansing, with Enclosure

My dear Mr. Secretary:          The White House 27 January, 1917

I have read the enclosed with the greatest emotion. It seems to me a very sober and significant document. I would be very much obliged if you would be kind enough to tell me what form of acknowledgment you think it would be wise for me to return.

Cordially and faithfully yours,     Woodrow Wilson

TLS (SDR, RG 59, 763.72119/458, DNA).


E  N  C  L  O  S  U  R  E


## From Francis Johnson[1]

Dear Mr. President:          London, E. C. January 6th, 1917.

I am directed by the National Administrative Council of the Independent Labour Party to send, with deep respect, their expression of profound gratitude to you for your noble and momentous action in addressing to the belligerent Powers your Note on the question of Peace. My Council, who speak with a special knowledge of public opinion in Great Britain, particularly among the working classes, desire to assure you that your action is gratefully appreciated by the sober and responsible sections of the British people. They know that the critical and unsympathetic response which has been accorded to your Note by certain journals in this country does not represent the feelings of the British Nation. The desire to see this terrible War brought to an end at once is widespread among all classes, and your appeal has raised a fervent hope that negotiations may be begun now which will lead to a settlement on such terms as will be just and honourable to all the Countries involved, and which will begin the formation of a League of Nations for maintaining Peace, to which idea you have given such valuable support.

My Council earnestly hopes that you will continue your great effort to bring the belligerent Nations together, and they pray that a speedy success will reward you. You have already, by your Note, rendered the greatest service to humanity, and by the continuance of your efforts in this direction, you will earn the undying gratitude of this and succeeding generations.

Believe me, dear Mr. President, your obedient servant,

Francis Johnson.

TCL (SDR, RG 59, 763.72119/458, DNA).
[1] Secretary of the Independent Labour party.

## To Miles Poindexter

My dear Senator:            [The White House] 27 January, 1917
I would be very much obliged to you if you would read the enclosures.[1] I quite recognize the fact that the matter they concern does not fall in any way under federal jurisdiction, but the facts, if correctly and fully stated, are so shocking in themselves that I would like very much to know whether the statements are true or not. I would be very glad to cooperate in any way that I properly could to correct an injustice so great as this seems to be if you think there is any channel through which it can be corrected.
With much respect,
Cordially and sincerely yours,   Woodrow Wilson

TLS (Letterpress Books, WP, DLC).
[1] Wilson's letter and enclosures cannot be found in the Poindexter Papers, ViU.


## To Joseph Patrick Tumulty

Dear Tumulty:            [The White House, Jan. 27, 1916]
I would be very much obliged if you would send this correspondence to Mr. Hurley with the suggestion that I think there is a great deal in what Mr. Kent says and that I would like him to tell me once more what he thinks possible.
The President.

TL (WP, DLC).


## To James Hamilton Lewis

My dear Senator:            [The White House] 27 January, 1917
Thank you for your courtesy in telling me the result of the caucus so far as the strike legislation was concerned. I am sincerely gratified to learn that the caucus is willing to modify the measures as you indicate.
Cordially and sincerely yours,   Woodrow Wilson

TLS (Letterpress Books, WP, DLC).


## From Robert Lansing, with Enclosure

My dear Mr. President:            Washington January 27, 1917.
I send you a memorandum of a conversation I had with the Japanese Ambassador[1] day before yesterday. Will you kindly

return the memorandum with any comments upon it which you may desire to make?

Faithfully yours,   Robert Lansing.

TLS (SDR, RG 59, 893.51/1743, DNA).
  [1] Aimaro Sato, Japanese Ambassador to the United States since October 30, 1916.

E N C L O S U R E

## A Memorandum by Edward Thomas Williams

MEMORANDUM.        January 25, 1917.

The Japanese Ambassador called upon the Secretary of State and said that the British Ambassador had mentioned to him a conversation with the Secretary relating to cöoperation between Americans and Japanese in loans and industrial enterprises in China.

In reply to an enquiry from the Japanese Ambassador the Secretary stated that the American Government was not opposed to cöoperation between Americans and Japanese in China provided the parties interested desired to cöoperate, that the United States had no political ambitions in the Far East and therefore had no reason to oppose such cöoperation. He stated furthermore that the American Government welcomed such cöoperation when free from political designs because it tended to the promotion of international friendship. Where cöoperation, however, was sought to promote political objects it rather tended to arouse suspicion than to promote friendship.

One thing, the Secretary said, the American Government could not approve—that was the cöercion of China.

The conversation was frank and friendly upon both sides.

The Ambassador enquired about the proposal to cöoperate in railway building in Manchuria.

The Secretary replied that the Ambassador must be aware that the American Government recognized that Japan had special interests in Manchuria. Although no declaration to that effect had been made by the United States yet this Government had repeatedly shown a practical recognition of the fact and did not desire to do anything there to interfere with Japan's interests.

"But," asked the Ambassador, "was not the proposal made by the American Minister in Peking?" The Secretary said he did not know of it. "Was it not done then in accordance with instructions from the Department of State?" asked the Ambassador. The Secretary said that he did not recollect any such instruction.

(Comment by E.T.W. No such instruction was given, but in a recent telegram, concerning the Japanese protest against the American contract to improve the Grand Canal in *Shantung*, the American Minister at Peking was instructed that the Department saw no objection to cöoperation between Americans and Japanese *elsewhere*, provided China were willing, but that the American Government considered the improvement of the Grand Canal an exceptional undertaking that should remain solely American—referring to its connection with the Famine Relief scheme of the American Red Cross. It is presumed that the American Minister, acting upon this suggestion, may have proposed as an alternative to participation in canal improvement the cöoperation in Manchuria. As a matter of fact, however, the cöoperation in railway building in Manchuria had been discussed previously by Mr. Straight and the Japanese interested.)

The Secretary called the attention of the Ambassador in this connection to the difference between Manchuria where Japan's special interests were conceded and Shantung where no such special interest was recognized.

The Japanese Ambassador said that Germany had claimed special interests in Shantung. The Secretary replied that the United States had never recognized such claim.

The Ambassador then asked what the attitude of this Government was towards the suggested cöoperation of American bankers with the Consortium (the international group that made the Reorganization Loan of 1913.)

The Secretary said that he could not approve such cöoperation for the reason that it appeared to be a political combination interfering with China's sovereign rights. He believed that generally speaking international cöoperation in China was a good thing but it should be free from political motives.

E.T.W.

Correctly reported, Robert Lansing 1/27/17

TI MS (SDR, RG 59, 893.51/1743, DNA).

## From Edward Mandell House

Dear Governor:                    New York. January 27, 1917.

I wrote you rather hastily last night after my conversation with Wiseman and there are some things I wish to add.

The other day he told me in the deepest confidence that there was some ground to think that the Pope might be able to get Austria to consent to a separate peace.

Yesterday, Wiseman thought, if a conference were held it might be advisable to hold it in Spain, giving as a reason that it would be remote from intrigue which he feared would be rampant at the Hague. I did not take to the suggestion kindly and told him that Spain was too distant and it would be too inconvenient. I thought if the Hague was open to the objections he mentioned, Christiania or Stockholm would be better than Spain. He did not press the matter. But taking his former conversation with that of yesterday, it seems to me likely that a trade is going on with the Vatican and Austria (with the approval of the allies) looking to the holding of the peace conference in a Catholic country and a country favorable to Austria, and perhaps with Alphonso as sponsor. I shall watch this lead closely and try to follow it further.

I do not want you to think that anything that Wiseman said when he returned from Washington reflected his own views. He had been saturated with the unfriendly attitude of Spring-Rice and, for the moment, it warped his vision. Wiseman seems to be a sincere liberal and a devoted adherent to the principles of democracy. He is working intelligently in the direction we desire. For instance, he is cabling to his government the favorable editorials like those in the World, and is trying to give them a different viewpoint from that which they must necessarily get from Spring-Rice.          Affectionately yours,   E. M. House

TLS (WP, DLC).

## From David Lawrence

My dear Mr. President:          [Washington] January 27, 1917

I feel encouraged by your cordial response in the Colombian matter to draw your attention to some helpful things that might be done *at once* with respect to Mexico.

I gather from what is being said in the public prints that it is not only the intention of the Government to withdraw Pershing[1] but to send Ambassador Fletcher. These two things must be of inestimable value to the de facto government. Let us reap the greatest benefit from our act by making a friendly statement of policy toward Mexico—something that will emphasize the word-and-deed combination of our policy. Irrespective of what may ultimately be the turn of events in Mexico, such a statement will be an important contribution to the record in the case as revealing the benevolence of our actions.

I have written you a great deal about Mexico from time to time. I have lately written a good deal more publicly about it. I never have hesitated in the past nor shall I in the future to say that your Mexican policy in principle is the greatest of your achievements for while many a statesman may point to fine words spoken, while other nations may profess a friendliness for weaker peoples, we have actually given a demonstration of our high-mindedness when selfishness might have dictated another and easier course.

When I say that your policy has been great in *principle*, I mean that those entrusted with the execution of it have been clumsy and narrow-visioned. In Ambassador Fletcher, I think we have the first man who has the *savoir faire* and the necessary insight to deal with the Mexicans. But his efforts will be retarded if he is not sent under conditions favorable to Mexico and in an atmosphere of friendliness. It is precisely to create that atmosphere that I would suggest a statement at this time covering our recent and present action with respect to Mexico. I would like to see emphasized—not necessarily in the United States—but in the press of Mexico something concrete that we have done for the good of Mexico. Most everything that has come out of the Government contained always a sort of mental reservation, a sort of warning for the future, a veiled intimation that was probably prompted by a consideration for our own public opinion. Such warnings and intimations can be most effectively delivered informally or through an Ambassador—not public statements.

I know that many of our newspapers look cynically at the withdrawal of the Pershing expedition. Those newspapers have not learned the fundamental principles of fairness for they assume that everything American is right and everything foreign is wrong and never alter the premise. There may have been something irregular about the Pershing expedition—our entry without specific permission—but our course was dictated by self-preservation, the highest rule in international law, for the de facto forces were not at the time capable of preventing the raids.

Many things have been accomplished by the Pershing expedition. Our army, for one thing, has learned a great deal about preventing raids, we have a fairly good intelligence system; we shall not be caught napping again as at Columbus (at least I hope so for in my years of experience with our army on the border I cannot understand Slocum's failure to use his own men for intelligence purpose, particularly when the hostility of the forces close to the border was a matter of such common knowledge at the time).

We are in a position, therefore, to protect our side of the line. We must faithfully discharge the obligations of neutrality by making it impossible for the dozens of juntas which infest our border states even to exist. They are not in the same class with political refugees who obtain asylum so as to forward the cause of liberty. They are conspiring to obstruct a government on which our own government is pinning its hopes for a solution of the Mexican problem. Let us make our moral support more practical in this regard. In a public statement or otherwise something also ought to be done to get the state authorities of Texas, New Mexico and Arizona interested in frustrating the activities of their own officials, so often corrupt and unscrupulous, so often themselves responsible for the hatreds that breed border raids.

But whatever pronouncement that is issued must emphasize in a practical way our friendliness for the de facto Administration. We cannot cast doubt upon the sincerity of our own words by withholding for example arms and ammunition from the constituted government. We must also send our consuls and consul-generals at once not only as an evidence of friendliness but as an assistance to our nationals and as a means of keeping the people of the United States better informed as to conditions. Our consular service in Mexico heretofore has been miserably incompetent. If you could personally see some of the men I have seen, you would have no wonder as to the reasons for the frequent failure of our representations.

I do not mean to reflect in the example I am about to give on the character or ability of the men at present handling our affairs in Mexico City and Queretaro but they are young and *do not carry weight* with the Mexican government. Certain features of the proposed Constitution are causing uneasiness to foreign interests. We have no one to impress our point of view on the Mexicans. Ambassador Fletcher ought to be there this very day to handle that question because it involves property rights for such a long period ahead. There are other problems which need immediate consideration and treatment by competent hands. Concretely, I would suggest that these things be done within the next week:

1. That Ambassador Fletcher be ordered to Mexico with a full staff and with sufficient ceremony to impress the Mexicans that an Ambassador from the United States is coming.

2. That a public statement of policy be issued by you announcing the withdrawal of Pershing and the intention to send Fletcher; that this statement frankly discuss the accomplishment of the Pershing expedition briefly as indicated above and avow our friendship for Mexico and our earnest hope that the de facto government, about to become a de jure government through an

election, will be able to restore peace and order and bring Mexico back to the position she once occupied in the Pan-American family of nations. We should emphasize that while we may not have understood the complex problems of internal politics that have delayed the coming of domestic peace, we are anxious to do our part from the outside to sustain Mexico's sovereignty and stimulate her growth. We are, in other words, withdrawing Pershing and sending our Ambassador to renew diplomatic relations because we believe it to be for the good of Mexico, because it will give the de facto government a prestige in the world which it could not have if the United States, its nearest neighbor, maintained troops on its soil or hesitated to send an Ambassador to reestablish the channels of diplomacy.

We can point out that we are doing these things of our own volition, unselfishly and with no motive except the desire that our acts shall remove any obstructions which may have existed to the growth of the de facto government or the restoration of constitutional government. Reciprocity, however, is a fundamental principle in foreign relations. American public opinion gives its sanction to the acts of its government, to the cause of friendship for the de facto government in the confident expectation that where the legitimate rights of Americans are concerned the de facto government will on its part deal with them in a spirit of justice, fairness and unselfishness. We can expect that the protection of Americans and their property will not fail in the light of our ren[e]wed evidences of friendliness to be a subject of practical solicitude with the Mexican government.

It seems to me that the time is ripe for a "new deal" with respect to Mexico. One year is not a long time for us to wait for the reestablishment of constitutional government. Such a complete disintegration of authority as Mexico has witnessed cannot be remedied in a year—and it is just that long since we recognized Carranza. Personally I should think two and three years would not be a long time to wait. One thing is evident—Mexico is moving ahead, not rapidly but slowly. It is enough that Mexico is moving ahead, that conditions are better politically than they were a year ago, that municipal authority is alread[y] reconstructed in many cities and that state governments are being rehabilitated. Villa is on a huge raiding expedition—the kind of disorganized warfare that always precedes the formation of a real revolt in Mexico. If we assume a passive attitude, his friends in this country—all the reactionaries—will continue to work zealously for him. He will with difficulty organize a real revolution because with the withdr[a]wal of Pershing he will be deprived of an issue, and the

people of Mexico are tired of fighting for abstractions. If we un-
equivocally express a friendliness for Carranza and show that we
intend to make it a "go," it will strike discouragement to the plotters and in a short time Villa's raiding columns will be scattered,
though it will take another year to rid the country in the north
of his bandits. It will take an army much larger and better
equipped than anything Carranza can hope to get in six months
under the most favorable conditions to hem in the bandits in that
wild northern country. But we cannot afford to be passive. The
sequel of our recognition a year ago of the de facto government
must be a moral support that is practical, something that will
make business men in Mexico who have hesitated to order goods
for long periods of time because they believed intervention or
some other change of policy was due any day forget these doubts
and convince them that the United States means to put all of its
power behind the de facto government to make it stand. For
whatever becomes of the individual at the head of it, we must not
lose sight of the fact that a government has been created within
the last year and that the structure must be supported and encouraged irrespective of our likes or dislikes of the present personnel.

I suppose I am like a great many persons who write to you on
Mexico—I feel that if my suggestions are acted upon, the problem
will be soon on the way to a solution. I say simply this: let us go
the limit in friendly acts and words, let us have a competent per-
sonnell to express our purposes and conduct our business, let us
eliminate threats and warnings in our public statements that
make the Mexican discount our good words and remember only
our veiled intimations, let us do it Mexico's way for once and
await the outcome. There is plenty of time and opportunity, the
Lord knows, for the other kind of policy, the impetuous course
that so many of our selfish and mistaken people have lately been
advocating.

With best wishes, I am,

Sincerely yours,   David Lawrence

TLS (WP, DLC).
  1 Baker, on January 18, had ordered Pershing to begin the withdrawal. It was
completed on February 5.


## Robert Lansing to Joseph Patrick Tumulty

PERSONAL AND PRIVATE:

Dear Mr. Tumulty:          Washington January 27, 1917.

I am returning the telegram of His Holiness, the Pope, to the
President, with the following comment:

We have had no diplomatic relations with the Vatican and therefore no direct communication between the Papal See and this Government has ever taken place. Prior to this time no Pope has ever, as far as I can learn, addressed the President directly— having always done so through the Papal Legate in this country, or one of the Cardinals. To reply directly to the telegram would undoubtedly raise some difficult questions with the Italian Government.

You perceive that the telegram has caused an embarrassing situation. My suggestion would be that you, as the Secretary to the President, address a communication either to the Papal Legate or to Cardinal Gibbons, stating that the President had received the telegram and that you are authorized to communicate, with the person to whom you write, that the advices of this Government are that one of the prelates in danger in Mexico is reported to be in hiding, while the other is under arrest; but that it is stated that money is being collected for their defense and that they will be given opportunity to clear themselves of the charges made against them. It might be added that this Government is doing everything possible for the safety of these Churchmen.[1]

I think this is the best way out of the embarrassment caused by the action of His Holiness in addressing the President direct.

Very sincerely yours,    Robert Lansing

TLS (WP, DLC).
[1] A pencil notation on this letter reveals that Tumulty wrote to the Apostolic Delegate, the Most Rev. Giovanni Bonzano, on January 27. Tumulty's letter is missing in WP, DLC. See also G. Bonzano to JPT, Jan. 29, 1917, TL (WP, DLC).


## George Rublee to Edward Mandell House, with Enclosure

Dear Colonel House:                    [New York] January 27, 1917.

I enclose the letter I promised. It was not a pleasant one to write, but desiring as much as I do the success of the Commission I think I ought to state the truth as I see it.

You asked me one question the other day which I should have answered more fully. It was whether there was likelihood of opposition by the present membership of the Commission to the new members if they were strong, able men who knew what they were about and agreed on a policy. I said I thought there would be no trouble. Perhaps I ought to have said that this was my hope.

Mr. Harris wants to do the right thing. He would not be likely to make up his own mind by independent thought about matters coming before the Commission, because he has had little experience in such matters, and his interest is mainly in politics. He would take the advice that he trusted, and I believe he would support new members of the sort I am supposing.

I am rather inclined to think Mr. Parry would do so too, but I am not quite sure. He seems to mean well, works hard and loves detail. But he has not a firm grasp of the big questions. He is timid and wants to lean on somebody. I should never expect to find him standing out alone. He would be likely to choose to stand where he thought the more powerful force in the long run would be found.

I cannot predict what Mr. Davies would do. I have told you that I do not regard him as a sound lawyer. He is facile, vague and optimistically confident, but he is not thorough and is without well grounded knowledge either of law or of business. He wants to control the Commission and has a good deal of rather childish vanity. He is one of the reasons why I think two lawyers should be appointed and why one, however good, would not be enough.

If two of the type I have suggested were appointed I should hope that Mr. Davies might fall in line and perhaps be stimulated to take hold of his job and work harder at it than he has.

Sincerely yours    George Rublee

My address is 22 East 11th. St., New York.

ALS (WP, DLC).

E  N  C  L  O  S  U  R  E

## George Rublee to Edward Mandell House

Dear Colonel House:                    New York January 26, 1917.

At your request I am putting in writing the substance of my talk with you about the situation in the Trade Commission.

Mr. Hurley recently told me that the President was still thinking of nominating me as a member of the Commission. If this is true, I deeply appreciate his confidence in me and belief in my ability. I had thought that it would be really worth while, aside from any consideration personal to me, to make a fight against "senatorial courtesy" if there were any reasonable chance of securing my confirmation. But Mr. Hurley's resignation has weakened the Commission so much that its re-organization ought not to be delayed by re-opening the controversy about me. There are so many great matters engaging the attention of the country and of Congress, and the end of the session is so near that probably either the nomination would again fail of confirmation or no action would be taken. My principal interest is in the success of the Commission, and the need of strengthening it is so immediate, that in my judgment further consideration of me should be dropped and two men of the highest ability and fitness should without delay be appointed to fill the vacant places.

The condition of the Commission is very serious and I am greatly concerned about its future. The truth is that the Commission has not yet made a record to justify its existence and to fulfill the expectations of those who hoped it might become an agency of great benefit to the public. There is still a chance for it to make good, but I think that success depends upon the appointment of two men of very unusual capacity, who may be able to work in harmony. Unless appointments of this character are made, I fear there may be a collapse. Already in Congress and elsewhere among men who have some information there is a growing impression that the Commission is weak and inefficient. If any inquiry should be made I apprehend that there would come to light a condition of disorganization, failure to settle fundamental questions of policy and inability to dispatch business promptly. This would produce a very damaging impression. If the Trade Commission were discredited the effect would be not only to jeopardize a very promising experiment in the regulation of big business, but the whole idea of regulation by commission in other fields as well would suffer. The danger is that the public might condemn the idea as impracticable, losing sight of the fact that the failure was due to the incapacity of those who were charged with the duty of carrying it out.

The weakness of the Commission is most apparent on its legal side. The Commission has done very little in the way of clarifying or using its power to prevent unfair methods of competition. A large number of applications for action by it have accumulated since it was created and many matters and questions that ought to have been disposed of a year or more ago, are still pending. This is the principal reason why I urged the appointment of two thoroughly qualified lawyers rather than one lawyer and one business man. I know that there is a prejudice against lawyers and a feeling that the business world would be better satisfied if a conspicuous business man were appointed. This consideration, I believe, is heavily outweighed by the need of converting the Commission into an effective body capable of finding itself and of doing the work for which it was created.

At the outset the Commission had and it still has a number of very delicate fundamental legal problems to solve which no business man can deal with without guidance and which only lawyers of rather extraordinary flexibility of mind, soundness of judgment and large experience in business affairs can handle. The powers of the Commission are expressed in general terms, leaving their application entirely to the discretion of the Commission. The Commission must determine the limits of its jurisdiction. On the one hand it ought to avoid a useless invasion of the province of the courts by undertaking things which the courts do as well, if not better than the Commission could, and on the other hand it must avoid clashing with the Department of Justice. It must devise and apply a new method of procedure so as to exercise its quasi-judicial functions with the greatest promptness and certainty. It must so make up its records, findings and reports that they will bear scrutiny by the courts. In analyzing the results of its economic investigations and in recommending legislation to Congress it must be soundly advised in regard to existing law and must analyze and weigh the consequences of its proposals. These are all matters in regard to which a business man going on the Commission would have to rely for guidance upon experienced lawyers. He would not find such guidance in the Commission as it is now constituted, and however able he might be he would be likely to make mistakes which would serve as precedents and be difficult of correction. The Commission has to map out and chart a new field and then lay out its course. This work can only be done by a creative, imaginative lawyer versed in affairs. Mr. Justice Brandeis is an eminent example of the type of man to be sought. Another reason why two lawyers are needed on the Commission is that the Commission has no chief counsel and the limitation of salary imposed by Congress is such that no suitable man can be secured to serve as chief counsel.

You have asked me to suggest names. Under the law only one of the appointments can go to a Democrat.

Among the Republican lawyers whom I know one man is so much the best qualified for the place that I shall suggest no other. He is Edward B. Burling,[1] of Chicago. He is a Republican of the Progressive kind but has never been active in politics. He is a man of the highest character and standing at the Chicago Bar and has all the needed qualities—an open mind of the finest quality, good judgment, great legal ability, the right point of view, and long experience in large affairs. One of his clients, Mr. Cyrus McCormick is, I believe, a friend of the President. I know that Mr. McCormick would be very glad to give the President his opinion of Burling, both as a lawyer and as a man of business. Inquiry might also be made of Mr. Hurley, Mr. Charles Crane,

Mr. Walter Fisher,[2] Mr. Frank Scott[3] of Chicago, or of any prominent Chicago lawyer.

The Democratic names I have in mind are Mr. Raymond B. Stevens of New Hampshire and Mr. Edward F. McClennen, of Boston,[4] the ablest of Mr. Brandeis' former partners.

Mr. McClennen is a very able lawyer of high standing and reputation at the Boston Bar and has been long engaged in large business affairs. He is a thoroughly competent man and if he should accept the place it would only be from a wish to render public service. Mr. Justice Brandeis could tell the President all about him.

The President knows Mr. Stevens well. While he has not had the business experience of Burling and McClennen, he is so familiar with the Trade Commission Act, is so imbued with its spirit, is so able and fair, and has so proved his quality as Chief Examiner of the Commission that I believe him to be entirely qualified.          Sincerely yours,   George Rublee

TLS (WP, DLC).
  1 Edward Burnham Burling.
  2 Walter Lowrie Fisher, Secretary of the Interior, 1911-1913; now a lawyer of Chicago.
  3 Frank Hamline Scott, lawyer.
  4 Edward Francis McClennen.


Count Johann Heinrich von Bernstorff
to Theobald von Bethmann Hollweg

Washington, den 27. Januar 1917.
Ankunft: den 28. Januar 1917.

Nr. 239. Im Anschluß an Radiogramm Nr. 120 [60][1] und Telegramm Nr. 238.[2]

House bat mich spontan im Auftrage Wilsons, ihn zu besuchen und sagte mir das folgende als offiziellen Auftrag des Präsidenten:

Wilson anbietet zunächst vertraulich Friedensvermittelung auf Grund seiner Senatsbotschaft, d.h. also ohne Einmischung in territoriale Friedensbedingungen. Als *nicht* vertraulich betrachte Wilson sein gleichzeitig an uns gerichtetes Ersuchen um Mitteilung unserer Friedensbedingungen.

House entwickelte mir folgenden Gedankengang des Präsidenten: Unsere Feinde hätten ihre unmöglichen Friedensbedingungen offen ausgesprochen. Darauf habe Präsident in direktem Gegensatz hierzu sein Programm entwickelt. Nunmehr seien auch wir moralisch verpflichtet, unsere Bedingungen bekanntzugeben, weil unsere Friedensabsichten sonst als nicht ehrliche angesehen werden würden. Nachdem Euere Exzellenz Herrn Wilson mitgeteilt hätten, daß unsere Friedensbedingungen gemäßigte seien und daß wir auf die zweite Friedenskonferenz eingehen wollten,[3] glaube Präsident, daß er mit seiner Senatsbotschaft unseren Absichten entsprochen hätte.

Wilson hoffe, daß wir ihm Friedensbedingungen mitteilen würden, welche hier und in Deutschland veröffentlicht werden dürften, damit sie unbedingt in der ganzen Welt bekannt würden, wenn wir nur in ihn Vertrauen hätten, sei Präsident überzeugt, daß er dann die beiden Friedenskonferenzen erreichen könne. Er wäre besonders erfreut, wenn Euere Exzellenz gleichzeitig erklären wollten, daß wir bereit seien, auf der Basis seiner Senatsbotschaft in die Konferenzen einzutreten. Motivieren ließ sich unsere Erklärung dadurch, daß Wilson uns jetzt direkt um unsere Friedensbedingungen gebeten hat. Präsident meint, die an (Gruppe fehlt.) gerichtete Entente-Note braucht als Bluff nicht in Betracht gezogen zu werden. Er hoffe bestimmt, Friedenskonferenzen zustande zu bringen und zwar so schnell, daß unnötiges Blutvergießen der Frühjahrs-Offensiven verhindert werde.

Wie weit Euere Exzellenz Wilson entgegenkommen wollen und können, läßt sich von hier aus nicht beurteilen. Indeß bitte ich dringend, folgendes vortragen zu dürfen. Wenn jetzt ohne weiteres U-Bootkrieg begonnen wird, wird Präsident dies als Schlag ins Gesicht betrachten und Krieg mit den Vereinigten Staaten ist unvermeidlich. Hiesige Kriegspartei wird Oberhand gewinnen und Beendigung des Krieges m.E. unabsehbar sein, da Machtmittel der Vereiningten Staaten trotz allem, was man dagegen sagen kann, sehr groß sind. Andernfalls, wenn wir auf Wilsons Vorschlag eingehen, allein Pläne trotzdem an der Hartnäckigkeit unserer Gegner scheitern, wird es dem Präsidenten sehr schwer werden, gegen uns in den Krieg zu gehen, selbst wenn wir dann uneingeschränkten U-Bootkrieg anfangen. Es handelt sich also vorläufig nur um einen Aufschub von kurzer Dauer, um unsere diplomatische Stellung zu verbessern. Ich (2 Gruppen unverständlich.) mich allerdings zur Ansicht, daß wir jetzt durch Konferenzen einen besseren Frieden erreichen werden als wenn sich die Vereinigten Staaten unseren Feinden anschließen.

Da Kabelgramme stets mehrere Tage brauchen, bitte um umgehende drahtlose Weisung, falls telegraphischer Erlaß 157 am 1. Februar nicht auszuführen ist.          Bernstorff.

T telegram (Der Weltkrieg, No. 23, geheim, Die Friedensaktion der Zentralmächte, 4058/910778-80, GFO-Ar).

¹ The number of this radiogram was corrected in the journal of messages received. See André Scherer and Jacques Grunewald, eds., *L'Allemagne et les Problèmes de la Paix* (2 vols., Paris, 1962-66), I, 684. Telegram No. 60, January 26, was in reply to Bethmann Hollweg's telegram 157, January 16, which instructed Bernstorff to tell the American government on February 1, 1917, that Germany was introducing unrestricted submarine warfare. Telegram No. 60, transmitted in English, reads as follows: "Your 157, most urgent! After having had very important conference request most urgently postponement till my next two messages received. Suggest reply by wireless." Wilhelm A. von Stumm, Under State Secretary, replied to telegram No. 60 in Berlin's telegram No. 63, January 29, "Regret postponement impracticable." These telegrams are printed in the collection of hearings of the German Constituent National Assembly, *Die Deutsche Nationalversammlung im Jahre 1919/20: Beilagen zu den Stenographischen Berichten über die öffentlichen Verhandlungen des Untersuchungsausschusses der Verfassunggebenden Deutschen Nationalversammlung. 2. Unterausschuß. Beilage 1, Aktenstücke zur Friedensaktion Wilsons 1916/17* (Berlin, 1919), p. 72 (Doc. No. 68), and p. 74 (Doc. No. 70).

² It was a shorter version of telegram No. 239; for the text, see *ibid.*, p. 76 (Doc. No. 73).

³ Bernstorff had conveyed this information in the conversation reported in his telegram No. 212, January 16, 1917, on the basis of Zimmermann's instruction described in n. 1 to that telegram. Bernstorff's telegram is printed at Jan. 16, 1917, Vol. 40.

T R A N S L A T I O N

Washington, January 27, 1917.
Received: January 28, 1917.

No. 239. Further to Radiogram No. 120 [60] and Telegram No. 238.

On behalf of Wilson, House, without prior arrangement, invited me to visit him and told me the following as the President's official message:

Wilson offers, in the first place, confidential mediation for peace on the basis of his message to the Senate, i.e., accordingly, without becoming involved in the territorial conditions of peace. Wilson regards as *not* confidential his simultaneous efforts directed at us to reveal our peace conditions.

House set forth for me the President's train of thought as follows: Our (Germany's) enemies have publicly expressed their impossible peace conditions. The President has developed his program in direct opposition to this. Now we too are under moral obligation to state our conditions, for otherwise our peace aims will be seen as not honorable. After Your Excellency told Mr. Wilson that our peace conditions were moderate and that we were willing to participate in the second peace conference, the President believes that with his message to the Senate he has met our aims.

Wilson hopes that we will impart to him our peace conditions, which could be published here and in Germany, so that they could be known unconditionally throughout the world. The President is convinced that, if we just will confide in him, he can then achieve both peace conferences. He would be especially pleased if, at the same time, Your Excellency would declare our readiness to take part in the conferences on the basis of his message to the Senate. The reason given for our declaration would be that Wilson has now asked us directly for our peace conditions. The President believes that the Entente's note addressed to [him?], being a bluff, need not be taken into account. He certainly hopes to bring about the peace conferences and, indeed, quickly enough to prevent unnecessary bloodshed in the spring offensives.

From here we cannot judge how far Your Excellency is willing and able to go to meet Wilson. However, I urgently request permission to express the following. If submarine warfare is now begun without further ado, the President will take this as a slap in the face and war with the United States cannot be avoided. The war party in this country will gain the upper hand and in my view the end of the war will be unforeseeable, because—despite all that can be said to the contrary—the power and resources of the United States are very great. On the other hand, if we accept Wilson's proposal, and if, nevertheless, the plans then break down through the obstinacy of our enemies, the President will find it very hard to go to war against us, even if at that time we were to begin unrestricted submarine warfare. For the present, then, it is only a matter of a short delay in order to improve our diplomatic position. In any case I [hold] the view that we shall attain a better peace through the conferences than if the United States joins our enemies.

Since cablegrams regularly require several days, I request an immediate instruction by wireless, in case telegraphic instruction No. 157 is not to be carried out on February 1.

Bernstorff


## A Veto Message

The White House,

*To the House of Representatives:*          *January 29, 1917.*

I very much regret to return this bill (H.R. 10384, "An act to regulate the immigration of aliens to, and the residence of aliens in, the United States") without my signature. In most of the provisions of the bill I should be very glad to concur, but I can not rid myself of the conviction that the literacy test constitutes a radical change in the policy of the Nation which is not justified in principle. It is not a test of character, of quality, or of personal fitness, but would operate in most cases merely as a penalty for lack of opportunity in the country from which the alien seeking admission came. The opportunity to gain an education is in many cases one of the chief opportunities sought by the immigrant in coming to the United States, and our experience in the past has not been that the illiterate immigrant is as such an undesirable immigrant. Tests of quality and of purpose can not be objected to on principle, but tests of opportunity surely may be.

Moreover, even if this test might be equitably insisted on, one of the exceptions proposed to its application involves a provision which might lead to very delicate and hazardous diplomatic situations. The bill exempts from the operation of the literacy test "all aliens who shall prove *to the satisfaction of the proper immigration officer or to the Secretary of Labor* that they are seeking admission to the United States to avoid religious persecution in the country of their last permanent residence, whether such persecution be evidenced by overt acts or by laws or governmental regulations that discriminate against the alien or the race to which he belongs because of his religious faith." Such a provision, so applied and administered, would oblige the officer concerned in effect to pass judgment upon the laws and practices of a foreign Government and declare that they did or did not constitute religious persecution. This would, to say the least, be a most invidious function for any administrative officer of this Government to perform, and it is not only possible but probable that very serious questions of international justice and comity would arise between this Government and the Government or Governments thus officially condemned should its exercise be attempted. I dare say that these consequences were not in the minds of the proponents of this provision but the provision separately and in itself renders it unwise for me to give my assent to this legislation in its present form.                    Woodrow Wilson.[1]

Printed in *Message from the President of the United States* . . . (Washington, 1917).
[1] There is a WWsh draft of this message in WP, DLC.

## From William Charles Adamson

Washington, D. C.

Dear Mr. President:                    January [29] 30, 1917.

Considering the intense and patriotic interest that you manifest in the situation I think you ought to know every material thing that happens. For fear you don't get it straight I want to write you exactly what occurred at Philadelphia in the conclusion of the debate Saturday night between the Railroad Brotherhoods and the other side. Mr. Frank Trumbull, Chairman of the Association of Railroad Organizations, and Mr. Lee, one of the members of his Organization, were present and debated the cause of the Managers and Presidents. Mr. W. G. Lee and Mr. Stone represented the Brotherhoods. I presided over the meeting and prevented unpleasantness by diffusing a lot of humor throughout the proceedings and had a very good meeting.

Just before adjournment Mr. W. G. Lee arose and called me as the presiding officer and Chairman of the Committee on Interstate and Foreign Commerce to witness that he offered to Mr. Trumbull and the Railroad Companies the following Proposition—"The Brotherhoods will guarantee that there shall never be another strike, nor any further trouble on their part, if the Railroad Companies will agree to submit the whole matter to the President, all agreeing to do just what the President suggests in adjusting the matter, and the Brotherhoods will faithfully do just what the President concludes."

There was no reply from the railroad officials. Just what bearing this will have on the situation you can judge as well as I can, but it appears to me that unless the Railroad Companies make a proper response it will prejudice them very much in the eye of the public, because everybody knows that you could adjust this matter in twenty-four hours if they would submit it to you.

With high regards and best wishes, I remain,

Yours truly,   W C Adamson

TLS (WP, DLC).

## To William Charles Adamson

My dear Judge:          [The White House] 29 January, 1917

Your letter just received has given me a great deal to think about. That certainly was a most extraordinary incident at Philadelphia and it is to me very significant indeed that the gentlemen representing the railway managements did not respond to Mr. W. G. Lee's offer, which was extraordinarily generous and, I should have supposed, perfectly safe to both sides.

Thank you very warmly for letting me know about it.

Cordially and sincerely yours,   Woodrow Wilson

TLS (Letterpress Books, WP, DLC).

## To Charles William Eliot

My dear Doctor Eliot:        [The White House] 29 January, 1917

I am taking the liberty of writing to you as one of the trustees of the Carnegie Foundation for Peace to ask whether it would or would not in your opinion be possible and wise to get the consent of the Foundation to back my recent address to the Senate up with a systematic propagation of the ideas and the implicit programme which it embodies.

I feel that the task of the moment is the rousing of a great body of opinion to very definite thought and purpose, not only in this country but in the countries most immediately involved in the present terrible struggle, and it has occurred not only to me but to many who have spoken to me that the Carnegie Endowment might at the present moment find a very great opportunity.[1]

Cordially and sincerely yours,   [Woodrow Wilson]

CCL (WP, DLC).

[1] Wilson wrote much the same letter, *mutatis mutandis*, to several other trustees of the Carnegie Endowment for International Peace—Cleveland H. Dodge, Oscar S. Straus, John Sharp Williams, John W. Foster, Samuel Mather, Andrew J. Montague, and George Gray. He also wrote to Secretary Houston and asked him to use his influence with Robert S. Brookings, also a trustee.

## To John Palmer Gavit

My dear Gavit:        [The White House] 29 January, 1917

Your letter of the twenty-sixth has cheered me very much and I thank you for it from a full heart. The real people I was speaking to was neither the Senate nor foreign governments, as you will realize, but the *people* of the countries now at war.

I am very sorry indeed to hear that you have not been well. Take care of yourself and stay until you come back really cured.

Cordially and faithfully yours,   Woodrow Wilson

TLS (Letterpress Books, WP, DLC).

## To Atlee Pomerene

My dear Senator:        [The White House] 29 January, 1917

Again I have gone very thoroughly into the question of the District Judgeship in Ohio and this is the result:

There is, I think, no choice between Mr. Young[1] and Mr. Westenhaver,[2] and perhaps very little choice between Mr. Young and Mr. Leighley,[3] on the score of legal equipment and ability as a practicing lawyer, but the more I inquire about these gentle-

men the more clear it becomes to me that the real *progressive* of
the three is Mr. Westenhaver. If he has faults of temperament,
I feel that we ought to risk them rather than continue the stiff-
ness of the federal courts with regard to forward-looking measures and hopeful changes in the point of view of the law.

I need not say that I am not saying this as any criticism on the
character of either Mr. Young or Mr. Leighley. I know just the
type they belong to, because I have been associated with such
men very often. Their minds have been trained by their practice
and by their associations, and they are conscientious conservatives. I cannot quarrel with their opinions, nor even with their
attitude, but I do feel that it is my duty to prefer another sort in
appointments of this kind at this time.

With warmest regard,

Cordially and sincerely yours,   Woodrow Wilson

TLS (Letterpress Books, WP, DLC).
[1] William Elmore Young, lawyer of Akron.
[2] David Courtney Westenhaver, lawyer of Cleveland.
[3] Per Lee Alvin Lieghley, not Leighley, judge of the Court of Common Pleas,
Cleveland.

## From Norman Hapgood

Dear Mr. President:                    London, W. Jan 29 [1917]

The inclosed report is sent, as you will see, at Professor
Masaryk's[1] request. He is the leader of the Independent Bohemia
party and is now under sentence of death. He it was who proved
that the documents adduced to prove the complicity of the Serbian Government in the plots alleged in the Friedjung trial[2] were
forgeries. I myself am not for an independent Bohemia, but I
think Professor Masaryk deserves a hearing. I inclose also their
map.

The leader of the Poles here, Mr. Dmowsky,[3] wants to unite
Bohemia with Poland.

Mr. Seton-Watson[4] thinks the only relation between Bohemia
and Poland should be mere[ly] an arrangement that will give
Bohemia access to open water.

Other high authorities on Austria and the Balkans, such as
George Young[5] and Noel Buxton, favor merely local autonomy
for Bohemia, without breaking up the Empire.

Probably you know that the French, who wrote the reply of the
allies to you, put in the words Chekho-Slovaks afterward, in order

to bring in the question of Bohemia without letting most Americans know what they were doing.

Hoping you are feeling very well indeed

Yours sincerely　Norman Hapgood

ALS (WP, DLC).

1 Tomáš Garrigue Masaryk, born March 7, 1850, in Hodonín, Moravia. Educated at the Universities of Vienna (Ph.D., 1876) and Leipzig. Married Charlotte Garrigue of Brooklyn, N. Y., in 1878 and adopted her surname as his middle name. Professor of Philosophy at the Czech University of Prague, 1882-1914. Author of important scholarly books on such diverse subjects as the sociology of suicide, Marxist theory, and Russian thought. Masaryk gradually became a publicist for and leader of the Czech and Slovak nationalist movements and an inspirational leader of other minority groups within the Austro-Hungarian Empire. Deputy in the Austrian Reichsrat, 1891-1893 and 1907-1914. Spent four months on a lecture tour of the United States in 1902 under the auspices of Charles R. Crane. Went into exile shortly after the outbreak of the First World War. At this time, Masaryk was in London and was chairman of the Czechoslovak National Council and a lecturer at King's College. Standard biographies of Masaryk are Paul Selver, *Masaryk: A Biography* (London, 1940), and Edward Polson Newman, *Masaryk* (London, 1960). A good summary of Masaryk's London years by a close friend is Robert W. Seton-Watson, *Masaryk in England* (Cambridge and New York, 1943).

The enclosed "report" (accompanied by T. G. Masaryk to N. Hapgood, Jan. 27, 1917, ALS [WP, DLC]) was Tomáš G. Masaryk, *At the Eleventh Hour: A Memorandum on the Military Situation* (London, 1916). This pamphlet carried the notation "Strictly Confidential" on the title page and the date "7th January 1916" in the preface. Masaryk discussed the military situation and strength of the Central Powers as compared to that of the Allies. He concluded that the alliance dominated by Germany was in many respects stronger and certainly more unified in purpose than the rather loose coalition of the Entente. The war and the future of Europe would be decided on the battlefield. Hence, the Allies, in order to win, would have to provide far more manpower to their armies than heretofore. However, they also needed something else totally lacking at present—a grand plan for the future of Europe to match the Pan-German *Drang nach Osten*. Masaryk argued that the Allies' grand plan should be to establish viable independent Polish, Bohemian, and southern Slavic states to serve as buffers against Germany. The full text of *At the Eleventh Hour* is reprinted in Seton-Watson, *op. cit.*, pp. 153-202.

2 Heinrich Friedjung, an eminent Austrian historian and publicist, published in the Vienna *Neue Freie Presse*, March 24, 1909, an article which said that certain Croatian and Serbian political leaders within the Austro-Hungarian Empire had conspired with the government of Serbia to create a greater Serbian state. The persons implicated brought a libel suit against Friedjung. In a sensational trial in Vienna in December 1909, abundant evidence and expert testimony revealed that the documents on which Friedjung had based his article were blatant forgeries; even Friedjung himself was driven to admit in court that some of them were fraudulent. Friedjung refused to state the source of the documents, but it had been clear from the beginning that they could have come only from the Austrian Foreign Ministry, and many observers believed that the then Foreign Minister, Count Alois Aehrenthal, was personally involved. Masaryk, an authority on Slavonic languages, testified as an expert against the authenticity of the documents. The most thorough study of this affair remains Robert W. Seton-Watson, *The Southern Slav Question and the Habsburg Monarchy* (London, 1911), pp. 200, 202-206, 209-87. More concise accounts appear in Selver, *op. cit.*, pp. 220, 224-33, and in Arthur J. May, *The Hapsburg Monarchy, 1867-1914* (Cambridge, Mass., 1951), pp. 384-85.

3 Roman Dmowski, leader of the National Democratic party, a right-wing Polish nationalist organization.

4 Robert William Seton-Watson, the leading English-language authority on the politics and history of the Austro-Hungarian Empire and its constituent national groups.

5 George Young (1872-1952), former career diplomat, at this time involved in intelligence work in the British Admiralty; author of *Nationalism and War in the Near East* (Oxford, 1915).

## From Thomas Davies Jones

My dear Mr. President:                    Chicago January 29, 1917.

I am very deeply gratified to receive your letter of the 26th instant, and I wish I could feel that I am free to accept the offer. Let me tell you very briefly the obstacles:

There is the stiffest kind of work ahead of the Tariff Commission. While I do not feel the encroachments of age, the calendar tells me that those encroachments cannot be far off. Anything like thoroughgoing work on details of costs, on schedules, tariffs and rates has always cost me an inordinate amount of labor. My mind never has worked freely on that sort of thing. I am not advancing the plea of laziness, but lack of adaptability to a certain class of work, which grows upon me with age. The work of that Commission, if it be well done, will involve familiarizing oneself with a multiplicity of details which cannot safely be relegated to subordinates. You do not need to be told that it is through subordinates that sinister influences usually get in their work.

My other difficulty is also a personal one and is rather serious. You will take it for granted that any one accepting a position on that Commission would divest himself absolutely of all connection of every sort with business interests to which the tariff is a consideration, however slight. No matter what the formal requirements of the position may be, I would not consider the acceptance of the place on any other basis. I have been for over thirty years up to my neck in zinc business. So far as official connection is concerned, either as director or as an officer of the New Jersey Zinc Company or its subordinates, the matter would be quite simple, because I have not been active in the business for many years, but the bulk of whatever property I have accumulated is involved in zinc, and unfortunately the zinc business is rather a narrow specialty and there is no real market for zinc stock, and I simply could not divest myself of my interest without affecting the welfare of others whose welfare is to me a matter of real importance. I do not want to overemphasize this difficulty. I think I am capable of putting aside such considerations if they alone stood in the way of performing needed, important public service, and if I felt that I had any special aptitude for the service to be performed. The first of the reasons above given is to my mind the decisive reason.

The possibility of a contest over my confirmation would not weigh with me in the slightest. I would be sorry to involve you in another controversy, but that is a matter which you have evidently considered. But for reasons which I have above briefly stated, I feel that I ought to decline the offer which you so kindly make.

I can honestly say that I appreciate your opinion of me which has led you to offer me this very important position more highly than the distinctions of office.

Faithfully yours,   Thomas D. Jones

TLS (WP, DLC).


## Theobald von Bethmann Hollweg to Count Johann Heinrich von Bernstorff[1]

Berlin, den 29. Januar 1917.

65. Antwort auf Telegramm 239. Bitte dem Präsidenten Dank Kaiserlicher Regierung für seine Mitteilung aussprechen. Wir bringen ihm volles Vertrauen entgegen und bitten ihn, dasselbe auch uns zu schenken. Deutschland ist bereit, die von ihm vertraulich angebotene Vermittlung zur Herbeiführung einer direkten Konferenz der Kriegführenden anzunehmen und wird seinen Verbündeten das gleiche empfehlen. Wir bitten unsere Annahme ebenso wie das Angebot ganz vertraulich zu behandeln.

Öffentliche Bekanntgabe unserer Friedensbedingungen ist jetzt unmöglich, nachdem die Entente Friedensbedingungen publiziert hat, die auf Entehrung und Vernichtung Deutschlands und seiner Bundesgenossen hinauslaufen und vom Präsidenten selbst als unmöglich bezeichnet werden. Als Bluff können wir sie nicht auffassen, da sie vollkommen mit den Reden übereinstimmen, die feindliche Machthaber nicht nur vorher sondern auch nachher gehalten haben, und sich genau mit Zielen decken, um derentwillen Italien und Rumänien überhaupt in Krieg eingetreten sind, auch was die Türkei anlangt den von England und Frankreich vertraglich an Rußland gemachten Zusicherungen entsprechen. So lange diese Kriegsziele unserer Gegner öffentlich aufrecht erhalten werden, würde öffentliche Bekanntgabe unserer Friedensbedingungen als Zeichen nicht vorhandener Schwäche unvertretbar sein und nur zur Verlängerung des Krieges beitragen. Um Präsidenten Wilson einen Beweis unseres Vertrauens zu geben, teilen wir ihm, jedoch ganz ausschließlich für seine Person hiermit die Bedingungen mit, unter denen wir bereit gewesen *wären* in Friedensverhandlungen einzutreten,

falls die Entente unser Friedensangebot vom 12. Dezember v. J.
angenommen hätte:

"Rückerstattung des von Frankreich besetzten Teils von
Oberelsaß.

Gewinnung einer Deutschland und Polen gegen Rußland
strategisch und wirtschaftlich sichernden Grenze.

Koloniale Restitution in Form einer Verständigung, die
Deutschland einen seiner Bevölkerungszahl und der Bedeutung
seiner wirtschaftlichen Interessen entsprechenden Kolonial-
besitz sichert.

Rückgabe der von Deutschland besetzten französischen
Gebiete unter Vorbehalt strategischer und wirtschaftlicher Grenz-
berichtigungen sowie finanzieller Kompensationen.

Wiederherstellung Belgiens unter bestimmten Garantien für
die Sicherheit Deutschlands, welche durch Verhandlungen mit
der belgischen Regierung festzustellen wären.

Wirtschaftlicher und finanzieller Ausgleich auf der Grundlage
des Austausches der beiderseits eroberten und im Friedensschluß zu restituierenden Gebiete.

Schadloshaltung der durch den Krieg geschädigten deutschen
Unternehmungen und Privatpersonen.

Verzicht auf alle wirtschaftlichen Abmachungen und Maßnah-
men, welche ein Hindernis für den normalen Handel und Ver-
kehr nach Friedensschluß bilden würden, unter Abschluß entspre-
chender Handelsverträge.

Sicherstellung der Freiheit der Meere.[2]

Die Friedensbedingungen unserer Verbündeten bewegten sich,
in Übereinstimmung mit unseren Anschauungen, in gleich
mäßigen Grenzen.

Wir sind ferner bereit, auf der Basis der Senatsbotschaft des
Präsidenten Wilson in die von ihm nach Beendigung des Krieges
angestrebte Internationale Konferenz einzutreten."

Euere Exzellenz wollen dem Präsidenten diese Mitteilungen
bei Übergabe der Note über den verschärften Ubootkrieg[3] machen
und gleichzeitig folgendes bemerken:

Wenn sein Angebot nur wenige Tage vorher erfolgt wäre, hätten wir den Beginn des neuen Ubootkrieges vertagen können.
Jetzt sei es hierzu trotz bester Dispositionen aus technischen
Gründen leider zu spät, da umfassende militärische Vorberei-
tungen getroffen, die nicht mehr rückgängig zu machen und
Uboote mit neuen Instruktionen bereits ausgelaufen seien. Form
und Inhalt der feindlichen Antwortnote auf unser Friedensangebot und die Note des Präsidenten seien derart schroff gewesen,
daß wir angesichts des uns auf's neue angekündigten Kampfes

auf Leben und Tod die Anwendung des besten zu schneller Kriegsbeendigung geeigneten Mittels nicht mehr hinausschieben und Verzicht darauf vor unserem eigenen Volke nicht hätten verantworten können!

Wie die Instruktion wegen verschärften Ubootskrieges ergibt, sind wir jederzeit bereit, den Bedürfnissen Amerika's nach aller Möglichkeit Rechnung zu tragen. Wir bäten den Präsidenten, seine Bemühungen trotzdem aufzunehmen respektive fortzusetzen und erklärten uns zur Einstellung des verschärften Ubootkrieges bereits, sobald volle Sicherheit dafür geboten sei, daß die Bemuhüngen des Präsidenten zu einem für uns annehmbaren Frieden führen würden.          gez. von Bethmann Hollweg.

T telegram (Der Weltkrieg, No. 23, geheim, Die Friedensaktion der Zentralmächte, 4058/910835-9, GFO-Ar).

1 Bethmann Hollweg had been excited by the renewed hope of peace held out by Bernstorff's dispatch No. 239. However, Emperor William and his military advisers were not at all enthusiastic, and, in an Imperial Conference at Pless on January 29, they informed Bethmann that the intensified submarine campaign had to go forward. Nevertheless, they permitted Bethmann to send the following telegram. See Link, Campaigns for Progressivism and Peace, pp. 284-88.

2 It should be noted here that, as recently as January 4, Bethmann Hollweg had included much more severe terms of peace in a draft of instructions to Bernstorff which he discarded in favor of a more generalized document prepared by the Foreign Office. Ibid., pp. 255-56.

3 See the two memoranda printed as part of the Enclosure with RL to WW, Jan. 31, 1917.

T R A N S L A T I O N

Berlin, January 29, 1917.

65. Reply to Telegram 239. Please express to the President the thanks of the Imperial Government for his message. We offer him complete trust and ask him to grant us the same. Germany is ready to accept the mediation he offers in confidence for bringing about a direct conference of the belligerents and will recommend the same course to its allies. We ask that our acceptance be treated in strictest confidence just as the offer itself.

Public announcement of our peace conditions is now impossible, after the Entente has publicized its peace conditions, which amount to the dishonor and destruction of Germany and its allies, and which the President himself has characterized as impossible. We cannot regard them as a bluff, for they agree completely with the speeches of the enemy rulers both before and after; they coincide in general with the aims for which Italy and Rumania have entered the war; and, as regards Turkey, they correspond also to the assurances granted by treaty to Russia by England and France. So long as these war aims of our enemies are openly maintained, open publication of our peace conditions would be unwarrantable as a sign of a weakness that does not exist, and this would only prolong the war. To give President Wilson a sign of our trust, we now state—but exclusively for him personally— the conditions under which we *would have been* ready to undertake peace negotiations, had the Entente accepted our peace offer of December 12 of last year:

Restitution of the portion of Upper Alsace occupied by France.

Establishment of a strategically and economically secure frontier of Germany and Poland against Russia.

Colonial restitution in the form of an understanding that Germany is to secure colonial possessions in keeping with the numbers of its population and the importance of its economic interests.

Return of the French territory occupied by Germany with the proviso that there be strategic and economic boundary rectifications as well as financial compensations.

Restoration of Belgium under specific guarantees for Germany's security, to be determined through negotiations with the Belgian government.

An economic and financial settlement based on exchange of the territories which were conquered by both sides and are subject to restitution on the conclusion of peace.

Compensation for German firms and private persons damaged by the war.

Renunciation of all economic arrangements and measures which, after peace is established, would pose obstacles to normal trade and traffic; this to be achieved by concluding appropriate trade treaties.

Guarantee of the freedom of the seas.

The peace conditions of our allies, in agreement with our conceptions, fall within equally moderate limits.

We are ready, moreover, on the basis of President Wilson's message to the Senate, to enter into the international conference he is working for to follow the end of the war.

Your Excellency will give the President this information when you present the note about the intensified submarine warfare, and will at the same time state the following:

If his offer had come only a few days earlier, we could have delayed the onset of the new submarine war. Now, unfortunately, despite best intentions, it is for technical reasons too late, because comprehensive military preparations that cannot be recalled have gone into effect, and submarines have already gone out with new instructions. The form and content of the enemy notes in reply to our peace offer and to the President's note were so harsh that—in view of the life and death struggle declared anew against us—we can no longer put off using the best means for ending the war quickly, nor can we be responsible to our own people for failing to use them.

As the instruction on intensified submarine warfare points out, we are always ready to make allowance for American needs as far as possible. We ask the President, despite everything, to resume or continue his efforts, and we declare ourselves ready to discontinue the intensified submarine warfare as soon as we can be sure that the President's efforts will bring a peace acceptable to us.                    Bethmann Hollweg

## Remarks at a Press Conference

January 30, 1917

Mr. President, have you selected a new successor for Mr. Martin[1] as Vice-Governor of the Philippines?

No, I haven't found a man.

The report is published this morning that Governor Harrison was to resign, and that Governor Glenn[2] was to succeed him?

That is made up. I know nothing of either. I have seen in the papers, and I think a friend of Governor Harrison told me, that he was likely to resign because he felt that he had been there as long as the situation justified. I haven't received any communication from him.

Have you received a communication for a six months' leave from him?

Yes, I believe that has been received. I am not sure of that, but I think that that is true. He is certainly entitled to it by this time.

Have you started on your Inaugural Address yet?

No, I have got to sit up all night soon, some time, to do that.

Mr. President, will it be a short one similar to the one you delivered last time?

[1] Henderson S. Martin, of Kansas, who had just resigned. Martin, a lawyer of Marion, had managed the Democratic campaign in Kansas in 1912. Wilson, after the election of 1912, was reported to have spoken of Martin to a member of the Kansas delegation in Congress as follows: "There is a tall, black-haired young fellow out in your state. I can't remember his name but he told me to lay off Roosevelt or I would lose Kansas. I did as he told me and I carried Kansas. Get him in here. I think I can use him." Shortly thereafter, Wilson appointed Martin as Vice-Governor of the Philippines. Kansas City *Times*, July 11, 1935.

[2] Robert Brodnax Glenn, Governor of North Carolina, 1905-1909.

I honestly don't know. I haven't thought about it one way
or the other.

Mr. President, can you give us a clear insight into the legislative
situation?

I wish I could, Mr. Oulahan.[3] I don't know the details of it.
So far as one can judge in the interpretation of things, it is
going as well as could be expected.

Aren't they rather banking on the supposition up there that you
are not disposed to call an extraordinary session of Congress
and have taken advantage of that?

I don't think so, because I haven't told anybody I felt that
way. The way I feel about an extra session depends entirely
upon what is done at this session, so I am suspending judgment.

You wouldn't like to take us more fully into your confidence?

I am not taking you because I can't make up my mind one
way or the other until I see whether the horse is before the
cart.

Is the proposed railroad program working out toward a compromise?

I think not. It is working out towards an act.

Towards an act. Towards the lines you want?

Essentially as I suggested.

Mr. President, your world peace league plan you unfolded to the
Senate seems to give the United States a certain interest in the
possible future quarrels of Europe. It occurred to me that if the
European nations would be given a reciprocal interest—

My dear boy, do you suppose I am going to tell an answer?
If you want to find out, attend the conference that brings
this thing about. I don't know anything about it.

Mr. President, it has been published that we have sent to some
Latin American countries a new trade treaty as a result of the
financial conference. The story is printed yesterday.

That may be so. I don't know of it. That may have been done
in a regular diplomatic conference to clear up doubts and
points, but I really know nothing about it. If so, it is probably
just details that need clarification.

Has any progress been made, Mr. President, in the oil leasing
situation?

I don't see any. I wish I did. Things are tied up on that just
about as badly as on anything that has been discussed, be-

[3] Richard Victor Oulahan, chief Washington correspondent of the *New York
Times*.

cause there are wide differences of view—very genuine differences. And I haven't seen any common ground yet myself.
Is it a subject on which you could express a view?

> I might express one after I have one that would be service-
> able, but I haven't been able to see the way out myself.

The Secretary of the Navy seems to be thoroughly convinced of
the vital interests of the navy in the situation.

> There is no doubt about that. The navy has the most vital
> interest.

And he takes the view that there has been found no means by
substitution to protect those interests. It must be in California or
not at all?

> Well, of course, it is only in those fields that we know just
> what we are dealing with. The other fields are undeveloped,
> if they exist. And the Secretary of the Navy's feeling is that
> the navy is not so much interested in getting a royalty in the
> shape of money on oil as in knowing that there is a reserve
> of oil in the earth for future development, because our navy
> has not been equipped to burn oil to any great extent yet.

That necessity has impressed itself upon you?

> I think it is very obvious, yes. But that, unfortunately, does
> not settle this leasing question, because the leasing arrange-
> ments ought to go through, and yet the navy's interest ought
> also to be safeguarded.

Mr. President, have you found a tariff board yet—all the members?

> To tell the truth, I have had several declinations. That is
> what is holding me up. You see, as I explained once before,
> it is asking a good deal of the type of man I want to give
> up his other business connections and come here on $7,500
> a year.

Mr. President, has Ambassador Fletcher been ordered to his post
yet?

> I believe not.

Do you contemplate sending him?

> I believe very soon, yes.

Has the Department of Justice reported, Mr. President, on the
equities of these various claims?

> No, it has not. It has intimated to me that it would take a
> microscope to find them, but that is only my conclusion.
> That is not what they have said. They have not reported at
> all.

Mr. President, there is a story being printed today that there is some kind of negotiation or communication passing between the State Department and the German government with reference to arming merchant vessels.[4]

> There are no communications passing about that just now.

Or with the British government?

> Or with the British government.

The armed ship question is one which you can't discuss?

> No, it is not. It is a very complicated question, to tell the truth.

Could you tell us whether you are contemplating making any pronouncement as to the government's policy in the future on that question?

> No, except in the sense that it will, in time, become a practical question.

But no announcement would be made until a definite occasion?

> No, I suppose not. I really hadn't answered that question even in my own mind.

Mr. President, have you found a successor for Mr. Baker as a member of the shipping board?

> No, I haven't. Of course that took me very much by surprise, and I haven't had time to look around yet. . . .

Mr. President, on the proposals of the brotherhoods, with reference to a commission which will investigate grievances in the railroad program, have you given that act a thought?

> Yes, I have given that act and all the other suggestions that have been made—I have just put them all before the two committees of the Senate and House and asked their advice about them, and I haven't received it yet.

Mr. President, Judge Adamson told me that, if a representative of the public were added to such a commission, it would meet with his approval. Would it meet with yours?

> I didn't get that impression from my conversation with him. Of course, that wouldn't amount to anything. It would simply mean that they meet here to decide anything. My idea, instead of having representatives of the two sides and then appoint an umpire between them, would be just to appoint an umpire by himself to begin with. That is just a snap, horseback judgment.

Mr. President, will you have occasion to do anything further about the increase of salaries of government employees?

> The committee of the employees visited me yesterday at the Capitol and presented a very formidable looking petition. I haven't had time to examine it yet, except the language. All

---

[4] About this issue, see RL to WW, Jan. 12, 1917, Vol. 40.

the signatures I have examined. And it is largely, I understand—everybody understands—a matter of finance. With
the tremendously increased expenditures of the government,
it is a very serious matter whether we could finance a general increase.

You would, as I understand, favor an increase of the smaller
salaried men?

That depends on the budget, whether I would or would not.
I have to be a housekeeper.

They seem to have reported something of that sort.

No, I told them that, having lived on a salary myself, I understood the situation they were in, and that I would give
it, of course, my most friendly consideration.

Some of us would like to get your help along the same line.

I told them that, once, a committee of a bankers association
asked me to address them on the elasticity of the currency,
and I told them I supposed they assumed me an expert, but
I knew how elastic it was from personal experience.[5]

Mr. President, we are still very much interested in the New York
Post Office.

So am I.

Have you taken the matter up lately?

No, I haven't. I am thinking of hiring another man besides
mine. I haven't got enough.

Senator Lewis is worrying a good deal about the Chicago and
New York offices.

Yes. I worried about it so much, perhaps he can take it off
my mind.

Will the new government down in Costa Rica be recognized?[6]

I don't know the circumstances there enough to answer that.

Mr. President, is there any information you wish to describe to
us that we haven't touched on this morning?

No, I think not.

Mr. President, can you say anything about the cabinet? There
was a story yesterday that four members would not be in the
cabinet after March fourth.

All that is "guff." I don't know who is interesting himself in
that, but it is "guff."

Does that apply also to the Diplomatic Corps?

In general terms, yes. Somebody is trying very hard to get

[5] In an address to the New York State Bankers' Association. See the news
report printed at Dec. 19, 1902, Vol. 14; also the address, "The Banker and the
Nation," printed at Sept. 30, 1908, Vol. 18.
[6] About this matter, see RL to WW, Feb. 7, 1917.

the Secretary of State out of the cabinet. I don't know who
that somebody is, tending to business which is not his own.

JRT transcript (WC, NjP) of CLSsh (C. L. Swem Coll., NjP).

## To Edward Albert Filene[1]

My dear Mr. Filene:          [The White House] 30 January, 1917

Your letter of the twenty-ninth[2] interests me and gratifies me
very much. I think that the work that you have been doing ought
to yield very valuable fruit.

The only thing I have to suggest is that I think that it would be
a mistake, so far as our influence in the foreign countries is concerned, to press for any particular plan. I have carefully put forth
only the idea, no particulars, with the feeling that it could be best
achieved by leaving the whole question of organization and detail
to the international conference which I hope will some day meet
to determine the ways and means of concerted action in the support of peace. If we leave this field clear, we can hope for the
ultimate acceptance of the idea and still have the most favorable
possible atmosphere. At present the opponents of the measure are
rejoicing in setting up men of straw and knocking them down,
and all the men of straw are particular plans and details.

Cordially and sincerely yours,   Woodrow Wilson

TLS (Letterpress Books, WP, DLC).
  1 Merchant, reformer, and philanthropist of Boston.
  2 Filene's letter is missing.

## To Joseph Patrick Tumulty

Dear Tumulty:          [The White House, Jan. 30, 1917]

I doubt very much whether it would be wise to do this.[1] I
think that if the Poles begin to congratulate me on this matter in
this public fashion, it would create the impression that I believe
the whole thing is likely to be settled by our dictum or influence.
I would very much like the intimation conveyed to them that,
deeply as I appreciate their desire, I believe that their cause can
be served best by postponing interviews of this sort.

The President.

TL (WP, DLC).
  1 I. V. Stanley Stanislaus to JPT, Jan. 27, 1917, TLS (WP, DLC). Ignatius
Valerius Stanley Stanislaus, a chemist of Philadelphia, requested an "audience"
with Wilson at which representatives of the Polish National Defence Committee would present a "Memorandum endorsing the President's position made
public in his memorable speech to the United States Senate."

## To David Lawrence

My dear Lawrence:          [The White House] 30 January, 1917

Your letter of January twenty-first has given me a great deal to think about and I thank you for it sincerely. I hope you will always feel free to suggest.

In haste          Cordially yours,   Woodrow Wilson

TLS (Letterpress Books, WP, DLC).

## To Franklin Knight Lane

My dear Mr. Secretary:     [The White House] 30 January, 1917

Thank you warmly for your action in the matter of the clear-listing order.[1] I think that things can now go forward without further hitch.

With warmest regard,
                         Faithfully yours,   Woodrow Wilson

TLS (Letterpress Books, WP, DLC).
[1] That is, the decision made by Clay Tallman, Commissioner of the General Land Office, in regard to the claims of the Honolulu Consolidated Oil Co. in Naval Petroleum Reserve No. 2, about which see FKL to WW, June 1, 1916, Vol. 37, and FKL to WW, Jan. 23, 1917, Vol. 40. Wilson, on January 27, had requested that Lane have the clear-listing order withdrawn in order to permit further consideration of the case. WW to FKL, Jan. 27, 1917, TLS (Letterpress Books, WP, DLC). Lane replied on January 29, saying that he had done so. FKL to WW, Jan. 29, 1917, TLS (WP, DLC). However, Lane never actually ordered a hearing. See T. W. Gregory, "The Honolulu Case," Feb. 27, 1919, T MS, WP, DLC.

## From Edward Mandell House

Dear Governor:                    New York. January 30, 1917.

I notice Baruch in his testimony today,[1] said that I asked him to make suggestions for the Federal Reserve Bank directorship here.

I simply write to let you know that McAdoo telephoned me to ask Baruch to make a suggestion and wondered what I thought of Untermyer for the place. I called Baruch up and told him of McAdoo's request and asked him to communicate with him direct.

                         Affectionately yours,   E. M. House

Bernstorff has just called me up to say that he is sending over by messenger tomorrow, a *very important* letter. I asked him if it was an answer. He replied: "a partial one."

TLS (WP, DLC).
[1] Baruch was testifying at the so-called leak investigation, about which see P. Ritter to A. Hoffmann, Dec. 28, 1916, n. 11, Vol. 40.

## From the Diary of Breckinridge Long

Tuesday Jan 30 [1917]

This morning I called on Tumulty and asked to see the President and made an appointment for 12:30 which I kept. I saw the President only for a few moments, but took that opportunity to thank him for the confidence reposed in me.[1] He was very cordial and gracious & said "I wanted to appoint you"—emphasizing the "wanted"—when I was in the middle of a sentence thanking him for the appointment. He held my hand—and held it firmly—the whole time we were talking, and his face lighted up with an expression of real pleasure at seeing me. That reads foolishly—but it is how I observed & it was a real pleasure to feel that way—& to continue to feel that way—in speaking to a person for whom I have the most infinite regard.

Hw bound diary (B. Long Papers, DLC).
[1] Wilson had appointed him as Third Assistant Secretary of State, to succeed William Phillips.

## Four Letters to Robert Lansing

My dear Mr. Secretary,          The White House. [Jan. 31, 1917]

Thank you for letting me see this memorandum.[1] I think the position you took the right one throughout the conversation.

Faithfully Yours,   W.W.

WWTLI (SDR, RG 59, 893.51/1743, DNA).
[1] That is, the Enclosure printed with RL to WW, Jan. 27, 1917.

My dear Mr. Secretary,          The White House. 31 January, 1917.

It is a shame for me to have treated Page in this way.[1] The truth is, I have not known just what course to pursue, whether it was best to retain him until the end of the war or to let him retire now. What is your advice? I shall be writing him immediately.

Faithfully Yours,   W.W.

WWTLI (R. Lansing Papers, NjP).
[1] Lansing had just reminded Wilson, probably by telephone, that he, Wilson, had never answered Page's no. 5391 of December 29, 1916, in which Page had offered to resign and asked Wilson whether he wanted him to stay on as Ambassador to the Court of St. James.

My dear Mr. Secretary,          The White House. 31 January, 1917.

Allow me to return Mr. Gerard's letter with my thanks.[1]

It is odd how his information seems never to point to any con-

clusions whatever; but in spite of that his letters are worth reading and do leave a certain impression.

Faithfully Yours,   W.W.

WWTLI (SDR, RG 59, 123 G 31/52½, DNA).
  1 Printed as an Enclosure with RL to WW, Jan. 23, 1917, Vol. 40.

My dear Mr. Secretary,      The White House. 31 January, 1917.

This is, to my mind, quite the most puzzling and difficult question we have had to deal with.[1] It is becoming pretty clear to me
that the British are going beyond the spirit, at any rate, of the
principles hitherto settled in regard to this matter and that the
method in which their ship captains are instructed to use their
guns has in many instances gone beyond what could legiti-
mately be called defense. It appears that they have more than
once attacked. The question is more whether their guns have been
*used* only for defense than whether they exceed in calibre what
would reasonably constitute armament for defense and whether
their being mounted in the bow is a presumption that they are to
be used for offense. I would be glad to know the progress of
your own thought in this matter.

Faithfully Yours,   W.W.

WWTLI (SDR, RG 59, 763.72111/4470½, DNA).
  1 Wilson referred to J. H. von Bernstorff to RL, with enclosures, Jan. 10, 1917,
printed as an Enclosure with RL to WW, Jan. 12, 1917 (first letter of that date),
Vol. 40.

## From Robert Lansing, with Enclosure

PERSONAL AND PRIVATE:

My dear Mr. President:      Washington January 31, 1917.

I enclose in compliance with your request of January 24th,
supplemented by your letter of today, a memorandum of views
on the subject of armed merchant vessels.[1] From the standpoint
of abstract right as well of accepted legal rules I am convinced
that the conclusions reached are just and should control our
policy in dealing with this vexed and dangerous question.

Of course the whole matter boiled down is this: Since a
belligerent has the right to capture or destroy private owned
merchant ships of enemy register, such ships are entitled to
defend themselves from certain loss to their owners, and their
treatment as public ships because they carry an armament

adequate to protect them from destruction can find no warrant in the rules of naval warfare or in justice.

I feel that we ought without delay to reach a very definite conclusion as to this matter because everything indicates the intention of the German authorities to treat all armed merchant vessels as ships of war. The press is industriously circulating this view and I understand it is getting its material from the German Embassy. Gerard's reports all point the same way; and the memorandum sent me by the German Ambassador on January 10th (Enclosure B)² makes it very evident that the stage is being set for a new act on the part of his Government. In fact everything is being done to prepare the American public for a more vigorous submarine war on commerce.

If we let the German memorandum go unanswered it will be alleged that we have accepted their interpretation of our declaration of March 25, 1916 (Enclosure C),³ and that we are, therefore, *particeps criminis.* Nothing we can say later will remove the impression on our own people that though fully warned we permitted Germany to proceed in her announced purpose of treating armed merchant vessels as warships. For that reason I deem it essential that a very definite attitude should be at once reached.

Furthermore, if the German Government carries out her manifest plan to renew ruthless submarine attacks I believe that the consequences will be irreparable so far as peace is concerned. Not only will the Entente powers be so enraged as to refuse to consider any overtures, but, if we with previous knowledge fail to do all we can to prevent it, your influence over them, I fear, will be seriously impaired, and the very hope of peace will be extinguished.

I believe this is a time to state to Germany frankly and with the greatest firmness our views and to impress them with the possibility of an actual break in our relations if they attempt to carry forward their plan. In dealing with that Government our greatest success has come when they saw we would not recede or compromise. I think this is a time to adopt that course. If we do not, we may expect, in my opinion, a critical situation especially if American citizens are killed or imperiled.

You may see, Mr. President, from what I have written that I am greatly agitated over the present state of affairs. I am indeed more anxious than I have been since the SUSSEX affair. In many ways this is even a greater crisis as so much depends on nothing being done which will prevent the movement toward peace, and that movement will, I am firmly convinced, come to an end if submarine war of a reckless sort is renewed by Germany.

I enclose also for your consideration a report of the Neutrality Board on this subject (Enclosure D)[4] which is referred to in my memorandum (Enclosure A).[5]

Faithfully yours,   Robert Lansing.

P.S. Since writing the foregoing the German Ambassador has been to see me and has left me a communication accompanied by two memoranda (Enclosure E), which shows the prognostications were right, and we are face to face with the gravest crisis presented since the war began. I think that as soon as you have read these papers we should have a conference to determine the course to be taken.                    RL.

TLS (SDR, RG 59, 763.72111/4443, DNA).

[1] RL, "Armed Merchantmen," TS memorandum (SDR, RG 59, 763.72111/4443, DNA). As Lansing states in the following paragraph, this lengthy memorandum affirmed, through detailed, legalistic reasoning, the right of armed merchant ships to resist capture or destruction. The memorandum's specific conclusions were that vessels under governmental commissions or orders to use force without restraint, vessels with officers in the service and pay of the government, vessels carrying a naval flag, and vessels named in a country's naval list should be treated as warships. All other armed vessels should be treated as merchantmen "so long as they leave port under an assurance of their government that they are not to operate aggressively, and so long as there is no reason to doubt their faithful compliance with the assurance." However, to avoid criticism by "the other belligerent," Lansing recommended that limitations be placed on the armament of merchantmen. In accordance with the recommendation of the Joint State and Navy Neutrality Board (see n. 4 below), Lansing suggested that a merchant vessel be permitted to mount up to four guns no larger than six inches in caliber, each to be manned by one officer and a number of men equal to the inches of caliber, these gun crews not to be in the active armed forces of their nation.

[2] Printed as an Enclosure with RL to WW, Jan. 12, 1917 (first letter of that date), Vol. 40.

[3] *Memorandum on the Status of Armed Merchant Vessels . . . March 25, 1916*, printed as an Enclosure with WW to RL, April 24, 1916, Vol. 36.

[4] James Harrison Oliver and William Bartlett Fletcher to RL, Jan. 26, 1917, TS memorandum (SDR, RG 59, 763.72111/4443, DNA). These members of the Joint State and Navy Neutrality Board reached the conclusions on the armament of merchant vessels which Lansing stated in his memorandum (see n. 1 above).

[5] Lansing attached the following Hw memorandum to the foregoing documents: "These papers the President handed back to me after a conference at the White House (Jany 31, 1917, 8:45-10:30 pm). The German note of Jany 31st with 2 memoranda were the subject of discussion and its receipt made the subject of the letter and memorandum on armed merchant ships unnecessary of consideration. The President, however, indicated that he was in doubt as to the soundness of the memorandum of the 30th. 2/1/17. Robert Lansing."

ENCLOSURE

Count Johann Heinrich von Bernstorff
to Robert Lansing

Handed to me by German<br>
Amb. at 4:10 pm Jany 31, 1917 RL

(ENCLOSURE E)

TRANSLATION.

Washington D. C.,

Mr. Secretary of State,                    January 31, 1917.

Your Excellency were good enough to transmit to the Imperial Government a copy of the message which the President of the United States of America addressed to the Senate on the 22, inst. The Imperial Government has given it the earnest consideration which the President's statements deserve, inspired as they are, by a deep sentiment of responsibility. It is highly gratifying to the Imperial Government to ascertain that the main tendencies of this important statement correspond largely to the desires and principles professed by Germany. These principles especially include Selfgovernment and equality of rights for all nations. Germany would be sincerely glad if in recognition of this principle countries like Ireland and India, which do not enjoy the benefits of political independence, should now obtain their freedom. The German people also repudiate all alliances which serve to force the countries into a competition for might and to envolve them in a net of selfish intrigues. On the other hand Germany will gladly cooperate in all efforts to prevent future wars. The freedom of the seas, being a preliminary condition of the free existence of nations and the peaceful intercourse between them, as well as the open door for the commerce of all nations, has always formed part of the leading principles of Germany's political program. All the more the Imperial Government regrets that the attitude of her enemies who are so entirely opposed to peace makes it impossible for the world at present to bring about the realization of these lofty ideals. Germany and her allies were ready to enter now into a discussion of peace and had set down as basis the guaranty of existence, honor and free development of their peoples. Their aims, as has been expressly stated in the note of December 12, 1916, were not directed towards the destruction or annihilation of their enemies and were according to their conviction perfectly compatible with the rights of the other nations. As to Belgium for which such warm and cordial sympathy is felt in the United States, the Chancellor had declared only a few weeks previously that its annexation had never formed part of Germany's intentions. The peace to be signed with Belgium was to provide for such conditions in that country, with which Germany desires to maintain friendly neighborly relations, that Belgium should not be used again by Germany's enemies for the purpose of instigating continuous hostile intrigues. Such precautionary measures are all the more necessary, as Germany's enemies have repeatedly stated not only in speeches delivered by their leading men, but also in the statutes of the economical conference in Paris, that it is their intention not to treat Germany as an equal, even after peace has been restored but to continue their hostile attitude and especially to wage a systematical economical war against her.

The attempt of the four allied powers to bring about peace has failed owing to the lust of conquest of their enemies, who desired to dictate the conditions of peace. Under the pretence of following the principle of nationality our enemies have disclosed their real aims in this war, viz. to dismember and dishonor Germany, Austria-Hungary, Turkey and Bulgaria. To the wish of reconciliation they oppose the will of destruction. They desire a fight to the bitter end.

A new situation has thus been created which forces Germany to new decisions. Since two years and a half England is using her naval power for a criminal attempt to force Germany into submission by starvation. In brutal contempt of International Law the group of Powers led by England does not only curtail the legitimate trade of their opponents but they also by ruthless pressure compel neutral countries either to altogether forego every trade not agreable to the Entente-Powers or to limit it according to their arbitrary decrees. The American Government knows the steps which have been taken to cause England and her allies to return to the rules of International Law and to respect the freedom of the seas. The English Government, however, insists upon continuing its war of starvation, which does not at all affect the military power of its opponents, but compels women and children, the sick and the aged to suffer, for their country, pains and privations which endanger the vitality of the nation. Thus British tyranny mercilessly increases the sufferings of the world indifferent to the laws of humanity, indifferent to the protests of the Neutrals whom they severely harm, indifferent even to the silent longing for peace among England's own allies. Each day of the terrible struggle causes new destruction, new sufferings. Each day shortening the war will, on both sides, preserve the life of thousands of brave soldiers and be a benefit to mankind.

The Imperial Government could not justify before its own conscience, before the German people and before history the neglect of any means destined to bring about the end of the war. Like the President of the United States the Imperial Government had hoped to reach this goal by negotiations. After the attempts to come to an understanding with the Entente-Powers have been answered by the latter with the announcement of an intensified continuation of the war, the Imperial Government—in order to serve the welfare of mankind in a higher sense and not to wrong its own people—is now compelled to continue the fight for existence, again forced upon it, with the full employment of all the weapons which are at its disposal.

Sincerely trusting that the people and Government of the United States will understand the motives for this decision and its necessity, the Imperial Government hopes that the United States may view the new situation from the lofty heights of impartiality and assist, on their part, to prevent further misery and avoidable sacrifice of human life.

Enclosing two memoranda regarding the details of the contemplated military measures at sea, I remain

etc.    J. Bernstorff.

### MEMORANDUM.

After bluntly refusing Germany's peace offer the Entente-Powers, stated in their note addressed to the American Government, that they are determined to continue the war in order to deprive Germany of german provinces in the West and the East, to destroy Austria-Hungary and to annihilate Turkey. In waging war with such aims, the Entente-Allies are violating all rules of International Law, as they prevent the legitimate trade of Neutrals with the Central Powers, and of the Neutrals among themselves. Germany has, so far, not made unrestricted use of the weapon which she possesses in her submarines. Since the Entente Powers, however, have made it impossible to come to an understanding based upon equality of rights of all nations, as proposed by the Central Powers and have instead declared only such a peace to be possible, which shall be dictated by the Entente-Allies and shall result in the destruction and the humiliation of the Central Powers, Germany is unable further to forego the full use of her submarines. The Imperial Government, therefore, does not doubt that the Government of the United States will understand the situation thus forced upon Germany by the Entente-Allies' brutal methods of war and by their determination to destroy the Central Powers, and that the Government of the United States will further realize that the now openly disclosed intentions of the Entente-Allies give back to Germany the freedom of action which she reserved in her note addressed to the Government of the United States on May 4, 1916.

Under these circumstances Germany will meet the illegal measures of her enemies by forcibly preventing after February 1, 1917 in a zone around Great Britain, France, Italy and in the Eastern Mediterranean all navigation, that of neutrals included, from and to England and from and to France, etc. etc. All ships met within that zone will be sunk.

The Imperial Government is confident that this measure will result in a speedy termination of the war and in the restoration of peace which the Government of the United States has so much at heart. Like the Government of the United States Germany and her allies had hoped to reach this goal by negotiations. Now that the war, through the fault of Germany's enemies, has to be continued, the Imperial Government feels sure that the Government of the United States will understand the necessity of adopting such measures as are destined to bring about a speedy end of the horrible and useless bloodshed. The Imperial Government hopes all the more for such an understanding of her position, as the neutrals have under the pressure of the Entente-Powers, suffered great losses, being forced by them either to give up their entire trade or to limit it according to conditions arbitrarily determined by Germany's enemies in violation of International Law.

MEMORANDUM.

From February 1, 1917, all sea traffic will be stopped with every available weapon and without further notice in the following blockade zones around Great Britain, France, Italy and in the Eastern Mediterranean.

*In the North*: The zone is confined by a line at a distance of 20 seamiles along the Dutch coast to Terschelling fire ship, the degree of longitude from Terschelling fire ship to Udsire, a line from there across the point 62 degrees north 0 degrees longitude to 62 degrees north 5 degrees west, further to a point 3 seamiles south the southern point of the Faroe Islands, from there across point 62 degrees north 10 degrees west to 61 degrees north

15 degrees west, then 57 degrees north 20 degrees west to 47 degrees north 20 degrees west, further to 43 degrees north, 15 degrees west, then along the degree of latitude 43 degrees north to 20 seamiles from Cape Finisterre and at a distance of 20 seamiles along the north coast of Spain to the French boundary.

*In the South*: The Mediterranean. For neutral ships remains open: The sea west of the line Pt. del'Espiquette to 38 degrees 20 minutes north and 6 degrees east, also north and west of a zone 61 seamiles wide along the Northafrican coast, beginning at 2 degrees longitude west. For the connection of this sea zone with Greece there is provided a zone of a width of 20 sea miles north and east of the following line: 38 degrees north and 6 degrees east to 38 degrees north and 10 degrees east to 37 degrees north and 11 degrees 30 minutes east to 34 degrees north and 11 degrees 30 minutes east to 34 degrees north and 22 degrees 30 minutes east.

From there leads a zone 20 seamiles wide west of 22 degrees 30 minutes eastern longitude into Greek territorial waters.

Neutral ships navigating these blockade zones do so at their own risk. Although care has been taken, that neutral ships which are on their way toward ports of the blockade zones on February 1, 1917, and have come in the vicinity of the latter, will be spared during a sufficiently long period it is strongly adviced to warn them with all available means in order to cause their return.

Neutral ships which on February 1, are in ports of the blockaded zones, can, with the same safety, leave them if they sail before February 5, 1917, and take the shortest route into safe waters.

The instructions given to the commanders of german submarines provide for a sufficiently long period during which the safety of passengers on unarmed enemy passenger ships is guaranteed.

Americans, en route to the blockade zone on enemy freight steamers, are not endangered, as the enemy shipping firms can prevent such ships in time from entering the zone.

Sailing of regular American passenger steamers may continue undisturbed after February 1, 1917, if

  a) the port of destination is Falmouth

  b) sailing to or coming from that port course is taken via the Scilly Islands and a point 50 degrees north 20 degrees west.

  c) the steamers are marked in the following way which must not be allowed to other vessels in American ports: On ships' hull and superstructure 3 vertical stripes 1 meter wide each to be painted alternately white and red. Each mast should show a large flag checkered white and red, and the stern the American national flag.

Care should be taken that, during dark, national flag and painted marks are easily recognizable from a distance and that the boats are well lighted throughout.

d) one steamer a week sails in each direction with arrival at Falmouth on Sunday and departure from Falmouth on Wednesday

e) The United States Government guarantees that no contraband (according to German contraband list) is carried by those steamers.

T MSS (SDR, RG 59, 763.72/3179, DNA).

## James Watson Gerard to Robert Lansing

Berlin (via Copenhagen) January 31, 1917.

4961. Confidential. Giving more details of my conversation with Zimmermann last night.

He said that he and I must work hard now to keep peace between Germany and America. I said yes but it was rather late and apparently a sudden decision. He said yes, that it had been much discussed in the last two weeks and that that was the reason for his constant trips to Great Headquarters but that now even the Chancellor had come round; that the military and naval people had forced this and said that America could do nothing; that the Foreign Office had warned them and done what it could and was on record against this step. But he said it was their last chance as Germany could not hold out a year on the food question but that what finally decided them was *not*[1] the nasty answer to Wilson of the Allies showing that it is impossible to make peace. That he realized that it was a very serious step and would probably bring the whole world into the war but that Germany had this weapon and must use it no matter what the consequences were.

End conversation.

There is no doubt but that Germany believes that Americans are a fat, rich race without sense of honor and ready to stand for anything in order to keep out of war and Americans in Germany, particularly creatures like von Wiegand and Schuette[2] of Chicago DAILY NEWS, have encouraged them in this belief. The Germans think and newspapers have published that the President's peace moves are inspired by fear only. Please do not give out my conversation with Zimmermann which was confidential. I think the reasons for the hasty decision, First, the desire to torpedo ships carrying grain from Argentina; Second, food situation here; Third, threatened great Allied offensive; Fourth, public demanding use of submarine weapon and contempt and hate for America. I expect note tonight.                           Gerard.

T telegram (SDR, RG 59, 763.72/3170, DNA).
  1 The decoder was not sure that this word was included in the message.
  2 Oswald Francis Schuette.


## Count Johann Heinrich von Bernstorff
## to Edward Mandell House

My dear Colonel House:

Washington, D. C.
January 31, 1917.

I have received a telegram from Berlin,[1] according to which I am to express to the President the thanks of the Imperial Government for his communication made through you. The Imperial Government has complete confidence in the President and hopes that he will reciprocate such confidence. As proof I am to inform you in confidence that the Imperial Government will be very glad to accept the services kindly offered by the President for the purpose of bringing about a peace conference between the belligerents. My Government, however, is not prepared to publish any peace terms at present, because our enemies have published such terms which aim at the dishonor and destruction of Germany and her allies. My Government considers that as long as our enemies openly proclaim such terms, it would show weakness, which does not exist, on our part if we publish our terms and we would in so doing only prolong the war. However, to show President Wilson our confidence, my Government through me desires to inform him *personally* of the terms under which we would have been prepared to enter into negotiations, if our enemies had accepted our offer of December 12th.

"Restitution of the part of Upper Alsace occupied by the French.

Gaining of a frontier which would protect Germany and Poland economically and strategically against Russia.

Restitution of Colonies in form of an agreement which would give Germany Colonies adequate to her population and economic interest.

Restitution of those parts of France occupied by Germany under reservation of strategical and economic changes of the frontier and financial compensations.

Restoration of Belgium under special guarantee for the safety of Germany which would have to be decided on by negotiations with Belgium.

Economic and financial mutual compensation on the basis of the exchange of territories conquered and to be restituted at the conclusion of peace.

Compensation for the German business concerns and private persons who suffered by the war. Abandonment of all economic agreements and measures which would form an obstacle to normal commerce and intercourse after the conclusion of peace, and instead of such agreements reasonable treaties of commerce.

The freedom of the seas."

The peace terms of our allies run on the same lines. My Government further agrees, after the war has been terminated, to enter into the proposed second International Conference on the basis of the President's message to the Senate.

My Government would have been glad to postpone the submarine blockade, if they had been able to do so. This, however, was quite impossible on account of the preparations which could not be canceled. My Government believes that the submarine blockade will terminate the war very quickly. In the meantime my Government will do every thing possible to safeguard American interests and begs the President to continue his efforts to bring about peace, and my Government will terminate the submarine blockade as soon as it is evident that the efforts of the President will lead to a peace acceptable to Germany.

The motives of my Government for beginning the submarine blockade are the following: After bluntly refusing Germany's peace offer the Entente Powers stated in their note addressed to the American Government that they are determined to continue the war in order to deprive Germany of German provinces in the West and the East, to destroy Austria-Hungary and to annihilate Turkey. In waging war with such aims, the Entente-Allies are violating all rules of International Law, as they prevent the legitimate trade of Neutrals with the Central Powers, and of the Neutrals among themselves. Germany has, so far, not made unrestricted use of the weapon which she possesses in her submarines. Since the Entente Powers, however, have made it impossible to come to an understanding based upon equality of rights of all nations as proposed by the Central Powers, and have instead declared only such a peace to be possible, which shall be dictated by the Entente-Allies and shall result in the destruction, and the humiliation of the Central Powers, Germany is unable further to forego the full use of her submarines.

The Imperial Government, therefore, does not doubt that the

Government of the United States will understand the situation thus forced upon Germany by the Entente-Allies' brutal methods of war and by their determination to destroy the Central Powers and that the Government of the United States will further realize that the now openly disclosed intentions of the Entente-Allies gives back to Germany the freedom of action which she reserved in her note addressed to the Government of the United States on May 4, 1916.

I am always at your disposal if I can be of any service.

Yours very sincerely,   J. Bernstorff.

P.S.   I could not get the translation of the official answer to the President's message ready in time to send it to you. I was in such a hurry to give you the above most important news; namely that the Blockade will be terminated, if a conference can be brought about on reasonable terms.

CCL (WP, DLC).
1 T. von Bethmann Hollweg to J. H. von Bernstorff, Jan. 29, 1917.

## From John Hollis Bankhead

Dear Mr. President:                    [Washington] 31 January, 1917

Your letter of the 26th instant with reference to the Shields Water Power Bill was received, and I thank you very much for the suggestions contained. I am endeavoring to put them into effect. I have had a conference with Mr. Sherley, and have his assurance that he will assist in bringing together the six members of the House, whom you name, for a conference, as you suggest, either Thursday or Friday of this week. At present two of them are in New York with the "Leak" Committee.

In the conference between Mr. Sherley and myself no attempt was made to arrive at any agreement, but we merely discussed some avenues through which we might approach the subject in the conference to be held later.

If you conclude that you may be of further service in bringing about an agreement between the House and Senate, I will greatly appreciate it if you will do it. It seems to me if all the gentlemen you name will approach the situation with a purpose of working out a solution that will be fair and just to the Government it should by all means be done. If you will pardon the suggestion I regard this question among the most important legislation now before Congress. I need not enter into an argument to satisfy your mind of that situation.

Please help us all you can.

Sincerely yours,    J H Bankhead

TLS (WP, DLC).


## From Walter Lippmann

Dear Mr. President:                    [New York] January 31, 1917.

At the suggestion of Secretary Baker I am sending you a new edition of my book, which contains an attempt at explanation of some of the outlines of foreign policy as they seem to be developing.[1] I should not have sent you a copy if he had not suggested it and I do not in the least expect you even to look at it.

You may be interested in seeing a portion of a letter which I received last Saturday from Mr. H. G. Wells.[2] The letter of course was written before your address to the Senate and it contains the following suggestion:

"In my forthcoming book 'War of the Future,' I suggest what I call a 'Third Party' solution of the war, i.e. a solution not from the point of view of victory but from the point of view of Right. Why should you not try to get out in America what I might call an American Peace Idea, the peace the American mind would like * * *? Tell both sides plainly what neutral minds think is a just settlement. So far as the war goes I think I have now a fairly strong grasp of the situation. On the west and generally the Germans are beaten. The first half of 1917 will—in spite of our generals—demonstrate that. The boundaries will be drawn by a rather ascendant but not completely ascendant *Western* Europe. But the big treaty, the League to Enforce Peace, the broad *general* settlement has to be made by all the world."

The good effects of your move grow more evident as time goes on. Everywhere I hear even among political opponents an extraordinary enthusiasm and affection for what you have done.

Sincerely yours,    [Walter Lippmann]

CCL (W. Lippmann Papers, CtY).

[1] A new, popular editon of *The Stakes of Diplomacy*, originally published in New York in 1915, was advertised in *The New Republic* of February 3, 1917. Henry Holt & Company wrote as follows: "Walter Lippmann's informed interpretation of President Wilson's peace policy is embodied in a new preface to Mr. Lippmann's latest book, The Stakes of Diplomacy. The book considers, in Mr. Lippmann's clear fashion, just those matters with which the world is now so anxiously concerned: a league to enforce peace; national patriotism and

international relations; the removal of 'backward' nations as international danger spots, etc."

2 H[erbert]. G[eorge]. Wells, who had recently written articles for *The New Republic*.

## Two Letters from Edward Nash Hurley

Dear Mr. President:                 Washington January 31, 1917.

The most important convention ever held in this country in connection with foreign trade was held last week in Pittsburgh under the auspices of the National Foreign Trade Council. Over 1,000 business men, most of them small manufacturers, attended the convention and showed so much interest in foreign trade that I was very much encouraged and felt that we are gradually laying aside our provincialism in this direction.

The Federal Trade Commission has presented facts showing the absolute necessity for the Webb bill, and I sincerely hope that you will find it consistent to urge the Senate further to enact this desirable legislation.

Respectfully yours,   Edward N. Hurley

Dear Mr. President:                 Washington, January 31, 1917.

Mr. Tumulty has transmitted to me Congressman Kent's letter addressed to you, dated January twenty-sixth, which was in reply to my letter to you of January eighteenth. Congressman Kent and I had a conference yesterday, which was continued this morning with Congressmen Garner and Borland[1] also present, on the proposed investigation of the meat packing industry.

They said they were under the impression that the Federal Trade Commission did not wish to investigate this matter. I assured them that we were here to take orders, and that when Congress appropriated sufficient funds and directed us to do the work we would be glad to do it.

When Congressman Kent cited paragraph (d) of section 6 of the Federal Trade Commission Act it gave me the impression that what was desired was a prosecution under the antitrust laws, and this is obviously a matter which comes primarily within the jurisdiction of the Attorney General, and could be reached as it was in the case of Swift & Company v. United States, 196 U.S. 375. It appears, however, from our conferences that Congressman Kent had in mind a general investigation of wider scope.

I pointed out to the Congressmen that the Department of Agriculture is in a better position to conduct this proposed investigation, so far as the range and farm conditions are concerned, but that we are prepared, if directed by Congress, to investigate the production and distribution of the meat packing industry of the country.

My proposal of a departmental committee, in my letter to you of January 18, 1917, was predicated not so much on the possible inadvisability, at present, of a general investigation which would furnish no immediate relief and possibly might be nullified when half completed by a return of more normal conditions, as on the impression given me by Congressman Kent that Congress would not appropriate the money needed for the proposed investigation. I therefore tried to devise a method by which the investigation could be made through the available machinery of the government.

Congressmen Kent, Garner and Borland, however, stated this morning that they could get the appropriation, and it seems to me, therefore, that the proper thing for us to do is to await action by Congress.          Very truly yours,   Edward N. Hurley

TLS (WP, DLC).
1 William Patterson Borland, Democratic congressman from Missouri.


## John Howard Whitehouse to Edward Mandell House, with Enclosure

My dear Colonel House,          [New York] 31st. Jany., 1917.

This extraordinary news is staggering. The first essential is time for consideration. The position is only hopeless if panic supervenes. May I see you early tomorrow. In the meantime I send the enclosed memorandum which the President may care to have. I am certain that the general position in England, as regards the President's action, has been improving, and that the spirit of the President's address to the Senate has met with increasing favour. It will be a supreme tragedy if in view of this the war is to be resumed on a more horrible scale than ever, and perhaps extended.          Ever yours   J. H. Whitehouse

TLS (WP, DLC).


### E N C L O S U R E

31st. January, 1917.

I desire to submit the following suggestions in view of the new situation created by the German note to America published in this evening's papers. I do so under the obvious disadvantage of having only the newspaper reports to guide me but as every moment may be of urgent importance I send this memorandum on the assumption that the German note is correctly given in the papers tonight.

1. If America is suddenly forced into this war by the unrestricted submarine warfare now threatened by Germany it would be a vital disaster alike for England, America, and humanity. It would mean the continuance of the war perhaps for years on a scale of unthinkable horror, with ultimate results which no one can foretell.

2. The first thing to secure therefore is time for consideration. If the war is to be extended, at least let the panic decisions of 1914 be avoided.

3. One way to secure this would be for the President to demand that Germany should not depart from the pledges she had given him; and that further consultation should take place. This was not the time for Germany to make new threats. The Allies had outlined terms to the President in response to his invitation. He had outlined to the Senate the principles upon which he could assist in order to reach a permanent peace. It was now for Germany to submit either in public, or to him in private, a statement of the terms she suggested. The President could then judge as to the possibility of a just and permanent peace through negotiation.

4. Germany's note may be the result of absolute panic. A little delay will show if this is so. If she is willing to place herself in the hands of the President, in the light of his address to the Senate, peace ought still to be within measurable distance. If her proposals and attitude can be adequately ascertained by the President I am convinced that great good might result by an immediate secret mission to the English government.

5. But if all steps which may be taken fail to bring the belligerents together, or to prevent the possible extension of the war, I earnestly submit that before considering any other action, the President should make a definite and reasoned offer of mediation to the whole of the belligerent countries.

J. Howard Whitehouse

TS MS (WP, DLC).


## From the Diary of Colonel House

The White House, Washington. February 1, 1917.

I arrived in Washington on time and went directly to the White House and had breakfast alone. Soon after breakfast the President appeared and we were together continuously until two o'clock. I handed him Bernstorff's letter and he read it aloud. He saw at once how perfectly shallow it was. Bernstorff's protestations were almost a mockery when the substance of the cable from his Government was considered.

The President said Lansing was preparing a communication to Bernstorff, citing our notes and theirs in the Sussex case, and their promise of May 4th. This was being prepared for the purpose of giving Bernstorff his passports if it was thought advisable.

The President was sad and depressed and I did not succeed at any time during the day in lifting him into a better frame of mind. He was deeply disappointed at the sudden and unwarranted action of the German Government. We had every reason to believe that within a month the belligerents would be talking peace. Wiseman and I had already discussed how it could be begun and the Germans, on the surface, seemed eager for it. The German people, I am sure, feel as they appear to, but there is some devilish machinations in governmental or military circles back of it all. It may be that it is to save the Hohenzollern Dynasty; it may be to save the military caste; it may be that the Civil Government desires to save its face, but I feel certain that there is an inhuman and selfish purpose back of it all.

The President said he felt as if the world had suddenly reversed itself; that after going from east to west, it had begun to go from west to east and that he could not get his balance.

The question we discussed longest was wh[e]ther it was better to give Bernstorff his passports immediately or wait until the Germans committed some overt act. When Lansing came this discussion was renewed and we all agreed that it was best to give him his passports at once, because by taking that course, there was a possibility of bringing the Germans to their senses. If we waited for the overt act, they would believe we had accepted their ultimatum. I had in mind, too, the effect it would have on the Allies. We would not be nearly so advantageously situated if we waited as if we acted promptly.

The President was insistent that he would not allow it to lead to war if it could possibly be avoided. He reiterated his belief that it would be a crime for this Government to involve itself in the war to such an extent as to make it impossible to save Europe afterward. He spoke of Germany as "a madman that should be curbed." I asked if he thought it fair to the Allies to ask them to do the curbing without doing our share. He noticeably winced at this, but still held to his determination not to become involved if it were humanly possible to do otherwise.

We sat listlessly during the morning until Lansing arrived, which was not until half past eleven o'clock. The President nervously arranged his books and walked up and down the floor. Mrs. Wilson spoke of golf and asked whether I thought it would look badly if the President went on the links. I thought the American people would feel that he should not do anything so trivial at such a time.

In great governmental crisis of this sort the public have no conception what is happening on the stage behind the curtain. If the actors and the scenery could be viewed as a tragedy like this is being prepared, it would be a revelation. When the decision has been made, nothing further can be done until it is time for the curtain to rise. This will be when the President goes before Congress to explain why he is sending the German Ambassador home. Meanwhile we were listlessly killing time. We had finished the discussion within a half hour and there was nothing further to say. The President at last suggested that we play a game of pool. Toward the end of the second game Lansing was announced. The President, Lansing and I then returned to the study.

Lansing was so nearly of our mind that there was little discussion. He read what he had written and we accepted it. The President showed him the German communication which the German Ambassador had made through me. Lansing took it to have a copy made and then left.

The President asked if I thought he ought to call a Cabinet meeting today. I thought it was not necessary; that he could call it tomorrow at the usual time, since it had been decided that Bernstorff should not be given his passports until Saturday morning. The President had promised Senator Stone, Chairman of the Foreign Relations Committee, that he would not give Bernstorff his passports without first notifying him, Stone. Stone is in St Louis and the President has telegraphed him to come at once to Washington.[1]

We speculated upon how the Cabinet would stand. He thought the only ones who would dissent from the program agreed upon would be Burleson. Daniels, he thought, would be passive; McAdoo for immediate and drastic action; Baker and Gregory would agree with our program in toto; Lane would be for war, and Houston for somewhat more drastic action than had been determined upon.

In talking with Burleson and McAdoo later in the day, I found he was correct in his judgment. Much to my surprise, Lansing agreed with the President and me that if we could possibly retain the Austrian Ambassador, we should do so. I advised the President to begin at once with Tarnowski and see whether we could not make peace proposals through the Austrians. I believe we have made a mistake in confining ourselves so wholly to the English and the Germans, for they are the real belligerents and the most stubborn of them all. This conflict comes down so largely to a question of supremacy between these two nations that neither one will likely listen to a reasonable peace unless their allies force them to it.

T MS (E. M. House Papers, CtY).
    1 Stone returned to Washington on February 2. Wilson, immediately after a lengthy meeting with the cabinet on that date (about which see J. Daniels to WW, Feb. 2, 1917, n. 1), went to the Capitol and arrived there about 5 P.M. He talked with Stone for about half an hour in the office of the Senate Foreign Relations Committee. Then Wilson went to the President's Room, while Stone rounded up as many senators as he could find. Sixteen Democrats came at about 5:30 and sat in a semicircle around the President. Except for Atlee Pomerene of Ohio, they all represented southern and western states and included some of the hitherto most ardent champions of neutrality in the upper house. There were no Republicans only because the Senate had adjourned and the pages could find none.
    Wilson opened the discussion by saying that he had come "seeking light"—to hear senatorial opinion on what seemed to be, as he put it, the three choices open to the American government: (1) an immediate break with Germany; (2) postponement of a break until Germany had committed an overt act against *American* rights, and (3) a redefinition of American policy, with a final warning that a German offense would lead to rupture in diplomatic relations. He wanted to know the pulse of the Senate in this gravest crisis in American history, Wilson went on. He wanted each man to speak his mind frankly, with the welfare of the nation and civilization at heart. Stone and Lewis said that they favored assuming that the Germans did not really intend to sink American ships without warning. They would, they added, meet any such violation of American rights with immediate severance of relations. All other senators who spoke said that it was obvious what the Germans were going to do and that the President should break relations at once. They argued that this was the only dignified course and said that they were sure that their constituents would applaud such action. The conference ended at a little after 7 P.M. Each senator shook Wilson's hand on leaving and assured him that he would be sustained by a unanimous Senate whatever course he followed. Link, *Campaigns for Progressivism and Peace*, pp. 297-98, and *New York Times*, Feb. 3, 1917.

# A Memorandum by Louis Paul Lochner

### INTERVIEW WITH PRESIDENT WILSON—FEB. 1, 1917.[1]

The President looked haggard and worried. I said to him that much of what I had intended to say was changed by the most recent move of Germany. He nodded to this and said it was most surprising. He stated it may change the whole world (if I remember correctly). I said that the move was all the more distressing to me because our last emissary to Germany had brought back word from Berlin, from Zimmerman, that even the successes in Roumania would not enthrone the war party, and that indeed the military was well in check. The President replied, "But it is this very party that smashed through Roumania that evidently has control now." I then said whether there was anything that our modest organization could do to help in this crisis. He said, "no, I don't see anything. I am merely trying all day to think, and not to form any hasty judgment."

I then took up the work of our conference, and said that I wanted him to know our work in its main outlines, and then to request him to state whether there was anything in our program that was in any way embarrassing to him.

First I took up our propoganda of the idea of a league of nations, ever since he made his speech before the League to Enforce Peace. I showed how we had gotten prominent professors and publicists to express themselves in syndicated articles. Next came the German peace note, and again we promoted interviews in which the stress was laid upon the guarantees after the war. The[n] came the President's peace note, and now we urged all our societies and affiliations to cable him. I handed him the copies of cables, and asked him whether he had received them. He said he was afraid that many had not reached him. He thereupon looked them over for some minutes.

Next I spoke of the proposed Review,[2] and gave him the prospectus. He studied this for awhile, and then said that the one thing he could advise us to guard against, in discussing the guarantees of the future, was that of losing ourselves in details of the machinery of the future organization of the world, rather than sticking to the principles, such as he outlined in his speech to the Senate. "The minute you discuss details, the main issue is clouded and the discussion diverted. Besides, would it not be well to leave something to those who will gather around the council table to agree upon the form of such a league?" He stated further that one's ideas often changed as a result of a conference.

I next took up our scientific work and handed him Dr. Lie's report.[3] This, again, he perused with interest, and when I told him what use was to be made of the material, he nodded approvingly.

The next point was the reasons for our urging a neutral conference. I stated that I could quite understand now why he was in favor of mediation by the United States alone, but that nevertheless in neutral Europe we had to put forward the idea of a joint conference as a "counter-irritation" to the policy of the Activists. It would not have done for us to urge any single neutral of Europe to mediate, for the European neutrals are too small. I then dwelt upon the success of our August demonstrations, and showed him how, for instance, in Sweden we had held 408 meetings in a week in as many cities. In this the President seemed greatly interested.

Now while these petitions did not move the neutrals to act together, I continued, yet their great practical value became evident when he, Pres. Wilson, issued his peace note. We immediately telegraphed to our centers, asking that now the neutrals be urged to support the President of the United States. The Swiss Government, I said, acted to our certain knowledge as a result of the pressure our petition had brought to bear. Similarly in Scandinavia I soon received a wire that the three Northern Governments would support the President. The President manifested the deepest interest in all this. He did not *say* anything, as he evidently wanted me to talk, but he nodded repeatedly approvingly.

Next I asked him about the work here in America. Ought Mr. Ford to support any particular movement, or in what way could he help?

The President replied that he, as head of the nation, could not advise anybody to identify himself with any particular movement; that for instance the League to Enforce Peace had tried to get him to make a statement identifying himself with them, but that he had to decline, as the League stood for a definite program, while he was advocating principles.

These points, however, he said should be made clear to the people of the United States by every conceivable means: First, the desirability of the United States actually joining such a league; secon[d]ly, the insistence of the United States, before joining, upon acceptance of the principles he enunciated, principles which, he said, he felt sure he could guarantee because they were absolutely American principles. "This I know for certain, that each and every one of them is an American principle."

Continuing, he said that the Senate had read all sorts of things into his speech that he never said—which illustrated concretely his point of before, namely, the danger of giving too many details. If this is true of the simple principles he enunciated (argued Mr. Wilson), how much more would it not be true if an elaborate, detailed program were to be submitted for discussion.

Finally, the President said, there was a suggestion in the reply of the Entente—he did not say that the Entente reply meant that, but simply *might* mean it—that past history would have to be undone before his program was realizable. The President was insistent that he did *not* attempt in any way to undo past history, and that this point should be clearly understood.

I then told him of the plans under way in Switzerland for a meeting of influential men in March, who wished to discuss his program and then bring pressure to bear upon their Governments (the neutral governments of Europe) either to endorse the President's program *in toto*, or else to make known in how far they had indorsed it. The President said he had not heard of this meeting, and that it might do much good. I explained to him that it was not governmental in scope, but that it was being engineered by the Central Organization for a Durable Peace. If my memory does not fail me, the President said in connection with the above re-mark—namely, that such a meeting might do much good, words to the effect that "unless these new complications change every-thing." He evidently sees the gravity of the situation.

I concluded somewhat as follows: "I felt, Mr. President, that before I return to Europe you should know just what we are doing abroad."[4] The President replied, "Except for what you told me, I must confess that I have not been able to keep abreast of your work." "Then, Mr. President, is there anything in our work as out-lined that you regard as in any way harmful or as embarrassing your work?" To which the President replied, "There certainly is not. Of course, I know only what you have presented now. But as outlined by you, I see where much good is possible." (I cannot vouch for the exact words, but think I am reflecting him cor-rectly.)

I rose to go and said that I hoped most sincerely that out of this situation which now confronts us, grave though it be, the Presi-dent might find a peaceful way. "Thank you," he said warmly and shook hands. Then, when I was just opening the door, he called after me, "if it can be done, I certainly wish it with all my heart."

Louis P. Lochner.

CC MS (L. P. Lochner Papers, WHi).

[1] Wilson saw Lochner in the Oval Office at 4 P.M., immediately after House had departed for New York.

[2] A periodical, to be called *Post Bellum*, which would deal with the prob-lems of peacemaking and world organization. It was to be the organ of the Neutral Conference for Continuous Mediation, the group sponsored by Henry Ford and which employed Lochner. See Barbara S. Kraft, *The Peace Ship: Henry Ford's Pacifist Adventure in the First World War* (New York and London, 1978), pp. 250-51, 261.

[3] Mikael Lie, a Norwegian, consultant on international law to the Nobel Institute. At this time, he was working in conjunction with the Neutral Con-ference for Continuous Mediation on the preparation of an agenda for a future peace conference of the belligerent nations, and his report dealt with the assignment of position papers for this purpose. *Ibid.*, pp. 213, 214, 250.

[4] As it turned out, Lochner did not return to Europe at this time. On February 7, Ford informed Lochner through an intermediary that he was closing down all of his peace activities as of March 1 and that Lochner's services were to be terminated on that date. *Ibid.*, pp. 267-68.

## To Edward Nash Hurley

My dear Hurley:                    [The White House] 2 February, 1917

Thank you for your letter of January thirty-first. I am pressing the Webb Bill as warmly as I can and think there is some prospect of its going through.

In haste

Cordially and faithfully yours,    Woodrow Wilson

TLS (Letterpress Books, WP, DLC).


## To Charles Stedman Macfarland

[The White House]

My dear Doctor Macfarland:              2 February, 1917

Your letter of the thirty-first[1] has given me a great deal of cheer. Just now it looks as if the cause of peace were all but desperate, but words of encouragement such as you are generous enough to send help immensely in these dark hours.

Cordially and sincerely yours,    Woodrow Wilson

TLS (Letterpress Books, WP, DLC).
[1] It is missing in all collections.


## To Thomas Davies Jones

My dear Friend:              The White House 2 February, 1917

Of course, I am dreadfully disappointed, but not disappointed in you. I think you reason the case out in a way that is unanswerable and I accept the decision, distressing as it is to me to think that I shall not realize my earnest hope that I was to have you here associated with me in Washington. Every time I come to your mind, I value its counsel all the more.

There is a lawyer in Chicago whom his friends refer to as Ned Burling. Can you tell me something about him? He has been suggested, not for the Tariff Commission, but for the Trade Commission, and I would like to know something about his qualifications and, incidentally, what his politics are.

In haste, with the warmest regard and deep appreciation of your generous attitude of friendship.

Cordially and sincerely yours,    Woodrow Wilson

TLS (Mineral Point, Wisc., Public Library).

## To William Jennings Bryan

My dear Mr. Bryan:        The White House 2 February, 1917

Your letter to me about my address to the Senate has given me the deepest gratification, as I am sure you must have known that it would. It was generous of you to write it. I hope with all my heart that something can be worked out that will assure the world of peace and justice.

In haste

Cordially and sincerely yours,   Woodrow Wilson

TLS (W. J. Bryan Papers, DLC).


## From Josephus Daniels

Dear Mr. President:        Washington Feb. 2, 1917.

I was glad to hear you say you could not at this time fully trust anybody's judgment in this crisis, not even your own,[1] for my feeling that we are the trustees of the civilization of our race is so strong that the possibility of becoming involved in the world's struggle makes me unable to sleep. After returning to the Department I had a long talk with Admiral Benson. Of course I told him nothing of your views or the cabinet discussion, but found he had the same abhorrence of becoming enlisted with either side of combatants that you expressed. His view is that if we lose our equipoise, the world will be in darkness. He expressed the hope that you would find a way to avert the calamity. It must oppress you to feel that those of us who would help feel our inability. I thought you would like to know Admiral Benson's strong feeling, much stronger than I can express. Many civilians are more inclined to accept what they call the "logic of war" than the ablest of military men.

My feeling is that you are acting not only for our country alone but for all neutrals, and that an expression of a strong desire that all neutrals should act in concert would have a salutary effect on the whole world, and show that your position was in keeping with your address to the Senate.

Sincerely yours,   Josephus Daniels

ALS (WP, DLC).

[1] The cabinet had met from two thirty to four forty-five that afternoon. About this meeting, see Lansing's memorandum printed at Feb. 4, 1917; F. K. Lane to G. W. Lane, Feb. 9, 1917; David F. Houston, *Eight Years with Wilson's Cabinet, 1913 to 1920* (2 vols., Garden City, N. Y., 1926), I, 227, 229-31; and Link, *Campaigns for Progressivism and Peace*, pp. 296-97.

## From Edward Mandell House, with Enclosure

Dear Governor: New York. February 2, 1917.

I am enclosing a copy of a letter which I have sent Bernstorff.

I talked with Wiseman this morning and while he took it for granted that you would send Bernstorff home, he expressed the hope that some way would be found to keep Tarnowski. He believes it might be possible to continue peace negotiations through him, and in a much more favorable way than through the German Government for whom the Allies have such an abiding distrust.

Do you not think it would be advisable for Lansing to get in touch with Tarnowski as early as possible in order to inform him that he is not to share Bernstorff's fate.

The sending of Bernstorff home may after all prove to be to the general advantage. Let us hope that this is true.

Affectionately yours, E. M. House

TLS (WP, DLC).

## ENCLOSURE

## Edward Mandell House
## to Count Johann Heinrich von Bernstorff

Dear Count Bernstorff: [New York] February 2, 1917.

Upon receipt of your letter of January 31st I thought it advisable to take it to Washington and hand it to the President in person.

The President is deeply disappointed at the sudden turn in the situation. It seemed as if peace was near by and could be reached by concessions here and there on both sides.

The action of your Government in regard to its submarine policy has made it impossible to carry peace negotiations further at present.

Even if the submarine issue had not been injected the proposals that your Government make are, in effect, no proposals at all. They are nullified by the expression "the terms under which we would have been prepared to enter into negotiations, if our enemies had accepted our offer of December 12th."

The suddenness with which the new undersea warfare was put into force makes it impossible for the President to propose mediation.

I cannot tell you how deeply I regret the turn matters have taken, for there was every reason to believe that within a short time the belligerents would be discussing peace.

Sincerely yours,    [E. M. House]

CCL (WP, DLC).


## From Robert Lansing, with Enclosure

PERSONAL AND CONFIDENTIAL:

My dear Mr. President:          Washington February 2, 1917.

I send you some thoughts on Germany's broken promise and the crime of submarine warfare, which I put down in writing last evening. These express my real views, which of course are given no publicity.          Faithfully yours   Robert Lansing.

TLS (WP, DLC).


### E N C L O S U R E

February 1, 1917.

This Government has been compelled to sever diplomatic relations with the Imperial German Government. For two years it has with patience and forbearance endeavored through negotiations to persuade the Imperial Government to refrain from the illegal and inhuman methods employed by its submarine commanders in their depradations upon neutral as well as enemy commerce. Its efforts have failed. Its patience has gone unrewarded. It is true that for the past nine months these methods have been modified in accordance with an assurance given this Government in response to the demand which it made after the sinking of the cross-channel steamer SUSSEX, but the act of the Imperial Government was not the abandonment of the lawless methods employed, which was demanded by this Government, it was only a postponement until Germany could materially augment its fleet of submarines and could train men to man them. This the Imperial Chancellor has publicly declared,[1] thus stamping the assurance given to this Government as an intentional subterfuge to gain time to perfect its plans of destruction. To practice such deceit upon this Government which trusted and relied upon the solemn promise of the German Government invites the contempt as well as the indignation of all right-thinking men.

Not only has the German Government violated the sanctity of its word but it proclaimed its purpose of a renewal of lawless methods only eight hours before such renewal went into effect. No reason can be given, no excuse offered which can satisfactorily explain the arrogance and insolence of a notice of this sort to neutral powers, the lives and property of whose citizens are placed in jeopardy without warning and, therefore, without opportunity to avoid the dangers, which have so suddenly and unexpectedly been decreed by the German Government over wide areas of the high seas. It is difficult to characterize such indifference to neutral rights in temperate language or to refrain from expressing the sense of outrage and resentment which is aroused by so flagrant a breach of every principle of honor and every instinct of humanity.

The methods of submarine warfare, previously practiced and the return to which has now been formally announced, invite the condemnation of civilization. In the wars of the past, even in the more barbarous periods of history, it will be hard to find examples of inhumanity parallel to the cruel and wanton slaughter of men, women and little children peaceably traversing the high seas. The brutalities perpetrated in the heat of battle, during the sack of city captured by assault, or in revenge for comrades slain find, in exceptional circumstances, possible excuse in the aroused passion and excitement of conflict; but the cold-blooded deliberation of the submarine commander skulking undersea and seeking to surprise a vessel laden with defenseless human beings and to destroy them regardless of their age and sex, regardless of their nationality, regardless of law and humanity, is a type of brutality which finds a counterpart only in that which made the pirate an international outlaw and which exists among those tribes of savages which are yet untouched by civilization.

A crime against humanity is a hundredfold more atrocious when its perpetrator has attained a high state of intellectual development. It becomes in such circumstances a premeditated reversion to barbarism, which no nation in this enlightened age can permit and expect to retain the respect of civilized nations. A government which allows such outrages by its military and naval forces and still more a government which encourages such wanton acts of inhumanity ought not and ought not to expect to be treated as a government representative of the dignity of a great people. It has lost caste among the governments of the world, and will be shunned as one dead to all moral sense. No government with a lofty conception of the sanctity of human rights or with a high regard for national honor can consistently maintain intercourse with a government which not only defends cruelty but applauds and rewards the agents who carry out its infamous policy.

The United States had endured much at the hands of Germany's ruthless naval commanders prior to the period of relaxation which followed the SUSSEX affair. It had seen its citizens, peaceably traveling on the high seas with a feeling of security that their rights would be respected, hurled to sudden death by an exploding torpedo launched from a German submersible. It had seen them torn and mangled by gun-fire as they sought to escape from a doomed vessel. It had seen them forced into frail open boats on rough seas suffering and even dying from exposure and hopeless of ever reaching the shore a hundred miles away. Not men alone bore these outrages, but delicate women and infants have been the victims of the German submarine officers who have committed these crimes without mercy and apparently without remorse.

The Government of the United States, restraining the natural impulse to allow the intense indignation caused by these horrors to direct its conduct, did not permit itself to believe that the Imperial Government, when the full enormity of these deeds were brought home to it, would not suppress so merciless and inhuman a method of warfare, if that Government really represented the thought and moral sentiment of the people of Germany. When the assurance of an abandonment of these brutal methods was given in May, 1916, this Government felt that its judgment was right, its policy of forebearance had been vindicated, its confidence in the moral character of the German Government warranted. It is, therefore, with astonishment and a deep sense of wrong that it received the declaration that indiscriminate and ruthless warfare was to be renewed with increased vigor against the commercial vessels of neutrals as well as against those of Germany's enemies.

Faith in the word of the Imperial Government is at an end. Contempt has supplanted respect. Hope for an amicable adjustment of differences has vanished. Today the eyes of the American Government and people are opened; they see the true character of the ruling power in Germany in all its falsity and brutality. It can no longer be treated as a government which is controlled by justice or right or honor. It has forfeited the regard once given to it, and has made of Germany through its dishonorable acts an outcast among the nations.

With a government, which has thus imposed upon a confiding people the verdict of outlawry, for it is the German people who must bear this penalty because they permit such a government, all intercourse must cease. Trust is the essential quality which makes international relations possible. The Government of the United States does not and cannot trust the Imperial German Government. Deceived and humiliated it has but one course to pursue and that is to denounce as outlaw the government which has treated it with contempt, has imposed upon its good will, has done to death its citizens, has ignored the most sacred rights, and has presumed in spite of all this that the United States would submit to its arrogance and insults rather than come to an open breach of friendly relations.

The situation can no longer be tolerated. The time for patience has passed. The United States would feel itself dishonored to pretend that it now has esteem for the Imperial Government or to attempt to maintain with that government the friendly intercourse which exists between governments possessing mutual sentiments of respect and good will.　　　Robert Lansing.

TS MS (WP, DLC).
[1] A reference to Bethmann Hollweg's statement on January 31 to the Main Committee of the Reichstag. *New York Times*, Feb. 2, 1917.


## From Robert Lansing

PERSONAL AND PRIVATE:

My dear Mr. President:　　　　Washington February 2, 1917.

I have been considering deeply and I believe without emotion the present crisis and just what course should be taken. The results are as follows:

I am firmly convinced that we must without taking any preliminary step break off diplomatic relations by sending Bernstorff and his suite home and by recalling Gerard and closing our Embassy at Berlin.

The next step is less clear and requires very careful thought before it is adopted. There seem to be two courses open to us.

*First*: To follow the severance of diplomatic relations by announcing to Congress this action with a statement that this Government must consider Germany to be an international outlaw, and that it would be necessary to warn Americans to keep away from the seas infested by its piratical craft.

*Second*: To follow up the severance of relations by announcing to Congress this action with a statement that Germany has forfeited every consideration by reason of her breach of faith, that the full criminality of her previous acts is revived and that no other honorable course remains but for this country to employ every resource which it possesses to punish the guilty nation and to make it impotent to commit in the future crimes again humanity.

The first course has certain advantages in that, while we would not be at war, we would be in a position to do certain things which we cannot do now consistently with strict neutrality. Furthermore it would give time for consideration as to the advisable steps to be taken afterward for I feel convinced that Germany will not declare war on the breaking off intercourse. As to the suggested warning of Americans, we could do it with propriety if we declare Germany outlaw, something which could not be done as long as we treated her as a friend. It has this disadvantage, which requires very careful consideration and may make it inadvisable, namely, that it will accomplish the very purpose which Germany sought a year ago by keeping American ships and citizens from going to Great Britain and her allies. So that it would result in Germany obtaining by threat of lawless action what she was unable to obtain through friendly negotiation.

The second course has these advantages. It amounts to a frank declaration that an outlaw Government is an enemy of mankind, and will show that the present military oligarchy must be eliminated for the sake of civilization and the future peace of the world. It will influence other neutrals far more than the less vigorous course and will, in my opinion, induce them to follow such action, which I do not think they will do unless they are certain we are willing to go the limit. It will leave us some friends after the war. It will do more to end the war than anything that can be done. It will give this country a prominent place in the peace negotiations which will prevent unjust treatment of the Central Powers and will be decidedly for their interests. It will give tremendous moral weight to the cause of human liberty and the suppression of Absolutism. It will remove all charge of weakness of policy and satisfy, I believe, our own people. (This latter advantage is not of great importance but the benefit of popular support is not to be ignored.)

In brief these are my views as to the two courses open to us if severance of diplomatic relations takes place.

Faithfully yours,   Robert Lansing.

TLS (WP, DLC).

# From Harry Augustus Garfield, with Enclosure

*Personal*

Dear Mr. President:                    Williamstown Mass. Feb. 2/17

This is hastily done & therefore not satisfactory to me. I am sending it to a fire-eating member of our Faculty in the hope of showing him the larger view. My heart is with you in this fearful hour. With the utmost of confidence in your calm & wise leadership, I am,

With high & affectionate regard,

Faithfully yours,    H. A. Garfield.

ALS (WP, DLC).

ENCLOSURE

If Germany insists on her right to sink American ships and take American life, as stated in her note of January 31, the Administration will be compelled forthwith to sever diplomatic relations. If Germany actually puts into practice her declaration as a matter of right, we shall (may?) be forced into the war. It is needless to say that the same course must be pursued if England or any of the belligerents takes the same position.

But the Administration should employ every last resource to prevent this catastrophe. Our sovereign rights are of high importance. But there is something more important than insisting upon our rights or aiding either of the belligerents or punishing any of them, namely, the creation of a union of the states of western civilization, whether called a union, a concert, or a league, and however constituted to foster the social and racial and industrial relations now existing between the several states.

If by insisting, stubbornly, upon our own rights, or upon our right to go to the aid of another nation if we so desire, or to assist another nation in its effort to right a wrong, we destroy the possibility of forming such a union, concert, or league, or postpone its consummation for years to come, we shall have sacrificed the more important for the less important duty resting upon us.

With a view to the formation of such an international state or league, it is clearly our duty, as the most powerful of the neutral nations, to keep out of the war if it is at all possible. We ought, therefore, to subordinate national rights and racial sympathies and curb righteous indignation to the accomplishment of this high aim. It will be a test of the moral courage of our people whether we succeed in thus subordinating rights of a lower order to those of a higher, under these circumstances.

The only practical way of subordinating our sense of injury to the perception of this high duty is by keeping steadily before our minds, freed from passion, the value of our services to Europe if we succeed in keeping out of the war. Only by maintaining as far as possible friendly relations with both England and Germany shall we be able to make ourselves ready when peace comes to contribute in the most effective way to the rehabilitation of Europe.

The service that we shall be able to render by keeping out of the war will far exceed any contribution we could make by an actual participation in hostilities. Indeed we can be of no great military assistance either on land or sea. To go into the war against the Entente Allies would be a serious blow to them, for an important source of food supply and munitions would thereby be cut off. On the other hand, to go into the war against the Central Allies would help rather than hurt their cause, for then there would be no question as to the relation of the submarines of the Central Powers to our merchant and passenger ships.

The people of the United States are in grave danger of being swept off their feet because of failure to perceive the superiority of the international over the national problem. Rights and duties such as are involved in this war are relative, not absolute. To argue as many do that to delay the enforcement of national rights, much less to waive any of them, particularly those involving the lives of American citizens, must inevitably lead to the sacrifice of all our rights is a reductio ad absurdum. This was the argument in support of honor and the duel, yet the sense of honor has survived the duel and men are less likely to insult one another than formerly. To say that we ought scrupulously to insist upon the punishment of violators of sovereign rights, even to making war when human lives are involved, is to say that we ought to march troops into the state whose authorities have failed to punish lynching. But we do not for civil war is a greater evil than lynching and does not prevent it.

T MS (WP, DLC).

## Paul Ritter to Arthur Hoffmann, with Enclosures

III.4 Friede.

Herr Bundesrat,                    [Washington] den 2. Februar 1917.

Meine beiden gestrigen chiffrierten Kabel 67 und 68 erfordern wenig weitere Erklärung.

Ich habe nach Erhalt Ihres Kabels No. 47 die Senatsrede Wilson's genau durchgangen und ich glaube in der Uebersetzung diejenigen Punkte hervorgehoben zu haben, auf welche Sie sich beziehen.

Die Audienz ist mir sofort bewilligt worden. Der Präsident sah sehr niedergeschlagen aus und sagte mir, dass ihm der neueste deutsche Schritt als vollkommene Ueberraschung gekommen sei. Ich las ihm Ihr Kabel vor (Beilage 1) und knüpfte einige persönliche Bemerkungen daran (Beilage 2).

Herr Wilson erwiderte, dass ihm dies sehr interessant sei und er wollte wissen, ob Sie bei der Absendung schon Kenntnis von der neuen deutschen Aktion gehabt haben. Ich sagte, dass dies der Fall gewesen sein dürfte und bat ihn, mir seine Antwort unter dieser Annahme zu geben. Der Präsident äusserte sich, dass ihm dies heute unmöglich sei, zuerst müsse die Antwort an Deutschland festgelegt sein. ("Any comment on this question is to be delayed until the German question is answered.")

Was die Stellungnahme der hiesigen Regierung gegenüber Deutschland sein werde, vermöge er mir jetzt unmöglich zu sagen. Er wisse es selbst nicht. Sein Prinzip sei immer gewesen nichts zu überstürzen ("to let cool off things"), und er glaube, dass ein Entschluss frühestens nächste Woche gefasst werde. Er beauftragte mich, sobald eine Rückäusserung von Ihnen, ob Sie heute die Vorschläge genau noch wie vor drei Tagen aufrechterhalten, eingetroffen sein werde, wieder bei ihm vorzusprechen.

Die gestrige Audienz ist vom hiesigen diplomatischen Corps, welches sie natürlich mit der Blockadefrage in Zusammenhang brachte, als sehr wichtig vermerkt worden, besonders da die Botschafter und Gesandten gestern den ganzen Tag bei Staatssekretär Lansing antichambrierten, ohne ihn sehen zu können.

Herr Wilson war äusserst zuvorkommend. Die würdige Art und Weise, wie der Präsident sich über Deutschland äusserte, rechtfertigte keineswegs die Aussage der gestrigen Abendblätter, (Beilage), dass Graf Bernstorff seine Pässe innert 48 Stunden zugestellt erhalten werde.

Die Zeitungen melden, dass die deutsche Besatzung gestern den in Charleston internierten Dampfer "Liebenfels" gesenkt habe, und dass auf anderen Dampfern die Maschinen unbrauchbar gemacht werden, um zu verhindern, dass die Schiffe eventuell durch die Vereinigten Staaten in Gebrauch genommen würden. Ich lege Ihnen heute nochmals eine Liste der hier internierten 93 deutschen Dampfer (601,287 Tonnen) bei.

Gestern abend ist der neue Oesterreich-Ungarische Botschafter Graf Tarnowski in Washington angelangt. Er ist mit dem holländischen Dampfer "Noordam" anstandslos nach New York gefahren.

Ich trete heute nicht weiter auf die deutsche Frage ein. Wer weiss wann dieser Bericht in Ihre Hände gelangt.

Die Amerikaner haben ihre Truppen aus Mexico zurückgezogen. Von einer Bestrafung Villas redet niemand mehr und es ist anzunehmen, dass für jenes Land, wenn es von den Vereinigten Staaten endlich in Ruhe gelassen wird, in absehbarer Zeit auch wieder bessere Zeiten kommen werden. (Der schweizerischen Presse entnahm ich kürzlich mit Erstaunen, dass schweizerische Kapitalien in der Höhe von 80 Millionen Franken in Mexiko angelegt seien.)

Japan hat—geschickt wie immer—auch die jetzige kritische Lage der Vereinigten Staaten benützt, um gestern durch seinen Botschafter Protest gegen von den Staaten Idaho und Oregon geplante antijapanische Gesetzesvorschriften betreffend Landerwerb zu erheben.

Ich beehre mich, Herr Bundesrat, Sie darauf aufmerksam zu machen, dass die Nationalbank, II. Department, in Bern, auf den New Yorker "Commercial and Financial Chronicle" abonniert ist und denselben regelmässig durch die Gesandtschaft zugestellt erhält. Es ist dies eines der best informierten Wochenblätter, das Ihnen und andern Departementen als Nachschlagewerk (wie zum Beispiel gestern Ihre Anfrage, die spanische Friedensnote betreffend) manchmal rasch dienen könnte. Die heute an die Nationalbank abgehende Nummer enthält u.A. den Text der Senatsansprache des Präsidenten (pag. 316). Einen Artikel: "Mr. Wilson's speech on Peace Conditions" (pag. 294). Ferner "President Wilson on principles which would serve to enlist United States in Peace Federation" (pag. 315). "President Wilson's Peace League compared with the holy Alliance["] (pag. 317). "Developments growing out of the alleged Leak in peace proposals" (pag. 322), "Resignation of Expresident Taft as Head of Worlds Court" (pag. 335), "German Consul General at San Francisco sentenced for neutrality violation" (pag. 331), "Retrospect of 1916["] (pag. 303), etc.

Genehmigen Sie, Herr Bundesrat, die Versicherung meiner ausgezeichneten Hochachtung.                    Ritter

CCL (E2200, Washington 9, Vol. 1, Swiss Federal Archives).

E N C L O S U R E     I

Please convey to President Wilson thanks of the Federal
Council for the new step made in favor of peace through his
address to Senate. Bring home to him the question whether the
cause of peace could not be promoted mightily if the fundamental
principles of the international concert, of which his address
speaks, were discussed and prepared in a conference of neutrals,
primarily on the basis of a program to be outlined by him. Attrac-
tion of the belligerents to consideration of this question is presumably not attainable today for practical purposes. But should
it not be prepared now, there is danger that, after peace between
belligerents is concluded, international organisation adjourn "ad
Calendas Graecas."

E N C L O S U R E      I I

You said that you felt sure that the American Nation shall
have a voice in de[te]rmining whether the peace terms shall be
made lasting or not by the guarantees of a universal covenant &
that the judgement be spoken now not afterward, when it may
be too late, upon what is fundamental & essential.

The Federal Council evidently & fully realizes the significance
of your endeavor to arouse the American Nation to its responsa-
bility in this grave problem, and desire to cooparate practically
in the endeavors so eloquently voiced by you. The Federal Council therefore suggests that you outline a definite program, laying
down the fundamental principals of the international concert to
be made the basis of deliberation by the neutral nations in anticipation of general negotiation.

CC MSS (E2200, Washington 9, Vol. 1, Swiss Federal Archives).

T R A N S L A T I O N

III.4 Peace.

Mr. Federal Councilor,                    Washington February 2, 1917.

My two encoded cables 67 and 68 of yesterday require little
further explanation.

After receiving your cable No. 47, I have gone through Wilson's speech to the Senate carefully and I believe I have stressed
in the translation the points that you mention.

The audience was granted me immediately. The President seemed very downcast and told me that the latest German step had come to him as a complete surprise. I read him your cable (Annex 1) and added a few personal observations (Annex 2).

Mr. Wilson replied that it interested him very much, and he wished to know whether, when you sent it, you already knew about the new German action. I said that this might well be the case and asked him to give me his reply on this assumption. The President said that he could not do this today, for first the reply to Germany must be decided. ("Any comment on this question is to be delayed until the German question is answered.")

At present he cannot tell me what position the government here will take toward Germany. He himself does not know. His principle always has been not to rush things ("to let cool off things"), and he believes that a decision will be reached next week at the earliest. He charged me to see him again as soon as I learn from you whether you still stand by the proposals today just as you did three days ago.

My audience yesterday has been considered very important by the diplomatic corps here, which naturally relates it to the blockade question, especially since the ambassadors and ministers spent the whole day yesterday in Secretary of State Lansing's antechamber without ever being able to see him.

Mr. Wilson was extremely friendly. The dignified way in which the President spoke about Germany in no way justifies the statements in last night's newspapers (enclosed) that Count Bernstorff will receive his passports within forty-eight hours.

The newspapers report that yesterday the German crew sank the steamer "Liebenfels," which was interned at Charleston, and that the machinery on other steamers had been rendered unusable, in order to prevent possible use of the ships by the United States. I enclose again a list of the 93 German steamers (601,-287 tons) interned here.

The new Austro-Hungarian Ambassador, Count Tarnowski, arrived in Washington last night. He came to New York without incident on the Dutch steamer "Noordam."

I shall say no more on the German question today. Who knows when this report will reach you?

The Americans have recalled their troops from Mexico. No one speaks any more of punishing Villa, and we can expect that, when at last the United States leaves the country in peace, it might within the foreseeable future enjoy better times. (In a word the Swiss press astonishes me, since Swiss capital to a value of eighty million francs is invested in Mexico.)

Japan, clever as always, has taken advantage of the present critical situation of the United States to lodge a protest yesterday through its ambassador against the anti-Japanese legislation planned by the states of Oregon and Idaho on acquiring land.

I have the honor, Mr. Federal Councilor, to bring to your attention that the Nationalbank, Department II, in Bern, subscribes to the New York "Commercial and Financial Chronicle" and regularly receives it through this legation. It is one of the best-informed weekly papers and can often serve you and the other departments as a reference work, as for example your inquiry yesterday about the Spanish peace note. The number going today to the Nationalbank contains, among other things, the text of the President's speech to the Senate (p. 316); an article, "Mr. Wilson's speech on Peace Conditions" (p. 294); also "President Wilson on principles which would serve to enlist United States in Peace Federation" (p. 315); "President Wilson's Peace League compared with the holy Alliance" (p. 317); "Developments Growing out of the alleged Leak in peace proposals" (p. 322); "Resignation of Ex-President Taft as Head of Worlds Court" (p. 335); "German Consul General at San Francisco sentenced for neutrality violation" (p. 331); "Retrospect of 1916" (p. 303); etc.

Accept, Mr. Federal Councilor, the assurance of my highest respect.                                                Ritter


## From John Sharp Williams

My dear Mr President:          Washington, D. C. [Feb. 3, 1917]

I understand that after I left the Capitol yesterday you expressed [the desire] to get views of Senators. This emboldens me to write mine and in my own hand, as I do not care to risk leaks.

1st.   Break off all diplomatic relations with Germany

2nd.   "   "   "   "          "          "   any of her allies who follow up her declaration with a similar one.

3rd.   Put marines on all German interned or merchant ships in our ports to prevent their being scuttled to block our harbors & remove their officers and crews not as prisoners but as "our guests."

4th.   Advise our merchant ship to carry batteries fore and aft for defense & ask Congress to give the Navy department authority to furnish them with guns of suitable calibre & men to handle the guns.

(5)    Ask Congress for money and authority to purchase or com-

mandeer abundantly motor motors [boats], suitable for meeting and overcoming submarines & guns & torpedo tubes for them—motor boats of proper size & character to serve as submarine destroyers.

6    Announce that our merchant ships will be convoyed by motor boats & where advisable by cruisers

(7)    Inform Germany through the Swiss Minister to Berlin of what we have done & that it is a course taken solely as precautionary and defensive and not as an act of war & that war or peace lies in her hand. We seek peace but if she attacks one of our ships thus convoyed we shall regard it as a declaration of war & meet that declaration in the only way that a self-respecting people can.

It is folly to await an overt act before breaking off diplomatic relations—breaking off may possibly though not probably prevent the overt act.

I write shakily and I fear not too legibly. I have not yet fully recovered from my last illness.

Above are my views: I have stated them to several Democratic members Foreign relations Committee & to one leading Republic[an] & to six or eight other Senators & all of them approved.

But whatever course you take to meet an insolent threat of ferocious terrorism, I am with you hand, heart, & soul.

With expressions of regard,      John Sharp Williams

P.S. Since writing the above I learn that you have already taken the first step and broken off diplomatic relations. Hurrah for you. Your friend more than ever even

John Sharp Williams

ALS (WP, DLC).


## An Address to a Joint Session of Congress

3 February, 1917.

Gentlemen of the Congress: The Imperial German Government on the thirty-first of January announced to this Government and to the governments of the other neutral nations that on and after the first day of February, the present month, it would adopt a policy with regard to the use of submarines against all shipping seeking to pass through certain designated areas of the high seas to which it is clearly my duty to call your attention.

Let me remind the Congress that on the eighteenth of April

last, in view of the sinking on the twenty-fourth of March of the cross-channel passenger steamer SUSSEX by a German submarine, without summons or warning, and the consequent loss of the lives of several citizens of the United States who were passengers aboard her, this Government addressed a note to the Imperial German Government in which it made the following declaration:

"If it is still the purpose of the Imperial Government to prosecute relentless and indiscriminate warfare against vessels of commerce by the use of submarines without regard to what the Government of the United States must consider the sacred and indisputable rules of international law and the universally recognized dictates of humanity, the Government of the United States is at last forced to the conclusion that there is but one course it can pursue. Unless the Imperial Government should now immediately declare and effect an abandonment of its present methods of submarine warfare against passenger and freight-carrying vessels, the Government of the United States can have no choice but to sever diplomatic relations with the German Empire altogether."

In reply to this declaration the Imperial German Government gave this Government the following assurance:

"The German Government is prepared to do its utmost to confine the operations of war for the rest of its duration to the fighting forces of the belligerents, thereby also insuring the freedom of the seas, a principle upon which the German Government believes, now as before, to be in agreement with the Government of the United States.

"The German Government, guided by this idea, notifies the Government of the United States that the German naval forces have received the following orders: In accordance with the general principles of visit and search and destruction of merchant vessels recognized by international law, such vessels, both within and without the area declared as naval war zone, shall not be sunk without warning and without saving human lives, unless these ships attempt to escape or offer resistance.

"But," it added, "neutrals can not expect that Germany, forced to fight for her existence, shall, for the sake of neutral interest, restrict the use of an effective weapon if her enemy is permitted to continue to apply at will methods of warfare violating the rules of international law. Such a demand would be incompatible with the character of neutrality, and the German Government is convinced that the Government of the United States does not think of making such a demand, knowing that the Government of the

United States has repeatedly declared that it is determined to restore the principle of the freedom of the seas, from whatever quarter it has been violated."

To this the Government of the United States replied on the eighth of May, accepting, of course, the assurances given, but adding,

"The Government of the United States feels it necessary to state that it takes it for granted that the Imperial German Government does not intend to imply that the maintenance of its newly announced policy is in any way contingent upon the course or result of diplomatic negotiations between the Government of the United States and any other belligerent Government, notwithstanding the fact that certain passages in the Imperial Government's note of the 4th instant might appear to be susceptible of that construction. In order, however, to avoid any possible misunderstanding, the Government of the United States notifies the Imperial Government that it can not for a moment entertain, much less discuss, a suggestion that respect by German naval authorities for the rights of citizens of the United States upon the high seas should in any way or in the slightest degree be made contingent upon the conduct of any other Government affecting the rights of neutrals and noncombatants. Responsibility in such matters is single, not joint; absolute, not relative."

To this note of the eighth of May the Imperial German Government made no reply.

On the thirty-first of January, the Wednesday of the present week, the German Ambassador handed to the Secretary of State, along with a formal note, a memorandum which contains the following statement:

"The Imperial Government, therefore, does not doubt that the Government of the United States will understand the situation thus forced upon Germany by the Entente-Allies' brutal methods of war and by their determination to destroy the Central Powers, and that the Government of the United States will further realize that the now openly disclosed intentions of the Entente-Allies give back to Germany the freedom of action which she reserves in her note addressed to the Government of the United States on May 4, 1916.

"Under these circumstances Germany will meet the illegal measures of her enemies by forcibly preventing after February 1, 1917, in a zone around Great Britain, France, Italy, and in the Eastern Mediterranean all navigation, that of neutrals included, from and to England and from and to France, etc., etc. All ships met within the zone will be sunk."

I think that you will agree with me that, in view of this declaration, which suddenly and without prior intimation of any kind deliberately withdraws the solemn assurance given in the Imperial Government's note of the fourth of May, 1916, this Government has no alternative consistent with the dignity and honour of the United States but to take the course which, in its note of the eighteenth of April, 1916, it announced that it would take in the event that the German Government did not declare and effect an abandonment of the methods of submarine warfare which it was then employing and to which it now purposes again to resort.

I have, therefore, directed the Secretary of State to announce to His Excellency the German Ambassador that all diplomatic relations between the United States and the German Empire are severed and that the American Ambassador at Berlin will immediately be withdrawn; and, in accordance with this decision, to hand to His Excellency his passports.

Notwithstanding this unexpected action of the German Government, this sudden and deeply deplorable renunciation of its assurances, given this Government at one of the most critical moments of tension in the relations of the two governments, I refuse to believe that it is the intention of the German authorities to do in fact what they have warned us they will feel at liberty to do. I cannot bring myself to believe that they will indeed pay no regard to the ancient friendship between their people and our own or to the solemn obligations which have been exchanged between them and destroy American ships and take the lives of American citizens in the wilful prosecution of the ruthless naval programme they have announced their intention to adopt. Only actual overt acts on their part can make me believe it even now.

If this inveterate confidence on my part in the sobriety and prudent foresight of their purpose should unhappily prove unfounded; if American ships and American lives should in fact be sacrificed by their naval commanders in heedless contravention of the just and reasonable understandings of international law and the obvious dictates of humanity, I shall take the liberty of coming again before the Congress, to ask that authority be given me to use any means that may be necessary for the protection of our seamen and our people in the prosecution of their peaceful and legitimate errands on the high seas. I can do nothing less. I take it for granted that all neutral governments will take the same course.

We do not desire any hostile conflict with the Imperial German Government. We are the sincere friends of the German people and earnestly desire to remain at peace with the Government which speaks for them. We shall not believe that they are hostile to us unless and until we are obliged to believe it; and we purpose nothing more than the reasonable defense of the undoubted rights of our people. We wish to serve no selfish ends. We seek merely to stand true alike in thought and in action to the immemorial principles of our people which I sought to express in my address to the Senate only two weeks ago,—seek merely to vindicate our right to liberty and justice and an unmolested life. These are the bases of peace, not war. God grant we may not be challenged to defend them by acts of wilful injustice on the part of the Government of Germany![1]

Printed reading copy (WP, DLC).
    [1] There is a WWsh draft of this address in WP, DLC. The shorthand draft conforms largely to the final version, except (1) Wilson omitted the quotations from the diplomatic correspondence between the two governments in his shorthand draft; (2) he added the statement about other neutrals breaking relations to his final version; and (3) he added the following sentences in the last paragraph of his final version: "We wish to serve no selfish ends. We seek merely to stand true alike in thought and in action to the immemorial principles of our people which I sought to express in my address to the Senate only two weeks ago,—seek merely to vindicate our right to liberty and justice and an unmolested life. These are the bases of peace, not war."
    Since Wilson did not dictate this address to Swem, he presumably wrote it on his own typewriter and sent it to the Public Printer. The WWT copy does not seem to have survived.


## To David Franklin Houston

My dear Houston:        The White House 3 February, 1917

Here is a letter from Kent which explains itself.[1] I would like your advice very much.

Do you not think it would be well to make the inquiry broader than he suggests? I would be very much obliged if you would suggest to me a form of request to the Trade Commission defining the scope and purpose as clearly as possible.

Just the best way to get the necessary appropriation perhaps you can tell me better than anyone else.

In haste
        Cordially and faithfully yours,   Woodrow Wilson

TCL (RSB Coll., DLC).
    [1] W. Kent to WW, Jan. 26, 1917.

## To John R. Mott

My dear Doctor Mott:          The White House 3 February, 1917

No telegram that I have received has given me such gratification as that of yesterday signed by yourself, Cleveland Dodge, Elliot Wadsworth, Frederick Alcott,[1] C. A. Coffin,[2] W. L. Honnold, and Herbert Hoover.[3] The spirit of it is, I hope, the spirit of America itself and makes me feel stronger and more certain of the course to pursue.

With warmest regard and gratitude,

Faithfully yours,    Woodrow Wilson

TLS (J. R. Mott Papers, CtY-D).
[1] Swem misspelled these names. They were Eliot Wadsworth and Frederick Walcott.
[2] Charles Albert Coffin of the General Electric Co.
[3] The telegram, which obviously commended Wilson's address to Congress, is missing. However, on February 5 Hoover sent Tumulty a letter signed by himself and Wadsworth and addressed to Wilson, in which they described a recent meeting of members of the principal relief organizations. Those present had been the signers of the telegram, that is, Wadsworth (American Red Cross), Mott (Y.M.C.A.), Hoover and Honnold (Belgian Relief Commission), Walcott (Rockefeller Foundation), Dodge (Armenian Relief Commission), and Coffin (American Relief Clearing House). This group had concluded "that it would be very desirable, as a matter of preparedness, to take early steps for the formation of a great national relief fund, to meet the present crisis at home, this fund to be raised primarily for the American Red Cross and secondarily for other relief measures at home and abroad." H. C. Hoover and E. Wadsworth to WW, Feb. 5, 1917, TLS (WP, DLC). Hoover asked Tumulty to bring the matter to Wilson's early attention. H. C. Hoover to JPT, Feb. 5, 1917, TLS (WP, DLC).

## To Walter Lippmann

My dear Lippmann:          [The White House] 3 February, 1917

Thank you warmly for the copy of your "Stakes of Diplomacy." I shall take the greatest pleasure in looking it through and shall expect a great deal of profit from doing so.

The extract from Mr. Wells' letter which you were kind enough to copy into yours is extremely interesting, particularly since it so closely coincided with some of the things at any rate that I was trying to do.

In haste, with warmest regard,

Cordially and sincerely yours,    Woodrow Wilson

TLS (Letterpress Books, WP, DLC).

## To Anita McCormick Blaine

My dear Mrs. Blaine:          The White House 3 February, 1917

I have read your telegram with the most solemn interest.[1] I wish that I could see some way that would accomplish what you evidently have in mind, but, unhappily, I have been dealing so intimately and so long with the German authorities that I feel that any course except the one I am pursuing today would be practically useless. It is a hard decision to come to, but one which has been forced upon me. I believe the other things that you have in mind must be delayed until some better opportunity offers.

In haste, with the warmest regard,

Cordially and sincerely yours,   Woodrow Wilson

TLS (A. M. Blaine Papers, WHi).
¹ The telegram is missing. Earlier, Mrs. Blaine had asked Wilson about the advisability of convening an international congress of women at the same time and place as the peace conference. Anita M. Blaine to WW, Dec. 19, 1916, ALS (WP, DLC). Wilson had replied on December 28, 1916, that, in his judgment, it would be "distinctly a hindrance and not a help for outside bodies bent upon influencing the result to meet at the same time and place with the conference or whatever other body may assemble for the settlement of the issues of the present war." WW to Anita M. Blaine, Dec. 28, 1916, TLS (Letterpress Books, WP, DLC).

## From Newton Diehl Baker, with Enclosure

(CONFIDENTIAL)

Dear Mr. President:                Washington, February 3, 1917

I inclose for your eye a copy of the dispatch which I have just sent General Wood.

Respectfully yours,   Newton D. Baker

TLS (WP, DLC).

### E N C L O S U R E

Washington. February 3, 1917

Delay muster out of Delaware troops and any others not yet mustered out until further orders. Question of calling any troops into the Federal service will be determined later. It is reported here that the Governors of New York and Connecticut have called out State troops for local use. The President deems it imperative that no troops under Federal control be stationed or used in a manner which will excite apprehension or suggest anticipated trouble, and especially that no basis should be given for opinion abroad that we are mobilizing. The breach of diplomatic relations does not justify such action and if taken it might be gravely misconstrued.                Newton D. Baker

TC telegram (WP, DLC).

## From Walter Hines Page

*Personal and Confidential*

Dear Mr. President:                    London. Feb. 3. 1917

For a long time I have been hoping that an opportunity wd. come some day for me to explain to the British Gov't the disadvantage of having Spring Rice in Washington, especially in times like these. I recall that House and I once talked it over here.

Well, such an opportunity did come a week or more ago and I very frankly (and, I hope, kindly) told Mr. Balfour the whole truth. I hear now, quite definitely but not officially, that a change is soon to be made.          Yours sincerely,   Walter H. Page

ALS (WP, DLC).


## From Warren Worth Bailey, with Enclosure

My Dear Mr. President:    Washington, D. C. February 3, 1917.

I am taking the liberty of sending you the enclosed telegram, just received, from George Foster Peabody of New York, hoping that it may interest you at this crucial juncture. I can not but feel that the sentiment which responded to Mr. Bryan's great appeal last night in the metropolis is indicative of that prevailing throughout the United States. There must be some other way out of this terrible situation than that of an appeal to the sword.
          Yours respectfully,   Warren Worth Bailey

TLS (WP, DLC).


### E N C L O S U R E

New York NY Feb 2 17

This message entirely my own thought and not suggested. Bryan made one of his greatest speeches tonight to over seven thousand people, seven-eighths voters, who were magnificently responsive to every one of many superb arguments. He was splendid in the heartiest praise at great length of the great message of the President through the Senate to the world. He left here midnight to stop over at Washington. I hope the President receives the report direct from him of the wonderful sentiment of this meeting.          George Foster Peabody.

T telegram (WP, DLC).

## Robert Lansing to All Missions of the United States in All Neutral Countries

Washington, February 3, 1917.

(Send to Madrid first)

You are instructed to notify immediately the Government to which you are accredited that this Government, in view of the recent announcement of the German Government of its intention to renew indiscriminate submarine warfare, has no alternative but to pursue the course laid down in its note to the German Government on April 18, 1916. It will, therefore, recall the American Ambassador and his suite at Berlin and will forthwith deliver to the German Ambassador here passports for him and his suite.

You will also say that the President is reluctant to believe that Germany will actually carry out the threats made against neutral commerce, but, if it is done, the President will ask from Congress authority to use the national power to protect American citizens engaged in peaceable and lawful errands on the high seas. The course taken is, in the view of the President, in entire conformity with the principles enunciated by him in his address to the Senate on January 12th (22), and he therefore believes that it will make for the peace of the world if the other neutral powers can find it possible to take similar action to that taken by this Government.

Immediately make full report by telegraph of the reception of this announcement and of suggestion as to similar action.

Lansing.

T telegram (SDR, RG 59, 763.72/3199a, DNA).

## From Walter Hines Page

London, February 4, 1916 [1917].

5595. PERSONAL TO THE PRESIDENT.

Your prompt action after your patient efforts to avoid a rupture will strengthen our national character and build up our national unity at home. In Europe it will put us in the highest esteem of all nations including even the people of the Central Powers; it will shorten the war; it will preserve to us our proper high place in the family of great powers; it will immeasurably advance the influence of democracy and it will give you the lead with your constructive programme in insuring peace hereafter.

Mrs. Page thinks this telegram too impersonal. So it may be, but I am afraid to let myself go.                    Page.

T telegram (SDR, RG 59, 763.72/3198, DNA).

## From Edward Mandell House, with Enclosure

Dear Governor:                    New York. February 4, 1917.

Here is a letter which came from Bernstorff this morning.

I am told that he wants to go to Cuba instead of home. They seem to be fearful not only of the voyage but of their reception in Germany. I think it would be a mistake to allow him to remain in the Western Hemisphere if it can be avoided. Even if he did not foment trouble, it would be thought that he was doing so.

If actual war occurs (which I hope and pray it may not) could I not be of more service to you if you placed me on your Staff, letting me help wherever the pressure was greatest?

I know how deeply you feel the present crisis. You should remember, though, that you have done everything that could humanly be done to avert it. If war comes, it will not be a war of your making nor, indeed, will it be a war just begun, therefore, no more lives will be lost than if we remained out, and the possibilities for directing a wholesome peace will be enormously increased.

If Germany does not soon succeed in her submarine warfare she will be insistent upon peace, and if the Allies do not succeed as they expect, they too will consent to a conference. I therefore believe the war is in its last phase and I beli[e]ve that the action you have taken may be all for good.

Your affectionate,   E. M. House

TLS (WP, DLC).

### E N C L O S U R E

## Count Johann Heinrich von Bernstorff to Edward Mandell House

Washington, D. C.

My dear Colonel House:                    February 3, 1917.

Many thanks for your letter.[1] You know how I feel about the matter, so I need not tell you. However, I do not believe that my Government intended to nullify the peace terms I mentioned to you. I understand those terms to be our present ones, and that they will only be changed, if the submarine warfare leads to decisive results.

I do not wish to close this letter, without expressing to you my most cordial thanks for the kind assistance you have always given me during the last years of stress. I shall never forget the friendship you have shown me.

Yours very sincerely,   J. Bernstorff.

TCL (WP, DLC).
¹ EMH to J. H. von Bernstorff, Feb. 2, 1917, printed as an Enclosure with EMH to WW, Feb. 2, 1917.

## A Memorandum by Robert Lansing

MEMORANDUM ON THE SEVERANCE OF<br>DIPLOMATIC RELATIONS WITH GERMANY.

February 4, 1917.

During the forenoon of Wednesday, January 31, 1917, the German Ambassador telephoned my office and arranged an interview for four o'clock that afternoon. He did not indicate his purpose and my own idea was that he probably desired to talk over confidentially the terms on which Germany would make peace.

That afternoon I was working on a letter to the President in regard to the arming of merchant vessels on the ground that Germany was undoubtedly preparing to renew vigorous submarine warfare. Before I had completed the letter the German Ambassador was announced.

When he entered my room at ten minutes after four I noticed that, though he moved with his usual springy step, he did not smile with his customary assurance. After shaking hands and sitting down in the large easy chair by the side of my desk he drew forth from an envelope, which he carried, several papers. Selecting one he held it out saying that he had been instructed to deliver it to me. As I took the paper he said that he had had for convenience an English translation made. He then handed me three documents in English consisting of a note and two accompanying memoranda.

He asked me if he should read them to me or if I would read them to myself before he said anything about them. I replied that I would read the papers, which I did slowly and carefully for as the nature of the communication was disclosed I realized that it was of very serious import and would probably bring on the gravest crisis which this Government had had to face during the war. The note announced the renewal on the next day of indiscriminate submarine warfare, and the annulment of the assurances given this Government by Germany in the note of May 4, 1916, following the SUSSEX affair.

While I had been anticipating for nearly three months this very moment in our relations with Germany and had given expression to my conviction in the public statement which I made concerning our note of December 18th, for which I had been so generally criticized, I was nevertheless surprised that Germany's return to ruthless methods came at this time. I knew that all her shipyards had been working to their full capacity in constructing submarines for the past seven months and that thousands of men were being trained to handle their complex mechanism, but I assumed that on account of the difficulties of using submarines in northern waters during midwinter the campaign would not begin before March and probably not until April. It was therefore with real amazement that I read the note and memoranda handed me. I can only account for the premature announcement of indiscriminate warfare on the ground that the food situation in Germany had reached such a pass that the Imperial Government had to do something to satisfy public opinion.

As I finished my deliberate perusal of the papers, I laid them on the desk and turned toward Count Bernstorff. "I am sorry" he said, "to have to bring about this situation but my Government could do nothing else."

I replied, "That is of course the excuse given for this sudden action, but you must know that it cannot be accepted."

"Of course; of course," he said, "I understand that. I know it is very serious, very, and I deeply regret that it is necessary."

"I believe you do regret it," I answered, "for you know what the result will be. But I am not blaming you personally."

"You should not," he said with evident feeling, "you know how constantly I have worked for peace."

"I do know it," I said, "I have never doubted your desire or failed to appreciate your efforts."

"I still hope," he said speaking with much earnestness, "that with a full realization of Germany's situation your Government will in justice decide that the notification of blockade is entirely warranted."

I answered him that I could not discuss the merits until I had thoroughly digested the documents, but I would say that the first reading had made a very bad impression, and that to give only eight hours notice without any previous warning of intention was in my opinion an unfriendly and indefensible act.

He exalimed [exclaimed], "I do not think it was so intended; I am sure it was not."

"I regret that I must differ with you," I replied, "but this has come so suddenly that I am sure you will understand I do not wish to discuss the matter further."

"Of course, of course; I quite understand," he said rising and extending his hand which I took with a feeling almost of compassion for the man, whose eyes were suffused and who was not at all the jaunty care-free man-of-the-world he usually was. With a ghost of a smile he bowed as I said "Good afternoon" and turning left the room.

Immediately on his departure I called in Polk and Woolsey, and read the communication which I had received. We all agreed that the only course which seemed open was to break off diplomatic relations. I think we all expressed indignation at the shortness of the notice and the repudiation of the SUSSEX assurance.

I telephoned to the White House and found the President was out. I then wrote him a short letter transmitting the papers, and sent it by Sweet to the White House, who between five and five-thirty left it with the usher to be put in the President's hands as soon as he returned. Through some confusion with other papers the President did not get the papers until after eight o'clock. He then telephoned me to come to the White House.

From a quarter to nine until half past ten we conferred in his study beneath the picture of Secretary Day and the French Ambassador signing the preliminaries of peace with Spain. Throughout the conference I maintained that we must pursue the course which we had declared we would pursue in our SUSSEX note of April 18, 1916, namely to break off relations with Germany if she practiced ruthless submarine warfare; that any lesser action would be impossible; and that the only question in my mind was whether we ought not to go further and declare that the actual renewal of indiscriminate submarine attack affecting our citizens or ships would be considered by us to be an act of war.

The President, though deeply incensed at Germany's insolent notice, said, that he was not yet sure what course we must pursue and must think it over; that he had been more and more impressed with the idea that "white civilization" and its domination in the world rested largely on our ability to keep this country intact, as we would have to build up the nations ravaged by the war. He said that as this idea had grown upon him he had come to the feeling that he was willing to go to any lengths rather than to have the nation actually involved in the conflict.

I argued with him that, if the break did not come now, it was bound to do so in very short time, and that we would be in a much stronger position before the world if we lived up to our declared purpose than if we waited until we were further humiliated. I said that if we failed to act I did not think we could hold up our heads as a great nation and that our voice in the future would be treated with contempt by both the Allies and Germany.

The President said that he was not sure of that; that, if he believed that it was for the good of the world for the United States to keep out of the war in the present circumstances, he would be willing to bear all the criticism and abuse which would surely follow our failure to break with Germany; that contempt was nothing unless it impaired future usefulness; and that nothing could induce him to break off relations unless he was convinced that viewed from every angle it was the wisest thing to do.

I replied to this that I felt that the greatness of the part which a nation plays in the world depends largely upon its character and the high regard of other nations; that I felt that to permit Germany to do this abominable thing without firmly following out to the letter what we had proclaimed to the world we would do, would be to lose our character as a great power and the esteem of all nations; and that to be considered a "bluffer" was an impossible position for a nation which cherished self-respect.

There was of course much more said during our conference. The President showed much irritation over the British disregard for neutral rights and over the British plan (asserted by Germany) to furnish British merchant ships with heavy guns. I told him that so far as proof of this we had none, but it seemed to me that Germany's declaration in any event justified such a practice. He replied that he was not certain that the argument was sound but he did not think it worth while to discuss it now in view of the present crisis.

After some further talk it was agreed that I should prepare a note to Bernstorff setting out the breach of faith by Germany and breaking off diplomatic relations. This was to be a tentative draft and a basis for further consideration of the subject.

On returning home I immediately prepared a draft in rough form, and the next morning (Thursday) redrew it in my own handwriting using for the quoted parts clippings from the printed correspondence. (This note with practically no changes was the one finally sent.)

Although many diplomats called at the Department I denied myself to them all as I did not care to discuss the situation. However I had to see Senator Hitchcock, who in the absence of Senator Stone was the ranking Democrat on the Committee of Foreign

Relations. He suggested that we ask the belligerents of both sides for a ten-days armistice. I asked him what good that would do. He said "To gain time." "Well, and then what?" I asked. He had nothing to offer and I told him that I did not think that it would get us anywhere, but that, even if there was some benefit to be gained, I was sure that Germany would decline and the Allies would probably do the same. He went away in a dispirited frame of mind, saying that he saw no other way of avoiding the trouble.

At noon on Thursday (the 1st of February) I went over to the White House and with Col. House, who had arrived early that morning, conferred with the President for about an hour in his study. We went over substantially the same ground, which the President and I had covered the night before. The Colonel, as is customary with him, said very little, but what he did say was in support of my views.

I went further in this conference than I did in the previous one by asserting that in my opinion peace and civilization depended on the establishment of democratic institutions throughout the world, and that this would be impossible if Prussian militarism after the war controlled Germany. The President said that he was not sure of this as it might mean the disintegration of German power and the destruction of the German nation. His argument did not impress me as very genuine, and I concluded that he was in his usual careful way endeavoring to look at all sides of the question.

When I left the conference I felt convinced that the President had almost reached a decision to send Bernstorff home. It was not any particular thing which he said but rather a general impression gained from the entire conversation. At any rate I felt very much better than I had the night before when the President's tone of indecision had depressed me. Probably I misjudged him because he did not at once fall in with my views, which were certainly radical.

Thursday evening I wrote out at considerable length an arraignment of Germany on her submarine methods and the faithlessness of the German Government in giving its assurance of May 4, 1916, in the SUSSEX case. I wrote it as I felt without softening the harshness of my thoughts, and, as I intended to send it to the President, I wished him to know exactly how I felt.

The next morning (Friday, the 2nd) I read to Mr. Polk my arraignment of Germany, which he heartily approved, and then sent it to the President. Three times that morning the President and I conferred over our private wire. We discussed the issuance of passports, the sailing of American ships for the "danger zone" and the possibility of securing identic action by other neutrals in case of a break with Germany.

At 2:30 Friday afternoon the Cabinet met and sat until 4:45. The entire time was given to a discussion of the crisis with Germany. The discussion was very general although it was chiefly confined to the subjects which the President and I had been over in our conferences.

I felt all the time that, while the President was holding back in the traces, he was not unwilling to be urged forward by argument favoring a strong policy. He appeared to be resisting the idea of a break with Germany. In this he was supported by Secretary Wilson, and Burleson seemed more or less sympathetic. All the rest were united in support of severing relations, McAdoo and Houston being particularly outspoken. I am not at all sure that the President urged his arguments in good faith. I do not mean anything invidious by this, only that I have often seen him in Cabinet meetings oppose action, which I was sure he favored, in order to draw out arguments on both sides. Indeed I am morally certain his mind was made up when he came to the meeting.

Just at the close of the session he read the note which I had drafted saying that if it seemed best to sever relations it was proposed to send this note which avoided a general attack on lawless submarine warfare and dealt only with Germany's broken promise.

I think that the part of the discussion which most deeply shocked some of the members was the President's comment on a remark which I made concerning the future peace of the world. I said that I was convinced that an essential of permanent peace was that all nations should be politically liberalized; that the only surety of independence for small nations was that the great and powerful should have democratic institutions because democracies were never aggressive or unjust. I went on to say that it seemed to me there could be no question but that to bring to an end absolutism the Allies ought to succeed, and that it was for our interest and for the interest of the world that we should join the Allies and aid them if we went into the war at all.

To this the President replied, "I am not so sure of that." He then went on to argue that probably greater justice would be done if the conflict ended in a draw. This did not make so painful an impression on me as it did on others who heard it, for I was sure it was done to draw out arguments. Furthermore I knew that the President agreed with me about democracy being the only firm foundation for universal peace.

When we left the Cabinet room some of my colleagues remarked that I seemed very cheerful. I told them I was cheerful for I was sure that it would all come out right. They shook their heads dubiously and said that they could not see it that way.

Friday was a day of extreme tension. From morning till night officials and newspaper men were fairly on tiptoe with suppressed excitement. Fully eighty of the correspondents were present at my interview in the morning, and they were swarming in the corridors when I returned to the Department at five o'clock. I slept soundly that night feeling sure that the President would act vigorously.

Saturday morning (the 3rd) soon after I reached the Department Polk and I discussed the situation. He was doubtful and distressed, and I assured him that I was certain the President would act that day.

A little after ten Senator Stone, who had arrived from the West on Friday noon and had taken part in the conferences which the President held in his room at the Capitol soon after the Cabinet meeting, came in, but as I had just been summoned by telephone to the White House we had only a word together.

At 10:30 I reached the President's study and we conferred for half an hour. He told me that he had decided to hand Bernstorff his passports and to recall Gerard, and that at two o'clock that afternoon he would address Congress laying before them in a little more elaborate form the substance of the note which I had drafted together with a statement that he would come before them again and ask for powers in case Germany should carry out her threats. I congratulated him on his decision saying I was sure that he was right and that the American people almost to a man would stand behind him.

It was arranged that at the hour when the President began his address to Congress Count Bernstorff would receive his passports. I told the President that in view of the routine preparation of the note and passport and of the necessity of getting of telegrams to Berlin and neutral countries inviting their identic action, it would be impossible for me to go to the Capitol at two o'clock. He replied that he understood perfectly and that in any event the essential part of his address was in the note which I had drafted.

On leaving the White House I met Tumulty in front of the Executive Offices. He had just returned from the Capitol, where he had been to arrange for the President's appearance there at two o'clock. I then hurried over to the Department, called in Polk and Woolsey and later Phillips and Sweet. The necessary papers were prepared as rapidly as possible and I read and signed them. Everything was carried through according to schedule. At two the President spoke at the Capitol in the House of Representatives. Three minutes before two Woolsey delivered the note and passports to Count Bernstorff at the Embassy; and the necessary telegrams were put on the wires.

Even so serious an act as the severing of diplomatic relations with Germany was a great relief from the intense anxiety of the two preceeding days. From the reception of the German notification Wednesday afternoon I had felt that such action was the only possible one to take and to preserve the Honor, dignity and prestige of the United States. I did not really doubt but that the President would ultimately reach the same conclusion, but I feared that the delay would create the impression that he was wavering and undecided. When, therefore, he announced his decision on Saturday morning I was thankful that the period of uncertainty was over, that the die was cast, and that Germany's insolent challenge had been met with firmness. That it would be received with the universal approval by the American people was not a matter of doubt. Whatever may be the consequences no other course was open to a self-respecting nation.

T MS (R. Lansing Papers, DLC).

## Chevalier Willem Louis Frederik Christiaan van Rappard to the Netherlands Foreign Ministry

[Washington] 4. febr 1917

Tel 125 J'apprends de source autorisée que President des Etats-Unis a reçu aujourd'hui en audience privée mon collègue de Suisse chargé des interets allemands aux Etats-Unis. point. On m'assure qu'il s'agirait d'une dernière tentative de paix emanant du conseil fédéral. point. J'ignore toutefois les termes. point. Si vous connaissez par Legation Berne les termes de cette proposition, et si vous croyez pouvoir les appuyer peut-être qu'une action commune aurait encore quelque effet. point. Ce n'est qu'à contre coeur que Etats-Unis entrent en guerre avec Allemagne.

Rappard

Hw telegram (540/532, NFM-Ar).

T R A N S L A T I O N

[Washington] Feb. 4, 1917

125. I have learned from an official source that today the President of the United States received in private audience my

Swiss colleague, who is in charge of German interests in the United States. I am told that it concerned a last attempt at peace by the Federal Council. I do not know the terms, however. If you have learned the terms of this proposition through the Legation in Bern, and if you believe that you can support them, it may be that a common action could still have some effect. Only with the greatest reluctance would the United States go to war with Germany.                                                        Rappard

## To Nelson C. Durand[1]

My dear Mr. Durand:        [The White House] 5 February, 1917

I wish with all my heart that I might be present to take part in celebrating Mr. Edison's seventieth birthday. It would be a real pleasure to be able to say in public with what deep and genuine admiration I have followed his remarkable career of achievement. I was an undergraduate at the University when his first inventions captured the imagination of the world, and ever since then I have retained the sense of magic which what he did then created in my mind. He seems always to have been in the special confidence of nature herself. His career has already made an indelible impression in the history of applied science and I hope that he has many years yet before him in which to make the record still more remarkable.[2]

Cordially and sincerely yours,    Woodrow Wilson

TLS (Letterpress Books, WP, DLC).

[1] Vice-president and general manager of the Ediphone Division of Thomas A. Edison, Inc., and one of Edison's early associates in the development of the incandescent lamp and in the development of electronic recording.

[2] Some 1,800 employees of Thomas A. Edison, Inc., celebrated Edison's birthday with him on February 10 in the Edison Storage Battery Building at West Orange, N. J. There were no speeches, but Wilson's letter was read. *New York Times*, Feb. 11, 1917.

## From Robert Lansing

Dear Mr. President:        Washington February 5, 1917

The British Ambassador called upon Mr. Phillips this morning and asked that you be advised privately that he had received a message from the Duke of Devonshire, Governor-General of Canada, expressing, not only on his own behalf but on behalf of both parties and the people of Canada, the intensity of their feeling of admiration for the course which you have taken.

Apparently it is the policy of the British Government to suppress to a considerable extent the press reports of the tremenduous enthusiasm in the British Empire, not only in Government circles but in all classes of society including the labor element, fearing that the outburst of enthusiasm, which has in fact occurred, if advertised too much, might not be desirable from the point of view of this country. Sir Cecil Spring Rice therefore has informed the Duke of Devonshire that his message to you is being communicated unofficially through me.

With assurances of respect, etc., I am, my dear Mr. President,
Faithfully yours,   Robert Lansing.

TLS (SDR, RG 59, 763.72/3312C, DNA).

## From Edward Mandell House

Dear Governor:                    New York. February 5, 1917.

Von Weigand, the one time World correspondent at Berlin and now attached to the American, contemplates returning to Germany within a few days. If he cannot get to Germany he will go to Holland.

He believes if the German people could know just what is in your mind and what you have tried to do for peace, it would make a vast difference in the situation. He thinks he is in a position to get this information to them through the German press.

Just how trustworthy von Weigand is, I do not know. Gerard does not like him, but since he has interviewed the Kaiser, the Crown Prince, the Chancellor, Hindenberg, the Pope and practically everyone else in high position, both in Germany and Austria, I judge he has standing among them.

Thank you for enclosing me the cables from Stovall.[1] I shall attend to the matter at once.

Your affectionate,   E. M. House

I am seeing a great many people of the press and am trying to guide them and *calm* them.[2]

TLS (WP, DLC).
[1] Telegrams 470, 478, and 481 from Bern, Jan. 13, 25, and 29, 1917, together with Lansing's telegrams 351 and 361 to Bern, Jan. 16 and 27, 1917, and Gerard's telegram from Berlin, Jan. 26, 1917, which was sent as Egan's telegram 4934 from Copenhagen, Jan. 26, 1917. These telegrams bear no file numbers. They conveyed a report to Stovall by I. (or J.) Gumpertz, a Swiss national living in Hamburg, to the effect that he had been approached by several prominent Germans "with the object of enlisting his cooperation in a plot to assassinate the President of the United States" (telegram 470). Stovall reported in telegram 478 that Gumpertz stated under oath before the Secretary of Legation that the proposal had been presented in Hamburg in August 1916 by Max Schultz, a commercial agent, and, further, "that Schultz was acting for a number of prominent Germans in Hamburg whose names he will not reveal; that all were members of the German all Deutsch Party [Alldeutscher Verband]; that he is greatly worried over his own participation in this plot; that he had virtual-

ly agreed, should the President be reelected, to proceed to the United States to carry out this plot, but now that he has revealed it to the American authorities he desires only to be released from his criminal agreement and to ensure his personal safety; that Schultz has a brother in the United States who might be secured to carry out this plot." Stovall, who earlier was not fully convinced of Gumpertz's credibility, noted that Schultz now appeared to be telling the truth. Lansing's two messages were requests for further information. Stovall's telegram 481 stated that Gumpertz had never known the name or address of Schultz's brother in the United States. Telegram 4934 reported that the American Consul General in Hamburg knew the Gumpertz family personally and would try to get further information. Wilson sent copies of these telegrams to House with an undated pencil notation: "Dear House—Here are the despatches I said I w'd get for you. W.W." Wilson had presumably discussed the matter with House at the White House on February 1. ALI, c. Feb. 4, 1917, with the six listed telegrams enclosed (E. M. House Papers, CtY). House's diary for February 6, 1917, includes the following: "Chief Flynn of the Secret Service was my first caller. I gave him some cablegrams from our Minister at Berne telling of a plot to assassinate the President and giving the name of a German in New York who was concerned in it. Flynn and I went over the situation carefully as to possible disturbances here which might arise in the event of a break with Germany."

2 EMHhw.


## From Cleveland Hoadley Dodge

My dear President                    New York. February 5th 1917

It had to come and you must be happy to have the long agony over. How wonderfully the country has risen to the occasion

For we, who have been surrounded by men for months, who didn't approve of you (to say the least) it is a source of great joy to now hear, without a dissenting voice, a great chorus of praise, and the admission that you have known better than they, and have done all along the right thing.

Dark days may be ahead of us, and when I think of my dear ones in Turkey,[1] I am naturally a little anxious, but I feel in the bottom of my soul that you couldn't have done otherwise.

May God bless & keep you and give you new strength for all that is ahead!

With love to all the family

Yours affectionately    C H Dodge

ALS (WP, DLC).
[1] His son, Bayard Dodge, and Bayard's wife, Mary Williams Bliss Dodge. Bayard Dodge was connected with the American University of Beirut.


## Robert Lansing to Walter Hines Page

Washington, February 5, 1917.

4395   Confidential and personal for Ambassador.

Under extreme pressure of present situation President has been unable to consider your communications in regard to your resignation. He desired me to inform you that he hopes that at the present time you will not press to be relieved from service, that he realizes that he is asking you to make a personal sacrifice but believes that you will appreciate the importance in the crisis which has developed that no change should be made. I hardly need to add my personal hope that you will put aside for the present any thought of resigning your post.          Lansing

T telegram (SDR, RG 59, 123 P 14/54a, DNA).

## Frederic Courtland Penfield to Robert Lansing

Vienna via Berne, Feb. 5, 1917.

1683.   Following addressed to Secretary of State at the request of Minister for Foreign Affairs:[1]

"The Imperial and Royal Ambassador Count Tarnowski has conveyed to me the kind words which you were good enough to express to him concerning Austria-Hungary[2] and I hasten to transmit to you on that account my very best thanks.

I need not say I, too, would be very pleased if the diplomatic relations between us and the United States could be maintained intact. But in order to obtain that result I must above all once again ask the Government of the United States to take into consideration the position in which we are placed.

We have declared—openly and honestly—that we only wage a war of defense, that is, that we are ready to negotiate honorable conditions of peace—a peace without victory. These proposals we are still determined to maintain. The basis, according to which there should be neither victor nor loser, was suggested by Mr. Wilson himself and it is now up to Entente to accommodate themselves to that basis as we did. As long as the Entente will not give up the programme published in their last note, a programme which aims at the dismemberment of Austria-Hungary, it is impossible for us to talk about peace, and we are forced to defend ourselves with every means at our disposal.

A technical modification of the submarine war is impossible. First of all an exchange of views with our allies would be necessary to that purpose. Moreover—and this is the chief reason—the numerous submarines which have left their ports cannot be reached by any orders.

The point of the question is, it seems to me, that Mr. Wilson who proposed a peace without victory should now feel morally obliged to use his influence with the Powers of the Entente to make them accept that basis as we accepted it. The President has all the qualities to achieve this—on account of his high position, the personal esteem he enjoys all through Europe and on account of the possibility for the United States, by cutting off the requisites of war, to induce the Powers of the Entente to conform themselves to Mr. Wilson's point of view.

I trust that the President of the United States will continue the work of peace he began in a spirit of impartiality and I sincerely hope that he will induce the Powers of the Entente to accept, like us, the American point of view, that there should be neither victor nor loser and that the peace concluded should be an honorable one for both sides—a lasting one for the whole world.

Should the President follow this line of conduct not only the terror of the submarine war, but war in general would come to a sudden end and Mr. Wilson's name will shine with everlasting letters in the history of mankind.

I beg to request you kindly to bring the above as well as the answer you might send me to the notice of Ambassador Count Tarnowski.   (Signed) Czernin.["]          Penfield.

T telegram (SDR, RG 59, 763.72/3243, DNA).
1 Count Ottokar Czernin (von und zu Chudenitz), who had become Foreign Minister of Austria-Hungary on December 23, 1916.
2 Tarnowski had made his first call as Ambassador-designate at the State Department on the morning of February 3, and Lansing had talked with him about the desirability of maintaining diplomatic relations between the United States and Austria-Hungary. See RL to F. C. Penfield, Feb. 4, 1917, *FR-WWS 1917*, I, 112-13.

## Chevalier Willem Louis Frederik Christiaan van Rappard to the Netherlands Foreign Ministry

[Washington] 5. 2. 17.

127.   Mon telegramme 125. J'apprends que Suisse avant rupture entre Etats-Unis et Allemagne a proposé à Amerique une reunion de neutres pour etablir ligne de conduite de tous les neutres lorsque pendant prochain pourparler de paix les grands problèmes de droit international seront discutés. point. Suisse observait qu'il serait advantageux si pendant ces discussions les neutres presentaient front uni et pas divisés entre eux. point. Après rupture President des Etats-Unis a pris initiative en demandant à Suisse si elle maintenait sa proposition même après les derniers evenements. point. Hier Ministre de Suisse est allé assurer President que son Gouvernement maintenait sa proposition qu'il voyait même dans conditions actuelles raison de plus

pour la maintenir. On me dit confidentiellement que bientôt President agira d'une facon ou autre sur cette proposition.

Rappard

Hw telegram (552/540, NFM-Ar.).

TRANSLATION

[Washington] 5. 2. 17.

127.  With reference to my telegram 125. I have learned that, before the breach of relations between the United States and Germany, Switzerland proposed to the United States a meeting of neutrals to decide on a course of action for all the neutrals when great problems of international law are discussed in the next peace negotiations. Switzerland pointed out that in these talks it would help if the neutrals presented a united front and were not divided among themselves. After the breach, the President of the United States took the initiative by asking if Switzerland still supported its proposal even after the latest events. Yesterday the Swiss Minister went to reassure the President that his government maintained its proposal and in existing circumstances saw even more reason to do so. I have been told confidentially that the President will soon act one way or the other on the proposal.                    Rappard

## Two Letters to Robert Lansing

My dear Mr. Secretary,     The White House.   6 February, 1917.

I am glad that the British authorities are showing this kind of good taste and good judgment.[1]

I wonder if there is any need of my making personal acknowledgement? Perhaps it would be best for the Department to make acknowledgement for me.       Faithfully Yours,   W.W.

WWTLI (SDR, RG 59, 763.72/3312½, DNA).
[1] See RL to WW, Feb. 5, 1917.

My dear Mr. Secretary,     The White House.   6 February, 1917.

I entirely agree with this suggestion so far as Panama is concerned.[1]

In the case of Cuba[2] I have this question in my mind: might not such action on her part be used as an excuse by Germany for an early attack upon her, or the seizure of a naval base there, on the pretext that Cuba was in effect hostile? It might be to Germany's advantage, in other words, to declare war on Cuba (or make it without declaring it) before taking action against us. A base for her submarines on this side the sea would be most convenient. What do you think?[3]   Faithfully Yours,   W.W.

WWTLI (SDR, RG 59, 763.72/3314½, DNA).
[1] That is, that Panama be asked to break off relations with Germany and expel the German consuls. RL to WW, Feb. 5, 1917, CCL (SDR, RG 59, 763.72/3203, DNA).
[2] RL to WW, Feb. 5, 1917, CCL, with W. E. Gonzales to RL, Feb. 4, 1917, T telegram (SDR, RG 59, 763.72/3207, DNA).
[3] A Hw note by Lansing, dated February 7, 1917, and attached to Wilson's letter, reads: "Saw the Cuban Minister and advised him that it would be unwise for Cuba to break off diplomatic relations with Germany. He said that he would so advise his Govt."

## To Robert Lansing, with Enclosure

My dear Mr. Secretary,    The White House.   6 February, 1917.

This appeals to me. I would like your advice as to the best way in which to give the assurance.[1]

Faithfully Yours,   W.W.

WWTLI (SDR, RG 59, 763.72113/1238, DNA).
[1] See the statement printed at Feb. 8, 1917.

## E N C L O S U R E

## William Gibbs McAdoo to Robert Lansing

Dear Mr. Secretary:            Washington February 6, 1917.

The enclosed telegram to the Comptroller of the Currency[1] is submitted for your consideration. We are getting this morning from various quarters reports that German citizens in this country are withdrawing deposits from the banks under the apprehension that in case of war there will be confiscation or sequestration of their funds. Will you please give this matter consideration so that we may discuss it at the Cabinet meeting this afternoon? It may become necessary for this Department to issue a formal statement on the subject, in order to allay apprehension. I suppose our treaty obligations with Germany will determine this question.          Faithfully yours,   W G McAdoo

TLS (SDR, RG 59, 763.72113/1238, DNA).
[1] It is missing.

## To Frank Foxcroft[1]

My dear Mr. Foxcroft:          [The White House] 6 February, 1917

I have all my reading life valued THE LIVING AGE very highly and every Christmas a year's subscription to it is my favorite Christmas present to friends at a distance. My own subscription lapsed not because of any lack of appreciation, but simply because I found that as practical duties pressed more and more upon me it was less and less possible for me to read anything systematically, as I used to read THE LIVING AGE.

I know that you will appreciate my hesitation to receive so interesting a gift,[2] but I would be delighted to have you put my name again upon the subscription list and send me a bill for it. I would like to show my appreciation of the very unusual journal.

Cordially and sincerely yours,    Woodrow Wilson

TLS (Letterpress Books, WP, DLC).
   [1] Editor of (Littell's) *The Living Age* since 1896.
   [2] Foxcroft's letter offering to renew Wilson's subscription is missing.

## To Cleveland Hoadley Dodge

Personal.

My dear Cleve:          The White House 6 February, 1917

Your letter of February fifth has strengthened my heart and comforted me greatly. There never was a time when the messages of real friends were more welcome and more needed.

I have thought more than once of your dear ones in Turkey with a pang of apprehension that was very deep. Fortunately, there is always one of our vessels there, inadequate though it may be, and I hope with all my heart that we can manage things so prudently that there will be no real danger to the lives of our people abroad. Still, I know how very anxious you must be and my heart is with you.

I wonder, my dear Cleve, whether, if a change were made at London, it would be possible for you to consider taking the Ambassadorship there? This question is not based upon any immediate prospect of a change, because it would be unwise to change in the midst of the present critical condition of affairs, but with a view to having a very certain knowledge of what it would be possible for me to do in case a change should ultimately come. I hope with all my heart that you would find that it was possible for you to consider it.

Always, with warmest messages from us all,

Affectionately yours,    Woodrow Wilson

TLS (WC, NjP).

## To Edward Mandell House

My dear House,          The White House. 6 February, 1917.

Your letter about the suggestion made by von Weigand has just been handed to me. Tumulty has also just told me of a conversation he had with von Weigand in which V. W. represented that Lansing's determination not to allow representatives of German papers to be present at his interviews with the newspaper men would prevent his attempting the right interpretation of our attitude and actions to the German people.

Being present when Lansing sees the newspaper men would not serve him in *interpreting* anything. I have suggested to him, through Tumulty, that he see you at such times as you can see him and get his interpretations from you, if you are willing, it being understood that he is not to quote you but merely to get his guidance and leads from you. Are you willing? It might serve a useful purpose if he can do it well and do it in time.

I note with genuine delight your recent suggestion that I place you "on my Staff." I will with the deepest pleasure and alacrity place you wherever you are willing to be placed,—as I am sure you know. But just what have you in mind? If you have thought anything out, please let me know as soon as possible what it is. I am eager to know.

In inevitable haste, with warmest messages from us all,
          Affectionately Yours,   Woodrow Wilson

WWTLS (E. M. House Papers, CtY).


## From Walter Lippmann

Dear Mr. President:          New York City February 6, 1917.

I was deeply touched to receive a letter from you written last Saturday, and I do not want to take any more of your time than is absolutely necessary. There are two matters, however, that we have talked over here and have very much at heart and that we want to put before you:

The first is that if it becomes necessary to raise a considerable army a recruiting campaign should be avoided. Any army that would be raised would probably be unready to fight before the war was drawing to its close, and the purpose of producing the army would really be for emergencies and to give the country a sense of security. We feel that it would be almost impossible to raise such an army by voluntary enlistment, and there is no prospect of immediate service in view of the present condition of the labor market, except by a newspaper campaign of manufactured hatred that would disturb and distract the morale of the nation. It has always seemed to me that the experience of England in her recruiting campaign acted like poison. We here have never up to this time been believers in compulsory military training, but in view of the immediate facts that seems to be the only orderly and quiet way to accomplish what may be the necessary result. Our idea was to make the training compulsory; call up two or three classes and then make foreign service voluntary.

The other matter is the question of a censorship. We feel very strongly that in this country in view of the temper of the people, the usual military censorship would be of great danger and we were hoping that you could see your way to putting it in civilian control, under men of real insight and democratic sympathy. The danger in America from the press will be far less the danger of the conventionally unpatriotic than it will be the danger of those who persecute and harass and cause divisions among our people. It will be more important to control untruth than it will be to suppress truth as is done so much in Europe. In case of war the protection of a healthy public opinion in this country will be of the first importance. And after talking over the matter we feel that if he could be spared the ideal man to take charge of a censorship would be Secretary Lane. I hope you will pardon the liberty of my suggesting this to you.

I need hardly tell you I suppose that The New Republic and all of us here are entirely at your disposal.

Warmly yours,   Walter Lippmann

TLS (WP, DLC).


## From Albert Shaw

[New York] February 6, 1917

I approve and support your efforts to avoid war. Great grievances do not always necessitate warfare. The status of belligerency would be seriously perplexing in view of our diplomatic record. Both sides have planted mines illegally in arbitrary zones of public water. Your peace proposals of last month represent American sentiment. Americans should avoid danger zones for brief period while you endeavor to promote adjustment. I find war sentiment very limited while disposition to support your policies is quite unanimous. Your efforts as neutral more needed in the world than anything that belligerency could accomplish.

Albert Shaw

CC telegram (WC, NjP).

## From Walter Hines Page

London, February 6, 1917.
5616.   Confidential to the Secretary and President.

I called on the Prime Minister yesterday. In a private unofficial talk he said that it would be an affectation to conceal his pleasure at our diplomatic break with Germany. He began immediately to talk about the probability of war following. I reminded him that the United States are arranging peace and that war was not in my vocabulary. He replied that it was well to look a little ahead in a private conversation. He hoped that in no event would our supply of ammunition to the Allies be curtailed, that a much larger supply of steel could be got from the United States which munition factories here badly need and he asked earnestly about our merchant shipbuilding activities. "Are your shipyards on the Great Lakes doing their utmost? Vast numbers of small ships are now needed and whoever owns a ship can get rich and this condition will not soon change." I reminded him that supplies for belligerents concerned the belligerents, shipbuilding, private concerns in the United States and not our Government. But such reminders in no way stopped his rapid talk. He continued, "If you are drawn into the war I shall be glad for many reasons but especially because your government will then participate in the conference that concludes peace. (   ?   ) I especially desire this because of your President's cool and patient and humane counsel which will be wholesome for us all." Then he asked, "Is there any way we can serve you? I have already directed our Army Chief of Staff (Robertson)[1] and the first Sea Lord (Jellicoe)[2] to give you all possible information out of our experience that you may ask for. You will find them communicative to you at any time," and he asked if any other Departments of his government could serve us, "if so come and see me at any time and I will open the way." Perhaps you will send me definite suggestions or instructions on this point.

Lloyd George is decidedly not a spent force, but the most active and inspiring mind that I know in England, with the most energetic and vivid imagination. He and Balfour have both been most cordial but since our diplomatic breach even more communicative than before. They open all doors more widely and the latch string is easier to find. I have already cultivated both Robertson and Jellicoe. Public as well as official opinion continues to become more cordial. It has not lacked in essence of friendliness but it was becoming fearful lest we should wander from the road of practical action. Now both the government and the press understand and heartily appreciate your whole wise and patient course. I think the expectation is general that the Germans will force war on us, but even if they should not, they regard our present attitude with genuine but restrained satisfaction.          Page.

T telegram (SDR, RG 59, 763.72/3234, DNA).
  1 Gen. Sir William Robert Robertson, Chief of the Imperial General Staff.
  2 Admiral Sir John Rushworth Jellicoe.


## Walter Hines Page to Robert Lansing

London, February 6, 1917.

5611. CONFIDENTIAL, and personal for the Secretary. Your 4395, February 5, 4 p.m. At any sacrifice I am happy to serve here until after the end of the war and I am making my arrangements to stay for this period.

I have no wish to be relieved from service since the President wishes me to remain; and I beg you to do me the favor of expressing personally to him my grateful appreciation of this fresh proof of his confidence which I hope I can continue to justify. I also thank you heartily for the evidence of your sympathetic approval.

Page.

T telegram (SDR, RG 59, 123 P 14/55, DNA).


## To Edward Mandell House, with Enclosure

My dear House,          The White House. 7 February, 1917.

Here is a despatch I meant to put in my letter last night. Here is a much more definite statement of terms, supplying what Bernstorff's left to inference!

In haste,          Affectionately,   Woodrow Wilson

WWTLS (E. M. House Papers, CtY).


ENCLOSURE

Berlin via Copenhagen, February 4, 1917.

4994   Confidential. Chancellor sent for me last night at six and I was with Zimmerman at supper later for two hours. Both seemed very much worried over attitude America and continually asked me for news and begged me to help keep peace. Chancellor said the Allies had refused to make peace when Germany wanted to and that President had Germany's peace terms and so there was nothing left to do but use all means at hand. I said that member of Reichstag had told me that matter might be arranged if food allowed in. Chancellor (*) modest terms would have been misunderstood.[1] I finally got him to tell me what those terms are: Germany to give up Belgium but retaining so-called guarantees such as railroads, forts, a garrison, ports, commercial control, et cetera; a slice of France through rectification of frontier; will only give back a small part of Servia, and Bulgaria can do as she likes with Roumania and everybody must pay indemnities to Germany, et cetera. If Bernstorff has given President any other terms he is fooling him, but do not quote me to Bernstorff.

Zimmerman said he had often thought of telling me of the pending action in the ten days before February first but knew I would only say it was impossible and would lead to a break but that they hoped by taking the action first that we would stand for it as the situation had been altered by the peace talk and anyway that we wanted peace.

Suggest if you decide make any threats threaten war. Germans not afraid of break of diplomatic relations which simply means they can go ahead and do what they please and attack us if they win. Chancellor spoke of the great hatred the military and naval people have for America. Even if there is war German military calculate they can starve England before America can do anything. These people have only one God—Force.    Gerard.

(*) *Omission.*

T telegram (E. M. House Papers, CtY).
  [1] This sentence in the copy of this telegram in the State Department files (RG 59, 763.72/3213, DNA) reads as follows: "Chancellor said it was too late and that nothing but peace on admirably modest terms would do."


## To Robert Lansing, with Enclosure

My dear Mr. Secretary:        The White House 7 February, 1917

Thank you for the enclosed. I would be very much obliged if you would suggest the wisest way for me to acknowledge this interesting communication.

Cordially and sincerely yours,    Woodrow Wilson

TLS (SDR, RG 59, 860c.01/10, DNA).

E N C L O S U R E[1]

[Warsaw, c. Jan. 31, 1917]

The Provisional Council of State in the Kingdom of Poland, who by the Manifesto of the sovereigns of the Central Powers given on November 5th, 1916, has been called to restore the Polish state, has taken knowledge of your address with the deepest gratification. For the first time since the outbreak of the war has the head of a mighty neutral power, who at the same time is the highest representative of a great nation, declared officially that according to his conviction an independent State of Poland is the only right way to solve the Polish question as well as a necessary preliminary condition for a lasting and just peace. For this wise and noble recognition of the rights of the Polish nation, the provisional Council of State, that form the nucleus of the Government of the future state, begs to express to you, Mr. President, his deepest gratitude and highest esteem, in his own name as well as in the name of the Polish people.

Kronmarschall W. Niemojowski.[2]

TC telegram (SDR, RG 59, 860c.01/10, DNA).

[1] Sent to Wilson in RL to WW, Feb. 5, 1917, TLS (WP, DLC). Lansing wrote that he had received the telegram in a note from Bernstorff of February 1.

[2] Waclaw Jósef Niemojowski, a large landholder in Poland and grandson of Bonawentura Niemojowski, a leader of the Polish national movement against Russia in 1831. Waclaw J. Niemojowski had been elected Crown Marshal of Poland on January 15, 1917, by the Provisional Council. Pending the choice of a ruler or regent, he was to serve as head of the Polish state. Bogdan Graf von Hutten-Czapski, *Sechzig Jahre Politik und Gesellschaft* (2 vols., Berlin, 1936), II, 324-27.

# From Robert Lansing, with Enclosure

PERSONAL AND CONFIDENTIAL:

My dear Mr. President:          Washington February 7, 1917.

I enclose to you a memorandum on Costa Rica prepared by Mr. Stabler, concerning which I spoke to you a few moments ago on the telephone. Accompanying the memorandum are two telegrams which will be sent if they meet with your approval.

Faithfully yours,   Robert Lansing.

TLS (SDR, RG 59, 818.00/105½, DNA).

E N C L O S U R E

MEMORANDUM        February 6, 1917.

*The Overthrow of the Government of Costa Rica
by the Minister of War, Federico Tinoco,
January 27, 1917.*

On Sunday, January 28th, Mr. Walter Penfield, the local attorney for the United Fruit Company, called Mr. Stabler at his residence shortly after two p.m. and informed him that he was in receipt of a telegram from the New York offices of the Fruit Company, embodying a telegram from their representative in Costa Rica to the effect that President Gonzales[1] had been overthrown by his Minister of War, General Tinoco,[2] by a coup d'etat, and was in asylum in the American Legation, and that Tinoco had control of the troops. Mr. Penfield also read Mr. Stabler a later telegram in which it was stated that there had been no bloodshed in the seizure of the Government; that the people of the country were in sympathy with the movement, and that it was hoped that the United States would not intervene.

Mr. Penfield stated that the American Minister at San José[3] had wished to send a cipher telegram to the Department, via the Fruit Company's wireless station, but that the company had informed him that it could not do so as it would be a violation of the neutrality laws of both the United States and Costa Rica to send a wireless message in cipher. The Department is now having an investigation made of this refusal on the part of the Fruit Company to send a cipher message for the American Minister and will bring the matter forcibly to the attention of the company if it is shown that the company is at fault.

On Monday the 29th a cable was received from Minister Hale, dated the 27th,[4] informing the Department of Tinoco's act and saying that he had given asylum to the President, the President of the Senate[5] and to Castro Quesada, Costa Rican Minister to Washington, and that President Gonzales had asked that no recognition be given by the United States to Tinoco and that assistance be sent to him from the Panama Canal by the American authorities to give protection to the legal government.

Several further cablegrams were received of Jan. 29th and 30th from the Minister and from the Consul at San José,[6] the gen-

[1] Alfredo González Flores.          [2] Federico Tinoco Granados.
[3] That is, Edward Joseph Hale.     [4] Printed in *FR 1917*, p. 301.
[5] Máximo Fernández.
[6] Several messages from Hale and from Consul Benjamin Franklin Chase are printed in *FR 1917*, pp. 301-305.

eral purport of which was that quiet prevailed and that martial law had been established and that Gonzales was still asking aid of the United States in reestablishing the legal government. Later the Minister cabled saying that there was great excitement on account of rumors of the approach of American war ships and that if ships had been sent they should be ordered back as their presence would have a bad effect.[7]

As all cablegrams from the Legation confirmed the fact that the machinery of Government was proceeding as usual and quiet prevailed, the Department thought it best to ask for a full report on Tinoco's coup d'etat and to caution the Minister against taking any action which might be construed as granting recognition to any new government, and therefore cabled him along these lines.[8]

On Feb. 2d the Minister cabled the Department stating that arrangements were being made to call for elections and to establish, through legal means, a constitutional government.[9]

Mr. Pacheco,[10] the representative of General Tinoco, called at the Department on Feb. 2d, with his attorney, Mr. Van Dyke,[11] but Mr. Stabler informed them that he was unable to receive them, as he had received no instructions from the Secretary to see them. Mr. Van Dyke then wrote, stating that Tinoco did not ask for recognition at this time but wished assurances on the part of the Government of the United States that it had no intention of intervening in Costa Rica at this moment. No reply has as yet been sent to this communication.

On January 29th Mr. W. H. Field, of the firm of Montealegre & Bonilla, coffee exporters of San José, Costa Rica, and New York City,[12] called at the Division of Latin American Affairs, being introduced by Mr. Canova, Chief of the Mexican Division. Mr. Field, it is understood, has had many years' experience in Latin-American matters, and particularly in connection with Costa Rica. He said he desired to give the Department all the information he had in his possession in regard to the coup d'Etat of Tinoco. He said that he had no political interests whatsoever. He

[7] E. J. Hale to RL, Jan. 29, 1917, *ibid.*, p. 303.

[8] RL to E. J. Hale, Jan. 30, 1917, *ibid.*, p. 304.

[9] E. J. Hale to RL, Jan. 30, 1917, T telegram (SDR, RG 59, 818.00/65, DNA). Despite the difference in dates, this is the message to which Stabler refers.

[10] Leonidas Pacheco, lawyer, who represented the Sinclair oil interests in Costa Rica.

[11] Harry Weston Van Dyke, lawyer of Washington, author and translator of several books on Latin American countries.

[12] Woolsey Hopkins Field, who was and remained for several years the "most active propagandist" for González Flores in the United States. Dana G. Munro, *Intervention and Dollar Diplomacy in the Caribbean, 1900-1921* (Princeton, N. J., 1964), p. 459.

said that Federico Tinoco was of the upper class of Costa Rica, clever, unscrupulous and forceful; that he and his brother were murderers and extremely dangerous.

Mr. Field further stated that Gonzales, who had come into the Presidency after the resignation of the President elected by the Congress,[13] was not popular in Costa Rica; that his attempt to reform the land and income tax laws had made him very unpopular. He stated that he thought that the arrangement was probably made with Tinoco by the dissatisfied element, which he said was in the great majority in the country, that he should make this coup d'etat and then call for elections and the President would be elected legally.

Apparently the announcement, upon his arrival in Costa Rica, by Mr. Castro Quesada, Costa Rican Minister to Washington, that he had come to assist at the election of President Gonzales, inflamed the Costa Rican people, since according to the Constitution a President cannot succeed himself.

Mr. Field went on to say that President Gonzales granted to an American citizen, Herbert Noble, the rights to certain important water ways in Costa Rica on the San Juan River, which if the Nicaraguan canal were ever built, would have a very strategic position. These concessions were ostensibly for a pineapple plantation. Noble turned these rights over to Chandler & Co. of New York, who have been acting for the German Government in the sale of German bonds in the United States, which fact was known to the Government of Costa Rica at the time that it named them as its financial agents.

Mr. Field went on to say that he did not consider that the government of the United States could take any steps to reestablish Gonzales in office, nor did he feel that the Government of the United States should recognize the Government set up by Tinoco, who was not worthy of recognition, and that the best policy to pursue would be to wait until a Government was established by law and then grant recognition.

He said that Tinoco had attempted to draw money on deposit with the Irving National Bank and one or two other corporations.

He was advised by Mr. Stabler that this government would take no hurried step in granting recognition to any government in Costa Rica, and therefore he thought it safer for the New York firms not to give money to Tinoco or any other person in Costa Rica until they belonged to a duly recognized government.

Mr. Field felt that if Tinoco did not endeavor to run himself, Congress would elect Francisco Aguilar, a prominent lawyer of

13 González had succeeded Ricardo Jiménez Oreamuno in 1914.

Costa Rica, with an independent fortune, who has never before entered into politics. Apparently he is one of the best men in Costa Rica.

Mr. Field addressed a letter to Mr. Stabler, dated Jan. 31st, in which he transmitted a list of the Cabinet which it is reported that Tinoco has selected. It is of interest to note that Carlos Lara, who is selected as Minister for Foreign Affairs, is a relation by marriage of Mr. Minor C. Keith, Vice President of the United Fruit Co.[14] Lara is also connected by marriage to Tinoco. Joaquin Tinoco, slated for Secretary of War, a brother of Federico, has been charged with several murders.

Mr. Field promised to give the Department further information when possible in regard to conditions in Costa Rica, requesting that his communications and name be kept strictly confidential.

The coup d'etat of Tinoco may possibly be connected with the general Central American revolutionary plot, which it is believed on good authority is being elaborated with ardor by certain professional revolutionists amongst whom are Maximo Rosales of Honduras, and Irias[15] of Nicaragua. The plot is directed against Chamorro[16] in Nicaragua through a revolution headed by Irias and the Liberals, who may be supported by Costa Rica, and against Estrada Cabrera,[17] through a revolution in the North of Guatemala, aided by Carranza from Mexico, and a revolution to the South from Honduras if Rosales is able to overthrow President Bertrand[18] and set up an enemy of Estrada Cabrera.

According to a cablegram from Mr. Long,[19] it would appear that the present President[20] and government of Salvador are very much disturbed by Tinoco's coup d'etat, as they feel that Gonzales and Quesada were working with them against Nicaragua and United States in the dispute over the canal treaty.

From the United Fruit Company's evident desire to inform this Department immediately of Tinoco's coup d'etat and its insistence that the United States should not intervene and also in view of the fact that they did not apparently desire to cooperate with the American Minister in sending his cipher message to the Department and also on account of the connection by marriage between Mr. Keith and Tinoco, it would seem that the Fruit Com-

14 Minor Cooper Keith, long associated with business affairs in Costa Rica, who had founded the United Fruit Co. in 1899.
15 Julían Irías.
16 That is, Emiliano Chamorro Vargas, former Nicaraguan Minister to the United States, who had just been inaugurated as President of Nicaragua.
17 Manuel Estrada Cabrera, President of Guatemala.
18 Francisco Bertrand, President of Honduras.
19 Boaz Walton Long, United States Minister to Salvador.
20 Carlos Meléndez.

pany must at least have known about Tinoco's plot, if it has not aided and abetted him in it. If this is true, it would appear that the Fruit Company should be given clearly to understand that its interference in Central American politics must cease immediately or it will be made public that the United States considers that it is not worthy of its diplomatic protection in Central America. This would undoubtedly curb the activities of the Fruit Company along revolutionary lines.

There is no question that Tinoco, aside from the illegality of his action, is absolutely unsuited to be given any recognition by this Government, as he is an unscrupulous character.

It appears that Tinoco's brother-in-law is the Austrian consul in Costa Rica,[21] but it is understood that he has become a Costa Rican citizen, in order to escape the British blacklist.

The proximity of Costa Rica to the Canal is an important factor on account of the present situation, and it is felt that great care must be exercised in taking any step. Undoubtedly the Government of Gonzales was backed by German influence as can be seen from their having made Chandler & Co. their agents in New York and it is understood that a great deal of the propaganda against the United States and Nicaragua, on account of the canal treaty was paid for by German agents.

It is necessary to have in Costa Rica a government which is friendly to the United States, but on the other hand the example which Tinoco has set would have a far reaching, baneful effect on the revolutionary parties in the other states of Central America and I feel that a strong policy must be pursued.

In view of the condition which has been brought about by Tinoco's act and the uneasiness felt by Chamorro in Nicaragua and which is also apparent in Honduras, that the peace of Central America is insecure, it is felt that the President's Latin American policy enunciated by him in 1913, should again be brought clearly to the notice of all Governments in Central America and particularly to the people of Costa Rica; that Tinoco be advised that the United States will not give recognition to him or to any government which he may form, since he came into power through a revolutionary, illegal and unconstitutional act and that recognition will only be granted to a government which is constitutionally formed.                                    Stabler.

TS memorandum (SDR, RG 59, 818.00/105½, DNA).
[21] K. W. Wahle, who had been Austrian consul at San José since 1896.

# To Robert Lansing, with Enclosures

My dear Mr. Secretary,          The White House. 7 February, 1917.

I am much obliged for this memorandum and entirely agree with Mr. Stabler's conclusions. The sooner the intimation he suggests giving to the American Fruit Company is given the better. Their implication lies on the very surface of all the circumstances. A word to Mr. Untermyer, who seems to speak as their attorney, might give them immediate pause.

I think the telegram to San José ought to be made a little stronger. It ought to instruct the Minister to say to Tinoco that no government set up by *him* will be recognized, and no government which he takes part in originating or organizing, and that no contracts made by any citizen of the United States with such a government will be recognized by this Government as valid. We cannot be too explicit or too downright. I hope the message will go at the earliest possible moment.

Faithfully Yours,   W.W.

WWTLI (SDR, RG 59, 818.00/106½, DNA).


ENCLOSURE          I

Washington, February 7, 1917.

You are instructed to state to the government of the country to which you are accredited that it is desired that the following statement be made public—QUOTE—The Government of the United States has viewed the recent overthrow of the established government in Costa Rica with the gravest concern and considers that illegal acts of this character tend to disturb the peace of Central America and to disrupt the unity of the American Continent. In view of its policy in regard to the assumption of power through illegal methods, clearly enunciated by it on several occasions during the past four years, the Government of the United States desires to set forth in an emphatic and distinct manner its present position in regard to the actual situation in Costa Rica which is that it *will not give recognition or support* to any government which may be established unless it is clearly proven that it is elected by legal and constitutional means. END QUOTE.

Lansing[1]

T telegram (SDR, RG 59, 818.00/79a, DNA).

[1] Lansing sent this instruction on February 9, 1917, as a circular telegram to the United States legations in Guatemala, Honduras, Nicaragua, and Salvador (SDR, RG 59, 818.00/79a, DNA).

E N C L O S U R E     I I

Amlegation, San José.          Washington, February 6, 1917.

You will ask for an unofficial interview with General Tinoco and inform him that you have been instructed to hand him for his information a copy of a cablegram which has been sent to the American Legations in the other four Central American capitals for presentation to the respective governments and you will state to him that the friendship of the government of the United States for the Republic of Costa Rica has been such for so many years that it is most earnestly desired by this government that nothing may occur which might injure this relationship; that the desire which this government has of seeing the will of the people prevail in governmental matters in Costa Rica has forced it to the conclusion that no government except such as may be elected legally and established according to the Constitution shall be considered entitled to recognition.

Following is text of cablegram to other countries in Central America: . . .[1]

T telegram (SDR, RG 59, 818.00/79b, DNA).
   [1] Lansing sent this telegram to San José on February 9, 1917. He added the following concluding paragraph: "CONFIDENTIAL. You will further make it plain to General Tinoco that no government set up by him will be recognized, and no government which he takes part in originating or organizing, and no contracts made by any citizen of the United States with such a government will be recognized as valid."


## To Walter Lippmann

My dear Lippmann:          [The White House] 7 February, 1917

The two matters you speak of in your letter of February sixth are certainly of capital importance and I find myself in general agreement with you about both of them. I shall certainly try to work something out in that spirit at any rate, and thank you sincerely for your thoughtful suggestions.

   In haste

          Cordially and sincerely yours,   Woodrow Wilson

TLS (Letterpress Books, WP, DLC).


## A Draft of a Letter to William Julius Harris[1]

Sir:                                    Feb. 7, 1917

An adequate supply of food products is a matter of concern to the Nation at all times. It is of peculiar importance at present.

Our domestic food supply is normally very large and has become increasingly varied. In some respects it has steadily expanded and has kept pace with the increasing population. Unfortunately this is not true, *however,* of a number of important staple products, including certain cereals and particularly meats. While the population of the Nation has increased 26,000,000 since 1900, the production of the two leading cereals, corn and wheat, while tending to increase, has shown only a slight advance; and that of the meat products in the same period has shown an increase of only 3,500,000,000 pounds,—a decrease of 29 pounds *per capita.*

⟨Unquestionably⟩ Much can be done, and is being done, to change this situation through improved methods of production and through the control or eradication of plant and animal diseases. But there are problems also of distribution; and, in some respects, the problems presented in this field are the more difficult. Only recently have official agencies been created to deal systematically with this side of ⟨agriculture⟩ *the difficulty.* Much work has been done and, considering the limited nature of the powers under which it has been conducted, no little headway has been made, particularly in obtaining and diffusing useful information. Nevertheless, it is not yet clear in many directions just what the nature of the difficulty is or what measures should be adopted to effect fundamental improvements. Many necessary facts are not available, and it is question⟨ed⟩*able* whether any single agency of *the* government at present possesses the requisite power and equipment to secure the information needed to enable *both* public and private instrumentalities to render their fullest service to the people. It is obvious that there will be no sufficient incentive to enlarge production if there does not exist an unobstructed and economical system of distribution. Unjustifiable fluctuations in prices are not merely demoralizing; they inevitably deter adequate production.

It has been alleged before Committees of the Congress, and elsewhere, that the course of trade in important food products is not free, but is restricted and controlled by artificial and illegal means. It is of the highest public concern to ascertain the truth or falsity of these allegations. No business can be transacted effectively in an atmosphere of suspicion. If the allegations are well-grounded, it is necessary that the nature and extent of the evils and abuses be accurately determined, so that proper remedies, legislative or administrative, may be applied. If they are not true, it is equally essential that the public be informed, so that unrest and dissatisfaction may be allayed. In any event, because of the grave public interest*s* ⟨with⟩ which the food supply ⟨is⟩ affect⟨ed⟩*s*, the efficient performance of the duties imposed upon agencies of the Government requires that all the pertinent facts be ⟨secured⟩ *ascertained*. To this end, the powers of such agencies should be made adequate, if in any respect they are now deficient.

Pursuant to the authority conferred upon me by the Act creating the Federal Trade Commission, therefore, I direct the Commission, within the scope of its powers, to investigate and report the facts relating to the production, ownership, manufacture, storage, and distribution of foodstuffs and the products or by-products arising from or in connection with their preparation and manufacture; to ascertain the facts bearing on alleged violations of the anti-trust acts, and particularly *upon the question* whether there are manipulations, controls, trusts, combinations, conspiracies, or restraints of trade out of harmony with the law *or the public interest*.

I am aware that the Commission has additional authority in this field, through the power conferred upon it to prevent certain persons, partnerships, or corporations from using unfair methods of competition in commerce. I ⟨recognize⟩ *presume* that you may see fit to exercise that authority, upon your own initiative, without direction from me.

The Department of Agriculture has been engaged for several years in studying problems of distribution. I have noted that it has been proposed in the Congress to add ⟨somewhat⟩ to the funds of the Department and give it larger powers to conduct its investigations. As its activities will touch phases of the problem I am calling to your attention which may not be covered by your inquiry, and may furnish information of great importance for the purposes contemplated, I shall direct that Department to cooperate with you in this enterprise.

For the adequate prosecution of the inquiry by both your Commission and the Department of Agriculture, it is essential that sufficient funds be available. I accordingly request that you furnish me at the earliest possible moment an estimate for a appropriation, if one is needed, to supplement existing appropriations, to enable you successfully to carry out the investigation.

A copy of this letter is being sent to the Secretary of Agriculture, with the direction that his Department cooperate with you and with the request that he furnish an estimate for the funds needed by his Department.[2]

TMS (WP, DLC).

[1] This draft was prepared by Secretary Houston. Words in angle brackets deleted by Wilson; words in italics added by him.

[2] This was sent as WW to W. J. Harris, Feb. 7, 1917, TLS (Letterpress Books, WP, DLC). The "a appropriation" was corrected to read "an appropriation."

## From Edward Mandell House

Dear Governor:                    New York. February 7, 1917.

Of course, I shall be glad to see von Weigand and guide him as best I can. Lanier Winslow, one of Gerard's secretaries, tells me that he thoroughly mistrusts von Weigand so I shall be careful in talking with him.

Jusserand called this morning but I got nothing of value from him.[1]

My thought about being on your Staff was that I could form a little bureau to make your burden less heavy in the event of war. It would necessitate our moving to Washington for the time being and I would be at your disposal day and night.

I would have Gordon Auchincloss and several others so you could have trustworthy messengers at all times and for any purpose. I think this could be done without hurting the sensibilities of anyone. However, we can talk about it when I am next in Washington.

If Austria holds to Germany's new submarine policy, if I were you, I would send the whole lot home with the Germans. I have another plan to suggest to you which Wiseman and I think might prove more effective than if Tarnowski were retained. It may not be workable but Wiseman thinks it might be.

Your affectionate,   E. M. House

TLS (WP, DLC).

[1] A somewhat curious statement. Actually, House and Jusserand had quite a long and friendly talk. House told the Ambassador that, upon receipt of the German note, Wilson had called him, House, to Washington and had done only what House advised him to do ("et n'a rien fait que sur son avis"). Then the two men talked at length about how the United States could best help the Allies if she entered the war. J. J. Jusserand to the Foreign Ministry, received Feb. 8, 1917, T telegram (Guerre 1914-1918, États-Unis, Vol. 505, pp. 70-71, FFM-Ar).

## From Josephus Daniels

My dear Mr. President:        Washington, February 7, 1917.

The following is a message that Mr. George Barthelme[1] was permitted to send via the Sayville wireless station to the KOELN-ISHE ZEITUNG:[2]

Koelnishe Zeitung, Koeln Langasse

February fifth from high sources whose identity cannot disclose, I (am urged almost implored) have been requested to convey to German people and government idea that message must not be construed as indicating any desire on part government people for war (with Germany). Strongest attention called to following passage:

"I refuse believe is intention to do in fact what they warned us they will feel at liberty to do. Only overt act can make me believe it even now."

Further following sentence:

"If this inveterate confidence should unhappily prove unfounded, I shall take liberty coming again before Congress ask authority use any means necessary for protection our seamen people."

These passages widely construed first as expressions of confidence some way out might be found, second not containing any war threat notwithstanding language used. General opinion is President could do nothing else but sever relations to make good former note. Now up to Germany provide an opening: first thing necessary avoid everything which makes maintenance friendly relations impossible, particularly refrain from destruction American ships, then make clear misunderstood terms German note—that no unrestricted submarine warfare contemplated but only blockade confined within narrowest limits compatible with necessary military aims. Even within those limits greatest care taken not to interfere with innocent American commerce and every precaution taken to limit destruction of neutral ships carrying contraband, and of enemy vessels, to ships and cargo, but safeguarding wherever possible lives passengers crews as was recent practice. Then propose joint commission for negotiation code governing blockade and submarine (~~warfare~~) generally, such offer inducing delay and made as special token ancient friendship two countries. Then consider possibilities provided in Hensley resolution[3] for calling conference powers, which possibilities closed by hasty action. Some explanation about sailing of only four especially marked American ships would remove extremely bitter impression created by this wholly incomprehensible proviso, hurting national pride as nothing else. My informants assure most emphatically country is not for war. Will be for war only when forced into. Only certain very small circles clamoring for hostilities, but huge majority praying for peace with honor. Feel it my solemn duty to inform you about these sentiments and opinions entertained by men of highest standing, noblest character, responsible position, loftiest ideals and thoroughly good will. Should you deem advisable to exert influence of our great paper, do so to find way out of situation, not yet unavoidably pregnant with gravest possibilities. I honestly believe country just anxiously waiting for one more good word.                    Georg Barthelme

Note:    Words in parenthesis have been stricken out.

Faithfully yours,    [Josephus Daniels]

CCL (J. Daniels Papers, DLC).
 1 Washington correspondent of the *Kölnische Zeitung*.
 2 About this dispatch, see G. W. Kirchwey to RL, Feb. 12, 1917, printed as an Enclosure with RL to WW, Feb. 17, 1917, and Link, *Campaigns for Progressivism and Peace*, p. 318.
 3 About which, see WW to C. H. Levermore, March 28, 1916, n. 1, Vol. 36.

## From Newton Diehl Baker

Dear Mr. President:                  Washington, February 7, 1917

This is a memorandum of the steps taken by the War Department so far in the present emergency:

1. I have caused a plan to be worked out to put into operation, by which, upon a given signal, the Government use of the entire telegraph and telephone systems of the country will be preferred and, to the extent necessary, exclusive of all private business.

2. In cooperation with President Willard of the Baltimore & Ohio, representing the railroads, I am having all anticipated needs for transportation systematized and proper relations created between the personnel of the railroads and this Department, so that there will be no loss of time should need arise.

3. All Bureaus and Divisions of this Department are preparing estimates of supplies necessary to be bought and arrangements necessary to be made in the event of an order being given to increase the Regular Army and National Guard to war strength, and undertake the training of a large volunteer force for which purpose the anticipated volunteer force has been tentatively fixed at 500,000 men. The details of their enlistment, transportation, equipment and training are being reduced to written statements and orders to avoid confusion should such a plan be determined upon.

4. We are making immediate purchases in anticipation of pending appropriations for supplies, such as clothing, shoes, foodstuffs, tentage, etc. to the fullest amount possible. The contracts, however, will not be signed until the Appropriation Bill is passed, but the time will be saved of advertisement, receipt of bids, and determination of awards, all of which are usually deferred until after the passage of the Bill.

5. The Ordinance Department has been directed to operate all arsenals immediately on a two-shift basis, that being upon a maximum efficiency of operation, and in order to secure the necessary trained mechanics the Department of Labor has been

asked to cooperate. This will be valuable in any event, since the appropriations made last year are ample to cover the output of the arsenal so operated, and the result will not increase our supply beyond the adopted program.

6. I have ordered torpedo nets for all harbors on the Atlantic Coast except those provided with such nets by the Navy Department.

7. I have placed all the facilities of the War Department, engineers, personnel, arsenals, etc. freely at the disposal of the Navy in any way in which our cooperation will be helpful.

8. We have completed a somewhat long-drawn effort to purchase land at Montauk Point for the protection of New York Harbor and are installing in temporary form additional coast defenses there.

I have endeavored in every way possible to have these steps carried out without publicity in order not to give rise either to excitement in our own country or misconstruction abroad.

Respectfully yours,    Newton D. Baker

TLS (WP, DLC).

## From Newton Diehl Baker, with Enclosure

Dear Mr. President:              Washington. February 7, 1917

If the inclosed dispatch to Governor-General Harrison meets with your approval, I will send it at once.

Do you think it would be advisable for me to issue to the newspapers a statement as follows?:

In the harbors of Manila and elsewhere in the Philippine Islands, and at Colon, Panama, the German merchant vessels were discovered to have had certain parts of their machinery removed and in some instances evidences of preparation for the sinking of these vessels had been made. Solely for the purpose of protecting the several harbors and other shipping and property therein, steps have been taken to prevent damage, but none of the ships have been seized by the Government of the United States and in all cases the commanders and crews have been informed that the Government of the United States has made no seizures, claims no right to the vessels, and does not deny the right of the commander and crew to destroy the vessels if they see fit, so long as the destruction is accomplished in a way which will not obstruct navigable port waters or injure or endanger other shipping or property. The breach of diplomatic relations between the Governments of the United States and Germany has not changed the relation of these ships or their crews to the Government of the United States or forfeited their right to our hospitality, and the steps taken are limited to necessary police regulations to prevent injury to the property of others or the obstruction of harbor waters.

I have cabled to Colonel Morrow[1] at the Panama Canal as shown by the copy of the dispatch sent you last night.[2] As soon as I receive a reply from him, I will forward it for your information. Respectfully yours, Newton D. Baker

TLS (WP, DLC).
[1] Lt. Col. Jay Johnson Morrow, U.S.A., Engineer of Maintenance, and, at times, Acting Governor, of the Panama Canal.
[2] NDB to J. J. Morrow, Feb. 6, 1917, CC telegram, enclosed with NDB to WW, Feb. 6, 1917, TLS (WP, DLC).

## E N C L O S U R E

Washington. February 7, 1917.
Harrison, Manila. (URGENT, CONFIDENTIAL)

It is of utmost importance that it be made plain that German merchant ships have not been seized and that crews are not in any sense imprisoned or interned but that steps taken are purely for the protection of the harbor and other shipping. Suggest that you inform German Consul that the Insular Government claims no interest in ships and will permit their crews to take them out of the harbor and destroy them if they desire, but cannot permit their destruction in the harbor or at places where other shipping will be endangered. Also that officers and crews of the ships be accorded all the rights and privileges of other foreigners temporarily resident in the Islands and be made to understand that their movements are entirely unrestricted, subject only to the common obligation of all to obey the law.

T MS (WP, DLC).

## From Newton Diehl Baker, with Enclosures

My dear Mr. President: Washington. February 7, 1917.
I inclose a letter from Mr. Taft and a copy of my response.
Respectfully yours, Newton D. Baker

TLS (WP, DLC).

ENCLOSURE     I

## William Howard Taft to Newton Diehl Baker

**PERSONAL**

My dear Mr. Secretary:     New Haven, Conn February 6th, 1917.

I have your very cordial note of February 3d, and thank you for your kindly approval of what I said at the dinner of the National Chamber of Commerce on Friday night. The President and you and your colleagues of the Cabinet have a very grave responsibility, and any man is lacking in proper patriotic feeling who is not willing to do everything to help you. I presume you have definite ideas as to the legislation which you desire in respect to the army. I have been a great deal troubled as to what Congress would do and what Congress ought to do. I have gradually forced myself into the conviction that we must have a mild form of conscription or compulsory military service, by which every young man between 19 and 24 shall be required to serve one year with the colors. I know this will meet with great opposition, and probably you and the President do not fully approve it, but I believe that any other method of raising an army will prove in the end to be disappointing, and that this has not only the advantage of furnishing a constant source for trained men to be called back into the service, but it is usefully educational in the discipline that it will afford and in the emphasis that it will give to the obligation which each individual owes to the government—an obligation which, I regret to say that in these days of prosperity and comfort is lost sight of. I presume it will not be adopted, however. What I fear is that we shall have such a mushroom growth of volunteer regiments as we had in the Spanish War, at great expense, and with no training that ultimately inured to the benefit of the military service of the United States. I presume the remarks I have made on this subject may bring down on my head a great deal of criticism, but my convictions are so clear that I am content. Meantime we propose to press the League to Enforce Peace. If anything could ever satisfy the American people of the necessity for such a League, it is the condition in which we find ourselves now. The President once said that in the next war there will be no neutrals. His remark was so true that it seems likely to apply to this one. Indeed the lesson of the present situation is the necessity for the political organization of the world to stop the spread of a local war into a general conflagration.

Please present my felicitations to the President on his presentation of the issue to Congress, and on the unanimous response that it evoked from the American people.

Sincerely yours,   Wm H Taft

TLS (WP, DLC).


E N C L O S U R E     I I

## Newton Diehl Baker to William Howard Taft

PERSONAL AND CONFIDENTIAL.

My dear Mr. President:          [Washington] February 7, 1917.

I have your very generous letter of the 6th, and thank you for writing me so fully on these difficult subjects and at this trying time.

The problem presented by the crisis which the country now faces, coming at a time when there was country-wide discussion of a change in our fundamental military policy, is beset with more than normal difficulties. As you have, of course, observed there has been throughout the entire nation a disposition to accept in some form universal service, but the difficulty about it is that as yet nobody has been able to write out the details of a universal service law which the head of a family could apply to his own situation and reason about with knowledge as to just how it would affect him and his family. Should it come to pass that we must immediately embark in extensive preparations for war, the country would, I think, stand unitedly back of the President in any program adapted to that end, but there would undoubtedly be great suspicion aroused if compulsory service were suggested at the outset and before any opportunity to volunteer had been given. Unfortunately, a number of men have already suggested that this would be a good emergency to make use of to get compulsory service, and a belief in the country that the administration was making use of this emergency for the indirect purpose of accomplishing this fundamental change in our military policy, rather than resorting to it because it was needed, would raise troubles which ought not to be added to those we already have. Fortunately, it is not within the range of probability that we could repeat the volunteer system of the Spanish War, or at least repeat its errors. There, we had hastily to assemble men and send them untrained to the front. Since that time we have all learned a great deal about the essentials of training, and should we have a large volunteer force, there would be time for its training according to approved standards without the losses sustained in the training camps in this country in '98.

I shall take great pleasure in conveying your message to the President, and I can express, in anticipation, his hearty reciprocation of your kindly sentiments and his appreciation of your helpful and patriotic cooperation.

Cordially yours,    Newton D. Baker.

CCL (WP, DLC).


## From Francis Griffith Newlands

My dear Mr. President:                    [Washington] February 7, 1917.

I have been confined to my room for the past week with bronchitis and am out for the first time today for a few hours only.

I had a conference yesterday with Senator Robinson who informed me that he is positive that none of the Republicans, with the exception of three or four, will sustain the strike suspension provision, and that not over half the Democrats will. There are only four Democrats on the Senate Committee who can be relied upon to support the strike suspension provision. It might be persuasive if upon one of your visits to the Capitol you would take occasion to confer with the Democratic members of the Committee on this subject.

In the hope that the House Committee might report favorable action on your recommendation regarding the suspension of the right of strike during the period of investigation, I concluded to delay the report of the Senate Committee until the House Committee should act. The Bill just reported by Mr. Adamson does not contain the strike suspension feature, but does follow the Senate measure, of which I had sent him a copy, in making it a penal offense to hinder or obstruct or delay the makeup, dispatch or operation of trains in interstate commerce. I attach much value to this.

The House Bill adds to the Mediation Act Section 12, which provides that where a controversy arises which cannot be settled through mediation and conciliation or by voluntary arbitration in the manner provided in the Act, the President shall be notified by the Board of Mediation and Conciliation and shall thereupon add to it four members, two from representatives of employes and two from representatives of railroad officials, and that the Board so constituted shall make the investigation and report. The only objection which I can suggest to this is that possibly the participation of the standing members of the Board of Mediation in controversies coming under the jurisdiction of the enlarged Board and their identification with heated controversies may subsequently render them unacceptable to the brotherhoods as mediators and conciliators and that thus much of the benefits of mediation and conciliation may be lost.

I am just told, however, by Mr. Adamson over the telephone that the Bill which he has reported has the unanimous support of his Committee and that it meets with your approval, and with this understanding I will, unless I hear something from you to the contrary, immediately present it to the Senate Committee for consideration.

I am,      Very sincerely yours,      Francis G. Newlands

TLS (WP, DLC).

## From James Woodrow

My dear Cousin Woodrow:          Columbia, S. C. Feb. 7, 1917.

All of us are exceedingly concerned and interested in the outcome of our present condition, and we feel deeply for you in this crisis. It is a wonderful satisfaction to know that we have a strong hand and a steady head guiding us and our destinies.

It has been rather pathetic to see my grandmother[1] during the last few days. She is thinking of you and the Country all the time. All day Sunday and most of Monday you would see tears running down her cheeks and then she would ask some question or other about you. The only thing that has seemed to give her any satisfaction or comfort is the gratifying stand all the people of the Country have taken. She seems very much better now, however.

Please know that, no matter what the outcome is, I am at your call for any service whatsoever and wheresoever you may wish.

All of us here are well. We are hoping and praying for your guidance and protection. With love and best wishes to you and all, I am,          Affectionately yours,      James Woodrow

TLS (WP, DLC).
[1] Felexiana Shepherd Baker Woodrow, "Aunt Felie."

## A Statement[1]

[Feb. 8, 1917]

It having been reported to him that there is anxiety in some quarters on the part of persons residing in this country who are the ⟨citizens⟩ *subjects* of foreign states lest their bank deposits or

other property should be seized in the event of war between the
United States and a foreign nation, the President authorizes the
statement that all such fears are entirely unfounded. The Government of the United States will in no circumstances take advantage of a state of war to take possession of property to which
international understandings and the recognized law of the land
give it no just claim or title. It will scrupulously respect all private rights alike of its own citizens and of the ⟨citizens⟩ *subjects*
of foreign states.

WWT MS (WP, DLC).
    [1] Words in angle brackets deleted by Lansing; words in italics inserted by
him.


## To Walter Hines Page

Washington, February 8, 1917

4421.   The President directs that you lay the following before
the leading members of the British Government in strictest confidence and begs that you will press the points it contains with all
the earnestness and directness you would use were they your own
personal views. He speaks of the leading members of the Government rather than of the Foreign Office because he does not intend
this as in any sense an official but only as a personal message
and wishes you to ascertain informally what he might expect
should he make the proposals here foreshadowed officially to the
Foreign Office.

The President knows that peace is intensely desired by the Teutonic powers, and much more by Austria than by any of her allies
because the situation is becoming for many reasons much graver
for her than for the others. He is trying to avoid breaking with
Austria in order to keep the channels of official intercourse with
her open so that he may use her for peace. The chief if not the
only obstacle is the threat apparently contained in the peace
terms recently stated by the Entente Allies that in case they succeeded they would insist upon a virtual dismemberment of the
Austro-Hungarian Empire. Austria needs only to be reassured on
that point, and that chiefly with regard to the older units of the
Empire. It is the President's view that the large measure of autonomy already secured by those older units is a sufficient guarantee of peace and stability in that part of Europe so far as national and racial influences are concerned and that what Austria
regards as the necessities of her development, opportunity, and
security to the south of her can be adequately and satisfactorily
secured to her by rights of way to the sea given by the common
guarantee of the concert which must in any case be arranged if

the future peace of the world is to be assured. He does not doubt that Austria can be satisfied without depriving the several Balkan states of their political autonomy and territorial integrity.

The effort of this Government will be constantly for peace even should it become itself involved, although those efforts would not in the least weaken or slacken its vigorous action in such a case. The President still believes and has reason to believe that, were it possible for him to give the necessary assurances to the government of Austria, which fears radical dismemberment and which thinks that it is now fighting for its very existence, he could in a very short time force the acceptance of peace upon terms which would follow the general lines of his recent address to the Senate regarding the sort of peace the United States would be willing to join in guaranteeing. He is urgently desirous that the Entente Governments should make it possible for him to present such terms and press them for acceptance. The present enthusiastic support which the people of the United States are giving his foreign policy is being given it is very evident because they expect him to use the force and influence of the United States, if he must use force, not to prolong the war, but to insist upon those rights of his own and other peoples which he regards and they regard as the bases and the only bases of peace.

Lansing.[1]

T telegram (SDR, RG 59, 763.72119/483A, DNA).
[1] There is a WWsh and a WWT draft of this telegram in WP, DLC.


## To Josephus Daniels

My dear Daniels,                The White House. 8 February, 1917.

So many people who want to run our foreign affairs for us are trying to communicate with the German Government that it has occurred to me that they might try to employ the wireless stations, which are under the control of your Department. I hope that you will very carefully guard against that and issue very strict and definite orders about it. There is extreme danger in everything of that kind. Impressions are apt to be made which will be so misleading as to make war more rather than less likely, by leading the German authorities to a wholly wrong impression,—especially as they know that no messages go through that we do not officially let through.

I hasten this over to you, because it is a matter which I had omitted to cover in our conferences.

Faithfully yours,    Woodrow Wilson

WWTLS (J. Daniels Papers, DLC).

## To Francis Griffith Newlands

My dear Senator:          [The White House] 8 February, 1917

Thank you very much for your letter of February seventh. I hope that you will follow the course you indicate, though I trust that the amendment which I know Senator Underwood will offer will meet with the approval and support of the Committee. Without it the Act is most imperfect.

The House Committee having been unwilling to put in the suspension clause, I think we had better push through the rest of the legislation, notwithstanding.

I am glad to infer from your letter that you are better.

Cordially and sincerely yours,   Woodrow Wilson

TLS (Letterpress Books, WP, DLC).

## From Robert Lansing, with Enclosures

My dear Mr. President,          Washington February 8, 1917.

I return "Bases of Peace" which I received yesterday afternoon together with some notes which I prepared last night. My endeavor was to criticize and raise objections for the purpose of discussion and not with an idea of opposition since I am wholly in accord with the purposes of the four articles.

Faithfully yours   Robert Lansing

ALS (WP, DLC).

### E N C L O S U R E     I

#### BASES of PEACE—

#### I.

Mutual guarantee of political independence,—absolute in all domestic matters, limited in external affairs only by the rights of other nations.

#### II.

Mutual guarantee of territorial integrity.

#### Note.

The application of this guarantee to the territorial arrangements made by the terms of the peace by which the present war is ended would, of course, necessarily depend upon the character of those arrangements, that is, their reasonableness and natural prospect of perman[en]cy; and would depend, so far as the participation of the United States is concerned, upon whether they were in conformity with the general principles of right and comity set forth in the address of the President to the Senate on the twenty-second of January last.

## III.

Mutual guarantee against such economic warfare as would in effect constitute an effort to throttle the industrial life of a nation or shut it off from equal opportunities of trade with the rest of the world.

### Note.

This would, of course, not apply to any laws of any individual state which were meant merely for the regulation and development of its own industries or for the mere safeguarding of its own resources from misuse or exhaustion, but only to such legislation and such governmental action as could be shown to be intended to operate outside territorial limits and intended to injure particular rivals or groups of rivals.

## IV.

Limitation of armaments, whether on land or sea, to the necessities of internal order and the probable demands of cooperation in making good the foregoing guarantees.

### Note.

PROVIDED the nations which take part in this covenant may be safely regarded as representing the major force of mankind.

GENERAL NOTE: It is suggested that it would not be necessary to set up at the outset any permanent tribunal or administrative agency, but only an Office of correspondence through which all matters of information could be cleared up, correspondence translated by experts (scholars), and mutual explanations and suggestions interchanged. It would in all likelihood be best to await the developments and suggestions of experience before attempting to set up any common instrumentality of international action.[1]

WWT MS (WP, DLC).
[1] There is a WWsh draft of this document in WP, DLC.

E N C L O S U R E     I I

*Notes on "Bases of Peace," Feby 7, 1917.*

*Article I.*

Would it be better to insert "equal" before the word "rights" in the last line.

*Article II.*

Does this provide for the adequate expansion of territory as a result of increased population or an accumulation of capital desiring investment in territory under national control? That is, should not some provision be made for future colonization?

So far as the American nations are concerned—and I think the same is true of Russia with its vast undeveloped territories and Great Britain with its great colonial possessions still but partially settled—a provision of this sort could be applied without danger of being disturbed for many decades, but is the same true of such populous countries as Belgium, France, Germany, Italy, Holland, etc.?

Is it possible to make a rigid and permanent delimitation of territory which will not in a short time be the source of trouble from the pressure of population? Will not such conditions cause aggression from necessity and in no sense from material ambition or improper motives? Is it possible to provide some elasticity as to territory which will furnish an outlet for surplus populations?

I do not think that the conditions for the application of a *world* treaty are the same as the conditions for the application of a Pan-American treaty.

I have no suggestion to offer now as the problem seems to me to require very careful study. I am merely raising here possible objections to the present terms of this Article.

*Article III.*

Does this provision apply to "economic warfare" by a single state against another state? If it does, then the power to retaliate for unjust commercial legislation or regulation by one nation, which though general in terms operates in practice against only one other nation, would be lacking and prevent the injured party from protecting itself from injustices. I assume the basic thought in this article is to prevent such international combinations as the Entente Allies had in mind during the Paris Economic Conference which, as I understand, proposed to unite their nations in preferential trade facilities after the war so that they would benefit first the Allies, second friendly neutrals, and third other neutrals, leaving the Central Powers commercially isolated or at least greatly handicapped in trade opportunities.

I am afraid that in its present form the article would be difficult of application. Who would be the judges as to the purpose of an economic war between states? Whose duty would it be to assume to judge of this matter? And whose duty would it be to enforce the guarantee after the authorized party had decided that action was necssary? This article seems to me much more difficult of practical application than either of the two preceding articles.

As a matter of fact I have never felt that the proposed plan of the Paris Conference could be carried out. Such a combination, even if attempted, would by the natural laws of trade fall to pieces in a short time.

Would it not be as efficacious and less difficult of application to enter into a mutual agreement not to form any international combination or conspiracy to interfere with the commercial enterprises or to limit the equal trade opportunities of any nation? This would not deprive a single state of the power to act in its own interests, but would prevent the united or identical action of two or more nations.

*Article IV*

This seems to me the most difficult of all the articles for proper application. So much depends on the geographical location of territorial possessions and their relation to one another, to the state of civilization attained in colonies, to the proximity of semi-civilized nations, to the restlessness of populations due to lack of intellectual development, to political oppression, to industrial injustice, to other causes of domestic unrest.

In limited and settled populations with liberal institutions the difficulties would be easily overcome, but in the larger states where domestic peace depends on an adequate force to suppress uprisings that force might in the hands of an ambitious and unscrupulous government be a very grave menace to small neighboring states.

I am sure that you will understand I am not arguing against the article. I believe in it but I am endeavoring to raise in my own mind the possible difficulties of the practical operation of the provisions if they should be adopted.

Who would determine what armament a nation was entitled to maintain? What would be the basis for limitation? How would an increase or decrease be determined if conditions changed? How would a proper limitation be enforced, and who would determine when enforcement should take place?

These questions are to me very perplexing and very real, and I cannot feel that they should remain unanswered until after the proposal of such an article as this. They will have to be answered some time and better before that the nations are committed because they would then be a source of endless controversy and of possible discord.

*General Note*

As to this note I have no comment. It seems to me sound and to offer the best agency possible under present international conditions.                          Robert Lansing

HwS MS (WP, DLC).


## From Edward Mandell House, with Enclosure

Dear Governor:                          New York. February 8, 1917.

Paul Kellogg of the Survey has asked me to enclose you this memorandum which was prepared by Ralph G. Hays, Professor of History at Columbia.[1] It is intended to give historical precedents for enforcing the claims of a nation without actually going to war.[2]

Thank you for enclosing me Gerard's last cable. The peace terms are preposterous and either indicate a gigantic bluff or a better state of affairs than is generally supposed to exist there.

Cardeza,[3] Penfield's secretary, has just landed. He gives me an intelligent resume of conditions in Austria.

There is a general demand for peace. The Austrians and Hungarians are at swords point and the government does not dare call Parliament together. Many of its members are in jail. There is great antagonism between the Germans and Austrians, but Germans largely officer the Austrian troops.

Food conditions are bad but he thinks it is possible to go through another winter. There is a shortage of metals which is perhaps their most serious problem. The florin is now worth nine to the dollar as against about four seventy-five before the war. There is little ill feeling against America.

Willcox called this afternoon. He goes to Washington tonight and hopes to see you in order to offer the services of his organization. I hope it will be possible for you to give him a few minutes of your time, for we had no more valuable aid in the campaign than he gave as Chairman of the Republican Committee.

Your affectionate,   E. M. House

TLS (WP, DLC).
¹ He meant Carlton Joseph Huntley Hayes, distinguished historian of modern Europe.
² Hayes published an expanded version as "Which? War without a Purpose? Or Armed Neutrality with a Purpose?" *The Survey*, XXXVII (Feb. 10, 1917), 535-38.
³ Thomas D. M. Cardeza.

## E N C L O S U R E

## Memorandum on Constructive Action if Confronted by Alternative of War.

1. That a league of armed neutrals is a better harbinger of future world solidarity than a league of belligerents.
2. That this is the third great maritime war in history, and
3. That such leagues were formed in the two earlier ones, when invasion of neutral rights at sea became intolerable.
4. That this did not involve the neutrals in those wars, even though neutral naval convoys engaged attacking vessels in defense of the merchantmen.
5. That it did not entangle them in the war even though a belligerent declared war on the neutrals. They simply ignored this.
6. That this joint action of defense laid the basis of neutral rights at sea, and ushered in a new stage of international law.

### Precedents.

Revolutionary Era—When France and Spain were at war with England, Russia, Denmark, Sweden, Prussia, Austria and Portugal formed an armed neutrality to—

1. free passages of neutral ships from port to port and along the coasts of combatant nations,
2. inviolability of an enemy's goods in neutral ships with the exception of such goods as were contraband of war, and
3. exact definition of a blockaded port, a merely nominal (paper) blockade, that is, one not enforced by a sufficient number of ships of war at the vicinity of the specified harbor, being declared inadmissible.

Napoleonic Era—When in the midst of Franco-British conflict, the Baltic powers revived their armed neutrality.

Also, more pertinent to America, the instance in 1798 when the United States to protect our rights at sea, broke off diplomatic relations with France, and Congress authorized American frigates to capture French vessels guilty of depredations on American commerce. Actual naval engagements were fought, but no formal declaration of war was made; and within a year France backed down.

However indecisive the armed neutrality leagues were at the time, they crystalized neutral sentiment, ultimately led to a revision of rules of naval warfare in line with the principles they laid down, and paved the way in the Paris Declaration of 1856 and the London Declaration of 1909, for the international law which, since the outbreak of the European war, it has been Mr. Wilson's concern to maintain with an enduring patience.

Unlike earlier proposals for conferences of neutral nations, this would not entangle us in timid co-operation in mediating the European war; but would organize concerted action in a definite field. Concensus of neutral opinion and a community of neutral interests might be brought about by cable, no less than by conference; and the program would not be halted by the failure of any neutral, or group of neutrals, to come in.

Prof. Hays' paper (in Col. House's hands) takes up the procedure of such a league with respect to a declaration of principles (1) contraband, (2) blockade, (3) convoy, and (4) submarine warfare; and their enforcement, giving examples.

### Advantages.

1. That such joint action would not involve delay. In instituting the first league, Catharine the Great invited others to join with Russia but went alone the first six months.

2. That by laying a framework and invitation to joint action, it would lift the course at the outset to the plane of organized maintenance of common rights.

3. That it will not throw 100 million people into the world war, and so wipe out the last great civilized area, unswept by hatred, which is the world's last great reservoir of goodwill and resources for the generous purposes of reconstruction.

4. That it would not put us at war with a country whose offenses, however outrageous, are not due to enmity of us and ours.

5. That we should not irremediably lose our opportunity to champion real *neutral* rights against *belligerent* intentions.

6. That, in a sense, it would be "extending the Monroe Doctrine to the sea," and conceivably the first to associate themselves

in the concerted action would be the South American powers which, because of their food supplies, are taken more seriously in Europe than heretofore.

7. That it would not involve us in accepting the views of the Entente Allies as to the freedom of the seas, in sending expeditionary force or conscripted army to the trenches of Flanders and the Somme, or in agreeing to make peace only in concert with belligerent allies.

8. That it would not destroy our great moral power in maintaining peace under provocation, as a presage of settling international disputes by methods other than those which have wrecked Europe.

9. That it would not forfeit our supreme vantage ground as the one strong neutral from which conceivably great mediatory steps can be taken in bringing in peace without victory.

10. That it would make us first and foremost of a group of neutral nations rather than the last and least of the belligerents, in the day of settlement.

T MS (WP, DLC).


# Lillian D. Wald to Joseph Patrick Tumulty, with Enclosure

Dear Mr. Tumulty:                    New York. February 8th, 1917.

I am quite sure that it is better to send the memorandum[1] to the President than to take up his time in a necessarily brief interview.

I am enclosing the proposals that he was good enough to suggest that I should send to him with a further note of explanation. As the matter if valuable at all should be considered immediately, may I beg you to give him the notes without delay.[2]

Our anxieties are with the President. His friends hardly sleep at night or rest by day in their ardent desire to help him sustain his high moral plane and to keep out of the war.

With much appreciation of you[r] quick response to the telephone communication sent to you, I am

Very sincerely yours,    Lillian D. Wald

TLS (WP, DLC).
  [1] She enclosed a copy of Hayes' memorandum, just printed, and galley pages of Hayes' article in *The Survey*, just cited.
  [2] Wilson wrote to Tumulty: "Colonel House also sent me a copy of Professor Hayes' suggestions, and I have already communicated them to the Secretary of State. They will, of course, receive the most careful consideration, and I am very much obliged indeed to Miss Wald for sending them. I hope you will tell her so." WW to JPT, c. Feb. 9, 1917, TL (WP, DLC).

# From Lillian D. Wald

Dear President Wilson:          New York February 8th, 1917.

Mr. Tumulty conveyed your message to me and I beg to present the memorandum embodying certain proposals to you without delay. Professor Hayes was called because of a great emergency to California and Mr. Paul Kellogg and I have tried to condense the suggestions he made and to have them fit into the situation as we understand it to be at the present time.

We are very well aware that to a great historian these facts are known, but your friends have thought deeply upon this matter and hope that they have something that may be of suggestive value to you.

We believe that public opinion would sanction concerted protection in an extreme crisis and a league of Neutrals thus might very natrually [naturally] and convincingly pave the way for America's taking part in such a league of the nations as you yourself laid before the Senate in your notable address. "It might lay the bogey of entangling alliances."

The principles of this address are ones which the lesser Neutrals, especially those of the Americas, would take to heart. And these principles could conceivably be re-enunciated by the United States at the outset as things which other Neutrals could be asked to jointly stand for in the councils of the world along with those principles of international rights for which they would be asked to jointly act on the high seas.

It would not necessarily call for a formal break with Germany by any of the other Neutrals subscribing to its principles.

It would not seem necessarily to involve questions of right of travel on belligerent ships but would concern itself primarily with Neutral navigation.

It could be put over as an affirmative American act at once, without waiting for or being dependent upon what Germany does or does not do from now on; and in the absence or subsequent flagrant violation of the principle of humanity its joint civil as distinct from its joint naval elements would make it the harbinger of the new international organization.

May I on this occasion report to you that I followed up without delay your suggestion of securing direct action from Mr. Carnegie, but I am sorry to say that he is unable to transact any business at all and therefore could not at the present time communicate with the officials of his various peace societies. This is a

matter of deep regret because plans should be made for an organized effort to get the principles of your great message before
every citizen of the United States.

Very faithfully yours,    Lillian D. Wald.

TLS (WP, DLC).


# From Newton Diehl Baker

My dear Mr. President:          Washington. February 8, 1917.

I have your suggestion of February 7th,[1] with regard to calling
a meeting of the Council of National Defense and the Advisory
Committee to collate and act upon the various offers which are
coming so generously to the government from manufacturers and
others to place their services and facilities at the disposal of the
Government.

A steady stream of these offers is pouring into the War Department, and I am having them all courteously acknowledged and
preserved for consideration should occasion arise. Practically all
of the manufacturing establishments represented in these offers
are tabulated and their facilities catalogued in the industrial survey made by Mr. Coffin,[2] which includes, as I understand it, every
industrial enterprise in the country doing a business equal to
$100,000 a year, and one element of the Coffin survey includes an
expression of the part of the plant as to whether it would be willing, upon call, to use its facilities for the government either in
the line of its regular manufacture or in other lines to which its
appliances could be more properly diverted in the event of emergency.

Unless you entertain a different view, I should hesitate to call
a meeting of the Council and Advisory Commission at this time,
for the following reasons:

1. Such a call would undoubtedly cause comment, and might
   lead to the suggestion of immediate and active preparations
   on the part of the country, which up to this time we have
   been able to avoid. I can see advantages on both sides of
   this question.
2. There is no new thing for the Council of National Defense
   to do at the present moment, and the first question it would
   have to consider would be the one which nobody can answer, as to whether hostilities are likely.
3. Should the situation become more grave, very far-reaching
   plans ought to be made at the outset, and it would then be
   wise to call the Commission and have them devote consid-

erable time to such plans, and publish a matured program dealing with the whole question of supply in the nation.

Such questions, however, if taken up now, would cause anxiety if they became known. Incidentally, it may be important for you to know the organization of the Council has been attended with some confusion, and it has been difficult to work out the proper limits of its activity, so as not to duplicate work already being done in the established Executive Departments.[3] I am a little afraid that to summon the Council and Commission to a present meeting, and have no more definite task for them than a direction to the Director to collate and acknowledge these offers, would seem premature to the members of the Commission.

If these views meet with your approval, I suggest that an acknowledgement in the following sense be sent to all such offers:

"Your generous and patriotic offer has been received. The War and Navy Departments and the Council of National Defense are actively considering these matters, and should the gravity of the present situation be increased, they will at once notify you of the best mode of cooperation. Your offer will be placed before them for consideration."

Respectfully yours,    Newton D. Baker

TLS (WP, DLC).
[1] WW to NDB, Feb. 7, 1917, TLS (Letterpress Books, WP, DLC).
[2] About this, see the press release printed at Oct. 10, 1916, Vol. 38. Howard Earle Coffin, a member of the Advisory Commission of the Council of National Defense, was also chairman of the Committee on Industrial Preparedness of the Naval Consulting Board.
[3] For an account of the early activities of the Council and Advisory Commission, including a meeting with Wilson on December 6, 1916, see Frankin H. Martin, *Digest of the Proceedings of the Council of National Defense during the World War*, Senate Doc. No. 193, 73d Cong., 2d sess. (Washington, 1934), pp. 51-98.

## From Cleveland Hoadley Dodge

My dear Friend & President        New York February 8th 1917

How can I thank you enough for your very kind letter, with your words of cheer about conditions in Turkey.

What you say about the position in London has completely flabbergasted me. It is needless to say that your mere thought of me, in that connection, has touched me deeply, as an evidence of your confidence and esteem. I fully realize that the post there is one of the most important in the world, & for that reason, it ought to be filled by the ablest man in the United States, who has had the training & experience fitting him to cope with all the complicated questions which will arise. I have enough sense to know my own limitations. While I have some of the necessary qualifications, I am wofully lacking in others which are essential. No one could serve the country & you more loyally, but there are others who would serve just as loyally & much more capably.

I am glad to see by the morning paper that Mr. Page has consented to stay on, & trust that he will remain for a long time. If the economic question still worries him I hope we can relieve his mind of any anxiety. Owing to the war, he has had less entertaining & a reduction in other expenses, so that he has not needed as much as we at one time anticipated. Although I have a definite understanding with his son that he should call on me whenever he needs funds, he has not recently asked for as much as at first. Perhaps it is because he does not want to be under obligations to anyone, but if that is the case you can surely disabuse his mind of any such idea. Unless his son has told him, & he swore he wouldn't, I do not think he knows where the money comes from. If later on, you find that he insists on resigning, you may find the right man to succeed him, whose decision to accept might depend on the financial aspect & in that event, I want to assure you that I will consider it an honor & pleasure to help out to the fullest extent, by providing any amount which may be needed.

In addition to my feeling that I am not sufficiently qualified for the post, I must tell you very frankly that I do not think my health would stand the strain. When I had my breakdown eight years ago, my heart was pretty well knocked out, and the experts told me that I must be very careful to lead a regular life and avoid dinners & functions & late hours. By doing this I get on very well, but I know that the stress & responsibility at London would be disastrous, and moreover my dear wife's increasing deafness would be a great handicap.

There is however one insuperable objection which makes it impossible for me to even consider your generous proposal. When I hitched my wagon to a star, long ago, I did so, as you well know, purely from love of you & my country, without any thought or desire for personal advantage. Four years ago I made a solemn vow that I would never ask or accept anything from you, except your friendship—that you have accorded me in rich measure, and it has been & is a priceless possession. Although I have been publicly assailed & charged with having bought special privileges by my campaign contributions, it has been a source of peculiar pride and satisfaction to know that I have kept my vow and that I can look anyone in the eyes. If you should offer me the richest plum in your gift, and I should accept it, the bloom would all disappear, and the genial critics would have the time of their lives, with *apparent* justification for anything they might say. Even if I were willing to stand the racket for myself, I could not consent to your being subjected to the kind of abuse which you would surely receive and which many righteous souls would feel that you justly deserved. Just think what I would have to live down, if I should go to St James (not to mention my bad golf)

No, my dear old friend, I will do anything in my power to help you in these critical times, but I can help you better in other ways than this

When I started I did not mean to inflict on you such a long and egotistical letter, and I hope you will forgive me. If I could only bear some of your awful burdens I should be happy, but I can at least stand on the side lines & cheer you on.

God bless you in all the critical hours, sure to come! !

Mrs Dodge joins me in warm regards & love for you & Mrs Wilson

Ever devotedly & sincerely your friend

Cleveland H. Dodge

ALS (WP, DLC).

## From George Howe III

Dear Uncle Woodrow,          Chapel Hill [N. C.] Feb. 8, 1917

Is there any way I can be of assistance to you—or to the country —in these critical times? I am at your service whenever you may call—and you know my devotion. I do not refer to possible soldiering, though when a call comes for forty-year-olders I shall respond, but to service which the present moment may demand & which requires extra men. I know it is a bad thing to be a nephew, but I am also a good citizen. Particularly, I am thinking of your part in it all and my heart is full of the desire to be near you to offer any sort of aid I am capable of that will make the pressure easier to sustain. How can I help? If in any way, feel no hesitation in sending for me.

With best love to all,   George Howe

ALS (WP, DLC).

## To Robert Lansing, with Enclosures

My dear Mr. Secretary,      The White House. 9 February, 1917.

The Swiss minister is pressing for a reply to the suggestion of his government.[1] He is a very diligent and pressing gentleman!

What would you think of replying to him in the sense of the enclosed memorandum?

I have tried my hand at a restatement of the BASES. What do you think of the result? All that we can hope for is to agree upon definite things and rely on experience and subsequent exchanges of treaty agreement to develop and remove the practical difficulties.                              Faithfully Yours,    W.W.

WWTLI (SDR, RG 59, 763.72/3261½, DNA).
[1] That is, the Swiss proposal for a "conference of neutrals," the text of which is printed as an Enclosure with P. Ritter to A. Hoffmann, Feb. 2, 1917.


E  N  C  L  O  S  U  R  E      I

Points to be made in reply to the suggestion of the Swiss Federal Council.

The probable physical impossibility of holding an actual conference.

The embarrassments which it is now evident many neutral governments would feel in seeming to come together to influence the present course of events.

The desirability, nevertheless, of a frank interchange of views.

SUGGESTION, therefore, that the Swiss Federal Council communicate to the Government of the United States its views as to any present feasible course of cooperative action and any common bases upon which neutrals might at this time draw together in a League of Peace. The United States would be very glad in its turn, or at the invitation of the Council, to submit its own views on these vital and important subjects.


E  N  C  L  O  S  U  R  E      I  I

### BASES of PEACE.

#### I.

Mutual guarantee of political independence,—absolute in all domestic matters, limited in external affairs only by the equal rights of other nations.

#### II.

Mutual guarantee of territorial integrity.

Note.

The application of this guarantee to the territorial arrangements made by the terms of the peace by which the present war is to be ended would, of course, necessarily depend upon the character of those  arrangements, that is, upon their reasonableness and natural prospect of permanency; and, so far as the participation of the United States in the guarantee is concerned, would depend upon whether they were in conformity with the general principles of right and comity which the President set forth in his address to the Senate on the twenty-second of January.

Such a guarantee would not affect natural expansion peaceably accomplished.

## III.

Mutual agreement not to take part in any joint economic action by two or more nations which would in effect constitute an effort to throttle the industrial life of any nation or shut it off from fair and equal opportunities of trade with the nations thus in concert or with the rest of the world.

Note.

This would of course not apply, as its terms indicate, to the laws of an individual state intended for the regulation and development of its own industries or for the safeguarding of its own resources from misuse or exhaustion, but only to cooperative action between states intended or which would operate to injure particular rivals or groups of rivals.

## IV.

Mutual agreement to limit armaments, whether on land or sea, to the necessities of internal order (including, of course, the internal order of an empire) and the probable demands of cooperation in making good the foregoing guarantees and agreements.

Note.

PROVIDED the nations which take part in these covenants may reasonably be regarded as representing the major force of mankind.

GENERAL NOTE. It is suggested that it would not be necessary to set up at the outset any permanent tribunal or administrative agency, but only an office of correspondence through which all matters of information could be cleared up, correspondence translated by competent scholars, and mutual explanations and suggestions exchanged. It would in all likelihood be best, in this matter of executive organization, to await the developments and lessons of experience before attempting to set up any common instrumentality of international action.

WWT MS (SDR, RG 59, 763.72/3261½, DNA).

## To Robert Lansing, with Enclosures

My dear Mr. Secretary,      The White House. 9 February, 1917.

These and earlier telegrams about the possible action of China make my conscience uneasy. We may be leading China to risk her doom.

Have you been sending any replies to Reinsch's messages? It seems to me that if we suffer China to follow us in what we are now doing we ought to be ready to assist and stand by her in every possible way consistent with her and our engagements in the East. What she has asked through Reinsch has not been unreasonable, but can we count on the Senate and on our bankers to fulfill any expectations we may arouse in China?

I would very much like to have your thoughts and your advice. We cannot keep them conjecturing. We ought to answer their questions at once.         Faithfully Yours,   W.W.

WWTLI (SDR, RG 59, 763.72/3275½, DNA).

### E N C L O S U R E   I

Peking, Feb. 6, 1917.

February 6, 1 P.M.

I have discussed Department's circular of February 3, 1 P.M.,[1] with the President,[2] Minister for Foreign Affairs,[3] Premier,[4] and Minister of Finance.[5] Cabinet meeting took place today but no decision yet arrived at.

I have been questioned on the following points relating to eventuality of China's being drawn into the war in consequence of taking the action suggested: first, could assurances be given that Chinese arsenals and military forces would not come under foreign control; second, could assurances be given that China would be admitted to full membership in the peace conference; third, what would be relations of the Powers now entering the war to the London agreement not to make separate peace? I confined myself to conjectures but should be assisted by having your instructions on these points.

Our influence with the Chinese has been markedly impaired by the publication of the proposed cooperation with Japan in the canal projects, more particularly because the Japanese reports have given rise to the belief that the Americans took the initiative in seeking Japanese assistance.

British Chargé d'Affaires[6] made to me the surprising statement that the attitude of Japan would probably be decisive of the question of China's following the American proposal. Considering the Chinese fear of the Japanese it is to be apprehended that opposition on the part of the latter would determine China to remain passive.

Please keep me informed of the action of other neutral powers which would also influence China.                    Reinsch.

T telegram (SDR, RG 59, 763.72/3230, DNA).
1 That is, RL to all missions of the United States in all neutral countries, Feb. 3, 1917.
2 Li Yuan-hung.
3 Wu T'ing-fang.
4 Tuan Ch'i-jui.
5 Ch'en Chin-t'ao.
6 Beilby Francis Alston.


ENCLOSURE II

Peking, Feb. 6, 1917.

February 6, 11 P.M.
Strictly confidential.

The Cabinet met again today and the Minister of Finance informs me that the sentiment in favor of joining the United States is gaining strength phenomenally. He intimates that the chief obstacle to such action is the fear concerning arsenals. If I can be authorized to give to the Chinese Government the assurance that ten million dollars gold will be loaned from American sources to improve arsenals and that the United States Government will agree to funding of its portion of Boxer indemnity in long term bonds and to urge the same course upon the allied powers, I feel assured that the Chinese Government will forthwith associate itself with the American action. The former is the more important. Should the arrangement for funding the indemnity require action by Congress it is possible that the Chinese Government might be persuaded to act upon the assurance that the administration would at some opportune time recommend appropriate legislation to that effect.

The Chinese officials recognize the justice of the cause espoused by the United States as well as the desirability of China's associating itself with the measures taken, but they will not act unless they can have effective assurances that their national independence will be safeguarded by the United States as by the means suggested above, which would be a very moderate amount of support.                                              Reinsch.

T telegram (SDR, RG 59, 763.72/3245, DNA).


E N C L O S U R E    I I I

Peking, Feb. 7, 1917.

February 7, 6 p.m.

STRICTLY CONFIDENTIAL.

My telegram of February 6, 11 p.m.

In a further (#) Minister of Finance stated that the Chinese officials are increasingly disposed to associate their government with the action of the United States but are deterred by the fear that evident necessity for more adequate military organization might lead the Japanese Government to seek from the Allies mandate to supervise such organization: and that to avert the possibility of Japan's creating such a situation the Chinese Government considers it to be of the utmost importance to have some assurance that means will be provided to enable it to undertake the requisite measures independently with American financial assistance and guidance. In view of his urgent request for some immediate assurance on which the decision of the government can be made, before other influences can be interposed, I shall feel justified in addressing the Minister for Foreign Affairs as follows, if it appears that by doing so without delay a favorable decision may be obtained: "I have recommended to my Government in the event of the Chinese Government's associating itself with the President's suggestion the Government of the United States should take measures to put at its disposal funds immediately required for the purposes you have indicated, and should take steps with a view to such a funding of the Boxer indemnity as would for the time being make available for the (purposes?) of the Chinese Government at least the major portions the current indemnity installments: and I have indicated to you my personal conviction that my government would be found just and liberal in effecting this or other such arrangements to enable the Chinese Government to meet the responsibilities which it might assume upon the suggestion of the President. I should not be wholly frank with you however if I were to fail to point out that the exact nature of any assistance to be given or any measures to be taken must be determined through consultation of various administrative organs, in some cases including reference to Congress, in order to make effective such arrangements as might have been agreed to between the executive authorities of the two governments: and I therefore could not in good faith make in behalf of my government any definite commitments upon your suggestions at the present time.

I do however feel warranted in assuming the responsibility of assuring you in behalf of my government that by the methods you have suggested, or otherwise, adequate means will be devolved to enable China to fulfill the responsibilities consequent upon associating itself with the action of the United States, without any impairment of her control of her military establishment and general administration." I venture the hope that this action which I shall take only under imperative immediate necessity will meet your approval and that my position in this matter may be strengthened by authorization to affirm the acceptance by our government of the principle of affording China such financial assistance as Great Britain for example has given Russia.

Reinsch.

T telegram (SDR, RG 59, 763.72/3256, DNA).

E N C L O S U R E    I V

Peking, Feb. 8, 1917.

February 8, 12 p.m. STRICTLY CONFIDENTIAL.

In the strictest confidence the representatives of France, Great Britain, and Russia[1] express earnest hope that China will associate itself with the action of the United States but all feel precluded from making any official statement because of the necessity of consulting the wish of Japan which may as in 1915 be opposed to China's taking any part in the war.

After daily deliberations the Cabinet have sent word to me that they will send a note to Germany strongly disapproving submarine policy and declaring that they will break off diplomatic relations if it is persisted in: they are ready to take this action on condition that I give them the assurances reported in my cipher telegram February 2, 12 midnight[2]: they offer in return the assurances that any action on the part of Germany which the

United States takes as a casus belli they will regard as occasion for severing diplomatic relations. I do not propose to give the assurances unless this Government associates itself more fully with the action of ours but I urgently request your instructions whether I might do so if no more satisfactory action by China could be induced by any other means.                    Reinsch.

T telegram (SDR, RG 59, 763.72/3270, DNA).
  [1] That is Alston; the French Minister to China, Alexandre Robert Conty; and the Russian Minister in Peking, Prince Nikolai Aleksandrovich Kudashev.
  [2] The decoder's mistake. Reinsch obviously referred to his telegram of February 7, 6 P.M. There is no Reinsch to RL of February 2, midnight.


## To Robert Lansing

My dear Mr. Secretary,       The White House. 9 February, 1917.

I think you will be interested to read this letter from House and the accompanying memorandum.[1]

Please let me have them back when you have read them.
                    Faithfully Yours,   W.W.

WWTLI (SDR, RG 59, 763.72/3355½, DNA).
  [1] That is, EMH to WW, Feb. 8, 1917, with its Enclosure.


## To Harry Lane

My dear Senator:          [The White House] 9 February, 1917

There are a great many important interests depending upon the passage of the general Alaska fisheries bill[1] and I am writing to ask if you would not be good enough to put your shoulder behind it and assist in putting it through. It is a most important measure. It would stop the present waste of food fishes and restrict existing monopolies of fishing rights in a way which I think would be distinctly for the public benefit.

          Cordially and sincerely yours,   Woodrow Wilson

TLS (Letterpress Books, WP, DLC).
  [1] About this measure, see W. C. Redfield to WW, Dec. 30, 1916, Vol. 40.


## To Albert Sidney Burleson

My dear Burleson:          The White House 9 February, 1917

I wonder if it would be convenient for you to see Representative Frank Clark of Florida, the Chairman of the Public Buildings and Grounds Committee, and tell him how sincerely interested I am in having the bill for the purchase of Monticello reported

out? The members of the D.A.R. have been canvassing the House
and Senate very earnestly in this matter and feel confident that
the bill would pass if reported out. I have once written to Mr.
Clark[1] but nothing seems to have come of it, and I don't like to
write again.

Always          Faithfully yours,   Woodrow Wilson

TLS (A. S. Burleson Papers, DLC).
[1] Wilson's letter is missing.

## To William Royal Wilder[1]

My dear Wilder:          [The White House] 9 February, 1917

Why bills are held up in the Senate is almost always a matter
of mystery, and I do not know just what is holding the Porto
Rican Bill back, but I have been constantly interested in it and
you may be sure that if it is passed, I will very carefully consider
Hamilton's[2] claims, though I must frankly say that his conduct
since going to Porto Rico has not been wise and has made a bad
impression on the Department of Justice. Not that they have any
doubt of his honesty, but they have a great deal about his practical sense.

In haste          Sincerely yours,   Woodrow Wilson

TLS (Letterpress Books, WP, DLC).
[1] Wilson was replying to W. R. Wilder to WW, Feb. 8, 1917, TLS (WP, DLC).
[2] That is, their classmate, Peter J. Hamilton, federal district judge in Porto
Rico.

## To James Woodrow

My dear Jimmie:          [The White House] 9 February, 1917

Thank you for your letter of February seventh. I have time for
only a line of acknowledgement but it is a line of grateful affection. Please give my love to Aunt Felie and tell her not to worry
too much; we will all combine to try to do the best possible in the
circumstances.

In haste          Faithfully yours,   Woodrow Wilson

TLS (Letterpress Books, WP, DLC).

## From Stephen Samuel Wise

[Dear Mr. President:]          [New York] February 9, 1917

I have not written to you during these days of crisis because I
know you would be overwhelmed by messages from those who do

not perhaps realize the importance of sparing you at such a time as this. I merely write now in order to tell you that I thanked God for your leadership of the nation.

On Sunday morning, in my pulpit, I shall say that the country must stand behind you and will stand behind you. You have kept us in the paths of peace as a result of your high statesmanship and as a result of that infinite patience worthy of the head of a great and free people.

The time has come for the American people to understand that it may become our destiny to have part in the struggle which would avert the enthronement of the law of might over the nations.

Speaking on Sunday morning on "America's Lincoln and Wilson's America," I shall have great joy in saying, not only of the President of the United States but of an honored and cherished friend, that, as Washington was the father of the nation and Lincoln later became its savior, so in this time of world crisis the American people was led by a man whose name is hereafter to be bracketed with the names of Washington and Lincoln, equal to the genius of the spirit of America and worthy to become the champion and servant of humanity.

[Faithfully yours,    Stephen S. Wise]

Printed in Carl Hermann Voss, ed., *Stephen S. Wise: Servant of the People* (Philadelphia, 1969), pp. 74-75.

## George Wilkins Guthrie to Robert Lansing

Tokyo, February 9 1917.

STRICTLY CONFIDENTIAL. Chinese Minister[1] here has this morning sent word to me in the strictest confidence through a member of Legation staff that his Government has determined in accordance with the President's suggestion to sever diplomatic relations with Germany in the immediate future and to recall her Minister at Berlin forthwith. The Minister by instruction of his Government asked me to advise him as to whether he should in my opinion inform the Japanese Foreign Office before the step is taken. He asked also for information as to probable course of the United States in the event of war being declared between the United States and Germany. On latter point I sent word to him that my belief was that the Senate of the United States in such a contingency would at first at least confine its participation in the hostilities to naval and material assistance to the Entente Powers. As to the first point after careful consideration I answered that I believed the contemplated action of China was entirely independent of Japanese and would be taken at the suggestion of the President of the United States; I felt therefore that it should be taken, to be most effective, without any prior notification to the Japanese Government.

The Minister did not come in person in order to avoid the possibility of his communication to me coming to the knowledge of the Japanese authorities.

The Minister sent me word that owing to pressure in Peking the Chinese Foreign Office had cabled to its representative[s] in the allied capitals and Washington for assurances as to position of China after such a step and would not act until satisfactory answers were received.                                                      Guthrie

T telegram (SDR, RG 59, 763.72/3275, DNA).
¹ Chang Tsung-hsiang.


## Paul Samuel Reinsch to Robert Lansing

Peking, Feb. 9, 1917.

February 9, 12 midnight. My telegram of February 8, 12 midnight. Chinese Government has now replied to the following effect to my note in pursuance of your telegram:

"Chinese Government being in accord with the principles set forth in Your Excellency's note and firmly associating itself with the Government of the United States, has taken similar action by protesting energetically to the German Government against the new measures of blockade. Chinese Government also proposes to take such action in the future as will be deemed necessary for the maintenance of the principles of international law." It has at the same time addressed to German Minister¹ note of protest expressing the hope that the proposed measures will not be carried out and adding that "In case contrary to its expectations its protest be ineffectual, the Government of the Chinese Republic will be constrained to its profound regret to sever the diplomatic relations at present existing between the two countries."

SPECIAL GREEN

STRICTLY CONFIDENTIAL. It is also making to me by a note verbale the following confidential communication interpreting the note quoted above:

"In case an act should be performed by the German Government which should be considered by the American Government as sufficient cause for declaration of war between the United

States and Germany, the Chinese Government should at least break its diplomatic relations with Germany."

This identification with the policy of the American Government, though conforming incompletely with its action already taken, appears to be the utmost that can be immediately obtained in view of strong German influences and apprehensions of other dangers and obstacles. In order to bring it about, I found it imperatively necessary to give the assurances referred to in my cipher telegram February 7, 6 p.m. which however I have pointed out apply to the consequences of action taken concurrently with the United States.

The strongest exertion of influence and persuasion was necessary to obtain this result in the face of numerous unfavorable factors. The most potent (at?) [factor] in our favor was the confidence felt by the Chinese in the aims of the American Government and their reluctance to fail to respond when invited to associate themselves with its action.

I beg to request that my telegram of February 6, 1 p.m. be considered strictly confidential.                    Reinsch.

T telegram (SDR, RG 59, 763.72/3383, DNA).
1 Paul von Hintze.


## Franklin Knight Lane to George Whitfield Lane[1]

My dear George,                    Washington, February 9, 1917

I am going to write you in confidence some of the talks we have at the Cabinet and you may keep these letters in case I ever wish to remind myself of what transpired. A week ago yesterday, (February 1st), the word came that Germany was to turn "mad dog" again, and sink all ships going within her war zone. This was the question, of course, taken up at the meeting of the Cabinet on February 2nd. The President opened by saying that this notice was an "astounding surprise." He had received no intimation of such a reversal of policy. Indeed, Zimmermann, the German minister of Foreign Affairs, had within ten days told Gerard that such a thing was an "impossibility." At this point Lansing said that he had good reason to believe that Bernstorff had the note for fully ten days before delivering it, and had held it off because of the President's Peace Message to Congress, which had made it seem inadvisable to deliver it then. In answer to a question as to which side he wished to see win, the President said that he didn't wish to see either side win,—for both had been equally indifferent to the rights of neutrals—though Germany had been brutal in taking life, and England only in taking property. He would like to see the neutrals unite. I ventured the expression that to ask them to do this would be idle, as they could not afford to join with us if it meant the insistence on their rights to the point of war. He thought we might coördinate the neutral forces, but was persuaded that an effort to do this publicly, as he proposed, would put some of the small powers in a delicate position. We talked the world situation over. I spoke of the likelihood of a German-Russian-Japanese alliance as the natural thing at the end of the war because they all were nearly in the same stage of development. He thought the Russian peasant might save the world this misfortune. The fact that Russia had been, but a short time since, on the verge of an independent peace with Germany was brought out as evidencing the possibility of a break on the Allies' side. His conclusion was that nothing should be done now,—awaiting the "overt act" by Germany, which would take him to Congress to ask for power.

At the next meeting of the Cabinet on February 6th, the main question discussed was whether we should convoy, or arm, our merchant ships. Secretary Baker said that unless we did our ships would stay in American ports, and thus Germany would have us effectively locked up by her threat. The *St. Louis*, of the American line, wanted to go out with mail but asked the right to arm and the use of guns and gunners. After a long discussion, the decision of the President was that we should not convoy because that made a double hazzard,—this being the report of the Navy,—but that ships should be told that they *might* arm, but that without new power from Congress they should not be furnished with guns and gunners.

The President said that he was "passionately" determined not to over-step the slightest punctilio of honor in dealing with Germany, or interned Germans, or the property of Germans. He would not take the interned ships, not even though they were being gutted of their machinery. He wished an announcement made that all property of Germans would be held inviolate, and that interned sailors or merchant ships could enter the United States. If we are to have war we must go in with our hands clean and without any basis for criticism against us. The fact that before Bernstorff gave the note telling of the new warfare, the ships had been dismantled as to their machinery, was not to move us to any act that would look like hostility.

[Sincerely yours,   F. K. Lane]

Printed in Anne Wintermute Lane and Louise Herrick Wall, eds., *The Letters of Franklin K. Lane, Personal and Political* (Boston and New York, 1922), pp. 233-35.
¹ Brother and former law partner in San Francisco of Franklin K. Lane.

## Two Letters from Robert Lansing

PERSONAL AND PRIVATE:

My dear Mr. President:          Washington February 10, 1917.

Thank you for letting me see Colonel House's letter of the 8th with Professor Hays' memorandum on armed neutrality, which I herewith return.

Colonel House's information from Cardeza confirms our reports as to the Austrian situation.

Phillips had a long talk last evening with Tarnowski. The latter said that his Government is most anxious to avoid breaking off relations and hoped that we could find some subject for conversations. I think this can be done, as Austria last spring complained of the illegal attacks of French submarines and we can ask an explanation of their attitude then and now, thus providing a reasonable basis for discussion.

If we could meanwhile persuade the Entente Governments to so modify their peace terms that Austria would not feel that they meant the dismemberment of that Empire, I believe something might be done to lessen Austrian dependence on Germany. If any means could be found to weaken their alliance, it would be a decided step toward peace. Of course this is a hope rather than an expectation, but I think that it is worth trying, since we know the desperate internal situation of Austria and also because from now on our intercourse with Austria's representative here will not be under the influence of the German Ambassador.

If these suggestions meet with your approval I would like to know it in order that the machinery may be set in motion.

Faithfully yours,   Robert Lansing.

TLS (WP, DLC).

My dear Mr. President:          Washington February 10, 1917.

Your note of yesterday's date relating to the telegrams from Reinsch has led me to hold back the attached telegrams which I was just about to send to Peking and Tokyo.

I am disposed to believe that if China should break off diplomatic relations with Germany and war should result the fears of the Chinese Government would be only too sure to be realized, for if China attempted to improve her defences Japan would probably consider any strengthening of China's military forces a menace that would justify her in demanding control of arsenals and command of the troops. It would be of immense advantage to China to be permitted to create an army of sufficient size to defend her territories and put an end to foreign encroachments. It would also undoubtedly be to our advantage, but if we encourage such an effort I feel confident we shall have to be prepared to meet Japanese opposition.

China knows that she cannot afford to allow Japan to take charge of her forces and that she dare not undertake military improvement without Japanese consent.

I shall await your direction before telegraphing Reinsch and Guthrie.          Faithfully yours,   Robert Lansing.

TLS (SDR, RG 59, 763.72/3270, DNA).


## To Robert Lansing, with Enclosures

My dear Mr. Secretary,     The White House. 10 February, 1917.

Thank you for letting me see the enclosed telegrams. I have suggested a few changes and additions.

I think that it would be well to let Reinsch tell the Government of China how sincerely we desire to help China and that we are constantly trying to shield her against the selfishness of her neighbor. I do not want them to get the idea that we are unappreciative of their present willingness to stand with us, which is singularly generous and enlightened.

Faithfully Yours,   W.W.

WWTLI (SDR, RG 59, 763.72/3275, DNA).


E N C L O S U R E     I

Washington, February 9, 1917.

Amembassy, Tokyo. Your cipher telegram of February 9, two p.m.

The Department believes that Chinese Government is well advised to consult its representatives in allied countries before severing diplomatic relations with Germany. Ignorance of Japan's attitude suggests caution. The unwillingness of other important neutrals to follow lead of United States should also ⟨perhaps⟩

have consideration. *This government does not wish to lead the Government of China into additional danger.*[1]

T telegram (SDR, RG 59, 763.72/3275, DNA).
[1] Wilson added this sentence; he also excised the "perhaps."


ENCLOSURE   I I[1]

Washington, February 10, 1917.

Amlegation, Peking. Your cipher telegrams of February 6, one p.m. and eleven p.m.

The American Government highly appreciates disposition of China but *does not wish to lead it into danger. It* regrets *practical* inability to give any *present* assurances. Unwillingness of any other important neutral to follow American example ought ⟨perhaps⟩ to be *very gravely* considered *by China, who should in prudence avoid isolated action.* The Chinese Government, therefore, ⟨might⟩ *would* do well to consult its representatives in the allied countries. Ignorance of Japan's attitude also suggests caution.

Following for your informal use.

The Department fear hasty action by China might lead to the foreign control of arsenals and forces which China apprehends. British Chargé's remark would seem to indicate British willingness to acquiesce in Japanese view.

T telegram (SDR, RG 59, 763.72/3230, 3245, DNA).
[1] Words in angle brackets in the following document deleted by Wilson; words in italics added by him.


# From Robert Lansing, with Enclosure

[Washington] 2/10/17

For your special consideration

Robert Lansing

ALS (WP, DLC).


ENCLOSURE

New York, February 10, 1917.

Confidential.

Unless you instruct us to the contrary we intend to despatch the American line steamship PHILADELPHIA from Liverpool to New York on or about February fourteenth and the American steamship FINLAND from Liverpool to New York a day or two later.

Both these steamers are unarmed and will carry passengers and cargo, possibly also mails.

We feel that the Government should arrange for their protection through the war zone.

For reasons that you will appreciate we are making no public announcement of these sailings.

INTERNATIONAL MERCANTILE MARINE CO.<br>P. A. S. Franklin,[1] President.

TC telegram (WP, DLC).
  [1] Philip Albright Small Franklin.


# From Josephus Daniels

Dear Mr. President:                    Washington. Feb. 10, 1917.

The only guns that can be placed in private hands are three inch guns at Bethlehem. The St. Louis would require 6 inch guns and we can find none except those belonging to the Navy, provided as a reserve to be used on merchant ships if made naval auxiliaries. In the survey of ships, the Operations department scheduled 6 in guns for the St. Louis and ships of that type. The owners of that ship say they cannot go out with guns of less range. The new German submarines carry 4 inch. Our 6 inch guns have a range of about 6 miles while the range of the 3 inch guns is about 3 miles.

Three of the ships of Mr. Franklin's company are in English waters. I have heard he has applied to the English Admiralty to equip them with 6 in guns before they leave, but he has received no answer. There seem to be no 6 inch guns available. In fact none in this country except in the Navy's possession. In the plan for use of the St. Louis and sister ships in case of war we had provided to equip them with 6 guns of 6 inch type. It has been suggested that we might let that ship and other like ships have two such guns. That seems the only thing that can be done if those ships are equipped with effective guns.

Sincerely,   Josephus Daniels

ALS (WP, DLC).

# From Josephus Daniels, with Enclosure

Dear Mr. President:                     Washington. Feb. 10, 1917.

I am enclosing a memorandum submitted by Mr. Roosevelt after his visit to New York with his suggestion as to the course he recommends.                     Sincerely,     Josephus Daniels

ALS (WP, DLC).

E N C L O S U R E

February 10, 1917.

### Memorandum for the Secretary:

1. I find that we have six 6-inch guns (Mark IX, 44 calibers long) which are regularly held for the American Line Steamer "St. Louis."

2. I have talked to Admiral Earle[1] and find that we have no authority to sell serviceable ordnance material and, while these guns are somewhat old, it would be in the nature of a subterfuge to condemn them and sell them as condemned material at present. Under the law, however, guns may be *loaned* provided a suitable bond be given.

3. Frankly I believe that an intolerable situation is beginning to arise. After my investigations in New York yesterday it is clear that American ships cannot get guns suitable for arming themselves except from the Government, and I believe the position of the American Line is well taken—that they cannot square it with their consciences to let their passenger ships leave New York without some protection, either convoyed or armed.

4. The situation is now this: The Navy has enough guns to let the American Line and other larger ships have two large guns for each ship (It is really a fact that the 3-inch guns are too small for use against submarines). I would suggest that we can properly loan these guns with their mounts and ammunition, the work of installation and mounting of the guns to be done by the owners of the vessels. This I am confident they can do themselves.

5. May I ask that you send this memorandum to the President, as I believe it points a way out of the difficulty of asking the authority of Congress? The special point I would make is that the only available guns are in the possession of the United States Government. If we refuse to let this source become available to private companies we close absolutely the only door open to them.

We have taken the position that it is entirely proper for merchant ships to arm if they so desire. We can, therefore, by loaning these guns give them the only opportunity to get them and they themselves would be entirely responsible for the installation and handling of the guns after they are on board. In case this should be approved it would take four or five days' work before the vessels could be made ready to sail and in the meantime, as you know, everything is held up.          Franklin D Roosevelt

TS MS (WP, DLC).
[1] Rear Admiral Ralph Earle, Chief of the Bureau of Ordnance.

## From Edward Mandell House

Dear Governor:          New York. February 10, 1917.

The Dutch Minister[1] called this morning. He said one reason your call to the neutrals had no response was because the neutrals had been trying to get you for two years to cooperate with them and that you had refused until a crisis arose.

He thinks if you would call a neutral conference at Washington with the suggestion that the Ministers act as representatives, you could get the neutrals to join the United States in formulating a plan of action directed against violations of sea rights.

I have a notion that this plan was suggested to him by Bernstorff, than whom he has no closer friend among the Diplomatic Corps.

Knowing that Rappard would take whatever I told him back to Bernstorff, I used the opportunity to advantage. I gave him some idea of the potential power of this country both from a military, financial and industrial viewpoint, and told him that if we were pushed into war, the efforts of even England would be insignificant in comparison to what we could and would do.

If this country continues to present a united front so that all the predictions of the German Government are unverified, and if England can hold down the submarine warfare to a minimum, Germany, I think, will go to pieces before long.

The food situation there is so bad that the civil government was forced into adopting the military and naval undersea warfare through pressure of the people. If it fails, there will be a general collapse.

I believe the main thing you have to consider now is the maintenance of your strong position (since we broke with Germany) with the Allies, for this is necessary if you are to exert an influence towards a peace that is worthwhile.

I was informed yesterday that England had diverted 250 000 rifles from Europe to India. The order was changed yesterday. I am wondering why. Is there revolution in India, or is it to arm troops for European service, or is it to send them more safely into Mesopotamia.

I am enclosing an article by Lincoln Colcord which I believe will interest you.[2] If you have not time for it all please read the last two or three paragraphs in which he speaks of you. Brougham is trying to liberalize the Ledger, and if he can get Curtis' consent, he will use in the editorial staff not only Colcord, but Creel and Miss Tarbell. Colcord's idea is to make it the Manchester Guardian of America.        Affectionately yours,    E. M. House

P.S. Rappard wanted me to ask you to let him come to see you informally. Not as a Minister, but as a private citizen in order to talk over his plan for a neutral conference.[3]

TLS (WP, DLC).
[1] That is, Chevalier Willem Louis Frederik Christiaan van Rappard.
[2] Lincoln Colcord, "Danger of Junkerism Drawing U. S. Into War," Philadephia *Public Ledger*, Feb. 10, 1917, "Special Telegram" from Washington, dated February 9. It began:

Now that we have definitely and sharply broken off diplomatic relations with Germany and while we are waiting in suspense for that "overt act" which the President hopes may not occur, but the possibility of which it is well for us to face without evasion, we have time to think what the war really means, to analyze its causes, to estimate at their face value the forces which are drawing us into the world disaster and to forecast broadly the result of our precipitation in the conflict both upon the issues involved and upon a future international polity.

At the start, it behooves us not to underestimate the weaknesses of our position. I do not refer to physical weaknesses, but to weaknesses inherent in the emotions which are now daily gaining headway with us. It behooves us still to bear in mind the same set of factors which we saw in operation a week ago to remember that because Germany has suddenly become black the Allies have not as suddenly become white, that because junkerism has triumphed in Germany it has not necessarily been defeated in England; and, above all, it behooves us to take stock of our own junkerism and to watch it closely during the days that are to come. It behooves us to realize that the call of patriotism may be utilized to cloak various aims. It behooves us in so far as humanly possible to depend upon reason rather than upon emotion, to determine the validity of arguments and impulses, to separate what is false from what is true.

Either willfully or from a native lack of understanding, a great many men in the public eye of America during this critical period seem not to have grasped the essentials, the very fundamentals, upon which the President has based his thought and action from the beginning of the European war. A large share of public opinion in the United States adverse to the President's course has been created not alone on the strength of antagonistic partisan feelings, but also on a basis of genuine misconception of his point of view.

Perhaps the President has been at fault for not explaining himself more fully, but on the whole he doubtless has chosen the part of wisdom in letting his policies finally speak for him. A man with such policies can afford to wait. President Wilson's one fairly outright and radical expression, his speech before the Senate on January 22, met with violent misinterpretation both at home and abroad. But even in the short time that had elapsed between its delivery and its sudden eclipse by the crisis of German submarine warfare, the President's words were having remarkable effect, and his views were well on the way toward a fuller and more sympathetic understanding.

By one speech he had succeeded in reviving liberalism throughout the world.

I feel that I know with some degree of clearness the mind of the Administration upon several of these mooted points. The following brief summary will be an attempt to cover in a few paragraphs a range of subjects which would require volumes for their adequate elucidation.

Colcord then pointed out that the era of acute industrialism had taken western civilization unawares, and that the great world war had brought further drastic changes. The existing literature of socialism, economics, political economy, and history was insufficient to explain what was happening; recent developments were founded upon aims of material rather than spiritual progress, and they stressed possession instead of creativity. Labor's philosophy was as erroneous and as frankly predatory and materialistic as capital's philosophy. The theories of ultra-democracy were as fallacious as the theories of autocratic materialism. Instead, there was need for a new social politics based on the spirit of nationalism. Germany had already imposed on the world its theory and ideal of the state, and in some way it had derived spiritual values from its industrialism and given its people something to work for. The ideal of the state had come to stay, and the world needed "unit sovereign States, each one representing for its constituents an ideal to work for, to profit, to be proud of and to die for in case of aggression." These nationalisms need not be aggressive but could, rather, be highly competitive and yet in perfect harmony. A wrong financial system and tradition had hindered democratic America and Britain from making progress in this direction; important governmental functions had become vested in forces (such as banks and newspapers) whose object was the benefit of a special class rather than the whole community. These forces contributed to a conservatism of opinion and action that tended to discourage initiative and deaden the creative energies of the community. These same conservative forces, looking abroad to new territory and nonindustrialized lands for the fulfillment of their reactionary financial dreams, also provided the main support for the spirit of imperialism which animated western civilization. "Under the pressure of their own tightening markets, they follow the lure of big and safe money in the undeveloped regions of the world." The system depended on expansion and conquest, and the next step in the old tradition of imperialism was to secure foreign privilege by sovereignty. Colcord went on:

We are now fairly well able to define the junker. The junker is the reactionary, the conservative, the hidebound standpatter, the rampant imperialist. He is always a great believer in militarism wherever he may be found. He is an exponent of arbitrary force as opposed to reason and understanding. The junker, too, is the man who profits by war, who strives to bring about war from his own selfish motives, who does all he can to maintain war after it has been brought about. We know that every nation contains many such men. In short, junkerism is nothing but the ancient and selfish creed of special privilege.

From this viewpoint President Wilson has watched the war in Europe with troubled gaze. He has seen clearly that it is a new war, an absolutely different kind of war from any that has ever taken place before, a war for which there are no comparisons or precedents, a war which must be spoken of in new phrases and estimated in new terms. He sees that it is the first great test of an industrialized world community, and that so far in this test all of the old traditions and systems have broken down. In such a vision there is no thought of belittling the spiritual factors—the heroism of Belgium, the nobility of France, the sterling determination of England or the spirit of service of Germany.

War has a spiritual value whose equivalent has not yet been supplied in times of peace by an industrialized world; a spiritual value whose profound reaction is plainly to be seen throughout Europe today. It may be that only through war can the true organization of human forces be accomplished. It may well be that America today needs war more than she knows.

But there are other factors to be considered—anguish, destruction, impoverishment of stock and all the enormous debts of spirit and material for the future to pay. The war in Europe seems to have got beyond its legitimate bounds, beyond control. It is a Frankenstein's monster, pulling down the structure of the modern world. And in spite of spiritual values, in spite of high purposes and glorious sacrifices, we see this war everywhere gradually playing into the hands of the reactionaries, strengthening the grip of junkerdom upon a distraught and desperate humanity. Everywhere liberals tend to become conservatives, the rule of reason is threatened and the passions of men are loosed in force and power.

And now America stands on the brink of war. The issue is plain; our honor is involved. Our word was given, and must be upheld. If we enter the war we will have been forced into it by German junkerdom.

But the worst of it is that American junkerdom will be delighted, too. One has only to look about him these days to see the forces which make for war, which assume that war is inevitable, which will have war whether or no. They are the same forces which the other day so violently disapproved of the President's speech before the Senate. They are the forces which, if war comes, will make the most of the call of patriotism. We must watch them closely then, lest we serve to contribute only another arm to the octopus of world junkerdom. It is well for us, and perhaps for the whole issue, that we have in our chief post of authority one of the most uncompromising liberals the world has ever seen.

# Pleasant Alexander Stovall to Robert Lansing

Berne, Feb. 10, 1917.

501.    Referring to my telegram number 488 of February 5th, Noon.[1]

I have received from Dr. Hoffman, Chief of the Swiss political Department, a supplementary and definitive reply to my note of February fourth. The following is a translation of this reply.

"Mr. Minister.

By my note of February fifth I had the honor to inform Your Excellency that before determining definitely in regard to the declarations of the German Government relative to the blockade, the Swiss Federal Council desired to enter into communication with the other neutral States of Europe which are in situation analogous to that of Switzerland. I added that the Federal Council desired first to draw the attention of President Wilson to Switzerland's peculiar attitude prescribed by its principles as a state of complete and perpetual neutrality, principles founded on its constitution, on ancient traditions and on the will of its people.

The Federal Council today can only refer to Switzerland's declaration of neutrality dated April [August] four, nineteen fourteen, of which all foreign Governments were informed at the time of its promulgation. On that date the Federal Assembly and the Federal Council announced their firm determination not to deviate in any manner whatsoever from the principles of neutrality, so highly cherished by the Swiss people and in such perfect conformity with their aspirations, with their institutions, with Switzerland's situation in regard to other States, and which the guaranteeing powers expressly recognized in eighteen fifteen. This is the reason the Federal Council and the Federal Assembly have expressly declared that, during the duration of the war, the

Swiss confederation will maintain and will defend its neutrality and the inviolability of its territory by all the means in its power.

The events of the present war have fortified the Federal Council in its conviction of the necessity for the maintenance of a strict and loyal neutrality and have furnished the proof that, today as in eighteen fifteen, the true interests of European politics are furthered by the entity and independence of Switzerland. Switzerland will maintain this neutrality as long as the independence and integrity of its territory, its honor and its vital interests are not attacked.

The Federal Council must again draw the attention of President Wilson to the unusual geographical situation of Switzerland entirely surrounded by belligerents, and which would certainly become, the moment that Switzerland ceased to be neutral, the theater of the general war.

Regardless of how difficult Switzerland's economic situation may become because of the threatened blockade and regardless of the degree in which the effective execution [of] the blockade may run counter to the principles of international law, the Federal Council cannot however decide to follow President Wilson in his demarches regarding the Imperial German Government which have been made necessary by a state of affairs entirely special. Consequently the Federal Council has confined itself to a protest and has reserved all its legal rights resulting from the execution of the blockade announced by the Imperial Government should this blockade prove to be contrary to neutral rights as recognized by the general principles of international law. In particular the Federal Council has reserved all its legal rights in the event that the effective execution of the blockade proving incomplete, should the means used by Germany and its allies result in the destruction of Swiss citizens or of Swiss property.

In submitting the present communication to Your Excellency in reply to your note of February fourth, nineteen seventeen, I take this occasion to present to you assurances of my high consideration. (signed Hoffman)."                    Stovall.

T telegram (SDR, RG 59, 763.72/3294, DNA); printed in *FR-WWS 1917*, I, 127-28.

    1 P. A. Stovall to RL, Feb. 5, 1917, T telegram (SDR, RG 59, 763.72/3231, DNA). It included a translation of the first Swiss reply to Stovall's note of February 4, which had conveyed the message contained in the circular telegram of February 3, printed at that date. The substance of the first Swiss note is recapitulated in the first paragraph of the second Swiss note, printed here.

## Paul Samuel Reinsch to Robert Lansing

Peking, February 10, 1917.

February 10, 1 p.m. Strictly Confidential.

My telegram of February 9, 12 midnight. The result obtained through the action of the Chinese Government is that it has un-equivocally associated itself with the policy of the United States in defense of international right. In accordance with confidential understanding it has bound itself to further action should the United States declare war; in this case it would be incumbent upon the United States to assist the Chinese Government in carry-ing its responsibilities. The Chinese Government has therefore committed itself to the leadership of the United States in this momentous matter. The dicision of the Chinese Government is understood as an entry upon a definite foreign policy and is highly approved of by the allied representatives here who are now free to express their indorsement of the fait accompli.

The action was made possible by the united support of the younger republican leaders in the government and parliament as against inertia of the mandarinate, the strong influence of Ger-many especially with the military leaders, and the fear of Japa-nese disapproval. In the action as taken all parties are now united.                                             Reinsch.

T telegram (SDR, RG 59, 763.72/3289, DNA).

## Robert Lansing to Paul Samuel Reinsch

Washington, February 10, 1917.

*Not to be distributed.*

Until further instructed avoid giving any promises or as-surances and take no other action in regard to matters mentioned in your cipher telegrams of February 6, one p.m. and eleven p.m., February 7, six p.m. and February 8, 12 midnight. Matter under consideration.                                          Lansing

T telegram (SDR, RG 59, 763.72/3270, DNA); printed in *FR-WWS 1917*, I, p. 408.

## Franklin Knight Lane to George Whitfield Lane

[Washington] February 10 [1917]

Yesterday we talked of the holding of Gerard as a hostage.[1] Lansing said there was no doubt of it. He thought it an act of war in itself. But did not know on what theory it was done, except that Germany was doing what she thought we would do. Germany evidently was excited over her sailors here, fearing that they would be interned, and over her ships, fearing that they would be taken. I said that it seemed to be established that Germany meant to do what she said she would do, and that we might as well act on that assumption. The President said that he had always believed this, but thought that there were chances of her modifying her position, and that he could do nothing, in good faith toward Congress, without going before that body. He felt that in a few days something would be done that would make this necessary.

So there you are up to date—in a scrappy way. Now don't tell what you know. Ned[2] is flying at Newport News. He sent me a telegram saying that the President could go as far as he liked, "the bunch" would back him up. Strange how warlike young fellows are, especially if they think that they are preparing for some usefulness in war. That's the militaristic spirit that is bad. Much love to you and Frances.[3] Give me good long letters telling me what is in the back of that wise old head.                F.K.

Printed in Lane and Wall, eds., *The Letters of Franklin K. Lane*, pp. 235-36.

[1] The German Foreign Office had informed Gerard that he and his staff would not be permitted to leave Germany until definite information had been received regarding arrangements for the departure of Count von Bernstorff and his staff from the United States. The American embassy in Berlin would not be permitted to communicate with its consuls until it had information from the State Department about the disposition of German consuls in the United States. J. W. Gerard to RL, Feb. 5, 1917, *FR-WWS 1917*, I, 587.

In reply (through the Spanish Ambassador at Berlin) the United States Government expressed surprise at the German government's attitude and stated that complete arrangements had been made for the departure of Count and Countess von Bernstorff, the embassy staff, and all German consuls in the United States on *Frederick VIII* on February 13. RL to Joseph E. Willard, Feb. 6, 1917, *ibid.*, p. 587-88.

[2] Franklin Knight Lane, Jr.

[3] Presumably the wife of George W. Lane.

# From Edward Mandell House

Dear Governor:                New York. February 11, 1917.

It may sometime be useful to you to know about the relations of Spring-Rice with his government.

Wiseman and Gaunt tell me that Northcliffe, aided by Carson and Curzon, want him removed. They (Wiseman and Gaunt) admit that he is temperamentally unfit for the place but they believe, as I do, that he is infinitely better than any Northcliffe product that might be sent over to replace him.

The one thing that has fretted me in the break with Germany is the character of support you have been getting from the alienated Americans. However, it will not be long before they will all be yelping at your heels as hard as ever. It is difficult to believe you are right when you have such opinion with you, and I shall feel more comfortable when they are barking at you again.

Your affectionate,    E. M. House

P.S. I hope you are watching Bryan and his endeavor to muddy the waters. I am told that he is back of the German-Swiss proposal of yesterday[1] and that he purposes staying in and around Washington to direct a propaganda.

TLS (WP, DLC).
  [1] About this, see RL to WW, Feb. 12, 1917.

## From Francis Griffith Newlands

My dear Mr. President:          [Washington] February 11, 1917.

I send you herewith two clippings from the Congressional Record, which will explain themselves; one relates to the proposed railroad legislation and the other to the waterway legislation.

Regarding the railroad legislation, I have to say that there are so many matters of urgency now before the Senate, that it will be difficult for me to get consideration of the proposed railroad legislation unless I have your active cooperation.

Recently Mr. Overman has reported from the Judiciary Committee a number of measures intended to meet possible conditions of war.[1] He has appealed to me to give him the right of way, which I am reluctant to do, unless you are of the opinion that the measures which he is urging are of more pressing importance.

As to the waterway legislation, I have to say that the friends of the flood control bill have been making a thorough organization for its early consideration in the Senate. They have, apparently, the friendly aid of the Steering Committee, and they are making every effort, by personal solicitation and otherwise, to secure the early consideration of the Flood Control bill.

The difficulty with this bill is that it is simply a perpetuation of the old policy of piece-meal,—commonly called the spoils system—legislation, which has been so barren of results in the past, and against which I have been contending for twelve years with the support of Mr. Roosevelt, Mr. Taft, yourself and every Secretary of War during these three administrations, with the exception of Mr. Garrison, who stood for the exclusive jurisdiction of

the Engineer Corps of the Army and not for the principle of coordination of Departments and Services. You know how vigorously the Cabinet Committee appointed by you has cooperated
with me in this matter, resulting in my introducing a modified
bill which left out the large and continuous appropriations called
for in my original measure, and simply presented, with a modest
appropriation, the plan of organization provided by it.

I had supposed that the collaboration of Senator Ransdell and
Secretary Baker and myself towards the close of the last Session
had resulted in an adjustment satisfactory to all concerned,
which would involve as a substitute for the Flood Control bill the
acceptance of my bill with provisions including the lower Mississippi River project and the Sacramento River project as accepted
and approved projects under the general plan, but at this Session
Mr. Humphreys[2] has declined to accept this proposal, declaring
that it would involve the loss of the bill in the House, and, accepting this view, the friends of his bill in the Senate are urging
the passage of the Flood Control bill without variation or amendment.

They have endeavored to induce me to acquiesce in this by assuring me that they would put my measure on the River and
Harbor bill, and this they have done. My answer to it is that this
does not satisfy me; that the House may reject it as it did several
years ago, and that my only recourse is to fight all piece-meal
legislation until the adoption of a general scheme of legislation is
forced.

You have no idea what constant watchfulness this contention
requires. Friends of a general reform are rarely as active as the
beneficiaries of an existing abuse, and the spoils system, both as
to public buildings and rivers and harbors has such a hold upon
Congress that it is very difficult to loose it.

You will observe that Senator Jones of Washington announced
that, unless he changed his mind, he would make a point of order
against the amendment to the River and Harbor bill embracing
a general plan of waterway development. He has informed me
since that, while he has been sympathetic with my general views
regarding waterway development, he does not believe in a Cabinet
Commission which, he thinks, may lead to political abuses. He
prefers a non-partisan engineering commission, and, if the
amendment is changed so as to provide for this, he will make no
objection. My answer was that the coordination of the various
Departments and services was of the highest importance, and
that the creation of an outside commission with powers to bring
them into coordination would be to create an imperium in im-

perio, and would be likely to produce confusion. I urged that the engineers of the proposed commission would be the working force, and that the Cabinet Committee would simply consider general policies, and, after their adoption, would bring their departments and services into harmonious cooperation with them.

I did not convince Mr. Jones, however, and the shortness of the time, of course, can make the opposition of such men as Mr. Jones and Mr. Kenyon very potential. I can say that both of them have been in sympathy with the reform which I am urging, and I should like very much to conciliate them.

I think that I will endeavor to get the Cabinet Committee together tomorrow, and suggest that, instead of providing for a cabinet commission, we will simply put in the bill a general power, authorizing the President to bring into coordination the various Departments and services of the Government that relate to the control, development and utilization of water and the investigation of water resources, and to appoint such boards, commissions, etc. as he deems necessary for that purpose, with a view to their cooperation with similar organizations in the various States for the full and comprehensive development of our waterways. This could give the President a free hand to perfect an organization before the next Session of Congress, and to report plans for the approval of Congress. This plan might satisfy Mr Jones.

I write you thus fully in order that you may be informed regarding the situation and make such suggestions as you deem advisable.    Very sincerely yours,    Francis G. Newlands

P.S. I will add that Mr Underwood has been authorized to add his provision as a Committee amendment

TLS (WP, DLC).
    1 Overman, on February 8, had reported to the Senate fourteen bills which, among other things, defined and provided punishment for espionage, perjury designed to influence foreign governments or to assist foreign governments in disputes with the United States Government, impersonation of foreign officials, efforts to damage ships engaged in foreign commerce, fraudulent use of official seals, and conspiracy to injure or destroy the property in the United States of any government with which the United States was at peace. Other bills in the group authorized the regulation and inspection of foreign ships, regulated the issuance and use of passports, enforced neutrality regulations, authorized seizure of munitions used illegally, regulated the conduct and movements of interned soldiers and sailors of belligerent nations, and provided for the issuance of search warrants and seizure of property thereunder. *Cong. Record*, 64th Cong., 2d sess., 2819-21. Four days later, Overman announced that he had consolidated these fourteen bills into a single one, S. 8148, which the Senate passed on February 20 under the amended title, "A bill to punish espionage and acts of interference with the foreign relations, the neutrality, and the foreign commerce of the United States, and better to enforce the criminal laws of the United States, and for other purposes." *Ibid.*, pp. 3075, 3665. On February 28, Edwin Yates Webb, chairman of the House Judiciary Committee, reported S.

8148 favorably (with minor amendments) to the House of Representatives, but the House did not complete action on it before the end of the Sixty-fourth Congress. *Ibid.*, p. 4563.

2 Benjamin Grubb Humphreys, congressman from Mississippi.

## Chevalier Willem Louis Frederik Christiaan van Rappard to the Netherlands Foreign Ministry

[Washington] 11. 2. 17.

Tel 153   J'ai eu hier interessante conversation avec Colonel House à New York qui m'a parlé d'un desir attribué au President des Etats Unis de convoquer d'urgence toutes les nations neutres à Washington afin de deliminer si possible un programme commun pour tous les neutres. point. Ce programme serait ensuite soumis à tous les belligerants et pourrait conduire à negociations de paix. point. Il va sans dire que ce projet du President tomberait si Allemagne per acte contre bâtiment americain sans avertissement préalable pousserait Etats Unis dans un etat de guerre avec Allemagne point. J'ai fait entrevoir au Colonel que si toutes nations neutres participeraient, je croyais bien que Gouvernement neerlandais aussi disposé à se joindre aux autres. point. Je vous tiendrai informé.                                           Rappard

Hw telegram (637/577, NFM-Ar.).


T R A N S L A T I O N

[Washington] 11. 2. 17.

Telegram 153.   I had an interesting conversation yesterday in New York with Colonel House, who attributed to the President of the United States a desire to convoke at Washington all the neutral nations, on an urgent basis, to outline if possible a common program for all of them. This program would then be submitted to all the belligerents and might lead to peace negotiations. It goes without saying that the President's project would collapse if Germany, by acting against an American ship without prior warning, should push the United States into war. I informed the Colonel that if all the neutral countries participated, I was sure that the Netherlands government would also be disposed to join the others. I will keep you informed.          Rappard

## To Edward Mandell House

My dear House,          The White House. 12 February, 1917.

The enclosed despatch turned up with others to-day, in a batch sent over from the Department of State.[1] I know nothing of the matters to which it refers but what it itself says. I send it because it seems to afford a clue through which to follow up the Schultz lead in the other despatches I sent you. It will, obviously, have to be used with the utmost caution, since it would not do to let the matter here disclosed be generally known and its use might give a premature alarm to persons whom it is very necessary that the Department of State should keep within their reach and control.

I feel as you do about the character of the support I am now receiving from certain once hostile quarters. You notice the suggestion is being actively renewed that I call their crowd into consultation and have a coalition cabinet at my elbow. It is the *Junkerthum* trying to creep in under cover of the patriotic feeling of the moment. They will not get in. They have now no examples of happy or successful coalitions to point to. The nominal coalition in England is nothing but a Tory cabinet such as they are eager to get a foothold for here. I know them too well, and will hit them straight between the eyes, if necessary, with plain words.

Give yourself no uneasiness about the Swiss-German move: it will not work. They must renew and carry out the pledge of last April if they want to talk to us now,—or else propose peace on terms they know we can act upon.

Warmest messages from us all.

Affectionately Yours,   Woodrow Wilson

WWTLS (E. M. House Papers, CtY).
   [1] WHP to RL, Feb. 10, 1917, T telegram (E. M. House Papers, CtY). Page reported on cooperation with British authorities regarding the activities of German agents in the United States and on two American journalists in Holland who were apparently employed by German agents. The telegram mentioned one Schultz, "German spy-master in Antwerp." Wilson thought that there might be a connection between this Schultz and the Max Schultz who was reported to have been involved in Hamburg during the previous summer in a plot to assassinate Wilson. See EMH to WW, Feb. 5, 1917, n. 1.

## From Robert Lansing, with Enclosures

PERSONAL AND PRIVATE:

My dear Mr. President:          Washington February 12, 1917.

Mr. Polk reported to me that the Swiss Minister on Saturday called at the Department and in my absence saw him. The Minister said he had received a reply to a suggestion which he had made that he might do something here to prevent war between this country and Germany. He stated in substance what is contained in the enclosed memorandum, and Mr. Polk said he would submit the matter to me.

I told Mr. Polk Sunday morning when he told me of the interview that I wished to have the statement in writing and until then would make no comment. He saw the Minister and as a result Sunday night I received the enclosed note and memorandum.

Prior to seeing Mr. Polk the newspapers were informed that Germany had taken steps to open a discussion with the United States as to means for preventing war. Both Mr. Polk and I denied this Saturday afternoon but it appeared under prominent headlines in all the Sunday papers. When the Swiss Minister was asked if he had given this out he denied having done so, and no one in the State Department knew of the interview of the Minister with Mr. Polk, excpet [except] Mr. Polk and I. There seems to be one conclusion as to the source of the newspaper reports and that is the German Embassy which is in constant communication with the press.

As to the memorandum of the Swiss Minister I think that there is little to say. Of course we cannot for a moment consider negotiations either formal or informal unless the German Government ceases its present ruthless methods and returns to the *status quo ante* the proclamation of January 31st, and that the memorandum declares they cannot do. Of course they knew that we would not accept such a condition as appears in the memorandum and, when it was sent, they knew that there could only be a refusal to an overture on that basis.

I believe that the purpose of this movement had nothing to do with an actual desire to open negotiations, but was intended for public consumption in this country and as an aid to those who are endeavoring to stir up opposition to the Government's continuing to take a firm and unyielding attitude toward the present ruthless conduct of Germany. The wording of the memorandum, the publicity given the idea that the German Government was ready to negotiate before we knew of it, and the extension of the statement in the press beyond the exact language of the memorandum, all indicate the design of embarrassing this Government by putting it in the light of refusing to consider overtures of arrangement voluntarily offered by Germany. It is apparently done to convey the impression that Germany is willing to do anything to prevent war but that you are not willing to listen to them, being determined to go forward. The attempt is to throw the responsibility on you in case hostilities cannot be averted.

I am convinced that the whole scheme was hatched here in Washington, and that not only Bernstorff had much to do with it but also I am ashamed to say that I believe that he has been assisted by certain Americans who are antagonistic to your policy and who will go to almost any lengths in order to force you to recede from the firm position which you have taken. I have heard in the last few days some things which have aroused my intense indignation against certain people and which, if true—and the evidence seems very strong, smacks of treason. I do not wish to write of these matters but will tell you when I see you.

It seems to me that the only answer which can be made to the memorandum is to say that no discussion or negotiation can take place except upon the condition precedent that the proclamation of January 31st be annulled; and that, when that has been done, this Government is prepared to consider any subjects which the German Government desires to propose for discussion. I also think that the memorandum and our answer should then be made public, in order that the people may have no erroneous impression as to the character of the German overture, and we may counteract the effect which has possibly resulted from the insidious statements published by the Germans here and those who are aiding them to arouse opposition to the Government.

Faithfully yours,   Robert Lansing

TLS (SDR, RG 59, 763.72/3262½, DNA).

ENCLOSURE I

## Frank Lyon Polk to Robert Lansing

My dear Mr. Secretary:          Washington February 10, 1917.

The Swiss Minister just called and left with me the answer of the Swiss Government to the President's Note, which merely states their position.

He also gave me a suggestion of an agreement he communicated for the German Government which would construe the treaty of 1799. This can wait.

After he had presented these two documents, he said he had just received a telegram from the Swiss Government which was an answer to a suggestion made by him that he might be able to do something here to prevent war between Germany and this country. I took down the part of the telegram he read, which was as follows:

They, the German Government, "will be willing to negotiate

on any point the United States may ask provided (or except) that the blockade against England be maintained."

I pointed out that this seemed to imply that they would be satisfied with a blockade against England alone. He said he did not know anything about that; he had merely read the message as given in the telegram. I said of course I could not speak for you, but it seemed to me at first glance that they had excepted the one question on which the President had based his breaking off of diplomatic relations.

I asked if he had any suggestions and he said he had none, but he thought possibly something might be discovered which would save the situation, or that we might think of some point that we wished to discuss.

I told him I would submit the matter to you at once, so you could take it up with the President if you thought it desirable.

Yours sincerely,   Frank L Polk

TLS (SDR, RG 59, 763.72/3262½, DNA); printed in *FR-WWS 1917*, I, 125.


E  N  C  L  O  S  U  R  E      I  I

Washington, D. C. February 11, 1917.
Memorandum.

The Swiss government has been requested by the German government to say that the latter is, now as before, willing to negotiate, formally or informally, with the United States, provided that the commercial blockade against England will not be broken thereby.                                    P. Ritter

TS memorandum (SDR, RG 59, 763.72/3263½, DNA); printed in *FR-WWS 1917*, I, 126.


## To Robert Lansing

My dear Mr. Secretary,    The White House. 12 February, 1917.

I am obliged to concur in your conclusions with regard to this matter. I suggest that you reply to the Swiss Minister in the following sense:

I am requested by the President to say to you, in acknowledging the memorandum which you were kind enough to ⟨bring to the Department⟩ *send me*[1] on the ⟨tenth⟩ *eleventh* instant, that the Government of the United States would gladly discuss with the German Government any questions it might propose for dis-

cussion were it to withdraw its proclamation of the thirty-first
of January, in which, suddenly and without previous intimation of any kind, it cancelled the assurances which it had given
this Government on the fourth of ⟨April⟩ *May* last, but that it
does not feel that it can enter into any discussion with the German Government concerning the policy of submarine warfare
*against neutrals* which it is now pursuing unless and until the
German Government renews its assurances of the fourth of
⟨April⟩ *May* and acts upon the assurance.[2]

Faithfully Yours,   W.W.

WWTLI (SDR, RG 59, 763.72/3264½, DNA).
  [1] Words in angle brackets deleted by Lansing; those in italics added by him.
  [2] This was sent as RL to P. Ritter, Feb. 12, 1917, CCL (SDR, RG 59, 763.72/
3263½, DNA); it is printed in *FR-WWS 1917*, I, 129.


## From William Julius Harris

Dear Mr. President:          Washington February 12, 1917.

In further reply to your letter of the 7th instant,[1] directing this
Commission to investigate the facts relating to the production,
ownership, manufacture, storage and distribution of foodstuffs
and the products thereof, and to any violations of the antitrust
acts in respect thereto, an estimate for an appropriation is submitted in compliance with your directions.

The estimate for appropriation submitted herewith is for the
sum of $400,000 to be available immediately, and to continue
available until expended.

An estimate for this specific investigation is made for the reason that the amounts already appropriated for the current fiscal
year are insufficient to enable the Commission to initiate this
investigation, while the amounts estimated for the next fiscal
year were made for the carrying on of other work, already imposed upon this Commission by resolutions of Congress, or in accordance with its organic act.

The Commission, in making and submitting this estimate, is
in complete concurrence with your views as to its urgent public
necessity, and realizes the wide scope, complex character and
magnitude of the investigation required. It involves the entire
business of producing, manufacturing and marketing the vast
volume and varied classes of foodstuffs and food products of this
country and includes, among other things, the ascertainment of
the facts regarding alleged violations of the antitrust laws in
respect thereto.

The Commission is also mindful of the fact that, through such investigation or otherwise, there may be disclosed various practices prohibited by law which it is the duty of this Commission to prevent, and it begs to assure you that it will give earnest attention thereto.

The cooperation of the Department of Agriculture in this work, according to your direction, is heartily welcomed by this Commission, which is aware of the fact that that Department has already obtained extensive information on this subject, and, through its various activities, is in a position greatly to assist the Commission in collecting further information pertinent to this investigation. A conference has already been had with the Secretary and with a committee from his Department, and such consideration has been given to the character and scope of the work as the time has permitted. The Department of Agriculture, as this Commission is advised, will submit a separate estimate for such additional appropriation as it may require for the proper prosecution of its part of this investigation.

The estimate of this Commission, referred to above and enclosed herewith, is submitted for your approval and for transmission, if approved by you, to the Secretary of the Treasury for submission to Congress as provided by law, with such recommendation as you may deem it advisable to make.[2]

Very respectfully, Wm J. Harris

TLS (WP, DLC).
[1] W. J. Harris to WW, Feb. 9, 1917, TLS (WP, DLC), was a preliminary reply.
[2] Wilson approved the estimate and sent it to the Treasury on February 13.


## From Newton Diehl Baker

Dear Mr President:                    Washington. February 12, 1917

I asked Colver[1] whether he would consent to the consideration of his name and held out no assurance of appointment so as to leave you free. He is willing to accept. I enclose his letter.[2] In it he qualifies *only* for the democratic vacancy.

I told him I thought you would like to credit the appointment, if made, to St Paul Minnesota, rather than to any more eastern place of residence. A part of his letter is responsive to that. He asks to be notified in advance of his name being sent in, if possible, so that he can inform his business associates. I can reach him by long distance telephone if you desire. The print-paper inquiry suggestion seems unimportant as that inquiry is substantially completed and will be through before he could be confirmed.                    Respectfully   Newton D. Baker

ALS (WP, DLC).
¹ William Byron Colver of St. Paul, Minn., editor-in-chief of Clover Leaf Publications of that city.
² W. B. Colver to NDB, c. Feb. 11, 1917, ALS (WP, DLC). Colver wrote that he would be glad to serve on the Federal Trade Commission. He regarded the tariff as "the paramount issue in national affairs" and had "always been opposed to the Republican theory of Protection." "So I am a Democrat," he added. Colver also pointed out that a controversy was pending before the commission between newspaper publishers and print-paper manufacturers and that he was a publisher and a stockholder in various newspaper corporations.

## From Harry Lane

My Dear Mr. President:        Washington, D. C. Feb. 12, 1917.

I am in receipt of your esteemed favor of the 9th inst., in regard to the Fisheries Bill.

I am glad that you are interested in securing a bill which will put a stop to the present waste of food and restrict monopolies of fishing rights.

The new bill will be reported in a few days and will accomplish this purpose and I have reason to believe that it will not only meet with the approval of the members of the House, who formerly opposed it and the objections to it in the Senate also I think will be overcome.

I hope you will permit me to use your letter in confidence to the members of the Committee to further this purpose.

Thanking you for writing to me and with assurances of my desire to aid you in securing the early passage of this measure, I am,                Yours very truly yours,    Harry Lane

TLS (WP, DLC).

## From William Kent

Dear Mr. President:        [Washington] February 12, 1917.

I was greatly pleased with your letter of instructions to the Trades Commission. I believe the Commission, as now constituted, is in favor of doing desirable work and that with the authority which doubtless will be granted to the Market Bureau, there will be such cooperation as will bring about increased production of food and a better and cheaper system of distribution.

It seems obvious that, granted initiative, constructive ability and adequate funds, the Federal Trades Commission may be made equally important or even more important to the public welfare than the Interstate Commerce Commission.

The twilight zone created by the common law and the Sherman

act must be explored and mapped out by a body differing in function from the Department of Justice.

The task of encouraging free competition and of breaking down abuses and wrongs, is by no means parallel in its entirety with the duties of prosecution. I do not believe that people can be forced to compete against their wills, but that they should be enabled to compete freely, in any and all of the elements that go into the making or distributing of products.

It is a sad commentary on the chaotic state of business relationships, that there does not exist either a body of law or a tribunal that has been able to define in advance, the limitations upon business cooperation and combination, a function that has been satisfactorily exercised for the railways by the Interstate Commerce Commission.     Yours truly,   [William Kent]

CCL (W. Kent Papers, CtY).


## To William Kent

My dear Mr. Kent:          The White House 13 February, 1917

I am glad you approved of the letter of instructions to the Trade Commission.

I did not write it myself. I got the Secretary of Agriculture to prepare it for me, because I knew that he was familiar with the whole field in a degree that I was not, but I was very glad to sign so adequate a letter, which was just what I wanted him to prepare for me.

Cordially and sincerely yours,   Woodrow Wilson

TLS (W. Kent Papers, CtY).


## To Thomas Davies Jones

My dear Friend:          The White House 13 February, 1917

I am heartily glad you think William B. Carlile a good selection for postmaster in Chicago,[1] and I am thankful that at last we have found a man whom the Senators are willing to take and who is highly qualified for the position. It is a load off my mind.

In haste          Faithfully yours,   Woodrow Wilson

P.S. Your full letter about Mr. Burling[2] I am really grateful for. It tells me just exactly what I wanted to know and tells it in just the candor and fullness I knew you would employ. W.W.

TLS (Mineral Point, Wisc., Public Library).
1 Wilson had nominated William Buford Carlile as Postmaster of Chicago on

February 9. Senator Lewis said in Washington that night: "Of course, I shall support Mr. Carlile. I could not do otherwise. Several days ago when the president flatly told me he no longer could consider a German-American for the office, as I had insisted all along he should do, he presented me with a list of names of prominent Chicagoans and asked me to make a selection. I told him any of the men would do." Chicago *Tribune*, Feb. 10, 1917. Jones had written to express his pleasure at Wilson's selection of Carlile. T. D. Jones to WW, Feb. 10, 1917, TLS (WP, DLC).
    ² T. D. Jones to WW, Feb. 5, 1917, TLS (WP, DLC).


## To Newton Diehl Baker

My dear Baker:            The White House 13 February, 1917
    I am heartily glad to hear of Colver's decision. I shall try to act upon it at once.
    In haste
            Cordially and sincerely yours,    Woodrow Wilson

TLS (N. D. Baker Papers, DLC).


## To Stephen Samuel Wise

My dear Rabbi Wise:        The White House 13 February, 1917
    Your generous letter of February ninth brings with it a breath of friendship and encouragement for which I am deeply grateful. I must in conscience demur to your generous estimate of me and of what I have done, but I accept it joyously as coming from your heart and feel a very deep pride in having such a friend.
            Cordially and sincerely yours,    Woodrow Wilson

TLS (MWalA).


## To Duncan Upshaw Fletcher

My dear Senator:         [The White House] 13 February, 1917
    I am so deeply interested in the Alaska General Fisheries Bill that I write to ask if it will be possible for it to pass at this session. The measure so directly affects the food supply of the country, both in respect of quantity and quality, and would so effectually put an end to certain mischievous monopolies now existing that I think it is of the utmost consequence that it should be passed as soon as it is practicable to pass it.[1]
            Cordially and sincerely yours,    Woodrow Wilson

TLS (Letterpress Books, WP, DLC).
    [1] Wilson sent an identical letter to Joshua W. Alexander, chairman of the Committee on Merchant Marine and Fisheries, House of Representatives: WW to J. W. Alexander, Feb. 13, 1917, TLS (Letterpress Books, WP, DLC).

## To George Howe III

My dear George:          [The White House] 13 February, 1917

It was like you to offer to help and you may be sure I would have known you were ready, whether you had said so or not. You may be equally sure that if there is anything I need to call on you for, I would not hesitate to call. I am sure you know how you have always enjoyed my confidence as well as my affection. I pray God there may be no need to call for you, but every voice of helpfulness like yours is welcome to me at a time like this.

We are all well and all unite in warmest messages.

Affectionately yours,   Woodrow Wilson

TLS (Letterpress Books, WP, DLC).

## From Robert Lansing, with Enclosure

PERSONAL AND PRIVATE:

My dear Mr. President:          Washington February 13, 1917.

From a newspaper correspondent who is I believe reliable comes the information that he has found in visiting the Entente Embassies here a change of sentiment in the last day or two as to the desire that this country should be drawn into the war. It now seems, according to this informant, that they are as anxious now to have us keep out as a few days ago they were anxious to have us come in. The conclusion drawn from his conversation with various members of the Embassies was that they had decided that they did not want this Government to take part in the peace negotiations because we would be too lenient with Germany.

I do not know what was said to him and I only give you his opinion as of interest without attempting to value it.

There is, however, this: You may recall that last spring, when the SUSSEX affair was being discussed, I said that I could see a possible reason for Germany's wish to have us in the war as her antagonist if she was convinced that she would be defeated or could not win, and that was, that when the peace was negotiated we would be a generous enemy and favor moderate terms, so that she would be protected from the hatred of the Allies.

The present viewpoint of the Embassies would seem to be the complement of that idea.

Faithfully yours,   Robert Lansing

Mr. Page's 5665, which is enclosed, appears to be contrary to the viewpoint of the Embassies here          RL.

TLS (WP, DLC).

E N C L O S U R E

LONDON February 11, 1917

5665.  THE FOLLOWING IS STRICTLY CONFIDENTIAL FOR THE
PRESIDENT AND THE SECRETARY OF STATE ONLY.

Your 4421, February eight, midnight.

I immediately sought the Prime Minister with whom I had an
interview yesterday afternoon. I reminded him of the purely personal and private nature of our conferences and told him that I
now had a most important subject to put before him at the President's command in this personal and private way.

I first told him the general substance of your telegram. He welcomed it and before I could mention details he answered every
question I had prepared to ask him. The following is the substance of and in part the phraseology of his talk.

He knew that Austria was very eager for peace. She really
never wanted war and surely there is no animosity between the
British and the Austrians. The new Emperor was especially weary
of a war that he had not made but had inherited. Besides Austria
was obliged to stop in any event. If the Teutonic Powers won she
would be a vassal of Germany which would be worse for her than
an Entente victory. Austria is now generalshiped and managed by
Germany. Her very armies are commanded by Germans. She
suffers most from economic pressure. "I know she wants to quit."

Lord Gray [Grey] said to me months ago when I first asked for
the safe conduct of the new Austrian Ambassador— "We no longer
consider that Austria exists except as a convenient German fiction for Germany dictates her policies, changes her Cabinet and
commands her armies."

Mr. George continued—"Of course the Austrian Emperor wishes
as far as possible to save his Empire. We have no objection to his
retaining Hungary and Bohemia. We have no policy of sheer dismemberment but we must stand by the nationals of our allies,
such as the Roumanians, the Slavs, the Servians and the Italians.
Their just demands must be met by the principle of nationality."

But neither the British Government nor its allies could under
straitened circumstances lose Italy as an ally. The blockade of
Germany might be broken on the Austrian side. German troops
and German officers who now hold the Austrian armies together
could be released to strengthen the German line in more important places. (The?) present military, submarine and economic
conditions ( * ) even receive a formal offer of peace from Austria.
The time for that has passed and has not yet come again. Present

conditions must first change. The premeditated retirement of Austria from the war might bring especial disadvantages to the Entente. Austrians released from the Army would go to Germany and be added to German productive power. Austria is now an increasing military and economic burden to Germany and Germany will probably give in sooner with the load of Austria on her back than if Austria were out of the war.

The Prime Minister repeated that the British had not the slightest animosity to the Austrians whose future freedom in fact they wished to safeguard. The present question is purely a question of military expediency regarding the war as a whole and the removal from Germany of the burden of Austria now would add to the strength of Germany. "For these and other reasons," the Prime Minister continued, "we cannot now even receive formally any peace offer from Austria nor authorize any discussion of peace with her on our behalf. We must look at the war as a whole, but if the President should see fit, acting for himself, to receive specific and concrete proposals from Austria, and should be able and willing to transmit them to me through you in private confidence, I should, at the earliest moment, inform you when the time had come for us formally to receive and consider. I shall be willing and in fact very glad to have such proposals proceed on the principles laid down in the President's recent speech to the Senate. Free access to the sea may present difficulties but I should try to remove them."

After the foregoing general declarations by the Prime Minister I put to him seriatim the several questions and propositions contained in your telegram.

*One. Question:* If the President should transmit officially to the British Government a specific and concrete proposal of peace from Austria what might he expect under present conditions?

*Answer:* The British Government could not now receive it without risk of weakening the Entente's military and economic pressure and position.

*Two. Question:* Would the Entente Governments consent that assurance be conveyed by the President to the Austrian Government that the older units of the Empire will not be taken from it?

*Answer:* The British Government could not under present conditions authorize any to Austria. The British Government sees no reason to dismember Austria by removing Hungary and Bohemia but the peoples of the Entente Governments, such as Slavs, Roumanians, Serbs and Italians, as well as Bosnia and Herzegovina must by the principle of nationality be freed from Austrian control, but the British Government cannot now authorize any representations on its behalf.

*Three. Question*: Could Austria have a guarantee of free access to the sea if she should lose her Adriatic coast line?

*Answer*: This principle is not objectionable but there may be practical difficulties which, however, it may be possible to overcome when the time to discuss this subject arrives.

A necessary inference from the whole conversation is that the only proposal for peace that the British Government would officially receive under existing conditions is a *bona fide* proposal officially made by Germany at least as specific and concrete as the terms that the Entente Powers set forth in their note to the President. Nothing else will be officially received until the issue of the submarine campaign and of the forthcoming great battle in France is decided. The Prime Minister then spoke with warmth and admiration of the President substantially as follows: "We want him to come into the war not so much for help with the war as for help with peace. My reason is not mainly the military nor naval nor economic nor financial pressure that the American Government and people might exert in their own way against Germany; grateful as this would be I have a far loftier reason. American participation is necessary for the complete expression of the moral judgment of the world on the most important subject ever presented to the civilized nations. For America's sake, for our own sake, for the sake of free Government, and for the sake of democracy, military despotism must now be ended forever. The President's presence at the peace conference is necessary for the proper organization of the world which must follow peace. I mean that he himself must be there in person. If he sits in the conference that makes peace he will exert the greatest influence that any man has ever exerted in expressing the moral value of free Government. Most of the present belligerents will have suffered so heavily that their judgment also may have suffered and most of those that win will want some concrete gain, old wrongs righted, or boundaries changed. Even Great Britain, who wants nothing for herself, will be prevented from returning the German colonies. South Africa and Australia will not permit the giving back of lands that would make them neighbors to German subjects and give Germany secret submarine bases throughout the whole world. The United States wants nothing but justice and an ordered freedom and guarantees of these for the future. Nobody therefore can have so commanding a voice as the President. Convey to him this deep conviction of mine. He must help make peace if the peace made at the conference is to be worth keeping. American participation in the war would enable him to be there and the mere moral effect of this participation would shorten the war, might even end it very quickly."

The present Government is unique in English history. The Cabinet, which is constantly in session, now consists of only five men—the Prime Minister, Curzon, Milner, Bonar Law and Henderson.[1] Curzon sneers at the United States, Milner is in Russia, Bonar Law, I know, holds the same opinions on these large subjects as George and Henderson's business is only to keep organized labor quiet. The Prime Minister, by public consent, is nearer to a dictator than any man in England since Cromwell. For reasons, therefore, not only of good form but also of principle I was obliged to ask his consent to speak to any other member of the Government. There is a practical reason also. Anyone to whom I may have spoken would at once have repeated what I said or asked to the Prime Minister. He replied—"No. Speak to no one else for the present. I will take a few into my confidence and tell you whenever there be anything to tell."

I met Minister Balfour at dinner last night and from a remark he made to me I suspect the Prime Minister had told him of this conversation of a few hours before.                                        Page

( * ) Apparent omission

T telegram (SDR, RG 59, 763.72119/488, DNA).
   [1] Arthur Henderson, secretary of the Labour party and its leader in the House of Commons; president of the Board of Education (a cabinet position), 1915-1916.


## From Edward Mandell House, with Enclosures

Dear Governor:                                        New York. February 13, 1917.

Flynn[1] is in Washington today looking after the Bernstorff party. He will return here tomorrow and I will take up with him further the matters mentioned in the cable from Page.

I will also take it up with Gaunt of the British Intelligence Department and will see that it is kept quiet. Flynn is already working on the Stovall cable you sent last week. This makes that situation more possible of solution.

I am enclosing you a letter from Hoover which I had him write for your information. He believes that unless Whitlock is gotten out of Belgium, trouble of some sort will certainly follow.[2]

How would it do to have Whitlock come home for a vacation and look him over for London in the event a change is made there? It would be a popular appointment and he has the qualities necessary to interpret your policies to the British people which is almost all that is needed in an ambassador at this time.

I am enclosing a letter from Miss Tarbell which I am sure will be of interest.

I also enclose a copy of a letter from Lord Bryce and the article from the Westminster Gazette[3] to which he refers.

Affectionately yours, E. M. House

P.S. Gaunt has just left. He tells me that he has the name and address of Schultze and will work along with Flynn. Gaunt also told me that in his opinion our battleships that are now at Guantanamo should be immediately recalled and seek the protection of our harbors. He thinks one of the first things the Germans will do will be to send submarines over here and try to destroy several of our battleships which will be easy to do if we are not alert. He has already told this to Franklin Roosevelt but whether he has acted upon it I do not know.

TLS (WP, DLC).

[1] That is, William James Flynn, Chief of the Secret Service Division, Department of the Treasury.

[2] Hoover's letter is missing, but for documents relating to Whitlock's and the Belgian Relief Commission's difficult situation following the imposition of new blockade measures and the break in diplomatic relations between the United States and Germany, see FR-WWS 1917, I, 628-64.

[3] The editorial (clipping, WP, DLC) in the London Westminster Gazette, Jan. 23, 1917, "His Own Interpretation," suggested that Britons avoid polemics regarding Wilson's speech to the Senate on January 22 and instead take Wilson's views on "peace without victory" on his own terms. The article asked whether Wilson had any undisclosed information to justify his assumption that the Central Powers would actually agree to such a peace. It concluded as follows: "The ideals which President WILSON sets before us are so remote from Prussian militarism that their realisation necessarily carries with it the extinction of the German tyranny. His general idea of the world at peace, with the reign of law established, and all nationalities, great and small, living in freedom and security, carries with it the consequence that he can only get what he wants if we at the same time get what we want. We frankly do not know what he means by the 'freedom of the seas,' but in all other respects his aims are our aims, and his ideals our ideals. No man who is interested in these aims and ideals can be disinterested in the terms of peace; and no peace can secure them which does not, in our opinion, carry with it the defeat of our enemy."

ENCLOSURE I

# Ida Minerva Tarbell to Edward Mandell House

Des Moines, Iowa.
My dear Colonel House:
February 8, 1917.

I have been speaking in Illinois and Iowa for the last three weeks. I have made some observations in this time on the way that the people out here were taking the new developments, first in regard to Peace and second in regard to the break with Germany. It has seemed to me that possibly I ought to report them to you, and that you would know whether they would be of any interest or use to the President.

I take it that it is quite unnecessary for me to say that personally I feel that the President's message to the Senate was a very great document, and admirably timed to produce a profound effect. It was very interesting to me to see how all sorts of people I met in travelling discussed it gravely, as if it had for the first time phrased what many of them had only half worked out in their minds. I am convinced that that message is going to be taken by the people of the country as a call to a new National obligation. In the talking I have been doing out here I have repeatedly referred to it, and have seemed to detect that there was a very profound feeling towards it in my audience.

There is no question at all that an overwhelming majority of the people are behind the President in the break with Germany. There is no question at all but that this Middle West will turn out to a man. I have been talking with all sorts of people, hotel bell boys, trainmen, women in various public places, and the general sentiment seems to be that the men will go. I am told today here in Des Moines that there are long lines waiting to enlist. There is no excitement, no disturbance, but if the time comes they will go about their fighting as simply and naturally as they are going about their daily work. It is all very impressive and very fine to me. You somehow know you can count on the country.

The women are asking everywhere what they can do. If it comes to war, and the Administration contemplates any organization of women for any purpose and you think I am needed of course you can count upon me. I am hoping against hope that it will not come to war, but whatever happens these people here will put in all they have.

This is probably carrying coals to Newcastle but I thought it worth taking the chance.

Very sincerely yours,    Ida M. Tarbell.

ENCLOSURE II

## James Viscount Bryce to Edward Mandell House

Forrest Row, Sussex
Dear Colonel House:                                January 24, 1917.

As you might not otherwise see it, I enclose the most temperate editorial which I have seen in our press on the President's most impressive speech to the Senate.

We warmly appreciate its spirit, and we should like to see the attainment of the conditions which he lays down as preconditions to a League of Peace, and as necessary to ensure stability, contentment and good will in this distracted Europe. But we do not see how these are to be attained with such a Government as Germany has at present, a Government which goes on showing its utter disregard of justice and humanity by its slave-raiding and other cruelties in Belgium, and by its entire contempt for the faith of treaties and other international obligations and duties.

There is no peace movement in this country. There would be, but for the conduct of the German Government. Their latest doings in Belgium have created as strong a feeling in the working classes over England against a peace which would not secure the fullest reparation to Belgium as in any other class.

Is there any chance that Germany would yield up Lorraine, and Austria the Trentino, and the Turks Armenia? If there is I wish we knew of it. Yet without these concessions, could there be stability and security in Europe?

I am,                    Sincerely yours,    James Bryce.

TCL (WP, DLC).


## From Moorfield Storey and Others

Dear Mr. President:            New York City February 13, 1917.

The officers and members of this Association respectfully request that in your coming inaugural address you say something against the barbaric system of lynching which prevails in various parts of this country.

Public sentiment on the question is rapidly becoming aroused, as is shown by the editorials in the leading newspapers of South Carolina and Georgia, by the action taken by the Governors of Kentucky and South Carolina, and by letters from leading Southern men. While it is true that this crime under our system of government can be punished only by the local authorities, the disgrace falls upon the nation as a whole, and we can never effectively address the world on great moral questions so long as this stain upon our civilization is permitted to continue.

We feel that you can do a great deal to help the cause of civilization and good government, and to hold up the hands of those who are trying to prevent mob violence in the United States by some strong expressions in your inaugural, and we respectfully request that you will take this matter into serious consideration.

Very truly yours,   NATIONAL ASSOCIATION FOR THE
ADVANCEMENT OF COLORED PEOPLE.
Moorfield Storey President.
John Hurst[1] Vice-President.
J. E. Spingarn Chairman of the Board.
Oswald Garrison Villard Treasurer.
W. E. B. Du Bois Director of
Publications and Research.
Archibald H. Grimké,[2] President,
District of Columbia Branch.

TLS (WP, DLC).
[1] Haitian-born bishop of the African Methodist Episcopal Church; he lived in Baltimore at this time.
[2] Archibald Henry Grimké, author and lawyer of Washington.

## To Robert Lansing, with Enclosures

My dear Mr. Secretary,      The White House. 14 February, 1917.

Thank you for letting me see the enclosed letter to you from Nelso[n] Page. I am sending you herewith a letter from him to me which is intended as a supplement.

Faithfully Yours,   W.W.

WWTLI (SDR, RG 59, 763.72/3170½, DNA).

ENCLOSURE          I

## Thomas Nelson Page to Robert Lansing

PRIVATE AND CONFIDENTIAL

My dear Mr. Secretary,                Rome January 22, 1917.

Night before last I was called on by a gentleman who had received from the Vatican a very interesting memorandum in regard to the views of the latter on the Allies' note to the President

in reply to his note of December 18th, although more specifically
it related to Mr. Balfour's note of explanation and endorsement
of the Allies' note.[1] The substance of this memorandum I sent
you in a confidential telegram yesterday morning[2] and I am writing you this so that you may show it to the President. I gave the
substance of the memorandum in my telegram, but there were
one or two interesting things mentioned by the gentleman in
question which were not in the written memorandum. This memorandum was first written out and given him, but the next morning he was recalled and was given permission to copy the memorandum, but had to leave the original, as indeed he had been
told he must do, when it was first handed to him. He was told that
Poincaré, when Minister in 1912 promised Russia, in consideration of her support in [of] France, that she should have Constantinople and the Straits, and that after Poincaré was elected President, he confirmed this promise in writing. Also, that when in the
autumn of 1914 the conference of the Allies took place in London
at the time, I think it was, when England secured the promise
from the Allies that no one would make a separate peace but that
all would stand together to the end, Russia presented Poincaré's
written engagement,—that she should have Constantinople and
the Straits,—and England had to yield to secure her engagement
not to make a separate peace.

I have read in the press in the last few days that the Vatican
got the Spanish Ambassador to Washington[3] to call on the President and assure him of the Vatican's entire sympathy with his
recent move to ascertain the terms of the Allies in the hope of
leading eventually to peace, yet at the same time the press here
has been commenting constantly on the Pope's entire abstention
from any reference to the President's step in the locution which
the former made here the day before Christmas and his failure in
such a discourse to refer to the President has been generally accepted as evidence that he did not approve of the President's step.
On the side many have drawn the inference therefrom that the
Pope is working with Spain to be, if possible, selected as the ar-
biter when the peace conference shall assemble, but in any event
to be recognized and have a seat in that conference. I have given
you the information which has come to me, not because I do not
appreciate the futility of the curiously antiquated sort of intriguing diplomacy which it exemplifies, but because I think it shows
very clearly that the Vatican is working with all its power for
Austria. The contention set forth in the memorandum which
came to me and which I telegraphed you is undoubtedly true; the

handing over to Russia of all the provinces therein listed[4] with the cession of Constantinople and the Dardanelles will undoubtedly give her tremendous, if not overwhelming, power in Europe and make her very strong in the Orient. The whole tone of this memorandum, however, is against England and, incidentally, her allies, who accede to this programme. It was said, indeed, in the memorandum that England does not dare to present the true program which she has in mind to Europe and therefore has violently protested against the cruelty of the Turks against the Armenians, et cetera.

The gentleman told me that the Vatican keeps, he believes, absolutely informed of every move that is made in the whole field of present diplomacy and he believes that the Vatican knows just what terms Germany and Austria would be willing to make peace on. I am sure that the Vatican used certain influences during the last electoral campaign in America, on account of the President's attitude with regard to Mexico, to withdraw from the President the support of representatives of the church in America.

The newspapers here are filled all the time with stories of the troubled conditions existing in Germany and Austria. Thoughtful men, however, who are not swayed by prejudice think that Germany can hardly be starved out, but the very general impression is that Austria is in a very bad way indeed. I myself, remembering the days of my childhood in the South, am skeptical as to the people's being forced to yield because of the scarcity of even the necessaries of life.

I have written the foregoing to you, not only for yourself, but thinking this the most confidential way to have it reach the President.

Believe me, my dear Mr. Secretary, always,

Faithfully yours,   Thos. Nelson Page

TLS (SDR, RG 59, 763.72/3170½, DNA).

1 It is printed as an Enclosure with W. G. Sharp to RL, Jan. 10, 1917; Balfour's note is printed as an Enclosure with C. A. Spring Rice to the Department of State, Jan. 16, 1917, both in Vol. 40. The notes are also printed in *FR-WWS 1917*, I, 6-9 and 17-21, respectively.

2 T. N. Page to RL, Jan. 21, 1917, T telegram (SDR, RG 59, 763.72/3149, DNA). It is printed in *FR-WWS 1917*, I, 22.

3 Juan Riaño y Gayangos.

4 All of Poland, the Dardanelles, Kurdistan, Armenia, Romanized Nia, and Galicia.

ENCLOSURE I I

## From Thomas Nelson Page

My dear Mr. President:                    Rome January 22, 1917

I have written a letter to the Secretary Mr. Lansing by this pouch which it may interest you to see and I will not repeat anything that I said in that letter.

The unknown quantity in the present problem, here at least, seems to be Russia. No one here appears to know just what is going on there. The Russians themselves say that Russia is getting ready for a great move and that she will be able to save Roumania; that the change will take place very soon, et cetera. They also declare that Russia is absolutely determined to carry the war through to complete victory. I am sensible myself that there at least seems to be, not only considerable ignorance here among the representatives of the other Allies as to what Russia is doing or can do; but also some anxiety on this point. According to what we read and hear here, the Russian cabinet appears to be in a constant state of change, or "crisis," as they say here. Ministers succeed Ministers with startling rapidity, without any one here knowing precisely why. One thing, however, appears reasonably certain, that Russia has recently been on the verge of making some sort of separate accommodation, if not actually a separate peace, and the whole matter of the Dardanelles and Constantinople has come out in consequence of this fact. As my telegram of yesterday stated, Russia seems to be in a fair way of getting from the other Allies a hand sufficiently free to give her a very preponderant position as regards, not only Eastern and Southeastern Europe; but even the Orient itself. I draw from this the conclusion that it was necessary to make large concessions to Russia, either to secure her continued co-operation or to make it appear worth while to her to face the conditions in which she finds herself and to put forth extraordinary efforts.

There seems a general impression here that Germany may be in a bad way, economically, but that Austria is certainly in an exceedingly bad way. I incline to the opinion that the Memorandum to which I have referred in my letter to Mr. Lansing, was brought to my attention because of the untoward condition in which Austria-Hungary is at present and the apprehension that Russia may become absolutely preponderant in Southeastern Europe.

As you will have heard, the recent Conference here of the Prime Ministers of the Allies, excepting that of Russia,—with their leading military representatives, besides deciding on an answer to your Note, decided also to create a mobile army the size of which is set at anywhere from three-quarters of a million to a million men, composed of forces of all the Allies to be used wherever occasion demands. In pursuance of this, considerable numbers of French troops have been coming into Italy,—whether for use in the Balkans or for use in Italy along her northern battle front, I have not so far been able to ascertain. Some say one thing, some another. It was, however, in consequence of this proposed mobile army, no less perhaps than in consequence of the alleged increase of German Austrian forces along the Swiss northern and western frontier, that Switzerland the other day decided to mobilize the greater part of her troops. The press here, as in the other Allied countries, makes the claim that this mobilization is entirely against Germany and Austria, while I see the latter say it is against the Allies. I think it may be said with certainty that it is not against the Allies solely that Switzerland has mobilized. I know that the Swiss Government made representations to the Allies that the step was not taken with any hostile intent against them. It was taken to protect Switzerland's neutrality from aggression on either side. This is the real fact and I understand that Switzerland now feels pretty well assured that neither side in the great combat will undertake to do that which will fling the whole weight of her force, which although small by modern reckoning, is pretty compact,—against them.

I learn from the best authority here that Switzerland at present, although very short of supplies, has sufficient for her immediate needs. A short time ago there was a great discussion among the Allies as to whether Switzerland should be permitted to export anything into Germany, which she imported, and that England was for excluding her right to export anything whatever. She was obliged, however, to yield to the extent of permitting the exportation of what is called here "agrume," that is, fruits such as oranges, lemons, citron, etc. and possibly certain vegetables such as onions, inasmuch as Sicily and Southern Italy, where these fruits are the principal staple of production and export, absolutely demanded it, and Italy herself stated that it was necessary to make this concession.

Switzerland, as you know, has been a great producer of condensed milk, cheese, butter, etc. and I learn that there is great apprehension lest, owing to the inability to get a continuance of imports of winter feed for the cattle, they will have to be killed, in sufficient numbers at least to injure seriously this source of her supply.

I have been much troubled recently to find how far Italy has

appeared to think it necessary to yield to what I cannot but think
is a sort of dictatorship on the part of England with regard to certain very important necessaries of life here for which Italy is
entirely dependent on importations, such as coal, grain, steel,
etc. There is a very apparent propaganda in progress and not a
great deal that is American escapes the interference on the part
of these British propagandists in one way or another, the general
method being that which dates back to the earliest days of Rome,
of whispers that these American representatives have Austrian
connections and are really working not in Italy's interest.

I took the matter up informally with the Minister of Foreign
Affairs.[1] He, however, gave me to understand that, with regard to
the particular articles as to which I approached him,—coal, grain,
steel,—Italy had no choice. It was a matter of necessity for her to
fix prices in order to secure a guarantee of the quantities of these
staples necessary for her existence. My contention with him was
that America could not compete if the prices were that at which
they were fixed; but that if she were left to take her chance of
finding a market, she would bring coal, etc. to Italy. The Minister
said that this was a war measure and was necessary for the reasons he gave me, as otherwise the war could not continue; but he
said it would not be continued after the war.

The text of your address of this afternoon before the Senate
arrived here in sufficient time to have it put in proper shape to
deliver, according to instructions, this evening at the hour of its
delivery in Washington, and I have made an appointment with
the Minister of Foreign Affairs for that purpose. At the same time
I am having to-day careful translation made from English into
Italian, so that if necessary I may send it with the English text
for publication in the press here.

Your Note of the 18th of December suffered very much I think
from the somewhat inexact translation made here at the Foreign
Office, and I attribute a part of the virulence of attack made on it
here in the press, to this translation.

I do not, however, mean to attribute too large a part of this attack to this cause, for I feel sure that the cue came from the outside and I believe that it was given because there was a serious
apprehension that the suggestion of Peace might weaken the
power of the Allied countries.

The position that was allowed to be taken that you had declared
the two sides to be of similar merit was so manifestly without
foundation that I feel very well assured that no representative of

---

[1] Baron Sidney Sonnino.

any Government who read your note, really believed what the press declared.

I think it quite possible that at the very beginning some of them suspected that Germany had asked you to intervene in some way; but certainly they were soon disillusioned and I do not think that this view was ever entertained by Baron Sonnino. A certain amount of mischief has resulted from the efforts of certain American busy-bodies who have undertaken a sort of propaganda to create in the minds of representatives of the Allies as well as in the public mind, the impression that you and your administration speak rather for a fraction than for the whole of the American people. Even the complete reversal of their prophecy that you would not be re-elected, has not entirely failed to stop them and there is so much ignorance here as to America that their propaganda is at times really mischievous.

Immediately after your Note came out, I heard from one of the Ministeries here a reference to the impression which had been made by the impertinent activities of the man who in Paris is the sort of head and front of this propaganda[2] and more recently the press has occasionally had a reference to the opinion of Americans of standing who are critical of the position which you have set forth in your note.

I cannot close this without expressing to you the enormous interest which your address before the Senate set for this afternoon has for me. It is a very high note which you have struck. I do not see how it could be higher. I shall await with breathless interest its effect. I do not mean its immediate reception; but its subsequent influence on the present world conflict and its consequences. Whether the world is ready for it or not remains to be seen. In any event, it is nearer to a declaration of the principle of right, based on the highest ethical foundation, than anything that I remember in any State paper, of which I have knowledge.

Believe me, my dear Mr. President, always with the greatest regard and the sincerest friendship, yours,

Thos Nelson Page

TLS (SDR, RG 59, 763.72/3171½, DNA).
[2] He probably referred to Robert Bacon.

## From Robert Lansing

PERSONAL AND PRIVATE:

My dear Mr. President:        Washington February 14, 1917.

I find that I have overlooked replying to your letter of the 7th enclosing a translation of a communication of the Provisional

Council of State in the Kingdom of Poland addressed to you, and asking a suggestion for a reply thereto.

It is my belief that in the present circumstances it would be unwise to make any reply for the reason that it might be miscon-strued—whichever way answer is made.

The communication is herewith returned for your file.

Faithfully yours,   Robert Lansing

TLS (WP, DLC).


## From Robert Lansing, with Enclosures

My dear Mr. President:              Washington February 14, 1917.

I have received the enclosed letter of the 13th from Senator Stone transmitting a resolution introduced by Senator Saulsbury in regard to the use of our ports by belligerent warships.

Senator Saulsbury called to see me yesterday morning and showed me the proposed resolution asking my views in regard to it. I told him that of course I could not endorse the resolution, but that under certain conditions it might be useful.

He asked me if it would embar[r]ass the Government if it was introduced. I told him I did not think it would if it was referred without debate to the Foreign Relations Committee. He said that he intended to do that.

I repeated to him that he must not consider anything I had said as endorsing the resolution or approving its introduction. He said that he understood that.

I took this course because I saw that the Senator was very desirous to introduce the resolution, and I thought that it could be better handled if it was referred to the Committee as it could then be suppressed or held without action for the time being.

Senator Stone's letter will have to be answered, however, and I should like to have your instructions before replying.

Faithfully yours,   Robert Lansing.

TLS (SDR, RG 59, 763.72111/4527½, DNA).


E N C L O S U R E     I

## William Joel Stone to Robert Lansing

Dear Mr. Secretary:              [Washington] February 13 1917.

At the request of Senator Saulsbury, I have directed the Clerk of this Committee to forward you, for any comment you might care to make thereon, his Resolution presented this morning; copy of which is herewith enclosed.

Sincerely yours, Wm. J. Stone

TLS (SDR, RG 59, 763.72111/4520½, DNA).

## E N C L O S U R E   I I

Resolution, by Mr. Saulsbury of Delaware.

An act to discourage the violation of international law upon the high seas.

Whenever a state of war exists between two or more nations with whom the United States are at peace and one or more of the belligerents shall upon the high seas enter upon, engage in or permit a course of warfare or use a method not justified or warranted by the laws of war as generally accepted or as construed by this Government, the ports, harbors and waters of the United States may, as freely as in time of universal peace, be resorted to, used and frequented by the warships or other vessels of any other belligerent, however armed, for the possible purpose of capturing, destroying, resisting or escaping from any vessel of the belligerent or belligerents engaged in such unwarranted course of warfare, or using such illegal methods.

Provided, before the ports, harbors and waters of the United States may be so resorted to, used and frequented, the President shall by proclamation declare that proper occasion has arisen therefor under the terms of this act.

T MS (SDR, RG 59, 763.72111/4520½, DNA).

## From Edward Mandell House, with Enclosure

Dear Governor: New York. February 14, 1917.

Here is a copy of a letter from Hoover in which he outlines his idea of the best way to serve in the event of war with Germany. I think you will agree with most of his suggestions.

If No. 9 is adopted, Hoover would undoubtedly be the best man for that place.[1] Affectionately yours, E. M. House

TLS (WP, DLC).
[1] Wilson sent a copy of Hoover's letter to Baker with this comment: "Here is a letter so pertinent to the inquiries now being made by the Council on National Defense that I am taking the liberty of sending it to you for consideration. It comes from a very experienced man." WW to NDB, Feb. 16, 1917, TLS (WP, DLC).

## Herbert Clark Hoover to Edward Mandell House

Dear Colonel House:          New York.   13, February, 1917.

Apropos of my conversation with you this morning, my own views as to immediate steps to be taken in case we go to war with Germany are as follows:

1. I trust that the United States will enter into no political alliance with the Allied Governments, but will confine itself to naval and military cooperation.

2. The first step for such cooperation would be to bring to bear the whole weight of our naval, shipping and other resources to supply England, France and Italy with food-stuffs and munitions.

3. It will probably be necessary for us to open to them all the facilities of which we are capable to enable them to finance such purchases in the United States.

4. Although, as you know, I have no sympathy with the food-blockade of Germany, this measure has proceeded to such a length that from a military point of view it is necessary that it should be now continued to the end and we would therefore need address ourselves to the reenforcement of it at every point. You are also aware that the Allied Governments have found themselves embarrassed by the necessity of bending to the demands of this country in connection with trade with the Northern neutral governments. As a consequence, a considerable leakage of their native food-supplies filters into Germany from these quarters, but by cooperation with the Allied Governments in the restriction of permits for the shipment of food-stuffs from this country to these neutral powers, we could no doubt further restrict the native supplies now going into Germany.

5. It would probably be necessary for this government to direct as much American shipping to the assistance of the Allies as possible, but we can go no further if we join with the Allies, by pressure upon neutral shipping to serve the Allies. For instance, if we cooperate with the Allies in refusing coal to shipping except upon terms that they serve the Allies beyond their regulated self-needs, we can force a great deal of neutral shipping into the service of the Allied Governments. There are other means by high pressure that can be directed to this end as well.

6. I do not wish to pretend to any naval or military experience but two suggestions of this character are impressed upon my mind. The first is that the protection of overseas shipping is a matter for mosquito craft; that it is dangerous to undertake this

work with large naval units; and that American submarines are a defensive weapon and therefore that the most of our naval construction should be devoted to the creation of a mosquito surface fleet for safeguarding commerce. The second military suggestion that I have in mind is that the French Army has passed the zenith of its strength and its formations are diminishing with its casualties. As you know, it is the most skilled army in Europe. Furthermore, for the American people to put an expeditionary force into Europe presents many difficulties, not only as to transport and the long time required in preparation, but it has political difficulties in association. If, on the other hand, this country were opened to recruiting for the French or other Allied Armies, and if the Government gave a stimulus by the provision of pensions etc., I am confident that a large body of men could be recruited and sent, simply as man-power to France. These men, put into the training depots in Europe would be ready for front-line work within four or five months, and they would form a nucleus upon which a skilled army could be subsequently built up if we desired to go further in the matter. This would free us from the provision of all the impedimenta involved in an expeditionary force.

7. It appears to me that the political situation which will eventuate out of this war makes it absolutely necessary that this country should not only be protected by a large defensive force, but that we should have a force in being when peace approaches. As our terms of peace will probably run counter to most of the European proposals, our weight in the accomplishment of our ideals will be greatly in proportion to the strength which we can throw into the scale.

8. It appears that the world will be faced with a food shortage before the next harvest and that some measures will be necessary for the control of food consumption in this country, if we are adequately to supply the Western Allies. Such measures do not need to take the form of rationing the people, or any drastic measures of that character, but there are many indirect methods of repressing food-consumption, such as the suppression of the consumption of grain and sugar for brewing and distilling purposes, and a long list of other measures with which we are well familiar.

9. All such measures involve a large amount of intimate military, naval and economic cooperation with the Western Allies. If we attempt it by the use of the usual chain of Ambassadors through the Foreign Offices to other departments and back and forth again to the State Department in Washington, it will be

hopeless of practical and effective results. It seems to me the only proper solution would be to establish a branch of the American Government in Europe, headed by a man of Cabinet rank, and equipped with a proper expert staff of Commissioners, in order that direct access should be had by the American Government to every official and department in Europe, with influence, and without red-tape.　　　　Yours faithfully,　Herbert Hoover.

TCL (WP, DLC).


## From Paul Samuel Reinsch

Dear Mr. President:　　　　　　　　Peking, February 14, 1917.

By associating herself with the United States in the matter of the protest against German submarine warfare[1] China has again shown her trust in American aims and policies. An opportunity is afforded to us to strengthen international justice and security by basing all questions of China's international politics upon the same ground as supports your action in the submarine controversy, namely,—the strengthening of international right by the creation of a community feeling among independent states for the mutual respect of that right.

The act of China has already visibly diminished the danger of having China made a pawn of the selfish game of politics regardless of her rights of independent development. If the American Government can follow this up quietly with judicious and firm support of the position of China as an independent nation, especially in the matter of preserving her control of her own military establishment, the security of the world will be greatly stren[g]thened. Should China in following the lead of the United States be eventually involved in the war, a moderate amount of American financial support will be necessary in order to make her assistance effective and in protecting her against falling under outside domination.

These matters are of such far-reaching importance for the immediate and future security of our own country that I may feel it necessary to suggest that certain phases of the question be submitted to you directly for your decision. I am writing this note only to express to you my earnest conviction that the opportunity is at hand for the solving of the Chinese problem for a long time to come in a manner consistent with our national safety and the fundamental rights of China without coming in direct conflict with the position and legitimate interests of other nations.

With the highest regard and the best wishes for your continued well-being, I am, dear Mr. President,

Faithfully yours,    Paul S. Reinsch.

TLS (WP, DLC).
[1] The Chinese cabinet had recently endorsed the action of the United States
Government in breaking relations with Germany. It had also notified the German
government that China would sever relations with Germany if she pursued all-
out submarine warfare. *New York Times*, Feb. 11, 1917.


## From Duncan Upshaw Fletcher

My dear Mr. President:          [Washington] February 14, 1917.

Your note of the 13th inst., regarding the Alaska Fisheries Bill
has been received.

I have frequently urged action in this matter and yesterday
Senator Lane, Chairman of the Committee on Fisheries introduced a bill, copy of which I am enclosing, S-8242. It has also
gone to the Secretary of Commerce and I am assured as soon as
his report is received the Committee will take action. There would
seem to be no need of hearings because the bill introduced,
S-8242, is the result of hearings on the subject already had. I also
enclose for comparison a copy of the House bill, H.R. 17499,
which is pending there. Senator Lane tells me that Judge Alexander and all parties concerned approve of the measure as expressed in his bill, S-8242. It is quite a long bill and it will be
difficult to get it up for consideration on account of the unprecedented jam in the Senate, but we shall do our best to pass it.

If there are any changes or amendments advised by the Department they will no doubt come to us shortly and probably will
not be such as to cause delay.

Very sincerely,    Duncan U. Fletcher.

TLS (WP, DLC).


## From Edwin Grant Conklin

Princeton, New Jersey
My dear President Wilson,                    February 14, 1917

I am enclosing herewith a copy of a letter from Professor A.
Brachet of the University of Brussels who is now an exile in
Paris.[1] This letter was written, as you will see, to Professor E. B.
Wilson of Columbia University and he thought that it showed so
deep an appreciation of your address to the Senate that he for-
warded it to me. I am making bold to send it on to you with the

thought that you may be pleased to know that your notable address has made so great an impression upon a distinguished Belgian scientist. In common with most forward looking men throughout the world, I also was thrilled by your noble address, which seems to me one of the most notable public utterances ever made by any of our Presidents.

I realize how great is the pressure upon your time and energy and I beg of you not to take the time to acknowledge this note.

Sincerely and faithfully yours,   E. G. Conklin

TLS (WP, DLC).
[1] Albert Brachet to Edmund Beecher Wilson, Jan. 24, 1917, TCL (WP, DLC). Brachet wrote that Wilson's address to the Senate of January 22 had made a very profound impression upon him and that he could scarcely believe that a statesman, representing one of the leading powers of the world, could dare to pronounce words of such elevated thought in which the ideal truth of humanity was expressed so clearly. Europe was chained by its long history and could not envisage a new future. President Wilson was right. The New World could bring to an old continent ideas and points of view free from the remains of feudalism which still remained among most of the European powers: "En faisant cela il nous aura rendus un service aussi grand que tous ceux que l'Europe a pu lui rendre dans la passé."

## From Charles Sumner Hamlin

Dear Mr. President:               Washington February 14, 1917.

I send you herewith copy of a telegram and letter received from Mrs. J. Malcolm Forbes,[1] of Milton, Massachusetts, asking if I can give her some confidential advice as to whether she ought to sustain or oppose the "good" work of the Emergency Peace Committee. I hate to trouble you at this time, but thought you ought to know of this correspondence. Mrs. Forbes is President of the Massachusetts Branch of the Woman's Peace Party and for the last ten years she has been very prominent in advocating peace. In fact, I am led to believe that she has expended very large sums of money in helping along this movement. You will also probably remember that she did splendid service towards your re-election in the campaign. In fact, I know of no woman in the country that has done as much towards your election as has she.

I can appreciate fully that very likely you would not care to express an opinion on this subject, but if there is anything you would care to have me say I will be glad to talk with her, expressing, of course, only my personal views colored by such information, if any, as you care to give me.

My personal feelings are that this movement is calculated to do anything rather than to help your splendid efforts in the cause of peace and I am sure that a word from me will bring Mrs. Forbes out in active opposition.

Please do not take the trouble to answer this note unless there is something you would care to have me say to her.

Believe me,

Very sincerely yours,    Charles S. Hamlin

TLS (WP, DLC).
¹ Rose Dabney (Mrs. J. Malcolm) Forbes, a widow. The enclosures were Rose D. Forbes to C. S. Hamlin, Feb. 12, 1917, T telegram, and Rose D. Forbes to C. S. Hamlin, Feb. 13, 1917, TCL, both in WP, DLC.

## To Robert Lansing

My dear Mr. Secretary,    The White House. 15 February, 1917.

The proclamation by the President here contemplated would, in effect, be a proclamation of outlawry against the naval representatives of a Government with which this Government would be at peace, and would beyond all doubt be considered so unfriendly an act as virtually to amount to a declaration of war. To vest such a power in the President would, therefore, be in fact (whatever the theory or intention of the Act) to depute to him the power to declare war. That would clearly be unconstitutional, virtually if not technically, and I think very much better and more direct ways of bringing on war would be preferable to this.

I would be glad if you would let Senator Stone have a copy of this letter when you reply to his inquiry.

Faithfully Yours,    Woodrow Wilson

WWTLS (SDR, RG 59, 763.72111/4527½, DNA).

## To Robert Lansing, with Enclosure

My dear Mr. Secretary,    The White House. 15 February, 1917.

I shall be very glad to discuss this delicate matter with you this afternoon at 2:30, if you can come over to the House at that time.

Faithfully Yours,    W.W.

WWTLI (SDR, RG 59, 763.72/3314½, DNA).

E N C L O S U R E

## From Robert Lansing

PERSONAL AND PRIVATE:

My dear Mr. President:        Washington February 14, 1917.

I send you a letter which has just been received from the Sun Company, of Philadelphia¹ relative to the arming of their vessels in English ports, with the aid of the British Government. Since the letter was received the Company has telephoned that the British Government is willing to supply the guns, provided our Government does not object.

This raises a new problem in the matter of arming merchant vessels. I would not favor allowing them to receive guns without our consent, and, at the same time, I am very doubtful as to whether we should give consent. This is but one additional perplexity to the many which are presented by the existing situation.

I think it would be well if you could arrange to let me see you sometime tomorrow (Thursday) in order that certain of these questions may be answered in accordance with the policy which you have in mind. If you can arrange this will you please let me know by telephone?

Faithfully yours,   Robert Lansing.

TLS (SDR, RG 59, 763.72/3314½, DNA).
    ¹ H. C. Carr to the State Department, Feb. 13, 1917, TLS (SDR, RG 59, 763.72/3315, DNA). Carr was assistant to J. Howard Pew, president of the Sun Co. of Philadelphia, producers and shippers of petroleum and petroleum products.


## To Charles Sumner Hamlin

My dear Mr. Hamlin:      [The White House] 15 February, 1917

I am warmly obliged to you for calling my attention to your correspondence with Mrs. J. Malcolm Forbes. I share with you the feeling that the work which societies such as the one she has been connected with have hitherto been doing can in the present circumstances, if continued, do nothing but harm by creating the impression that there are divided counsels amongst us. I am sure that Mrs. Forbes will believe me when I say that I am doing everything that I honorably can to keep the country out of war, and I think that the best way to support my efforts just now is to show that the whole country, at any rate the thoughtful element of it, is back of me. I would be very much obliged if you would convey some such counsel to Mrs. Forbes, whom I very much admire and who I am sure will be moved by the highest patriotic purposes.

Cordially and sincerely yours,   Woodrow Wilson

TLS (Letterpress Books, WP, DLC).

## To Claude Augustus Swanson

My dear Senator:          [The White House] 15 February, 1917

It was a great pleasure to see you the other night and to see you looking so well after your illness.

You looked so unusually fit that I am wondering if I may without seeking to overtax you speak again of my very great interest in the bill for the purchase of Monticello. Apparently, the ladies of the D.A.R. who are interesting themselves in this matter have been so active among the members of both houses that the passage of the bill could be counted on if it were reported out favorably.     Cordially and sincerely yours,     Woodrow Wilson

TLS (Letterpress Books, WP, DLC).

## To Brand Whitlock

My dear Mr. Minister:          [The White House] 15 February, 1917

I warmly appreciate your generosity in sending me a copy of the medal struck in your honor and the very interesting portrait. I shall value them both as reminding me constantly of a friend whom I greatly value and admire. What you say about myself and the work we are all engaged in together makes me very proud and very grateful.[1]

Things are thickening so about you in Belgium that it may not be very long before I see you again, but whether I see you or not, you will, I am sure, realize my warm friendship and the high value I place upon your own.

Cordially and sincerely yours,     Woodrow Wilson

TLS (Letterpress Books, WP, DLC).
[1] B. Whitlock to WW, Jan. 20, 1917, Vol. 40.

## From the White House Staff

The White House
Memorandum for the President:          February 15, 1917.

Senator Saulsbury telephoned this afternoon to say that he would be glad to have a talk with the President concerning the advisability of including his bill—permitting the use of United States waters by the vessels of the belligerents engaged in hunting down submarines—as an amendment to Senator Overman's Omnibus Bill concerning spies, breaches of neutrality, etc. Senator Saulsbury asked that the President be advised that he has had some talk with Secretary Lansing on this subject without committing him in any way. The Senator stated that no one knew of these talks with Mr. Lansing. The Senator would be glad to see the President about this matter any time the President cared to fix. He did not, however, wish to take the President's time unless the President considered it worth while.[1]

TL (C. L. Swem Coll., NjP).
[1] There is no record of a meeting between Wilson and Saulsbury on this subject.

## Frederick Dixon to Edward Mandell House

*Private.*                                    Boston, Massachusetts.
Dear Colonel House:                        February 15, 1917.

Here is a piece of information for you, just for whatever it may be worth, and I am not sure it may not be worth something, unless I am merely carrying coals to Newcastle.

The day after the break with Germany I traveled from Washington to New York in the same car as Mr. Bryan. I had a long talk with him on the subject of what had happened. He made no secret that his policy was utterly opposed to the President's, both on the subject of the break and on the subject of the league for peace. On the subject of the league for peace he declared that it would involve this country in war immediately, on the continent. On the subject of the break he declared that it never should have taken place, and that it was quite unnecessary. He was, it seemed to me, quite bitter on the subject, and it is here the interesting part comes in. He went on to insist that if the President should go to Congress for further powers, he would demand a referendum in order to repudiate any such action.

I do not know how far he seriously would go, nor have I anything like your knowledge of how far his influence would stretch, nor have I any idea whether it was a mere ebullition of the moment, or whether in practice he would really carry out such a thing. He made it quite clear to me then, however, that he would thwart the President's policy as far as ever he could.

Yours very sincerely,   Frederick Dixon.

TCL (WP, DLC).

## To Edwin Grant Conklin

My dear Professor Conklin:   The White House 16 February, 1917
It was certainly thoughtful of you to send me Professor Brachet's letter to Professor E. B. Wilson. It is indeed delightful to

get such evidences of the impression made by my address to the Senate which, alas, had too little practical effect.

I am greatly cheered by your own words and thank you for them from the bottom of my heart.

In haste

Cordially and sincerely yours,   Woodrow Wilson

TLS (E. G. Conklin Papers, NjP).


## To Duncan Upshaw Fletcher

My dear Senator:          [The White House] 16 February, 1917

I am warmly obliged to you for your kind reply to my letter of the thirteenth and am sincerely glad to know that there is some prospect of the passage of a satisfactory fisheries bill with regard to Alaska.

Cordially and sincerely yours,   Woodrow Wilson

TLS (Letterpress Books, WP, DLC).


## From Joshua Willis Alexander

Dear Mr. President:       Washington, D. C. February 16, 1917.

I beg to acknowledge receipt of your letter of the 13th instant. I note your deep interest in the Alaska Fisheries Bill, and your earnest wish to have it passed at this session.

I regret to say the outlook for the passage of the bill is not bright. I share your wish to pass the bill, and will do all in my power to that end. There are many obstacles in the way.

I have had frequent conferences with the Secretary of Commerce and the Commissioner of Fisheries, and they are fully informed about the situation.

Sincerely yours,   J. W. Alexander

TLS (WP, DLC).


## From Newton Diehl Baker, with Enclosure

My dear Mr. President:       Washington. February 16, 1917.

I inclose copies of several telegrams showing renewed raiding activity on the border.[1] It seems to be agreed that we cannot afford adequate protection to the border by merely staying on our own side and resisting bandits after they have crossed. I think

General Funston ought to be instructed to pursue these bodies, and suggest orders to him as shown in the accompanying memorandum. If you prefer to see me about this, I can of course come at your call. No orders have been sent, and none will be sent, without your approval.

Respectfully yours,   Newton D. Baker

TLS (N. D. Baker Papers, DLC).
  1 Alonzo B. Garrett (Consul at Nuevo Laredo, Mexico) to RL, T telegram, Feb. 15, 1917; F. Funston to H. P. McCain, T telegrams 4596 and 4597, Feb. 16, 1917; all in the N. D. Baker Papers, DLC.


E N C L O S U R E¹


MEMORANDUM for                                    Washington.
The Adjutant General:                       February 16, 1917.

The Secretary of War directs the following instructions be telegraphed, in code, to the Commanding General, Southern Department.

The Secretary of War directs that in the event of the repetition of such raids by Mexican bands crossing the border into the United States as were reported in your numbers 4596 and 4597, you will take action as follows: You will direct the nearest commanding officer of U. S. troops who has a suitable and sufficient force for the purpose to immediately pursue the raiding band with a view to its capture or destruction. The limit of pursuit will be three days' march by whatever means of transportation is used. If organized troops of the *de facto* government are met, ⟨the pursuit will be turned over to them⟩ *the American force shall withdraw after giving all information of value to the de facto commander*. If sufficient American force is not at hand or near the place of raid, you will have it collected from the nearest available stations provided it can cross the border in pursuit not later than seven days after the raid and provided ⟨there is reasonable belief⟩ *subsequent information subsequent to the raid shows* that the raiding band can be struck within three days after crossing. Where it is probable that such movement will result in hostile collision with *de facto* government troops, it will not be made without specific instructions of War Department.

Major-General, Chief of Staff.

T MS (N. D. Baker Papers, DLC).
  1 Words in angle brackets in the following document deleted at Wilson's instruction; words in italics (except the first and third *de facto*) added by Baker at Wilson's instruction during a meeting in Baker's office at 4:30 P.M. on Saturday, February 17.

## From Francis Griffith Newlands

My dear Mr. President:                [Washington] Feb. 16, 1917.

I send you herewith my report on the labor legislation, and call your attention particularly to pages 4 and 5.[1] I think I have already informed you that the Committee has authorized the acceptance of Mr. Underwood's measure as an amendment to the bill.

The Chiefs of the Railroad Brotherhoods appeared before the Committee yesterday and presented their objections to the bill. They expressed lack of confidence in the Board of Mediation and Conciliation and made statements on this line which I understand are to be presented to you.

I am making a continuous effort to secure consideration but conditions are not very encouraging.

Believe me,      Sincerely yours,      Francis G. Newlands

TLS (WP, DLC).

[1] 64th Cong., 2d sess., *Senate Report No. 1025. . . . February 10, 1917.* In it, the Commerce Committee reported favorably to the Senate the bill (S. 8201) to amend the Railway Mediation Act of 1913. Wilson's address to a joint session of Congress of December 5, 1916 (printed at that date in Vol. 40), had included six recommendations concerning management, labor, and the railroads. Newlands' report quoted the relevant portions of the address and noted that Congress had already enacted some of Wilson's recommendations or was in process of doing so. The committee, however, was "divided upon the subject of suspending the right of strike and lockout during the period of investigation and a reasonable time thereafter." A majority of the committee held that the right to strike had been "a potent factor in the betterment of the wages and conditions of labor" and that "it would not be wise, for the present at least," to modify or suspend it. A minority, including the chairman, recognized that the strike was labor's only effective weapon, but believed that "the advance of civilization requires the substitution of reason for force in all contentions between the State and the individual and between man and man, as well as between nations." The minority accordingly held that it was "the duty of Congress in its control of interstate commerce" to provide for a fair tribunal, and that, once this tribunal was created, "the right of strike, as well as the right of lockout, should be suspended." This, they believed, was particularly true in the field of interstate transportation. The committee as a whole was unwilling to suspend the right to strike, however, and for this reason it "felt it all the more incumbent upon them to protect the instrumentalities of transportation from any hindrance or obstruction." The committee, therefore, provided that anyone who "knowingly and willfully by physical force or threats or intimidation" obstructed the United States mail or orderly movement (including railways) in interstate or foreign commerce, or who trespassed for this purpose on property of a common carrier, should be deemed guilty of a misdemeanor. This provision was not to be construed to modify or repeal Sections 6 or 20 (the labor provisions) of the Clayton Act. The committee also supported Wilson's recommendation that power be given to the Executive, in case of military necessity, to take control of those railways required for military use.

## Franklin Knight Lane to George Whitfield Lane

My dear George,                [Washington] February 16, [1917]

That letter and proposed wire were received and your spirit is mine—the form of your letter could not be improved upon—and you are absolutely sound as to policy.

At the last meeting of the Cabinet, we again urged that we should convoy our own ships, but the President said that this was not possible without going to Congress, and he was not ready to do that now. The Navy people say that to convoy would be foolish because it would make a double target, but it seems to me the right thing to risk a naval ship in the enforcement of our right.

At our dinner to the President last night he said he was not in sympathy with any great preparedness—that Europe would be man and money poor by the end of the war. I think he is dead wrong in this, and as I am a member of the National Council of Defense, I am pushing for everything possible. This week we have had a meeting of the Council every day—the Secretary of War, Navy, Interior, Commerce, and Labor—with an Advisory Commission consisting of seven business men. We are developing a plan for the mobilization of all our national industries and resources so that we may be ready for getting guns, munitions, trucks, supplies, airplanes, and other material things as soon as war comes—*if not too soon*. It is a great organization of industry and resources. I think that I shall urge Hoover as the head of the work. His Belgian experience has made him the most competent man in this country for such work. He has promised to come to me as one of my assistants but the other work is the larger, and I can get on with a smaller man. He will correlate the industrial life of the nation against the day of danger and immediate need. France seems to be ahead in this work. The essentials are to commandeer all material resources of certain kinds (steel, copper, rubber, nickel, etc.); then have ready all drawings, machines, etc., necessary in advance for all munitions and supplies; and know the plant that can produce these on a standard basis.

The Army and Navy are so set and stereotyped and stand-pat that I am almost hopeless as to moving them to do the wise, large, wholesome job. They are governed by red-tape,—worse than any Union.

The Chief of Staff[1] fell asleep at our meeting to-day—Mars and Morpheus in one!

To-day's meeting has resulted in nothing, though in Mexico, Cuba, Costa Rica, and Europe we have trouble. The country is growing tired of delay, and without positive leadership is losing its keenness of conscience and becoming inured to insult. Our Ambassador in Berlin is held as a hostage for days—our Consuls' wives are stripped naked at the border,[2] our ships are sunk, our people killed—and yet we wait and wait! What for I do not know. Germany is winning by her bluff, for she has our ships interned in our own harbors.

Well, dear boy, I'm not a pacifist as you see. Much love,

Frank

Printed in Lane and Wall, eds., *The Letters of Franklin K. Lane*, pp. 236-37.

[1] General Scott.

[2] In a dispatch to the United Press from Paris, Carl W. Ackerman reported on February 15 that Gerard had been held in Germany for several days against his will, and that a few weeks earlier he had protested that the Germans were searching the wives of American consuls at the border. Ackerman wrote that, at Warnemünde alone, the wives of three prominent officials had been totally stripped, bathed with acids, and examined, because they were suspected of carrying documents. Officials in Washington on February 15 confirmed that they had received such reports "about two months ago." *Washington Post*, Feb. 16, 1917. No reports of indignities by search and detention had come to the State Department since its protest against such practices was sent to Berlin just before diplomatic relations were broken off. *New York Times*, Feb. 18, 1917.


## Remarks to the Gridiron Club[1]

[Feb. 17, 1917]

Mr. Toastmaster and gentlemen: We have had an evening of various and interesting entertainment, and I am going to ask you to excuse me from making the vain attempt to add to so delightful an evening. The things that I am constantly thinking about are not at present things that are suitable to discuss, and I would not try to lead your thoughts away in a vain attempt to speak upon other topics. And yet I would be doing violence to my own feeling if I did not express my gratitude to you for the gracious reception you have given me and my sincere appreciation to the Gridiron Club for a delightful evening, in expressing which sentiment I am sure I am expressing yours.

T MS (C. L. Swem Coll., NjP).

[1] Which met at the New Willard Hotel. Thomas Francis Logan, Washington correspondent for the *Philadelphia Inquirer*, was the toastmaster.


## To William Joel Stone

My dear Senator:          The White House 17 February, 1917

I take the liberty of writing to ask you if it will not be possible to press the pending treaty with Colombia again for ratification. I must admit my surprise that there should be any objection to its consideration or to immediate action upon it in view of the unusual circumstances of the moment.

The main argument for the treaty and for its immediate ratification is, of course, that in it we seek to do justice to Colombia and to settle a long-standing controversy which has sadly interfered with the cordial relations between the two republics. In addition to that argument which should be conclusive, there is this only too obvious consideration, that we need now and it is possible shall need very much more in the immediate future all the friends we can attach to us in Central America, where so many of our most critical interests center.

I would very much like your advice as to this matter. It seems to me that those who oppose this treaty must be thoughtless of the present situation.

Cordially and faithfully yours,    Woodrow Wilson

TLS (RG 46, Records of the U. S. Senate, Senate 65B-B1, DNA).


## To Francis Griffith Newlands

My dear Senator:          [The White House] 17 February, 1917

I thank you sincerely for your letter of yesterday and its enclosures. I am distressed to learn that you feel discouraged about the progress of the railway legislation. Is there anything you think I could do?

In haste

Cordially and sincerely yours,    Woodrow Wilson

TLS (Letterpress Books, WP, DLC).


## To Henry French Hollis

My dear Senator:          [The White House] 17 February, 1917

I am distressed about the miscarriage of your efforts to have me see the heads of the brotherhoods. What happened is this:

I was told they were to be here only on Thursday, and on Thursday it was impossible for me to see them. Then ensued an interval in which I did not know that efforts were being made to bring us together, and before I knew about it again they were gone.

I am certainly very sorry and I hope that you will understand it and will be gracious enough to explain it to them.

Cordially and sincerely yours,    Woodrow Wilson

TLS (Letterpress Books, WP, DLC).

# From Robert Lansing, with Enclosures

PERSONAL AND PRIVATE:

My dear Mr. President:        Washington February 17, 1917.

I send you a letter which I have received from Doctor Kirchwey, and which I thought you would find of interest in connection with the activities of the pacifists. Will you please return it after you have read it?        Faithfully yours,   Robert Lansing

TLS (SDR, RG 59, 763.72/3353½, DNA).

ENCLOSURE        I

# George Washington Kirchwey to Robert Lansing

My dear Mr. Secretary:        New York, Feb. 12, 1917.

I take pleasure in complying with your request to submit to you a statement of my connection with recent unofficial efforts to bring about such modifications of the German submarine warfare as might lead to a restoration of friendly relations between our government and that of Germany.

Believing that the action of the German Government in promulgating the new submarine policy was due, in some measure at least, to its failure to understand the attitude and policy of our government and people, and fearing that the action of the President in severing diplomatic relations would be interpreted by the German Government and people in the usual sense, as a mere preliminary to an act or declaration of war on our part, or as indicating that we, as a people, had gone over to the "war party," it seemed to me that it might be useful to remove such misconceptions if they existed.

I had no thought of playing any part in the situation when I arrived in Washington, Sunday morning, Feb. 4, but circumstances quickly placed me in a position where, as it appeared to me, I could not refuse to accept the responsibility of taking action along the lines above indicated.

A German newspaper correspondent, Dr. George Barthelme, representing the Cologne Gazette, who had called on me for the purpose of securing an interview with Mr. William J. Bryan, was induced to abandon that purpose and to prepare in its stead a dispatch which might have the effect of enlight[en]ing the German people and Government as to the attitude and purpose of the American Government and people. He gladly accepted the task and later in the day submitted the matter to me for criticism and correction. I rewrote it in large part, the matter marked in the enclosed copy of the dispatch having been written by my hand, and all the rest, with the exception of the opening and closing paragraphs, having been suggested by me.

As the wireless via Sayville was no longer open to Dr. Barthelme, I undertook to see Secretary Daniels with a view to having the embargo lifted, and accordingly did so on the following day (Tuesday morning, Feb. 6.). The Secretary heard me with apparent interest and read the dispatch with care, after which he called Admiral Benson into conference with us and submitted the dispatch to him. Both officials expressed their satisfaction with the tone and substance of the paper but suggested a few changes in phrase[o]logy and the elimination of some matter which Dr. Barthelme had quoted from Mr. Bryan's published "Statement to the American People" (Feb. 4.).[1] The changes suggested seemed to me wise and on the same evening the corrected dispatch was submitted to Admiral Benson. The enclosed copy (marked No. 1)[2] represents this final form of the dispatch as it was submitted by Dr. Barthelme for transmission to his newspaper. I learned subsequently from Admiral Benson that before passing it he made a further change in the first sentence. (Probably deleting the two words "almost implored," to which I had previously taken exception).

It may be proper for me to add that I took the action above outlined without consultation with anyone except as stated, and in particular that Mr. William J. Bryan had no part in nor any knowledge of the affair. It is true I obtained from him a formal note of introduction to Secretary Daniels, but without giving him any information as to my purpose except that I desired to see the Secretary in order to ascertain whether the wireless service via Sayville was still available for the transmission of regular newspaper dispatches to Germany.

In the meantime I had sought and obtained, Sunday afternoon, February 4th, an interview with Count von Bernstorff, in order to secure as trustworthy information as possible as to the probable effect of the severance of diplomatic relations between the German and American Governments on the question of peace and war between the two countries. As President of the American Peace Society it seemed to me of the utmost importance to secure such information in order that the Society might be in a position to act promptly and intelligently in an effort to secure united, prudent and patriotic action by the numerous and influential peace organizations of the country in the crisis confronting the nation, and especially to forestall any unwise, precipitate action by any pacifist groups that we might be able to influence.

As I feared would be the case, Count von Bernstorff took the view that the severance of diplomatic relations between the two countries made war inevitable. He was of the opinion that the German Government and people could put no other construction on the President's act. I urged the contrary view, that unless the Imperial Government was bent on war with the United States (which, he assured me, was not the case) it might still be possible to avert that calamity by inducing the German Government, even at the last moment, to modify its program of submarine warfare in such a way as to make it acceptable to our government. Finally the Count accepted my view of the situation and referred me to Dr. Paul Ritter, the Swiss Minister, to whom the interests of Germany had been committed.

I was unable to secure an interview with Dr. Ritter until Tuesday morning, Feb. 6, when the opportunity was afforded me of laying the matter before him. I found that Count von Bernstorff had already enlisted his interest in the cause and that Dr. Ritter was quite willing, in the interest of his own government and people, who were, as he pointed out, vitally concerned in the avoidance of war between the two great powers, as well as in the general interests of peace and good will, to make an effort to secure the good offices of his government to that end.

At his suggestion I drafted a note embodying my views, as they had been expressed to him and previously to Count von Bernstorff, as to the attitude of the Government and people of the United States and as to the steps that might be taken by the Imperial German Government to avoid war between the two countries.

This note, a copy of which I enclose (marked No. 2) I submitted to Dr. Ritter, and it was, as I am informed, made the subject of a conference on the same day (Tuesday, February 6) by Dr. Ritter, Count von Bernstorff and Dr. Barthelme, and approved by them. I am also informed that it was somewhat condensed and, possibly, otherwise altered for transmission, but that its substance and effect were carefully preserved, and that it was then transmitted to the Swiss Government on the evening of that day.

I desire to add that in this, as in the matter of the newspaper dispatch, I acted solely on my own initiative and without consultation with anyone, save that I reported from time to time to Mr. Arthur Deerin Call, the Secretary of the American Peace Society. In particular I wish to state that Mr. William J. Bryan had no cognizance of my plans or proceedings and to my personal knowledge had no communication, direct or indirect, with Count von Bernstorff or Dr. Ritter.

Meanwhile, Tuesday afternoon, I had made several efforts to see you, but the Cabinet meeting and subsequent conferences in which you were engaged made it impossible for me to do so. However, in the evening I saw Secretary Baker at the War Department and gave him a full account of my activities as well as of the motives that had inspired them—of all of which, I am happy to say, he expressed complete approval. The following morning (February 7) I had the pleasure of seeing you and of submitting a resumé of the matter.

I know that you do not need any assurance from me that in all the proceedings above recounted I have had no aim but to serve the highest interests of our country—its honor and dignity as well as its peace—and to further, as far as it might lie in my power to do so, the aims and policy of the President and of your high office.

With sincere appreciation of the opportunity you have afforded me of submitting this detailed statement of my efforts in this crisis of our national life, I have the honor to be

Yours very sincerely,   George W. Kirchwey

TLS (SDR, RG 59, 763.72/3353½, DNA).

[1] Bryan's statement, released on February 3, said that the American people were opposed to entering the war on either side and were "not willing to surrender the opportunity to render a supreme service to the world as a friend to all and peacemaker when peace is possible." *New York Times*, Feb. 4, 1917.

[2] It is printed in JD to WW, Feb. 7, 1917.

E  N  C  L  O  S  U  R  E        I  I

Wireless via Sayville, Feb. 6, 1917.

With the approval of Count Bernstorff, I urgently recommend immediate transmittal of following to Imperial German Government.

American public opinion strongly supports President in his actions and sentiments but strongly averse to war, which however will inevitably result from serious overt act. Tension will relax as time elapses without such act. Such forbearance coupled with reasonable modifications of announced blockade would afford American Government welcome opportunity to restore friendly relations. Slight modifications already announced have produced good effect. New announcement should make clear that no unrestricted submarine warfare contemplated but only blockade confined within narrowest limits compatible with necessary military

aims and even within those limits greatest care taken not to interfere with innocent American commerce and every precaution
taken to limit destruction of neutral ships carrying contraband
and enemy vessels to ship and cargo, safeguarding wherever possible lives of passengers and crews. Not impossible that constructive proposals allowing time to elapse and demonstrating sincerity and reasonableness of Imperial Government might prove
acceptable—as that the two governments institute a joint commission, perhaps in conference with other neutral powers affected, for negotiation of a code governing blockade and submarine warfare generally, or suggestion for a conference of
powers authorized in Naval Appropriation bill (1916).[1]

Extreme gravity of situation would seem to warrant earnest
representations to above effect to Imperial German Government.

T MS (SDR, RG 59, 763.72/3353½, DNA).
  [1] That is, the Hensley Resolution, about which see WW to C. H. Levermore,
March 28, 1916, n. 1, Vol. 36.

## From Key Pittman

My dear Mr. President:          [Washington] February 17, 1917.

I beg that you permit me to add to your burdens by submitting
for your consideration a letter on behalf of the application for
pardon that I am informed has been made upon behalf of Maury
I. Diggs and Drew Caminetti, convicted of a violation of the Mann
White Slave Act, and which conviction has recently been sustained by the Supreme Court.[1]

I frankly confess that my efforts in this behalf are urged by my
strong friendship for Mr. Anthony Caminetti and his wife. It is
their suffering that appeals to me more deeply than any suffering
the guilty parties may have endured in the past or may be compelled to submit to in the future.

While I do not agree with the majority opinion of the Supreme
Court, it would not only be useless but improper to request any
action based upon an argument in opposition to such decision.
This case was a test case. Before final decision by the Supreme
Court, many able lawyers publicly declared that the acts committed by said defendants did not constitute a crime under the
Mann Act, and therefore the guilty parties could be excused if
they did not consider such acts criminal. The same excuse, of
course, cannot be extended to any person committing a similar
act in the future, as the law is now definitely construed. These
men, in my opinion, however, are entitled to be treated as first
offenders under a new Act, and with that leniency that is deemed

to bring about the best practical results under the circumstances.

I do not contend that these men committed no crime, because they did commit a moral crime whether it was covered by the Mann Act or not, and for such crime they deserve punishment. I believe that they have received a greater punishment than they would have suffered had they pleaded guilty without trial and had served their terms in the penitentiary. The mortification, the humiliation and the notoriety that was given to them and to their families, the intense agony of their parents month after month and year after year, the suspense, the alternate hope and despair during a long period of time, have, in my opinion, been a sufficient punishment to accomplish every purpose of punishment under the law.

I sincerely hope that you will extend to these young men such leniency as in your mature judgment and superior sense of justice seems meet and proper.

I beg to remain, Mr. President,

Very sincerely and obediently yours,   Key Pittman

TLS (WP, DLC).
¹ About this case, see EAW to WW, July 30, 1913, n. 4, Vol. 28.

## To Robert Lansing

My dear Mr. Secretary,     The White House. 19 February, 1917.

I have always had a good opinion of Professor Kirchwey and have no reason to doubt that he did what he did in this instance with the best intentions, but it was certainly a most extraordinary performance, take it in all its aspects.

Faithfully Yours,   W.W.

WWTLI (SDR, RG 59, 763.72/3354½, DNA).

## To Thomas Watt Gregory

[The White House]

My dear Mr. Attorney General:     19 February, 1917

I had a conversation the other day with Senator Swanson and in the course of it he made a very interesting suggestion about settling the controversy concerning the oil lands of California.¹ I did not have time to go into it fully with him but it interested me enough to lead me to ask you whether you were yourself convinced that it was a practicable and right way out. The Senator said that he had discussed it with you and you seemed to be favorably impressed.

If you are favorably impressed with it, I will be very much obliged if you would consult Daniels and Lane about it and see whether it affords a ground for agreement.

Cordially and faithfully yours,    Woodrow Wilson

TLS (Letterpress Books, WP, DLC).
    1 See T. W. Gregory to FKL, Feb. 21, 1917, printed as an Enclosure with T. W. Gregory to WW, Feb. 26, 1917.


## From Robert Lansing

PERSONAL AND PRIVATE:

My dear Mr. President:              Washington February 19, 1917.

I had a long talk this morning with the deposed President of Costa Rica who was introduced by his Minister.[1] He made upon me a most favorable impression as a man of high motives and real patriotism.

The causes of the rebellion appear to be chiefly two, the avarice of Tinoco and his family and the opposition of certain interests to the numerous reforms in taxation and fiscal matters which the President supported and carried through. He appears to have been a real progressive in his ideas and sought to give the poorer classes a better chance than they have had before. He told me that the hostility of the privileged rich and the ignorance of the poor were the immediate cause of his overthrow together with the great confidence which he had placed in the loyalty of Tinoco.

I told him that we would not recognize Tinoco or any government growing out of the revolution and that privileges or concessions granted by such government would not be supported by this Government. He seemed very much pleased by this statement, and said that he was very grateful as a Costa Rican but he was strongly opposed to any intervention on our part. He did not seek to be reseated as President; all he wished was the restoration of constitutional government. If that could be done without him he was entirely satisfied.

Following your expressed willingness to see the President I asked Mr. Phillips to arrange a time when he could call upon you. I will be interested to know if he makes upon you the same favorable impression which he made upon me.

Faithfully yours,    Robert Lansing

TLS (SDR, RG 59, 818.00/106½A, DNA).
    1 That is, Alfredo González Flores and Manuel Castro Quesada.

# From Robert Lansing, with Enclosure

PERSONAL AND PRIVATE:

My dear Mr. President:          Washington February 19, 1917.

I send you for your consideration a communication which was handed to me today by the Minister of Ecuador.

Faithfully yours,   Robert Lansing.

TLS (WP, DLC).

# ENCLOSURE

# Rafael Héctor Elizalde to Robert Lansing

TRANSLATION.

Mr. Secretary of State,          Washington, February 19, 1917

I have the honor to inform Your Excellency that I have received the following telegram from my Government:

"Quito. February 17, 1917. Minister of Ecuador, Washington. We have answered the cablegram from Mexico:[1] The initiative that we the American countries took to secure the union of all in the matter of maintaining the rights of neutrals and allaying the rigors of war, is proof of the conviction they entertain that individual action is fruitless, as joint action will be fruitful. What is lacking is to determine in what form joint action is to be exercised. That may be determined through the immediate meeting of American Congress in Uruguay, for instance, for the purpose of agreeing upon measures likely to guarantee the rights of the continental neutrality and allay the rigors of the struggle. Officially lay this idea before the Secretary of State of the United States and the American representatives at the capital where you reside and ask them to forward it to their respective Governments. Minister of Foreign Relations."

The text of the above inserted telegram will have shown to Your Excellency the object of this note, in the sense of submitting to Your Excellency's Government's consideration the idea of an immediate meeting of an American Congress on continental cooperation in maintaining neutral rights and alleviating as far as possible the rigors of war.

None of the reasons on which my Government bases its proposition at the present time or which lead it to believe that it may bear at this juncture the results of American Continental Union which it promotes will surely escape Your Excellency's high ability.

Should Your Excellency's Government lend its weighty patronage to the defensive and altruistic undertaking the proposition implies, it may be presumed that the most complete success will very soon crown the joint efforts of all the American peoples.

I avail myself of this opportunity to reiterate to Your Excellency the assurance of my highest and most distinguished consideration.                                        R. H. Elizalde.

T MS (WP, DLC).
    [1] It contained Carranza's proposal to the neutral governments that they join in inviting the belligerent powers, "in common accord and on the basis of absolutely perfect equality," to end the war either by their own efforts or through friendly mediation by the neutrals. If this effort did not succeed within a reasonable time, Mexico proposed that the neutrals should then sharply reduce the conflagration by refusing deliveries to the belligerents and suspending commercial relations with them. The note was directed primarily to the United States, Argentina, Brazil, Chile, Spain, Sweden, and Norway. For a translation of this proposal as presented to the United States by the Mexican Consul General at San Francisco in Charge of Mexican Interests, temporarily at Washington, see Ramón P. De Negri to RL, Feb. 12, 1917 (SDR, RG 59, 763.72119/468, DNA); printed in *FR-WWS 1917*, I, 44-46.

## From Edward Mandell House

Dear Governor:                            New York. February 19, 1917.

Filene has asked me to write you concerning the plan which he proposed in a recent letter to you. I discouraged the idea as I am afraid such a movement would create opposition in the belligerent countries and for reasons which are apparent.

If they want to do anything of this sort it might be done individually through correspondence with friends on the other side. They are perfectly willing to drop it or go ahead as you may indicate.

I have gotten Colcord to write an article concerning the peace conference which I think you will approve. It is to be published not only in the American papers but in the London Times and Nation and the Manchester Guardian.[1]

My idea is to get them thinking about the only feasible way that a conference can be held to accomplish satisfactory results. The object also is, of course, to outline a plan which will call for you to sit as president of the congress.

I have been working fitfully for sometime trying to get the Carnegie peace group[2] to cooperate with those that believe in a league to enforce peace rather than in Mr. Root's "World Court League."[3] Root, Nicholas Murray Butler and Pritchett[4] are the directing spirits and are, I am told, inclined towards the Root plan.

John Sharp Williams, Schmidtlapp,[5] Oscar Strauss and some

others favor a league. Mr. Taft is willing to try to convert Root and Butler provided he knows that you approve. He does not want anything from you direct, but if you will say to me that you would like to have him go ahead, it can be arranged verbally without mentioning your name.

I think it is important, for they have some $600,000. I am told at their disposal, and if they got up a contrary propaganda it would muddy the waters.[6]

Will you not advise me as to this?

Affectionally yours,    E. M. House

TLS (WP, DLC).
[1] Colcord never published this article.
[2] That is, the Carnegie Endowment for International Peace.
[3] The American Society for Judicial Settlement of International Disputes, founded in 1910. In 1915 and 1916, William Howard Taft was honorary president, Theodore Marburg was president, and Root was vice-president. For a discussion of Root's abstention from the League to Enforce Peace, see Ruhl J. Bartlett, *The League to Enforce Peace* (Chapel Hill, N. C., 1944), pp. 43-44.
[4] That is, Henry Smith Pritchett.
[5] Jacob Godfrey Schmidlapp, not Schmidtlapp, banker and manufacturer of Cincinnati; treasurer of the American Society for Judicial Settlement of International Disputes.
[6] Actually, Wilson had already done this on his own. See WW to C. W. Eliot, Jan. 29, 1917, and n. 1 thereto.


# From Henry French Hollis

[Washington]

Dear Mr. President:                    February Nineteen 1917

I have your letter of February 17th regarding the Heads of the Railroad Brotherhoods.

When Messrs. Stone, Carter, Sheppard and Lee[1] called to see me Thursday afternoon at 2 o'clock, they expressed their earnest desire to see you, and explained to me in detail their reasons for this desire. I was strongly impressed with the importance of their visit and was exceedingly anxious to have you see them. I told them so and did my best to arrange a meeting.

At about 3 o'clock Thursday (February 15) I talked to Mr. Tumulty by telephone. He explained that the reason you could not see the Brotherhood Heads on Thursday was because of illness.[2] I then explained my anxiety to have them see you on Friday and told him that they would wait over one day for that purpose. Mr. Tumulty seemed to appreciate the importance of the meeting and assured me that he would try to arrange it for some time on Friday.

I understood that Mr. Tumulty would communicate with me Friday morning about the matter. Not hearing from him Friday morning, I called him on the telephone at about 11 o'clock, and he informed me that he had been unable to get an answer from you, but he would make another effort. At about 1 o'clock (Friday) I called up the White House again and was informed by Mr. Forster that Mr. Tumulty had gone over to the White House in person to try to arrange the meeting. I informed Mr. Forster that the matter was very important and I hoped for a reply within an hour.

At about 2 o'clock I tried to talk to Secretary McAdoo by telephone, but he was about to start for a Cabinet meeting so I did not reach him. I impressed upon Secretary McAdoo's clerk the importance of my message and at about half past three Secretary McAdoo telephoned me. I explained to him in considerable detail why I considered it important for the Brotherhood Heads to see you, and he evidently shared my anxiety.

A 6 o'clock I had received no message of any sort and I could not even tell the Brotherhood Heads whether they could see you on Saturday if they remained over another day, so I felt obliged to let them leave for Cleveland, where important business awaited their return.

I was in touch with these men while I was at Chicago during the past campaign, and I know their faith in the Administration. They have honored me by reposing similar confidence in me. It was with the keenest regret that I permitted them to depart for Cleveland Friday night without any definite word of any sort from the White House. I felt, however, that I had exhausted my powers.

They did not do or say anything to indicate that their feelings were injured: on the contrary, they were very generous in their appreciation of the weighty international problems that now engross your attention. I naturally emphasized this side of it.

The Heads of the four Brotherhoods desired me to convey to you the information they gave me regarding the present status of railroad legislation and to explain the particular reasons why they desired to see you. I realize the difficulty of transmitting in any adequate form the ideas they expressed to me, but I shall be happy to do my best if you can find it convenient to see me.

Sincerely yours,   Henry F. Hollis.

TLS (WP, DLC).
    1 That is, Warren Sanford Stone, William Samuel Carter, Lucius Elmer Sheppard, and William Granville Lee, heads, respectively, of the brotherhoods of locomotive engineers, locomotive firemen and enginemen, railway conductors, and railway trainmen.
    2 Wilson certainly was not ill. He was extremely busy all that afternoon and evening.

# From William Bauchop Wilson

My dear Mr. President:          Washington February 19, 1917.

I am submitting herewith a draft of a bill for the adjustment of labor disputes in the transportation systems of the country,[1] prepared along the lines suggested in my letter to you of November 29, 1916.[2] I believe that if it can be put into effect, it will prevent strikes and lockouts by removing the motive, make progress possible without the use of such instrumentalities, and at the same time conserve the rights and liberties of all persons concerned.

May I not briefly state my attitude of mind in approaching this subject-matter in order that you may more clearly understand the object sought to be attained by the various provisions of the proposed bill. I have been opposed to compulsory arbitration because I did not believe that any man or set of men should be compelled to work for the profit or convenience of any other man or set of men. All other objections are economic and incidental, although some of them are nevertheless serious.

All progress heretofore made by the wage-workers through their collective activities has been brought about by destroying the equities. To illustrate: The shorter work-day has not been obtained by reducing hours of labor from ten to eight per day in every part of the same industry or occupation at the same time. The object has been attained by grasping the opportunity existing in some locality to compel some particular employer or employers to concede a shorter work-day, and then utilizing the accomplishment as a leverage to force similar concessions from other employers. But in the meantime the competitive equality of the employer granting the shorter work-day has been destroyed. In any system of arbitration the tendency is toward equalization with the highest existing standards for the workers as the ultimate basis upon which the equality should rest. With a continuing system of arbitration the lowest would in time be brought to an equal standard with the highest. When that point is reached the progress would be extremely slow, because the economic pressure would have to be sufficient to lift the entire load at once instead of lifting it a piece at a time, as the previous practice has been. In dealing with the railway situation, if the hours of labor are definitely placed upon an eight-hour basis or less, it would be one or two generations before there could possibly be any serious demand for change, and we might well leave the solution of that part of the problem to those who would have to deal with it at that time.

In any system of continuous arbitration the final protection of the wage-workers against unfair decisions would be the standard of living, which is flexible and may be raised or lowered and the workmen still live, while the employer would have as his final protention [protection] the clean cut inflexible line between profit and loss, which he would be able to show definitely from his cost accounts. This would result in giving a greater measure of protection to the employers than to the employees against the possibility of unfair decisions.

The first objection cited involves a serious question of human liberty which no majority should have the right to invade. I realize, however, that when all the people are cut off from their food supply and starvation confronts them, they are not going to stop to consider whose rights are invaded or whose liberty is destroyed. They are going to find means of securing food. They will take the most direct road whether that happens to be the right way or the wrong way. For that reason it would seem the part of wisdom to carefully work out the problem when no crisis exists with a view to conserving both the freedom of the workers and the food supply of the people. The other two objections are purely economic and may with perfect propriety be dealt with in such a manner as will best protect the general walfare [welfare].

These thoughts have been borne in mind in the preparation of the measure which I submit for your consideration. It is proposed to create a system by which nothing can be gained by striking. Other machinery is provided by which progress can be made. The worker is left free to work or not work, individually or collectively, and the employers to dismiss their workmen individually or collectively, but the motive for strikes and lockouts is destroyed. I feel sure that with a measure of this character on the statute books strikes and lockouts would never occur over a sufficiently large area to seriously impair the transportation facilities of the country, and the end would be reached not by crushing the workers but by giving them a different method of adjusting grievances. It is presumed that if Congress has the power to create a Commission to regulate rates, so long as they are not confiscatory, it would have the same power to create a Commission to regulate any of the component parts of rates, such as wages. The further thought has been in my mind that the cost of any of the component parts of rates cannot be confiscatory, but only the rates as a whole. When the Interstate Commerce Commission fixes a rate that is not confiscatory, the law gives it all the force and effect of a contract between the shipper and the transportation company without there having been an actual meeting of minds between them. This principle is utilized.

One of the arguments used against Government ownership of

railroads is that it would create an army of Government employees located throughout the country in such a manner as to
wield undue influence over the Members of Congress, thereby enabling them to compel Congress to grant wages and other conditions of employment out of all just proportion to the value of
their services. With the method of wage adjustment provided in
this bill, an effective buffer would, in the event of Government
ownership, be erected between the railway employees and the
legislative branch of the Government which would very materially reduce any danger that might arise from that source.

I have made a few marginal comments on the bill for its
further elucidation.[3]

If the measure appeals to you, I would be pleased to discuss it
further with you.            Faithfully yours,   W B Wilson

TLS (WP, DLC).
[1] "A Bill to Create a Commission on Industrial Arbitration, and for other
purposes," T MS (WP, DLC). This bill created a United States Industrial
Arbitration Commission of nine members to be appointed by the President of
the United States for staggered terms and to represent, equally, railroad employers, railroad employees, and the public. The commission's purpose was to
arbitrate disputes between employers and employees engaged in interstate
transportation. The bill authorized the commission to hold hearings and to
compel testimony on disputes under investigation. Then the commission would
prepare its findings and issue an order or orders for the adjustment of the
dispute, such order or orders to have the same force "as would a contract made
and executed by and between the same parties upon the same subject-matter."
Such orders would be filed with the federal district court in which the dispute
occurred. Either party could appeal the decision of the district courts. The bill
further forbade employers and employees to make any kind of contract or agreement upon any matter in dispute while the commission conducted its investigations. In the adjustment of disputes, the commission should base all its orders
on the supposition of an eight-hour day or less, and the commission might order
extra pay for overtime. United States attorneys were to see to the recovery of
back pay by employees, and "the order or orders of the Commission shall be
conclusive evidence of the rate or rates of wages or compensation properly and
lawfully payable to the wage-earners within the recognized division of labor
specified in such order or orders, from and after the operative date originally
fixed by the Commission." Normally, the commission's orders would run for
three years; however, the commission could change its order or orders before
the expiration of the three-year term if an "emergency or extraordinary condition" arose. Nothing in this act should be construed to require workers to
render labor without their consent or to require employers to continue in employment or refrain from dismissing any workers, either individually or collectively.
[2] WBW to WW, Nov. 29, 1916, Vol. 40.
[3] They were separate "Legends," or explanatory notes.

## From John Franklin Fort

                                        Newark, New Jersey,
My dear Mr. President:                   February 19, 1917.
The telegram of Mr. Tumulty, just received, advising me that
you had sent my name to the Senate as a member of the Federal
Trade Commission, was a most profound and delightful surprise.

I am unable to express my deep appreciation of your generous consideration. If I am confirmed and enter upon the duties of the office, for which you have so kindly selected me, it will be my constant aim to fill the position with fidelity, and I hope I shall never give you cause to regret your act in naming me.

With warm personal regards, believe me,

Gratefully yours,   John Franklin Fort

TLS (WP, DLC).


## Sir Cecil Arthur Spring Rice to the Foreign Office

Washington, Feb. 19, 1917.

My tel. No: 426 (Feb 15).

Following from Sir R. Crawford: "As the result of conversations with Secretary of the Treasury and with Governor of the Federal Reserve Board I am able to announce that, with the consent of the President, the Federal Reserve Board and the Comptroller of the Currency have been authorized to encourage the National Banks to participate in taking up an issue of British Exchequer Bonds to a total of 250 million dollars, the proceeds to be used in financing exports from the United States to the United Kingdom. The rate of interest suggested is 6% or a lower rate if that should be found feasible. Holders of bonds to have option of requesting payment of principal and interest at 30 days notice after one year at reduced rate of interest, say 4½%, or after 18 months at 5%. No collateral to be deposited but a gold reserve representing 20% of the issue outstanding to be kept at Ottawa to provide for redemption of any bonds presented for redemption before maturity. The figures suggested as to interest and gold reserve are maxima and subject to any modification which may be agreed on.

"It should be understood that in these conversations H.M.G. have not been committed to the foregoing or to any proposal. My object has been to secure a reversal of the attitude of the U.S.G. towards our financial transactions in this country and to obtain their support and consent to an operation sustained on the credit of H.M.G. and without the deposit of collateral on the scale hitherto required for our issues in this country. The foregoing proposal now submitted for your consideration is the outcome of my representations that the time had come when the U.S.G. should themselves recognize that they had serious interest in the financing in part of the enormous supplies we were purchasing from this country, and that I should be authorized to convey a message to H.M.G. that these considerations had at last been recognized by the U.S.G.

"I hope that my action may receive the approval of H.M.G. I am handing over the further handling of this matter to Sir H. Lever[1] and Mr. J. P. Morgan. It is understood that the Exchequer Bond issue if approved by you will be submitted to the U. S. Treasury as a proposal from Messrs. J. P. Morgan and Co., and that it will afford an opportunity to the Federal Reserve Board to withdraw from the position they took up over the Treasury Bills last October. The Board will accordingly issue a statement indicating why they are supporting this proposal in preference to an issue of Treasury Bills on the lines contemplated in October last."

Lever is in Washington and has been informed. I will telegraph again. Meanwhile I hope I may tell R.C. how much you appreciate his exertions.

T telegram (FO 115/2258, pp. 185-86, PRO).
[1] Sir Samuel Hardman Lever, an accountant who had worked for many years in New York; in 1915, he became a cost accountant in the Ministry of Munitions. He had just returned to the United States as a special representative of the British Treasury to act as liaison with J. P. Morgan & Co.

## To Robert Lansing

My dear Mr. Secretary,     The White House. 20 February, 1917.

I am glad you had this talk with the ex-President[1] and formed a favourable impression of him. His explanation of the revolt is just what had formed in my own mind out of such information as had reached us.

I will be willing to see him, of course, as you request.[2] It will add nothing to what we already know, but it may make an impression in certain quarters which it is desirable to make.

Faithfully Yours,    W.W.

WWTLI (SDR, RG 59, 818.00/107½, DNA).
[1] That is, Alfredo González Flores of Costa Rica.
[2] Wilson received González Flores at the White House at 2 P.M. on February 21.

## To Joseph Patrick Tumulty

Dear Tumulty:               [The White House, c. Feb. 20, 1917]

The Church seems to me a very queer unit to build a defense league of any kind on (I think our ministers are going crazy) and I would be very much obliged if you would explain to Mr. Flynn[1] how impossible it is for me to do what he asks without writing to practically every organization of the country.

The President.

TL (WP, DLC).
1 The Rev. John William Flynn, minister of the Methodist Episcopal Church of Bernardsville, N. J. He had written to Wilson to request a "word of greeting" that might be read at an "Inauguration Service" on March 4 in connection with the organization of the men of the township into a "defense" league of some kind. J. W. Flynn to WW, Feb. 19, 1917, ALS (WP, DLC).

## To Robert Lansing

My dear Mr. Secretary,     The White House. 20 February, 1917.

I would very much like your opinion on this question: Might it not be a good thing (if not for the situation in the world at large, at least for the situation in the Americas) to acquiesce in this plan and take part in a conference such as it proposed?[1] Would it not serve to shoulder out any sinister influences now at work in Latin America, or likely presently to be set afoot, for example in Colombia? It is the psychology of the thing, chiefly, that I have in mind, rather than any concrete result it might accomplish.     Faithfully Yours,     W.W.

WWTLI (WP, DLC).
1 That is, the suggestion of the Ecuadorean government conveyed in R. H. Elizalde to RL, Feb. 19, 1917, printed as an Enclosure with RL to WW, Feb. 19, 1917 (second letter of that date).

## To William Bauchop Wilson

My dear Mr. Secretary:     The White House 20 February, 1917

At the earliest possible moment you may be sure I shall give very careful study to the draft of a bill to create a commission on industrial arbitration and for other purposes, which you were kind enough to send me in your letter of yesterday. I have been in constant touch with the committees of the House on this subject and feel that it would be fruitless to propose a new measure at this session. I fear that no action of any kind will be taken and that fear is associated with very great anxiety as to what may be the result. I hope that you will send a copy of the draft bill to Judge Adamson and to Senator Newlands. I am sure they will wish to study it at the same time that I do.

In haste, with warmest cordiality,

Sincerely yours,     Woodrow Wilson

TLS (LDR, RG 174, DNA).

## To Thomas Francis Logan

My dear Logan:          [The White House] 20 February, 1917

Your letter of the eighteenth was very generous.[1] It made me feel uncomfortable to disappoint the diners the other evening at the Gridiron dinner, because I am afraid that all confidently expected a speech, but if they are all as generous as you are, I need not be worried. I was glad to be there and liked very much indeed the wholesome character of the whole thing with the vein of seriousness running beneath everything.

Cordially and sincerely yours,    Woodrow Wilson

TLS (Letterpress Books, WP, DLC).
[1] It is missing.


## To Eda Blankart Funston

My dear Mrs. Funston:    [The White House] 20 February, 1917

May I not tell you with what genuine grief I have learned of the death of your distinguished husband?[1] I feel confident that I am expressing the feeling of the whole country when I say that we have lost in him an officer of unusual gallantry, capacity and loyal devotion to the interests of the country. He has repeatedly in very recent months proved his ability to handle situations of unusual delicacy and difficulty with discretion and success.

May I not express my warm personal sympathy for you in your irreparable loss?

Cordially and sincerely yours,    Woodrow Wilson

TLS (Letterpress Books, WP, DLC).
[1] General Funston had died suddenly of a heart attack on February 19.


## To George Howe III

My dear George,          The White House. 20 February, 1917.

You are quite right.[1] I hope that you will get into communication with Mr. Wintersteen and, through him, take charge of the settlement of your mother's estate.

I have had many twinges of conscience about my own neglect of this important matter, which ought, in fairness alike to Annie and to all concerned, to have been attended to long ago; and you are generous to understand as you do what has diverted me, not only from this but also from all private business of my own.

I am enclosing the note to me which dear Sister dictated on her death-bed and, along with it, the memorandum you were kind enough to send me last October.[2]

I stand ready to take up all the debts at any time that they become embarrassing, as I am sure you know. Please let Mr. Wintersteen know this.

I have paid Sister's debt to the Princeton Bank and now hold the securities which she had deposited for it. I will turn them over to the administrator so soon as he is appointed. Please let Mr. Wintersteen know this, too.

I am writing, as always nowadays, in haste; but I am sure, my dear boy, that you know what is in my heart and can read it without words.

Affectionately Yours,    Woodrow Wilson

All join me in the most affectionate messages.    W.W.

WWTLS (WP, DLC).
  [1] Howe's letter, to which this is a reply, is missing.
  [2] These enclosures are missing.


## From Walter Hines Page

London, Feb. 20, 1917.

5714. The following is strictly private for the President and Secretary only:

Since my 5665 February 11th., I have seen the Prime Minister three times. He has discussed the subject with some of his associates as he promised me that he would and modified his first views and recommendations. He has just told me and authorized me to telegraph you that if you formally submit a peace commission proposal on behalf of Austria Hungary his Government will be glad to receive it formally and to consider it on its merits, on condition that every precaution be taken to insure the utmost secrecy, as if the Germans realize it they will stop. I reminded him of what he had said about his willingness not to disrupt the Austro-Hungarian Empire by the loss of its older units Hungary and Bohemia. He repeated what I reported in my above mentioned telegram on that subject.      Page.

T telegram (SDR, RG 59, 763.72119/8266, DNA).


## Franklin Knight Lane to George Whitfield Lane

Dear George,          Washington, February 20, [1917]

Another Cabinet meeting and no light yet on what our policy will be as to Germany. We evidently are waiting for the "overt act," which I think Germany will not commit. We are all, with the exception of one or two pro-Germans, feeling humiliated by the situation, but nothing can be done.

McAdoo brought up the matter of shipping being held in our ports. It appears that something more than half of the normal number of ships has gone out since February 1st, and they all seem to be getting over the first scare, because Germany is not doing more than her former amount of damage.

We were told of intercepted cables to the Wolfe News Agency, in Berlin, in which the American people were represented as being against war under any circumstances—sympathizing strongly with a neutrality that would keep all Americans off the seas. Thus does the Kaiser learn of American sentiment! No wonder he sizes us up as cowards! . . .                    F.K.L.

Printed in Lane and Wall, eds., *The Letters of Franklin K. Lane*, p. 238.

## To Key Pittman

My dear Senator:                    [The White House] 21 February, 1917

I wish I could follow my heart in the cases of Mr. Diggs and Mr. Caminetti, for my heart does ache for Mr. and Mrs. Caminetti, but I feel so strongly that all the virtue there is in the Mann Act would go out of it if I exercised executive clemency in this case that I am obliged to harden my heart and do nothing.

I am sure that you will sympathize with me and will know how to understand my action.

Always
                    Cordially and faithfully yours,    Woodrow Wilson

TLS (Letterpress Books, WP, DLC).

## To William Joel Stone

My dear Senator:                    The White House 21 February, 1917

Thank you warmly for your letter of February twentieth.[1]

Rather than to keep you waiting, I asked Mr. Forster to tell you over the 'phone yesterday that I was quite willing that you should give my letter to you about the Colombia treaty publicity along with a statement of your own.

Changing the subject for a minute, let me say that the papers were entirely wrong in saying that I went up to the Capitol the other day to consult the Senators about an extra session.[2] I went

up on a miscellany of small errands with individual Senators, and
that question was discussed merely in passing.

In haste, with warm regard,

Faithfully yours,    Woodrow Wilson

TLS (RG 46, Records of the U. S. Senate, Senate 64B-B1, DNA).
  [1] W. J. Stone to WW, Feb. 20, 1917, TLS (WP, DLC).
  [2] Late Saturday afternoon, February 17.


## To Henry French Hollis

My dear Senator:              [The White House] 21 February, 1917

Thank you for your letter of the nineteenth.

At my request, the Secretary of Labor is sending to Senator
Newlands the draft of a bill which is drawn in the spirit of the
whole body of organized workers and if Senator Newlands can
let you see that bill, I would be very much obliged if you would
read it and form a judgment as to how nearly it meets the views
expressed to you by the heads of the brotherhoods, before you
and I have the conference which you suggest and which I should
welcome.

Cordially and sincerely yours,    Woodrow Wilson

TLS (Letterpress Books, WP, DLC).


## From Walter Hines Page

London, Feb. 21, 1917.

5725.    The following is strictly private for the President and
the Secretary only:

My 5714 February twentieth. There are two facts that might
have been and perhaps ought to have been emphasized more
strongly in that telegram. One is the Prime Minister's fear of
publicity. I assured him that extraordinary precautions would be
taken. The other fact is the earnestness with which any proposal
officially received will be considered.

The Prime Minister's first mood has been completely changed,
it was shared and urged as nearly as I can find out chiefly by
* * * * but the Navy in particular and presumably the Army are
anxious to cause the possible detachment of Austria Hungary
and their pressure I believe changed the Prime Minister's first
view.

If this can be accomplished they will expect a very much

earlier end of the war. Your efforts will be fully and generously appreciated.                                    Page.

* * * * Undecipherable groups. Repetition requested.

T telegram (R. Lansing Papers, NjP).


## From Robert Lansing, with Enclosure

Returned to me by Prest.
3 pm Feby 22/17 RL.

PERSONAL AND PRIVATE:

My dear Mr. President:           Washington February 21, 1917.

I enclose a memorandum which I have prepared on the subject of arming merchant vessels, with particular reference to the question of supplying guns and trained men to American vessels visiting the "danger zone." The memorandum also includes a brief reference to the conflict of right, duty and expediency which it seems to me must be considered in determining upon a definite policy.            Faithfully yours,    Robert Lansing.

The Prest said to me that I did not include [in] the memo. a course of action. I told him that I had not intended to do so, that I wished to lay before him my conception of the principles involved and the questions which were raised in my mind by the situation, but that the question of right policy lay with him.
RL Feby 22/17.[1]

TLS (SDR, RG 59, 763.72/3468½, DNA).
[1] RLhw.

MEMORANDUM ON THE ARMING OF MERCHANT VESSELS.

February 20, 1917.

The arming of merchant vessels of belligerent nationality and the arming of merchant vessels of neutral nationality rest rest [sic] upon two different principles.

A belligerent merchant vessel's right to carry an armament and to employ it in resisting attack by an enemy ship arises primarily from the fact that a merchant vessel and its cargo are under the recognized rules of naval warfare proper prize of an enemy who may seize and confiscate them. As the vessel is not under the direct protection of the armed forces of its government when traversing the high seas, it may rightfully defend itself from seizure and thus attempt to prevent its owner from suffering a total loss by reason of its capture. If the rule as to private property on the high seas was the same as that applicable to private property on land so that it would be immune from confiscation without just indemnity, it is probable that forcible resistance would be declared to be illegal; but as long as the present rule of prize exists the right of defense cannot justly be denied to a belligerent merchant vessel.

A neutral merchant vessel's right to carry and use an armament arises primarily from two facts, first, the defenseless character of a commercial vessel, and second, that, as a rule, there is no protection furnished by a government to its merchant vessels on the high seas against piracy or any other form of lawlessness imperiling human life. It is manifestly impossible for a government to give full protection to its merchant marine in all parts of the globe and, therefore, its merchant vessels are warranted in being prepared against lawless attacks and in resisting lawless assailants. It is the same primitive law of self-defense that justifies an individual in arming and defending himself from a highwayman in a region which is known to be without police protection.

Neutral property on the high seas is by the laws of naval warfare immune from confiscation by a belligerent unless it has through the voluntary act of the owner become tainted with enemy character. Against the exercise of the belligerent right of visit and search to determine the character of its cargo a neutral merchant vessel has no right to resist by force, since if it is engaged in innocent trade it cannot lawfully be seized and confiscated. If, however, a neutral merchant vessel is attacked by methods which ignore the rule of visit and search, the immunity of innocent cargoes, and the safety of human life, it possesses the right of self-defense whether the lawless attack is made by a public or a private ship. The essential element of this right of defense is the duty, as well as the right, to protect human life, the protection of the property being incidental and subordinate to the more important object. As to the loss of innocent neutral property, whether it be vessels or cargoes, there is an adequate remedy through the enforcement by diplomatic or judicial processes of indemnities.

If an illegal attack is made upon a neutral merchant vessel under the direct order of a belligerent government, the primitive right of self-defense ought not by reason of that fact to be annulled or abridged. To deny the right of resistance in such circumstances would amount to legalizing illegality and to subordinating neutral right of safety to life on the high seas to the arbitrary will of belligerents.

If the orders issued by a belligerent government to its naval vessels are flagrantly in violation of the laws of naval warfare which give protection to the lives of neutrals traversing the high seas in neutral bottoms (not to mention belligerent merchantmen) and if, by notifying neutral governments that "all ships within" a certain portion of the high seas "will be sunk," the threat is made that neutral ships and cargo will be destroyed without regard for the safety of the persons on board the vessels, there would seem to be no valid reason for a neutral government to refuse to allow its merchant vessels to carry armaments and to use them to defend themselves from the lawless attacks threatened. To compel a merchant vessel to proceed on its voyage without means of defense, when it is notorious that the laws of naval warfare protective of human life will be disregarded by a belligerent, would come near to making the neutral government an accessory in the crime and in any event encourage the offending government to continue with free hand its reprehensible practices. It would seem to be the duty of a neutral government to give full sanction to and to advise its merchant vessels to arm and resist illegal attacks of such nature.

With the right of a neutral merchant vessel to arm and to use its armament to protect the lives of the persons on board if lawlessly attacked, the question arises as to the duty of a neutral government to provide the guns and gun crews necessary to equip its merchant vessels for defense against the announced illegal purposes of a belligerent.

This question viewed from the standpoint of abstract right offers little difficulty as there can be no doubt but that a government should defend, if it is able, its merchant vessels on the high seas from all forms of outlawry and particularly so if the lives of the persons on the vessels are imperilled. The practical means would be to furnish an armament and trained men to man it. Such a course would be based on the same principle as convoy except that the vessel would be subject to the belligerent right of visit and search. However, if a belligerent government gave notice which in effect amounted to a declaration that the right of visit and search would not be exercised, the very presence of a belligerent armed vessel would be a menace to human life, and warrant the use of an armament to ward off attack.

From the standpoint of expediency the question can be less readily answered. A belligerent government having announced its purpose to employ lawless methods of attack against all vessels regardless of nationality or of the safety of the persons on board, might consider resistance by an armament furnished by a neutral government and served by gunners from its navy to be a hostile act amounting to a *casus belli*. It would certainly entail a certain measure of danger of creating a state of war between the neutral and the belligerent.

On the other hand if the purpose of the announced policy of lawlessness is to prevent by threats as well as by force neutral vessels from entering a certain zone on the high seas which they have a right to traverse in safety, the failure to provide arms and trained men for defense would accomplish that purpose, if unarmed vessels should refrain from entering the zone on account of fear of the threats made and especially if they could not obtain an efficient armament from other sources than the government.

Where the duty of a neutral government lies in such circumstances is not entirely clear. The right to aid its merchant vessels to protect the lives of the persons on board while traversing the high seas seems certain, but if the exercise of the right is a menace to the peace of the nation ought the right to be exercised? If refraining from the exercise of the right encourages lawlessness and accomplishes the purpose of the lawbreaker ought it not to be exercised? If the failure to exercise the right increases the peril to human life and prevents neutrals from entering certain portions of the high seas through fear of lawless attacks should the neutral government exercise its right if by so doing it will lessen the peril and remove the fear of travelers?

In dealing with a situation in which a neutral government's obligations are manifestly complex and conflicting it is necessary to have in mind the maintenance of rights, the national honor and prestige, the future consequences of resistance or of non-resistance to lawless acts from the domestic as well as the foreign standpoint, the probability of a state of war resulting in any event, whatever policy is adopted, the effect of a severance of diplomatic relations upon the probable outcome, the expediency of awaiting an actual loss of life before acting, the effect of delay of action upon domestic popular support, the effect of immediate action upon the public mind, the effect of non-action upon the commerce and industry of the neutral, these and other subjects should be carefully considered and weighed before a policy is determined upon.                                    Robert Lansing.

TS MS (SDR, RG 59, 763.72/3468½, DNA).

# From Robert Lansing, with Enclosure

My dear Mr. President,          Washington February 21, 1917.

I enclose a draft of telegram to Ambassador Penfield in line with our conversation over the telephone today. I have avoided any mention of the submission of a peace commission proposal as it seems to me it would be advisable to try out the temper of the Austrian Government before going as far as that.

As the Department is closed tomorrow I will be at my house.

Faithfully yours,   Robert Lansing.

Handed to me by the Prest. Feby 22/17 together with telegram corrected. RL

ALS (R. Lansing Papers, NjP).

E N C L O S U R E[1]

Approved by Prest
and handed to me at
3 pm Feby 22/17.   RL

Department of State, Feby 22, 1917. 5 P.M.

*Strictly confidential* for the Ambassador to decipher.

(Paragraph). When there is opportunity for you to see the Minister of Foreign Affairs alone you may say to him, provided the occasion seems suitable, that you have received information from the highest authority which convinces you that in arranging terms of peace the Allied Governments have no desire or purpose to disrupt the Austro-Hungarian Empire by the separation of Hungary and Bohemia from Austria unless a continuance of the war causes a change of conditions; that undoubtedly a definite assurance of this might be obtained through this Government, if the Austrian Government (indicated a desire) *indicating a desire for an early peace, wished* that you *should* act secretly to that end; and that you would be pleased to convey to this Government any comments, suggestions or proposals in regard to this subject which the Austrian Government may be pleased to make, it being understood that whatever exchanges may take place will be treated in the strictest confidence.

(Paragraph). You should make it perfectly clear to the Minister of Foreign Affairs before making the foregoing statement that you are about to give him information of the most confidential character and that you rely upon him to prevent it from becoming known for if it should through mischance become public or reach any other government you would be compelled to repudiate it.

(Paragraph) In view of the secrecy which should be preserved in this matter you will in no circumstances commit anything you may say to writing or permit any notes to be made in your presence. You may however, if you wish, show this telegram to Grew[2] impressing upon him the importance of absolute secrecy.

(Paragraph) The President relies upon you to use the greatest discretion in this delicate negotiation and hopes that you may soon be able to report in strict confidence the result of your interview.                                    Lansing.[3]

Hw MS (SDR, RG 59, 763.72119/10094a, DNA).
[1] Words in angle brackets deleted by Wilson; words in italics added by Wilson.
[2] Joseph C. Grew, following his departure from Berlin, had just taken up a new assignment as Counselor of the embassy in Vienna.
[3] This telegram is printed in FR-WWS 1917, I, 57-58.


## From Robert Lansing, with Enclosure

Dear Mr. President:        Washington February 22, 1917.

I have the honor to enclose herewith a copy of a wireless message which was received by the Navy Department through the Commander of the American war vessel at Santiago and sent by the American Consul at that port.

Will you be good enough to give me such directions as you may desire concerning the reply to be made to this telegram.

I am, my dear Mr. President,
                Very sincerely yours,    Robert Lansing.

TLS (WP, DLC).


ENCLOSURE

February 21, 1917.

The below quoted despatch relative to the present condition here is forwarded to President Wilson on the request of the entire Chamber of Commerce of this city, Quote: Honorable President of the United States, Washington, D. C. The military authorities that effected the coup d'etat on the twelfth instant and rule this capital have maintained complete order guaranteeing thus far lives and property.[1] They endeavor also to reestablish the normal economic life but in order to accomplish this rapidly without the complete ruin of the present crop it is necessary in the judgment of the commercial and producers classes to have diplomatic mediation of your Government. With this object in view said commercial and producers elements assembled today in the Chamber of Commerce of this city unanimously resolved to solicit of you as a good friend of Cuba to interpose your good offices to obtain rapidly the desired end. If present conditions prevail immense damage and loss will surely be cause[d] that can be easily avoided by your timely mediation.

Santiago, February 20, 1917, Signed Badell, President, Jose Hall, Secretary. Unquote Griffiths, Consul.[2]

T telegram (WP, DLC).

[1] A few weeks earlier, on January 22, the American Minister in Havana, William Elliott Gonzales, had warned the State Department that the Cuban political situation was "critical and dangerous." The intense rivalry between the Conservative party of President Mario García Menocal and the Liberal party of Dr. Alfredo Zayas was likely to lead to a revolution even more bitter than the one of 1906. Lansing supported Gonzales in urging all parties to avoid the use of force, but the garrison at Santiago de Cuba seized the town government and arrested the governor and other officials on February 12 for not proceeding constitutionally in the conduct of contested elections. On the following day, General José Miguel Gómez, the former President of Cuba, a Liberal, was reported to be leading a force of several thousand rebels in Camaguey. On the basis of these and other reports, Lansing, also on February 13, instructed Gonzales to have the following statement published throughout Cuba:

"The Government of the United States has received with the greatest apprehension the reports which have come to it to the effect that there exists organized revolt against the Government of Cuba in several provinces and that several towns have been seized by insurrectionists.

"Reports such as these of insurrection against the constituted Government cannot be considered except as of the most serious nature since the Government of the United States has given its confidence and support only to Governments established through legal and constitutional methods.

"During the past four years the Government of the United States has clearly and definitely set forth its position in regard to the recognition of governments which have come into power through revolution and other illegal methods and at this time desires to emphasize its position in regard to the present situation in Cuba. Its friendship for the Cuban people, which has been shown on repeated occasions, and the duties which are incumbent upon it on account of the agreement between the two countries force the Government of the United States to make clear its future policy at this time." RL to W. E. Gonzales, Feb. 13, 1917, FR 1917, p. 356.

A special dispatch of February 13 to the New York Times reported that Wilson and his advisers were awaiting developments in Cuba before taking further action and that Gonzales had been instructed to report any further events promptly so that, if American intervention became necessary under the provisions of the Platt Amendment, this could be carried out promptly and efficiently. Tentative plans were being made by the United States Army to send 5,000 to 7,000 troops to Cuba, if needed, New York Times, Feb. 14, 1917.

Lansing, after further consultations with Wilson, on February 18 sent another telegram to Gonzales, which read in part:

"1. The Government of the United States supports and sustains the Constitutional Government of the Republic of Cuba.

"2. The armed revolt against the Constitutional Government of Cuba is considered by the Government of the United States as a lawless and unconstitutional act and will not be countenanced.

"3. The leaders of the revolt will be held responsible for injury to foreign nationals and for destruction of foreign property.

"4. The Government of the United States will give careful consideration to its future attitude towards those persons connected with and concerned in the present disturbance of peace in the Republic of Cuba." RL to W. E. Gonzales, Feb. 18, 1917, *FR 1917*, p. 363. Gonzales was instructed to make this telegram public.

2 Pearl Merrill Griffith.

## From Walter Hines Page

Dear Mr. President:                                    London. 22 Feb. 1917.

I telegraphed so fully about my interviews with Lloyd George concerning a possible Austrian peace proposal that I need write only certain minor illuminative incidents. At my first interview I expressed my astonishment at his conclusion—that Austria was a greater hindrance to Germany as an ally than she would be as a neutral. To my arguments he simply repeated his conclusion—with amazing rapidity. The most hopeful thing that I could then induce him to say was that he wd. take some of his associates into his confidence and tell me when there was anything more to say. But on top of this he forbade me to mention the subject to any members of the government "for the present." That for the time being baulked me. It was as if an Ambassador at Washington had taken up a subject with you, had got your answer and had askd. leave to discuss it with members of your Cabinet. If you had said 'No,' he wd. of course have been silenced on the penalty of forfeiting your confidence, if he had gone further. It occurred to me, then, that perhaps I had made a mistake in going to him first. Yet any other course wd. have been discourteous to him after his request that I shd. take up with him informal subjects of high importance; for he is practically Dictator. All that was left me to do was to pursue him relentlessly since I cd. pursue nobody else—or to give it up; and I had no idea of resting with the answer he had given me.

The very next day I had what seemed a piece of good luck. I was invited by a member of the Government to dinner a few evenings later—"the Prime Minister will come." After dinner I talked again with Lloyd George. "Nothing to say further yet," he said. "I haven't had a chance to go over the subject with the men I had in mind." Then I got up a little dinner myself for him, to which I invited the Jellicoes, the Bryces and several other couples of high degree. Again I askd. him "What news?" He shook his head. I took him aside and remarked on the ease with which great men and great governments make great mistakes. Lloyd George is perhaps the easiest man to talk with (not necessarily to convince) of all men that hold high places. He has little dignity.

He has no presence, except as an orator. He swears familiarly on easy occasion. But he has as quick a mind and as ready speech as any man that I ever encountered. It is impossible to realize that his casual deliverances are the Voice of the British Empire. After more talk, in which he had injected an oath or two, I made bold to say, "Good God! Prime Minister, have you forgotten that the whole object of the war is to reduce Europe to peace, and here may be peace that you are rejecting—how do you know?" But I got no satisfactory response. This was my third interview.

I still refused to believe that this was to be the end of the matter.—Now queer accidents happen when you keep steadily on one quest and see many people and hear much talk; and by accident I found out that Curzon was opposed to discussing peace with anybody and had talked with the Prime Minister and that Jellicoe was eager for peace with Austria and had not been able to talk with the Prime Minister on the subject. That very night I dined with Lord Salisbury. Lady Curzon was there—without Lord Curzon. Lady Curzon, by the way, married just a month to his Vice-Regal Pomp, began her amazing life as an Alabama girl[1] and you can yet distinguish the Alabama intonations in her speech as you now and then hear the oboe in an orchestra. She married an Argentine fortune and a year or two ago buried her husband,[2] drink having killed him, and, knowing Curzon's weakness for rich American women, proceeded to capture him and thus become a Countess. ["]Where's your husband?" I askd. her. "He had to spend the evening with the Prime Minister." That sounded somewhat discouraging.

The next day was Sunday. I recalled that Admiral Jellicoe left his ceaseless watch at the Admiralty every Sunday afternoon at five o'clock and went home to meet his friends at tea. At five o'clock, therefore, Mrs. Page and I were there to pay our respects. I cd. not yet mention the subject to the Admiral, but I gave him a chance to mention it to me. Not a word did he say about it. He told me only that fishing (for submarines) was pretty good—that's all.

A full week had passed and I had got no further than I had got at my first interview. I resolved to go and see the Prime Minister again at his office. I rehearsed my arguments, which seemed to me irrefutable and I was determined to fight to the last ditch. To my surprise, he yielded at once—gracefully, easily, almost unbidden. He had somewhat modified his views, he said—provided, provided, provided the greatest secrecy could be maintained. By this emphasis he gave me the cue to his thought and mood.

The German proposal of a peace-conference a little while ago, which, because no terms were named, was regarded by the British as a trick, steeled the nation and the Government in particular against all peace-talk till the Spring campaign and the submarine war decide something. The very word 'peace' was banished from the English vocabulary. Lloyd George himself in several speeches had declared that there could yet be no peace —no thought of peace. This was his state of mind when I first brought up the subject and the state of mind of the nation. Peacemen had been hooted in the House of Commons and suspected peace-meetings had been dispersed by the police. His emphasis on secrecy made his fear plain. No doubt if he cd. announce Austria's surrender, that wd. be a great stroke. But if it got abroad that he were "dickering" with Austria or anybody else about peace, he wd. lose his Dictatorship over night. He was afraid of the subject. But having discussed this particular possibility of eliminating Austria, with some of his colleagues, he "had somewhat changed his view."

I feel the necessity to be on my guard with Lloyd George. Perhaps I do him wrong. Of course his political enemies (and he has many and fierce enemies) say that he is tricky and untruthful. They are not good witnesses: no doubt their judgment is unfair. But he is changeable—mercurial. He reaches quick conclusions by his emotions as well as by his reason—he reasons with his emotions. He has been called the illiterate Prime Minister, "because he never reads nor writes." He is the one public man in the Kingdom who has an undoubted touch of genius. He has also the defects of genius. He has vision and imagination, and his imagination at times runs away with him. That's the reason he's the most interesting man here—an amazing spectacle to watch. He compels admiration but does not compel complete confidence. I wish I instinctively had the same unquestioning and unshakable confidence in him that I have in Edward Grey whose genius is all the genius of character. A Scotch friend of Lloyd George was defending him the other night in a little group of men who expressed fear of his emotional adventures, and one of them asked about his truthfulness. "Oh, he's truthful— perfectly truthful. But a Scotchman's truth is a straight line. A Welshman's is more or less of a curve." But how this Kingdom has waked up under his leadership! There's something ramshackle and slipshod about him and his ways and his thought. But he has organized England, man-power, pound-power, mind-power, will-power, as perhaps no man ever did before.

The situation, therefore, so far as the mood of this Govern-

ment is concerned, is just as good as it wd. have been if the Prime
Minister had given the answer we wanted when I first brought
the subject to him—only a week was lost because of this extraordinary man's extraordinary mood and of his extraordinary
attitude to me whereby he had me bound to secrecy on pain of
becoming a traitor to him; and his extraordinary attitude to me
comes of his admiration for you and from his wish to have
you at the Conference that will make peace.

Now, of course, I have talked with others. Mr. Balfour is
eager to see a proposal from Austria, provided he can believe
it to be a genuine proposal. He and others have some fear of the
hand of Germany in it—fear that it may be a trick. But the answer
that the Prime Minister gave me at my last interview is the
answer of the Government. They will give thorough and appreciative attention to any proposal that come.

Very heartily Yours,   Walter H. Page

ALS (WP, DLC).
 1 Grace Elvina Trillia Hinds Duggan Curzon, Lady Curzon, originally from
Decatur, Ala.
 2 Alfred Duggan, who had been the owner of a large ranch in Argentina.


## From Robert Lansing, with Enclosures

PERSONAL AND PRIVATE:

My dear Mr. President:          Washington February 23, 1917.

I told you yesterday of a conversation which I have had with
the Swiss Minister in regard to the overture of Germany looking
toward further negotiations. I enclose to you a copy of a
memorandum of the conversation which I had with him.

Faithfully yours,   Robert Lansing.

TLS (WP, DLC).


E N C L O S U R E     I

MEMORANDUM OF CONVERSATION WITH THE SWISS MINISTER.

February 21, 1917.

The Swiss Minister called this afternoon and after attending
to some other matters I told him that I was perplexed by a
statement regarding the overture which he had sent to me on
Sunday the 11th on behalf of Germany. I then read to him the
annexed telegram received from Berne. He listened very intently
and when I had concluded I said: "It would appear, Mr. Minister,

that the overture was suggested originally by you. Is that correct?"

The Minister appeared very nervous and after some hesitation said: "I will tell you the whole story." He then proceeded to relate in substance the following:

Diplomatic relations were broken off on Saturday, February 3rd. On Monday, the 5th, Count Bernstorff telephoned him that Dr. Kirchwey was coming to see him (Dr. Ritter) with a message to be sent through Berne to Berlin and that he approved of the message. Dr. Kirchwey called to see him and showed him the wireless message which had been sent by Bartelme and asked him to send identically the same message to Berlin via Berne. Dr. Ritter replied that he had not yet been authorized to act for the German Embassy and in any event he could see no use in repeating the same suggestions already made by wireless. He finally agreed to send a message stating that "with the approval of Bernstorff" he suggested some steps toward negotiations being taken along the lines of the Bartelme message and asking his government to repeat the suggestion to Berlin.

Either on Friday evening, the 9th, or Saturday morning following, (I am not sure which time he gave) he received the communication, the substance of which was in the paper which he sent me Sunday evening, the 11th. It came from his Government which transmitted it from Berlin. About ten o'clock on Saturday morning, the 10th, he showed the message or gave a copy of it to Prince Hatzfeldt.[1] About noon Draper[2] of the Associated Press called to see him stating that he had the substance of the overture for negotiations which he (Ritter) had received. Draper repeated what he had learned and the Minister saw that Draper did in fact have the substance, though Draper assured him that he had not obtained it from Bernstorff. The Minister was convinced that Hatzfeldt had told Draper.

The next that the Minister knew of the matter was that he read a statement in regard to the message in the afternoon paper on Saturday, and as he had made an appointment to see Mr. Polk at six o'clock that evening he determined to present the overture orally to him, which he did, and after Mr. Polk had communicated the substance to me, he, upon Mr. Polk's stating on Sunday morning that I wished him to put it in writing, did so and sent it to me that afternoon.

Upon the completion of his narrative, which was told in a disjointed and nervous way, and was rather hard to follow, I said to him: "So, Mr. Minister, this plan of an overture originated here in Washington?"

"Yes," he answered, "it was all done with the approval of Count Bernstorff."

"Dr. Kirchwey appears to have acted as his agent in this matter," I said.

"Yes," he replied, "Count Bernstorff asked me by telephone to send a message, which Dr. Kirchwey would come and see me about. I found it just like the Bartelme wireless message so another was made suggesting following the advice in that message." The Minister said further he would show me the original, and something about a memorandum or paper in Bernstorff's handwriting. I did not understand and obtained no further light although I questioned the Minister about it. I did not press the matter as I feared that it might arouse suspicions in his mind and prevent his showing me the original papers.

The Minister said, on taking his leave, that now that he had fully explained the matter he hoped that no blame could be attached to him and that he wished I would find it possible to let the newspapers know that he had not acted improperly. I told him that if he would show me the originals I had no doubt some statement could be made. He repeated that he would bring me the papers.                                                      Robert Lansing

CC MS (WP, DLC).
  1 Hermann, Prince von Hatzfeldt-Trachenberg, Second Counselor of the German embassy in Washington.
  2 Norman Draper, correspondent for the Associated Press.


E N C L O S U R E    I I

Berne, Feb. 19, 1917.

545. Highly confidential.

The press of the French speaking cantons of Switzerland has criticised the Swiss Minister at Washington for his activities in behalf of the German offer to secure, without withdrawing thr [the] threat of indiscriminate submarine warfare, a renewal of diplomatic relations with the United States. The basis of these criticisms is that it is not clear that Doctor Ritter's proposal originated with the German Government in the form in which it was presented by him. A semi-official communique issued yesterday in Berne reads as follows: "The steps taken by Minister Ritter at Washington tending to a renewal of negotiations between the German Government and that of the United States have been undertaken without instructions from the Swiss

Federal Council or from the Political Department. It will be readily understood that no explanations can be given at Berne as to correspondence between Berlin and Washington which the Federal authorities only transmit without naturally taking any responsibility whatsoever."

The German Government has issued through Wolff Bureau the following official communique regarding these pourparlers. This communique has been widely published in the neutral press of Europe and reads as follows: "The press has printed a Reuter's agency dispatch stating that the Berlin Government had requested Switzerland to inform the Washington Government that Germany remained disposed to negotiate with the United States in regard to the note establishing the blockade and the submarine war provided that the commercial blockade ordered against England were not interfered with by these pourparlers. The Reuter's Agency dispatch adds that the Government of the United States then communicated to Mr. Ritter, Swiss Minister at Washington, that it could not begin negotiations before Germany had renewed its promises made after the SUSSEX affair and had withdrawn its decision concerning the aggravation of the submarine war.

The following are the true facts upon which the Reuter's agency dispatch is based: The Swiss Government transmitted to the German Government a telegram from the Swiss Minister at Washington offering, if Germany consented, to serve as intermediary in pourparlers with the American Government in regard to the declaration of the blockade, as the danger of a German-American war could in this way be diminished. The Swiss Government has been requested to inform its Minister at Washington that Germany remained as before disposed to negotiate with the United States on condition that the commercial blockade against its enemies—not only against England—were not jeopardized by these negotiations. It is, generally speaking, scarcely necessary to say that Germany could not enter into negotiations of this character before diplomatic relations had been reestablished between Germany and the United States. Moreover the object of these pourparlers must be limited exclusively to certain concessions regarding the transportation of American passengers in order that the stoppage of importations from abroad established against our enemies by means of unrestricted submarine warfare be not weakened in any way whatsoever, even if diplomatic relations should be reestablished. This was all clearly set out in its response to the Swiss Minister at Washington. As has already been repeated by official circles, Germany will not reconsider its resolution to completely stop by submarines all importations from abroad by its enemies.' "                    Stovall.

T telegram (WP, DLC).

# From Robert Lansing, with Enclosure

PERSONAL AND PRIVATE.

My dear Mr. President:          Washington February 23, 1917.

In compliance with your request of yesterday I send you a copy of the so-called "Logan Act" which has been re-enacted as section five of the FEDERAL PENAL CODE of March 4, 1909.

Faithfully yours,   Robert Lansing.

TLS (WP, DLC).


E N C L O S U R E

## SECTION 5 OF THE FEDERAL PENAL CODE.

*Section 5.* Every citizen of the United States, whether actually resident or abiding within the same, or in any place subject to the jurisdiction thereof, or in any foreign country, (who) without the permission or authority of the Government, directly or indirectly, commences or carries on any verbal or written correspondence or intercourse with any foreign government or any officer or agent thereof, with an intent to influence the measures or conduct of any foreign Government or of any officer or agent thereof, in relation to any disputes or controversies with the United States, or to defeat the measures of the Government of the United States; and every person, being a citizen of or resident within the United States or in any place subject to the jurisdiction thereof, and not duly authorized (who) counsels, advises, or assists in any such correspondence with such intent, shall be fined not more than five thousand dollars and imprisoned not more than three years; but nothing in this section shall be construed to abridge the right of a citizen to apply, himself or his agent, to any foreign government or the agents thereof for redress of any injury which he may have sustained from such government or any of its agents or subjects.

(Section 5 of Federal Penal Code of March 4, 1909.)

T MS (WP, DLC).

## From Newton Diehl Baker

My dear Mr. President:        Washington. February 23, 1917.

I beg to quote the following message addressed to you received today from Governor Yager at San Juan:

Please accept for myself and the people of Porto Rico our appreciation and gratitude for your efficient and indispensable aid in securing the passage of the Porto Rican Bill.[1] We shall all make every effort to show ourselves worthy of your confidence. With hearty thanks.   Arthur Yager.

Very sincerely,   Newton D. Baker

TLS (WP, DLC).

[1] The House of Representatives passed the Jones-Shafroth bill, a new organic act for Porto Rico, in its final form on February 24, and the Senate approved it two days later. The bill conferred United States citizenship upon all Porto Ricans as a body and gave them an opportunity to renounce such citizenship within six months. The measure also incorporated a bill of rights and provided for executive, legislative, and judicial departments of government similar in many respects to those of the United States. The Governor would be appointed by the President of the United States, with the advice and consent of the Senate, and a Resident Commissioner to the United States would be elected by the citizens of Porto Rico. Intoxicating drinks and drugs would be prohibited one year after the Act went into effect, but this prohibition was subject to repeal by the voters within five years if they so desired. Voters should be citizens of the United States twenty-one years of age or over and have such additional qualifications as the legislature of Porto Rico might prescribe, except that there could be no property qualification for voting. Wilson approved the measure on March 2, 1917, as Public Law 368 of the Sixty-fourth Congress. 39 *Statutes at Large*, 951.

## From Henry Lee Myers and James Duval Phelan

Dear Mr. President:        [Washington] February 23, 1917.

There is one chance of passing the Leasing bill—that is by an agreement of all parties on the relief feature for oil operators in the Naval Reserve.

We would be obliged if you would suggest to the Departments affected the desirability of considering a compromise amendment.        Respectfully yours,   H. L. Myers

James D Phelan

TLS (WP, DLC).

## Robert Lansing to Pearl Merrill Griffith

Washington, February 23, 1917.

Your telegram forwarding statement of Chamber of Commerce of Santiago, addressed to President Wilson received. The President has instructed me to direct you to make the following statement in reply.

Taking the oath for a second time

Delivering the second Inaugural

The return to the White House

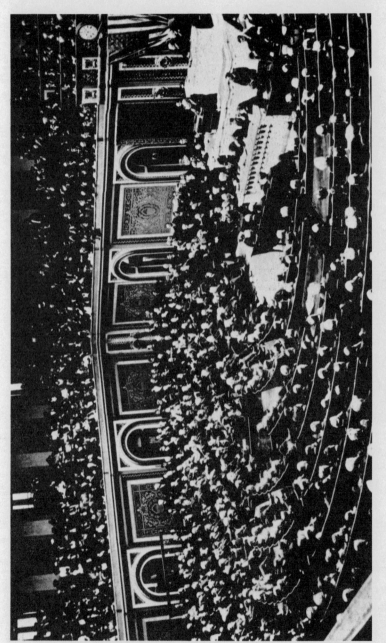

Delivering the War Message

The Government of the United States has clearly defined its position in the present armed rebellion against the Constitutional Government of Cuba and it will attribute any disturbance of economic conditions or ruin of crops to the action of those in rebellion against the Government. Moreover, it cannot hold communication with leaders of this rebellion while they are under arms against the Constitutional Government. No other question except the reestablishment of order throughout the Republic through the return of those in rebellion to faithful allegiance to the Government can be considered under the existing conditions.

The Government of the United States, as has been made known to the people of Cuba, will support only constitutional methods for the settlement of disputes and will exert every means in its power as the friend of the Cuban Republic, to effect such settlement, but, until those persons who have revolted against the Government lay down their arms, declare allegiance to their Government and return to peaceful pursuits, the Government of the United States can take no further step.   Lansing[1]

Printed in *FR 1917*, p. 366.

[1] This telegram and others relating to the crisis in Cuba were removed from the State Department files on January 9, 1943, by George M. Fennemore of the Division of Research and Publication of that department and were not returned.

## To William Gibbs McAdoo, with Enclosure

My dear Mac.,              The White House. 24 February, 1917.

Here is the language I suggest for all but the formal part of the Act or Joint Resolution, we discussed this morning. All that it needs is the addition of a provision as to the method by which the money is to be raised. Will you not get into touch with Burleson about it to get his advice as an old parliamentary hand, who knows the technicalities and the pitfalls?

Affectionately Yours,   W.W.

WWTLI (W. G. McAdoo Papers, DLC).

### ENCLOSURE

That the President of the United States be and is hereby authorized and empowered to supply merchant ships the property of citizens of the United States and bearing American registry with defensive arms, should it in his judgment become necessary for him to do so, and also with the necessary am[m]unition and means of making use of them in defence against unlawful attack; and that he be and is hereby authorized and empowered to employ any other methods that may in his judgment and discretion seem necessary and adequate to protect such ships and the citizens of the United States in their lawful and peaceful pursuits on the high seas.

The sum of one hundred million dollars is hereby appropriated to be expended by the President of the United States for the purposes herein stated; and also for the purpose of supplying adequate funds for the insurance of such ships against the risks of the present state of war (or whatever the phrase was in the existing war risk insurance act)[1]

WWT MS (W. G. McAdoo Papers, DLC).
[1] Following Wilson's address to Congress on February 26, printed at that date, Chairman Flood of the Foreign Affairs Committee introduced in the House of Representatives a bill which incorporated much of the first paragraph of this draft, appropriated $100,000,000 for defensive arms and for the Bureau of War Risk Insurance, and authorized the Treasury to borrow on the credit of the United States and to issue bonds up to the full amount appropriated. The text of the first paragraph was revised so as to authorize the President to "employ such other instrumentalities and methods as may in his judgment and discretion seem necessary and adequate to protect such ships and the citizens of the United States in their lawful and peaceful pursuits on the high seas." McAdoo had given copies of the draft to Flood and to Chairman Stone of the Foreign Relations Committee, who introduced a similar bill in the Senate. *New York Times*, Feb. 27, 1917. For information on the situation in Congress, see Link, *Campaigns for Progressivism and Peace*, p. 349.

## From Walter Hines Page

London, Feb. 24, 1917.

5747. My fifty-seven forty-six, February 24, 8 a.m.

CONFIDENTIAL. FOR THE PRESIDENT AND THE SECRETARY OF STATE.

Balfour has handed me the text of a cipher telegram from Zimmermann, German Secretary of State for Foreign Affairs, to the German Minister to Mexico,[1] which was sent via Washington and relayed by Bernstorff on January nineteenth. You can probably obtain a copy of the text relayed by Bernstorff from the cable office in Washington. The first group is the number of the telegram, one hundred and thirty, and the second is thirteen thousand and forty-two, indicating the number of the code used. The last group but two is ninety-seven thousand five hundred and fifty-six, which is Zimmerman's signature. I shall send you by mail a copy of the cipher text and of the de-code into German and meanwhile I give you the English translation as follows:

"We intend to begin on the first of February unrestricted submarine warfare. We shall endeavor in spite of this to keep the United States of America neutral. In the event of this not succeeding, we make Mexico a proposal of alliance on the following basis: make war together, make peace together, generous financial support and an understanding on our part that Mexico is to reconquer the lost territory in Texas, New Mexico, and Arizona. The settlement in detail is left to you. You will inform the President of the above most secretly as soon as the outbreak of war with the United States of America is certain and add the suggestion that he should, on his own initiative, invite Japan to immediate adherence and at the same time mediate between Japan and ourselves. Please call the President's attention to the fact that the ruthless employment of our submarines now offers the prospect of compelling England in a few months to make peace. Signed, ZIMMERMANN."

The receipt of this information has so greatly exercised the British Government that they have lost no time in communicating it to me to transmit to you, in order that our Government may be able without delay to make such disposition as may be necessary in view of the threatened invasion of our territory.

The following paragraph is strictly confidential.

Early in the war, the British Government obtained possession of a copy of the German cipher code used in the above message and have made it their business to obtain copies of Bernstorff's cipher telegrams to Mexico, amongst others, which are sent back to London and deciphered here. This accounts for their being able to decipher this telegram from the German Government to their representative in Mexico and also for the delay from January nineteenth until now in their receiving the information. This system has hitherto been a jealously guarded secret and is only divulged now to you by the British Government in view of the extraordinary circumstances and their friendly feeling towards the United States. They earnestly request that you will keep the source of your information and the British Government's method of obtaining it profoundly secret but they put no prohibition on the publication of Zimmermann's telegram itself.

The copies of this and other telegrams were not obtained in Washington but were bought in Mexico.

I have thanked Balfour for the service his Government has rendered us and suggest that a private official message of thanks from our Government to him would be beneficial.

I am informed that this information has not yet been given to the Japanese Government but I think it not unlikely that when it reaches them they may make a public statement on it in order to clear up their position regarding the United States and prove their good faith to their allies.                    Page.

T telegram (SDR, RG 59, 862.20212/69, DNA).
¹ Heinrich von Eckhardt.


## Franklin Knight Lane to George Whitfield Lane

My dear George,                    Washington, February 25, 1917

On Friday we had one of the most animated sessions of the Cabinet that I suppose has ever been held under this or any other President. It all arose out of a very innocent question of mine as to whether it was true that the wives of American Consuls on leaving Germany had been stripped naked, given an acid bath to detect writing on their flesh, and subjected to other indignities. Lansing answered that it was true. Then I asked Houston about the bread riots in New York, as to whether there was shortage of food because of car shortage due to vessels not going out with exports. This led to a discussion of the great problem which we all had been afraid to raise—Why shouldn't we send our ships out with guns or convoys? Daniels said we must not convoy—that would be dangerous. (Think of a Secretary of the Navy talking of danger!) The President said that the country was not willing that we should take any risks of war. I said that I got no such sentiment out of the country, but if the country knew that our Consuls' wives had been treated so outrageously that there would be no question as to the sentiment. This, the President took as a suggestion that we should work up a propaganda of hatred against Germany. Of course, I said I had no such idea, but that I felt that in a Democracy the people were entitled to know the facts. McAdoo, Houston, and Redfield joined me. The President turned on them bitterly, especially on McAdoo, and reproached all of us with appealing to the spirit of the *Code Duello*. We couldn't get the idea out of his head that we were bent on pushing the country into war. Houston talked of resigning after the meeting. McAdoo will—within a year, I believe. I tried to smooth them down by recalling our past experiences with the President. We have had to push, and push, and push, to get him to take any forward step— the Trade Commission, the Tariff Commission. He comes out right but he is slower than a glacier—and things are mighty disagreeable, whenever anything has to be done.

Now he is being abused by the Republicans for being slow, and this will probably help a bit, though it may make him more obstinate. He wants no extra session, and the Republicans fear that he will submit to anything in the way of indignity or national humiliation without "getting back," so they are standing for an extra session. The President believes, I think, that the munitions makers are back of the Republican plan. But I doubt this. They simply want to have a "say"; and the President wants to be alone and unbothered. He probably would not call Cabinet meetings if Congress adjourned. Then I would go to Honolulu, where the land problem vexes.

I don't know whether the President is an internationalist or a pacifist, he seems to be very mildly national—his patriotism is covered over with a film of philosophic humanitarianism, that certainly doesn't make for "punch" at such a time as this.

My love to you old man,—do write me oftener and tell me if you get all my letters.                                          F.K.L.

Printed in Lane and Wall, eds., *The Letters of Franklin K. Lane*, pp. 239-41.


## An Address to a Joint Session of Congress

26 Feb'y, 1917—1 P.M.[1]

Gentlemen of the Congress: I have again asked the privilege of addressing you because we are moving through critical times during which it seems to me to be my duty to keep in close touch with the Houses of Congress, so that neither counsel nor action shall run at cross purposes between us.

On the third of February I officially informed you of the sudden and unexpected action of the Imperial German Government in declaring its intention to disregard the promises it had made to this Government in April last and undertake immediate submarine operations against all commerce, whether of belligerents or of neutrals, that should seek to approach Great Britain and Ireland, the Atlantic coasts of Europe, or the harbours of the eastern Mediterranean, and to conduct those operations without regard to the established restrictions of international practice, without regard to any considerations of humanity even which might interfere with their object. That policy was forthwith put into practice. It has now been in active execution for nearly four weeks.

Its practical results are not yet fully disclosed. The commerce of other neutral nations is suffering severely, but not, perhaps, very much more severely than it was already suffering before the

[1] WWhw.

first of February, when the new policy of the Imperial Government was put into operation. We have asked the cooperation of the other neutral governments to prevent these depredations, but so far none of them has thought it wise to join us in any common course of action. Our own commerce has suffered, is suffering, rather in apprehension than in fact, rather because so many of our ships are timidly keeping to their home ports than because American ships have been sunk.

Two American vessels have been sunk, the *Housatonic* and the *Lyman M. Law*. The case of the *Housatonic*, which was carrying food stuffs consigned to a London firm, was essentially like the case of the *Fry*,[2] in which, it will be recalled, the German Government admitted its liability for damages, and the lives of the crew, as in the case of the *Fry*, were safeguarded with reasonable care. The case of the *Law*, which was carrying lemon-box staves to Palermo, disclosed a ruthlessness of method which deserves grave condemnation, but was accompanied by no circumstances which might not have been expected at any time in connection with the use of the submarine against merchantmen as the German Government has used it.

In sum, therefore, the situation we find ourselves in with regard to the actual conduct of the German submarine warfare against commerce and its effects upon our own ships and people is substantially the same that it was when I addressed you on the third of February, except for the tying up of our shipping in our own ports because of the unwillingness of our shipowners to risk their vessels at sea without insurance or adequate protection, and the very serious congestion of our commerce which has resulted, a congestion which is growing rapidly more and more serious every day. This in itself might presently accomplish, in effect, what the new German submarine orders were meant to accomplish, so far as we are concerned. We can only say, therefore, that the overt act which I have ventured to hope the German commanders would in fact avoid has not occurred.

But, while this is happily true, it must be admitted that there have been certain additional indications and expressions of purpose on the part of the German press and the German authorities which have increased rather than lessened the impression that, if our ships and our people are spared, it will be because of fortunate circumstances or because the commanders of the German submarines which they may happen to encounter exercise an unexpected discretion and restraint rather than because of

[2] She was, of course, *William P. Frye*, sunk by a German auxiliary cruiser on January 28, 1915.

the instructions under which those commanders are acting. It would be foolish to deny that the situation is fraught with the gravest possibilities and dangers. No thoughtful man can fail to see that the necessity for definite action may come at any time, if we are in fact, and not in word merely, to defend our elementary rights as a neutral nation. It would be most imprudent to be unprepared.

I cannot in such circumstance be unmindful of the fact that the expiration of the term of the present Congress is immediately at hand, by constitutional limitation; and that it would in all likelihood require an unusual length of time to assemble and organize the Congress which is to succeed it. I feel that I ought, in view of that fact, to obtain from you full and immediate assurance of the authority which I may need at any moment to exercise. No doubt I already possess that authority without special warrant of law, by the plain implication of my constitutional duties and powers; but I prefer, in the present circumstances, not to act upon general implication. I wish to feel that the authority and the power of the Congress are behind me in whatever it may become necessary for me to do. We are jointly the servants of the people and must act together and in their spirit, so far as we can divine and interpret it.

No one doubts what it is our duty to do. We must defend our commerce and the lives of our people in the midst of the present trying circumstances, with discretion but with clear and steadfast purpose. Only the method and the extent remain to be chosen, upon the occasion, if occasion should indeed arise. Since it has unhappily proved impossible to safeguard our neutral rights by diplomatic means against the unwarranted infringements they are suffering at the hands of Germany, there may be no recourse but to *armed* neutrality, which we shall know how to maintain and for which there is abundant American precedent.

It is devoutly to be hoped that it will not be necessary to put armed force anywhere into action. The American people do not desire it, and our desire is not different from theirs. I am sure that they will understand the spirit in which I am now acting, the purpose I hold nearest my heart and would wish to exhibit in everything I do. I am anxious that the people of the nations at war also should understand and not mistrust us. I hope that I need give no further proofs and assurances than I have already given throughout nearly three years of anxious patience that I am the friend of peace and mean to preserve it for America so long as I am able. I am not now proposing or contemplating war or any steps that need lead to it. I merely request that you will ac-

cord me by your own vote and definite bestowal the means and
the authority to safeguard in practice the right of a great people
who are at peace and who are desirous of exercising none but
the rights of peace to follow the pursuits of peace in quietness
and good will,—rights recognized time out of mind by all the
civilized nations of the world. No course of my choosing or of
theirs will lead to war. War can come only by the wilful acts and
aggressions of others.

You will understand why I can make no definite proposals or
forecasts of action now and must ask for your supporting authority in the most general terms. The form in which action may become necessary cannot yet be foreseen. I believe that the people
will be willing to trust me to act with restraint, with prudence,
and in the true spirit of amity and good faith that they have
themselves displayed throughout these trying months; and it is
in that belief that I request that you will authorize me to supply
our merchant ships with defensive arms, should that become
necessary, and with the means of using them, and to employ
any other instrumentalities or methods that may be necessary
and adequate to protect our ships and our people in their legitimate and peaceful pursuits on the seas. I request also that you
will grant me at the same time, along with the powers I ask, a
sufficient credit to enable me to provide adequate means of protection where they are lacking, including adequate insurance against
the present war risks.

I have spoken of our commerce and of the legitimate errands
of our people on the seas, but you will not be misled as to my
main thought, the thought that lies beneath these phrases and
gives them dignity and weight. It is not of material interests
merely that we are thinking. It is, rather, of fundamental human
rights, chief of all the right to life itself. I am thinking, not only
of the rights of Americans to go and come about their proper
business by way of the sea, but also of something much deeper,
much more fundamental than that. I am thinking of those rights
of humanity without which there is no civilization. My theme is of
those great principles of compassion and of protection which
mankind has sought to throw about human lives, the lives of non-
combatants, the lives of men who are peacefully at work keeping
the industrial processes of the world quick and vital, the lives
of women and children and of those who supply the labour which
ministers to their sustenance. We are speaking of no selfish
material rights but of rights which our hearts support and whose
foundation is that righteous passion for justice upon which all
law, all structures alike of family, of state, and of mankind must

rest, as upon the ultimate base of our existence and our liberty. I cannot imagine any man with American principles at his heart hesitating to defend these things.[3]

Printed reading copy (WP, DLC).
[3] There is a WWT undated outline; a WWsh draft with no composition date; and one WWT draft of this address in WP, DLC. Wilson's final WWT draft, which he sent to the Public Printer, is in the T. W. Brahany Coll., NHpR.

## An Unpublished Statement

[c. Feb. 26, 1917]

The following statement was given out by the President this evening:

A situation has developed in the Congress to which I deem it my duty to call the attention of the country in the plainest words. Every effort to legislate for the safety of the nation in these last hours of the Congress is being met by dilatory tactics on the part of certain ⟨Senators⟩ members of the House and Senate which are intended to make it impossible and to throw all action over until another Congress can be assembled and organized ⟨in which there will exist a most uncertain balance of parties and organization may be long delayed⟩. It should cause the gravest concern to everyone who knows anything of the real posture of our foreign affairs that it is in the power of a few men at this truly critical moment ⟨in⟩ when the fortunes of the nation may hang in the balance to put obstacles which may prove insuperable in the way of the immediate adoption of measures (notably the army and navy appropriation bills) whose main and only purpose is the national defence and which should be at once put into force. For myself I protest in the most earnest and solemn manner and in the name of the people themselves against this dangerous betrayal of the ⟨nation's⟩ country's most sacred interests. Nothing can excuse such action, and the partisan purpose by which it is apparently prompted evidently gives it the most sinister meaning. There is here injected into our politics, when the common safety should be the common interest of every man who professes to be a patriot, the most dangerous influence that could be conceived,—a sinister thing injected, not from the outside of our national circle, but at the very heart of it. I hope that the country will speak what it thinks.[1]

WWT MS (WC, NjP).
[1] Republican senators had already made it clear that they would filibuster on various bills in order to force Wilson to call a special session of Congress. See the *New York Times*, Feb. 26, 1917.

## To Edward Mandell House

My dear House,          The White House. 26 February, 1917.

Here is an astounding dispatch which I want you to see. We shall probably publish it (that is, let it be published) on Wednesday. In the meantime we are giving no intimation of it and have sent it to Fletcher at Mexico City to give Carranza a chance to say what he will about it.

Mrs. Wilson's sister, Mrs. Maury,[1] whom you met, I think, died this afternoon at her home in Roanoke, Virginia, as the result of a belated operation, and we are all deeply upset. Mrs. Bolling is here with us.

I hope you liked what I said to-day to the Congress.

In haste,      Affectionately Yours,   Woodrow Wilson

WWTLS (E. M. House Papers, CtY).
[1] Annie Lee Bolling (Mrs. Matthew H.) Maury.

## To William Julius Harris

[The White House]
My dear Mr. Commissioner:          26 February, 1917

I take the liberty of writing to ask that before you do anything toward making any arrangements about the investigation which you will probably be able to undertake of the food situation, you let me have a little talk with you if it is convenient. I have some suggestions I want to make.

Cordially and faithfully yours,   Woodrow Wilson

TLS (Letterpress Books, WP, DLC).

## From Thomas Watt Gregory, with Enclosures

*In re Senator Swanson's suggestion of settlement
of California Oil Land Problem.*

Dear Mr. President:      Washington, D. C. February 26, 1917.

Herewith I enclose copy of a letter addressed by me to the Secretary of the Interior on February 21st in regard to the above matter. A duplicate was sent to the Secretary of the Navy at the same time. I also enclose copy of a letter this day received from the Secretary of the Navy, dated February 26th,[1] and copy of another this day received by me from the Secretary of the Interior dated February 24th.[2] I likewise enclose copy of a letter I am sending to Senator Swanson.

I presume that there is nothing further for me to do.

Faithfully yours,    T. W. Gregory

TLS (WP, DLC).
  [1] JD to T. W. Gregory, Feb. 26, 1917, TCL (WP, DLC). Daniels reluctantly approved the Swanson compromise.
  [2] FKL to T. W. Gregory, Feb. 24, 1917, TCL (WP, DLC). Lane also approved the Swanson compromise; however, he thought that persons who had invested in lands outside the naval reserves should be given preference in the award of leases.

### E N C L O S U R E    I

## Thomas Watt Gregory to Franklin Knight Lane

My dear Mr. Secretary:          [Washington] February 21, 1917.

I am requested by the President to consult with you and Secretary Daniels respecting a suggestion made by Senator Swanson for a settlement of the oil land controversy in California. The President desires me to submit to you gentlemen the question of whether this suggestion affords ground for agreement.

The suggestion of Senator Swanson is as follows:

That any claimant, who either in person or through his predecessor in interest, entered upon any of the lands embraced within the executive order of withdrawal dated September 27, 1909, prior to July 3, 1910, honestly and in good faith for the purpose of prospecting for oil or gas, and thereupon commenced discovery work thereon, and thereafter prosecuted such work to a discovery of oil or gas, shall be entitled to lease from the United States any producing oil or gas well resulting from such work, at a royalty of not less than one-eighth of all the oil and gas produced therefrom, together with an area of land sufficient for the operation thereof, but without the right to drill any other or additional wells; provided, that such claimant shall first pay to the United States an amount equal to not less than the value of one-eighth of all the oil and gas already produced from such well; and provided further, that this act shall not apply to any well involved in any suit brought by the United States, or in any application for patent, unless within ninety days after the approval of this act the claimant shall relinquish to the United States all rights claimed by him in such suit or application; and provided further, that all such leases shall be made and the amount to be paid for oil and gas already produced shall be fixed by the Secretary of the Interior under appropriate rules and regulations.

This would afford substantial relief to all claimants, including assignees, who attempted in good faith to make locations after the withdrawal order in the mistaken belief that the order was invalid. In my judgment it would give them a far greater measure of relief than would be granted to them by a court of equity. It would give these persons a liberal portion of the fruits of their labor and investments while granting no relief to those guilty of fraud.

Senator Swanson tells me that the Naval Bill will probably come up on Friday, and he wishes to know before that time whether the three departments of the Navy, the Interior and Justice will acquiesce in the suggested adjustment. I am sending a duplicate of this letter to the Secretary of the Navy, and trust that I shall hear from both of you by the afternoon of Thursday, the twenty-second, so that I can notify the President and Senator Swanson of the result of the submission of the latter's suggestions. I feel that this is a matter falling peculiarly within the jurisdiction of the other two departments, the Interior because of its general jurisdiction over Government lands and the Navy because of its interest in the Naval Reserve. In case those two departments are satisfied with this suggestion, I shall make no objection to its adoption.          Faithfully yours,   [T. W. Gregory]

TCL (WP, DLC).


ENCLOSURE   II

## Thomas Watt Gregory to Claude Augustus Swanson

Dear Senator:                    [Washington] February 26, 1917.

Herewith I enclose copy of a letter written by me to the Secretary of the Interior on February 21st, in which I set out a suggestion made by you for a possible solution of the California oil land controversy. A duplicate of this letter was sent to the Secretary of the Navy on the same date. The letter as originally written without any pencil alterations is an exact copy of the letter sent and which I previously read to you over the telephone in order to be sure that it stated your suggestion accurately.

Subsequently, Secretary Lane suggested to me over the telephone that in the fourth line of the suggestion the words "after that date and" be stricken out so as to place all parties who entered upon the lands prior to July 3, 1910 on the same basis, instead of restricting the leasing privilege to those who entered between September 27, 1909, and July 3, 1910. After conferring with the Secretary of the Navy it was agreed that there was no real necessity for making any distinction, and that these four words could properly be stricken out. You will also find some pencil changes made in the last five lines of your suggestion, which merely serve to make the meaning a trifle more clear.

I also enclose herewith copy of a letter received this morning from the Secretary of the Navy in reply to my communication of the 21st, in which he signifies his acquiescence in your suggestion. I have likewise received this morning a letter from the Secretary of the Interior dated February 24th, in which he states that in so far as your suggestion relates to the naval oil reserves he will acquiesce in its passage; that it seems to go as far as the Secretary of the Navy is willing to go, and that he (the Secretary of the Interior) has always said that he would not undertake to determine or advise as to what policy the Government should pursue with respect to lands withdrawn for naval purposes. He says further that he thinks the provision made applicable to lands outside of the naval reserves should be more liberal, and that it might very well follow the suggestion made by Commissioner Tallman and Mr. Finney in their discussion before the Senate Committee and the Secretary of the Navy, which suggestion, he adds, will be found on page 104 of the proceedings of the special joint conference on H.R. 406.

On turning to this reference I find the suggestion of Mr. Tallman to be in the following language

"That upon relinquishment to the United States within 90 days after final denial or withdrawal of application for patent, of any claim asserted under the mining laws to any unpatented oil or gas lands included in an order of withdrawal or naval petroleum reserve No. 2, in the State of California, the claimant shall be entitled to a lease for each asserted mineral location of 160 acres or less, upon which such claim is based and upon which said claimant, his predecessor in interest, or those claiming through or under him have, prior to the date of this act, drilled one or more producing oil or gas wells, such lease to be upon a royalty of one-eighth of the production of oil or gas produced and saved therefrom after first deducting from the gross production such oil or gas as may be used in the development or operating of said lands, and otherwise on the same terms and conditions as other oil and gas leases granted under the provisions of this act: Provided, That within 90 days from the date of this act or of final denial or withdrawal of application for patent, the applicant for lease shall pay the United States for one-eighth of the oil or gas produced from the lands included in said claim subsequent to_____, at the current field price at time of production, which shall be in full satisfaction for all oil or gas extracted from said land prior to said lease: Provided further, That all royalties received under the provisions of this section from said naval petroleum reserve No. 2, whether in oil or money, shall be delivered or credited to the United States Navy: And provided further, That none of the provisions of this section or of this act shall be applicable to or affect lands or minerals included within the limits of naval petroleum reserve No. 1, in the State of California, or naval petroleum reserve No. 3, in the State of Wyoming."

The suggestion of Mr. Tallman would give to any person who up to the time of the passage of the bill had developed an oil or gas well (irrespective of when he entered upon the land or whether his claim was fraudulent or bona fide) the privilege of leasing each asserted mineral location upon a one-eighth royalty, such privilege to exist for 90 days after the final denial by the Land Department or withdrawal by the claimant of the application for patent. I am unable to approve this suggestion.

The President authorizes me to say to you that he has fully discussed with me your suggestion, contained in my above-mentioned letters of February 21st, and that it is the limit of liberality to which he is willing to go in dealing with these oil claimants.

I very much regret that I have not sooner been able to make you a full report in regard to this situation. The delay has been due to the necessity for discussion in detail of the terms of your suggestion with the other two Departments.

Sincerely yours,   [T. W. Gregory]

CCL (WP, DLC).


# From Edward Mandell House

Dear Governor:                    New York. February 26, 1917.

I believe your speech before Congress today will meet the approval of practically every American. The last two paragraphs are as fine as anything in the English language.

Henry White told me last night that Bernstorff said to him before he left that in sending him home you had done the only thing that could be done in the circumstances. He said that Bernstorff deeply regretted the action of his government believing that peace would have soon come through your efforts if they had not been interrupted.

Affectionately yours,    E. M. House

TLS (WP, DLC).

## From Josephus Daniels

Dear Mr. President:                    Washington. Feb. 26. 1917.

I cannot leave the Department without writing to say that your address to Congress heartened all Americans who hope and pray for peace while believing steadfastly in the protection of our rights upon the seas. Congress will give you the power, we will arm the ships, and the people will rejoice in the spirit which marked your address and the moderation which marks your actions. The hysterical talk one hears in Washington and New York does not represent the true public opinion any more than the expressions of those who are for peace at any price.

Sincerely,    Josephus Daniels

ALS (WP, DLC).

## From James Taylor Du Bois

To The President,                    Fellsmere, Florida February 26—17

Deeply impressed with your just and noble stand concerning the Colombian Treaty I take the liberty of briefly expressing my views.

I was the American Minister to Colombia under President Taft and my views are expressed in the inclosed document, parts of which I have marked in hopes that you might care to read them.[1]

It is of very grave importance that the United States should at once remove the unfortunate differences between our government and the Republic of Colombia caused by the violent separation of Panama. Colombia is the Northland of South America. She practically dominates the Canal and has two good harbors on the Atlantic and two on the Pacific. In times of stress she could do us infinite harm if allied to an enemy of the United States.

Colombia wants to be our friend. I lived among the Colombian people for two years. I know how they feel in this respect. They have faith in your love of Justice and fairness. Aside from an act of supreme Justice it would be great wisdom to settle our differences and this can be done, and completely done, by ratifying the Colombian Treaty as it was signed. The proposed modifications could not be accepted by Colombia, and this great nation would eventually deeply regret having asked her to accept them.

Colombia has been grieviously wronged and humiliated. A fair and just settlement with Colombia now will prove one of the most beneficent acts your administration has performed in the true and vital interests, not only of the American people, but also of the Western Hemisphere.

I am Mr. President,

Your obedient servant,    James T. Du Bois

ALS (WP, DLC).
[1] A printed pamphlet, *Ex-U. S. Minister to Colombia James T. Du Bois on Colombia's Claims and Rights*, n.p., n.d., but with text headed "Hallstead, Pa., July 1, 1914" (WP, DLC). Du Bois, who at various times had been a journalist, an officer in the Consular Service, and editor of the laws in the Department of State, wrote in the pamphlet that, since 1903, he had felt that the United States had treated Colombia unjustly. He expressed "profound esteem" for Theodore Roosevelt but said that no man was infallible. The people of Latin America, Du Bois went on, believed that the Panama incident was the only real injustice committed by the United States against them. The proposed treaty with Colombia would correct that feeling and "greatly change the sentiment that is now running heavily against us in all South America." Du Bois marked particularly the portions of his pamphlet which emphasized the wrongdoing of the United States Government and its obligation to make reparation to Colombia for that wrongdoing.

## From Albert Sidney Burleson

Mr. President,                                        [Feb. 27, 1917]

I have the House bill (with amendments proposed)[1] the purpose of which is to vest you with power and authority suggested in your message. Mr. Flood is at the end of the 'phone line awaiting suggestions.                                        Burleson

Let me see it, please    W.W.

ALS (A. S. Burleson Papers, DLC).
[1] During the afternoon of February 27, while the cabinet was meeting, Burleson was in the Capitol conferring with Stone, Flood, and other members of Congress about Wilson's proposed armed-ship bill. Members of the House Foreign Affairs Committee had proposed amendments to forbid the arming of merchantmen carrying munitions or any contraband and to omit the provision authorizing the President to use "other instrumentalities and methods." *New York Times*, Feb. 28, 1917.

## To Albert Sidney Burleson

[The White House, Feb. 27, 1917]

I hope very much that none of these amendments will be adopted. The original language was most carefully studied.

W.W.

ALI (A. S. Burleson Papers, DLC).

## To George Wilkins Guthrie

The White House

My dear Mr. Ambassador:                    27 February, 1917

Your words of approval of my address to the Senate on peace has[1] given me a great deal of pleasure.[2] You are certainly a most thoughtful friend to think of me on such occasions and let me know of the impression that is being made upon you in different surroundings and in a different atmosphere. It is of no small importance to me to have guidance of that sort.

We go breathlessly from day to day here trying to meet many things that press upon us, and I am only thankful that we have not made more mistakes than we have.

In haste, with the warmest regard and constant thought of your own services and difficulties,

Cordially and sincerely yours,    Woodrow Wilson

TLS (received from Thomas M. H. Blair).
[1] *Sic* in the Swem shorthand notebooks.
[2] Guthrie's letter is missing.


## To Richard Hooker

My dear Mr. Hooker:        [The White House] 27 February, 1917

Thank you warmly for your letter.[1] The two editorials which accompany it interest me very much indeed.[2] Our position with relation to other neutrals is admirably set forth, and I am delighted to find that you favor the idea of military service associated with vocational training. In the little trip I made a good many months ago into the Middle-West to speak in favor of preparedness, I made one or two references to that matter which were exactly to the same purport. I believe that that way lies the true solution of our problem, to associate military training with industrial training, with industrial training of course occupying the foreground and constituting the real interest of the men who are receiving the education.

I necessarily write in haste, but with warm appreciation.

Cordially and sincerely yours,    Woodrow Wilson

TLS (Letterpress Books, WP, DLC).
[1] It is missing.
[2] They were "Neutrals and Armed Neutrality Leagues," *Springfield*, Mass., *Republican*, Feb. 24, 1917, and "Training for War and for Work," *ibid.*, Feb. 18, 1917. The first argued that the refusal of the other neutral maritime nations, such as Spain, the Netherlands, and the Scandinavian countries, to join the United States in breaking diplomatic relations with Germany made it clear that they would neither actively support the United States if it went to war in defense of neutral rights nor join in a league of armed neutrality for the same purpose. "The United States, consequently," it concluded, "may as

well go it alone, as it has hitherto. The moral support of the entire neutral world we already have. . . . If we could not defend our own rights, we could no better succeed in defending specifically other nations' rights. If we do defend our own rights successfully, all neutrals will share in the triumph."

The second editorial suggested that the vocational training bill then awaiting the President's signature (about which see W. C. Redfield to WW, March 23, 1916, n. 1, Vol. 36) should be sent back to Congress so that provisions for some form of universal military training might be added to the measure. "Such a combination," it argued, "may offer the ideal solution in the long run, of the two problems of defense and of vocational training with wholesome but not militarizing discipline."


## To Jouett Shouse

My dear Mr. Shouse:        [The White House] 27 February, 1917

Thank you warmly for your letter of yesterday.[1] It gives me a great deal of genuine gratification.

I dare say, as I see things now, that it perhaps would have been well to go to Congress earlier, but you may be sure that I shall use every legitimate influence I can exercise to bring about a "show down" now.

Cordially and faithfully yours,   Woodrow Wilson

TLS (Letterpress Books, WP, DLC).
[1] It is missing in both WP, DLC, and in the J. Shouse Papers, KyU.


## To George Foster Peabody

My dear Mr. Peabody:        The White House 27 February, 1917

I am glad that you were here and heard my address to Congress yesterday, because I value your judgment about it.[1] It reassures me that you felt that it was so entirely right. These are days when none of us can feel absolutely certain of a correct judgment because there are so many things to stir passion and so many things to distress the mind and throw it off its right balance. Your letter has given me very deep and genuine pleasure and gratitude.

Cordially and sincerely yours,   Woodrow Wilson

TLS (received from Yaddo, Saratoga, N. Y.).
[1] Peabody's letter is missing.


## From Edward Mandell House

Dear Governor:        New York. February 27, 1917.

I am not surprised to read the despatch concerning the German proposal to Mexico. I have been satisfied for a long time that they have laid plans to stir up all the trouble they could in order to occupy our attention in case of eventualities.

I hope you will publish the despatch tomorrow. It will make a profound impression both on Congress and the country

I am distressed to hear the sad news about Mrs. Wilson's sister. Mrs. House will not go down with me Saturday, and had I not better stop elsewhere? I know you will tell me frankly as to this.

Affectionately yours,    E. M. House

TLS (WP, DLC).

## Robert Lansing to Walter Hines Page

Washington, February 27, 1917.

Your 5747, February 24, 1 p.m.

Referring to the penultimate paragraph of your telegram under reference, you will please convey to Mr. Balfour a message of thanks for this information of such inestimable value and add that the President has asked me to express his very great appreciation of so marked an act of friendliness on the part of the British Government.

For your information: Ambassador Fletcher has been instructed to take up the matter confidentially with General Carranza and his preliminary report indicates that perhaps it has not yet been presented by the German Minister. If telegram is published the source will be most carefully guarded. You will be kept informed.                                                    Lansing.

T telegram (SDR, RG 59, 862.20212/69, DNA).

## Frederic Courtland Penfield to Robert Lansing

Vienna (via Berne). February 27, 1917.

1730. Department's 1566, twenty-second.

I immediately entered upon the duty requested by your strictly confidential instructions and yesterday morning and this morning had lengthy discussions at my house with Minister for Foreign Affairs. Count Czernin is impressed with the communication verbally made to him, but feels that prohibition against "Any other Government" ever knowing of transaction must mean all Governments apart from Austria Hungary's Allies. With this understanding he today hands me this memorandum.

"Austria Hungary is always ready to end this war because she has always waged a defensive war. She however emphasizes the fact that she could only enter into negotiations for peace simultaneously with her Allies; that she must receive the guarantee that the Monarchy will remain intact; and finally the guarantee necessary to insure the cessation of propaganda on the part of her neighbors, propaganda which led to the assassination at Sarajevo.

The proposals made by Mr. Penfield to Count Czernin as well as those which may be made in future will remain secret; at the same time Count Czernin expects that his reply will remain secret also"

I can state that Minister for Foreign Affairs is keenly desirous of peace and agrees that it must eventually come through President Wilson. Czernin's bona fides and permanent confidence are certain. He thinks that Entente Governments are working for peace at Washington. If you can do so, please rush a telegram that may continue the negotiations. Grew was present at to-day's conference.

Must mention that as answer to my protest against certain journals abusing America and the President, Count Czernin caused the press to cease this altogether and for weeks nothing offensive has been printed. Two important Vienna journals have more than once appeared with editorial pages really benefited.                                    Penfield.

T telegram (SDR, RG 59, 763.72119/8389, DNA).


## From the Diary of Josephus Daniels

February Tuesday 27 1917

Cabinet today decided to send a division to Santiago, Cuba, to make demonstration to help Government against revolutionists[1] W said I am very free from G[erman] suspicions but so many things are happening we cannot afford to let Cuba be involved by G plots.

Benson did not think it necessary but—

I said to Lansing "You are never happy except when you are breaking up naval operations—'Manouevering[' "]

W: Gerard's remark to von Jagow who said to G "If there is war bet. G & US, you will find there are 500,000 German reservists ready to take up arms for mother country & you will have civil war." G replied "I do not know whether there are 500,000 or not. But we have 500,001 lamp posts & every man who takes up arms against his country will swing from lamp-post.["]

L repeated there was rumor that 500 German Reservists had

gone to Mexico to make trouble  Also McAdoo 200 Japs to make
munitions. Wilson, W B Strange that G & Japs both going to Mex
seeing they are at war.

Discussed resolution for arming ships

Bound diary (J. Daniels Papers, DLC).

1 Wilson, through Daniels, authorized Admiral Henry T. Mayo, commander
in chief of the United States Atlantic Fleet, to take all necessary steps to protect
American and foreign lives and property in Cuba. Under this authority, a
naval force of 250 men was landed at Guantánamo City on February 27, and
other forces were available. It was reported that Wilson and his advisers viewed
recent events in Cuba with "grave concern" and considered that the Platt
Amendment and the several American occupations of Cuba warranted the
administration in taking very definite steps to maintain order and the integrity
of free government in Cuba. Unless earlier warnings were heeded, actual
intervention was considered probable. *New York Times*, March 1, 1917.

"During the revolution which took place in Cuba last winter it became
necessary to land marines and seamen from the vessels of the fleet at various
places in Oriente and Camaguey Provinces to protect American property from
the depredations of the rebel bands. The marine detachments of the *Connecticut, South Carolina, Michigan, Machias, Montana, New York, Texas,* and
*Olympia,* and the Forty-third, Fifty-first, and Fifty-fifth Companies of Marines,
from the *New Hampshire, Vermont,* and the *Maine,* served ashore at different
times during the period from March 1 to May 24, 1917, and the landing force
was reinforced by a battalion of marines consisting of the Seventh, Seventeenth, and Twentieth Companies." Report of the Major General Commandant
of the United States Marine Corps, Washington, October 10, 1917, printed in
*Annual Reports of the Navy Department for the Fiscal Year 1917* (Washington,
1918), p. 840.


## To William Riley Crabtree[1]

[The White House] February 28, 1917

May I not express my earnest hope that the Senate of Tennessee
will reconsider the vote by which it rejected the legislation extending the suffrage to women? Our party is so distinctly
pledged to its passage that it seems to me the moral obligation is
complete.                                    Woodrow Wilson

T telegram (Letterpress Books, WP, DLC).

1 Speaker of the Tennessee State Senate; real estate dealer and former
Mayor of Chattanooga.


## To Robert Lansing, with Enclosure

My dear Mr. Secretary,      The White House. 28 February, 1917.

This is a very interesting letter, which I return for your files.
Penfield always says something serviceable to our thought.

It's astonishing, however, is it not? how fast letters from
Europe become chronicles of ancient history.

Faithfully Yours,   W.W.

WWTLI (RSB Coll., DLC).

ENCLOSURE

## Frederic Courtland Penfield to Robert Lansing

STRICTLY CONFIDENTIAL

My dear Mr. Secretary:                    Vienna January 22, 1917

I certainly owe you an explanation for the lapse in my confidential letters, which is that with the demise of the Emperor Francis Joseph, the coming to the throne of Charles I, the changes in the Ministry of Foreign Affairs, the coronation at Budapest, and the several exchanges of Notes *re* Peace, I was never busier with matters that took much time and could not be slighted. And throughout the greater part of this period five of the six Secretaries have been ill. I doubt if a similar chapter of misfortunes ever confronted any servant of the Department of State. But, the Lord be praised, I have kept well and believe I have dealt appropriately with every official demand.

I have a few potent matters to communicate, which I briefly do as follows:

The last time I saw Baron Burián I found him in a mood for saying things that he would scarcely have uttered before his demotion from the Ministry of Foreign Affairs. He seemed resentful that the overture of the Central Powers for peace—a project that was really his own—had been vigorously denied by the Entente Allies. "Very well," he remarked, "we will now do in turn to each of our enemies what we have done to Rumania. It will be Italy's turn next." He did not advise me how this was to be accomplished.

At the Foreign Office a few days since the new Minister, Count Czernin, tried to draw from me an expression of opinion regarding the prospect of peace. I gave him so little satisfaction that he said to me, as if to conclude the topic, "Peace will not soon be with us, probably not before January 1st, 1918."

The scarcity of food in Austria and in Hungary is becoming alarming, while the anti-war agitation seems to be in danger of growing beyond the power of the authorities to suppress. The despair of the population is observable on every hand, especially since it has become an accepted fact that the Austro-German defeat of the Rumanians failed to produce the supplies of grain and petroleum that the people had been told would follow the fall of Bucarest. The booty was but trifling and is said to have gone chiefly to Germany and Bulgaria.

In my report six months ago I predicted that the crops then

being harvested would probably amount to 70 per cent. of normal. I now find that the estimate was too high, for the harvest was not in excess of 60 per cent.—a fact meaning privation in acute form to the civilian population. There is now little food for civilians, and nothing short of a miracle can carry the people over the next few months until the soil produces early vegetables.

March and April are certain to be months of great distress for millions upon millions of poor people. And if they survive the spring and summer, which they will in some manner do, the 1917 crops are certain to be much smaller than last year, for there are few horses and cattle left to furnish the essential fertilization of the soil, and nitrates and phosp[h]ates can in no manner be secured from oversea.

The armies of the Monarchy are better fed and provided for than the general population, otherwise they could not stand the demands of the campaigns.

Unfortunately the Dual Monarchy is in as sad a plight financially and economically as in its productivity.

It cannot be denied that Austria-Hungary is in a desperate situation. The people are subsisting on a quarter-portion diet, with meat, butter, eggs and milk seldom seen.

I am, my dear Mr. Secretary,

Yours very truly,   Frederic C. Penfield.

TLS (RSB Coll., DLC).


## To Robert Lansing

The White House.

My dear Mr. Secretary,                          28 February, 1917.

This, like Penfield's letter, begins to bear the aspect of ancient history, but it is out of the question to let such charges go uncontradicted, and this is unquestionably the right answer. It seems to me complete, and ought to make the persons who formulated the note of complaint ashamed of themselves.[1]

Faithfully Yours,   W.W.

WWTLI (SDR, RG 59, 763.72111 H 58/9½, DNA).
[1] The item under discussion was Department of State to the British embassy, Feb. 23, 1917, T MS (SDR, RG 59, 763.72111 H 58/11a, DNA). This lengthy document vigorously repudiated British charges that the United States had failed to take effective action to halt conspiracies originating on its territory by Germans and Indian nationalists against the British regime in India.

A News Report

[c. Feb. 28, 1917]
## A Visit to the President

About 150 delegates from the twenty-two leading peace societies of the United States met in New York City on February
22nd and 23d,[1] for a conference on the best coöperative means
of promoting international peace.

A committee reported recommendations for certain measures
to be adopted in the present emergency. One of these provided
for the sending of a delegation to interview President Wilson,
and urge upon him the unanimous desire of the conference that
he should continue to keep the country out of war and to settle
the existing disputes with Germany and Great Britain by peaceful means alone.

This delegation consisted of William I. Hull, chairman, Jane
Addams, Joseph D. Cannon, and Emily G. Balch.[2]

The President accorded the delegation an hour's interview on
the afternoon of February 28th. It was a time of very grave national tension, and the President talked most feelingly with the
delegation, but as he pledged its members to hold in entire confidence whatever he might say, no statement of his side of the
conversation can be given. It might be of interest, however, to
give in outline the message which the delegation presented to
him.

Dr. Hull emphasized a number of historical precedents for
the peaceful solution of exceedingly difficult international problems. Among these were the precedents set by Washington,
John Adams, Lincoln, and President Wilson himself. When the
French Revolution and the French Revolutionary War were raging in Europe, and a large portion of the American people
sympathized with France and desired to become its ally against
Great Britain, President Washington sent John Jay to England,
and succeeded in negotiating a treaty with England which settled some of the outstanding disputes between the two countries.
Jay was burned in effigy in America, and his treaty was extremely
unpopular—an unpopularity which Washington shared. In spite,
however, of the contumely which his political enemies heaped
upon Washington's head, the mature verdict of the American
people has been that Washington's greatness never shone brighter
than on this occasion.

Four years later when the great European tempest was still
raging, and even a majority of the President's own party under
the leadership of Alexander Hamilton were determined to fight

France, President John Adams sent commissioners to negotiate with the French Government. Although armed conflicts between French and American ships had already occurred upon the sea, Adams was successful in settling the dispute with the French Government. This was done in defiance of his own party, and indeed of his own cabinet, and cost him all chance of re-election to the Presidency; but he said in a letter written a score of years later that he would rather have inscribed upon his tombstone the words, "He kept the country out of war," than the record of any other event in his long and illustrious career.

The historic precedent set by President Lincoln in surrendering Mason and Slidell to the British at a time when the country deemed that they should be held at the risk of a war with England, and the settling of the *Alabama* claims by means of arbitration, were also recalled.

Finally, President Wilson's own success in keeping the country out of the European war, and in tiding over the Mexican crises by means of the conferences of Niagara Falls, Washington, and Atlantic City was recalled, and the conviction was expressed that the approval of these peaceful triumphs of the administration had been registered by the country at the last election.

In view of these and other notable precedents, Doctor Hull ventured to urge that two joint commissions of inquiry and conciliation should be appointed to negotiate with Germany and Great Britain, respectively, a *modus vivendi* relating to neutral rights and duties—possibly in line with the Declaration of London —until the end of the war. This attempt might seem especially helpful for the reason that both Great Britain and Germany have endorsed in principle the offer of the United States to investigate and settle by conciliatory means disputes which might arise between them; and also because such an offer would seem so reasonable to the *people* of the two belligerent governments that those governments could not well decline it.

Miss Addams emphasized especially the anxiety and distress of the German and Austrian immigrant families domiciled within our country, and mentioned several moving illustrations which had come to her personally in connection with her work at Hull House in Chicago. She quoted some of her immigrant friends as declaring that "Your President will not go to war, because he is a man of peace." She also expressed her conviction that our country cannot be precipitated into war by the "hyper-nationalism" which has forced the European belligerents into war, because of the cosmopolitan character of our American population; and she made a fervent appeal to the President that the great program of social legislation upon which his administration has made so splendid a beginning should not be sidetracked or destroyed by leading the country into a military means of settling international disputes.

Mr. Cannon, a representative of the miners, especially of those in the far West, reminded the President that all of the political parties in the recent Presidential campaign had endorsed the President's policy of keeping the country out of war, and he emphasized especially the overwhelming advocacy of the peace policy in the Democratic Convention, platform, and campaign; and finally he assured the President that only a small minority of the people were in favor of the war, and that the great majority of the American people would support unwaveringly whatever peaceful method the President decided upon for a solution of the outstanding questions with Germany and Great Britain.

Miss Balch expressed her conviction, on the basis of personal experience since the war began, that the German *people* were wholly adverse to war with the United States, and that if the President could decide upon some peaceful means of settling the dispute with their government, they would force their government to consider it.

After these preliminary statements were presented to the President, he entered into a very frank and earnest conversation with the delegation, in which he gave further convincing evidence of his earnest desire to find some peaceful means of settling our present international difficulties.[3]

At the end of the interview, Dr. Hull ventured to express on behalf of the New York conference the hope that the President would utilize the first suitable opportunity, preferably in his inaugural address, to bring before the world again his program for international organization and the limitation and reduction of armaments which he outlined in his address to the Senate on the 22d of January last, and which has already made so profound an impression upon the mind of the world.

Printed in the *Friends' Intelligencer*, LXXIV (March 10, 1917), 147-48.

[1] Where they formed the Emergency Peace Federation.

[2] Persons not identified heretofore were William Isaac Hull, Isaac H. Clothier Professor of History and International Relations at Swarthmore College, prominent Quaker leader and peace advocate, author of numerous studies of Quaker history and of international relations; Joseph D. Cannon, organizer for the Western Federation of Miners, Socialist party candidate for United States senator from New York in 1916; and Frederick Henry Lynch, secretary of the Church Peace Union of America and director of the New York Peace Society.

[3] Wilson met this delegation at 2 P.M. on February 28. Two of the participants later wrote their recollections of what Wilson had said. Hull remembered the following: "As for our informal discussion with President Wilson after the formal presentation of our points of view, I recall that he enumerated with great emphasis our various grievances against the Hohenzollern government . . .

and stressed repeatedly his conviction that it was impossible to deal further in peaceful method with that government. When I ventured to press upon him the possibility of making a successful appeal to the German people, over the heads of their government, he said that he considered that attempt impracticable. Finally, I recall with great vividness his tone and manner—a mixture of great indignation and determination—when he said: 'Dr. Hull, if you knew what I know at this present moment, and what you will see reported in tomorrow morning's newspapers, you would not ask me to attempt further peaceful dealings with the Germans.' " W. I. Hull to R. S. Baker, Oct. 10, 1928, TCL (RSB Coll., DLC).

Jane Addams recalled other facets of the encounter: "Professor Hull . . . , a former student of the President's, presented a brief résumé of what other American presidents had done through adjudication when the interests of American shipping had become involved. . . . The President was, of course, familiar with that history, as he reminded his old pupil, but he brushed it aside as he did the suggestion that if the attack on American shipping were submitted to The Hague tribunal, it might result in adjudication of the issues of the great war itself. The Labor man on the committee still expressed the hope for a popular referendum before war should be declared, and we once more pressed for a conference of neutrals. . . . The President's mood was stern and far from the scholar's detachment as he told us of recent disclosures of German machinations in Mexico and announced the impossibility of any form of adjudication. He still spoke to us, however, as to fellow pacifists to whom he was forced to confess that war had become inevitable. He used one phrase which I had heard Colonel House use so recently that it still stuck firmly in my memory. The phrase was to the effect that, as head of a nation participating in the war, the President of the United States would have a seat at the Peace Table, but that if he remained the representative of a neutral country he could at best only 'call through a crack in the door.' The appeal he made was, in substance, that the foreign policy which we so extravagantly admired could have a chance if he were there to push and to defend them, but not otherwise." Jane Addams, *Peace and Bread in Time of War* (New York, 1922), pp. 63-64.

# An Address to the President by Max Eastman[1]

Mr. President:                                    Feb. 28, 1917

I was especially eager to talk with you about this particular crisis, because your general international policy, announced in your address to the Senate advocating a league of the nations to ensure peace, has my fervent support and admiration. I am sure that with communication becoming continually more fluent and rapid all over the earth, with people all over the earth learning to read and translate each other's languages over-night, and with social and scientific and vast commercial combinations overspreading the boundaries of all nations, such a political union of the people for the protection of their common interests is inevitable. I am sure that whether the pre-prerequisite [sic] of peace without victory can be attained in this situation or not, in the lapse of time such a union will come nevertheless, and your "Declaration of Interdependence"—as we call it—will have an honored place in the histories of all nations.

I think of this union, and I believe you do, not exactly as the so-called "League to Enforce Peace," for it is utopian to hope that nations will go to war in distant parts of the earth merely because they have promised to. It is utopian to hope that the United States would promise to. But I think of it as a coming together, or congress, of representatives of the nations, who would arrange the terms of a reduction of national armaments, and possibly inaugurate an international government of the seas with a police power which would eliminate minor war-causes. Such an international government would automatically command a part of the instinctive loyalty which makes men in nations so bellicose. It would swing a vast body of sentiment to itself, and thus make nationalistic quarrels less agreeable to men's emotions at the same time that it furnished a mechanism for their settlement.

In my opinion, however, there is no single way of going toward this end. There are many steps that might lead to it, and any and all of them ought to be taken as they arise. Whenever international deliberation and international action are possible, there is an opportunity of moving toward the realization of your program. And in the present crisis, as it seems to me, the opportunity is peculiarly pressing and appropriate.

In the first place we have assumed and declared that we are representing the rights and interests of all the neutral nations of mankind. But we have no right to make that assumption or declaration unless we have conferred with the actual representatives, the governments of these nations, and have been to some extent at least delegated to represent them.

In the second place, even apart from our desire to be representative, I believe that our own best interest would be served by joining with other neutral governments, or as many of them as are in a position to join us, in a league of neutrality.

It would greatly strengthen the moral force of whatever position we might take toward the belligerent infringement of maritime rights.

It would diminish enormously the bellicose feelings which any emphatic position we took might stir up in the country whose military position suffered through it. Even assuming that the American republics are the only nations who would be entirely free to join in such a league, we can imagine that it would be difficult to make the people of Germany, for instance, feel a strong nationalistic anger toward a whole half of the earth.

Moreover it would undoubtedly tend to make our position more genuinely neutral. I am not unaware of the distinction between Germany's offenses against us, which involve loss of life, and England's which involve only loss of commercial values; but

I believe that if this country had happened to be genuinely neutral in feeling, had happened to contain as many and equally influential citizens who love Germany and desire her victory as who love England and desire hers, our protest against England might have been more severe and our demands of Germany, particularly in the matter of belligerent ships carrying munitions of war, less severe. And I believe that if we were acting in cooperation with a league of western republics, we should inevitably be led to act with a somewhat more genuine neutrality.

Perhaps I ought to say rather—if I express my true thought—that as the spokesman of such a league it would be possible for *you* to adopt a policy of even more genuine neutrality, and even more absolute determination to avoid war, than the patriotic emotions of the country will allow you to adopt in the purely nationalistic disagreement with Germany which now exists.

I know that you have the sense of war's futility and almost universal failure to accomplish those ends of civilization and justice for which men think they undertake it. You have the historian's knowledge and more than the historian's imagination. The generality of men are lacking these qualities, and therefore I imagine that you must find yourself continually wondering how you can act upon your more fortunate sense of the true relations and consequences of things, without too far offending the more blindly instinctive patriotic passions of the people you serve. This problem will become infinately more acute if in pursuit of a policy of armed neutrality, actual shots are fired, or engagements occur between German and American ships, for with steel vessels sinking so quickly, and with cables and telegrams spreading the news, armed neutrality is a far more precarious state of fact than it was in the time of President Adams.

My suggestion to you therefore—if I may call it that—is that if you once established yourself in the position of leader and spokesman in a concerted action of a number of nations, you would be able to act much more extremely upon your own wisdom, without offending and seeming to misrepresent the will of the people. For the people would have an immense interest in such leadership, and a vast tolerance of the delay and deliberation that such concerted and truly democratic action would involve.

I believe that if, instead of inviting the other neutrals to imitate your foreign policy after it is accomplished, you would invite them to join you in the formation and enactment of a common policy, you might still guide us through this crisis without declaring an armed neutrality, or if an armed neutrality were declared, you might make it more genuinely neutral, so that it would become a step toward peace without Victory and the League of Nations, rather than a step toward our alliance with England in victory and an imperial domination of the globe that will certify the continuation of world wars into the future.[2]

T MS (L. D. Wald Papers, NN).
    [1] He was among a delegation from the American Union Against Militarism, headed by Amos Pinchot, which also included Lillian D. Wald and Paul U. Kellogg. This group met with Wilson immediately following the interview discussed in the previous document.
    [2] Nothing specific is known either about remarks of the other delegates or about Wilson's side of the exchange. The New York *Evening Post*, Feb. 28, 1917, reported on both meetings in a single sentence: "President Wilson told peace advocates who called on him to-day to protest against the steps he proposes in dealing with Germany, that the country was faced by a momentous problem in the present situation; that he always had been for peace, and would do everything within his power to maintain it."

## From Edward Mandell House

Dear Governor:                     New York. March 1, 1917.

The United Press people feel hurt beyond measure because the Associated Press were given the Zimmermann cable.[1]

Howard claims that he has never gotten anything of value from the Administration although he has placed his organization so entirely at its command.

Since the A.P. Has never shown any partiality for the Administration, I would suggest that the next sensation be given the U.P. Howard is also hurt because you have seen both Stone and Noyes[2] and have refused to see him. In view of the fact that there may be more disclosures from the same source I thought I had better call your attention to this.

Affectionately yours,   E. M. House

TLS (WP, DLC).
    [1] Wilson had given a copy of the Zimmermann telegram to the A.P. for publication in the morning newspapers on March 1. R. W. Howard to WW, March 1, 1917, TLS (WP, DLC), set forth the same complaint directly to Wilson. Howard declared that the United Press representative who called at the State Department on the evening of February 28 was told that there was nothing for publication, "even while the facts were being given to the Associated Press." Howard added that the failure to give the Zimmermann telegram to the U.P. had embarrassed not only the U.P. but also many newspapers in Japan, France, and South America which depended upon the U.P. for their American news.
    [2] That is, Melville Elijah Stone, general manager of the Associated Press, and Frank Brett Noyes, president of the Associated Press and publisher of the Washington *Evening Star*.

## A Memorandum

The following was dictated over the phone by Mr. W. J. Bryan, March 1, 1917.

My dear Tumulty:

I have just been reading a little book published by McClurg & Company, entitled "Napoleon in his own words."[1] I thought the President might be interested in something that Napoleon said in regard to peace without victory. It seems to me exactly in point with the President's appeal to the belligerent nations. Here is what Napoleon says:

"Peace ought to be the result of a system well considered, founded on the true interests of the different countries, honorable to each, and ought not to be either a capitulation or the result of a threat."

I underscore the last part of the sentence. This so strongly supports the President's appeal for a peace without victory that coming from so great a warrior as Napoleon I thought the President might be interested in seeing it.

Please give my regards to the President.

T MS (C. L. Swem Coll., NjP).
[1] *Napoleon in His Own Words, From the French of Jules Bertaut,* Herbert Edward Law and Charles Lincoln Rhodes, trans. (Chicago, 1916).

## To William Julius Harris

My dear Harris:                    [The White House] 2 March, 1917

To my surprise and distress, there seems to be some trouble about the appropriation for the food investigation. If it goes through, I shall be very glad to see the other Commissioners along with you for a little chat. I merely want to help in every way I can. I am doing what I can to get the appropriation. It would be very unfortunate for it to fail.

In haste
          Cordially and sincerely yours,    Woodrow Wilson

TLS (Letterpress Books, WP, DLC).

## To John Joseph Fitzgerald[1]

My dear Mr. Fitzgerald:        [The White House] 2 March, 1917

I know that in the rush of these last hours of the session you will forgive me if I call your attention to what seems to me the capital importance of passing an appropriation for the use of the Federal Trade Commission in the investigation of the food situation in the country and the cost of food. My own impression is that not all of the $400,000 asked for will be necessary, though I say this with considerable diffidence in view of the recommendation of the Commission itself. But I feel confident that the greater part of what is most necessary to be accomplished could be accomplished with an appropriation of, say, $250,000. I want to appeal to you very earnestly to see that this is added to the bill in order that a piece of work which the whole country is expecting of us may be performed.[2]

With apologies for troubling you, but feeling that it is justified by the importance of the object.

Cordially and sincerely yours,   Woodrow Wilson

TLS (Letterpress Books, WP, DLC).
[1] Wilson sent the following letter, *mutatis mutandis*, to Representatives Frederick Huntington Gillett, Republican of Massachusetts, and J. Swagar Sherley and Senator Thomas S. Martin.
[2] The appropriation recommended by Wilson failed to pass before the end of the session on March 4. However, an appropriation of $250,000 for the purpose discussed above was included in the sundry civil bill enacted by the Sixty-fifth Congress on June 12, 1917. 40 *Statutes at Large* 124.


## To Edward Douglass White

[The White House]
My dear Mr. Chief Justice:                    2 March, 1917

I hope that it will be possible for you without personal inconvenience to administer the oath of office to me in the President's Room at the Capitol on Sunday next at noon.

I am taking it for granted that I shall be there attending to the necessary last signatures, etc., of the session, and I would be very much complimented if you could yourself be there and do me this service.

Cordially and sincerely yours,   Woodrow Wilson

TLS (Letterpress Books, WP, DLC).


## To Daisy Allen Story

My dear Mrs. Story:                    The White House 2 March, 1917

I greatly regret to report that the objects in the way of the Monticello purchase have come to seem insuperable in these last hours of the session of Congress, though I know that you know that I have been deeply interested and have done what I could to

advance the measure. I dare not seek to interject anything now
because it is only too uncertain whether the appropriations bills
themselves will pass.

In haste, with warmest regard and sincere regret,

Faithfully yours,    Woodrow Wilson

TLS (WP, DLC).

## To William Dean Howells

Washn DC Mar 2 1917

May I not send my sincerest congratulations and best wishes
on your birthday[1] I am sure I am expressing the hope of the
whole country when I hope that you will have many very happy
returns of the day and that each year you will realize the honor
and admiration in which you are held    Woodrow Wilson

T telegram (W. D. Howells Papers, MH).
  [1] Howells had celebrated his eightieth birthday on March 1.

## From Clarence True Wilson[1]

Dear Mr. President:              Washington, D. C. March 2, 1917.

We learn that the Post Office Appropriation Bill which contains
two pieces of legislation for which the temperance forces of the
country including the great church bodies have been petitioning
for years, having passed both Houses of Congress by an overwhelming majority, has been dispatched to the White House for
executive action. The breaking down of the laws of the several
states by obnoxious liquor advertisements and interstate shipments had gone to such length that there was such a petition
for relief that Congress could not longer ignore it. Hence, the
vote of four and one-half to one in the lower House for the Anti-
Liquor Advertising Amendment and the Bone Dry Reed Amendment.[2]

Both the General Assembly of the Presbyterian Church and the
General Conference of the Methodist Episcopal Church had
prayed our National Executive Officers to cooperate with the efforts made by the Dry States to prevent the pumping of alcohol
into the veins of the body politic. We have ascertained that there
is no relief from this situation if the present Post Office Appropriation Bill should not receive the sanction of the President.
It is too late in the session to get relief from the conditions mentioned in any other way, therefore, as the officer designated to

represent the Methodist Episcopal Church in this behalf, a body of four millions of members with a constituency of ten millions, we earnestly pray your cooperation with the Dry States in the approval of this far-reaching and beneficent reform bill.

Most respectfully yours,    Clarence True Wilson

TLS (WP, DLC).
1 Methodist Episcopal clergyman, general secretary of the Board of Temperance, Prohibition, and Public Morals of the Methodist Episcopal Church, a leader in the drive for national prohibition.
2 The first of these amendments forbade the use of the mails to send advertisements or solicitations for alcoholic beverages into any state or territory of the United States where it was unlawful to advertise or solicit orders for such beverages. The second amendment, originally introduced by Senator James A. Reed, forbade the shipment of alcoholic beverages in interstate commerce into any state or territory which prohibited the manufacture or sale of such beverages. Wilson approved the Post Office appropriations bill, which included these amendments, on March 3. 39 *Statutes at Large* 1069.


## From Robert Henry Todd[1]

Sir:                         San Juan Puerto Rico. March 2, 1917.

The Municipal Council of San Juan has directed me to express to you the satisfaction felt by said body, representing the City of San Juan, on being acquainted of the fact that the Congress has passed a new Organic Act for Porto Rico, wherein the Portoricans are clothed with the high honor of American citizenship.

The Council is aware that this grant has been conferred through your efforts, and a vote of sincere thanks to you was adopted and recorded in the minutes of the day.

Very respectfully,    R. H. Todd

TLS (WP, DLC).
1 Mayor of San Juan.


## From Robert Lansing

My dear Mr. President,            Washington March 3, 1917.

How will this do for an instruction to Penfield? It was not an easy thing to draft in view of Count Czernin's memorandum.

Faithfully yours    Robert Lansing

ALS (SDR, RG 59, 763.72119/8389, DNA).

## To Robert Lansing, with Enclosure

My dear Mr. Secretary,            The White House. 3 March, 1917.

With the changes I have indicated in pencil, I think this will accomplish the most we are at liberty to attempt. The changes I suggest are intended to avoid the use of any words which might, either now or subsequently, be understood to indicate an attempt on our part to bargain with Austria-Hungary for her separation from her dominating ally. The word "arrangement" might be thought to wear that colour.

Faithfully Yours,    W.W.

WWTLI (SDR, RG 59, 763.72119/8389, DNA).

E N C L O S U R E[1]

Washington, March (3?), 1917.

Strictly confidential. To be deciphered by Ambassador. Your 1730, February 27th.

Assure Count Czernin that his confidence will be strictly observed and that all interchanges will remain secret.

Paragraph. You may further say to him that this Government appreciates the embarrassments of the Austro-Hungarian Government in discussing the desirability of obtaining assurances under present conditions. But, as the present seems opportune for that purpose while doing so at a later time, if certain events should take place, might be impossible or ineffective, this Government earnestly hopes that Count Czernin will reconsider the subject giving especial weight to the fact that conditions in the future may be far less favorable to Austria-Hungary than they are at present. It must be manifest to Count Czernin that this Government in again addressing him on a subject which can only be for the future welfare of his country is inspired by a disinterested desire to be helpful. It would be regrettable if certain ⟨arrangements⟩ *perfectly frank interchanges of intention* were not made before the progress of the war prevents even their consideration. This Government is loath to believe that Count Czernin is unwilling to obtain for his country certain advantages which this Government feels *might* be obtained under existing conditions which may not continue long and may not come again.

Lansing[2]

Hw telegram (SDR, RG 59, 763.72119/8389, DNA).
  [1] Words in angle brackets in the following document deleted by Wilson; words in italics added by him.
  [2] This was sent as RL to F. C. Penfield, March 3, 1917, T telegram (SDR, RG 59, 763.72119/8389, DNA); printed in *FR-WWS 1917*, I, 63-64.

# From Raymond Poincaré[1]

Paris, received March 3, 1917, 10:45 a.m.

Au moment où se renouvellent les pouvoirs de Votre Excellence, je me fais un plaisir de vous réitérer, avec mes vives félicitations, les souhaits que je vous exprimais au début de votre première présidence, pour votre bonheur personnel, pour la prospérité du peuple américain et pour le maintien de la traditionnelle amitié qui lie nos deux nations. Ces voeux trouvent dans les sentiments que les circonstances actuelles inspirent à la France entière un surcroit de force et de chaleur. Ce[s] ne sont plus seulement les souvenirs historiques, le respect héréditaire du droit, l'amour inné de la liberté, qui nous unissent à travers l'océan; c'est la conscience commune des grands devoirs que vous avez si éloquemment définis et que les Etats-Unis et la France ont à remplir envers l'humanité; c'est la necessité de défendre les principes moraux qui donnent seuls du prix à la civilisation; c'est la volonté d'assurer au monde, pour l'avenir, une paix juste el solidement garantie.          Raymond Poincaré.

T telegram (SDR, RG 59, 811.001W 69/261, DNA).
[1] Corrections from the original T telegram (Guerre 1914-1918, États-Unis, Vol. 505, p. 262, FFM-Ar).


T R A N S L A T I O N

Paris, March 3, 1917.

At the moment of the renewal of Your Excellency's administration, I give myself the pleasure of reiterating to you, with my lively felicitations, the wishes which I expressed to you at the beginning of your first administration for your personal happiness, for the prosperity of the American people, and for the maintenance of the traditional friendship which binds our two nations. These wishes find in the sentiments that the present circumstances inspire all over France an increase in force and warmth. They are not only the historical memoriès, the hereditary respect for law, [and] the innate love of liberty which unite us across the ocean; it is the common conscience of two great powers which you have so eloquently defined and which the United States and France have discharged toward humanity. It is the necessity of defending moral principles which alone are the prize of civilization. It is the desire to assure to the world a just peace on a solid basis for the future.

Raymond Poincaré.

# Jean Jules Jusserand to Aristide Briand

Washington, reçu le 3 Mars 1917, 12 h.50

M. BERGSON[1] me prie de transmettre à Votre Exc. le télégramme ci-apres:[2]

Monsieur LANE, Ministre de l'Intérieur avec qui j'ai eu plusieurs conversations, m'a dit avant-hier: "Vous avez réussi à convaincre M. MILLER dont l'influence est grande au Federal Reserve Board et ceci va probablement se traduire par des actes importants pour votre pays." Hier, M. MILLER m'a dit en effet, très confidentiellement, que certaines measures allaient sans doute être prises pour amener le public américain à preter directement son argent aux Alliés de sorte que nous n'aurons plus à fournir des gages quands nous emprunterons.

Je quitte Washington après avoir causé longuement avec le Président Wilson,[3] see ministres et divers membres de l'Administration et du congrès. Voici mon impression: on marche à la guerre, mais tandis que certains ministres la voudraient immédiatement et complète, le Président Wilson ne s'y décidera que lorsque les événements l'aurent rendue inévitable, parce qu'il tient à avoir derrière lui l'opinion encore divisée; dans l'Quest, beaucoup sont encore pour la paix à tout prix. Le Président veut ménager toutes les transitions avant d'arriver aux hostilités et il les ménagera probablement encore dans les hostilités elles-mêmes avant d'arriver à la guerre franche.

Si la guerre éclate, comme c'est probable, je ne sais si le Président et l'Amérique elle-même se proposerant les mêmes buts de guerre que nous et voudrent la défaite de l'Allemagne aussi complète. Cela dépendra des événements. Le Président Wilson m'a paru en tout cas faire siens les principes pour lesquels nous nous battons, mais il considère l'Angleterre comme luttant uniquement pour sa prépondérance commerciale qu'il ne semble pas soucieux d'assurer. De plus, il se fait une idée inexacte de l'état intérieur de l'Allemagne. Il croit que les Allemands sont las du militarisme prussien et peut-être du régime impérial. Je crains de n'avoir pas réussi à la détromper. BERGSON.                    Jusserand

T telegram (Guerre 1914-1918, États-Unis, Vol. 505, pp. 264-65, FFM-Ar).

[1] Henri Bergson (1859-1941), world-famous philosopher. He was awarded the Nobel Prize for Literature in 1928.

[2] According to Bergson's later account (1936), Briand, early in 1917, had asked him to undertake an official but unannounced mission to the United States. Various persons had told Briand that Bergson could be effective in presenting French views concerning the entry of the United States into the war to Wilson's entourage, and, perhaps, to Wilson himself. Any openly official approach might have a negative effect, it was feared, but a philosopher, well-regarded in America and speaking as a friend, might perhaps be heard. On

this basis, Bergson wrote, he visited Washington and New York from February to May 1917, and, by providential good fortune, soon became a friend of House, whom he described as Wilson's confidant and adviser, one who was "always heard, especially on foreign affairs, as Wilson knows nothing about Europe." In February and March, Bergson frequently saw House, who, he later wrote, deserved a statue in France for what he had done to bring about the indispensable American intervention in the war. This did not detract from his admiration for Wilson, Bergson added, but Wilson was "somewhat inacessible, on principle living in absolute solitude." If Wilson made an exception in his case, Bergson was able to tell Wilson some things which, as House said later, had made a real impression on him.

Bergson also became a friend of Lane, who was familiar with his philosophical writings, and had frequent conversations with him. Bergson told Lane that idealistic America could not help but enter the war. Bergson understood that Lane had relayed to Wilson some of what he had said, and, after the United States entered the war, Lane told Bergson: "You had much more to do than you realize in the President's decision."

Another reason for the mission, Bergson explained, was the French government's dissatisfaction with Jusserand's inability to remove the causes of Wilson's indecision. The French needed, above all, to show to the President, who was by nature an idealist, the unique opportunity that he now enjoyed to restore peace to the world and to open a new era in the history of mankind. Jusserand, Bergson noted, was too stiff to become an intimate of Wilson or to talk to him on terms of equality, and the Ambassador had failed to see that Wilson held a dangerously incorrect view of Germany. According to Bergson, Wilson told him in February 1917 that the Germans would soon bring the war to an end and get rid of their Emperor and government. In Wilson's words, "They have their bellies full." Bergson reported that he fought this view as hard as he could, "with an energy and insistence to which the President seemed unaccustomed." Bergson had the impression that the Germans were feeding Wilson false information in order to keep him neutral.

Given Wilson's "impenetrability," Bergson went on, one had to go to his entourage, especially House, to learn the deep causes of Wilson's indecision, which were religious and philosophical. Wilson had told House that, if he decided on war, God would hold him accountable for every American soldier killed. House told Bergson this, and also that he, House, had managed to remove these scruples by pointing out that, if the Americans did not fight Germany now, they would have to do so later at an even greater cost in lives. As for philosophical grounds for hesitation, these related to the incomparable role that the United States could play in Europe and the world by intervening to assure Allied victory. Wilson was interested in establishing machinery for peace, but he was mistrustful by nature, especially of official personages. Wilson asked whether one could find on either side anything other than national egoisms struggling with one another. He did not wish to be duped. Bergson thought that at first Wilson might even have considered France's desire for Alsace-Lorraine to be based on such egoism. Henri Bergson, "Mes Missions, 1917-1918," Vevey, Switzerland, Aug. 24, 1936, T MS (Papiers d'Agents, Bergson 1, 1ère Mission aux U. S. A., 1917-1918, FFM-Ar). Bergson's memorandum is reprinted in Henri Bergson, "Mes Missions (1917-1918)," La Revue Hommes et Mondes, III (July 1947), 359-75.

3 Bergson saw Wilson at the White House on February 19.

T R A N S L A T I O N

Washington, received March 3, 1917, 12:50 p.m.

No. 216. Mr. Bergson has asked me to transmit the following telegram to Your Excellency:

Mr. Lane, Secretary of the Interior, with whom I have had several conversations, told me the day before yesterday: "You have succeeded in convincing Mr. Miller, who has great influence in the Federal Reserve Board, and this will probably find expression in acts that are important for your country." Yesterday, Mr. Miller in effect told me, very confidentially, that certain measures will no doubt be taken to persuade the American public to lend its money directly to the Allies in such a way that we will no longer have to furnish security when we borrow.

I am leaving Washington after having talked at length with President Wilson, his cabinet members, and divers members of the administration and of the Congress. Here is my impression: They are marching toward war, but, while certain cabinet members wish to enter the war immediately and completely, President Wilson will not take this step until events have made it inevitable, because he still has opinion divided behind him; in the West, many persons still want peace at any price. The President wishes to manage all the transitions before deciding upon hostilities, and he will probably manage them even during actual hostilities, before reaching the stage of open war.

If war breaks out, as is probable, I do not know whether the President and America herself will propose the same war aims as ours and whether they would want as complete a defeat of Germany as we do. That will depend upon events. President Wilson appeared to me in any event to take as his own the principles for which we ourselves are fighting, but he considers England as struggling uniquely for her own commercial preponderance, which he does not seem eager to guarantee. Moreover, he has an inexact idea of internal conditions in Germany. He believes that the Germans are weary of Prussian militarism and perhaps of the imperial regime. I fear that I did not succeed in disabusing him of this idea. Bergson.                Jusserand

## From the Diary of Colonel House

Washington, March 3, 1917

Loulie and I came over here today for the Inauguration. There were many acquaintances on the train and I was not able to rest.

We drove immediately to the White House. After having tea with the President and Mrs. Wilson, the President and I went to his study where he read me his Inaugural Address. There was much to commend and nothing to criticise since it was a replica of his Senate Address of January 22nd.

We were much concerned about the action of the Senate regarding the bill to permit the arming of merchantmen, and little else was talked of.¹ There were some other house guests; consisting almost wholly of relatives. After dinner Mrs. Wilson and I had a confidential talk. She told me that she disliked McAdoo; that she had always disliked him. She considered him thoroughly selfish in as much as he would let nothing stand in the way of his ambition. In this she is pretty nearly right, although, by and large, he is an affectionate and generous friend. She asked what chance I thought he would have for the nomination for President. My opinion was that his chances were better than they had been, but it was too far off to speculate.

She said Mrs. Lansing had a lady ask her the other day if she knew the new way of spelling Lansing. Mrs. Lansing of course said no, and the lady proceeded to spell "H o u s e." Mrs. Wilson did not say what effect this had on Mrs. Lansing but I assured her it had none on Lansing himself. Lansing is a pretty big fellow in that way and does not seem to be disturbed by jealousy.

¹ Spurred by the publication of the Zimmermann telegram on March 1, the House of Representatives on that date, by a vote of 403 to thirteen, approved a bill which authorized the President to arm merchant ships, but omitted the clause of the original bill which permitted the President to use "other instrumentalities and methods" to protect American ships and citizens (see the Enclosure printed with WW to WGM, Feb. 24, 1917), and prohibited the War Risk Insurance Bureau from insuring ships carrying munitions. The Senate, on March 2, began debate on a stronger armed-ship bill approved by the Foreign Relations Committee on February 27. The senators discussed the measure for eight hours without any sign of a filibuster, until Senator Hitchcock asked unanimous consent to table the Foreign Relations Committee's bill and take up the measure adopted by the House. The Senate agreed to this and then recessed at 12:40 in the morning of March 3. The debate recommenced at 10 A.M. that same morning. Senator Stone made a four-hour speech against the bill and offered an amendment to prohibit the arming or convoying of ships carrying munitions but did nothing more to block action on the measure. However, by the early evening of March 3, it was clear that Senators Robert M. La Follette, George W. Norris, Albert B. Cummins, and Asle Jorgenson Gronna, Republican of North Dakota, were determined to prevent action on any armed-ship bill. They blocked every motion for unanimous consent to limit debate and vote and filibustered through the night and until noon on Sunday, March 4, when the Senate adjourned *sine die*. See the *New York Times*, March 2-5, 1917; *Cong. Record*, 64th Cong., 2d sess., pp. 4744-81, 4859-4919, 4977-5020; and Link, *Campaigns for Progressivism and Peace*, pp. 353-61 *passim*.

## A Statement

[*March 4, 1917*]

The termination of the last session of the Sixty-fourth Congress by constitutional limitation disclosed a situation unparalleled in the history of the country, perhaps unparalleled in the history of any modern Government. In the immediate presence of a crisis fraught with more subtle and far-reaching possibilities of national danger than any other the Government has known within the whole history of its international relations, the Congress has been unable to act either to safeguard the country or to vindicate the elementary rights of its citizens. More than 500 of the 531 members of the two houses were ready and anxious to act; the House of Representatives had acted, by an overwhelming majority; but the Senate was unable to act because a little group of eleven Senators had determined that it should not.

The Senate has no rules by which debate can be limited or brought to an end, no rules by which dilatory tactics of any kind can be prevented. A single member can stand in the way of action, if he have but the physical endurance. The result in this case is a complete paralysis alike of the legislative and of the executive branches of the Government.

This inability of the Senate to act has rendered some of the most necessary legislation of the session impossible at a time when the need of it was most pressing and most evident. The bill which would have permitted such combinations of capital and of organization in the export and import trade of the country as the circumstances of international competition have made imperative—a bill which the business judgment of the whole country approved and demanded—has failed. The opposition of one or two Senators has made it impossible to increase the membership of the Interstate Commerce Commission to give it the altered organization necessary for its efficiency. The conservation bill, which should have released for immediate use the mineral resources which are still locked up in the public lands, now that their release is more imperatively necessary than ever, and the bill which would have made the unused water power of the country immediately available for industry have both failed, though they have been under consideration throughout the sessions of two Congresses and have been twice passed by the House of Representatives. The appropriations for the army have failed, along with the appropriations for the civil establishment of the Government, the appropriations for the Military Academy, at West Point and the General Deficiency bill. It has proved impossible to extend the powers of the Shipping Board to meet the special needs of the new situations into which our commerce has been forced or to increase the gold reserve of our national banking system to meet the unusual circumstances of the existing financial situation.

It would not cure the difficulty to call the Sixty-fifth Congress in extraordinary session. The paralysis of the Senate would remain. The purpose and the spirit of action are not lacking now. The Congress is more definitely united in thought and purpose at this moment, I venture to say, than it has been within the memory of any men now in its membership. There is not only the most united patriotic purpose, but the objects members have in view are perfectly clear and definite. But the Senate cannot act unless its leaders can obtain unanimous consent. Its majority is powerless, helpless. In the midst of a crisis of extraordinary peril, when only definite and decided action can make the nation safe or shield it from war itself by the aggression of others, action is impossible.

Although, as a matter of fact, the nation and the representatives of the nation stand back of the Executive with unprecedented unanimity and spirit, the impression made abroad will, of course, be that it is not so and that other Governments may act as they please without fear that this Government can do anything at all. We cannot explain. The explanation is incredible. The Senate of the United States is the only legislative body in the world which cannot act when its majority is ready for action. A little group of willful men, representing no opinion but their own, have rendered the great Government of the United States helpless and contemptible.

The remedy? There is but one remedy. The only remedy is that the rules of the Senate shall be so altered that it can act. The country can be relied upon to draw the moral. I believe that the Senate can be relied on to supply the means of action and save the country from disaster.[1]

Supplementary Statement from the White House.

At the same time the President authorized the further statement that what rendered the situation even more grave than it had been supposed that it was, was the discovery that, while the President under his general constitutional powers could do much of what he had asked the Congress to empower him to do, it had been found that there were certain old statutes as yet unrepealed which may raise insuperable practical obstacles and may nullify his power.

Printed in the *New York Times*, March 5, 1917.
[1] There is a WWsh draft of the foregoing statement in WP, DLC.


# From Melancthon Williams Jacobus

My dear President Wilson:       Hartford, Conn. March 4th, 1917
    You have to day an opportunity for service to this Nation that has come to few Presidents in it's history.

Historically, Democracies have always found the strength that has carried them through their ordeals in the concentration of authority in their leaders—not in the distribution of it among their peoples.

As Nations they have never failed to pass away when their leaders have demitted their power of action to popular referendum; they have never failed to remain when their leaders have made that power the initiative of popular action

We have come now to where the question of our survival is at issue. Remember Lincoln and the habeas corpus act and crystallize our action by yours.

Yours faithfully   Melancthon W Jacobus

ALS (WP, DLC).


## From Chalmers Martin[1]

My Dear Tommy:                    Wooster, Ohio, March 4, 1917.

Somehow I just cannot let this day of your entering upon your second term pass without saying God bless you! Under other circumstances I could send you sincere but light-hearted congratulations. As it is, I recall with painful interest what you said to me when last I saw you, a little more than a year ago, of the diabolical plotting that was even then going on and of the grave conditions that made it dangerous for you to be absent from the capital for even the briefest time. But God has upheld and guided you through all that year of anxiety, and He will not forsake you in the one now beginning.

One cannot command the President of the United States, I suppose, but I charge you that this is not to be answered. If it affords you even a momentary comfort or courage, it has served its purpose. The White House waste basket must be of ample capacity. In with it!

Yours as always,   Chalmers Martin.

TLS (WP, DLC).
[1] Princeton 1879, Professor of Old Testament History and Literature at the College of Wooster.


## A Memorandum by Robert Lansing

MEMORANDUM ON THE MESSAGE OF ZIMMERMANN
TO THE GERMAN MINISTER TO MEXICO.

March 4, 1917.

On returning from White Sulphur Springs Tuesday morning, February 27th, Phillips handed me a confidential telegram re-

ceived the day before from London giving the English translation of a telegram from the German Secretary of Foreign Affairs
to the German Minister at Mexico City which had been forwarded
in cipher by Count Bernstorff under date of January 19th. The
cipher message had been obtained by secret agents of the British
Government and forwarded by them to London where it had just
been deciphered by means of a complicated German code in the
possession of the Foreign Office. Mr. Balfour gave the translation to Mr. Page expressing the hope that the source would be
concealed.

The fact that Mr. Balfour himself conveyed this information
to Mr. Page convinced me that it was genuine. Furthermore
the report from Mr. Page gave the numerals of the first and last
groups of the cipher message in order that we might find the
original at the telegraph office in Washington.

About ten o'clock Polk came into my office and we talked over
the substance of the telegram. He told me that on its arrival he
had at once taken it to the President who had shown much
indignation and was disposed to make the text public without
delay. Polk had advised him to await my return which he had
agreed to do. I also found that Polk with his usual promptness
had communicated with the Western Union officials and asked
them to search for and deliver the original to the Department.

At 11:30 I went to the White House and for an hour discussed
with the President the substance of the telegram and the way to
use it. The President said that he had been wondering how
Bernstorff got the message from Berlin and that the closing of
secret lines of communication with his Government made him
a little uncertain as to its authenticity.

I told him that I thought it could be easily explained, my
opinion being that it was done in the following manner: During
the early part of January Count Bernstorff at the instance of Col.
House had been laboring with his Government to obtain concrete
terms of peace. The Ambassador had complained of his inability
to communicate secretly and therefore freely with Berlin, which
he considered essential in order to accomplish his purpose. In
view of this reasonable statement we had consented very reluctantly to send messages in secret cipher for him through our
Embassy. This we did several times, permitting the German
Foreign Office to reply in the same way. On January 17th an ex-
ceptionally long message (some 1000 groups) came through
from Berlin. On the 18th this message was delivered to the
Ambassador. On the 19th the telegram from Bernstorff to Mexico was filed. From these facts I drew the conclusion that in

the long secret message delivered to him on the 18th was the message for the German minister besides other orders as to what to do in case of a severance of the diplomatic relations.

The President two or three times during the recital of the foregoing exclaimed "Good Lord," and when I had finished said he believed that the deduction as to how Bernstorff received his orders was correct. He showed much resentment at the German Government for having imposed upon our kindness in this way and for having made us the innocent agents to advance a conspiracy against this country.

I told the President that I thought it would be unwise for the Department to give out the telegram officially at this time as it would be charged that it was done to influence opinion on the bill for arming merchant vessels, but I thought it might indirectly be made public after we had confirmed the sending of the message by Bernstorff. To this the President agreed.

On returning to the Department I found Polk had obtained, after using considerable pressure, the original cipher message filed by Bernstorff. The Western Union were very unwilling to give it up but finally consented to do so. Nothing further was done that day.

Wednesday morning Bernstorff's cipher message to Mexico was cabled to London with the request that some member of the Embassy be permitted by the Foreign Office to decode it with German code, which they had. The President telephoned me over our private wire suggesting that we have a conference with McAdoo and Burleson as to making the text public and the best way to use it to get the greatest result in influencing legislation regarding the arming of merchant vessels. Later in the morning the President again telephoned saying McAdoo and Burleson were at the Capitol attending to pending bills and could not be reached.

A little before four that afternoon the President telephoned saying that he thought it was wise to give out the telegram for the morning papers and that he believed that it would be advisable for me to summon Senator Hitchcock, who had charge of the Arming Bill, to the Department and show him the message. I again suggested that the message be made public indirectly, that then when we were asked about it we could say that we knew of it and knew that it was authentic. I said that I could do this through a representative of the Associated Press. It was my opinion that this would avoid any charge of using the document improperly and would attract more attention than issuing it officially. With this plan the President agreed.

I at once telephoned Senator Hitchcock who arrived at the

Department twenty minutes later. I told him that we had obtained possession of a very important message from the German Foreign Office to its Minister in Mexico and I then read him the message without disclosing the source of our information. The Senator, who had pro-german tendencies, was greatly shocked and asked if I was sure that it was authentic. I answered that I could vouch for that, as the evidence was conclusive. He said that it would cause a tremendous sensation to make public so dastardly a plot. As the Senator left I said to him that he might tell Senator Stone of the contents of the message.

At about six that evening E. M. Hood[1] a correspondent of the Associated Press came to my house by appointment and I gave him a paraphrase of the telegram binding him to secrecy as to where he obtained it. He also agreed not to put it on the wires before ten o'clock, so that I should not be bothered by calls on the telephone as correspondents here would not get word of it until midnight.

The next morning, March 1st, the message of the German Secretary of Foreign Affairs was published in the papers and created a profound sensation throughout the country. Its effect on Congress was very marked. After a day given over to patriotic speeches the House by a vote of 403 to 13 passed the Arming Bill. The Senate debated a resolution introduced by Senator Lodge asking the President as to the authenticity of the Zimmermann message, a fact which I had admitted to the press correspondents at eleven o'clock that morning and which the President had also confirmed when questioned by Senator Swanson. The resolution was adopted about six that evening and the Presidents reply and my report were prepared by Woolsey and sent to me at the Italian Embassy where we were dining. I signed the report and arranged by telephone to have the clerk who brought the papers pass the guards at the White House. Within two hours after the passage of the resolution the President's reply transmitting my report unconditionally confirming the genuineness of the Zimmermann message was laid before the Senate.[2]

The next morning (Friday) Polk brought me a brief telegram from Page saying our copy of the cipher message obtained from the Western Union had been received, that instructions had been followed with success, and that text of deciphered message would follow. While I had never doubted the authenticity of the

[1] Edwin Milton Hood.
[2] WW to the Senate, March 1, 1917, enclosing RL to WW, March 1, 1917, printed in *Cong. Record*, 64th Cong., 2d sess., p. 4618. Lansing reaffirmed the authenticity of the telegram but said that it was incompatible with the public interest to divulge its source.

translation sent as it emanated from Balfour this corroboration by our own people was a relief.

That afternoon the German text of the deciphered message began to arrive, but its decoding was a slow process and there was no hope of getting it in accurate form that day.

At the Cabinet meeting at 2:30 p.m. the telegram was naturally the chief subject of discussion, but no inkling was given as to how it had been obtained. The concensus of opinion was that, if the German Government denied the genuineness of the message, the only thing to do was to assert that this Government was in possession of conclusive evidence that it was genuine, but to go no further. This statement could have been made most emphatically in view of the facts.

I had expected Zimmermann to deny the message and to challenge us to produce proofs. That would have been the politic thing to do because it would have put this Government in a dilemma in that we would have to make public the evidence or else refuse to do so simply affirming that the proofs were absolute but must be held secret. If we did not produce the evidence there would always be the charge that the whole thing was a fraud concocted to aid the passage of the Arming Bill, not by the Government but some other Government or some persons who had imposed upon us. Very many Americans, sympathizers with the Allies as well as sympathizers with the Germans would have believed this and blamed this Government for giving credence to so unbelievable a piece of folly as the message. To avoid this it might have been necessary to publish the proofs. If we did that the German government would have found out that we had access to its code and a channel for future information would have been closed. But, even under such necessity, we would have found it difficult, I fear, to have obtained the consent of the British Foreign Office to make the matter public, and of course without its consent we could not honorably have told the facts.

If I had been in Zimmermann's place I would have challenged this Government to prove its charge. It would have been a shrewd move. It is true, when I had been questioned by the newspaper correspondents Thursday morning, I had given the impression that to disclose the source from which the message had been obtained might endanger somebody's life. I did this in order to convey the idea that the text of the message had been obtained by purchase here or in Mexico or else from a spy in Germany. If that idea was accepted it would throw everyone, particularly the German Government, off the track and prevent any speculation from even approaching the real source. The British Government's secret would be safe.

Fortunately my suggestion was swallowed without question by the correspondents. The belief prevailed that Zimmermann had sent a *letter* to the German Minister at Mexico through the Embassy here, and that in some way the letter or a copy came into possession of the Department. The speculation was as to whether it was obtained in the United States, Germany or Mexico. There was never a suggestion that we had a cipher message of which we had the key. In the later discussion the German Government charged it up to "treachery."

Appreciating the probable denial by the German Foreign Office of the authenticity of the message I was naturally apprehensive of the effect on public opinion of a refusal to produce the proofs, which was the only course open if we kept faith with the British and that we were bound to do. It was, therefore, with profound amazement and relief when I read that Zimmermann on Saturday morning frankly acknowledged that the message, as printed, was genuine and attempted to justify his sending it.[3] It was a most unexpected course for him to take and showed him to be not at all astute or resourceful in dealing with a situation where he could have caused us serious embarrassment to say the least. He threw away a certain opportunity to put this Government in a weak defensive position or else to find out where we got the message. By admitting the truth he blundered in a most astounding manner for a man engaged in international intrigues. Of course the message itself was a stupid piece of business, but admitting it was far worse. It seems to me an amateur in diplomacy would have at once perceived the chance and denied the message. Zimmermann's course was a surprising example of incompetency and showed him to be a man of little ability. To blunder twice in such fashion ought to have been enough to cause his resignation.

Zimmermann's admission of the genuineness of the telegram is the end of the story—at least it is the end until Count Bernstorff now at sea reaches Germany when I presume the source of our knowledge will be discussed and discussed. The admission suppressed all the clamor of the German-American press about the message being faked and the unexpressed suspicion that it was fraudulent held by many other people. It is true that a few went so far as to declare that the admission was spurious in spite of the fact that it came by wireless through the Wolff Agency, the official news distributor of the German Government. Later the

[3] See, e.g., the *New York Times*, March 4, 1917.

submission of the matter to the Reichstag committee and its approval of Zimmermann's conduct silenced these doubters. A few other Americans, like Senator O'Gorman and former Representative Hermann Metz,[4] took the ground that Zimmermann's act was justified by the circumstances of the case and was the course which the United States would have taken if it had been in Germany's place. Neither of these pro-German groups are large or influential fortunately for the honor and welfare of this country.

On the other hand, the message and Zimmermann's unexpected admission have caused a tremendous sensation; the people all over the country are extremely enraged at the perfidy of the German Government in talking peace and friendship with this country and at the same time plotting a hostile coalition against it.[5]

T MS (R. Lansing Papers, DLC).
  [4] Herman August Metz, Democratic Congressman from New York, 1913-1915.
  [5] For the fullest account of the origin of the Zimmermann telegram and its reception by the Mexican government, see Friedrich Katz, *Deutschland, Diaz und die mexikanische Revolution: Die Deutsche Politik in Mexiko, 1870-1920* (East Berlin, 1964), and, by the same author, *The Secret War in Mexico: Europe, the United States and the Mexican Revolution* (Chicago and London, 1981), pp. 350-66.


# From the Diary of Thomas W. Brahany

Sunday, March 4, 1917

Woodrow Wilson began his second term as President of the United States at noon today. The oath of office was administered by Edward Douglass White of Louisiana, Chief Justice of the United States, in the President's room at the Capitol, at 12:04 P.M. No President had a more simple inauguration. Nobody was invited to attend. All the members of the Cabinet were present, but as far as I know, even they were not specially asked to attend. The Congress was in session all night, the House killing time, and the Senate killing the bill to authorize the President to arm merchant ships and take other measures to defend American rights at sea against German submarines. This bill passed the House a few days ago with only thirteen votes against it. I am quite ashamed that four of the thirteen votes were recorded by Wisconsin Representatives—Messrs. Cooper, Cary, Nelson and Stafford.[1] An overwhelming majority of the Senate favored the bill, but a small group of Republican Progressives led by Senators

  [1] Henry Allen Cooper, William Joseph Cary, John Mandt Nelson, and William Henry Stafford, all Republicans.

La Follette, Cummins, Norris and Gronna conducted a successful filibuster against its consideration. In this they were ably assisted by Senator Stone (Democrat) Chairman of the Committee on Foreign Relations. Because of Senator Stone's opposition, Senator Hitchcock was in charge of the bill. Until now the President has held Stone in high esteem, but his conduct the last few days has placed him in that class described by Mr. Roosevelt as "undesirable." Tumulty said the President told him this morning that he was "through with Stone." "I'll not even shake hands with him again," the President said to Tumulty. The President left the White House for the Capitol shortly before 11 o'clock. He was accompanied by Mrs. Wilson. I remained at the Executive Office, Forster going to the Capitol to look after the papers requiring the President's approval. The President reached the White House before 12:30. On their return Tumulty, Forster and Joe Murphy, the Chief of the Secret Service force at the White House, told me that the President was as "mad as a hornet" because uninvited persons crowded his room just before he took the oath. He seemed to resent especially the presence of Frank P. Glass, a Birmingham, Alabama, editor, who a few years ago was, for a short time, a U. S. Senator. The President remarked that "Glass is a very cheeky person." The President wants things to go according to schedule, and when he said he would take the oath "privately" on Sunday he meant *privately*. Joe Murphy said he was over his anger before he left the Capitol. None of the President's daughters was present to see the swearing in. Tumulty says that the Secretary of the Treasury, Mr. McAdoo, asked the President this morning if Mrs. McAdoo, (the President's daughter) might attend the oath-taking, and the President said "No." Tumulty thinks the President took this position because of his wish not to discriminate between members of the Cabinet. My own notion is that the President did not wish any woman other than Mrs. Wilson present. If Miss Wilson, Mrs. Sayre and Mrs. McAdoo had gone to the Capitol to see their father take the oath courtesy would have required them to ask all of [the] men and women who are White House guests, and the result would be a "function" at the Capitol. I imagine the President told the family that embarrassment would be avoided if all of them should stay at home. Even Colonel House, a White House guest, the President's closest friend didn't go to the Capitol. Mr. Glass was accompanied by a woman (his daughter,[2] I understand) and it may be that the presence of this uninvited woman was the fly in the ointment. Anyhow the

[2] The Editors have not been able to determine which of Glass's three daughters she was.

President was peevish and intimated to Tumulty that he would like some of these persons (nodding toward Glass and his companion) to leave. Instead Tumulty himself left and was not in the room when the oath was administered. Tumulty said the President told him he would at once call Congress in extraordinary session. The filibusterers killed not only the armed ship bill, but the army, sundry Civil and General Deficiency appropriation bills. The failure of the last named bill means that the soldiers serving on the Mexican border must want for their pay. The President has announced his purpose to retain all of his Cabinet Officers. The Republican press has poked a great deal of fun at the Secretary of the Navy, and we've had a dozen or more telegrams in the last week demanding that a strong man be appointed to succeed the affable Josephus. Up to 6 o'clock this evening, when I left the Executive Office, the President had not written the Inaugural Address which he is to deliver tomorrow at noon. Forster is at the office tonight in the hope that he may get a copy for the Public Printer. Among the bills signed by the President last night was the District of Columbia prohibition bill which goes into effect on November 1, next. On Friday last, Samuel Gompers, President of the American Federation of Labor, asked the President to veto the bill on the ground that the citizens of the District should be given a voice on the question of a wet or dry Washington. The President told him he felt the Congress was vested with police power for the District; and besides there was no machinery in the District to conduct a referendum. Following Gompers, three of the leading Democratic politicians of the District urged that the bill be vetoed. One of them was in the midst of a fervent plea in which he said "we beg you, Mr. President to show mercy," when the President interrupted, "Mercy to whom." "To the people of the District," stammered the orator. "Oh rats," said the President. I had twenty or more telephone calls this morning from persons who had heard reports that the bill was vetoed, with the exception of one all of them heaved a sigh of sorrow when I told them the bill had been signed.

This afternoon (March 4) the much advertised suffrage parade was held. For several months women have been standing just outside the two north gates of the White House grounds holding standards to which are attached yellow banners. These so called silent sentinels are members of the Congressional Union for women suffrage. They report at 10 o'clock and remain until 4:30. The first day they reported Tumulty, Forster and I held a Council of War and decided the best thing to do was to ignore them; that they would thrive on opposition. The White House policemen

were instructed accordingly. After the first few days the newspapers neglected them. On the first cold day of their vigil the
President told I. H. Hoover, Chief Usher at the White House to
tell the women that they could come to the lower corridor of the
White House if chilling blasts of the north wind made their outside station unbearable. It was a surprise message for the women,
who, when they saw Hoover coming thought he had an order
directing them to leave. None of the women took advantage of
the President's offer to come inside to get warm. Instead a negro
was employed to carry hot bricks to the gates for use on cold
days. The Congressional Union women are the militant branch
of the equal suffrage women. The President has on three or four
occasions received large delegations from the Congressional
Union, and his views on equal suffrage are perfectly well known.
In the last campaign most of the Congressional Union women opposed the President and some of their leaders were the chief
pedlars and promoters of the scandalous and utterly untrue
stories circulated in the middle and far west in reference to the
President's private life. Last week the Congressional Union and
the National Woman's party effected a merger. Resolutions were
adopted and it was desired that the resolutions adopted be presented to the President today. The President declined to see the
women. It was announced that thousands of them, some of the
press notices reading "at least 10,000," would march around the
White House this afternoon; that pickets would take their stand
and remain at attention for three or four hours. For nearly a week
Washington has "enjoyed" typical Inaugural weather,—rain,
sleet and wind. It was raining hard when the suffragists appeared
today. They were led by a band, and most of them carried banners. "Mr. President, how long must women wait for liberty,"
was a favorite banner slogan. I do not think there were more
than 500 women in line. The rain beat in their faces and the
wind played havoc with the banners. They presented a sorry
sight, but they went through with their program as well as they
could. In the grounds and in the streets were more policemen
than Washington had seen gathered ever before. It was not an
auspicious time for the militant ones to start trouble. The leaders
sought admission at several gates but each policeman of whom
inquiry was made politely told them "This is Sunday and the
White House grounds are closed to all visitors." The policemen
told them any papers they wished to leave would be sent to the
Executive Office. The marching and picketing continued for a
little more than an hour. It was not a successful day. The drizzle
had something to do with the fizzle.

As I write this (evening of March 4) a hard rain is falling and I am afraid bad weather is certain tomorrow. Joe Murphy made a bet this afternoon that the skies will clear before the President takes his public oath of office on the stand before the East front of the Capitol tomorrow. Joe has been with the President ever since his election four years ago. He says Woodrow Wilson is the luckiest man in the world, and Joe's bet is based solely on his belief that Wilson's luck is better in gambling odds than any prediction of the weather man. I don't think I shall go to the Capitol for the Senate and East front ceremonies. Mrs. Wilson sent tickets to Mrs. Brahany[3] and me, and from others I've received additional tickets. We're invited to the luncheon at the White House and have seats on the President's Reviewing Stand.

T MS (F. D. Roosevelt Papers, NHpR).
[3] Lucy Cahill Brahany.

## From the Diary of Josephus Daniels

1917 Sunday 4 March

Went to Capitol to see close of Congress. Adjourned without action. Lane, Bur, Baker & I suggested to President that he go before Congress & ask for passage of bill. B & B & L were enthusiastic. The dramatic setting appealed to them Pres. said "if I ought to have gone, should have gone sooner.["] Said he thought he ought to speak only when he could accomplish something & he thought it could not change the determination not to act. He convinced all he should not go.

Got pen with which President signed Naval bill

## From the Diary of Colonel House

March 4, 1917.

The day is dark and gloomy with high winds and floods of rain. The President and Mrs. Wilson started for the Capitol at 10.30. This was necessary in order that the President might sign the bills as they came in from Congress, and to be ready to take the oath of office at twelve o'clock. They asked me to go with them but I thought it best not to do so. I never like to be conspicuously in evidence. There is enough jealousy abroad without accentuating it unnecessarily. If in serving the public and the President I excite jealousy, I bear it with indifference, but I try to avoid it when there is nothing to be gained except some personal glorification.

When the President returned he showed much excitement, and was bitter in his denunciation of the small band of senators who undertook to use the arbitrary rules of the Senate to defeat the wishes of the majority regarding the arming of merchantmen. I suggested that he say to the public what he was saying to me, and to say it immediately. His answer was that he could not put it in his Inaugural Address because it would spoil the texture of it, but he would put it out in a few days. I urged him to do it now, giving it to the papers tomorrow morning in order to strike while the iron was hot. He wondered whether he could do it so quickly but said he would try.

He shut himself in practically all the afternoon and later produced the statement to be given out for publication in tomorrow morning papers. He called in McAdoo, Burleson and Tumulty after dinner to discuss it. They were unanimously in favor of the plan.

We discussed the formation of the new House of Representatives. The President is indifferent whether we control it or not believing that our control would be so narrow that it would perhaps be better not to have the responsibility. McAdoo differed from him. There are many arguments in favor of both positions.

## The Second Inaugural Address[1]

[March 5, 1917]

My fellow citizens: The four years which have elapsed since last I stood in this place have been crowded with counsel and action of the most vital interest and consequence. Perhaps no equal period in our history has been so fruitful of important reforms in our economic and industrial life or so full of significant changes in the spirit and purpose of our political action. We have sought very thoughtfully to set our house in order, correct the grosser errors and abuses of our industrial life, liberate and quicken the processes of our national genius and energy, and lift our politics to a broader view of the people's essential interests. It is a record of singular variety and singular distinction. But I shall not attempt to review it. It speaks for itself and will be of increasing influence as the years go by. This is not the time for retrospect. It is the time, rather, to speak our thoughts and purposes concerning the present and the immediate future.

Although we have centered counsel and action with such unusual concentration and success upon the great problems of domestic legislation to which we addressed ourselves four years ago, other matters have more and more forced themselves upon our attention, matters lying outside our own life as a nation and over which we had no control, but which, despite our wish to keep free of them, have drawn us more and more irresistibly into their own current and influence.

It has been impossible to avoid them. They have affected the life of the whole world. They have shaken men everywhere with a passion and an apprehension they never knew before. It has been hard to preserve calm counsel while the thought of our own people swayed this way and that under their influence. We are a composite and cosmopolitan people. We are of the blood of all the nations that are at war. The currents of our thoughts as well as the currents of our trade run quick at all seasons back and forth between us and them. The war inevitably set its mark from the first alike upon our minds, our industries, our commerce, our politics, and our social action. To be indifferent to it or independent of it was out of the question.

And yet all the while we have been conscious that we were not part of it. In that consciousness, despite many divisions, we have drawn closer together. We have been deeply wronged upon the seas,[2] but we have not wished to wrong or injure in return; have retained throughout the consciousness of standing in some sort apart, intent upon an interest that transcended the immediate issues of the war itself. As some of the injuries done us have become intolerable we have still been clear that we wished nothing for ourselves that we were not ready to demand for all mankind,—fair dealing, justice, the freedom to live and be at ease against organized wrong.

It is in this spirit and with this thought that we have grown more and more aware, more and more certain that the part we wished to play was the part of those who mean to vindicate and fortify peace. We have been obliged to arm ourselves to make good our claim to a certain minimum of right and of freedom of action. We stand firm in armed neutrality since it seems that in no other way we can demonstrate what it is we insist upon and cannot forego. We may even be drawn on, by circumstances, not by our own purpose or desire, to a more active assertion of our rights as we see them and a more immediate association with the great struggle itself. But nothing will alter our thought or our purpose. They are too clear to be obscured. They are too deeply rooted in the principles of our national life to be altered. We desire neither conquest nor advantage. We wish nothing that can be had only at the cost of another people. We have always professed unselfish purpose and we covet the opportunity to prove that our professions are sincere.

There are many things still to do at home, to clarify our own politics and give new vitality to the industrial processes of our own life, and we shall do them as time and opportunity serve; but we realize that the greatest things that remain to be done must be done with the whole world for stage and in coöperation with the wide and universal forces of mankind, and we are making our spirits ready for those things. They will follow in the immediate wake of the war itself and will set civilization up again. We are provincials no longer. The tragical events of the thirty months of vital turmoil through which we have just passed have made us citizens of the world. There can be no turning back. Our own fortunes as a nation are involved, whether we would have it so or not.

And yet we are not the less Americans on that account. We shall be the more American if we but remain true to the principles in which we have been bred. They are not the principles of a province or of a single continent. We have known and boasted all along that they were the principles of a liberated mankind. These, therefore, are the things we shall stand for, whether in war or in peace:

That all nations are equally interested in the peace of the world and in the political stability of free peoples, and equally responsible for their maintenance;

That the essential principle of peace is the actual equality of nations in all matters of right or privilege;

That peace cannot securely or justly rest upon an armed balance of power;

That governments derive all their just powers from the consent of the governed and that no other powers should be supported by the common thought, purpose, or power of the family of nations.

That the seas should be equally free and safe for the use of all peoples, under rules set up by common agreement and consent, and that, so far as practicable, they should be accessible to all upon equal terms;

That national armaments should be limited to the necessities of national order and domestic safety;

That the community of interest and of power upon which peace must henceforth depend imposes upon each nation the duty of seeing to it that all influences proceeding from its own citizens meant to encourage or assist revolution in other States should be sternly and effectually suppressed and prevented.

I need not argue these principles to you, my fellow countrymen: they are your own, part and parcel of your own thinking and your own motive in affairs. They spring up native amongst us. Upon this as a platform of purpose and of action we can stand together.

And it is imperative that we should stand together. We are being forged into a new unity amidst the fires that now blaze throughout the world. In their ardent heat we shall, in God's providence, let us hope, be purged of faction and division, purified of the errant humours of party and of private interest, and shall stand forth in the days to come with a new dignity of national pride and spirit. Let each man see to it that the dedication is in his own heart, the high purpose of the Nation in his own mind, ruler of his own will and desire.

I stand here and have taken the high and solemn oath to which you have been audience because the people of the United States have chosen me for this august delegation of power and have by their gracious judgment named me their leader in affairs. I know now what the task means. I realize to the full the responsibility which it involves. I pray God I may be given the wisdom and the prudence to do my duty in the true spirit of this great people. I am their servant and can succeed only as they sustain and guide me by their confidence and their counsel. The thing I shall count upon, the thing without which neither counsel nor action will avail, is the unity of America,—an America united in feeling, in purpose, and in its vision of duty, of opportunity, and of service. We are to beware of all men who would turn the tasks and the necessities of the Nation to their own private profit or use them for the building up of private power; beware that no faction or disloyal intrigue break the harmony or embarrass the spirit of our people; beware that our government be kept pure and incorrupt in all its parts. United alike in the conception of our duty and in the high resolve to perform it in the face of all men, let us dedicate ourselves to the great task to which we must now set our hand. For myself I beg your tolerance, your countenance, and your united aid. The shadows that now lie dark upon our path will soon be dispelled and we shall walk with the light all about us if we be but true to ourselves,—to ourselves as we have wished to be known in the counsels of the world and in the thought of all those who love liberty and justice and the right exalted.

Printed reading copy (WP, DLC).

　1 There is a WWsh draft, with no composition date, of this address in WP, DLC.

　2 In Wilson's shorthand draft this sentence reads: "We have been deeply injured and wronged by the governments of both sides upon the seas. . . ."

## Two Telegrams from Walter Hines Page

London, March 5, 1917.

5794. CONFIDENTIAL. For the President and the Secretary only. My 5644, February 9, 10 a.m. The financial inquiries made here reveal an international condition most alarming to the American financial and industrial outlook. England is obliged to finance her allies as well as to meet her own war expenses. She has as yet been able to do these tasks out of her own resources. But in addition to these tasks she cannot continue her present large purchases in the United States without shipments of gold to pay for them and she cannot maintain large shipments of gold for two reasons: first, both England and France must retain most of the gold they have to keep their paper money at par; and second, the submarine has made the shipping of gold too hazardous, even if they had it, to ship. The almost immediate danger therefore is that Franco-American and Anglo-American exchange will be so disturbed that orders by all the allied governments will be reduced to the lowest minimum and there will be almost a cessation of transatlantic trade. This will, of course, cause a panic in the United States.

The world will be divided into two hemispheres one of which has gold and commodities, and the other, which needs these commodities, will have no money to pay for them and practically no commodities of their own to exchange for them. The financial and commercial result will be almost as bad for one as for the other. This condition may soon come suddenly unless action is quickly taken to prevent it. France and England must have a large enough credit in the United States to prevent the collapse of world trade and of the whole of European finance.

If we should go to war with Germany the greatest help we could give the allies would be such a credit. In that case our Government could, if it would, make a large investment in a Franco-British loan or might guarantee such a loan. All the money would be kept in our own country, trade would be continued and enlarged till the war ends, and after the war, Europe would continue to buy food and would buy from us also an enormous supply of things to re-equip her peace industries. We should thus reap the profit of an uninterrupted, perhaps an enlarging, trade over a number of years and we should hold their securities in payment.

But if we hold most of the money and Europe cannot pay for re-equipment there may be a world-wide panic for an indefinite period.

Unless we go to war with Germany our Government of course cannot make such a direct grant of credit, but is there no way in which our Government might indirectly, immediately, help the establishment in the United States of a large Franco-British credit without a violation of armed neutrality? I am not sufficiently acquainted with our own Reserve Bank Law to form an opinion but if these banks were able to establish such a credit, they would avert this danger. It is a danger for us more real and imminent, I think, than the public on either side the ocean realizes. If it be not averted before its symptoms become apparent it will then be too late to avert it. I think that the pressure of this approaching crisis has gone beyond the ability of the Morgan Financial Agency for the British and French Governments. The need is becoming too great and urgent for any private agency to meet for every such agency has to encounter jealousies of rivals and of sections.

Perhaps our going to war is the only way in which our present preeminent trade position can be maintained and a panic averted. The submarine has added the last item to the danger of a financial world crash. During a period of uncertainty about our being drawn into the war, no more considerable credit can be privately placed in the United States and a collapse may come in the mean-time.                                                    Page.

T telegram (SDR, RG 59, 841.51/40, DNA).

London, March 5, 1917.

5795. For the President and the Secretary in greatest secrecy.

Mr. Balfour has given me the statement that follows with the request that I transmit it to you informally "even privately." His purpose in wishing you to know it is that you will understand proposed action, when it takes place and is published in the press, in order that no uneasiness may be felt regarding American ships. He has no plan to make such action general and these particular ships will be requisitioned with the consent of the owners. The whole matter will put the Danish Government in such a position that the most serious embarrassment and danger to Denmark would follow any publicity of the shipowners' consent. Following is the ststement [statement]:

"Owing to their fear of the German submarine warfare and also probably owing to political pressure put upon the Danish Government by the German Government Danish ships are refusing to put to sea. This is a serious matter for us partly because it enables the Germans to say that their submarine warfare has succeeded in preventing neutrals from entering the danger zone and partly because it prevents the Danes sending to this country that share of their agricultural produce which they have agreed to send. This has the secondary effect of making it likely that a larger quantity of produce will go into Germany.

We have been informed that Danish shipowners would be ready to sell their ships to British owners for the period of the war and thus enable them to be armed and to continue to sail and maintain the traffic of the seas but under Danish law this cannot be done by voluntary contract without the assent of the Danish Government and the German Government have, we have reason to believe, informed the Danish Government that if they do assent to any transfer of Danish shipping to the British flag they will regard it as an unfriendly action.

There is a certain amount of Danish shipping in British ports some of which is under charter to perform services of military importance to Great Britain and her allies. For instance, there are two Danish ships which are under contract to sail with coal cargoes for Italy which are urgently needed not only for ordinary civil purposes, but also for the maintainance of the manufacture of munitions in that country.

It seems that under recognized international law a belligerent power is entitled to seize neutral ships for military purposes. The rule is well stated in Article Six of the United States Naval War Code 'if military necessity should require it, neutral vessels found within the limits of belligerent authority may be seized and destroyed or otherwise used for military purposes but in such cases the owners of the neutral vessels must be fully compensated.'

The British Government have therefore decided to requisition such Danish ships as are urgently required for military purposes paying of course full compensation to the owners. They do not intend to exercise this power arbitrarily or extravagantly but they think that there can be no objection either in equity or in law to their requisitioning the two ships chartered to take coal for Italy to which reference has already been made and they have given directions to that effect."                    Page.

T telegram (SDR, RG 59, 763.72/3427, DNA).

# From Mario García Menocal

Havana Received March 5, 1917

Allow me to address you personally on the subject of the present peace disturbance in Cuba, to express to you once more my most sincere thankfulness for your several messages setting forth without leaving any room for doubt your high policy of upholding and supporting the Constitutional government here in the present unfortunate circumstances,[1] and to inform you that the only partial Presidential election pending now is that of a very few districts in Oriente Province, which you can be sure will be held pursuant to the laws in force on the subject as soon as Santiago is under regular government, which is expected to happen within very few days. This partial election will be effected notwithstanding that the Liberal candidate for the vice presidency[2] is in arms in the field against the government, and that the candidate for the presidency is notoriously one of the leaders of the outbreak in Santa Clara. The only other partial election which had to be held under the decisions of the Central Electoral Board and the Supreme Court, took place on the 14th ultimo, with strict pursuance to the provisions of the laws and after the government publicly announced that no act of coercion of violence would be tolerated, and there was none. This election, as all others, was held subject to legal protests and appeals to the courts. I only wish to add that in order to restore peace and maintain the present Constitutional government within the spirit of your noble policy, I only need that a very short time be given me to radically crush the outbreak which is now approaching its end, and I am confident that you will be the first to encourage me in my action against these chronic enemies of public peace.

Mario G. Menocal

T telegram (WP, DLC).
[1] Particularly RL to Consul Griffith, Feb. 23, 1917.
[2] Carlos Mendieta.

# From Cleveland Hoadley Dodge

New York.
My dear Old Friend and President          March 5th, 1917

You don't need any bouquets today, but I want to send just a word of cheer and greeting, as you start on your long four years voyage. Although you are sailing out to stormy seas, and the old Ship of State is a wee bit creaky, and some of her crew are rather mutinous, yet thank God, you have an heart of oak, and must feel today, as never before, that you have with you the wishes and prayers, not only of nearly all your own people, but those of nearly the whole world.

May God grant that your voyage may be prosperous and that after four years you may land safely and happily in a peaceful and spacious harbor. That you may be spared and strengthened in all that is before you is the earnest prayer of your devoted & affectionate friend                                    C H Dodge

ALS (WP, DLC).

## From Emily Greene Balch

New York N Y [March] 5 1917

May I express my gratitude for the way in which in your inaugural speech you strike again and again the note of international idealism and constructive peace The fact that I dread armed neautrality as a probable prelude to war and reject war as a tolerable policy even under far graver provocation that [than] we have suffered does not lessen my high hopes of the service to world peace which I believe you are destined to fulfill if this country does not become involved in the conflict

Emily Greene Balch.

T telegram (WP, DLC).

## From the Diary of Colonel House

March 5, 1917.

The family have been greatly alarmed as to the safety of the President. I tried to reassure them and partially succeeded. Loulie went with them to the Senate. I remained at home for the same reason I declined to go to the Capitol yesterday. I remained in the White House until lunch time when some two or three hundred guests, mainly of the official family, came for a buffet luncheon. I had difficulty in getting something to eat since there were so many people who insisted upon talking to me. I lead a retired life and avoid public functions to such an extent that the general public rarely get at me. When they do, they make full use of it.

Lansing wished to talk with me privately, and before luncheon was over I took him to my bedroom and we had an hour or more together. Then followed a succession of interviews. Gregory, McAdoo, Houston, Polk, Phillips, Franklin Roosevelt, etc. etc. My old friend Captain Bill McDonald came and it was a joy to be with him once more.

We had a quiet dinner and went upstairs to the oval sitting room to witness the fireworks. The family generally were at the main windows. The President and Mrs. Wilson sat by a side window, curtained off, and asked me to join them. The President was holding Mrs. Wilson's hand and leaning with his face against her's. We talked quietly of the happenings of the day and I spoke of my joy that we three, rather than the Hughes family, were looking at the fire-works from the White House windows.

Shortly after nine, the President suggested that we drive through the streets to see the illuminations. This turned out to be rather a risky adventure. There was no secret service man on the box, although a car with them followed. We had gone no distance before we were in a jam and the people, thronging the sidewalks and streets, recognized the President and sent up cheer after cheer. It was a dangerous moment, far more than anything he had gone through during the day. I sat with my automatic in my hand ready to act if the occasion arose.

When we returned to the White House, the President, Mrs. Wilson and I talked until eleven o'clock. There were a number of matters we had to discuss and decide which could not be done in the morning since he desired to have an early game of golf, and I intended to leave on the eleven o'clock train for New York.

Mrs. Wilson again expressed the hope that I would take the Ambassadorship to the Court of St James. The President said he had written Page that he would not make any change for the moment, but he was afraid Page had misconstrued it to mean that he would not make any change until the war was over.

We agreed upon the form of message which the President is to send to the meeting of the Commissioners from the Dominions of the British Empire who are to assemble soon in London.[1]

[1] See the Enclosure printed with W. Wiseman to C. A. Spring Rice, March 6, 1917. An imperial conference was to meet at London on March 20.

## From Robert Lansing

My dear Mr. President:                    Washington March 6, 1917.

As I told you this afternoon I have been studying the statute of 1819 (now Section 4295 of the Revised Statutes, copy enclosed)[1] which has been suggested as a possible restriction upon the arming of merchant vessels proceeding to the German "danger zone," and I am firmly convinced that it in no way restricts the power to arm against submarine attacks or affects the status of the vessel so armed.

In analyzing the statute I find the following reasons which are more or less technical for its not being applicable to the pending question:

1st. In excepting an armed public ship from attack by a merchant vessel, the ship excepted is that "of some nation in amity with the United States." It is significant that the customary words "peace and amity" are not used, only the word "amity." I would define "amity" to be "in friendly relations with." When diplomatic relations have been severed I do not think that it can be said that "friendly relations" exist or a state of "amity" exists. We are still at peace but not in amity with Germany.

2d. The law applies to "the commander and crew" of a merchant vessel. It would not apply to arms or an armed guard put on board such vessel by the Government, if that policy is determined upon.

3d. The statute is clearly *an enabling act* and *not a prohibiting act*. That is, it defines what a merchant vessel may do in case of aggression by a foreign private vessel, but it does not prohibit it from any act in relation to a foreign public ship. If it had a right to resist lawless conduct by a public ship prior to the passage of the statute, that right remained unimpaired.

4th. The act being without any provision for a penalty is effective and could not be enforced even if it could be construed as prohibitive. The absence of a penalty clause seems conclusive evidence that it is an enabling act and permissive in nature. If it was prohibitive there would be a penalty fixed.

Furthermore the statute when incorporated in the Revised Statutes was placed under the title of "piracy" and pertained, I assume, to the right to resist pirates. I do not consider that submarines can be so classed although their acts might be considered piratical. It is another form of lawlessness endangering life which is involved and to which the statute in question in no way applies. While a cursory reading of the provisions might raise a doubt as to the right of armed defense against a public ship, a study of the terms and purpose of the statute removes the doubt as entirely inapplicable to an illegal submarine attack.

In view, however, of the fact that the section of the Revised Statutes falls under the title of Piracy it is possible that private citizens may hesitate to arm their merchant vessels. It would not be at all unnatural if there was a measure of hesitancy.

There are two ways to meet this state of affairs: *First*, to issue a public statement declaring that the statute of 1819 does not apply to present conditions and that a merchant vessel has the right to arm and resist illegal attacks by submarines. *Sec-*

*ond*, for the Government to furnish guns and gun crews to merchant vessels sailing for the German "danger zone," which would remove any doubt of violation of a statute.

The first way has the disadvantage of placing the guns under the control of the master of a merchant vessel, who might not act with the discretion of a naval officer in using them. Furthermore, as the guns and ammunition can only be obtained from the Navy Department, the furnishing of the armament would appear to give official authorization to the merchant vessel to use it, and in no way relieve the Government of responsibility for its use.

The second way has the advantage of placing the armament under the control of naval gunners who could be given explicit orders as to its use. It would undoubtedly be far more efficient to have the guns handled in this way than under the direction of an inexperienced commander of a merchantman.

As to the propriety of furnishing naval guns and naval gunners to merchant vessels I have no doubt. On February 10, 1916, the German Government declared that it would consider armed merchant vessels to be public warships and not entitled to the treatment of private vessels of commerce. In view of this declaration I cannot see that it will give Germany any greater justification for lawless attack if the guns are directly operated by order of the Government than she would have if the ship's crew handled the armament under the captain's orders. It might be well, if it is decided to use naval guns and naval gunners, to direct particular attention to the German declaration.

As I pointed out in a memorandum submitted to you on February 22d, the employment of naval guns and gun crews would be in the nature of an armed guard to protect American lives, and would be based on the general principle of convoy, though differing in this, that the guard being on the vessel the belligerent right of visit and search would not be waived. In the present case, however, the German Government has announced its intention not to exercise the right and to sink all vessels on sight, so that a government armed vessel would have the indubitable right to use its armament on the approach of a German submarine. As the purpose of the arming would be to protect live[s] and not the cargo I do not see that the presence of contraband on board would affect the case. If the German submarines visited and searched the vessels the use of an armament by a vessel with or without contraband would be unjustified, but the declaration of a purpose not to observe the law, thereby imperiling life, removes any responsibility of the vessel to surrender or of the Government, which has armed it, to guaranty the innocent character of the cargo.

It seems to me that there is no more impropriety in placing armed guards on an American merchant vessel to preserve the lives of the persons on board than there is to land guns and blue jackets to protect the lives of American citizens on foreign soil when they are in danger of lawless attack. I do not know but the present case is even stronger because the sea is common to all nations and not subject to the sovereignty of any one nation. In fact the legal fiction that "an American vessel is American territory" might be applied. In that case the resistance of lawless acts would be like guarding the border from outlaws.

My own belief is that we would be in a stronger and more defensible position legally and accomplish better results if we frankly declared it to be our duty to place on every American merchant vessel sailing for the "danger zone" a naval guard with an armament sufficient to protect it from submarine attack, and that this practice would be followed regardless of the character of the cargo so long as the German Government menaced American lives by declining to exercise the right of visit and search and by attacking indiscriminately all vessels without regard to the safety of the persons on board.

Faithfully yours,   Robert Lansing.

TLS (WP, DLC).
1 Not printed.

## From Harry Augustus Garfield

*Personal*

Dear Mr. President:        Williamstown, Mass. March 6/17

I need hardly tell you with how much gratitude & hope I welcome your continuance in the high office to which you have again been inaugurated. May God grant you protection & guidance. With abiding trust in your leadership, I remain, as always,        Affectionately Yours   H. A. Garfield.

ALS (WP, DLC).

## From Julio Betancourt

Sir:        Washington, D. C. March 6th, 1917.

With the deepest regret I beg leave to state that sudden illness prevented me from taking part in the ceremonies incident to the induction of the new Administration, and, ensuing from that, my inability to deliver in person, to Your Excellency, in the name of my Government and in my own name, a message of cordial congratulayion and good-will.

I venture the hope that during Your Excellency's second administration the complete harmony and solidarity of the nations of this Continent shall become a living reality, thus embodying the essence of that true Pan-Americanism which has been so eloquently proclaimed by Your Excellency as the keynote of the Government's continental policy.

Allow me to state, further, that with the fullest confidence I look forward to an early renewal—through the ratification of the pending Treaty—of the sincere friendship that for so long prevailed uninterruptedly between Colombia and the United States.

Praying God to vouchsafe upon Your Excellency the blessing of a long and happy life, warmly cheered by the fortunate consummation of the noble objects which Your Excellency have sponsored for the good of all America, I remain,

Cordially yours,   Julio Betancourt

TLS (WP, DLC).

## From Newton Diehl Baker

My dear Mr. President:          Washington. March 6, 1917.

I take pleasure in advising you of the receipt of a cablegram from Governor General Harrison, at Manila, dated the 5th instant, containing the following message addressed to you jointly by Honorable Teodoro Yangco and Honorable Jaime C. de Veyra, newly elected Resident Commissioners from the Philippines:

"President Wilson: We consider your reinauguration a blessing for America. The world follows your policy with interest. Humanity wishes you success and both America and the Philippines rejoice over your great opportunity which will make you a preeminent figure in history. Lincoln's simile of a man crossing Niagara on a thread heavily laden could never be more fittingly applied than to you. May you be a worthy successor of that great statesman. Teodoro Yangco, Jaime C. de Veyra."          Very sincerely,   Newton D. Baker

TLS (WP, DLC).

# From the Diary of Josephus Daniels

1917 Tuesday 6 March

President called at Navy Dept. to talk over arming ships & dangers of sub-marines in American waters & about bringing the fleet North. He thought, in addition to arming, we ought to have 3 motor boats on each ship to be lowered in smooth seas & hunt submarines. When in England he saw the annual occasion where a shepherd would stand in a circle & by calls & whistles herd three sheep distant from him in a pen. It wasnt hard to manage 2, but very difficult with 3. They would expect a boat on each side of ship but the third boat would confuse them

# Sir William Wiseman to Sir Cecil Arthur Spring Rice, with Enclosure

Dear Sir Cecil:                          New York, March 6, 1917.

This letter will be in safe hands as it will be delivered to you by Furness.[1]

You will remember that I discussed with Beverly [House] the possibility of getting the President to make a written statement with regard to the relations between the United States and Great Britain and we decided that if I could get such a statement, I should send it to you to cable to the Foreign Office.

The accompanying statement has been produced in a somewhat different way. These notes were written by Beverly and myself. Beverly gave them to the President on Monday and they read them over together and the President said that they represented his views and he believed the views of the great majority of the American people and he authorized Beverly to let the Foreign Office have these notes as coming from him through any channel which was considered desirable. It is understood, of course, that it is not a state document.

I think it is much better that I should not communicate this to the Foreign Office, and I shall therefore not show it to anybody, but shall be glad if you think it is worth while to cable it to the Foreign Office and tell them how it originated.

Yours very sincerely,    W.W.

CCLI (W. Wiseman Papers, CtY).

[1] Marmaduke Furness, 2nd Baron Furness of Grantley, chairman of several British shipbuilding and shipping firms, at this time visiting the United States.

ENCLOSURE

RELATIONS BETWEEN THE UNITED STATES AND GREAT BRITAIN.

(1). It would be wrong to assume that there is any pronounced pro-Ally feeling on the part of the great mass of the American people. It would be certainly wrong to assume any pro-British sentiment.

(2). The overwhelming sentiment in the States has been a desire for peace and a horror of war. The Americans do not want to see the horrors of Europe repeated in their own country.

(3). The broader-minded and more intellectual people realise that the Cause of the Allies is on the whole the cause of Democracy, and that the spirit of Prussian militarism is perhaps the last great attempt of reactionary autocracy to dominate the civilised world. These thinking people are therefore sympathetic to the cause of the Allies.

(4). The Russian situation is not understood. It is not realised that Russia is struggling for domestic freedom at the same time that she is fighting a foreign war; that the success of the Germans would mean the success of the reactionary movement in Russia.

(5). Of the great Allied powers Great Britain is probably the least popular because all the war measures which have irritated the American people have been carried out by Great Britain as the representative of the Allies. In these, of course, are included the blockade, black-list, censorship, etc.

(6). Organized German propaganda in this country has been chiefly directed against Great Britain. Attempts have been made to stir up bad feeling and restart old quarrels which had been settled and forgotten long ago.

(7). The Irish question is one of the greatest obstacles to a good understanding. The Unionist side of the question is little understood and never presented. The only arguments heard are the stock-in-trade of the discontented Nationalists. There are, however, many reasonable and intelligent Americans of Irish extraction who feel very strongly on this subject, and who might be persuaded to lend their assistance with all honesty in the settlement of this question at the end of the war. Sensible opinion in the States would not expect the British to listen to Irishmen of the type of Devoy and O'Leary;[1] but the movement is given its greatest strength by the fact that reasonable honest citizens of the type of John Quinn[2] feel so strongly about it.

(8). Canada is feeling her strength, particularly from a military point of view, and every effort should be made to encourage good relations between the United States and Canada. All talk of Canada being absorbed into the States has ceased, and the Canadian people would bitterly resent any such suggestion now.

(9). The Mexican situation is full of difficulties and dangers, chiefly on account of German intrigues which will try to create bad feeling between the United States and Great Britain. Here again Great Britain must play the prominent part on account of her large interests and the big Canadian interests in Mexico. Careful handling of this situation should avoid all difficulties because the aims of the United States and Great Britain are identical, namely: to restore order and protect foreign lives and interests.

(10). Summarizing the position, it may be said that the people of the United States wish to be entirely neutral as far as the European war is concerned. The Administration, however, have always understood the causes of the war and have been entirely sympathetic to the Allies. The people are beginning to realise that it may not be possible for them to remain at peace with Germany. There is a feeling among the Americans that if they tolerate too much they will lose their prestige and authority as a world power. If the United States goes to war with Germany —which she probably will—it will be to uphold American rights and assert her dignity as a nation.

(11). It should be noted that some of our most fervent partisans in this country have done our cause much harm. Unintentionally, no doubt, they have drawn the whole question of the neutrality of the United States into domestic politics, which has been very much to the detriment of a proper understanding, and has hampered any common action between the two Governments.[3]

T MS (W. Wiseman Papers, CtY).

[1] John Devoy, editor and publisher of the New York *Gaelic-American*, longtime Irish revolutionary leader, who had been heavily involved in the plotting of the Easter Rising; and Jeremiah A. O'Leary, about whom see J. A. O'Leary to WW, Sept. 29, 1916, n. 1, Vol. 38.

[2] Distinguished lawyer and art collector of New York; an authority on modern Irish literature and drama.

[3] There is a slightly abridged version of this memorandum in the A. J. Balfour Papers, Add. MSS., 49740, British Library. Spring Rice cabled this memorandum to the Foreign Office on March 8. It was circulated to the King, the cabinet, Lord Robert Cecil, and others.

# Sir Cecil Arthur Spring Rice to the Foreign Office

Washington March 6th. 1917.

No. 600. Impression here to-day is that President will find some means of arming ships in spite of legal objections and majority of Cabinet advise this course. Navy Department is also in favour of it.

Friend of President[1] told me to-day that the latter's idea was to base appeal to the nation on absolute necessity, if processes of civilization are to continue, of putting an end to methods of Prussian Military Clique which are a return to the conditions of the stone age. He thinks the people can be brought to realize that this is a vital interest and that their reluctance to engage in the struggle (? can be) overcome by convincing them that it is not for the interests of a group of nations but of all the world. He also hopes that such an appeal would help to detach the mass of Germans especially here and in South Germany from their subserviency to Prussian clique.

I observed that the first and essential act in this programme was to undo the evil effects of President's attack on the credit of the Allies by the Federal reserve board manifesto. He promised to insist on this point.

Secretary of Treasury however still postpones action although he has promised to consider it favourably and Federal Reserve Board is unanimously in favour of issuing new notice.[2]

Could you speak to United States Ambassador at once?

President's friend has left.

---

T telegram (FO 371/3109, No. 49635, p. 279, PRO).

[1] Colonel House.

[2] The Federal Reserve Board did, indeed, on March 9, issue a statement which said that it by no means objected to the placing of foreign loans in the American market, and that it regarded them as "a very important, natural, and proper means of settling the balances created in our favor by our large export trade." This statement added that the board's warning of November 28, 1916, against purchase by American banks of Allied short-term notes had not been meant to reflect on any country's credit. The gold reserve of the United States, the statement went on, had been so augmented since November that there was now no reason why banks should not invest to a reasonable degree in foreign securities. The statement concluded by saying that American funds available for investment might, "with advantage to the country's foreign trade and the domestic economic situation, be employed in the purchase of such securities." *New York Times*, March 9, 1917. Wilson, Lansing, and McAdoo had discussed Page's telegram of March 5, No. 5794, on March 8, and McAdoo had conveyed the gist of the telegram to the Federal Reserve Board on the same day. Link, *Campaigns for Progressivism and Peace*, pp. 381-82.

## Franklin Knight Lane to George Whitfield Lane

Washington, March 6 [1917].

Well my dear George, the new administration is launched—smoothly but not on a smooth sea. The old Congress went out in disgrace, talking to death a bill to enable the President to protect Americans on the seas. The reactionaries and the progressives combined—Penrose and La Follette joined hands to stop all legislation, so that the government is without money to carry on its work.

It is unjust to charge the whole thing on the La Follette group; they served to do the trick which the whole Republican machine wished done. For the Penrose, Lodge people would not let any bills through and were glad to get La Follette's help. The Democrats fought and died—because there was no "previous question" in the Senate rules.

The weather changed for inauguration—Wilson luck—and the event went off without accident. To-day, we had expected a meeting of the Cabinet to determine what we should do in the absence of legislation, but that has gone over,—I expect to give the Attorney General a chance to draft an opinion on the armed ship matter. I am for prompt action—putting the guns on the ships and convoying, if necessary. Much love.          F.K.

Printed in Lane and Wall, eds., *The Letters of Franklin K. Lane*, pp. 241-42.


## From Robert Lansing, with Enclosure

PERSONAL AND PRIVATE:

My dear Mr. President:          Washington March 7, 1917.

Here is enclosed an extract from a mail dispatch from Ambassador Fletcher which I think you may find of interest—particularly the first paragraph on the second page.

Faithfully yours,   Robert Lansing.

TLS (WP, DLC).


### E N C L O S U R E

[Mexico City, Feb. 21, 1917]

"The Minister of Foreign Affairs, General Candido Aguilar, was absent from the city on my arrival. He returned on the 19th and I called upon him informally yesterday afternoon at the

Foreign Office. He is a young man slow of speech and of little experience in public affairs. He was noticeably nervous and embarrassed in the beginning of our interview. I thanked him profusely for the warm reception and courteous attentions I had received since my arrival at Nuevo Laredo, and made special mention of the kindness of Mr. Bridat and Captain Ochoa[1] who accompanied us from the border. He replied that it was very gratifying to his Government to have an American Ambassador accredited here, and hoped that the relations between our two Governments would continue to improve very rapidly, and assured me of his desire to do everything in his power to bring about this result. I replied along the same lines.

"With reference to my formal presentation he stated that General Carranza would be absent on an official visit until about the first of March, and that he would be glad to arrange for the formal presentation to him just as soon as possible after his return to the Capital. The Minister stated he would be glad in the meantime to transact with me such diplomatic business as might arise. He confirmed certain statements which he had made to Mr. Parker[2] earlier in the day with reference to the mining decrees referred to in my telegram of yesterday.[3] He distinctly stated that it was not the intention of the de facto Government to give a retroactive effect to its decrees nor to the constitution and laws made in pursuance thereof. He intimated that the new constitution contained provisions of a progressive and advanced character which the Government might find difficulty in carrying into immediate effect.

"He referred to the recent peace note of the Mexican Foreign Office and stated that General Carranza had particularly instructed him to ask me to inform you that the impression which certain newspapers had endeavoured to give to the effect that the note was pro-German, or anti-American, was entirely erroneous, and that the First Chief would be very sorry if our Government should receive such an impression, and wished to assure me that the note was inspired simply and solely by humanitarian motives and unselfish desire to have peace restored and to prevent, if possible, the extension of the war to include American nations.

"Our interview closed on an easy footing and General Aguilar begged me to treat with him in all matters concerning my mission on a basis of personal as well as official friendship."

T MS (WP, DLC).

1 Bridat cannot be identified. Captain Manuel Ochoa was a member of President Carranza's military staff.

2 Charles Bailey Parker, clerk in the American embassy, Mexico City.

352 MARCH 7, 1917

³ H. P. Fletcher to RL, Feb. 20, 1917, *FR 1917*, p. 1044. In response to an inquiry from Lansing (*ibid.*, p. 1043), Fletcher reported as follows: "Minister for Foreign Affairs states that he has no knowledge of any decree affecting rights of foreigners to real estate or mines to which such foreigners already have clear title, but that there are in existence decrees requiring the waiver of nationality in so far as concerns titles now under negotiation or to be acquired in the future. He has promised to send to the Embassy copies of such decrees. He further said that the legislation emanating from the new Constitution with respect to property rights would in his opinion in no wise prejudice present property rights and at the same time called attention to the article of the new Constitution which provides that no laws may be made retroactive."

## Two Letters from Robert Lansing

PERSONAL AND PRIVATE:

My dear Mr. President:          Washington March 7, 1917.

In regard to the communication from the Minister of Ecuador suggesting a meeting of American neutrals, which I sent you on February 19th and which you returned to me the following day, I feel that the time would not be opportune to pursue the suggestion at present. Conditions have materially changed since the Ecuadorean Government, on February 17th, made the proposal. Unless you feel there is something to be gained I will advise the Ecuadorean Minister that in view of present conditions the endorsement of the proposed Congress of Neutrals by this Government might be mis-interpreted and cause division of opinion among American republics.

Faithfully yours,   Robert Lansing

TLS (WP, DLC).

My dear Mr. President:          Washington March 7, 1917.

I return to you the interesting letter of Minister Reinsch dated January 10th. Matters have progressed considerably since this letter was written but I think that much of it is very well worth consideration.     Faithfully yours,   Robert Lansing

TLS (WP, DLC).

## From Lucius Elmer Sheppard and Others

Mr. President:          Cleveland, Ohio, March 7, 1917.

We feel obligated to officially advise you of our intention to again meet the National Conference Committee of the Railways, on March fifteenth, for the purpose of making another effort to adjust the pending eight-hour controversy.[1]

We are very hopeful of working out a satisfactory adjustment with the railroads, but if, while we are negotiating, our country should become involved in war, we want to assure you, as Chief Executive of the Nation, that we and the membership we represent can be relied upon to support you to the fullest extent, and that yourself and the Nation will have our hearty and full support.

We are, with great respect,

L. E. Sheppard

W. S. Stone

W. G. Lee.

W. S. Carter[2]

TLS (WP, DLC).

1 That is, the demand of the railway brotherhoods that the railroads implement the eight-hour day forthwith, even before the Supreme Court ruled on the constitutionality of the Adamson Act. See the *New York Times*, March 11, 1917, and Link, *Campaigns for Progressivism and Peace*, p. 392.

2 "Dear Tumulty: Please express my appreciation of this letter. The President." TL, n.d. (WP, DLC).

# From Newton Diehl Baker, with Enclosure

[Washington] March 7, 1917.

Memorandum for the information of the President:

The attached telegram from the Rev. Worth M. Tippy[1] is from one of the most prominent Methodist Ministers in America, a man of great eloquence, sweetness of spirit, and devotion to a ministry of service. He is at present the executive officer of a federation of churches of the country, and is a kind of interdenominational bishop, organizing the church activities of about 22,000 churches. I have always believed him to be almost a nonresistant. I send the dispatch because of Dr. Tippy's conservative character, though I do not know how much he has been affected by New York atmosphere since he left Cleveland to go there.                    Newton D. Baker

TS memorandum (WP, DLC).

1 The Rev. Dr. Worth Marion Tippy, executive secretary of the Commission on the Church and Social Service of the Federal Council of Churches of Christ in America.

E N C L O S U R E

New York, N. Y., Mar. 5, 1917

I regret to urge war but I think the time has come to go in with all our power. If your convictions allow, I wish you might rally the people about you [with] A statement favorable to action   the President needs to go ahead and lead resolutely.

Worth M. Tippy.

T telegram (WP, DLC).


## From Robert Bridges

Dear Mr. President:                    New York March 7 1917

Talcott[1] and I *walked* over from the Capitol to The White House, after the ceremonies, and so arrived too late to speak to you at the luncheon. We saw you in the glass case, and all of us thought you looked very well—Dan'l, Chang, Hiram,[2] Charley & I. Henderson[3] had a bad cold and had to go home from Balto. on Sunday and Mitchell[4] is not yet quite sure of himself.

But we had a beautiful time, all due to your kind foresight in putting us together on such a fine occasion. I wish you could have enjoyed the occasion as we did, instead of working. But it was a fine address! We read it with care, and Talcott gave it his political approval. We spent Sunday in Baltimore and had several meals together and the usual chaff. All the old jokes are good jokes—particularly when they are on Hiram!

You have an awful job, but you never were as strong as just now. I am malicious enough to ask some of my friends about their championship of Huerta! In the long run you are bound to come out right—and a lot of kickers are beginning to see the light.

But I just wanted to say how happy you made the crowd, and to wish you the good fortune of events which you so hugely deserve.

Good luck and good health and all good things for the New Term—which is the old troubles continued—for you always, Tommy, from      Your Friend always   Robert Bridges.

ALS (WP, DLC).
  [1] That is, Charles Andrew Talcott.
  [2] James Edwin Webster, William Brewster Lee, and Hiram Woods, Jr.
  [3] Robert Randolph Henderson.
  [4] Charles Wellman Mitchell.


## Jean Jules Jusserand to the Foreign Ministry

Washington, sans date reçu le 7 Mars 1917

No 235-236 Réponse à v. télégr. 282.

Le Président à qui j'ai exprimé les voeux du Gouvt. de la République,[1] a marqué en termes d'une grande cordialité combien il y était sensible. Il m'a parlé de la fâcheuse impression produite au dehors par certains passages de ses dernières notes, partiellement (gr. faux) où il parlait d'une paix sans victoire. "J'ai trouvé, dit-il, dans un article de revue, une expression qui aurait rendu bien mieux ma pensée; il y était question d'une paix scientifique. J'entendrais par là une paix où l'on ne verrait pas se reproduire l'énormité commise par les Allemands quand ils vous prirent l'Alsace-Lorraine. Nous ne devons pas souhaiter une paix qui créerait de nouvelles Alsaces-Lorraines."

Cette déclaration a, en tous cas, la grande importance de montrer qu'il est résolu à ce qu'on nous rende la nôtre.

Sur la similitude d'objet attribué aux deux groupes de belligérants dans sa note du 18 Décembre, il s'est défendu d'avoir pris à son compte une assertion dont, affirme-t-il, il avait voulu laisser la responsabilité aux hommes d'Etat des pays en cause.

J'ai rappelé que grammaticalement on pouvait s'y tromper, mais que naturellement sur une question de sens le dire de l'auteur de la phrase était décisif.

Sur la ligue pour le maintien de la paix qu'on pourrait créer aprè[s] la guerre il a déclaré n'avoir pas d'illusion et se rendre compte de la grandeur des difficultés. Il faudrait commencer par une entente, avec obligation de soumettre à une conférence des pays non directement intéressés les cas de différends internationaux. Peut être se créerait-il peu à peu des précédents qui déshabitueraient d'un recours aux armes. Ce serait une expérience à tenter. Il ne s'est pas exprimé d'une manière positive sur les recours possibles au moyen de coercition.

Faisant allusion à sa [la] note sur les conditions de paix,[2] je lui ai dit que, pour être agréable, le Gouvt. de la République était allé au delà de ce que, par crainte de raidir les résistances allemandes, j'aurais personnellement conseillé.

Il a répondu que cet effet ne s'était pas produit en Allemagne, mais peut-être en Autriche, pays sur lequel il s'est exprimé avec une modération marquée. Il parait estimer que sa mise en morceaux n'est pas souhaitable. Il devrait suffire suivant lui que les diverses races y reçoivent une autonomie si large qu'elles aient de quoi être satisfaites.

Un passage de son discours d'inauguration pouvant prêter à doute je lui ai demandé quelle portée il avait entendu donner à ce qu'il avait dit d'une limitation des armements.

Il a répondu qu'à son avis, ils devraient demeurer raisonnables, pour permettre non des guerres de conquête, mais la résistance à toute agression du dehors et le maintien de l'ordre en dedans. Un pays doit pouvoir défendre non seulement son territoire métropolitain mais encore ses colonies. Le Président m'a encore dit qu'il croyait que le Sénat aurait tôt fait d'adopter des réglements pour de clôture. Après cela il serait facile d'obtenir le vote des pouvoirs demandés pour la protection de la marine américaine. Les autorités légales du pays continuent du reste de discuter si le Président a réallement besoin d'un tel vote. La question est soumise à un nouvel examen de l'Attorney General et du Secrétaire d'Etat.                    Jusserand.

T telegram (Guerre 1914-1918, États-Unis, Vol. 505, pp. 280-81, FFM-Ar).
    1 R. Poincaré to WW, March 3, 1917.
    2 That is, the Anglo-French note in reply to Wilson's call for a definition of peace terms, printed in W. G. Sharp to RL, Jan. 10, 1917, Vol. 40.

T R A N S L A T I O N

Washington, n.d., received March 7, 1917, 2:55 p.m.
No. 235-236 in response to your Telegram 282.

The President, to whom I have just conveyed the felicitations of the government of the Republic, replied very cordially how much he appreciated them. He spoke to me of the false impression created abroad by certain passages in his latest notes, [particularly] where he spoke of a peace without victory. "I found," he said, "in a magazine article a term which would have expressed my thought better; that is, a scientific peace. I understand by that a peace in which one does not see reproduced the enormity committed by the Germans when they took Alsace-Lorraine from you. We must not want a peace that would create new Alsace-Lorraines."

This declaration has, in any event, the great importance of showing his resolve that our own shall be restored to us.

As for the similarity of aim attributed to the two groups of belligerents in his note of December, he denied being accountable for an assertion for which, he affirmed, he had wished to hold responsible the statesmen of the countries involved.

I replied that, grammatically, one could be misled, but that, in a question of meaning, the word of the author of the phrase naturally was decisive.

Regarding the league to maintain peace which might be created after the war, he said he had no illusions and recognized the magnitude of the difficulties. One should begin with an entente, with the obligation to submit cases of international differences to a conference of countries not directly interested. Perhaps there would thus be created, little by little, precedents that would break the habit of having recourse to arms. It would be an experience to try it. He did not express himself in a positive manner about possible recourses to means of coercion.

Alluding to the note on the conditions of peace I said to him that, in order to be agreeable, the government of the Republic, out of fear of stiffening German resistance, had gone further than I would personally have advised.

He replied that it had not had this effect in Germany, but perhaps in Austria, a country about which he expressed himself with notable moderation. He seemed to think that slicing it up was not desirable. It must suffice, according to him, that the diverse races there should receive enough autonomy to satisfy them.

One passage of his inaugural address being susceptible of doubt, I asked him what he had intended to convey in his remarks on the limitation of armaments.

He replied that it seemed to him reasonable to permit, not wars of conquest, but resistance to all aggression from outside and maintenance of order within. A country must be able to defend, not only its own metropolitan territory, but also its colonies. The President told me again that he believed the Senate would soon adopt rules for cloture. After that, it will be easy to obtain the vote for the powers requested for the protection of the American merchant marine. Meanwhile, the country's legal authorities continue discussing whether the President really needs such a vote. The question has been submitted to a new review of the Attorney General and the Secretary of State.

Jusserand.

## From the Diary of Thomas W. Brahany

Wednesday, March 7, 1917

Joe Murphy won his bet. The sun poked its nose through the clouds three hours before noon on March 5. Although a bit cold and quite windy the weather was bearable. The President left for the Capitol about 11 o'clock and returned to the White House about 1:30. There was no hitch in the programme, and no untoward incident of any kind. Mrs. Wilson, Senator Overman of North Carolina, and Representative Rucker[1] of Missouri rode with the President. The reception given the President was not violently demonstrative. This is not a time for wild cheering. The country is in a serious state of mind. I was told today that the figures show about 80,000 fewer persons passed through the Union Station than in the Inaugural period four years ago.

About 200 persons attended the buffet luncheon at the White House. Among the guests were Mr. and Mrs. B. M. Baruch[2] of New York. In the recent "leak" investigation held by the Rules Committee of the House, Baruch testified that he made about $500,000 by selling short U. S. steel the second week of December 1916. He had no information regarding the President's peace note of that period. He so testified and the Committee believed him. I am convinced he told the truth. He is one of the most daring and intelligent speculators in New York. In the last campaign he was an active Wilson partisan and one of the most liberal campaign contributors. Following the luncheon the President and Mrs. Wilson went to the Reviewing Stand. The parade was ended at 5:10—about three hours. Mrs. Brahany and I had fine seats in the President's section, in the row immediately back of Miss Bones and Mrs. Grayson. We were chilled after being in the stand for two hours and went to the Executive Office where we stayed until the colored Elks, District of Columbia Lodge, brought the parade to end by passing in review before the President. We had cards for the dancing party given that evening at the New Willard Hotel by the Vice President and Mrs. Marshall in honor of the Culver Cadets, escort for the Vice President, but Mrs. Brahany was fatigued and we did not attend.

On my arrival at the Executive Office on the morning of March 5, I learned that at 11 o'clock the night before the President had sent over the copy of his Inaugural Address. It was sent at once to the Public Printer and printed copies were handed to the newspapermen Monday morning. Sunday afternoon the President prepared a statement criticising the Senators who by their filibuster defeated the armed ship bill, and suggesting that the Senate adopt a cloture rule. This statement was given to the press last night and is the newspaper feature Monday morning.

We've received surprisingly few Inaugural congratulations not to exceed 1,000 letters and telegrams. About 500 letters and telegrams have been received approving the President's statement attacking the filibuster[er]s. Of course additional letters and telegrams will be received in the next few days. The press is practically united in its support and approval and many State Legislatures have adopted resolutions censuring "the little group of wilful men representing no opinion except their own." (I'm not sure this quotation is literally the phrase used in the President's statement.) While we've had relatively few messages of approval there is a notable absence of telegrams and letters of criticism in our correspondence of the last few days. Senator

Stone is in bad repute in the country and an influential portion
of the press (both parties) is suggesting he should not be permitted to hold the chairmanship of the Committee on Foreign Relations. A New York business man wrote the President today: I
have today written Robert M. La Follette. My letter in full is as
follows: "You are a national disgrace."

The President begins his second term in the same exclusive-
ness which marked the closing months of his first term. Hundreds of the Inaugural visitors wish to see him, but I doubt if he
will come to his office this week. The members of the Democratic
National Committee who came to Washington for Inauguration
were White House luncheon guests yesterday. The President saw
also the French and Japanese Ambassadors who brought Inaugural greetings from their countries. In the afternoon the President called on the Secretary of State and the Secretary of the
Navy. This morning the President sent for half a dozen Democratic Senators[3] with whom he talked over his suggestion that
the Senate rules be amended to limit debate. Late[r] he phoned
Tumulty that Dr. Grayson advised him to go to bed on account
of his cold. We've had a hard time today explaining to prominent
visitors that the President "is not seeing callers at this time." Yesterday a delegation of leading Slavonians called twice to see me.
They had come from the Middle West with handsomely en-
grossed resolutions approving the President and wished "one
minute only" to put these resolutions in his hand. I had to say
"No," but promised them a personal letter of acknowledgment
would be sent them by the President. The members of the Duck-
worth Club (75 strong) came from Ohio for the Inauguration
and made a fine showing in the parade. They are active and leading Democrats and had set their hearts on seeing the President
for a hand shake. Tumulty said of course he would arrange
it. One of my pleasant tasks today was to "explain" why it could
not be arranged. Tumulty ducked the Duckworths and others
for whom he promised to make hand shaking appointments,
most of his telephone trouble calls being switched to my receiver.
Late this afternoon Tumulty went to the Hotel Raleigh with Tom
McCarthy, U. S. Marshal for New York City. Charles Murphy,
leader of Tammany Hall, and a few other New York politicians
are to meet Tumulty in McCarthy's room. It is simply a courtesy
call, but Tumulty said he thought it best not to give it to the
press. Murphy has not asked to see the President. Four years ago
the Tammany delegation called on the President. Mr. Wilson
has not seen Murphy since that time, nor has he had any correspondence with him. He has no use for politicians of the

Murphy type. My personal callers today included Joseph Martin, Democratic National Committeeman for Wisconsin, and Mr. LaBudde,[4] Chairman of the Democratic State Committee of Wisconsin. They are strongly opposed to placing postmasters in the classified civil service. I told them to tell their troubles to the Postmaster General.

[1] William Waller Rucker, Democrat.
[2] Annie Griffen Baruch.
[3] James A. Reed, Robert L. Owen, Thomas J. Walsh, Claude A. Swanson, Hoke Smith, and Ollie M. James.
[4] Otto A. LaBudde.

## From Robert Lansing

PERSONAL AND PRIVATE:

My dear Mr. President:                    [Washington] March 8, 1917.

I know that you are giving constant and anxious thought to the course of action we should take in regard to arming merchant vessels, but I feel it my duty to express to you my personal views on the subject knowing that you will understand my motives in doing so.

It seems to me that we must proceed upon one of two hypotheses and should regulate our policy accordingly. These hypotheses are that we will ultimately be at war with Germany or that we will continue the present state of unfriendly peace.

As to the second hypothesis I can see no satisfactory outcome. Suppose we continue as we are, then Germany will have gained all she seeks by preventing American vessels from visiting the waters of the "danger zone" and meanwhile our people will become more and more incensed at German activities and intrigues until they turn against our own Government for failure to act under the greatest provocation. If delay in action is in the expectation or hope that Germany will declare war upon this country and relieve us of that grave responsibility, I am convinced that both expectation and hope will be vain unless we do something very definite which may be interpreted to be a *casus belli*. I think the German Government will be entirely satisfied to let the present situation continue and will do everything possible to avoid hostilities, feeling that by so doing this Government will be seriously embarrassed and placed in a very undesirable position before the American people. But can we afford to let matters stand as they are? If we do, what possibility is there for an improvement in conditions by continued inaction? I confess that I can see nothing to gain by a continuance of this situation so satisfactory to Germany and so unsatisfactory to us. I have considered the matter very carefully and endeavored to construct some result which will warrant a continuance, but I have failed.

Feeling the present state of affairs is hopeless for ultimate peace and being convinced of the impossibility of founding a policy on the hypothesis that we can remain at peace, it seems to me that we ought to proceed on the theory that we will in a short time be openly at war with Germany. If we assume that hypothesis our course is largely a matter of expediency taking chiefly into account what actions will appeal most strongly to the sense of justice and right of the American people and will most firmly unite them in support of the Government. I think that to be of first consideration at the present time.

My own belief is that prompt and vigorous action will do more than anything else to crystalize public support and unite the people behind the Government. As I read the public mind there is an impatient desire to go forward. The people will follow readily and whole-heartedly if a policy of action is adopted and pressed with vigor. I am firmly convinced that expediency as well as duty lies in action.

In view of the conclusion, which I have reached—and reached reluctantly in view of the great issue at stake—, I think that our merchant vessels should be sent out under armed guards, that announcement of this policy should be made immediately and the guns and men placed on the vessels as soon as possible.

I would not advise this course if I could see any possible benefit from delay, but I do not. On the contrary I think that delay is causing a wrong impression of the Government among the people, which, in view of the certainty of war at no distant day, ought to be avoided.

It is with hesitation I have written this letter, because I know that you are devoting your time to this greatest question of your Administration, but I felt that I would be derelict in my duty not to state frankly my views to you.

Faithfully yours,   Robert Lansing

TLS (Lansing Letterpress Book, SDR, RG 59, DNA).


## From Josephus Daniels

Dear Mr. President:          Washington. March 8. 1917.

If you should decide to have a civilian governor of the new Danish islands—or rather the Danish islands transferred to us, —it would seem to be advisable that the military force should be drawn from the Navy and the marines would be most suitable.

At present the Acting Governor of the islands[1] is a Danish Naval officer and is in command of the senior naval vessel in the islands. I had a conversation with Secretary Lansing and he is of the opinion that it is best for these islands to be under naval control.                    Sincerely    Josephus Daniels

ALS (WP, DLC).
  [1] Capt. Henri Konow, commander of the cruiser *Valkyrien*.

## A Memorandum by Josephus Daniels

Washington, March 8, 1917.

MEMORANDUM.

SUBJECT:—Governorship of Danish West Indies.

1. I wish to invite your attention to the desirability of appointing a naval officer to the Governorship of the Danish West Indies.

2. The studies of the General Board and of the Naval War College have brought out very clearly the great strategic importance to the Navy of the St. Thomas-Culebra region. This position is the natural outpost of the Navy in the Caribbean. It lies on the route from Europe to the Panama Canal, near the routes from Europe to all the Caribbean Sea and Gulf of Mexico and on the routes from our Atlantic Seaboard to South America. The United States cannot hope to command a position geographically better suited to strengthen all the measures of the Navy in defense of our interests in and near the Caribbean Sea. But this position, if it is to yield its full military value to the country, must be developed and expanded, so far as its military features are concerned, purely as an adjunct of the Fleet—a naval base. The position has no other military importance whatever. The islands were purchased with a definite *naval* mission in view, which was:

> To prepare the islands to support the operations of the Fleet and to deny their use to the ships of our enemies.

Fortifications, radio stations, docks, wharves, shops, all the facilities of a great naval center, if these are built at St. Thomas, will have no military importance except in so far as they are related to the possible activities of our Fleet. In time of war in the Atlantic the necessity for the closest possible cooperation between the Governor and the Commander-in-Chief of the Fleet is indisputable. No matter how complete the spirit of cooperation may be it will not render its full measure of support to the Government without the mutual understanding between ship and shore that comes through long association and similarity of training. The Army and the Navy both have the country's interests at heart, but they are trained in different schools, and have different viewpoints and widely different fields of activity. We have no right to expect, therefore, the best results unless naval officers are placed in control of naval duties and naval functions.

3. It is true that both the Army and the Navy must participate in the development of the islands as an outpost of the United States, but Army interest in the islands arises from naval needs. The primary interest is naval interest; the primary development must be a naval development. Unity of command with interest centered understandingly on our true mission in the islands is essential.

4. There are other aspects of the question than those that relate to preparedness. The history of the islands is a history of the coming and going of ships, a history of maritime commercial effort. The language and thought of the people is of ships and of the sea. Sea trade, sea law, sea customs,—all those activities with which the naval officer deals throughout his life are singularly prominent in the routine events of the islands. Within sight, almost within touch, of the islands lie other islands belonging to a foreign power. The nearness of these will call for a constantly tactful conduct of affairs to avoid every cause for international friction. The naval officer is trained in the school of experience to deal with foreign officials and to attain his ends through understanding their spirit, customs, and view points.

5. I recommend that the government of the Danish West India Islands be assigned to the Navy because:—

The usefulness of those islands to us is essentially *naval* usefulness.

Their military development will be exclusively for the Navy.

The sympathies and thoughts of the people are of the sea.

The peace time activities are with ships and navies and foreign as well as domestic interests, all of which the Navy is fitted specially to deal with.          Josephus Daniels

TS MS (WP, DLC).


## From Josephus Daniels

Dear Mr. President:          Washington. March 8. 1917.

I am sending herewith a memorandum of policy and rules regarding the matter of arming merchant vessels.[1] It was prepared in Operations and has been carefully considered by

Admiral Benson and other officers in Operations. I thought you would like to read it at this time.

Sincerely   Josephus Daniels

Additional ships have been assigned to duty on both coasts both North and South of Panama Canal and it is improbable anything in that section can escape their vigilance.

If we arm the ships it would seem wise to issue a statement as to the policy this Government would follow and the rules that would govern.   JD

ALS (WP, DLC).
[1] This document is missing, but see the Enclosure printed with RL to WW, March 9, 1917.

## From the Diary of Josephus Daniels

1917 Thursday 8 March

At night had message from Hoover at White House saying Mrs. Wilson wished me to call. Upon arrival she said she was a blind—that Pres. was declining to see anybody & that was why she called. He was suffering from cold.

We discussed arming ships Wished it all kept secret. Decided to arm ships. We had prepared regulations in event we armed & I had sent to him that afternoon. He suggested changes and particularly to omit "No ship shall go to rescue of ship attacked." England had adopted that rule after three ships were sunk that went to rescue of ship attacked. It seemed inhuman said President. Upon returning I called up Benson & Palmer,[1] & Benson went that night to N Y to see P S B [P A S] Franklin of American lines & arrange to have guns & armed guard put on all ships. He saw F, who thought visit & search should be permitted outside of zones. F called me up by telephone & wanted to know if he should arm Manchuria ready to sail.

[1] Rear Admiral Leigh Carlyle Palmer, U.S.N., Chief of the Bureau of Navigation.

## From the Diary of Thomas W. Brahany

Thursday, March 8, 1917

The President is still confined to his room—Dr. Grayson reports he is "on the mend," but his throat is sore and Grayson thinks it best he should have complete rest for another day. Many callers today who wished to see the President. A delegation of important men arrived this morning from Nebraska to invite the President to a semi-centennial celebration which is to be held in that State this summer. Senator Hitchcock is urging that the President see these men. I stood him off today, but will have a hard time with him tomorrow provided the President is able to leave his room and I am forced to admit this fact to the Senator.

## From the Diary of Chandler Parsons Anderson

March 8, 1917.

Mr. Harold Walker and Mr. Emory[1] of Kellogg, Emory & Cuthell, called this morning to confer with me with regard to the new Mexican Constitution. Mr. Walker brought a copy of it translated into English, which he had marked up to indicate the provisions most objectionable to the foreign interests in Mexico, which in effect amount to practical confiscation of all foreign owned interests there.

Mr. Walker said that the State Department was under the impression that the situation was not so serious as we regarded it, because the constitution provides that no retroactive law could be adopted, but an ex[a]mination of this provision shows that it applies only to laws adopted under the constitution in distinction from the provisions of the constitution itself, and most of the objectionable provisions of the constitution go into operation by their own force without legislation. He said that he thought that he had changed Mr. Polk's view on this point, but nevertheless, he was afraid that it was the intention of President Wilson to recognize Carranza as the de jure president of Mexico as soon as he was elected under the constitution, which would make it difficult for us to object to the validity of the constitution and to preserve American rights, which are jeopardized by its provisions.[2]

The President seems to be wholly lacking in interest in the protection of property and material interests, and is chiefly concerned with the establishment of a stable government in Mexico, on the theory of serving humanity. He also seems to be influenced in favor of recognizing Carranza by the hope of thereby bribing him to resist the German influences which have been recently exposed designed to force him into war with the United States.

They were in despair about the situation and asked me if there was not something I could do, or some course I could suggest,

in order to save the American interests. We discussed the various
elements and considerations entering into the question, and
particularly the question as to what action the British, French
and Spanish Governments were likely to take in regard to recognizing Carranza. Mr. Walker had not any definite information
about this, but I ascertained that he had been told by Mr. Holer,[3]
the new counselor of the British Embassy, as a matter bearing
upon this question, that Great Britain had a treaty with Mexico
which he thought would protect British interests against the
retroactive application to those interests of the new constitutional provisions. I then said that my experience had been that
the best way to obtain satisfactory action on the part of our
government was to work out before hand exactly what was
desired and present some practical suggestion as to how it should
be accomplished, with the terms already formulated in detail;
and that following that course, it seemed to me advisable that
we should prepare and agree upon some such suggestion in this
case; that what we wanted in this case was to prevent the
retroactive application of the new constitution; that they would
recall that at my suggestion we had first, some months ago, gotten the State Department to propose the adoption by the Mexican
constitutional convention of a clause declaratory that the constitutional provisions should not be retroactive; that the convention had failed to adopt this, and it was now too late to secure
any change in the constitution itself, but that it had occurred
to me in looking over the provisions of the constitution that an
opportunity was still open for accomplishing the end in view in
accordance with one of the provisions of the constitution, and
that provision was found in article 133, which states that all
treaties made, or which shall be made in accordance with the
constitutional requirements, shall be the supreme law of the
land. I therefore suggested that we should ask the State Department to make recognition of the new government dependent
upon the conclusion of a treaty with this government satisfactorily protecting American rights and property in Mexico against
the retroactive application of the constitutional provisions, and
that in view of Mr. Walker's statement that an existing British
treaty was regarded by Mr. Holer as sufficiently protecting British
interests in this respect, perhaps the simplest course for us to
pursue was to secure a treaty simply providing that the United
States should be entitled to favored nation treatment; that of
course, it would be safer and better for every reason if we could
secure a treaty protecting our rights independently of any other
treaty, and that we should aim to accomplish that if possible.

They were delighted with this suggestion, and thought it offered a satisfactory and practical solution of the whole question, and they asked me if I would take it up with the Department of State.

I said that I expected to go to Washington tomorrow with regard to other matters, and I said that I would be glad to make the suggestion to Polk, and talk to him about it.[4]

I said that I would also obtain from the British Embassy a copy of the treaty to which Mr. Walker referred in order to ascertain just what protection it afforded to British interests.

T MS (C. P. Anderson Papers, DLC).

[1] Dean Emery. Both were lawyers of New York.

[2] Most particularly, Article XXVII, which vested ownership of all mineral and oil subsoil rights in the Mexican people.

[3] That is, Thomas Beaumont Hohler.

[4] He wrote to Polk at once. See C. P. Anderson to F. L. Polk, March 8, 1917, TLS (SDR, RG 59, 812.011/57, DNA). Anderson also conferred with Lansing and Polk on March 10. See the extract from the Anderson diary printed at that date.

## A Statement

[*March 9, 1917*]

Secretary Tumulty stated in connection with the President's call for an extra session of Congress[1] that the President is convinced that he has the power to arm American merchant ships and is free to exercise it at once. But so much necessary legislation is pressing for consideration that he is convinced that it is for the best interests of the country to have an early session of the Sixty-fifth Congress, whose support he will also need in all matters collateral to the defense of our merchant marine.

Printed in the *New York Times*, March 10, 1917.

[1] Wilson, on March 9, issued a proclamation which called Congress into special session on April 16, 1917, at 12 o'clock noon, on account of "an extraordinary occasion." *New York Times*, March 10, 1917.

## Edith Bolling Wilson to Robert Lansing

My dear Mr. Secretary:                [Washington, March 9, 1917]

Mr. Wilson asks me to send you these papers, just received from the Secretary of the Navy, and asks if you will be kind enough to read them as soon as possible, and advise him which program you deem wise to follow.

He would be very much pleased if you could let him know in time to enable him to issue the orders today.

Cordially yours    Edith Bolling Wilson

ALS (SDR, RG 59, 763.72/3470½, DNA).

# From Robert Lansing, with Enclosures

My dear Mr. President:          Washington March 9, 1917.

I return herewith the papers from the Navy Department in regard to the arming of merchant vessels, which Mrs. Wilson was good enough to send me this afternoon.

As you know from my letters of the 6th and 8th I strongly advocate placing an "armed guard" on an American merchant vessel proceeding to the German "danger zone." I think that that policy would remove all question of constitutional right and executive power. It appears from the papers submitted that this method has not been considered in the three policies suggested by Secretary Daniels on which the three sets of regulations are based. It would seem, however, that they could readily be adapted to such a change.

After going over the policies stated and the regulations proposed I think that Policy No. 2 is the best from a legal standpoint, although it does not cover cases of illegal attack outside the zone. It is evident that to permit the people on board of a vessel to be placed in open boats at so great a distance from land as they would be if captured outside the zone would as seriously imperil their lives as if attacked without visit within the zone. I think it best to adopt Policy No. 2, with instructions allowing the armed guard to resist illegal attack outside the zone. In no circumstances would I favor No. 3.

In regard to the Regulations (or if issued to an armed Guard, Instructions) I do not feel competent to pass judgment upon them, but believe that with a definite policy adopted they can be worked out by the naval experts so as to be efficient and consistent with the policy. I think that it would be well to omit such positive statements as Regulation No. 2 (page 2). They would only serve to cause controversy. In Regulation No. 4 (page 3) I have also indicated a little more latitude to the armed guard.

I agree with Secretary Daniels that it is not practicable to proceed with this matter secretly, furthermore I do not think that it is politic to do so. My own view is that a public statement of the policy should be made very soon, tomorrow morning if possible, but the regulations (or instructions) should remain secret for the present. I enclose a suggestion for a public statement. In no event would I indicate that we had any choice of policies or that the protection is to be limited to the barred zones.

It is with very real gratification that I learn of your determination to adopt this course. It is so consistent with all you have said and so entirely right that I know it will meet with the approval of the American people.

Faithfully yours,   Robert Lansing

TLS (J. Daniels Papers, DLC).

## From Josephus Daniels

Dear Mr. President:            Washington. March 9, 1917.

Admiral Benson went over to New York last night to confer with Admiral Usher,[1] Mr. Franklin and others looking to carrying out the policy desired. The important question now seems to be which is the best policy to be adopted to carry into effect the arming of ships. There were three different methods outlined in the memorandum submitted to you yesterday. Briefly summarized, they are:

POLICY NO. 1.

Replies to the German threat to sink neutral vessels in designated zones of the high seas by assuming all German submarines on the high seas are attacking United States vessels and that merchant vessels of the United States consequently may fire upon German submarines wherever they are met on the high seas.

POLICY NO. 2.

Replies to the German threat to sink neutral vessels in designated zones of the high seas by assuming that all German submarines within those zones are attacking U. S. vessels and that consequently merchant vessels of the United States may fire upon German submarines wherever they are met within those zones, but that merchant vessels must grant to German submarines the right of visit and search in all other areas of the high seas.

POLICY NO. 3.

Replies to the German threat to sink neutral vessels in designated zones of the high seas by continuing to recognize the rights of German submarines to visit and search American merchant vessels, but authorizes those vessels to resist by force certain named unlawful acts of submarines.

I am enclosing redrafted copies of the memorandum submitted to you yesterday[2] giving in detail the three separate policies suggested. Policy No. one denies the right of German submarines to search and seizure, and if ships carrying contraband are to have guns and naval crews on board will it not be necessary to deny search and seizure? Otherwise, practically no goods could be transported and the orders from abroad could not be filled. Would not this practically tie up American ships from going through the barred zone? To be sure this would deny the belligerent right of Germany to visit and search anywhere on the high seas. This would, of course, be a departure from international law and usage. Germany and the world might say that, demanding observance of international law, we had ourselves failed to observe it. Of course, our answer would be that Germany's note that it would sink without warning justified our action. This would be sufficient answer, undoubtedly, if in your message to Congress you had not expressed the doubt that Germany would be guilty of that unprecedented act. I am calling your attention to what is involved in Policy No. 1 before you determine upon which course should be pursued.

Admiral Benson is strongly of the opinion that the first thing to be done would be to notify Germany that, in view of the declaration that she intends to sink our ships without warning in a certain zone, it is our purpose to arm our ships for protection. He believes if this information is imparted it is barely possible that Germany might not carry out her threat. If we deny the right of visit, Germany would declare that to be a warlike act, and that we were responsible for bringing on war. It is entirely probable that the next step would be war. If we must enter it to protect our rights and the lives of our people, I have felt we ought to do nothing to put the responsibility for this step upon our Government.

Last night I conferred with Admiral Palmer about the crews to man the guns. He has taken action, and sends this note which I thought you would like to read. It is as follows:

*Confidential.* March 9, 1917.

From: Bureau of Navigation.

To: Operations.

Subject: Arming merchant vessels with Naval gun crews and a Naval officer.

Before any action is taken the Secretary should know that the presence of U. S. sailors (and an officer) on merchant ships will probably be considered an act of war from the German viewpoint.

That it is most probable that a German submarine, knowing an American merchant vessel is armed, and has armed forces of the U. S. on board, for the definite and sole purpose of resisting attack of submarines, will attack without warning.

That the master of the merchant vessel and the Naval Officer will believe the German submarine will attack without warning, and therefore, for the safety of the vessel, passengers, U. S. sailors and crew, they will fire at the submarine on sight.

The Secretary should be fully informed on this subject before final steps are taken to place 50 U. S. sailors and officers on armed merchant vessels.

(Signed)    Leigh C. Palmer.

Admiral Benson is to telephone me how soon ships could leave and whether action can be taken without publicity. My own opinion is that it would be impossible to take the action without our own people knowing it for these reasons:

1. Passengers would not go on these ships unless they knew they were armed and had competent gun crews. Their families and friends would know they were going and publicity would be certain.

2. Shippers and all their employees would be busy loading the cargo, and this could not be kept secret.

3. The sending of the gun crew—40 or 50 on the larger ships —would be known on the ships or stations from which they are taken, and experience has shown how impossible such movements are to be confined to service channels.

The question arises, too, whether it would not be wisest to state that you had reached the conclusion that you had a right to arm the ships and would do so, making no statement as to the time or the method. I cannot resist the feeling that this would be the best course and meet public approval. If Germany wants war, she will try to sink in any event. If she wishes to avert war with us, there would be time to modify her orders to Naval commanders so they would not commit the overt act.

Admiral Benson will return this afternoon and I will send you tonight or tomorrow morning a statement from him after his talk with Mr. Franklin. It will take five days, after notice that ships are to be armed, for one to sail, and until I hear from you I will give no orders to arm them, but will have guns and crews ready for immediate action.

I suggest whether, when we undertake to arm the ships, it will not be necessary to secure some co-operation with the English or French to whose shores the ships are destined. The information comes to us that when a ship leaves New York, its route and time of arrival are cabled to the Admiralty and it is met and convoyed into port by destroyers or other craft through a lane traversed all the time by Naval craft. Suppose we send out an armed merchant ship, ought we not to secure some such convoy or protection when she nears port in the barred zone? This is a big question but is one that we probably must face. The English also on this side know when a ship is coming into an American port and keep ships over here to afford protection. Certain French and English Naval officers here have suggested to officers in our service that some character of co-operation would be necessary. Naturally they would expect us to patrol and convoy their ships coming into our ports if they protect and convoy our ships going into their ports. Such co-operation would be easy if we were at war with Germany, but as we are not at war, would not such co-operation make us regarded as an ally of the entente powers? The protection of our ships and their reaching ports in safety raises so many difficult questions, and the consequences are so grave, that I am trying to present them to you before the final order to arm is given, though, of course, they have been present in your mind during the whole controversy.

Sincerely yours,   Josephus Daniels

TLS (SDR, RG 59, 763.72/3470½, DNA).
    [1] Rear Admiral Nathaniel Reilly Usher, commandant of the New York Navy Yard.
    [2] This enclosure is missing.


E N C L O S U R E   I I

In view of the announcement of the Imperial German Government on January 31, 1917 that all ships, those of neutrals included, met within certain zones of the high seas, would be sunk without any precautions being taken for the safety of the persons on board, and without the exercise of visit and search, the Government of the United States has determined to place upon all American merchant vessels sailing through the barred areas an armed guard for the protection of the vessels and the lives of the persons on board.[1]

CC MS (J. Daniels Papers, DLC).
    [1] This statement was issued to the press on March 12.


## From Walter Hines Page

London, March 9, 1917.

Confidential, for the President and the Secretary only.

In reporting on the general feeling here I find that continued delay in sending out American ships, especially American liners, is producing an increasingly unfavorable impression. In spite of all explanations which are imperfectly understood here delay is taken to mean the submission of our Government to the German blockade. This is the view of the public and most of the press. There is a tendency even in high government circles to regard the reasons for delay which are published here as technicalities which a national crisis should sweep aside. British opinion couples the delay of our ships with the sinking of the LACONIA[1] and the Z. telegram and seems to be reaching the conclusion that our Government will not be able to take positive action under any provocation. The feeling which the newspaper despatches from the United States produce on the British mind is that our Government is holding back our people until the blockade of our ships, the Z. telegram, and the LACONIA shall be forgotten and until the British Navy shall overcome the German submarines. There is danger that this feeling harden into a conviction and interfere with any influence that we might otherwise have when peace comes.

So friendly a man as Viscount Grey of Fallodon writes me privately from his retirement: "I do not see how the United States can sit still while neutral shipping is swept off the sea. If no action is taken, it will be like a great blot in history or a failure that must grievously depress the future history of America."
Page.

T telegram (SDR, RG 59, 763.72/3458, DNA).

[1] A submarine had sunk *Laconia*, an armed Cunard liner, without warning off the Irish coast on February 25. Twenty Americans were aboard; two of them had died from exposure.

## From Edward Mandell House, with Enclosures

Dear Governor: New York. March 9, 1917.

Here are some extracts from letters which may be of interest.

What Frazier says is disturbing and I fear is true. If France should cave in before Germany it would be a calamity beyond reckoning.

I am glad that you continue to bring out the thought that in order to have peace, the people must have a voice in the direction of their governments. Sometime soon, when the occasion presents itself, I hope you will call attention to the fact that the violation of treaties and of other obligations has brought about international chaos. We are back to the Stone Age where might makes right. It has taken us thousands of years to reach some sort of social order, and until the same obligations are recognized internationally as they are between individuals, there can be no peace or order in the world.

In selecting a successor to Guthrie,[1] Vance McCormick occurs to me as he doubtless will to you. There is no more important post at this time than this and I hope you will disregard all political considerations and give it to the best man that can be found. McCormick has good sense, is in thorough sympathy with your ideals and has all the energy necessary to make a success and maintain good relations with Japan. Mr. Old, Manager of the Herald,[2] has already made the suggestion of McCormick although he does not know him personally. I mention this to indicate how his appointment would be received in other than democratic circles.  Affectionately yours,  E. M. House

I am anxious about this news of your illness. Do be careful until you have lost your cold.

TLS (WP, DLC).
[1] George Wilkins Guthrie had died suddenly of apoplexy on March 8, 1917.
[2] Josiah Kingsley Ohl of the *New York Herald*.

## E N C L O S U R E   I

# William Hepburn Buckler to Edward Mandell House

Dear Colonel House:        London. England. February 23, 1917.

The journalists' tea given by N. Buxton last Friday was chiefly interesting for the frank statement made by Welliver,[1] the new and pro-Entente correspondent of the "New York Sun," who said that England must not expect the U. S. to fight as an enthusiastic ally. If we "come in" at all, he thinks we shall fight in our own distant independent way, and we shall not, he feels sure, send any troops to Europe. If disappointment here is to be avoided, this kind of outspoken testimony is much needed.

The past week has been notable for the "field day" of the pro-negotiation group in the House of Commons on the 20th. The best speeches were those of Ponsonby, Trevelyan and Buxton.[2] The last scored a distinct success by securing from Mr. Long,[3] the Colonial Secretary, a repudiation of the recent speech in which he declared that the African Colonies could not be given back to Germany.

Ponsonby and Trevelyan have both told me that the quiet interest with which members listened to them—instead of leaving the House—was encouraging and very different from what their mood would have been even six months ago. Snowden's[4] speech actually lasted an hour, yet he met with few interruptions.

Latent pessimism is still, I should say, the prevalent feeling here, partly because of U-boat fears—which Carson's and Churchill's speeches in the recent Navy debate did little to allay—and partly because people are asking themselves whether the next three and a half months, in which the new war-loan will be spent, can possibly witness any great changes on the Western front. The state of Russian politics is also naturally causing much uneasiness.

The pro-negotiation people admit that as to our present position their feelings are somewhat divided. They all regret that we are no longer in direct touch with Germany, and wonder how far we shall be able to appeal to her through our Swiss-Spanish "long distance telephone."

The majority believe that the war would be prolonged by our appearing on the scene with our immense resources just when the war fever of the Entente is becoming exhausted—as they think it will be in the next few months. They therefore hope that we shall stay at peace.

On the other hand a few men like Buxton feel that we could do more good by "coming in" as a check on the Entente jingoes, and therefore wish for war.

The men whom I know in the Foreign Office expect little active support from us if we do go to war, but that they want us to go in is certain, partly for the immense moral effect, partly because of the benefits to the Entente which would automatically accrue from the mere fact of our belligerent state.

The confidence felt in the President's statesmanship is most striking. Ponsonby—who is an ex-diplomatist—tells me that a F. O. friend of his regards "Mr. Wilson and King Tino"[5] as the two greatest living diplomatists, because despite difficulties apparently insuperable they always come out on top.

I am sending you under separate cover a new book by Brailsford,[6] admirably written, which points out the great need in the "League of Nations" of some arrangement for future changes in territory etc. This is of all such problems perhaps the most knotty, but without it the League would be simply a scheme for insuring the "haves" against aggression from the "have nots."

Buxton and Sir E. Pears[7] have just told me that they are getting up a public meeting for March 19th—non-partisan as Lord Parmoor[8] will preside—to discuss the "straits" question, with its effect on American opinion.

Yours sincerely,   W. H. Buckler.

1 That is, Judson C. Welliver.

2 That is, Arthur Augustus William Harry Ponsonby, Charles Philips Trevelyan, and Noel Edward Noel-Buxton, leaders of the peace faction in the House of Commons.

3 Walter Hume Long.

4 Philip Snowden, Labour M.P., another leader of the peace faction.

5 Probably King Constantine of Greece.

6 Henry Noel Brailsford, *A League of Nations* (London and New York, 1917).

7 Sir Edwin Pears, lawyer for many years resident in Constantinople, expert on Turkish history and politics, at this time living in England.

8 Charles Alfred Cripps, 1st Baron Parmoor, eminent lawyer, opponent of British participation in the war, and advocate of world organization.

ENCLOSURE II

## Arthur Hugh Frazier to Edward Mandell House

Dear Mr. House:                    Paris, February 16, 1917.

You can well imagine how cordially the news of our break with Germany was received in France; the papers have been full of it ever since and they praise the attitude of President Wilson with a unanimity which is a little startling when contrasted with the tone of the same newspapers a few weeks ago.

Clemenceau's remarks were by far the most eloquent; he said that Mr. Wilson had reminded the entire world that there was such a thing as "le droit humain" ("Human" right is a very inadequate translation) which future generations would not again be able to ignore. The moral effect of our severance of relations with Germany has been enormous and I am firmly convinced that the French people, as distinguished from the official and governing classes, believe that they have found a champion in Mr. Wilson.

It would be idle to deny that the last few weeks have been a very severe trial for the French nation; the intense cold weather, coupled with a shortage of coal, have brought the war home to the civil population as never before; there can be no doubt that they are intensely sick of the war and only the thought that a peace at the present moment would be disastrous for the future holds them together; how long they will be able to hold out I do not know but they have nearly reached the limit.

Sincerely yours,   Arthur Hugh Frazier.

TCL (WP, DLC).

## From Josephus Daniels, with Enclosure

Dear Mr. President:                    [Washington] March 9th, 1917

Referring to your impression that fast small craft might wisely be placed on merchant ships going to England or France, I told you last night that Admiral Benson and Admiral Badger advised against it. This morning I had a talk with Admiral Taylor,[1] and am enclosing a memorandum prepared by him for your information.                    Sincerely    Josephus Daniels

Will you please return the picture of the boat because it belongs to Admiral Taylor's files.

ALS (J. Daniels Papers, DLC).
[1] David Watson Taylor, distinguished naval architect and engineer. At this time he was Chief Constructor, U.S.N., and Chief of the Bureau of Construction and Repair of the Navy Department.


E N C L O S U R E

Washington, March 9, 1917.
MEMORANDUM RELATIVE TO METHOD OF PROTECTING
MERCHANT VESSELS FROM ATTACKS BY SUBMARINES.

The best boats for the purpose that are available, or that could be obtained at short notice, would be sister boats of the Chingachgook. These are 60-ft. vessels of about 15 tons displacement, designed for a speed of 25 to 26 land miles, or in the neighborhood of 22 knots, in smooth water. The Department's data card for the Chingachgook, herewith, shows the appearance of this vessel.

As a rule, the trans-Atlantic cargo vessels could handle, without special arrangements, 5 tons only from a cargo boom. The ST. LOUIS, by special bracing of her booms, could handle 10 tons with a single boom, and her booms are so arranged that, for handling such boats, she could use two booms. These boats are not designed to be lifted in and out of the water, but could be handled by making special slings.

The Greenport Company, which built these boats, is supposed to have built them originally for Russia, but had them left on their hands. The Department's information is that it has now five boats similar to the Chingachgook and one additional boat which is completed except for the motors, which are expected about March 15th. This makes seven boats only, of this type, including the Chingachgook.

The ST. LOUIS could be fitted with cradles for two aft without serious difficulty. Two more could be carried forward, but it would be quite a job to build the necessary cradles to make them secure at sea. In rough weather, hoisting these boats in and out would be a difficult and dangerous undertaking.

There are practically no other small, high-speed boats available in the country at present capable of carrying guns up to the 3-pdr. caliber. There are a number of high-speed racing boats, but their construction is too flimsy to carry a gun of any size. The British have used a number of 80-ft. motor boats of about 30 tons displacement, as submarine chasers, but now consider that no boat would be satisfactory for that purpose less than 110 feet in length. The Navy Department submarine chaser plans are for 110-ft. vessels, smaller vessels being for auxiliary patrol, &c., but these are not expected to cope with submarines on an equal footing. The smaller vessels can carry only 3-pdr. guns, or thereabouts, whereas the German submarines carry 4-inch guns firing shot of more than 30 pounds in weight.

The size of boat that could be carried and hoisted in and out of a trans-Atlantic steamer could operate only in almost ideal conditions of weather and sea. The sea west of the British Isles, for practically two-thirds of the time, is more or less stormy and impossible of navigation by small craft at high speed. The so-called "danger zone" extends at least 300 miles off the west coast of the British Isles. Should a 20-knot passenger liner carry a number of small, high-speed motor boats and put them overboard at the outer limits of the danger zone, even if able to keep up with their ship in favorable conditions, they would lose from a third to a half of their speed under weather conditions which would not appreciably affect the large vessel, so that the large vessel would have to slow down unnecessarily, whereas the principal element of safety of vessels navigating the danger zone is to maintain as high a speed as possible, and above all things not to remain stationary for any length of time.

With several motor boats fitted with the racing type of engines, which must be used to give small vessels high speed, it is practically certain that one or more would have engine trouble and break-down, requiring the steamer to stop and pick them up or abandon them on the high seas.

The subject of carrying motor boats as pickets or lookouts to surround large vessels, has been discussed with a number of naval officers of experience, and they are unanimously of the opinion that the idea involves so many difficulties as to render it practicable only under exceptional conditions, and that in conditions normally to be expected, the undertaking would subject the vessel carrying them to greater danger, or compel abandonment of the boats on the high seas.

Some officers have suggested, as a possible means of protection of life, that three or more steamers of approximately the same speed, might travel in company, in some formation that would keep them near enough for mutual protection and assistance, but this also is not regarded as practicable. It may be recalled that, early in the war, a German submarine sunk a British cruiser, and when two sister vessels in the vicinity came to her assistance they were promptly sunk in turn by the same submarine, upon which the Admiralty issued orders that no naval vessel of military value was to attempt to succor a torpedoed vessel.                                        D. W. Taylor.

TS MS (J. Daniels Papers, DLC).


## From William Gibbs McAdoo, with Enclosure

Dear Mr. President:                    Washington March 9, 1917.

Mr. Vrooman[1] has explained to me fully why he feels unable to accept a position on the Tariff Commission. Just before Secretary Houston left town we discussed William Kent again and agreed that it would be well to put him on the Board if he could be induced to accept. I discussed the matter with Mr. Kent this morning and he has consented to serve if you want him to do so. I think this is a happy solution of the problem. It is, therefore, with great satisfaction and relief that I send you the recommendations for the Tariff Commission, and hope that you will be pleased with them. I would suggest that you send the nominations to the Senate at your earliest convenience if you approve them.                        Cordially yours, W G McAdoo

TLS (WP, DLC).
[1] That is, Carl Schurz Vrooman, Assistant Secretary of Agriculture.


E N C L O S U R E

## From William Gibbs McAdoo

Dear Mr. President:                    Washington March 9, 1917.

I respectfully recommend for appointment as members of the United States Tariff Commission, to be appointed by you under authority of the Act of Congress approved September 8, 1916, the following gentlemen:

For the twelve (12) year term:
    Mr. Frank W. Taussig, of Massachusetts, Independent;
For the ten (10) year term:
    Mr. Daniel C. Roper, of South Carolina, Democrat;
For the eight (8) year term:
    Mr. David J. Lewis, of Maryland, Democrat;

For the six (6) year term:
    Mr. William Kent, of California, Independent;
For the four (4) year term:
    Mr. William S. Culbertson, of Kansas, Republican;
For the two (2) year term:
    Mr. Edward P. Costigan, of Colorado, Progressive Republican.

The Act provides that not more than three of the members of the Commission shall be of the same political party. With the alignment I have suggested, there will be on the Commission two Democrats, two Independents, one Republican, and one Progressive Republican. For your further information I attach hereto a brief biographical sketch of each of the proposed members.[1]

Cordially yours,   W G McAdoo

TLS (WP, DLC).
[1] Not printed.

## From Edward Wright Sheldon

My dear Mr. President:        [New York] March 9th, 1917.

It gratified me profoundly to witness your second inauguration, and I wish to express to you personally my keen appreciation of your kind wish conveyed through Miss Bones that I should be present on that historic day. It was an occasion full of solemn significance, and the only regret it brought was that I had no chance to tell you how warmly my thoughts were with you, and to utter my Godspeed. In beginning your new term you have the soul of the whole country behind you, and in the universal desire to aid you and the common weal to the utmost, I most devoutly join.

The Director of the New York Public Library,[1] one of your staunch supporters, knowing of my intended visit to Washington, sent me the enclosed extract from a Harrisburg newspaper of November 1863, and thought it might amuse you.[2] It is a striking illustration of the fallibility in spirit and fact of contemporary journalistic criticism, and may suggest some recent analogies.

May I beg that you will offer to Mrs. Wilson my sympathy in her family grief?

Believe me, with affectionate regards,

Yours sincerely,   Edward W. Sheldon.

ALS (WP, DLC).
[1] Edwin Hatfield Anderson.
[2] It was a commentary on the Gettysburg Address in the Harrisburg, Pa.,

*Patriot and Union*, Nov. 24, 1863, which reads as follows: "The President succeeded on this occasion because he acted without sense and without constraint
in a panorama that was gotten up more for the benefit of his party than
for the glory of the nation and the honor of the dead. . . . We pass over
the silly remarks of the President; for the credit of the nation we are willing
that the veil of oblivion shall be dropped over them and that they shall no
more be repeated or thought of." T MS (WP, DLC).

## From the Diary of Josephus Daniels

March Friday 9 1917

President sick—no cabinet

Called to White House again to see President about armed
guard on ships. He had sent Lansing my memorandum of instruction. Should naval officer control or master? Or should they
agree? I thought if both must agree it might be debating society
& ship might be sunk waiting for decision.

Shall visit be permitted outside zone? That is required but
safety of passengers also required. If they conflict what? The
President say it was not to be permitted that they should be put
to sea in small boats 300 mi. from shore & German submarines
would not dare to tow them near to land. Therefore preservation
of life demanded leaving no chance by inaction outside of zone

Mayo to see Lansing & request him to see Spring Rice & request
protection of our ships near Great Britain as they protected their
ships

Danish West Indies

Taylor's statement about small boats seemed to convince the
President his idea was not practical

## From the Diary of Thomas W. Brahany

Friday, March 9, 1917

The President is much improved but did not leave his room.
The Postmaster General, after repeated efforts, succeeded in seeing the President shortly after 2 o'clock. A little later word came
that the President wished to see Tumulty. When Tumulty returned from the White House he brought word that the President wished a proclamation drafted convening the Congress in
extra session on Monday April 16. The proclamation was signed
and given to the press. At the same time Tumulty gave to the
press a statement setting out that the President is convinced he
has the right to arm American merchant ships. This was dictated
by the President but given to the press as a statement from

Tumulty. The President was propped up in bed when he dictated this statement and when he signed the extra session proclamation. Burleson is the man on whom the President depends largely for information regarding political matters having to do with Congress. I presume he told the President today that April 16 is the date most satisfactory to the leaders for beginning the extra session. Tumulty thinks Burleson is "in bad" with a great number of Democrats in the Congress. He is quick tempered, opinionated and domineering. Tumulty says he's awfully stingy. He is probably the richest man in the Cabinet. The fact that he keeps his small change in a pocketbook instead of loose in his pocket, is to Tumulty a sure sign that he's not let go of the first dollar he ever made. A stingy man always carries a pocketbook according to Tumulty.

## From Yoshihito

Tokio, March 10, 1917.

I desire to convey to you an expression of my profound sympathy in the loss which the American people have sustained by the death of his Excellency, the Honorable George Wilkins Guthrie, Ambassador of the United States. He has done so much to inspire confidence and friendship in the relations between our two nations and has so worthily represented his country to which he has devoted his faithful service up to the end.

Yoshihito.

T telegram (SDR, RG 59, 123 G 98/31, DNA).

## From Frank Lyon Polk, with Enclosure

My dear Mr. President:        Washington March 10, 1917.

I am sorry to bother you again, but the Secretary thought that you would prefer to see the attached telegram to Peking before it was sent.

You will recall that Mr. Reinsch reported the Chinese Government were very anxious to break off relations with Germany and laid down certain conditions. The impression we had here was that China was taking this opportunity to play a little international politics with a view to making friends here and in Europe who would be useful in its relations with Japan. My own feeling is that the last sentence of the telegram should be cut out so as not to shut the door entirely. While the chances of giving any assurances are remote, yet if we flatly say so at this time we would not be consulted further by the Chinese.

If you have an opportunity to look at this today or Sunday, and come to any conclusion, I could call at the White House and get the papers from Mr. Hoover.

Yours faithfully,   Frank L Polk

March 12, 1917

President returned telegram to China with last sentence cut out.   F.L.P.

TLS (SDR, RG 59, 763.72/3538½, DNA).


E N C L O S U R E


*Not for distribution*                    Washington, March 9, 1917.

Department's cipher telegrams of February 17, four p.m. and March 2, five p.m.

The Department appreciates action of China in awaiting the decision of this Government concerning the assurances which you proposed to give the Chinese Government on condition of action by it concurrent with that of the United States.

After careful reconsideration of the whole matter, this Government sees no reason to alter its decision communicated to you in the telegram of February 10, four p.m.

The Department is supporting China's efforts to obtain a loan in the United States. There are serious obstacles in the way but the approaching visit of Mr. Abbott[1] to Peking may possibly remove them.

The United States is not in a position to guarantee China a voice in possible conferences but desires China to have such a voice and in so far as practicable will use its influence to that end.

It must be understood, however, that this Government is not bidding against the Entente for adherence of China to American course of action. There appears to have been on the part of the Legation a misunderstanding of the President's circular invitation to neutral governments. All other important neutrals having declined that invitation the adherence of China without other powers would be insufficient for purpose originally intended. But the Department is of course deeply interested in the welfare of China and cannot but feel that if the Chinese Government will refuse to place itself in a position which will give others a reasonable excuse for demanding control of its military resources there will be no need to seek protection against such domination. ⟨In view of the above and seeing that China did not take concurrent action upon which condition your assurances were given you are instructed to withdraw them.⟩ Lansing.

T telegram (SDR, RG 59, 763.72/3397, DNA).
  [1] John Jay Abbott, vice-president of the Continental and Commercial Trust and Savings Bank of Chicago.

## From Frank Lyon Polk, with Enclosure

My dear Mr. President: Washington March 10, 1917.

I enclose a draft of a confidential despatch to Mr. Gonzales for your approval.

I have talked with the Secretary this morning, and while he is in agreement with the plan outlined, he thought that you would prefer to see it before it was sent. As you will probably recall, President Menocal suggested sending General Crowder down to make an investigation, and this telegram is merely pressing the suggestion made by him. Although Menocal has captured Gomez and other leaders, the danger is that small bands will continue operating unless they are given an opportunity to withdraw gracefully.

I sent for Mr. Ferrara's[1] representatives, and told him that it was his duty to return to Cuba and assist in restoring confidence in the Constitutional Government. I also told him to make it very clear that we could not permit him to continue his activities in this country.

If you will approve this telegram and return it to me this afternoon, I will send it at once.

Yours faithfully, Frank L Polk

TLS (SDR, RG 59, 837a/1195, DNA).
  [1] Orestes Ferrara, president of the Cuban House of Deputies and proprietor of *El Heraldo de Cuba*, at this time in New York as a propagandist for the Cuban Liberal party.

### E N C L O S U R E[1]

Washington, March 10, 1917

Confidential. You are instructed ⟨immediately⟩ to ask for an interview with President Menocal and to say that the situation in Cuba has been carefully considered by the President of the United States and the Secretary of State and that it is ⟨thought⟩ *suggested* that peaceful conditions may be sooner restored and further destruction of valuable property be prevented, if he should ask for an investigation and adjustment of the election question by General Crowder and other representative Americans, as was intimated by him to you; that this Government would be willing to lend its good offices to the Cuban people in this respect.

It is ⟨thought⟩ *suggested* that a proclamation embodying this request should follow the proclamation of President Menocal which was contained in your cable of March 8, 10 p.m.[2]

Lansing

I have made one or two alterations of words    W.W.

T telegram (SDR, RG 59, 837.00/1195, DNA).
    [1] Words in angle brackets deleted by Wilson; words in italics added by him.
    [2] W. E. Gonzales to RL, March 8, 1917, T telegram (SDR, RG 59, 837.00/1195, DNA); printed in FR *1917*, pp. 379-81. In this proclamation, Menocal said that the revolution had been broken, called on all rebels to lay down their arms, and promised that a free election would be held in the city of Santiago ten days after the reestablishment of constitutional government in that city.


## From the Diary of Chandler Parsons Anderson

March 10, 1917.

Had a talk with Bert Lansing this morning about the prospects of war and about what was being done in preparation for it, and he was very outspoken in expressing the conviction that war with Germany was inevitable. In regard to preparation, so far as the Department of State was concerned, he asked me to send in as soon as possible a memorandum covering the suggestions which I made to him two weeks ago as to the organization of the Liaison Board and the Committee of Information to answer inquiries, etc., etc. I promised to do this.

We also talked about Mexico, and he expressed considerable apprehension as to the reliability and trustworthiness of Carranza. I gathered, however, that the President was inclined to treat him with extreme friendliness and give him recognition as the de jure president in the hope of thereby purchasing his friendship. I told Bert that I hoped that it would not be necessary to go to that extent for that purpose, because if there was nothing more than that to hold Carranza by, I did not think that we would be able to compete with the promises which Germany seemed to be prepared to make. I said that this disposition on the part of our Government made it even more important than before for us to prevent the retroactive application of the new constitution to foreign owned property in Mexico. I then told him of the suggestion which I had written to Frank Polk the day before about making the recognition of Carranza conditional upon entering into a treaty with the United States protecting American interests against the objectionable provisions of the constitution. He said that he thought this would be an admirable plan and asked me to discuss it fully with Frank Polk.

In regard to the situation in the oil fields, the seriousness of which he thoroughly appreciates, he said that our government was entirely willing that General Peleyas[1] should be supplied with arms and ammunition from this country so long as the matter was not brought to the attention of the government, and that I might rest assured that the Administration would not prosecute any one who was assisting Peleyas so long as he remained friendly to the foreign interests in that region.

We also talked a little about the Costa Rican situation, and he said, and Frank Polk also said later, that the President was unwilling to recognize Tinoco as a de facto president, and that they were quite sure that he would refuse to recognize him even if he was elected at the coming election. I made no comment on this because I did not think it would be possible to impose any such limitations upon latin-american countries except by the general consent of those countries, which certainly could not be obtained at the present time, and as I have no authority to represent either faction in Costa Rica for this purpose, I had no excuse for going into the matter with the Department. I did ask both Bert and Frank, however, if they had in mind any plan which they could suggest as a solution for the present deadlock in their relations with Costa Rica, and we discussed that briefly, the conclusion being that the best thing to do would be to have all the factions agree upon some one to be elected president instead of Tinoco. . . .

Frank Polk lunched with me at the Club and we spent most of our time discussing the Mexican situation.

Frank said in the first place that he thoroughly agreed with my suggestion about negotiating a treaty and that he had been in despair about the situation and welcomed my suggestion, and hoped that I would work it out for them. He asked me to draft a form of treaty which would be satisfactory to the interests represented by me, which I told him I would do if after consultation with my clients I found that they wanted me to do it. He said that he was afraid that the President was set on recognizing Carranza because he thought that was the only way to prevent him from surrendering to German influence, and that he was afraid that the President would do this without making the necessary reservations as to the effect of the constitution upon foreign interests; and that in order to meet this he had instructed the solicitor's office to prepare a full memorandum showing the confiscatory effect of the objectionable provisions in the constitution if applied retroactively to foreign owned property in Mexico, and pointing out the ennormous value of the property involved and the destructive effect on material interest; and that he was having this done for the purpose of putting the question squarely up to the President himself, to make him responsible, and so that he would not act blindly. He said that my suggestion fitted right in with this plan, and gave him an opportunity to propose a practical solution, which he thought the President would eagerly accept.

¹ General Manuel Peláez, who controlled the petroleum-producing region between Tuxpan and Tampico.

## From Josephus Daniels

Dear Mr. President:          Washington. March 11, 1917.

Enclosed is a copy of tentative instructions to Armed Guard to be placed on American merchant ships. I have sent a copy to Secretary Lansing requesting [him] to make suggestions as to changes, omissions or additions. When he has given his suggestions and the regulations are approved in our Department I will send or bring over, as you like, a copy for your approval. Before waiting, however, for Secretary Lansing's suggestions I am sending you a tentative copy.¹ We are trying to cover the whole field and to so word the instructions so that if they should ever be published there will be no regulation contrary to the splendid spirit of our policy. It is easy for me to come to see you at any hour you desire. I hope you continue to improve.

Sincerely   Josephus Daniels

ALS (J. Daniels Papers, DLC).
¹ This enclosure is missing.

## Josephus Daniels to Robert Lansing

Dear Mr. Secretary:          Washington. March 11, 1917.

Enclosed are tentative regulations drawn up for the government of the Armed Guard to be placed on merchant ships. Will you be good enough to suggest any changes, additions or omissions that you think will be wise? We wish to send these instructions out on Monday. I will be glad to call to go over this matter if you desire.                    Sincerely,   Josephus Daniels

Please return enclosed with your suggestions.

ALS (SDR, RG 59, 763.72/3576¾, DNA).


## From Edward Mandell House

Dear Governor:                              New York. March 11, 1917.

Paderewski called yesterday to say that his compatriots are anxious to know your decision regarding their offer.[1] They have gone to considerable expense already in the renting of houses and a hotel at the place where they expect to undertake the training of the five hundred officers.

Paderewski told me at one time that at least fifty thousand Poles would enlist for service if called for.

I explained to him that you had been ill and had not had time to take the matter up with the Secretary of War.

I am happy to see from the papers that you are recovering rapidly.                    Affectionately yours,   E. M. House

TLS (WP, DLC).
[1] Paderewski had called on House on February 27 to present T. A. Starzynski and others to WW, Feb. 19, 1917, and T. A. Starzynski to WW, Feb. 27, 1917, both printed as Enclosures with WW to NDB, March 31, 1917 (first letter of that date).


## From Walter Lippmann, with Enclosure

Dear Mr. President,              Washington D. C. March 11, 1917

I am submitting a memorandum to you which was prepared after a conversation with Colonel House. The situation it is intended to meet contains these factors:

1. The very deep impression being made upon American opinion by the argument that the United States enforces its rights against Germany but not against Great Britain * * * see, for example the speech of the German Chancellor, February 27, 1917[1] and many speeches in Congress.

2. The fact that this discrimination, while it renders the German people hostile, has failed to win corresponding popular recognition in France, England and Canada; that it fortifies the anti-Administration elements in this country and confuses popular support by introducing a factitious elem[e]nt of "unfairness."

3. The inability of the pacifist forces to see the correlation between the peace program and warlike measures which may be necessary.

It has seemed to us (Mr. Croly and myself) that a statement by you was conceivable which might at one stroke accomplish a number of important things; might even have far-reaching consequences for good. These seem to us possible results of a statement along the lines of the attached memorandum:

1. Education of American opinion to the truth that the issue with Germany is not mere legalism or commercialism, but one arising out of America's vital interest in a just and lasting peace.

2. Revivification of the proposal of a league for peace.

3. Capture of liberal opinion in Allied countries.

4. Encouragement of German radicals to force a statement of terms, which might either

    a. Start international discussion

    b. or at least tend to divide German opinion

5. Warn our own jingo elements that American belligerency would still remain subordinate to liberal policy.

I have brought this memorandum to Washington in the hope that you will read it, and on the chance that you would be willing to see me for a few minutes about it. Forgive me if I have intruded. More than anything else it is a deep personal affection for you which prompts me.

Sincerely yours,    Walter Lippmann

TLS (WP, DLC).
¹ In a lengthy address to the Reichstag on February 27, Bethmann Hollweg defended recent German foreign and military policies, especially the all-out submarine campaign. He asserted that the United States had not been justified in breaking relations with Germany and cited numerous alleged examples of American partiality in favor of the Allies and against Germany. For an extensive report of his remarks, see the *New York Times*, Feb. 28, 1917.

E N C L O S U R E

MEMORANDUM.

It was the intention of the United States to remain neutral in this war, to share in the reconstruction and in the guaranties od [of] peace. During the course of the war the belligerents have asked America to forgo certain of its undoubted rights under international law.

Germany has requested the abandonment of at least two undoubted rights

the shipment of munitions
travel on the high seas and the safety of noncombatants.

Germany justifies her violent assault on American lives on the ground that America has not succeeded in sustaining certain commercial rights against Great Britain.

To this the United States replies that the rights of a neutral are not the possession of a belligerent. It feels entirely free to enforce its rights or suspend them temporarily in accordance with its national purposes. That purpose is simple and has been avowed. It consists in the organization of peace on the foundation of consent. To have suspended the right of shipment or travel could be justified only on the ground that Germany's purpose in the war is friendly to America's interest in international order. No assurance exists.

The controversy with Great Britain is suspended by the more immediate and irreparable injuries inflicted by Germany, by the intrigue and crime committed on American soil, by the refusal of Germany to disavow aggressive ambitions which if achieved would render the future peace of the world unstable.

In spite of all this it was the hope of the American Government that a peace could be negotiated without inflaming the whole world. The attempt to secure from Germany a statement of her principles failed to elicit a response, and America was forced to conclude that Germany is fighting for a victory subversive of the world system in which America lives.

Therefore, when Germany broke off the effort to reach some understanding by a proclamation of marine terrorism, America was forced more actively to uphold that portion of its rights which Germany was asking her to forgo in behalf of a victory for ends never revealed and justifiably regarded with suspicion.

The only victory in this war that could compensate mankind for its horrors is the victory of international order over national aggression. Whatever measures America takes will always be adapted to that end. It has no designs on Germany's life or her legitimate national development. It does not seek to humiliate the German people. It does not even propose to return upon them the grievous injuries inflicted by their government upon us.

But it does propose to resist the aggression which is touching America. It will not commit itself to any aggression upon Germany or her allies. It will reserve freedom of action for itself, and whenever Germany is ready to abandon aggression and enter a league of nations, America will be ready to discuss the matter through open diplomacy.

T MS (WP, DLC).

## From Josephus Daniels

Dear Mr. President:                    Washington. March 12, 1917.

Enclosed is a copy of the tentative draft of instructions with reference to Armed Guard upon merchant vessels. After it was prepared I gave it to Secretary Lansing and requested him to suggest any changes, additions and omissions. He has marked the omissions he recommends. I am sending it to you just as he handed it to me for your consideration.[1] Please note your wishes and if possible let me have instructions as you desire them changed so we can get them to our officers Tuesday night.

I hope you are quite well.

Sincerely,   Josephus Daniels

ALS (WP, DLC).
[1] This document is missing. For the revised version, see the memorandum by Daniels printed at March 13, 1917.


## To Josephus Daniels

My dear Mr. Secretary,       The White House. 12 March, 1917.

On the whole, I think Lansing's ammendments, omissions, and additions good. His idea as to the first part of this paper is, evidently, that it is not necessary in such a paper to state the *policy* of the Government, since the instructions embody that policy.

I would be very much obliged if you would give the most emphatic orders that no part of any of this is to be given even the least publicity. I should feel justified in ordering a court martial for disobedience to such an order.

In haste, with warmest regard,

Faithfully Yours,   Woodrow Wilson

WWTLS (J. Daniels Papers, DLC).


## From Robert Lansing, with Enclosure

PERSONAL AND PRIVATE:

My dear Mr. President:       [Washington] March 12, 1917.

I do not like the attitude which Mr. Carranza has taken, as indicated in this telegram from Ambassador Fletcher. I will take up immediately the matter of replying to his communication in regard to American neutrals.

Faithfully yours,   Robert Lansing

CCL (RSB Coll., DLC).

E N C L O S U R E

Mexico City Mar. 10, 1917.

CONFIDENTIAL. Returned last night from Guadalajara. Spent several days in the company of the First Chief who expressed a very sincere desire to arrange all matters which have arisen or may arise in a spirit of accommodation. On the subject matter of your number 10, February 26, eleven a.m.[1] he was extremely cautious. He said that Mexico had not received up to the present time from Germany any proposition whatever of alliance; that for his part his sincere desire was that the war should not come to this side of the Atlantic; that the peace note of Mexico[2] was based on this hope and upon the humane motive of helping as far as possible to reestablish peace and in compliance with the highest duties of self preservation and defense. He spoke at length of his great desire to have the neutral powers accept some plans, not necessarily his, which would bring peace and did not seem to fear Germany's future policy in case neutrals should or could impose peace at this time. He said that you had not replied to his note; that he hoped you would accept in principle and if you will so accept he would suggest that conference of all the neutral powers be called in Washington where all are represented diplomatically with a view to discovering the most convenient form of contributing to the early restoration of peace in Europe and he said it was immaterial whether the ideas proposed in his note should be adopted or others which the conference might deem more appropriate. In answer to my direct question as to his attitude in case Germany should propose an alliance he said that Mexico desires to avoid becoming involved in the war and again referred to his note but he avoided saying directly that such a proposition would be rejected. Personally I do not think Mexico would under present circumstances accept alliance referred to but I think First Chief wishes with[h]old categorical statement to that effect in the hope of inducing our Government to accept his peace proposals or a peace conference of neutrals.

While both he and Minister for Foreign Affairs were very careful and guarded in their utterances I gathered that their sentiments inclined somewhat toward Germany. As I was leaving the Minister for Foreign Affairs yesterday, in reply to my statement that I was rather sorry I would not be able to send to the President a frank and categorical statement of Mexico's attitude if an alliance with Germany should be proposed, he said that his Government wished to proceed step by step and that no doubt after a report [reply] had been received to their note the First Chief would confer with me again after having returned to the Capital next week, and he said that in any case Mexico's conduct would be just and correct whether any statement was made or not; that they believed that actions spoke better that [than] words.

Please advise me opportunely of any action on the Mexican note.                                                      Fletcher.

T telegram (RSB Coll., DLC).
    1 F. L. Polk to H. P. Fletcher, Feb. 26, 1917, T telegram (SDR, RG 59, 862.20212/70A, DNA); printed in *FR-WWS 1917*, I, 234-35. Polk stated the substance of the Zimmermann telegram to Fletcher and then gave him the following instructions:
    "You will at once see General Carranza or, if that cannot be arranged immediately, the Minister of Foreign Affairs. Read to him the substance of the German note and state that it is probable that the contents of this note will be made public in the United States immediately and suggest as your personal opinion that it might be well for the Mexican Government to make some comment.
    "CONFIDENTIAL MERELY FOR YOUR GUIDANCE. The Department does not feel that it can properly withhold from the public the text of this German message. Its publication, however, may cause great consternation and it is possible, unfortunately, that, with the intense feeling aroused, there may be included a degree of uncertainty in regard to the attitude of Mexico unless the Mexican Government can make some statement which might be published simultaneously tending to show their disinterestedness."
    2 About this matter, see R. H. Elizalde to RL, Feb. 19, 1917, n. 1, printed as an Enclosure with RL to WW, Feb. 19, 1917.

## James Hamilton Lewis to Robert Lansing

My dear Mr. Secretary:          [Washington] March 12, 1917.

Just as I had fully prepared to support my Resolution asserting executive power in the President to arm the ships,[1] and with your own good suggestion and aid had fortified myself,—I received a message in confidence from the President, transmitted through Senator Martin, stating that the President feared that my presentation of the question would awaken debate that would go to such extent and bring forth expressions of such nature, that at this time would embarrass and for the future might complicate the results we all hoped to achieve when the session begins,—or in the meantime, if events called for action previous to the meeting of the session.

The President was of the opinion that if I could forego the address at this time it might be to the advantage of the policies we are seeking to execute. Naturally I deferred to his wishes, and this note is only to explain to you why the presentation was not made by me according to the understanding I left with you gentlemen at the time you contributed your very kind aid to my undertaking.

With personal regards, Yours sincerely, Lewis

TLS (R. Lansing Papers, DLC).
[1] The Senate met in special session from March 5 to 16 for the purpose of debating the Treaty of Bogotá. As it turned out, it failed to give its consent to ratification. See Link, *Campaigns for Progressivism and Peace*, pp. 370-72.

## Paul Samuel Reinsch to Robert Lansing

Peking, March 12, 1917.

March 12, 1 p.m. STRICTLY CONFIDENTIAL.

The decision of the Cabinet to break off diplomatic relations with Germany has been communicated to both Houses of Parliament and indorsed in both by a vote of confidence. I am informed the decision is to be made effective tomorrow.

Premier still maintains that no commitment as to further action has been made: I have reason to believe, however, that he and an important faction have become thoroughly identified with Japanese intrigue and that the Japanese have furnished money and promised further assistance to be used in fortifying the position of those concerned. It is also becoming evident that a restoration of the Manchu monarchy is a part of this intrigue which if carried out is certain to cause grave difficulties and disturbances.

It is with deep regret that I have to state that the opportunity of the United States to avert these dangers to China and the world is irrevocably passing away and immeasurably greater exertion will be necessary in the future than would have sufficed in the immediate past to safeguard the situation. The reports of the recent decisive deliberations of the Cabinet show that the action of the American International Corporation, causing the Chinese to believe that Americans could not be safely trusted, has been damaging to our commercial interests.[1] But this handicap might have been overcome, if it had been possible to assure those who have confidence in our our leadership of our Government's readiness to do what it could to enable China to meet the responsibilities involved; but without any confirmation of even such general assurances, as I reported in my telegram of February 9, 12 midnight, they have no cogent alternative to offer to those won over to Japan and have to let the decision go by default. Reinsch.

T telegram (SDR, RG 59, 763.72/3483, DNA).
[1] About this matter, see Tien-yi Li, *Woodrow Wilson's China Policy, 1913-1917* (New York, 1952), pp. 186-90, and Noel H. Pugach, *Paul S. Reinsch: Open Door Diplomat in Action* (Millwood, N. Y., 1979), pp. 204-10.

# From the Diary of Josephus Daniels

1917 Monday 12 March

Sent to the President draft of orders to men on armed ships this afternoon, embodying suggestions from Lansing which would omit statement of policy. At ten o'clock received instructions from President approved as amended, with a note in which he wished me to give orders that nothing should be given out & he would wish any officer court-martialed who gave out any hint of instructions.


# A Memorandum by Josephus Daniels

### REGULATIONS

Governing the Conduct of American Merchant
Vessels on which ARMED GUARDS have been placed.

CONFIDENTIAL                              March 13, 1917.

1. Armed Guards on American merchant vessels are for the sole purpose of defense against the unlawful acts of the submarines of Germany or of any nation following the policy announced by Germany in her note of January 31, 1917. Neither the Armed Guards nor their arms can be used for any other purpose.

2. The announced policy of Germany, in her note of January 31, 1917, to sink all vessels that enter certain areas of the high seas, has led the Government of the United States to authorize Armed Guards on merchant vessels to resist any and all attempts of the submarines of Germany or of any nation following the policy announced by Germany in her note of January 31st, to put that policy into practice.

3. It shall be lawful for the Armed Guard on any American merchant vessel to fire upon any submarine of Germany or of any nation following the policy of Germany announced in her note of January 31, 1917, that attempts to approach, or lies within 4,000 yards of the commercial route of the vessel sighting the submarine, if the submarine is sighted within the zone proscribed by Germany.

4. No Armed Guard on any American merchant vessel shall fire at any submarine that lies more than 4,000 yards from the commercial route of the vessel sighting the submarine, except that the submarine shall have fired first.

5. No Armed Guard on any American merchant vessel shall take any offensive action against any submarine of Germany or

of any nation following the policy of Germany announced in her note of January 31, 1917, on the high seas outside of the zones proscribed by Germany, unless the submarine is guilty of an unlawful act that jeopardizes the vessel, her passengers, or crew, or unless the submarine is submerged.

6. No Armed Guard on an American merchant vessel shall attack a submarine that is retiring or attempting to retire either within or without the zone proscribed by Germany, unless it may be reasonably presumed to be manouevering for renewal of attack.

7. In all cases not herein specifically excepted the Armed Guard on American merchant vessels shall be governed by the principles of established international law and the treaties and conventions to which the Government of the United States is a party.

8. American merchant vessels are forbidden to pursue or search out the submarines of any nation or to engage in any aggressive warfare against them.

9. American merchant vessels shall make every effort compatible with the safety of the merchant vessel to save the lives of the crew of any submarine that may be sunk, or that submits, or is in distress.

10. American merchant vessels shall make every effort to avoid the submarines of Germany and of any nation following the policy of Germany announced in her note of January 31, 1917, while in the zones proscribed by Germany.

11. American merchant vessels shall display the American colors continuously at sea.

12. American merchant vessels should communicate with the Commandant of the Naval District before leaving a United States port to make sure of the latest information.

13. The safety of American merchant vessels requires that they obey all instructions of vessels of war of the United States.

ON SIGHTING A SUBMARINE IN THE PROSCRIBED ZONES

14. If a submarine is sighted beyond torpedo range, bring submarine abaft the beam and keep her there. If submarine attempts to close, bring her astern and proceed at highest possible speed.

15. If submarine is sighted close aboard forward of the beam, the greatest safety lies in changing course directly toward the submarine.

16. If submarine is sighted close aboard abaft the beam, the greatest safety lies in turning away from the submarine and proceeding at highest speed.

## ON OPENING FIRE IN DEFENSE
### AGAINST THE UNLAWFUL ACTS OF SUBMARINES

17. Hoist national colors before first shot is fired.

18. Once it has been decided to open fire, do not submit to the gun fire of a submarine so long as the armed guard can continue to fire.

19. Send all persons except bridge force and the armed guard below decks while vessel is under fire.

20. Watch out for torpedoes and maneuver to avoid them. If unable to avoid them, maneuver so that they will strike a glancing blow.

### THE ARMED GUARD

21. The Armed Guard is commanded by the Senior Naval Officer on board. He shall have exclusive control over the military functions of the Armed Guard and shall be responsible for the execution of all the regulations given herein governing the employment of the Armed Guard.

22. The military discipline of the Armed Guard shall be administered by the naval officer commanding the Armed Guard.

23. The Armed Guard shall be subject to the orders of the Master of the merchant vessel as to matters of non-military character, but the members of the Armed Guard shall not be required to perform any ship duties except their military duty, and these shall be performed invariably under the direction of the officer commanding the Armed Guard.

24. The decision as to opening fire or ceasing fire upon any submarine shall reside exclusively with the naval officer commanding the Armed Guard.

25. The enlisted personnel of the Armed Guard shall be quartered and messed together on board both in port and at sea, at the expense of the owners of the vessel, on which the Armed Guard is serving, in a manner satisfactory to the naval officer commanding the Armed Guard.

26. The naval officer commanding the Armed Guard shall take precedence next after the Master, except that he shall not be eligible for succession to the command of the ship. He shall be quartered and messed on board both at sea and in port, at the expense of the owners of the vessel on which he is serving, and in a manner appropriate to his precedence next after the Master.

27. The Master of the merchant vessel shall, on request of the commander of the Armed Guard, detail members of the crew to handle ammunition, clear decks, and otherwise supplement the service of the gun.

28. The naval officer commanding the Armed Guard shall be responsible for:

(a) The condition of the battery and its appurtenances.

(b) The training of the guns' crews and spotters, including members of the ship's force detailed by the Master to assist in the service of the guns.

(c) The readiness of the ship's battery at night.

(d) The readiness of the Armed Guard to perform its duties at all times.

(e) The continuous lookout near each gun by a member of the Armed Guard.

(f) The making of all reports required by the Navy Department.                                          Josephus Daniels

TS MS (SDR, RG 59, 763.72/3576¾, DNA).


## From Frederic Courtland Penfield

Vienna, via Berne, March 13, 1917.

1757. STRICTLY CONFIDENTIAL.

I have lost no time in further discussing with the Minister for Foreign Affairs, with secrecy and circumspection, the subject of your confidential instructions contained in telegrams 1566 February twenty second and 1580 March third. The Minister is keenly alive to the matter and four times has been in conference with me at my house. Naturally he has discussed matter with his Emperor with whom he has been two days visit to Hungary. To-day I have been with Count Czernin for an hour and in that time he announced a dozen times that a separate peace is out of the question. He gives me his complete confidence and he does not hesitate to speak feelingly of the good offices you are willing to use on Austria Hungary's behalf. The subjoined is an exact translation of a memorandum to-day handed me by Count Czernin made in his presence and read to him.

"Count Czernin repeats that he is disposed to enter upon conversations to end the war on condition that it is a question of a general peace and not a separate peace. It is absolutely out of the question to separate Austria Hungary from her Allies the Minister asserts with emphasis. Count Czernin states that he is convinced that none of the belligerent groups will be able to destroy its adversaries and that consequently it would appear desirable to put an end to slaughter which in any case will end sooner or later in an honorable peace for all the belligerents.

If the Entente maintains its proposal to enter upon free conversations which in every case must exclude a separate peace with Austria Hungary, Count Czernin would be disposed to send a man in his confidence to a neutral country to meet a representative of the Entente. The two gentlemen would discuss secretly and freely the basis and the conditions of negotiations for peace.

Furthermore Count Czernin has proposed that his representative as well as a representative of the Entente could meet on neutral territory to discuss there the lot of the prisoners of war, their exchange within possible limits, as well as other similar questions.

The matter is of such moment that Count Czernin asks what Entente belligerent is making the overture upon which your telegrams are based."

I have omitted nothing that might forward the instructions under which I have been working. No offer at this time can induce the Minister to debate any arrangement meaning a breaking away from Austria's Allies. There are rumors of Austria Hungary tiring of the overlordship of Berlin, but fear alone is enough to stifle any governmental expression of this.

Penfield.

T telegram (SDR, RG 59, 763.72119/10094, DNA).


## From Alice Edith Binsse Warren,[1] with Enclosure

Dear Mr Wilson,                    [New York] March 13th [1917]

The enclosed letter from the great suffrage leader to me I thought would interest you. It seems perhaps absurd at this moment, so full of worry and trouble—for literally you are carrying the world on your shoulders—to send you this tribute, but I send it—as I thought it might give you pleasure.

Very Sincerely,   Alice Warren

ALS (WP, DLC).
[1] Mrs. Schuyler Neilson Warren, active in the woman suffrage movement.


E N C L O S U R E

## Anna Howard Shaw to Alice Edith Binsse Warren

Florence Villa, Fla.

My dear Mrs. Warren,                    March 9th, 1917.

From what you said to me when I met you in New York, I am encouraged to write to you and especially as I re-read your letter which was sent from Oyster Bay in September, because I judge from what you said in New York that you thought perhaps I had forgotten you. I want to assure you that I have not and there has been scarcely a week since you were so kind to me in your home that I have not thought of you and of the pains you took to make me have a pleasant time and to meet such interesting women.

On re-reading your letter I find you are devoted to Mr. Wilson's policies and that you fear the Suffragists, because of Mr. Hughes' stand might flock to Mr. Hughes and oppose Mr. Wilson. Of course you know long ago that the only Suffragists who opposed Wilson, were known as the Congressional Union, which sent its women into the western States to fight Mr. Wilson's election and to try to defeat the democrats. This little branch of Suffragists do not belong to the National Association and never will so long as they keep up their semi-militant practice, and I assure you no woman in the country can feel worse than I do over the foolishness of their picketing the White House and the folly of their performance on inauguration day. But we have no power whatever over this little band. They make great boasts of vast thousands, etc. and by their boasts get a lot of news paper publicity. I have before me one of their announcements in regard to their plans for the inauguration and they start out by declaring that 10,000 enfranchised and unenfranchised women will march. Then long before inauguration day they came down to 1,000 women to be lead by Mrs. O. H. Belmont[1] and as it really happened on inauguration day there were 400 of them and I doubt if more than 10 or 15 were enfranchised women and Mrs. Belmont did not lead them. She undoubtedly told them she would as she frequently tells them that she will do a thing but does not, but by announcing that she is going to do it she gets all the advertising she wants and yet does not take the trouble of doing it and of exposing herself to either the weather or the ridicule.

I fully agree with you that Mr. Wilson intended just what he said at our National Convention at Atlantic City[2] and what is more he has lived up to his promise. He has done more for Suffrage during the month of February than all of the Presidents who have ever been in the White House before since the beginning of our Suffrage movement and what is more he has done it in an effective way and I believe he is sincerely fighting with us.

I am very glad to say, that while in my official position in the National Association I could not take sides for any political candidate, I still was able to use my influence with a lot of the prominent women in the west, so that a good deal of the folly of the Congressional Union in their campaign was nullified and no one rejoiced more than I over the election of Mr. Wilson, not because I am a democrat or because I care particularly for Mr. Wilson personally, but because I believe it would be the greatest possible help to the Suffrage movement.

I wanted to tell you this for fear you might not know how much women Suffrage appreciates the services Wilson is now rendering us and then I wanted to write to you anyhow. I have been wanting to for a long time and if I had remembered your New York address I would have done so.

I am sending this letter to the Head quarters, asking them to look up your address and forward the letter to you.

I want to enclose to you my valentine picture taken for my 70th birthday to let you see how well I look and to assure you I am quite fit for the splendid and active campaign upon which I am going to entire [enter] in two weeks, as soon as I leave here.

Affectionately,   Anna H. Shaw

Pardon this letter, I have a picked up stenographer, who knows nothing of our cause and mismatches his paper

TLS (WP, DLC).
¹ Alva Erskine Smith Vanderbilt (Mrs. Oliver Hazard Perry) Belmont.
² Wilson's speech to the National American Woman Suffrage Association, printed at Sept. 8, 1916, Vol. 38.


# Robert Lansing to Paul Samuel Reinsch

*Not to be distributed.*          Washington, March 13, 1917.

Your cipher telegram of March 12, one p.m. The Department can only repeat the statements made in its telegram of March 12, 3 p.m., but, while unable to give the assurances asked, the Department desires you to say to the Chinese Government that the American Government has learned with appreciation that China will support the United States in breaking off diplomatic relations with Germany and trusts that the assurance given you that no commitment as to further action has been made indicates an intention to await the movement of this Government. You may say too that it is reported in the United States from unofficial sources that there is intriguing in China for the division of that country between a republic in the south and a monarchy in the north, and that this Government strongly deprecates a revival at this time of monarchical schemes or the promotion of any movement tending to promote discord in China or loss of territory by the Republic. For your guidance it is important to bear in mind that the American Government is disposed to regard as inadvisable a declaration of war by China upon Germany at this time, if such declaration would mean the control of China's military resources by a foreign power.

Lansing

TS telegram (SDR, RG 59, 763.72/3483, DNA).

## William Bauchop Wilson to Joseph Patrick Tumulty

PERSONAL

My dear Mr. Tumulty:                    Washington March 13, 1917.

Referring to our conversation over the telephone concerning the railway situation, I have learned from sources that I consider reliable that the railway brotherhoods have determined upon the following policies:

The brotherhood chiefs will meet the representatives of the railway managers at New York on Thursday, the 15th instant. They will demand the establishment of an eight-hour schedule as the basis of operation of freight trains. If they fail to get an adjustment, within 24 hours after negotiations terminate, the members of the brotherhood on all roads centering in Chicago from the west, northwest and south will walk out. Within 48 hours after that the membership of the brotherhoods on the New York, New Haven and Hartford will walk out. Within 48 hours after that the membership of the brotherhoods on the Iron Mountain lines centering in St. Louis will walk out. Within 48 hours after that the membership of the brotherhoods on the B. & O. system will walk out; and so on at 48-hour periods until all of the great trunk lines of the country are involved, unless a settlement has been arrived at sooner. It is not the intention to call out the members operating passenger trains until the effect of the strike in the freight service is known, when, if they decide that the passenger men should cease work, sufficient notice will be given to enable people en route for any point to reach their destination. I have used the term "the membership of the brotherhoods will walk out" because they claim to have the situation so well in hand that it will not be necessary to issue any strike order, that plan of operation having been adopted for the purpose of heading off any writ of injunction to prevent issuance of a strike order.                    Cordially yours,   W B Wilson

TLS (WP, DLC).

## From the Diary of Josephus Daniels

March Tuesday 13 1917

At 6:30 signed instructions to Naval officers who command Armed Guard on merchant ships. Before doing so, submitted them to Attorney General & talked with the President & Secy. Lansing over telephone I signed ten copies which Palmer sent over to New York by officer. Benson, Roosevelt & I went over the instructions first. It was a rather solemn time, for I felt I might be signing what would prove the death warrant of young Americans and the arming of ships may bring us into war. To-night officers, armed with these instructions, started being admonished not to mention a word of their instructions.

No cabinet. President sick, but talked with him on phone

## To Yoshihito

[The White House] March 14, 1917.

I thank Your Majesty for your courteous and highly appreciated message of sympathy on the death of Mr. Guthrie, by whose demise the United States loses a valued citizen and Japan a sincere and constant friend, and whose lasting monument, I trust, will be the perpetuity of the present cordial relations and good understanding between the United States and Japan which he did so much to promote and had so much at heart.                    Woodrow Wilson.

T telegram (Letterpress Books, WP, DLC).

## To John Franklin Shafroth

[The White House] March 14, 1917.

May I not take the liberty of saying that it is my earnest hope that no legislation will be enacted by the General Assembly of Colorado which will impair or repeal directly or indirectly the Initiative and Referendum or Direct Primary laws. These are the instrumentalities by which government is brought nearer to the people and should be preserved.[1]  Woodrow Wilson.

T telegram (Letterpress Books, WP, DLC).
[1] This telegram largely repeated a draft received from Shafroth's office.

## From Robert Lansing

PERSONAL AND PRIVATE:

My dear Mr. President:          Washington March 14, 1917.

I enclose to you a draft of reply to General Carranza's note of February 11th inviting united action by the neutrals to bring about peace, and in the event of the non-acceptance of mediation by the belligerents to establish an embargo.

I hope that you can return this soon to me as I think we ought to reply to General Carranza.

Faithfully yours,   Robert Lansing.

TLS (RSB Coll., DLC).

## To Robert Lansing, with Enclosure

[The White House,
My dear Mr. Secretary          c. March 14, 1917]

This seems to me excellent. I have made only one or two verbal changes.          Faithfully   W.W.

ALI (RSB Coll., DLC).

### E N C L O S U R E[1]

Sir:

I have to request that you will have the kindness to transmit to the President-elect of the Mexican Republic[2] the following reply to the communication of February 11, 1917, addressed by him to you with instructions to deliver it to the Government of the United States.

In his note of February 11, 1917, the President-elect[3] proposes to all the neutral Governments that the

"groups of contending powers [in the present European conflict][4] be invited, in common accord and on the basis of absolutely perfect equality on either side, to bring this war to an end either by their own effort or by availing themselves of the good offices or friendly mediation of all the countries which would jointly extend that invitation. If within a reasonable time peace could not be restored by these means, the neutral countries would then take the necessary measures to reduce the conflagration to its narrowest limit, by refusing any kind of implements to the belligerents and suspending commercial relations with the warring nations until the said conflagration shall have been smothered."

The Government of the United States has given careful and sympathetic consideration to the proposals of the *de facto* Government, not only because they come from a neighboring republic in whose welfare *and friendship* the United States has a peculiar and permanent interest, but because these proposals have for their end the object which the President had hoped to attain from his discussion a few months ago of the aims of the belligerents and their purposes in the war. Of the futile results of the President's efforts at that time General Carranza is ⟨well⟩ *no doubt* aware. Instead of the conflict being resolved into a discussion of terms of peace, the struggle, both on land and on sea, has been renewed with intensified vigor and bitterness. To such an extent has one group of belligerents carried warfare on the high seas involving the destruction of American ships and the lives of American citizens, in contravention of the pledges heretofore solemnly given the Government of the United States, that it was deemed necessary within the past few weeks to sever relations with one of the Governments of the Allied Central Powers. To render the situation still more acute, the Government of the United States has unearthed a plot laid by the Government dominating the Central Powers to embroil not only the Government & people of Mexico but also the Government and people of Japan in war with the United States. At the ⟨very moment⟩ *time* this plot was ⟨being hatched⟩ *conceived*, the United States was at peace with the Government and people of the German Empire, and German officials and German subjects were not only enjoying but abusing the liberties and privileges freely accorded to them on American soil and under American protection.

In these circumstances, all of which were existent when the note under acknowledgment was received, the Government of the United States finds itself, greatly to its regret and contrary to its desires, in a position which precludes it from participating at the present time in the proposal of General Carranza, that the neutral Governments jointly extend an invitation to the belligerent countries to bring the war to an end either by their own effort or by availing themselves of the good offices or friendly mediation of neutral countries.

At the present stage of the European struggle, the superiority of the Entente Powers on the seas has prevented supplies from reaching the Central Powers from the Western Hemisphere. To such a degree has this restriction of maritime commerce extended that all routes of trade between the Americas and the continent of Europe are either entirely cut off or seriously interrupted. This condition is not new. In 1915 the Central Governments complained of their inability to ⟨receive⟩ *obtain* arms and ammunition from the United States while these supplies were being shipped freely to the ports of their enemies. The discussion of the subject culminated in the American note of August 12, 1915, (a copy of which is enclosed) to the Imperial & Royal Austro-Hungarian Government,[5] upholding the contention of the United States that its inability to ship munitions of war to the Central Powers was not of its own desire or making, but was due wholly to the naval superiority of the Entente Powers. Believing that this position of the United States is based upon sound principles of international law and is consonant with the *established* practice of nations, the President directs me to say that he can not bring himself to consider ⟨the⟩ *such a* modification of these principles or of this practice as compliance with General Carranza's proposal to suspend commercial relations with the warring nations would entail.

The President regrets, therefore, that, however desirous he may be of ⟨assisting⟩ *cooperating with* General Carranza in finding a solution of the world problem that is intruding itself upon all countries, he is, for the reasons set forth, unable at the present time to direct his energies toward the accomplishment of the lofty purposes of the President-elect[6] in the way suggested by his proposals. The President would not be understood, however, as desiring to impede the progress of any movement leading to the resumption of peaceful relations between all of the belligerents, and would not, therefore, wish the Mexican Government to feel that his inability to act in the present stage of affairs should in any way militate against the attainment of the high ideals of General Carranza by the co-operation of other neutral Governments in the use of their good offices and friendly mediation to bring about the end of the terrible war which is being waged between the great powers of Europe.

I am, Sir,                              Your obedient servant,[7]

T MS (RSB Coll., DLC).

[1] Words in angle brackets in the following document deleted by Wilson; words in italics (except *de facto*) added by him.

[2] Lansing's original text read: "the First Chief of the Constitutionalist Army in Charge of the Executive Power." Wilson wrote on the margin: "Is he not now President?" Lansing then corrected his error.

[3] Lansing originally wrote "General Carranza."

[4] Lansing's brackets.

[5] It is printed as an Enclosure with WW to RL, Aug. 5, 1915, Vol. 34.

[6] Lansing originally wrote "General Carranza."

[7] This was sent as RL to R. P. De Negri, March 16, 1917, CCL (SDR, RG 59, 763.72119/468, DNA) and is printed in *FR-WWS 1917*, I, 67-68.

# From Josephus Daniels

My dear Mr. President:          Washington. March 14, 1917.

The Wall Street Journal of March 10th had an article on the advance of price in steel which, of course, will greatly increase the cost of everything in the way of munitions and shipbuilding. So far, the Carnegie Company has given earlier deliveries to the Navy Department than any other company, and has given it a better price, but in view of the large program ahead of us and the fact that the prices they give us are only slightly lower than the prices charged the public, it gives us great concern.

I am sending it[1] not only from the standpoint of the Army and Navy but the public as well, showing that they are taking advantage of the present conditions to exact exorbitant prices from the public.     Faithfully yours,    Josephus Daniels

TLS (WP, DLC).
[1] The enclosure is missing.

# From Samuel Gompers

Sir:          Washington, D. C., March 14, 1917.

Because I appreciate the burden of responsibility that rests upon you in the nation's crisis I would hesitate to ask you to consider the enclosed matter if it were not of vital, immediate importance.

The letter enclosed[1] discloses a serious condition existing in Porto Rico and one which will materially affect the standing of our country not only in Porto Rico but in all Pan-America. The spirit of the letter carries conviction of the sincerity of the writer. There is no man in all Porto Rico who has done more to secure rights and opportunities for the masses of the people there than Santiago Iglesias. He is a man of intelligent understanding and vision and in close touch with the lives and problems of those who toil. The matter which he presents must receive immediate consideration and action if a great wrong is to be averted.

May I also call your attention to the fact that the people of many Latin-American countries regard the course which our Republic institutes in Porto Rico as a test of the idealism and the sincerity of our nation. Whatever is done in Porto Rico will affect the attitude of Pan-American countries toward our Republic.

I sincerely hope you will find a little time in the midst of your many pressing duties to consider the petition presented by the

authorized spokesman of the masses of Porto Rico and to give
it your favorable action.

Respectfully yours,    Saml. Gompers.

TLS (WDR, RG 350, BIA, Puerto Rico, DNA).
    1 Santiago Iglesias to S. Gompers, March 7, 1917, TCL (WDR, RG 350, BIA,
Puerto Rico, DNA). Iglesias charged that Governor Arthur Yager and his
executive council were opposed to the reforms called for by the recently enacted
organic act for Porto Rico and had no intention of implementing them. In
particular, they were opposed to organized labor and to its projected role in
the new government. Iglesias asserted that Yager had sought to circumvent
the requirements of the act by reappointing the "old bureaucrats" to the
temporary government which was to prepare the way for the coming elections
in July.


## From Frank Oscar Hellier

Dear Sir:                         Lumberton, N. C., March 14th. 1917

In behalf of the Presbyterian Church of Webster, Texas, permit me to express their appreciation of your gift of the Bale of
Cotton in the Warehouse of Mr. R. R. Dancy of Houston, Texas.[1]

This expression of their gratitude has been delayed for two
reasons, 1st that they might state the receipts, as the Houston
Chamber of Commerce are expecting to dispose of it for the
church,—and 2nd,—By my forced absence from home.

The disposal of the Bale is not yet accomplished and we feel
we can not longer delay the acknowledgement of your courtesy.
While we thank you most sincerely for your gift we appreciate
yet more the fact that amidst the extraordinary demands of
State at this time, you could pause for a few moments consideration of our little church and its needs. We recognise further that
it is your thoughtfulness of others that has given you your place
in the hearts of the nation.

Respectfully yours,    F. O. Hellier.

TLS (WP, DLC).
    1 See F. O. Hellier to WW, Jan. 17, 1917, Vol. 40.


## From Robert Lansing, with Enclosure

PERSONAL AND CONFIDENTIAL:

My dear Mr. President:          Washington March 15, 1917.

I enclose to you a very important cablegram which has just
come from Petrograd, and also a clipping from the New York
WORLD of this morning, in which a statement is made by Signor
Scialoia,[1] Minister without portfolio in the Italian Cabinet, which
is significant in view of Mr. Francis' report.[2] My own impres-

sion is that the Allies knew of this matter and I presume are favorable to the revolutionists since the Court party has been, throughout the war, secretly pro-German.

Faithfully yours,  Robert Lansing.

TLS (WP, DLC).
[1] Vittorio Scialoja.
[2] The brief news item in the New York *World*, March 15, 1917, reported that Scialoja had just returned from a conference of the Allied nations held in Petrograd. "The conference," Scialoja was quoted as saying, "afforded confirmation of the fact that, in accord with the Allies, the unshakable decision of the Emperor and the people of Russia is to continue the war to a victorious end, despite any possible internal political differences."

E N C L O S U R E

Petrograd, March 14, 1917.

1287. Unable to send a cablegram since the eleventh. Revolutionists have absolute control in Petrograd and are (#) strenuous efforts to preserve order, which successful except in rare instances. No cablegrams since your 1251 of the ninth, received March eleventh. Provisional government organized under the authority of the Douma which refused to obey the Emperor's order of the adjournment. Rodzianko,[1] president of the Douma, issuing orders over his own signature. Ministry reported to have resigned. Ministers found are taken before the Douma, also many Russian officers and other high officials. Most if not all regiments ordered to Petrograd have joined the revolutionists after arrival. American colony safe. No knowledge of any injuries to American Citizens.                          Francis.

CC telegram (WP, DLC).
[1] Mikhail Vladimirovich Rodzianko.

## From William Cox Redfield

PERSONAL AND CONFIDENTIAL

Dear Mr. President:          Washington March 15, 1917.

If I may accept the public prints, you are in touch, through the Secretary of Labor, with the railway strike situation. I do not feel, however, that I should be doing my duty as Secretary of Commerce if I did not express to you my views on this important subject. It directly affects our commerce, domestic and foreign, and that alone warrants my writing you.

In general, I am in sympathy with the objects sought by the brotherhoods. I believe it would be profitable, after the initial adjustments were over, to the railroad companies to concede much if not all the men demand. I regret indeed that the bettered working conditions sought are confined to those now most highly paid, and that the opportunity for advancement is not open to the larger numbers of the men paid much less, but upon whose faithful service the operation of the systems in large part depends. I regret that the railways seem unwilling to give the demands of the men fair trial in practice, and believe that such a course would commend them to public approval.

This said I must add that to advance a righteous cause at this juncture by stopping the transportation system of the country seems to me little short, if at all short, of the criminal. The ethics of that course would be more than doubtful at this time when thousands of our poorer fellows are suffering from the high prices for food, even were there no more vital question concerned. To deliberately advance one's righteous cause by the sufferings of fellow creatures not concerned in the controversy seems to me open to stern criticism on grounds of righteousness.

To add to this at a time when the nation is threatened with serious foreign complications the possibility that food and materials of all kinds may be delayed or stopped in transit when the nation may need them most, is to make a course of doubtful right one that is clearly wrong. It involves a deliberate offense against that safety of the people which is the supreme law. I venture to think it an intolerable thing that any personal claims, however well founded, of a small part of our people should be urged in such a way as to embarrass the whole of the nation in a time of public danger. It is no answer to say that by permission of a relatively few whose personal interests are involved the munitions and supplies needed to protect us all may freely pass. The confusion and uncertainty that the general stoppage of transit would involve would make the free movement of any selected portion of our traffic itself impossible. Naught could move with certainty where all was involved in disorder.

I respectfully suggest for your consideration the wisdom, in the event of the actual occurrence of the strike, of calling for volunteers to insure the operation of the transit systems of the country until the time of national emergency shall have passed. There are thousands of men of technical training, and many with railway experience, who could in a short time take the place of even the best of the men who might leave their places under the strike, and for those places which do not require specialized knowledge I think men would volunteer in numbers at least sufficient to mitigate the difficulty. There are thousands of young men, recent graduates from or about to leave our technical schools, who would, I believe, respond to a call from you as a patriotic duty, and thousands of others who would leave their occupations to serve in a like spirit.

It could be made clear that the particular questions in dispute were not concerned in the suggested call but that in time of national emergency it was impossible to permit that the transportation of the country should be held up for any cause.

It is assumed that the railway systems could and would accept the services of volunteers and would pay them. I think no expense to the Government need be involved. My thought is that if an appeal to the patriotism of the men immediately concerned should fail, the patriotism of the nation would protect itself against what would be in fact, though not in purpose, an attack upon the national security.

Yours very truly, William C. Redfield

TLS (WP, DLC).

## From Edward Mandell House

Dear Governor: New York. March 15, 1917.

Sir Cecil told Lodge the other day that the Allies were very anxious to have the Columbian Treaty go through and he hoped he would help. Lodge replied that he had gone too far in his criticism to help, but he promised not to obstruct and said he would be glad if it went through.

Lodge also told Sir Cecil that his (Lodge's) friends thought he had gone too far in his criticism of you during the campaign and that he was willing to admit it. I hope this indicates a resolution on Lodge's part to reform, but from what I see in the press it does not seem imminent.

I have been very distressed to hear of your continued illness. I have heard from you every day and I am glad you now seem on the road to a quick recovery. I have not written because I did not wish to bother you.

Affectionately yours, E. M. House

TLS (WP, DLC).

## From Robert Russa Moton

Dear Sir:                Tuskegee Institute, Alabama March 15, 1917.

I have not acknowledged your very kind letter of some weeks ago.[1] I did not think it wise to make any suggestions regarding the situation about which I wrote you, for the reason that I knew you have been very busy with other more weighty matters.

A number of people of prominence have approached me with reference to the attitude the Negroes would assume in case the country should go to war. I understand, also, that certain high officials of the Government have raised similar questions.

Notwithstanding the difficulties which my race faces in many parts of this country, some of which I called to your attention in my previous letter, I am writing to assure you that you and the Nation can count absolutely on the loyalty of the mass of the Negroes to our country, and its people, North and South; and as in previous wars, you will find the Negro people rallying almost to a man to our flag.

Whatever influence I may have personally, or whatever service I can render in or outside of the Tuskegee Institute I shall be glad to put at your disposal for the service of our country.

With very best wishes for your good health, and that you may be guided aright in all of this great responsibility which you are now carrying, I beg to remain,

Yours very sincerely,   R. R. Moton

TLS (WP, DLC).
[1] WW to R. R. Moton, Dec. 12, 1916, Vol. 40.


## Two Letters from William Bauchop Wilson
## to Joseph Patrick Tumulty

My dear Mr. Secretary:          Washington March 15, 1917.

Supplementing my note to you of the 13th instant relative to the railway-strike situation, I am advised that the statement made to you at that time is substantially correct. In the event of a failure to secure concessions today it is the intention of the brotherhoods to begin their strike operations in Chicago, as stated in that note. They may substitute the D. L. & W. for the New York, New Haven and Hartford and the Santa Fe for the Iron Mountain in the consecutive arrangement of their progressive strike, and will then center their activities on Pittsburgh.

I am advised that plans are being developed by the railway managers to have a number of the members of the railway brotherhoods sue out writs of injunction restraining the brotherhood chiefs, their aiders, abettors, associates, etc., from engaging in a strike, on the grounds that the strike vote taken last summer is void and of no effect at this time, and that the precipitation of a strike without authority would nevertheless result in those members who continue at work losing their membership in the brotherhoods, and their insurance, in which they have an equity, carried in those institutions would thereby be lost. How they expect to make such injunctions effective, if the plans of the brotherhoods have been so made that strikes will occur without the issuance of any strike order by the officers of the brotherhoods, I have not as yet been able to learn.

As soon as I learn anything further of importance I will communicate with you.          Cordially yours,   W B Wilson


*Personal*

Dear Mr. Tumulty:          Washington March 15, 1917.

With further reference to the railway-strike situation, I have just learned that the conference met this a.m. The brotherhoods presented a demand for all that the Adamson law gives them. After a brief parley the managers asked for an adjournment until 4 p.m., when the conference will reconvene and the managers make their reply. In the meantime the managers have secured two engineers, two conductors, two trainmen, residents of New York, and are prepared to sue out the writs of injunction mentioned in my note of this a.m. They have not as yet secured firemen to sue out writs. The managers are very doubtful about being able to make the writs effective, in view of the claim that the strike order has already been issued and that it will be obeyed unless instructions are sent by the chiefs directing the men not to strike.

Cordially yours,   W B Wilson

TLS (WP, DLC).

## To Robert Russa Moton

[The White House]
My dear Principal Moton:                    March 16, 1917

Accept my warm thanks for your kind letter of the fifteenth of March and allow me to tell you how deeply I appreciate your generous assurances.

Cordially and sincerely yours,   Woodrow Wilson

TLS (Letterpress Books, WP, DLC).

## From Joseph Patrick Tumulty

Dear Governor:         The White House. March 16th [1917].

I am afraid that there will be a great deal of criticism and censure levelled at the Administration unless something is done immediately, showing that we have taken a deep interest in the latest phase of the strike situation. I do not think that we can afford to sit down and wait for results of a nationwide strike. Public opinion will back you up in any effort you may make looking toward a settlement. I think a statement by you addressed to the whole country calling attention to the unyielding attitude of both sides would be helpful. It might bring these gentlemen to their senses.

If a strike should start at this time, God only knows how it might spread. I think you would be justified in your statement in characterizing the efforts of those who seem bent upon striking as acts of the highest treason.

Sincerely yours,   Tumulty

TLS (WP, DLC).

## To the National Conference Committee of the Railways

The White House. 16 March, 1917

I deem it my duty and my right to appeal to you in this time of national peril to open again the questions at issue between the railroads and their operatives with a view to accommodation or settlement. With my approval a committee of the Council of National Defense is about to seek a conference with you with that end in view. A general interruption of the railway traffic of the country at this time would entail a danger to the nation against which I have the right to enter my most solemn and earnest protest. It is now the duty of every patriotic man to bring matters of this sort to immediate accommodation. The safety of the country against manifest perils affecting its own peace and the peace of the whole world makes it absolutely imperative and seems to me to render any other choice or action inconceivable.                      Woodrow Wilson[1]

T telegram (Letterpress Books, WP, DLC).
[1] There is a draft of this telegram, with WWhw emendations, in the C. L. Swem Coll., NjP.

## From Elisha Lee

New York, March 16, 1917.

In harmony with the spirit of your message the National Conference Committee of the Railways will cooperate with the committee of the Council of National Defense in an earnest effort to avert the national calamity which would result from an interruption of railway traffic.                      Elisha Lee.

T telegram (WP, DLC).

## From Robert Lansing, with Enclosure

PERSONAL AND PRIVATE:

My dear Mr. President:      Washington March 16, 1917.

Yesterday, upon learning of the Russian revolution, I requested Mr. Crane to telegraph Professor Samuel N. Harper[1] of Chicago for his views concerning the uprising. I have just received from him the enclosed telegram which will give you some knowledge of the participants in the revolution and purpose sought by it.      Faithfully yours,   Robert Lansing

TLS (WP, DLC).
[1] Samuel Northrup Harper, Assistant Professor of Russian Language and Institutions at the University of Chicago, son of William Rainey Harper. Samuel N. Harper was a pioneer in Russian studies in the United States and had spent much time in Russia since 1904, most recently as an informal adviser to Ambassador Francis from June to September 1916. See Samuel N. Harper, *The Russia I Believe In: The Memoirs of Samuel N. Harper, 1902-1941*, ed. Paul V. Harper (Chicago, 1945).

### E N C L O S U R E

## Samuel Northrup Harper to Richard Crane

Chicago Ills 1917 Mar 16

Duma leaders last summer said confidently that revolution might become necessary and urged that I explain in such event

that of a political and not social character  They had tried
moral pressure for over a year to secure responsible government
Tried to gain ear of sovereign but unsuccessful despite fact that
army leaders cooperated here   Nicholas listened to small group
of reactionaries[,] to Empress who generally suspected of Pro-
germanism[,] and to recently removed Rasputin[1] alleged to be in
the employ of Germany stop Emperor retained in office Protopopoff[2] who publicly accused of being in touch with Germany
Demand for responsible government was primarily to eliminate
these so called pro Germans   At the same time the reactionary
members of government especially Minister of Interior Protopopoff was definitely attempting to disrupt public organizations
such as Zemstvo Union[,] Municipality Union[,] War Industry
Committees[,] and Peasant Cooperative Societies all working to
organize resourses of country for successful prosecution of war
Finally government was taking no adequate measures to prevent
avoidable food crisis in urban centers stop Demand for responsible government made by Duma was supported by Imperial
Council both elected [members] and members appointed by
Emperor such as late Ambassador Rosen[,][3] strong conservative   United nobility organization also supported but Emperor
appointed reactionary Golitsyn[4] whom nobody trusted and retained Protopopoff   During Duma session in November Minister
of War[5] came to Duma and publicly spoke for cooperation between government and Duma and this hailed at time as indicating that Duma supported by army stop Clear therefor that
Duma is supported by army [and by country as represented]
by public organizations such as Zemstvo Union   In new cabinet
Lvov[6] is president of Zemstvo Union and Guchkov[7] president of
central committee of all war industry committees   Such men
will be able to hold confidence of country and army and are
practical leaders of long administrative experience   Manuilov[8]
prominent Moscow public worker[,] university and newspaper
man   Shingarev[9] is one of most capable of Duma leaders and
chief helper of Milyoukovv[10] who is recognized leader of liberal
Constitutional Democratic Party   Nekrasov[11] is vice president of
Duma and active member of Municipality Union   Kerensky[12]
is a radical elected by workmen of Petrograd to Duma   Godnev
and Tereshchenko[13] are prominent Duma members stop The
previous efforts to persuade Emperor to trust people and the
appointment of regent indicate clearly that revolution was not
directed against dynasty stop Aim of Revolution as has been
aim of Duma for last year and half and also of public organizations is to create conditions that will make it possible for Rus-

sia to bring into force all her strength    Means therefor more
effective prosecution of war and war till victory and justified on
this ground[14]                          Samuel N Harper.

T telegram (WP, DLC).
[1] The notorious holy man and healer, Grigorii Efimovich Rasputin, who
had been murdered on December 30, 1916.
[2] Aleksandr Dmitrievich Protopopov, Minister of the Interior.
[3] Baron Roman Romanovich Rosen, career diplomat, Minister to Japan,
1897-1900, 1903-1904, and Ambassador to the United States, 1905-1911.
[4] Prince Nikolai Dmitrievich Golitsyn, Chairman of the Council of Ministers,
January-March, 1917.
[5] General Mikhail Alekseevich Beliaev.
[6] Prince Georgii Evgen'evich L'vov.
[7] Aleksandr Ivanovich Guchkov.
[8] Aleksandr Apollonovich Manuilov, Minister of Education in the provisional
government.
[9] Andrei Ivanovich Shingarev, Minister of Agriculture in the provisional
government.
[10] Pavel Nikolaevich Miliukov, Minister of Foreign Affairs in the provisional
government.
[11] Nikolai Vissarionovich Nekrasov.
[12] Aleksandr Fedorovich Kerenskii, Minister of Justice in the provisional
government.
[13] Ivan Vasil'evich Godnev and Mikhail Ivanovich Tereshchenko.
[14] Additions in square brackets in foregoing text from the edited version
in Harper, *The Russia I Believe In*, pp. 96-97.


## From John Franklin Shafroth

My dear Mr President,          [Denver, Colo.] March 16th 1917
    I want to thank you so much for your telegram concern-
ing the Initiative & Referendum and Direct Primary laws. I
closed my speech by reading your communication and the large
audience seemed almost to shake the roof of the Auditorium
with their applause and shouts of approval of your expressions.[1]
    Again thanking you for your kindness and trusting that you
have entirely recovered from your illness I remain
                         Yours truly   John F Shafroth

ALS (WP, DLC).
[1] Shafroth spoke at a nonpartisan mass meeting in the Auditorium in
Denver on March 14. The meeting was held to protest against a movement
in the Colorado legislature to emasculate the amendment to the state constitution which established the referendum and recall. *Denver Post*, March 15, 1916.


## From Newton Diehl Baker

PERSONAL.

My dear Mr. President:          Washington. March 16, 1917.
    I inclose a letter which came to me this morning,[1] suggesting
Raymond B. Fosdick for the Governorship of the Philippine

Islands. Of course, we have no means of knowing that Governor Harrison will not return, but I am wondering whether you would approve of my taking up with Fosdick the question of his accepting the Vice-Governorship. My admiration for him is very great, but as you know him more intimately than I do, I can add nothing to your knowledge in the matter.

Cordially yours,   Newton D. Baker

TLS (WP, DLC).
   [1] Adolphus Ragan to NDB, March 15, 1917, TLS (WP, DLC).


## From Edward Mandell House

Dear Governor:                         New York. March 16, 1917.

The State Department is having some trouble with Denman of the Shipping Board. Denman is determined to maintain American rights and in his attempt to do so is interfering with your foreign policy.

Polk and Lansing have tried to reason with him and it may be necessary for you to take a hand since the British are terribly upset. At this particular time it would seem the part of wisdom not to insist upon those things which we have heretofore allowed to go with a mere protest.

I am happy to know that you are so much better today.

Affectionately yours,   E. M. House

TLS (WP, DLC).


## From Robert Lansing

PERSONAL AND PRIVATE:

My dear Mr. President:          Washington March 16, 1917.

I enclose you a memorandum by Mr. Lorenzo Semple, of the firm of Coudert Brothers, New York, of a conversation which took place day-before-yesterday between Sir Richard Crawford and Mr. Denman of the United States Shipping Board.[1] I dislike very much at this time when you are not feeling well to trouble you with this matter, but the conversation was of such an extraordinary nature that I feel you should give it personal attention.

I have done everything that I could, as have Secretary McAdoo and Mr. Polk, to persuade Mr Denman to cease at the present time from his very aggressive attitude toward the British authorities. He is interfering very materially with the diplomatic situation and nothing can persuade him, apparently, to cease his activities, which are causing me very serious concern.

I learn that he is now taking up the matter of Canadian fisheries, which will further irritate the British Government at a time when we can ill-afford increased friction between the Governments. I am personally satisfied that Mr Denman has pro-German sympathies, or else anti-British feeling. It is most unfortunate that he cannot be persuaded to avoid attempted coercion in securing American rights because I am convinced his efforts will accomplish little good and may involve us in serious difficulties.

The morning papers report that Senator Stone has introduced a resolution in the Senate calling for certain information as to the transfer of vessels, which is presumed to be for the purpose of showing intention on the part of the Allied Governments to involve us in trouble with Germany. I fear, though I have no evidence, that Mr. Denman is responsible for resolutions of this sort, and will give information of a more or less confidential character to the anti-British members of the Senate and House. This in view of the approaching session of Congress would be unfortunate and materially interfere with the conduct of foreign affairs.

I hope that you will find it possible to do something to relieve us of the embarrassment of having the Shipping Board engage in the conduct of our foreign relations without regard to the greater issues which are at stake.

Faithfully yours,    Robert Lansing.

TLS (WP, DLC).
¹ L. Semple, TS MS (WP, DLC). The acrid exchange described by Semple took place at the Biltmore Hotel in New York on the morning of March 14. It centered on the so-called bunkering agreements then being imposed by the British government on neutral shipowners. The latter had to promise, in return for the privilege of purchasing British coal at any port, not to charter vessels to any person or company not approved by British authorities, not to do business with any country at war with Great Britain, to subject all their dealings with European neutrals to the supervision of the British government, and even to provide shipping facilities upon demand of the British Admiralty. About these agreements, see Link, *Campaigns for Progressivism and Peace*, p. 261.

Denman told Crawford that the signing of such an agreement by an American agent or shipowner was a direct violation of the act establishing the United States Shipping Board and constituted a misdemeanor, punishable by a fine of up to $25,000 for each such action. He further asserted that any British consular officer or any other person, including Crawford himself, who encouraged the making of such agreements, was liable to criminal prosecution for conspiracy to violate the laws of the United States, and he directly threatened Crawford with such a prosecution. Denman indicated that, if the British government ceased the policy of imposing bunkering agreements, past offenses would be condoned; otherwise, the law would be enforced.

Denman also asserted that the criminal laws of the United States had heretofore been enforced against Germans but not against the British. He went so far as to equate the imposition of bunkering agreements by British consular officials with the acts of a German consul in San Francisco who had been convicted of conspiring to destroy the Welland Canal.

Crawford heatedly defended both himself and his government against these various charges. Lorenzo Semple, the chronicler of the interview, recorded that he had directly disagreed with Denman's interpretation of both the shipping act and the criminal law and had criticized Denman's flouting of diplomatic etiquette.

## To Elisha Lee[1]

[The White House] March 17, 1917.

I am exceedingly glad that the conferences have been re-opened and that the prospect of a settlement looks brighter. I hope most earnestly, for the sake of all concerned and most of all for the sake of the nation, that the two parties will continue to draw closer together and that a little further conference will lead to the result the whole country hopes for and expects.

Woodrow Wilson.

T telegram (Letterpress Books, WP, DLC).
    [1] Copies of this telegram were addressed to Lucius E. Sheppard, Warren S. Stone, William G. Lee, and William S. Carter.

## To Frank Lyon Polk, with Enclosure

My dear Polk,          The White House [c. March 17, 1917].

I have taken the liberty of expanding this. Please let it go as soon as possible.          W.W.

ALI (F. L. Polk Papers, CtY).

### E N C L O S U R E[1]

Washington, March 17, 1917.

Amlegation Bogota

Department's February 28, 7 p.m.[2]

Senate adjourned at 3 p.m. yesterday until April 16. Consideration of the treaty was suspended until the extra session of Congress in April.

You may explain to Minister for Foreign Affairs that as extra session was called for April 16, there was but little time in special session of Senate for discussion of treaty and for that reason it was felt that there would be more chance of success in coming session of Congress. *The prospects of confirmation*

*were observed to be growing distinctly better under the in-*
*fluence of opinion in the country and it was felt to be wise to*
*let this influence mature, as it is expected it will now that the*
*significance of the treaty has been made clear at the session just*
*interrupted.*[3]

T and WWhw telegram (F. L. Polk Papers, CtY).
[1] Words in italics in the following document WWhw.
[2] RL to Chargé Perry Belden, Feb. 28, 1917, *FR 1917*, pp. 293-94. Lansing instructed Belden to inform the Colombian Minister of Foreign Affairs that a special session of the United States Senate had been called for March 5 in order to consider the Treaty of Bogotá. Belden was to urge that the Colombian government "refrain from taking any hurried step at this time in regard to withdrawal of its approval of the treaty."
[3] This was sent as RL to P. Belden, March 17, 1917, *ibid.*, p. 298.

## From Robert Lansing

PERSONAL AND CONFIDENTIAL:

My dear Mr. President:          Washington March 17, 1917.

This telegram from Mr. Penfield, No. 1757, March 13, 3 p.m.[1] (I enclose another copy as you have probably burned yours) seems to me to possess a possibility that something may be accomplished along the line suggested by Count Czernin, namely a secret meeting between a representative of the Allies and a representative of Austria-Hungary. If these two representatives come together to discuss general terms of peace, they may gradually drift into a discussion of a separate peace; and, if Austria-Hungary once permits her representative to talk even on that subject, I believe that something will have been gained.

It is my belief that the rumors reported in the last sentence of the telegram have substantial foundation, and that the Austrian Government is almost as fearful of its powerful ally as it is of its enemies. It seems to be in the unenviable position that its interests will be at the disposal of others however the war ends, in one case Germany will dictate, in the other the Entente Powers. As a matter of expediency, therefore, the Austrian Government may think it wise to come to some arrangement with the enemy before the war is decided, and takes this way of entering upon the subject. That is what I hoped and still hope. The keen interest shown by Count Czernin further encourages this hope.

I think that the insistence of Count Czernin, that a secret conference such as he suggests could only discuss the terms of a general peace, ought not to be considered as discouraging, because that is precisely what he should be expected to do. He must of necessity maintain an appearance of perfect loyalty to Austria's allies, not only to satisfy the Austrian sense of honor but also to avoid possible dangers from an enraged Germany in case the matter became public. That he is willing to engage in these *secret* conferences is, I think, very significant and ought to be encouraged. He must know that no single delegate of the Allies would discuss in any way terms of a general peace, especially with an enemy which could not control the other Central Powers. Knowing this these secret meetings must be proposed by Count Czernin for another purpose which, if it relates to peace, must have to do with terms affecting Austria-Hungary alone. A "separate peace" may be repudiated, but may be discussed nevertheless.

It seems to me that we ought to take the opening offered. We may accomplish nothing or we may accomplish more than we expect. If we fail, I do not see that anything has been lost. We will be no worse off than we are now.

We agreed, you will recall, to treat all communications from the Austro-Hungarian Government as strictly secret. The next step would seem to be to telegraph Penfield to ask Count Czernin if he would object to our making the suggestion of a meeting such as he proposed, to one of the Allied Governments, not as originating with Austria-Hungary but as originating here, explaining to him that, since the idea was his, we would not wish to appear to be violating our pledge of secrecy by even adopting the suggestion as our own unless he authorized us to do so. At the same time we should say that we cannot disclose our other correspondent as we are in that case also communicating in the strictest confidence.

Faithfully yours,   Robert Lansing.

TLS (WP, DLC).
1 F. C. Penfield to RL, March 13, 1917.


## From Edward Mandell House

Dear Governor:                      New York. March 17, 1917.

I want to suggest that you recognize the new Russian government as soon as England and France do so.

I think this country should aid in every way the advancement of democracy in Russia for it will end the peril which a possible alliance between Germany, Russia and Japan might hold for us.

You will come out of this war as its central figure, and largely because you stand easily to the fore as the great liberal of modern times. Your first inaugural address, your Mobile speech, and similar utterances have accelerated democracy throughout the world, and I am not too sure that the present outcome in Russia is not due largely to your influence.

Others have preached democracy, but you are the only potential ruler that has done so, and that makes the difference. The world at first failed to catch the significance and the difference between such utterances by you and by others not in authority.

Affectionately yours,   E. M. House

TLS (WP, DLC).


## From Harry Augustus Garfield

*Personal*                                    Williamstown,

Dear Mr. President:     Massachusetts March 17, 1917

Mr. J. S. Torrance,[1] whom you may recall as the writer of a letter concerning your Mexican policy[2] during the recent campaign, writes me under date of March 10 from Miami, Florida. He has just returned from Havana. He says concerning his visit: "I had an excellent opportunity while in Havana of learning some inside facts relative to revolutionary matters in the island. There is no doubt whatever but that notification from our government, that no regime inducted by force would be recognized by us, prevented the spread of and possible success of the Ferrara faction and the resulting bloodshed and increased destruction of property." As you may recall, Mr. Torrance thoroughly endorses your refusal to recognize government based on revolution and assassination.

It rejoices me to know that you are recovering rapidly from your severe cold. Your critics, even the bitter ones, prayerfully hope for your speedy recovery when you fall ill. I heard them the other night in New York. I am glad your health does not depend upon their prayers, which are too much like what Dr. Mark Hopkins described as "mere mutterings" born of fears for their own safety. Mr. Roosevelt's virulent nationalism and the pro-war spirit of the man with an interest are a serious menace. They are hardly to be distinguished from the sentiments of those who advocate submarine warfare even against neutrals. I suspect the chief difference is that our Hindenbergs and Krupps have not yet been subjected to the temptation of their German brothers. I still believe that our best service to the world will be performed if we defend ourselves, refusing to make anybody else's quarrel ours, doing nothing that does not make for greater liberty of men and surer cooperation between states.

With warmest regards, as always, I remain,

Faithfully yours,   H. A. Garfield.

TLS (WP, DLC).

[1] Jared Sidney Torrance, financier of Los Angeles.

[2] J. S. Torrance to H. A. Garfield, Oct. 5, 1916, TLS (WP, DLC), enclosed in H. A. Garfield to WW, Nov. 22, 1916, TLS (WP, DLC). Torrance had strongly endorsed Wilson's policy of nonrecognition of usurpers, such as Huerta, and Wilson's refusal to use military force against the Carranza government.

## From the Diary of Thomas W. Brahany

Saturday, March 17, 1917

The President was in his office yesterday, (March 16) for the first time since his inauguration. He saw a few persons at the White House the first of this week, and talked almost daily by telephone with Secretary Lansing. Some sensational stories regarding the President's health have been printed and we've received many letters and telegrams from his friends who [were] somewhat alarmed—at no time has he been seriously sick. Dr. Grayson reported to us daily. The President has had a bad cold and a sore throat—Grayson thought it best to take no chances and advised a complete rest. Secretary McAdoo, who by reason of his marriage to the President's youngest daughter, has more freedom of the White House than other members of the Cabinet, saw the President on Tuesday. He took up some official matters. Hoover reported McAdoo's visit didn't please the President, who didn't want to talk business. Hoover says he thinks McAdoo's call upset the President. He stayed too long and talked too much. We didn't look for the President to come to his office today. The four Railroad Brotherhoods are in disagreement with the Railroad Executives on the question of pay and hours of service and have called a general strike, the first group to quit work tonight. The President told Tumulty Thursday night that he had exhausted every remedy in this matter. Tumulty said the country would not be satisfied unless there was activity and interest shown by the administration to avert the strike. A strike now would be a national calamity. The Council of National Defense took up this matter yesterday morning and the President came to his office yesterday afternoon to talk over the situation with the Cabinet. Following the Cabinet meeting the President sent a telegram to the Brotherhood Chiefs begging them on patriotic grounds to accommodate their differences with the Railroad Executives. It was decided at the Cabinet meeting the Secretary of the Interior and the Secretary of Labor should leave at once for New York, as representatives of the President to try to compose the differences between the Brotherhoods and the Executives.

The first news of the revolution in Russia reached Washington yesterday. . . .

The Senate adjourned sine die yesterday. The President is greatly disappointed that no action was taken toward furthering ratification of the treaty with Colombia. We are all happy that Dr. Grayson's nomination to be a Rear Admiral has been confirmed. Everybody in the Executive Office likes Grayson.

## Two Letters from Robert Lansing

PERSONAL AND PRIVATE:

My dear Mr. President:          Washington March 19, 1917.

After considering carefully our conversation this morning I wish to say that I am in entire agreement with you that the recent attacks by submarines on American vessels[1] do not materially affect the international situation so far as constituting a reason for declaring that a state of war exists between this country and Germany. I think that these incidents, however, show very plainly that the German Government intends to carry out its announced policy without regard to consequences and to make no exception in the case of American vessels. It will, therefore, be only a question of time before we are forced to recognize these outrages as hostile acts which will amount to an announcement that a state of war exists.

I firmly believe that war will come within a short time whatever we may do, because the German Government seems to be relentless in pursuing its methods of warfare against neutral ships. It will not be many days, if past experience indicates the future, before an engagement will take place between one of our guarded steamships and a submarine. Whether that event will cause Germany to declare war or will cause us to recognize a state of war I do not know, but I do not think that we can successfully maintain the fiction that peace exists.

With the conviction that war is bound to come—and I have come to this conviction with the greatest reluctance and with an earnest desire to avoid it—the question seems to me to be whether or not the greatest good will be accomplished by waiting until some other events have taken place before we enter the conflict, or by entering now.

The advantage of delay would seem to be that in some future submarine attack on an American vessel the armed guard would with gun fire sink or drive off the submarine and by so doing induce the German Government to declare war upon us. If there is any other advantage I have been unable to imagine it. I am also convinced in my own mind that the German Government will not declar[e] war in any circumstances. Why should it? It will prefer to continue to wage war on us, as it is today, and at the same time keep our hands tied by our admitted neutrality. It can do everything practical to injure us and prevent us from doing many things to injure Germany. It would seem most unreasonable to expect the German Government to increase its difficulties by declaring the United States an enemy.

The advantages of our immediate participation in the war appear to me to [be] based largely upon the premise that war is inevitable. Of course if that premise is wrong what I say is open to question. I should add two other premises, the truth of which seem to me well established. They are that the Entente Allies represent the principle of Democracy, and the Central Powers, the principle of Autocracy, and that it is for the welfare of mankind and for the establishment of peace in the world that Democracy should succeed.

In the first place it would encourage and strengthen the new democratic government of Russia, which we ought to encourage and with which we ought to sympathize. If we delay, conditions may change and the opportune moment when our friendship would be useful may be lost. I believe that the Russian Government founded on its hatred of absolutism and therefore of the German Government would be materially benefitted by feeling that this Republic was arrayed against the same enemy of liberalism.

In the second place it would put heart into the democratic element in Germany, who are already beginning to speak boldly and show their teeth at their rulers. Possibly delay would not affect to a very great degree the movement, but I believe it would hasten the time when the German people assert themselves and repudiate the military oligarchy in control of the Empire.

In the third place it would give moral support to the Entente Powers already encouraged by recent military successes and add to the discouragement of the Teutonic Allies, which would result in the advancement of Democracy and in shortening the war. The present seems to be an especially propitious time to exert this influence on the conflict.

In the fourth place the American people, feeling, I am sure, that war is bound to come, are becoming restive and bitterly critical of what they believe to be an attempt to avoid the unavoidable. If there is a possibility of keeping out of the war, this attitude of the public mind would affect me not at all, but convinced as I am that we will in spite of all we may do become participants, I can see no object in adopting a course which will deprive us of a certain measure of enthusiastic support which speedy action will bring.

In the fifth place I believe that our future influence in world affairs, in which we can no longer refuse to play our part, will be materially increased by prompt, vigorous and definite action in favor of Democracy and against Absolutism. This would be first shown in the peace negotiations and in the general readjustment of international relations. It is my belief that the longer we delay in declaring against the military absolutism which menaces the rule of liberty and justice in the world, so much the less will be our influence in the days when Germany will need a merciful and unselfish foe.

I have written my views with great frankness, as I am sure you would wish me to do, and I trust that you will understand my views are in no way influenced by any bitterness of feeling toward Germany or by any conscious emotion awakened by recent events. I have tried to view the situation coldly, dispassionately and justly.

Faithfully yours,   Robert Lansing.

1 News had come on March 18 that German submarines had destroyed three American ships—*Vigilancia*, torpedoed without warning west of Bishop on March 16, with the loss of fifteen members of the crew; *City of Memphis*, sunk with no casualties off the Irish coast on March 17 after warning and evacuation of the crew; and *Illinois*, sent to the bottom by gunfire without warning off Alderney on March 18, one member of the crew wounded. See Link, *Campaigns for Progressivism and Peace*, pp. 396-97.

My dear Mr. President:          Washington March 19, 1917.

By the treaty of cession of August 4, 1916 we are bound to pay over to Denmark the twenty-five million dollars and take possession of the Danish West Indies before April 17th. That leaves us less than a month to make the arrangements for the formal delivery of the islands and payment of the money, which in view of the necessary communications with Copenhagen is a very short time. We ought to start without delay.

You have not indicated to me whether you have decided to have the War or Navy Department take control of the provisional government. That is of course the first question to be determined, because we must consult with the officials of the Department selected as to the formalities and the officers to administer the affairs of the islands. After this is decided I will name an official of the State Department to consult with an official of the other Department and also with the Danish Minister as to the procedure to be followed.

On account of the naval importance of the new acquisition as well as the marked efficiency shown by the naval officers in the conduct of affairs in Haiti and the Dominican Republic I personally favor the assignment of the duty of Government for the present to the Navy Department, although I realize that the War Department is especially equipped for administration of insular possessions. In voicing this opinion I do not intend to criticize in any way the War Department, which would undoubtedly do well in the administration of the civil government of the islands. My opinion is based on the fact that from the viewpoint of national defense the problems are essentially naval and that the administration of affairs and control of the public properties and improvements should be subordinated to the plans and purposes of the General Board of the Navy. I fear that with the War Department in control there might be failure to carry out these plans and purposes properly and there is always the possibility of friction as to the policies to be adopted.

I hope that you will be able to give me very promptly a decision in this matter as I feel that there is no time to lose in arranging for the formal delivery of the islands.

Faithfully yours,    Robert Lansing

TLS (WP, DLC).


## From Edward Mandell House

Dear Governor:                      New York. March 19, 1917.

Captain Gherardi, our Naval Attache at Berlin, who returned via Paris tells me that the French Admiralty and officers in the French Army told him that France badly needed steel billets, coal and other raw materials. They also told him that this war would be won by the nations whose morale lasted longest.

They estimated that the morale of the French troops was lifted 25% when the United States broke with Germany.

The strain upon the English to furnish materials for Russia, France and Italy has been so great that they are now unable to recruit for the army any further.

Everybody I have talked to connected with the English and French Governments tell me that if we intend to help defeat Germany that it will be necessary for us to begin immediately to furnish the things the Allies are lacking.

It has seemed to me that we should constitute ourselves a huge reservoir to supply the Allies with the things they most need. No one looks with favor upon our raising a large army at the moment, believing it would be better if we would permit volunteers to enlist in the Allied armies.

It seems to me that we can no longer shut our eyes to the fact that we are already in the war, and that if we will indicate our purpose to throw all our resources against Germany, it is bound to break their morale and bring the war to an earlier close.

Affectionately yours,   E. M. House

TLS (WP, DLC).


## Robert Lansing to Edward Mandell House, with Enclosure

My dear Colonel:                    [Washington] March 19, 1917.

I enclose you a copy of a *strictly confidential* dispatch received from Copenhagen under date of March 16th.

Of course it is all nonsense about Bernstorff denying the Carranza note. The effort seems to be to obtain knowledge of the source of our information. That the German Government will not get.

I would call your attention to the fact that the message is in our Green code and should be carefully protected.

I trust that Mrs. Lansing and I will be able to be with you next Saturday night, but the sudden turn of events as a result of the sinking of three American vessels may interfere with our plans.

I have just returned from a conference with the President. He is disposed not to summon Congress as a result of the sinking of these vessels. He feels that all he could ask would be powers to do what he is already doing. I suggested that he might call them to consider declaring war, and urged the present was the psychological moment in view of the Russian revolution and the anti-Prussian spirit in Germany, and that to throw our moral influence in the scale at this time would aid the Russian liberals and might even cause revolution in Germany. He indicated to me the fear he had of the queries and investigations of a Congress

which could not be depended upon because of the out-and-out
pacifists and the other group of men like Senator Stone.

If you agree with me that we should act now, will you not
please put your shoulder to the wheel?

                              Faithfully yours,   Robert Lansing

CCL (SDR, RG 59, 763.72/3528, DNA).


                    E N C L O S U R E

                              Copenhagen, March 16, 1917.

501. STRICTLY CONFIDENTIAL.

Department's telegram 273, March 12, 5 p.m.[1] Inexpedient to
employ Totten or Perkins.[2] Will you give me a free hand? Ought
to have a neutral in Germany.

Since Bernstorff's return, German officials insist that the Carranza note was a legitimate precaution. Bernstorff officially takes
this view, though he personally is trying for peace. German Legation here believes that military party will go to extreme lengths,
in spite of moderate attitude of Foreign Office. Zimmerman still
believes in a Japanese alliance.                      Egan.

T telegram (SDR, RG 59, 763.72/3528, DNA).
    [1] It is missing in the State Department files.
    [2] Capt. James Totten, U.S.A., military attaché at the American legation
in Copenhagen; and Cleveland Perkins, acting secretary of legation. They
were to be assigned to intelligence-gathering activities. RL to M. F. Egan,
March 20, 1917, T telegram (SDR, RG 59, 763.72/3528, DNA).


## From the Diary of Josephus Daniels

                              March Monday 19 1917

President called at Navy Department. I had asked to see him.
He called on me. Wished everything possible done in addition to
Armed Guards to protect American shipping, hoping this would
meet the ends we have in view. He had been urged to call Congress to declare war. He still hoped to avoid it and wished no cost
& no effort spared to protect shipping, putting efficacy above
prudence in the usual meaning of prudence. I asked Capt. Oliver[1]
to learn what English were doing to stop or lessen sub-marine
warfare. I told the President I would call General Board to consider every method to protect our shipping, it being paramount,
and send him their report. He was gratified that the strike had
ended as it had—eight hour law being upheld.[2] Approved working over eight hours in emergency, his approval being necessary.

Strongly approved my plan of putting educators rather than officers at head of non-military studies at Annapolis.

¹ Rear Admiral James Harrison Oliver, at this time director of the Office of Naval Intelligence. He had been promoted to flag rank on January 5, 1917.

² The mediators from the Council of National Defense—Secretaries Lane and Wilson, Samuel Gompers, and Daniel Willard—had conferred with the representatives of railroad labor and management in the Hotel Biltmore in New York all through Sunday, March 18, but to no avail. Lane telephoned the bad news to the White House at about midnight, and President Wilson responded with a dire warning that he was determined to prevent a strike at all costs. The railroad managers caved in thirty minutes later and authorized the mediators to grant whatever demands were necessary to prevent the walkout. The brotherhood presidents revoked the strike order a short time later. Both sides signed an agreement early in the morning of March 19 which gave union members ten hours' pay for eight hours' work and overtime pro rata, regardless of the Supreme Court's verdict on the Adamson Act. Link, *Campaigns for Progressivism and Peace*, p. 393.

A few hours later, the Supreme Court, by a majority of five to four, upheld the constitutionality of the Adamson Act. Chief Justice White, who spoke for the majority, affirmed that Congress had the power to establish an eight-hour day and that, faced by the threatened calamity of a nationwide railroad strike, Congress also had the power to prescribe minimum wages for a reasonable period of time, both to avert the calamity and to permit the contending parties time in which to agree upon a more permanent settlement. Wilson *v.* New, 243 U.S. 332.

## From the Diary of Thomas W. Brahany

Monday, March 19, 1917

Word was received late yesterday afternoon of the sinking by German submarines in the so-called danger zone of the American vessels, City of Memphis, Illinois and Vigilancia. Eighty-five Americans were aboard these three boats. The latest information is that fifteen men of the Vigilancia are missing. The general feeling here is that war with Germany is inevitable, and most of our callers today expressed a hope that the President would move forward three weeks the extra session of Congress, that is to say make the date March 26 instead of April 16. The President does not seem to be greatly perturbed. Early this morning he went to the Suburban Club where he played golf with Dr. Grayson. On his return he received the Secretary of State. After luncheon the President went to the office of the Secretary of the Navy where he talked for half an hour with Secretary Daniels. After the conference Daniels announced that the $150,000,000 bonds authorized by Congress a few weeks ago for emergency use would be immediately available. Late this afternoon the President received the Secretary of the Treasury. We didn't receive many telegrams today. Most of the messages relating to international affairs urged war with Germany. The office has been filled with newspapermen all day. Nearly all of them are

disappointed because the President didn't make an announcement to the country.

At noon today the Supreme Court, through Chief Justice
White, handed down a decision holding constitutional the so-
called eight hour law relating to railroads. Several weeks ago
Tumulty guessed this would be the Court's decision and so informed the President. The President said he thought Tumulty
was wrong. The railroad managers early this morning (shortly
after midnight) conceded the demands of the Brotherhoods and
the nation-wide strike scheduled to begin tonight was declared
off. There is a feeling of general relief in the country and the
railroad executives are being commended freely for their patriotic action. Samuel Gompers, President of the American Federation of Labor, one of the Committee of Four designated to confer
with the Brotherhood Chief[s] and the Executives didn't show
up in New York until Saturday night. He said he was in Atlantic
City and didn't know of his selection until Saturday afternoon.
When he failed to meet with his associates Friday night the
Washington office of the Associated press began an investigation
of his whereabouts. The trail led from sundry Washington bar
rooms to Atlantic City. Sam does this kind of things. Incidentally,
but pertinently, Sam called at the Executive Office about three
weeks ago and asked the President to veto the bill making
Washington a dry city.

## From Josephus Daniels

Dear Mr. President:                    Washington. March 20, 1917.

After the meeting of the cabinet I went to a meeting of the
General Board and discussed with its members the best means
of protecting our ships from the submarines. The net result of
all efforts to check submarines abroad is disappointing. Early
in the war, when they were small, England caught them in nets.
That method is not now deemed effective with the larger submarines. There is no effective method. The Board incorporates
its views in their letter enclosed.[1] The other suggestions, to which
reference is made in their letter, were embraced in the letter I
showed you some weeks ago. They advised bringing the fleet
to the Chesapeake (which has been ordered), mobilizing the fleet
(by bringing out all the navy militia) not needed now, increasing enlistments (which is being carried out) co-operation with
the allies and like suggestions.[2]

This is my original copy. Will you not return when you are
through with it?                    Sincerely,   Josephus Daniels

ALS (WP, DLC).

1 Senior Member Present (Charles J. Badger) to the Secretary of the Navy, March 20, 1917, CCL (NDR, GBR, File 425, Serial No. 689, DNA). The main portion of this memorandum follows:

"Of the measures advocated by the General Board in its letter of February 4, 1917, G. B. No. 425, Serial No. 666, especial attention is invited to the following which bear directly upon the protection of our commerce in transit between the United States and Europe:

"(a) Escort vessels to deep water from our ports and similarly from deep water to our ports;

"(b) Arrange with British and French governments for the convoy of our merchant ships through the barred zones;

"(c) Merchant ships to proceed on high seas from points of leaving and receiving escorts, depending upon their guns for protection, and upon changes of course to follow alternate routes;

"(d) Arrange with British and French governments a code of signals to be used in directing merchant ships as to routes to be followed and points of meeting escorts;

"(e) Establish a patrol of the Atlantic Coast;

"(f) Recruit up to the limit allowed by law for emergencies in order to provide crews for patrols and auxiliaries, and fill battleship complements which have been depleted to supply gun crews to merchant ships."

2 Senior Member Present (Charles J. Badger) to the Secretary of the Navy, Feb. 4, 1917, CCL (NDR, GBR, File 425, Serial No. 666, DNA).

## Thomas Nelson Page to Robert Lansing

Personal & Confidential

My dear Mr. Secretary,          Rome March 20th., 1917.

I am going to ask that you deliver this personally to the President.

A matter that has interested me greatly of late is the secret work of the Vatican relative to us and to the European belligerents. I have from time to time sent you telegrams referring to what has been going on as far as it has been brought to my notice. You will find from my telegram no. 800[1] and those following, that a gentleman came to me from the Vatican, that is of a way for the President to stop the war immediately by preventing the exportation of munitions of war and other supplies to any of the belligerents. It was full of praise of the President's fine idealism. When it was suggested by the gentleman who came to me that this might be regarded as an unfriendly act by the Allies, the reply was that we were always having questions arise between us and Japan, and that Governments could always arrange such matters, and we could make it appear that we thought it necessary in view of all this to reserve our products for ourselves.

Soon after that, the same gentleman came again, having been sent for to the Vatican, and presented the same ideas, rather more urgently and with rather less praise for the President. And this time it referred to our difficulties with Mexico as well as with Japan, and spoke of us in rather more positive terms.

The next time an actual message was written out, but not signed, for me to send to the President. I, however, declined to send such a message from the Vatican directly to our Government, but I later sent you for your information the substance of what had been told me.

Now again has come another, which my informant spoke of as another "Delenda est Carthago." It declares that "in well-balanced political circles of this Capital the following considerations are advanced:

"The position of President Wilson relative to the belligerent powers is not sustained from the point of view of International Law. It would have been much more logical and magnificently fine if he had really vindicated complete freedom of the seas, or the right of American citizens to trade with both groups of belligerents, carrying them not contraband of war but those products which on the basis of the Hague Conference do not constitute contraband of war. In this case the action of President Wilson would have been consonant with International Law, and he would have been followed by all the neutrals, and his figure in the history of the world would have towered gigantically.

"But now his position is not logical, because on one hand he says that he defends freedom of the seas while in reality he not only does not defend it, but yields to England's injunctions not to navigate to the Central Empires; therefore in reality he is not neutral."

You will observe the entirely different tone of this from former communications. At the same time there has appeared in a Jesuit journal published in Florence, a long article, signed "Catholicus," on the neutrality of the Pope, in which the Pope is declared to be the only true neutral, and that there is a manifest desire to abase his neutrality to the level of a cleverly calculated policy of interest,—to that indeed of many neutral states—"as to cite a classical example of selfishness, the United States who, have used their vaunted neutrality to gain millions and billions to the rhythmic beat of preparing ammunition which were used to scatter broadcast death and destruction throughout Europe—the sort of neutrality which no one has forbidden, no one has spoken against, and against whose base bargaining no one has lifted his voice in protest."

This and more is contained in this article, which is evidently intended to help secure for His Holiness that which is the prime wish of the Vatican—the internationalization of the law of guarantee[2] which at present is the work of Italy alone, and as a first step towards this a seat in the peace congress when it shall assemble.

By the way, I understand that the paper was shown by a rival paper in Florence to have had relations with the Austrian Jesuits in Gorizia about the time of the fall of that city.

It adds to my interest in the foregoing to have been informed a day or two ago that the Japanese Naval Attaché asked our Naval Attaché[3] if it were true that the Vatican had sent a man to me to try and prevent the sale of munitions to the Allies. The Japanese Naval Attaché is oddly enough a Catholic, and I am wondering how he got hold of this story, as no one knows it outside of my Secretary[4] who enciphered it. My Naval Attaché who knew nothing whatever about it, and knows nothing at this moment told him that it was not true.

Taking in connection the references in these several Vatican messages to me, to Japan and Mexico, with statements that appear from time to time in the press regarding the relations between the Vatican and the several Latin Roman Catholic Republics, I have a very strong suspicion that the German propaganda in these republics has had the good will and possibly more of the Vatican.

There was an interpolation in the Chamber here the other day, regarding a conspiracy which is said to have involved a considerable number of persons of standing, the expense of which was said to have been defrayed by a certain Mgr. Gerlach,[5] a Bavarian crony of His Holiness, who was harbored at the Vatican until a short time since when he slipped out of Italy into Switzerland. The answer to the inquiry was that the person mentioned was no longer in Italy and this was allowed to close the incident, but it is rumored and believed that this conspiracy had to do with the destruction of two Italian war-ships of the first class.

It is also rumored and believed generally that the recent breaking into the Austrian Consulate in Zurich resulted in the finding of important information, and although no one says publicly who committed the act, it is common talk here that much information was obtained favorable to Italy.

I am, my dear Mr. Secretary, with kindest regards,

Very sincerely yours, Thos. Nelson Page

TLS (SDR, RG 59, 763.72119/558½, DNA).

[1] Page's summary immediately following makes clear that he actually referred to his telegram No. 762, Dec. 26, 1916, quoted in n. 1 to T. N. Page to RL, Dec. 29, 1916, printed as an Enclosure with RL to WW, Jan. 23, 1917 (third letter of that date), Vol. 40. Page's letter of December 29 discussed the conversation in greater detail.

2 Following the annexation of Rome and the former papal states by the Kingdom of Italy in 1870, the government of that nation sought to define the position of the Pope and the Holy See in the territory which the Pontiff no longer ruled temporally by enacting the so-called "Law of Guarantees" on May 13, 1871. This act granted to the Pope, among other things, all the honors due a king, free communication with Catholics throughout the world, diplomatic immunities for foreign emissaries assigned to the Vatican, an annual income of over three million lira in perpetuity, and control over and tax-free status for the Vatican and Lateran palaces and Castel Gandolfo and the museums and libraries therein. Popes Pius IX (1846-78) and Leo XIII (1878-1903) utterly repudiated this settlement and refused to accept the financial offer or to recognize the law in any other way. However, Pius X (1903-1914) and Benedict XV gradually softened papal resistance to the act, and Benedict obviously hoped to strengthen its guarantees by internationalizing it in the peace settlement following the World War. *New Catholic Encyclopedia* (17 vols., New York, 1967-79), VI, 824; XII, 607-608.

3 Lt. Commander Charles Russell Train.

4 Arthur Bliss Lane.

5 The Rt. Rev. Rudolph Gerlach.

# A Memorandum by Robert Lansing

MEMORANDUM OF THE CABINET MEETING,
2:30-5 p.m. TUESDAY, MARCH 20, 1917.

The Cabinet Meeting of today I consider the most momentous and, therefore, the most historic of any of those which have been held since I became Secretary of State, since it involved, unless a miracle occurs, the question of war with Germany and the abandonment of the policy of neutrality which has been pursued for two years and a half.

Before describing the meeting it is necessary to go back a little in order to appreciate the situation when the Cabinet met.

On Sunday, March 18th, came word of the sinking by German submarines of the American merchant vessels, ILLINOIS, CITY OF MEMPHIS and VIGILANCIA. Two of these vessels were westward bound in ballast, and the reports indicated the loss of fifteen lives on board the VIGILANCIA.

On Monday morning (March 19th) I was summoned to the White House and for an hour the President and I sat in his study and debated the course of action which should be followed. The President said that he did not see that we could do more than we were doing in the way of protecting our vessels as already three of the American Line steamships had sailed for Europe with armed guards, each carrying four guns and forty men. I argued that war was inevitable, that I had felt so for months, and that the sooner we openly admitted the fact so much stronger our position would be with our own people and before the world. Of course much more was said along the same lines. I left the President without a definite impression as to what his decision would be. I was hopeful that he would see the future as I saw it, but was by no means certain. I felt that he was resisting the irresistable logic of events and that he resented being compelled to abandon the neutral position which had been preserved with so much difficulty.

Knowing the President's deliberate way of dealing with every question, no matter how critical it might be, and his preference for written statements which he could "mull" over, I wrote him a letter that evening on returning from a dinner at the Japanese Embassy, in which I set forth at some length my reasons for believing that he should at once summon Congress in extra session, lay before them a full statement of the wrongs we had suffered from Germany, and ask them to declare that a state of war existed and to enact the legislation necessary for active participation and national defense. This letter I sent to the President Tuesday morning.

From Sunday noon until Tuesday noon there was intense public excitement. Many of the newspapers clamored for war and inveighed bitterly at the President's failure to act. There was a general feeling that, if war did not come at once, it would come shortly, and that there was no valid reason for awaiting another outrage. I myself shared this feeling and was prepared to urge immediate action at the meeting of the Cabinet.

The corridors of the State Department and the Executive Office swarmed with press correspondents seeking to get some inkling of what would be done from passing officials. It was through these eager crowds of news-gatherers that I forced my way at half-past two Tuesday afternoon under a bombardment of questions, to which I made no reply, and entered the Cabinet room where all the other members had arrived.

Three minutes later the President came in and passed to his place at the head of the table shaking hands with each member and smiling as genially and composedly as if nothing of importance was to be considered. Composure is a marked characteristic of the President. Nothing ruffles the calmness of his manner or address. It has a sobering effect on all who sit with him in council. Excitement would seem very much out of place at the Cabinet table with Woodrow Wilson presiding.

After felicitating Secretaries Lane and Wilson on the success of their efforts at mediation between the railroad managers and the "Four Brotherhoods," the President said that he desired advice from the Cabinet on our relations with Germany and the course which should be pursued. He began with a review of his actions up to the present time pointing out that he had said to Congress on February 3rd that, while the announced policy of Germany had compelled the severence of diplomatic relations, he could not bring himself to believe that the German Government would carry it out against American vessels, but that, if an "overt act" occurred, he would come before them again and ask means to protect Americans on the high seas even though he thought he possessed the constitutional power to act without Congress. He said that the situation compelled him to do this on February 23rd and Congress had desired to adopt the measures, which he sought, but had been prevented, and that he had then acted on his own authority and placed armed guards on American vessels intending to proceed to the German barred zone.

He went on to say that he did not see from a practical point of view what else could be done to safeguard American vessels more than had already been done unless we declared war or declared that a state of war existed, which was the same thing; and that the power to do this lay with Congress.

He said that the two questions as to which he wished to be advised were—

Should he summon Congress to meet at an earlier date than April 16th, for which he had already issued a call?

Second. What should he lay before Congress when it did assemble?

He then spoke in general terms of the political situations in the belligerent countries, particularly in Russia where the revolution against the autocracy had been successful, and in Germany where the liberal element in the Prussian Diet was grumbling loudly against their rulers. He also spoke of the situation in this country, of the indignation and bitterness in the East and the apparent apathy of the Middle West.

After the President had finished McAdoo was the first to speak. He said that war seemed to him a certainty and he could see no reason for delay in saying so and acting accordingly; that we might just as well face the issue and come out squarely in opposition to Germany, whose Government represented every evil in history; that, if we did not do so at once, the American people would compel action and we would be in the position of being pushed forward instead of leading, which would be humiliating and unwise. He further said that he believed that we could best aid the Allies against Germany by standing back of their credit, by underwriting their loans, and that they were sorely in need of such aid. He felt, however, that we could do little else, and doubted whether we could furnish men.

McAdoo spoke with great positiveness in advocating an immediate call of Congress. His voice was low and his utterance deliberate, but he gave the impression of great earnestness.

Houston, who followed, said that he agreed with McAdoo that it would create a most unfortunate, if not disastrous, impression on the American public as well as in Europe if we waited any longer to take a firm stand now that Germany had shown her hand. He said that he doubted whether we should plan to do more than to use our navy and to give financial aid to the Allies; that to equip an army of any size would divert the production of our industrial plants and so cut off from the Allies much needed supplies; and he thought that we ought to be very careful about interfering with their efficiency. He concluded by urging the President to summon Congress at once because he felt that a state of war already existed and should be declared.

Redfield followed Houston with his usual certainty of manner and vigor of expression. He was for declaring war and doing everything possible to aid in bringing the Kaiser to his knees. He made no points which particularly impressed me; and, as he had so often shown his strong pro-Ally sentiments, I was sure his words made little impression upon the President.

Baker was the next to express an opinion and he did so with the wonderful clearness of diction of which he is master. He said that he considered the state of affairs called for drastic action with as little delay as possible, and that he believed Congress should meet before April 16th. He said that the recent German outrages showed that the Germans did not intend to modify in the least degree their policy of inhumanity and lawlessness, and that such acts could mean only one thing, and that was war.

Since we were now forced into the struggle he favored entering it with all our vigor. He advocated preparing an army at once to be sent to Europe in case the Allies became straightened in the number of their men. He said that he believed the very knowledge of our preparations would force the Central Powers to realize that their cause was hopeless. He went on to discuss the details of raising, equipping and training a large force.

I followed Baker and can very naturally remember what I said better and more fully than I can the remarks of others.

I began with the statement that in my opinion an actual state of war existed today between this country and Germany, but that, as the acknowledgement of such a state officially amounted to a declaration of war, I doubted the wisdom as well as the constitutional power of the President to announce such fact or to act upon it; that I thought that the facts should be laid down before Congress and that they should be asked to declare the existence of a state of war and to enact the laws necessary to meet the exigencies of the case. I pointed out that many things could be done under our present statutes which seriously menaced our national safety and that the Executive was power- less to prevent their being done. I referred in some detail to the exodus of Germans from this country to Mexico and Cuba since we severed diplomatic relations, to the activities of German agents here, to the transferrence of funds by Germans to Latin American countries, to the uncensored use of the telegraph and the mails, &c.

For the foregoing reasons I said that I felt that there should be no delay in calling Congress together and securing these necessary powers.

In addition to these reasons which so vitally affected our domestic situation I said that the revolution in Russia, which appeared to be successful, had removed the one objection to af- firming that the European War was a war between Democracy and Absolutism; that the only hope of a permanent peace be- tween all nations depended upon the establishment of demo- cratic institutions throughout the world; that no League of Peace would be of value if a powerful autocracy was a member, and that no League of Peace would be necessary if all nations were democratic; and that in going into the war at this time we could do more to advance the cause of Democracy than if we failed to show sympathy with the democratic powers in their struggle against the autocratic government of Germany.

I said that the present time seemed to me especially pro- pitious for action by us because it would have a great moral in- fluence in Russia, because it would encourage the democratic movement in Germany, because it would put new spirit in the Allies already flushed with recent military successes, and be- cause it would put an end to the charges of vacillation and hesitation, which were becoming general and bring the people solidly behind the President.

"The time for delay and inaction," I said, "has passed. Only a definite, vigorous and uncompromising policy will satisfy or ought to satisfy the American people. Of this I am convinced. We are at war now. Why not say so without faltering? Silence will be interpreted abroad as weakness, at home as indecision. I believe that the people long for a strong and sure leadership. They are ready to go through to the very end. If we enter this war, and there is not the slightest doubt but that we will enter if not today then tomorrow, the Government will lose ground which it can never regain by acting as if it was uncertain of its duty or afraid to perform that duty, a duty which seems to me very plain."

I said a good deal more in the same vein and urged the propriety of taking advantage of the aroused sentiment of the people since it would have a tremendous influence in keeping Congress in line. I said that I would not permit my judgment to be swayed by this sentiment but that as a matter of expediency in affecting congressional action it ought to be used. I must have spoken with vehemence because the President asked me to lower my voice so that no one in the corridor could hear.

The President said that he did not see how he could speak of a war for Democracy or of Russia's revolution in addressing Congress. I replied that I did not perceive any objection but in any event I was sure that he could do so indirectly by attacking the character of the autocratic government of Germany as manifested by its deeds of inhumanity, by its broken promises, and by its plots and conspiracies against this country.

To this the President only answered, "Possibly."

Whether the President was impressed with the idea of a general indictment of the German Government I do not know. I felt strongly that to go to war solely because American ships had been sunk and Americans killed would cause debate, and that the sounder basis was the duty of this and every other democratic nation to suppress an autocratic government like the German because of its atrocious character and because it was a menace to the national safety of this country and of all other countries with liberal systems of government. Such an arraignment would appeal to every liberty-loving man the world over. This I said during the discussion, but just when I do not remember.

When I had finished, Secretary Wilson in his usual slow but emphatic way said: "Mr. President, I think we must recognize the fact that Germany has made war upon this country and, therefore, I am for calling Congress together as soon as possible. I have reached this conviction with very great reluctance, but having reached it I feel that we should enter the war with the determination to employ all our resources to put an end to Prussian rule over Germany which menaces human liberty and peace all over the world. I do not believe we should employ half-measures or do it half-heartedly."

In view of the fact that Wilson had on previous occasions shown a disposition to temporize with the German Government and had opposed war because of submarine attacks, I was surprised at his frank assertion in favor of radical measures. There is this to be said of Secretary Wilson, he never speaks at haphazard; he is slow to express an opinion but very firm in it when it is once declared. When I have disagreed with him I have always had to acknowledge the soundness of his reasoning unless the subject was Labor, as to that he is biased. I consider him a valuable adviser because he is equipped with an abundance of commonsense.

Gregory, who had been listening with much attention although on account of his deafness I am sure only heard his neighbors at the table, gave it as his opinion that it was useless to delay longer, that the possibility of peace with Germany was a thing of the past, and that he was in favor of assembling Congress as soon as possible, of enacting all necessary legislation, and of pursuing as aggressive action toward Germany as we were able. He went on to speak of German intrigues here, of the departure of German reservists and of the helplessness of his Department under existing laws. He said that every day's delay increased the danger and Congress ought to be called on to act at once.

After Gregory had given his views the President said, "We have not yet heard from Burleson and Daniels."

Burleson spoke up immediately and said: "Mr. President, I am in favor of calling Congress together and declaring war; and when we do that I want it to be understood that we are in the war to the end, that we will do everything we can to aid the Allies and weaken Germany with money, munitions[,] ships and men, so that those Prussians will realize that, when they made war on this country, they woke up a giant which will surely defeat them. I would authorize the issue of five billions in bonds and go the limit." He stopped a moment and then added, "There are many personal reasons why I regret this step, but there is no other way. It must be carried through to the bitter end."

The president then turned his head toward Daniels who sat opposite Burleson and said: "Well, Daniels?" Daniels hesitated a moment as if weighing his words and then spoke in a voice which was low and trembled with emotion. His eyes were suffused with tears. He said that he saw no other course than to enter the war, that do what we would it seemed bound to come, and that, therefore, he was in favor of summoning Congress as soon as possible and getting their support for active measures against Germany.

Burleson had at previous meetings resisted an aggressive policy toward Germany, and he had, as late as the Cabinet meeting on Friday, the 16th, advocated very earnestly taking a radical stand against Great Britain on account of detention of the mails.

Whenever I had called attention to the illegal acts of Germany he would speak of British wrong-doings. I felt sure that he did this to cause a diversion of attention from the German violations of law. Possibly I misjudged him, and there was no such motive. His words at this meeting indicated hostility to Germany and a desire for drastic action, so I may have been mistaken.

As for Daniels his pacifist tendencies and personal devotion to Mr. Bryan and his ideas were well known. It was, therefore, a surprise to us all when he announced himself to be in favor of war. I could not but wonder whether he spoke from conviction or because he lacked strength of mind to stand out against the united opi[ni]on of his colleagues. I prefer to believe the former reason, though I am not sure.

The President said, as Daniels ceased speaking: "Everybody has spoken but you, Lane."

Lane answered that he had nothing to add to what had been said by the other members of the Cabinet, with whom he entirely agreed as to the necessity of summoning Congress, declaring war and obtaining powers. He reviewed some of the things which had been said but contributed no new thought. He emphasized particularly the intensity of public indignation against the Germans and said that he felt that the people would force us to act even if we were unwilling to do so.

Knowing the President's mental attitude as to the idea of being forced to do *anything* by popular opinion, these remarks of Lane seemed to me unwise and dangerous to the policy which he advocated. I could almost feel the President stiffen as if to resist and see his powerful jaw set as Lane spoke. Fortunately before the President had time to comment Lane kept on in his cool and placid way drifting into another phase of the subject which was more to the President's taste since it appealed to his conception that he must be guided by the principle of right and by his duty to this country and to all mankind. Thus what might have been a dangerous incident was avoided.

The foregoing is a brief outline of the debate which occupied over two hours and which frequently was diverted into other channels such as the effectiveness of armed guards on merchant ships, the use of patrol boats, German plots in Latin America, the danger of riots and vandalism in this country, the moving of interned vessels, the need of censors, &c., &c.

When at last every Cabinet officer had spoken and all had expressed the opinion that war was inevitable and that Congress ought to be called in extraordinary session as soon as possible, the President in his cool, unemotional way said: "Well, gentle-

men, I think that there is no doubt as to what your advice is.
I thank you."

The President, during the discussion or at the close, gave no
sign what course he would adopt. However as we were leaving
the room he called back Burleson and me and asked our views
as to the time of calling a session if he so decided. After some
discussion we agreed that to prepare the necessary legislation for
submission to Congress would take over a week and that, therefore, Monday, April 2nd, would be the earliest day Congress
could conveniently be summoned. I asked the President if he
would issue a proclamation that afternoon so it would appear in
the morning papers on Wednesday. He replied smilingly: "Oh,
I think I will sleep on it."

Thus ended a Cabinet meeting the influence of which may
change the course of history and determine the destinies of the
United States and possibly of the world. The possible results are
almost inconceivably great. I am sure that every member of the
Cabinet felt the vital importance of the occasion and spoke with
a full realization of the grave responsibility which rested upon
him as he advised the President to adopt a course which if followed can only mean open and vigorous war against the Kaiser
and his Government. The solemnity of the occasion as one after
another spoke was increasingly impressive and showed in every
man's face as he rose from the council table and prepared to
leave the room. Lane, Houston and Redfield, however, did not
hide their gratification, and I believe we all felt a deep sense of
relief that not a dissenting voice had been raised to break the
unanimity of opinion that there should be no further parley or
delay. The ten councillors of the President had spoken as one,
and he—well, no one could be sure that he would echo the same
opinion and act accordingly.

T MS (R. Lansing Papers, DLC).

## From the Diary of Josephus Daniels

1917 Tuesday 20 March

Cabinet discussed: Shall Congress be called earlier than April?
And what message shall be given? That was what was pro-
pounded by the President, who was grave. He pointed out that
he had told Congress he did not believe Germany would do what
it threatened; if so he would ask for power. G— had. He had the
power to put Armed Guard on ships & to use the Navy to protect.
He needed no other power, unless we should go the final step

and declare that Germany was waging war against us. He opposed G— militarism on land & E's militarism on sea. Both were abhorrent. He was disinclined to the final break. Spoke of the glorious act of Russians, which, in a way, had changed conditions, but he could not give that as reason for war. Asked cabinet's view. All declared for war except B & I, & the President said: "Burleson, you & Daniels have not spoken.["] B— said he thought we were already at war, & that unless President called Congress the people would force action. The Pres said "I do not care for popular demand. I want to do right, whether popular or not." It was a supreme moment in my life. I had hoped & prayed this cup would pass. But there was no other course opened, & I said our present attempt by Armed Guard could not be wholly effective & if it succeeded we must co-operate with English & let them convoy our ships while we patrolled this coast. Having tried patience, there was no course open to us except to protect our rights on the seas. If Germany wins, we must be a military nation.

President was solemn, very sad!!

## From the Diary of Thomas W. Brahany

Tuesday, March 20, 1917

Tumulty left for New Jersey at noon to attend the dinner given in his honor at Newark tonight. Responding to appeals from the newspapermen Tumulty went to the White House shortly before train time to get a line on the international situation for the guidance of the press. He returned empty handed. "There is nothing to announce," he reported to the waiting correspondents. The Cabinet—all members present—was in session from 2:30 until after 4 o'clock. Fully fifty newspapermen were in the outer Executive offices when the Cabinet adjourned. "Nothing to say," each cabinet officer reported. At the request of about a dozen of the leading correspondents, Forster saw the President and told him the newspapermen wished just a word for guidance in writing their dispatches. "The international situation was thoroughly discussed in all its phases," was the only announcement the President would authorize. Secretaries McAdoo and Lane, who are the best "news sources" in the Cabinet later in the evening let some of their newspaper friends know of the President's purpose to call Congress in extra session "not later than April 2." The President doesn't seem to be worried. He is planning to attend the vaudeville performance at Keiths Theatre tonight.

## A Proclamation

[Washington, March 21, 1917]

WHEREAS, public interests require that the Congress of the United States should be convened in extra session, at twelve o'clock, noon, on the second day of April, 1917, to receive a communication concerning grave matters of national policy which should be taken immediately under consideration;

Now, Therefore, I, WOODROW WILSON, President of the United States of America, do hereby proclaim and declare that an extraordinary occasion requires the Congress of the United States to convene in extra session at the Capitol in the City of Washington on the second day of April, 1917, at twelve o'clock, noon, of which all persons who shall at that time be entitled to act as members thereof are hereby required to take notice.

GIVEN under my hand and the seal of the United States of America, the twenty-first day of March in the year of our Lord one thousand nine hundred and seventeen, and of the Independence of the United States the one hundred and forty-first.

                                        WOODROW WILSON.

By the President:
Robert Lansing *Secretary of State.*

Printed copy (WC, NjP).


## From William Bauchop Wilson, with Enclosure

My dear Mr. President:          Washington March 21, 1917.

I am inclosing you herewith clipping from the New York Times of today in which the statement is made, "It is to be assumed that, in accordance with usage and precedent, the resignations of all his Cabinet officers have been placed in his hands."[1] If that course is in accordance with precedent I must plead guilty of having violated it. May I not explain, however, that on February 2d I had prepared my resignation to be placed in your hands and would have done so at that time but for the statement carried in the newspapers, said to emanate from the White House, that it was the intention of the President to retain his present Cabinet members.

Believe me, Mr. President, I have too high regard for the purity of your ideals, the sincerity of your motives, and the accuracy of your judgment to retard the progress of your policies by remaining in my present position, if doing so would in any manner impair the efficiency or value of your Administration. I would ask you, therefore, to accept this as my resignation, effective at any time when in your judgment a change is advisable.

I am inclosing you herewith the letter of resignation I had intended to send on February 2d.

With highest personal regards, I am,

Faithfully yours,    W B Wilson

TLS (WP, DLC).
¹ It is missing in WP, DLC. However, it was an editorial in the *New York Times*, March 21, 1917, entitled "The President's Cabinet." The editorial, without directly saying so, also clearly implied that the present cabinet members were unfit to conduct the government in the great emergency facing the country. "The imminence of war," it said, "lays upon him [the President] the imperative duty to consider how and where he may strengthen his council of advisers and executive chiefs. . . . The President owes it to himself, since the success of his Administration in a time of great trial may depend upon it. He owes it to the people, for if, as now seems probable, they are to be called upon to bear the heavy burdens and anxieties of war, there must not be added endless alarms arising from the doubt and fear that the men at the head of affairs are unequal to their tasks and responsibilities. . . . War is a business of the greatest seriousness, it demands for its direction and conduct the service of men of the first order of ability, men whose qualification may be summed up by saying that they must have the full confidence of the people. At such a time patriotism commands that the call to duty go forth to the country's great men, equally it commands them to answer the summons by acceptance."

E N C L O S U R E

## From William Bauchop Wilson

My dear Mr. President:          Washington February 2, 1917.

It has been very gratifying to me to have had the opportunity of service to my country and mankind under your direction. The association has been particularly pleasing because of the fact that even when divergent views on the details of any program have been frankly expressed, the relations between us have been the most cordial. I have been happy in the knowledge of the friendly feeling you have held toward me personally. I realize, however, that personal gratification and pleasant relations are but minor considerations in the selection of heads of departments for the purpose of carrying into effect the progressive policies you are developing.

In view of these reasons I trust you may feel as free to act in the selection of a Secretary of Labor for your second administration as if the circumstances I have referred to were not in existence and you were making an original appointment. May I not, therefore, place in your hands my resignation to take effect March 5, 1917.          Faithfully yours,    W B Wilson

TLS (WP, DLC).

## From John Rogers Commons

My dear President Wilson:                    Madison, March 21, 1917

I have just seen in to-day's paper a statement that the administration has under consideration plans for revenue so designed as to pay the expenses of the war out of income rather than by debts.[1] This is certainly a plan most heartily to be commended and any one who has read Professor Sprague's scholarly and scientific analysis of the subject[2] will at once agree that if the administration follows such a plan it will not only meet the popular demand of the country but will be scientifically correct.

With hearty support of the proposition, I am,

Sincerely yours,    John R Commons

TLS (W. G. McAdoo Papers, DLC).
[1] The *New York Times*, March 20, 1917, reported that McAdoo "had not given any thought" to the issue of bonds to finance the expenditure of $115,-000,000 authorized by Wilson on March 19 to forward naval preparedness. Such a bond issue was unnecessary. The report continued: "The money will be taken out of the general fund of the Treasury whenever it may be required for the preparedness work. Later, whenever the state of the Treasury is such that there is need to replenish it, provision will be made for the advertisement for bids for the bonds."
[2] Oliver Mitchell Wentworth Sprague, "The Conscription of Income," *The New Republic*, X (Feb. 24, 1917), 93-97. Sprague argued that financing of war through borrowing was both unjust and inefficient. It led to serious inflation and did not mobilize a country's resources with sufficient speed. A system of steeply graduated income taxes, together with sales taxes on some vital items such as sugar and gasoline, would cut civilian consumption drastically, avoid inflation, mobilize the nation's resources quickly, and place all citizens on an equal footing.

## From the Diary of Thomas W. Brahany

Wednesday, March 21, 1917

Early this morning the President telephoned Forster to come to the White House at once. On his arrival he outlined to him the draft of a proclamation convening Congress in special session on Monday, April 2. He authorized Forster to inform the newspapermen. The President and Dr. Grayson then left the White House for golf. On account of the bad weather they did not play, but a long motor ride being substituted. The proclamation was not signed until the President's return at 11 o'clock. It sets out that public interests require the convening of Congress on April 2 "to receive a communication concerning grave matters of national policy which should be taken immediately under consideration." The President didn't come to his office today. A few papers were sent to him for signature, including recess commission for members of the Tariff Commission. The President's desk is piled high with papers and letters, some of them of considerable importance. The President has dictated practically no letters since before his inauguration, but has signed some letters —not many—prepared for his signature. Apparently he is not in a working mood these days. He spends nearly all his time with Mrs. Wilson, reading, playing pool or visiting. The newspapermen are in the air as to what line they should take. They wish to know if the President intends to ask Congress to declare that a state of war exists between the U. S. and Germany, or if he will content himself with a statement of the recent submarine outrages and ask the authority of Congress to take such steps as may be necessary to safeguard American rights. Apparently members of the Cabinet don't know what the President plans to do. Late this afternoon Forster, responding to an appeal from eight or ten correspondents, went to the White House and submitted a request that the President see representatives of the press for a few minutes. The President declined to see them. He told Forster to say he hoped the newspapers would conjecture nothing except that obviously on the surface. The correspondents are very much put out. Many of them are repeating their former sarcastic references to "pitiless publicity." . . .

The President has the thrift of the Scotch race from which he is sprung. He always pays the exact change for his caddies, and he knows whether the club rules prescribe the fee to be 35 cents or 50 cents. He always pays the recognized fee, never adding a tip. Caddies understand there is nothing extra in the way of funds in working for the President, and there is no grand rush to carry his golf bag. I am led to make this observation by the fact that on yesterday the President signed an authorization to the Treasurer of the United States for the deduction of $125 a month from his salary warrant. Because of the constitutional provision that Congress shall not diminish the President's salary during his term, it was not necessary for the U. S. Treasurer who draws the President's salary warrant, to make any deduction on account of the income tax law, which was enacted after Mr. Wilson became President. The amended law enacted before March 4 applies to the salary of the President in his second term and on the President's salary of $75,000 a year the amount to be collected "at the source" is $125 a month. In signing the authorization yesterday for the withholding of this amount the President wished to make certain of what he was doing. He read twice, and very carefully, the blank order which he filled in and signed. He made no comment.

## To William Bauchop Wilson

My dear Mr. Secretary:        The White House 22 March, 1917

You made no mistake at all. I have told all the members of the Cabinet, and thought that you were present when I told them, that I did not want their resignations. I do not agree with either the spirit or the idea of the editorial from the New York Times. Every effort of that sort in other countries during the present war has been a conspicuous failure and I do not think that it would pay us to follow an example of that sort.

Moreover, I have learned to feel that the Cabinet has become a genuine team working in the spirit of the highest patriotism and with a genuine capacity which I have constantly admired. I had not the least thought of changing it.

With warmest appreciation of your own labors and the spirit in which they have been rendered,

Cordially and sincerely yours,    Woodrow Wilson

TLS (received from Mary A. Strohecker).


## To Julio Betancourt

My dear Mr. Minister:        [The White House] 22 March, 1917

Your letter of March sixth gave me a great deal of gratification. My illness has prevented my earlier acknowledgment of it. I understood entirely the reason of your absence from the ceremonies incident to the induction of the new administration, and I sincerely hope that your health is completely restored.

I echo very heartily your hope and your confident belief that the relations between the United States of America and Colombia will grow more and more cordial and intimate. They are based upon a genuine desire on both sides to promote the interests of true Pan-Americanism and I believe, as I am sure you do, that the real interests of all American countries lie together and not apart.

Cordially and sincerely yours,    Woodrow Wilson

TLS (Letterpress Books, WP, DLC).


## To Waldo Lincoln Cook[1]

My dear Mr. Cook:        [The White House] 22 March, 1917

I have for some time wanted to write to you to tell you not only how genuinely I have admired the editorials of the Springfield

Republican, which I have studiously read and pondered, but also
how much benefit and real guidance for my thought I have derived from them.[2] I know that most of them (perhaps all of those
to which I refer) come from your pen, and I would feel that I
had omitted a duty as well as a pleasure if I did not write to tell
you these things.

Cordially and sincerely yours,   Woodrow Wilson

TLS (Letterpress Books, WP, DLC).
[1] Associate editor and chief editorial writer of the *Springfield*, Mass., *Republican*.
[2] A reading of the editorials in the *Springfield Republican* from March 1 to
22, 1917, suggests that Wilson's comment was prompted by Cook's analysis of
the significance and implications of recent international events. Indeed, the
*Republican*'s cautious and judicious approach to problems of foreign policy
closely resembled Wilson's own pragmatic flexibility in his efforts to deal with
the rapidly changing international situation. Good examples of the *Republican*'s
examinations of recent events include the evaluations of the significance of
the Zimmermann telegram in "The German Plot," *Springfield Republican*,
March 2, 1917, and "America's Threatened Fronts," *ibid.*, March 3, 1917; the
discussion of Mexican-American relations in "First Chief Becomes President,"
*ibid.*, March 13, 1917; and especially the examination of the significance and
implications of the Russian Revolution in "Revolution in Russia," *ibid.*, March
16, 1917, "Russia and Peace," *ibid.*, March 18, 1917, and "America and the
Revolution," *ibid.*, March 19, 1917. The only specific proposal strongly set forth
by the *Republican* at this time was that the Wilson administration's policy
of armed neutrality be given an adequate trial, even in the face of such events
as the sinking of *Vigilancia*. This proposal appears particularly in "The U-Boat
Attacks," *ibid.*, March 20, 1917, and "Why Declare War," *ibid.*, March 21, 1917.
Another editorial on a more general subject which probably appealed strongly to Wilson was "Morbid Neutrality," *ibid.*, March 21, 1917. It argued that
Americans should not worry too much about charges that their neutrality was
one-sided or pro-Allied. "Neutrality," it declared, "is not a state of mind, to
be subjected to meticulous psychological analysis, but a perfectly definite and
official attitude, with recognized rights and prescribed duties. A nation in
deciding for war or for neutrality is not bound to search its heart to discover
whether in petto it is absolutely impartial. . . . What it has to deal with is an
actual situation involving innumerable complicated problems in law, in
equity, in the balance of power. All these have to be reduced to the single
supreme question of statesmanship—war, or peace?"

# To Ambrose Preece[1]

My dear Mr. Preece:          [The White House] 22 March, 1917

Illness has prevented my writing sooner to express the sincere
appreciation which Mrs. Wilson and I feel of your services in
driving the carriage which conveyed us to the Capitol on Inauguration Day and brought us back to the White House. We felt
that we were in very capable hands indeed, and I think that your
driving contributed to the dignity of the occasion.

Cordially and sincerely yours,   Woodrow Wilson

TLS (Letterpress Books, WP, DLC).
[1] Of New York, instructor of the Washington Riding and Hunt Club. The
*Washington Post*, March 6, 1917, called him "one of England's premier four-
horse drivers." "He has served," it continued, "under Queen Victoria, King
Edward and King George."

## To Edward Wright Sheldon

My dear Sheldon:              The White House 22 March, 1917

Your note of March ninth gratified me very much. I am sure you know that I would have replied to it sooner had I not been ill most of the time since Inauguration.

It was a genuine pain to me to be unable to see you and other dear friends during that busy day, but it was a comfort to feel that you were at hand and I thank you with all my heart for your generous letter.

Cordially and faithfully yours,   Woodrow Wilson

TLS (photostat in the RSB Coll., DLC).


## To Edward Parker Davis

My dear E. P.:              [The White House] 22 March, 1917

Your poem on my inauguration[1] has touched me more than I know how to say. I read it aloud to Mrs. Wilson and Miss Bones and they join with me in a feeling not only of admiration for the poem itself, but of deep gratification that the inauguration should have stirred such feelings in you about myself. I owe you, my dear fellow, a real debt of gratitude for the encouragement you have given me.

With warmest regards to you both,

Cordially and affectionately yours,   Woodrow Wilson

TLS (Letterpress Books, WP, DLC).

[1] "Woodrow Wilson, President. March 5, 1917," T MS (WP, DLC), enclosed in E. P. Davis to WW, March 17, 1917, ALS (WP, DLC).

It reads as follows:

"He stood upon the eastern gate,
Behind him rose the pillared dome
Of Liberty's enshrinéd home,
Around, his loyal people wait.

"Hes [His] speech was voice of human man,
His thoughts the words of living God;
Up to the heights where heroes trod
His dauntless spirit led the van.

"He gave a clear and thrilling call
To follow to the heights of right,
To join the great and solemn might
Before whose march oppression falls.

"He stood alone before the throng
In simple dignity of truth,
As David stood in holy youth
To smite the base, to slay the wrong;
His vision wide as spreading plain,

His strength the heights of fortressed hills,
His patience starlike, hope that fills
Men's thirsting souls like summer rain.

"His wingéd words flew far and wide,
Borne on the strong free rushing wind,
Heard by the finer sense that finds
God's voice in all the earth confides;
The flying clouds, the gleaming sun,
The charging armies of the wind,
The rushing stream all unconfined,
Springs vernal tumult just begun;
A new sweet freedom near at hand,
A hope of peace, a call for strength,
A tocsin ringing through the length
And breadth of all our waiting land.

"He stood upon the eastern gate,
High priest before the pillared dome
Of liberty's enshrinéd home,
And on his words our millions wait.

"He stood beside the flowing stream
His country's life poured through the banks
Of cheering thousands, rank on rank
They marched, a testament supreme
Of free young strength, of purpose fine,
Of steady courage, constant trust
That naught can dull, that naught can rust.
The sword of truth, the might divine.

"The trumpets answered to the wind,
And blew the call to arms on high,
The shining banners of the sky
Flung out the springtime of mankind;
That liberty is born again,
War's winter wasting to the end,
That we shall stand the world's great friend,
The ice of hate shall yield to rain
Of tears of mercy, strong and free,
The peoples of this war cursed earth
Shall wake to spring of better birth,
To golden days of liberty.

"He stood upon the eastern gate,
And led his people up to God;
He stood beside the marching flood
Of strong young life, and felt the fate
Of nations struggling to be free
Placed in our hands; he stands for you,
Strike down the false, put forth the true,
And stand with him, for liberty!"

## To Ella E. Martin Caminetti

My dear Mrs. Caminetti:     [The White House] 22 March, 1917

It tears my heart to have to say to you that I cannot see my way clear to pardon your son.[1] If I followed the dictates of my heart or allowed myself to be influenced by my genuine friendship for yourself and your husband, I would of course do it; but in matters of this sort it seems to me my imperative duty to leave personal feelings and connections out of the question entirely and look at the matter from the public point of view with regard to the influence it would have upon other cases. When I look at the case of your son from this point of view, it seems to me clearly my duty to withhold a pardon.

My heart goes out to you in genuine sympathy, my dear Mrs. Caminetti, and I cannot tell you what it costs me to write you this, but I am sure that you will understand that I am moved entirely by a sense of imperative duty.

Cordially and sincerely yours,   Woodrow Wilson

TLS (Letterpress Books, WP, DLC).
  [1] He was replying to Ella E. M. Caminetti to WW, March 20, 1917, ALS (WP, DLC).

## To James Duval Phelan

My dear Senator:          [The White House] 22 March, 1917

I cannot do better to show you how I have felt about the Caminetti case than send you a copy of my letter to Mrs. Caminetti which I have written today.[1] I must ask for your sympathy, and I sincerely hope that I will in the long run have your approval in this matter.

Cordially and faithfully yours,   Woodrow Wilson

TLS (Letterpress Books, WP, DLC).
  [1] Wilson was replying to J. D. Phelan to WW, March 20, 1917, ALS (WP, DLC).

## From the Diary of Colonel House

March 22, 1917.

The Attorney General is here for the day and I have been with him a large part of it. He lunched and dined with us, and we later went to see Henry Miller in the "Great Divide."[1]

Gregory told of the last Cabinet meeting. He thinks the President had no idea of calling Congress together earlier than the 16th but was persuaded to call it on the 2nd of April because of the unanimous opinion of the Cabinet that he should do so. He said Burleson remarked that the people wished this country to go into the war actively. The President replied that it did not make so much difference what the people wished as what was right. Burleson answered that if he were President and a situation like this arose, he would want the opinion of the people back of him.

The President gave no intimation to the Cabinet as to what he intended to do, but early next morning he called Congress for April 2nd. When Gregory telephoned yesterday at ten o'clock to tell me he would be in New York today, he did not then know that the President had made the call.

[1] A revival of William Vaughn Moody's play, *The Great Divide*, first produced in 1906. The drama, which centers upon a conflict between the puritanical repressions of the New-England-born heroine and the hedonistic freedom of the western hero, had been critically acclaimed as a great American play and had been a popular success, with many productions since its first appearance. The leading lady in the play was Gladys Hanson.


## From the Diary of Josephus Daniels

1917 Thursday 22 March

President: The present Russian Ambassador Bakhmeteff tried to have Prof Milukov removed as Professor. What will Milukov do to B? He must be uneasy.

When Benedict Arnold was given a roving commission to destroy he went South & met a N. C. man who was denouncing Arnold. "What" asked Arnold "would the people of N. C. do to Arnold if they captured him?" The unsuspecting N C said: "They would cut off the leg injured when he bravely followed Washington & give it an honorable burial. Then we would hang the balance of the d—rascal." This Apropos of seeing John Paul Jones's sword given by Willie Jones of N C

Mrs. W hangs on the Presidents stories & comments with enthusiasm—"Sweetheart"


## To Newton Diehl Baker

My dear Mr. Secretary,      The White House. 23 March, 1917.

This is entirely satisfactory to me,[1] except that I still prefer Charleston as the headquarters of the Southern Division because the main question in case of war will be, not so much transportation (at any rate in that part of the country) as coast defense, and because that is, for the present at any rate, much the most sedative place for the commander who is to be assigned to that Division.[2] I should think that that arrangement could without detriment be at least tried out.

I think this plan works out most satisfactorily and that it will make a good impression on the country.

Faithfully Yours,   Woodrow Wilson

WWTLS (N. D. Baker Papers, DLC).
¹ Wilson was replying to NDB to WW, March 22, 1917, CCL (N. D. Baker
Papers, DLC). Baker proposed to increase the number of military departments
into which the continental United States was divided from four to six. This
was to be accomplished by dividing the existing Department of the East into
the Department of New England, the Department of New York, and the
Department of the Southeast. Baker also proposed to make Atlanta, rather
than Charleston, the headquarters of the Department of the Southeast because
of its importance as a railroad center.
² General Leonard Wood. He went to Charleston.


## From Robert Lansing

PERSONAL AND CONFIDENTIAL:

My dear Mr. President:          [Washington] March 23, 1917.

After consultations with Senators Swanson, Knox and Lodge
I am convinced that the present Colombian Treaty could only
obtain senatorial consent by the acceptance of several amendments, which would require the assent of Colombia, and would
leave the finished treaty to my mind in a very confused and, if I
may use the term—inartistic form. Such amendments I feel
would also be viewed as criticisms of the Administration.

A careful canvass of the situation seems to assure thirty-seven
votes in opposition to the treaty even as amended by the Committee.

My suggestion is that, since in any event the treaty will require
further action by Colombia, the simplest and most expedient
method is to negotiate a new treaty. With that idea in mind I
send you a proposed draft.¹ This treaty I can guarantee will be
accepted by the Senate but of course I cannot speak for Colombia, though that Government will be very anxious to get the
twenty-five millions.

The most radical change is the omission of Article I of the
present treaty. I feel that in view of the proviso added by the
Senate Committee as to denial of criticism of any Administration
Article I means nothing. I understand that that proviso was a
concession to Senator Knox. Its effect, however, neutralizes every
expression of regret in Article I.

I enclose also a memorandum showing the original text, the
Senate amendments, and in typewriting and pen deletions the
proposed changes to be made in the old treaty.² The enclosed
clean draft on long paper incorporates all of these additions and
changes.

At your convenience I would like to talk the matter over with
you or to receive a memorandum on the proposed course of action and the enclosed draft.

                    Faithfully yours,   Robert Lansing

TLS (Lansing Letterpress Book, SDR, RG 59, DNA).

[1] Not printed. As Lansing indicates below, the new draft omitted entirely Article I of the original treaty which had expressed the "sincere regret" of the United States that "anything should have occurred to interpret or to mar" cordial relations between the two countries. To the article specifying the rights and privileges of Colombia in the use of the Panama Canal and Railroad, the new draft added a paragraph which stated that these provisions would not be operative in case of war between Colombia and the United States or between Colombia and Panama. In case of war between the United States and a country other than Colombia, the rights and privileges granted by the article were not to be used by Colombia "in any manner whatsoever to the advantage directly or indirectly of the enemy of the United States." Instead of the single lump-sum payment of $25,000,000 to Colombia called for by the original treaty, the new draft provided that the United States would pay over the money in five equal installments over a period of four and a half years. Under two new articles, Colombia was, first, to grant to the United States the exclusive right to construct another interoceanic canal over the Atrato River route or any other route through Colombian territory whenever the two nations agreed that such construction was desirable and, second, Colombia was to lease two small islands deemed important to the defense of the Panama Canal to the United States for 100 years, the lease to be renewable for similar periods as long as the United States might desire. T MS (Lansing Letterpress Book, SDR, RG 59, DNA). The original treaty is printed in FR 1914, pp. 163-64.

[2] This document is missing in both WP, DLC, and the files of the State Department.

## From Herman Bernstein

Dear Mr. President:                    New York March 23rd, 1917.

Permit me to congratulate you upon your wise and noble act of recognizing the new government in Russia, the government of the people.[1] The fact that America was first to recognize the New Russia officially will doubtless serve as a beautiful inspiration both in this country and in Russia. The men who are now at the head of the Russian government have been influenced by American ideals and guided by American traditions. The spirit of America is spreading abroad, and I feel that you have done more than any American President to extend the influence of American democracy.

With highest esteem and the best of wishes, I am,

Sincerely and faithfully yours,   Herman Bernstein.

TLS (WP, DLC).

[1] The United States recognized the provisional government on March 22, 1917.

## From Annie Wilson Howe Cothran

Dearest Uncle Woodrow,              N. Y. C. March 23rd, 1917.

I have thought of you so often and I love you dearly. I have not written you to tell you how much I appreciate your wonderful generosity to me and the two boys. The Princeton Bank debt has always hung like a cloud over mother and me and there is no way in the world in which you could have helped me more than by paying that off. I hope some day we three can pay you that debt each of us taking a third as our personal debt. Mr Wintersteen my lawyer asks me to secure either a list of the securities which you have from the Princeton Bank or the papers themselves to examine, and so, will you please, as soon as you can either send them direct to Mr Wintersteen or to me and I will forward them at once.

I have secured my decree for divorce at last. My papers came March 12th and I am free once more. I have not seen a word in any paper about it [and] am so pleased that it has been gotten in such a quiet dignified way. Arent you?

I am working hard again my siege of grippe having departed altogether at last. I have a concert engagement in St Louis Mo. April 13th. I sing at the St Louis Women's Club there. The reports from my manager out there are good. She writes our expenses are paid in receipts for the 13th. now. Everything else is clear profit! Wish me success.

With devoted love to you all, especially yourself,
devotedly yours,   Annie.

ALS (WP, DLC).


## Thomas Beaumont Hohler to Lord Hardinge,[1] with Enclosure

*Private.*

Dear Hardinge,                    Washington. March 23rd., 1917

Barclay[2] thought it might interest you to see the enclosed memo of a conversation I had on the 9th. with Col. House. Things are moving fairly quickly and last bag was not fully confidential, so it will be rather out of date.

It looks as if W. would in fact help us pretty *well*: almost all he can: but I think he will try not to be *technically* an ally. He's the most agile pussy-footer ever made, and when any serious decision is taken, always tries to unload the responsibility on to someone else, and has been doing so this time again. But it does seem as if the Huns had fairly driven him into a corner out of which he can't possibly wriggle!

Unpreparedness, except as far as money goes, is quite complete.

I am certainly lucky in arriving here at so interesting a moment. It is extraordinary how I never go to any country without bringing a war or a revolution along with me.

Yours very sincerely,   T. B. Hohler.

TCL (F/60/2/5, D. Lloyd George Papers, House of Lords Record Office).
  1 Charles Hardinge, Baron Hardinge of Penshurst, at this time Undersecretary of State for Foreign Affairs.
  2 That is, Colville Adrian de Rune Barclay, Counselor of the British embassy.

## E N C L O S U R E

### MEMORANDUM OF CONVERSATION WITH COLONEL HOUSE IN NEW YORK ON MARCH 9TH.

Colonel House had expressed the desire to see me in order to talk over Mexican affairs and I accordingly met him at his house last Friday (March 9th). We discussed the present very unsatisfactory conditions, taking into consideration the desirability and the practicability of giving not merely countenance and moral support, but active assistance to some other factor than that of Carranza, for we were agreed that the only hope, a very slender one, still existing was that Carranza might possibly pay heed to the advice which would be given him by the new United States Ambassador, but the probability, based on experience, was very high that he would not do so. Our heel of Achilles is our oil interests: they almost alone are susceptible of rapid and nearly irremediable damage: but, throughout, our interests are parallel and ought not to clash: at the present moment they must not be allowed to clash.

Colonel House was much impressed by the further danger to United States interests arising out of German intrigues. I said I had worked hard on enquiries into them in conjunction with Mr. Rogers, the American representative, and we had been able to ascertain but very little: up to the time I left Mexico there appeared to be no official or concerted action, only the activity of a small number of individuals. I could not say how serious the intrigues were now, though they certainly appeared to have become much more threatening, but again there appeared room to hope that they would not materialise, according to the Zimmermann note unless the United States entered into war with Germany.

He said that he considered this now practically certain. I said I had never been able to understand clearly how far it was in America's real interest to participate in the war, though of course it was clear that a defeat of the allies would place the United

States in a peculiarly disagreeable position, but this eventuality was in my opinion already eliminated. Nor could I understand how far war was really desired by the country. The Colonel replied that this was President Wilson's very difficulty: his sentiments were, he said, entirely with the Allies, but the critical thing was to judge the feeling of the country with nicety so as to enter the war without arousing civil strife here: his triumph would be if he could succeed in that, and the point seemed now attained. I said if the United States did enter, I was not clear how they would be able to help us, at all events unless they came in very soon, as my personal belief was that the end was almost in sight. He said he considered it certain that their entry would be early, but there must be the "overt act" first, and this he thought could hardly be delayed long. I thought this was rather a cumbrous way of putting a chip on one's shoulder, but he said it was indispensable for public opinion and for record.

I referred to fears I had heard expressed lest munitions, etc. should be held up from the Allies in order to arm American forces which would be in process of training: this would materially hamper the cause and so defeat the very aim which the United States would, in the eventuality, be pursuing. He said such a course had been insidiously insinuated to them from German sources, but it would not by any means be the case: heretofore the United States Government had allowed us to obtain munitions, credits and food: once the break came, they would "pump them in."

I think I am correct in stating that he said the United States could not afford to see the Allies beaten, but am not absolutely positive. He spoke at all events in that sense.

I said it had been a great pity that the President's phrase of "peace without victory" had been so much quoted as if it were a summary of his ideas instead of conveying, in isolation from its context, a very different thought. All the English had made such sacrifices that I doubted if there were one in a thousand that would accept any such ending, however much more sacrifice might be required to attain the victory. I thought this temper could not be too clearly understood. He replied that the press had made it amply clear though Mr. Wilson of course had referred to the destruction of the German nation, etc.

His tone was friendly in the highest degree, and while his degree of actual influence is doubtful, so long as he does in any way represent the President's ideas, his words were thoroughly satisfactory.                                        T. B. Hohler.

TC MS (F/6o/2/5, D. Lloyd George Papers, House of Lords Record Office).

# From the Diary of Josephus Daniels

March Friday 23 1917

When cabinet met, the President, grave within, told several stories before proceeding to business. Hope was expressed that Russian revolution would be permanent. "It ought to be good" said WW with a smile, "because it has a professor at the head." He seemed—in fact—stated his pleasure—that America was the first nation to recognize the new Russian government. Crane knew well the leading spirits & said they were men of ability and had the confidence of Russia.

Redfield, ought not to permit transfers from one Department to another. Small matter in time of great moment.

Burleson said it made him hot to read Gen. Wood's fulminations.[1] President spoke strongly of lack of loyalty by some Army & Navy officers. Said he came here without any prej[udice] vs Wood, but his conduct had been most reprehensible. Early in administration, W[ood] had to Dems criticized R[2] & to Reps criticized administration. Some member of cabinet asked Baker if Wood did anything but fulminate. "The most prodigiously busy man you ever saw" he replied. Asked if he had called W's attention to impropriety. "Yes" he said with a smile, "and he always acknowledges receipt of my letter.["] All laughed, Baker leading.

President said call for 87,000 men to fill up the Navy. Also use money for communications.

[1] Despite repeated warnings from Baker, General Leonard Wood had continued to speak out publicly for preparedness and universal military service and about the inevitability of American participation in the war. See, for example, the *New York Times*, Feb. 1, 9, and 11, and March 11, 13, 15, and 18, 1917.
[2] Theodore Roosevelt.

# To Josephus Daniels

My dear Mr. Secretary,          The White House. 24 March, 1917.

Thank you for the enclosed.

Somehow I cannot feel that this constitutes a very effective programme, but Unless I can suggest something better or something practicable in addition I have no right to criticize it.

The main thing is no doubt to get into immediate communication with the Admiralty on the other side (through confidential channels until the Congress has acted) and work out the scheme of cooperation. As yet sufficient attention has not been given, it seems to me, by the authorities on the other side of the water to the routes to be followed or to plans by which the safest possible approach may be made to the British ports. As few ports as possible should be used, for one thing, and every possible precaution thought out. Can we not set this afoot at once and save all the time possible?

Faithfully Yours,   Woodrow Wilson

WWTLS (J. Daniels Papers, DLC).

## From Joseph Patrick Tumulty

Dear Governor:               The White House March 24, 1917.

I have examined the editorials from the leading journals throughout the country and have gathered from them these impressions:

If we are driven into war by the course of Germany, *we must remain masters of our own destiny.*

If we take up arms against Germany, it should be on an issue exclusively between that Empire and this Republic;

And that the United States must retain control of that issue from beginning to end. (See New York Times editorial, March 22d, attached.)[1]

The consensus of opinion seems to be that the end of the war will be accomplished sooner if we go resolutely about it, in dead earnest, using all the energy we can immediately put forth in preparing ourselves swiftly to put all of our force into the struggle. That is the way to make the war short; that is the way to compel Germany to sue for peace, to convince her rulers and her people that she is defeated. (See New York Times editorial, March 22d, attached.)

As to preparations to meet the emergency, there are various opinions, but there seems to be an agreement on the following:

A stronger army than we now have in order that the land defence of this country may be adequately secured.

As the Springfield Republican says, "The times are such that no one should now be in the least doubt of the national need. The necessity for argument on that point was ended by the Zimmerman note proposing a German-Mexican-Japanese alliance against America."

Whether or not a large standing army can be procured now, it is imperative that we proceed *at once to enlist and train a large number of troops,* far beyond the force authorized by existing laws, and for that purpose Congress should give its authority. The duration of the war is uncertain, its issue must not be left in doubt, and we must be prepared to do our part, however

great, to put it beyond doubt. Moreover, there will be great hazards in the years following the war and we cannot with safety
pursue our policy of standing defenseless before the world, trusting to luck and our peaceful reputation. (See New York Times
editorial attached.)

The following are suggestions from the New York Times
editorial:

Financial aid to the Allies, probably in the form of a gift to
France. (N. Y. World suggestion also) Contributions of military and food supplies for the use of the nations more immediately involved.

Continuing, the New York Times editorial says:

"We must keep open the routes of trade to and from Great
Britain and her allies and in defending our commerce against
the submarine peril, we shall defend theirs. We must do our
utmost to destroy Germany's submarines. For that work it will
be necessary that we have naval bases on the British coasts. An
arrangement with the British Government to that effect would
necessarily imply the admission to our ports of British warships
for supplies and refitting. Those are rights mutually given between allies. It is probable, also, that the ships of our navy will
be able to take the place of British warships doing patrol duty in
Atlantic waters, relieving them for home service. And all the
time by the arming of merchantmen, by naval convoy, by fitting
out a large fleet of small craft for hunting down submarines, we
must maintain an uninterrupted outflow of our commodities
through the barred zone to British and French ports."

In discussing what our activities in the war should be, the
New York Evening Post editorial of March 22d suggests a certain degree of cooperation with the Allies. "If we are to endeavor
to keep the ocean open to legitimate commerce, it is obvious
that we should seek to make our efforts fit in with those of the
Allied navies. That is only common-sense. *Our patrols and
guard-ships would be more effective when added to those already
in existence. But this is a very different thing from putting our
navy outright under the orders of the British Admiralty.* The
United States may temporarily join hands with the Allies, for the
sake of better securing our aims, *but this country must not at
any time lose a free hand.* If we are driven into war by the course
of Germany, we must remain masters of our own destiny. It will
be for the United States to shape hostilities as it sees fit, to fight
until the objects of the war are attained, and then to make a
peace as advantageous as possible,—*all on its own decision.*"

Arguing for a free hand on the part of America, the New York

Evening Post says in its editorial of the 22d of this month (attached herewith): "The staring difficulties are too easily swept away. The way of allying ourselves with the other belligerents must be considered. For example, the Allies are bound together by a hard-and-fast treaty obliging each one not to make peace until all agree. Is the United States to put its name to that? Should we do so, and then Germany offer all that we have asked in order to settle our quarrel with her, we should have to go on fighting just the same, until England and France gave the word to lay down arms. But there is no likelihood whatever that the American people would wish to tie themselves up by any agreement of that kind. What, moreover, of Turkey and Bulgaria? Are we to declare war against those countries? We should have to, logically, if we went the whole figure of joining the Allies. Or, if we did join them in the full sense, their enemies would declare war upon us, though no direct controversy or other cause of war might exist between them and us. That is the sort of consequences it would be reasonable to expect to follow from leaping into the Entente before we looked. Nor can we fail, if we are prudent, to scrutinize the announced programme of the Allies before putting our names to it, and pledging to its execution our lives, our honor, and our sacred fortune. We have the sufficient detail in the reply of the Allied Governments to President Wilson. One item on their list is the expulsion of the Turk from Europe, and the turning over of Constantinople to Russia. That may be an end desirable in itself, but has the United States any call to fight for it? We should have to be ready to do so if we go in with the Allies up to the hilt. But is it not plain that, if it came to such a result, Uncle Sam would scratch his head and ask what he was doing in that galley? Another announced object of the Allies is the restoration of Alsace-Lorraine to France. But is that an American affair? We may approve of it, might hail it if it came, but are we to debar ourselves from making peace until that end is attained? The question answers itself. So does the question whether the United States ought to go to war for the purpose of dismembering Austria. That is distinctly on the programme of the Allies, but what have we to do with it?["]

Sincerely yours,   J. P. Tumulty

TLS (WP, DLC).
  1 He enclosed clippings of all the editorials mentioned in this letter.

## From Julio Betancourt

Sir:                          Washington, D. C. March 24th, 1917.

I have the honor to convey to Your Excellency, in the name of the Government and people of Colombia, the expression of profound gratitude for the noble and keen interest Your Excellency has unmistakeable displayed in favor of the Treaty which is awaiting the pleasure of the Senate.

In this connection the sad fact has come to my knowledge that a small group of Senators has set itself to prevent by all means the ratification of the aforesaid Treaty which, it must be owned, a certain section of the Press has chosen as its target to hurl absurd inventions and no less contemptible calumnies.

One of the means which that small group propose to make use of to prevent the final consummation of that act of simple justice, which Your Excellency has so earnestly endeavored to bring about, is to introduce certain reforms in the Treaty; reforms which, on the face of it, my country could not accept.

Urgent business calls me to New York city. I candidly hope that on my return home Your Excellency will be pleased to grant me, at my respectful request, an audience in order to reiterate in detail the purport of this letter.[1]

Please accept, Excellency, my best wishes for your personal welfare and the assurances of my highest consideration.

Faithfully yours,   Julio Betancourt.

TLS (WP, DLC).
[1] They were unable to find a mutually satisfactory time for a meeting.

## From Ella E. Martin Caminetti

My dear Mr. President,          [Washington] March 24, 1917

In acknowledging your favor of yesterday I wish to say that though disappointed and hopeless, I appreciate the force of your statement and will return to my humble and broken home satisfied that you have acted from the highest conception of your duty.

I sincerely regret that my troubles should have been forced on your attention when so many problems, vital to the Nation are at stake and demand your supreme care. Certainly one who can soothe grief such as mine, can and will master the impending crisis.

My prayers and feeble help are with you, dear Mr President, in your work for our people,

Faithfully Yours   E E Caminetti

ALS (WP, DLC).

## From the Diary of Josephus Daniels

1917 Saturday 24 March

Late in afternoon President and Mrs. Wilson called at Department—the first time she had been there. "Most beautiful office in W." She admired John Paul Jones' sword. President told of new head of affairs in Russia, Prof. Milukov. Invited to lecture by Crane at Univ of Chicago. Could not speak English, but promised to learn in a year. Attended meeting to plan reforms, put in jail for 1 yr, began to study English, & wrote his lectures in English painfully, & then reflected that though he wrote English he could not speak it. Resolved to learn & asked & obtained 3 months from jail to go to England. Strange to say granted & in that time learned to speak English well. Returned, went into prison, had to break in. Obtained interview with Prime Minister, who after long talk, was so pleased with him, he offered him Minister of Education. Declined because he was not in sympathy with spirit of Government. And now he is the head of the Russian Gov.

## From Edward Mandell House

Dear Governor:                        New York. March 25, 1917.

If it is convenient to you I will come down on Tuesday for there are some things I would like to talk over with you.

I particularly want to tell you and McAdoo of information I have regarding the Morgans and the effort that will probably be made to put them to the fore in the event any large international financing is to be done in conjunction with this country.

I got the enclosed memoranda[1] from a reliable source and expect in a day or two to be able to add to it. I showed it to Lansing, but, for the moment, it is important that it does not go further.

I am also enclosing you a letter from Frazier of our Paris Embassy[2] and a newspaper article by Hervé[3] which I am sure will interest you.

Will you not telegraph me upon receipt of this whether it is convenient for me to come or whether you would prefer another time.                        Affectionately yours,    E. M. House

TLS (WP, DLC).

[1] T MS dated March 23, 1917 (WP, DLC). As House's diary entry of March 23 reveals, the memorandum was written, or perhaps dictated, by Sir William Wiseman. It stated that information secured from the Austrian consulate in New York indicated that German submarines were cruising in American waters and that orders were being given in regard to German and Austrian ships interned in American harbors.

[2] A. H. Frazier to EMH, March 9, 1917, TCL (WP, DLC). Frazier enclosed the article discussed in n. 3 below and also commented upon the boost given to French morale by the American decision to sever relations with Germany.

[3] Gustave Hervé, "Scruples of Mr. Wilson," TC translation of article from *La Victoire*, March 7, 1917 (WP, DLC). Hervé used Wilson's second inaugural address to illustrate for his French readers his opinion that Wilson's "scruples" and "apparent hesitations" in regard to the European conflict were essentially political in nature. That is, according to Hervé, Wilson had to move slowly in order to preserve and strengthen the fragile unity of the conglomerate of ethnic groups which made up the population of the United States. "Read attentively his speech of yesterday," Hervé wrote, "it is that of a psychologist, of a realist, of a man of action. If he presides some day over the Congress of Nations, the Congress which will found as upon a rock—by the sword of the international police—the peace of the world, one will perceive that this shepherd of people is of the same timber of which were made, in the great days of the American Republic, the Washington and Abraham Lincoln."

## From John Palmer Gavit

Dear Mr. President:          Englewood, N. J. March 25, 1917.

It seems to me of vital importance that the United States should not declare war against Germany. We are in the position of dealing with outlaws, violators of every international decency. If they were Apache Indians, we should not declare war against them, nor recognize their declaration of war against us. We should defend ourselves, by whatever means might be necessary, even to the extent of a punitive expedition; but we never would establish a formal state of war.

I am not for non-resistance, or for peace at any price; but I am deeply anxious that when the record is made up it shall appear that the United States, throughout the war, never left its position save in self-defense, and then only to the extent that was absolutely necessary. A formal declaration of war justifies, or is construed to justify, many awful things in both countries; it creates "the enemy," by which is meant anybody who happened to be born within certain imaginary lines. It would lead to terrible things in our own population, some at least of which might be avoided.

Of course I know the legal and technical questions involved; I know that the Army gains status instanter upon the declaration of war; I know that the pro-Ally enthusiasts are anxious to have us actually fighting to our limit against Germany—to say nothing of those whose motives are less honest.

Nevertheless, when Congress meets next week I shall look for an utterance from you in line with what you have said before. I trust that never again in all time will the United States give utterance to that barbarism known as a declaration of war. It belongs in the category of the Apache's war-whoop and is not one whit more useful. Let us defend ourselves in such manner and by such means as may be necessary—nor would I have the defense half-hearted or ineffective—but let all the war-whooping be on the other side!

I consider that you have borne magnificently a burden under which most men would have broken long ago. Bear it yet a little while. If I can serve in any way, command me.

Sincerely,   John P. Gavit

Of course, in this I speak as an individual, representing nobody but myself.

TLS (WP, DLC).


## From the Diary of Colonel House

March 25, 1917.

Charles R. Crane and Mrs. Crane came to lunch. Sidney Brooks came just before lunch and S. R. Bertron just afterward. Crane goes to Russia on Tuesday and I wanted to talk over that situation with him, since he knows more about it than most. Bertron told of his recent interview with the President[1] and of his endeavor to get him to see the necessity for going into the war vigorously, if we went at all. He said he told him that people believed that he would not fight under any circumstances. He said the President flushed and declared it was not true.

[1] Bertron saw Wilson at the White House on March 23.


## To Edward Mandell House

The White House Mar 26th 1917

Will of course be delighted to see you Tuesday.

Woodrow Wilson.

T telegram (E. M. House Papers, CtY).


## To Harry Augustus Garfield

My dear Garfield:          The White House 26 March, 1917

I thank you sincerely for your letter of March seventeenth and the quotation from Mr. J. S. Torrance. You are always kind in sending me on these scraps of encouragement and enlightenment.

We think of you all very often and you may be sure with a great deal of affection.

In haste

Cordially and sincerely yours, Woodrow Wilson

TLS (H. A. Garfield Papers, DLC).

## To Anthony Caminetti

My dear Mr. Caminetti: [The White House] 26 March, 1917

May I not tell you and through you Mrs. Caminetti how deeply touched I have been by your[1] and her letters of last week? They are touched with a nobility and a sweetness of temper which I not only deeply admire but for which I am personally very grateful. I thank you both with all my heart.

Cordially and faithfully yours, Woodrow Wilson

TLS (Letterpress Books, WP, DLC).
[1] A. Caminetti to JPT, March 24, 1917, ALS (WP, DLC).

## To Annie Wilson Howe Cothran

My dear Annie: The White House 26 March, 1917

I wish I had time to write you a letter with my own hand, but I am sure you will understand. Your letter of appreciation about the Princeton indebtedness touched me very much. You may be sure that it was a pleasure to me to be able to do what I did.

I shall try to send a list of the securities at once to Mr. Wintersteen.

We are always so glad to hear of your success in making concert appointments and in satisfying your audiences. We missed you very much at inauguration time.

All join in warmest and most affectionate messages.

Affectionately yours, Woodrow Wilson

TLS (WP, DLC).

## From Newton Diehl Baker, with Enclosure

My dear Mr President: Washington. March 26, 1917

I enclose the answer from Colonel Ro[o]sevelt to my telegram about the Volunteer Division which he desired to form.[1]

May I, please, have it back?

Respectfully yours, Newton D. Baker

ALS (N. D. Baker Papers, DLC).

1 Theodore Roosevelt had sent a telegram to Baker on March 19 in which he requested permission to raise a volunteer division for immediate service at the front, "in view of the fact," as he put it, "that Germany is now actually engaged in war with us." Roosevelt proposed that, after six weeks of preliminary training in the United States, he should take the division to France for intensive training so that it could be sent to the front as soon as possible. He asked permission to assemble the division at Fort Sill, Oklahoma, and requested the War Department to furnish arms and supplies, as it had to the Plattsburg camps. Roosevelt would himself raise money to prepare the division until Congress had time to authorize a more permanent arrangement. The balance of his telegram outlined the composition of the division. He named specific officers of the regular army whom he wished to have as chief of staff and brigade commanders and added that he would later suggest the names of other regular army officers to hold the lesser commands of the division. TR to NDB, March 19, 1917, T telegram (N. D. Baker Papers, DLC).

Baker replied in the following telegram of March 20: "Your telegram March nineteenth received. No additional armies can be raised without the specific authority of Congress which by its act of February 27, 1906 has also prohibited any executive department or other government establishment of the United States to involve the government in any contract or other obligation for the future payment of moneys in excess of appropriations unless such contract or obligation is authorized by law. A plan for a very much larger army than the force suggested in your telegram has been prepared for the action of Congress whenever required. Militia officers of high rank will naturally be incorporated with their commands but the general officers for all volunteer forces are to be drawn from the regular army." NDB to TR, March 20, 1917, T telegram (T. Roosevelt Papers, DLC).

This exchange of telegrams is printed in Elting E. Morison *et al.*, eds., *The Letters of Theodore Roosevelt* (8 vols., Cambridge, Mass., 1951-54), VIII, 1164.

E N C L O S U R E

## Theodore Roosevelt to Newton Diehl Baker

Sir                  Sagamore Hill [Oyster Bay, N. Y.]. March 23d 1917

I have the honor to acknowledge the receipt of your telegram in answer to my telegram of the 19th, and will govern myself accordingly.

I understood, Sir, that there would be a far larger force than a division called out; I merely wished to be permitted to get ready a division for immediate use in the first expeditionary force sent over.

In reference to your concluding sentence I wish respectfully to point out that I am a retired Commander in Chief of the United States Army, and eligible to any position of command over American troops to which I may be appointed. As for my fitness for command of troops I respectfully refer you to my three immediate superiors in the field, Lieutenant General S. B. M. Young[1] (retired), Major General Samuel Sumner[2] (retired), and Major General Leonard Wood. In the Santiago Campaign I served in the first fight as commander first of the right wing and then of the left wing of the regiment; in the next, the big, fight as Colonel of the regiment; and I ended the campaign in command of the brigade.

The regiment, 1st United States Volunteer Cavalry, in which I first served as Lieutenant Colonel, and which I then commanded as Colonel, was raised, armed, equipped, drilled, mounted, dismounted, kept for two weeks on a transport, and then put through two victorious aggressive fights, in which we lost a third of the officers and a fifth of the enlisted men, all within a little over fifty days.

I have the honor to be,

Very respectfully yours    Theodore Roosevelt

ALS (N. D. Baker Papers, DLC).
1 Samuel Baldwin Marks Young.
2 Samuel Storrow Sumner.

## From Robert Lansing, with Enclosure

My dear Mr. President:          [Washington] March 26, 1917.

I would like to make a statement to the press, which would be in substance like the enclosed. There is much misapprehension on this subject and it seems to me the public should have [it] brought clearly to their attention.

I talked the matter over with Colonel House on Saturday and he thought such a statement would be very helpful.

Faithfully yours,    Robert Lansing

CCL (SDR, RG 59, 763.72/3593a, DNA).

ENCLOSURE

### PROPOSED STATEMENT TO THE PRESS

There seems to be a tendency in certain quarters, judging from newspaper reports, to show dissatisfaction with the President because he does not declare his position in regard to Germany or direct hostile acts against her. Some of these people criticize through ignorance and some in an effort to commit the Government before Congress meets next Monday.

Everyone who indulges in criticism of this character knows or ought to know that the power to declare war rests with Congress alone and that it would be highly improper for the President to say anything or do anything which infringes upon this constitutional power of Congress.

The course of silence which the President is following is the
only one consistent with his office. The American people ought
to understand that and not be influenced by radical partisans
who assert that President Wilson is undecided because he re-
fuses to declare his purpose or authorize an act of war against
Germany. They want him to usurp the powers of Congress and
are trying to force him to do so.

The people should not tolerate criticism of this sort.

T MS (SDR, RG 59, 763.72/3593a, DNA).


## From Robert Lansing

My dear Mr. President:            Washington March 26, 1917.

There is a policy which it seems to me should be determined
upon without delay as preliminary arrangements will have to be
made to carry it out. It is presented by the question, If a declaration of war against Germany or if a declaration of the existence
of a state of war is resolved by Congress what ought the Governments of Cuba and Panama to do?

It seems to me that we cannot permit Cuba to become a place
of refuge for enemy aliens. It would give them great facilities
for plots and intrigues not only against this country but against
the peace of Cuba. I have in mind the possibility of submarine
bases, the organization of reservists, the use of cables, etc., which
would be to my mind very serious and possibly disastrous. In
addition to this, if Cuba remained neutral, we could not use her
ports for our war vessels and that might result in a renewal of
the rebellious activities in the Island, which would be abetted by
the Germans there. To prevent this situation there seems to me
but one policy to adopt and that is to have the Cuban Government follow our action with similar action.

Both the Minister here[1] and Minister Desvernine[2] have stated
that they will do whatever we wish them to do. But we ought to
be prepared to tell them exactly what we want.

The Panama situation is not so easy to handle as the Government is less amenable. I feel, however, that it would be perilous
to permit Germans to be at liberty to go and come so near to the
Canal. It would be almost essential to have the Germans expelled
from the Republic. Furthermore, the laws of neutrality would
seriously embar[r]ass our people. These conditions could only be
avoided by Panama entering the war, if we become a party.

I think that I can influence the Panama Government to do

whatever we wish in the matter, but it will take a little time and requires preliminary work to accomplish it.

Please advise me at your earliest convenience as to your wishes, because delay may cause embar[r]assment and possibly a dangerous situation.

Faithfully yours,   Robert Lansing.

TLS (SDR, RG 59, 763.72/3759B, DNA).
[1] Carlos Manuel de Céspedes y Quesada.
[2] Pablo Desvernine y Galdos, Secretary of State of Cuba.


## From the Diary of Josephus Daniels

1917 Monday 26 March

4:30 p.m. President came when I was being interviewed by the press. Took a seat & did not know he was present. Said we must keep in close touch. Had letter from McAdoo opposing taking German ships & anchoring them in midstream.[1] Thought,[2] inasmuch as Germans had tried to destroy ships, they were now derelicts & ought to be taken in charge by Marines to prevent sinking and injury. Good to marry in the Navy—must be happy at least half of the time—for husband is away from home half the time

5 P.M. The President showed me letter from E.M.H. saying friend had informed him that Austrian had arrived on sub-marine—called upon Austrian consul who sent for Austrian Ambassador and gave him papers brought from Europe on sub-marine. He understood that the sub-marines had come over from Germany. I told Benson to send out All-Nav. wireless to be on the outlook.

[1] It is missing.
[2] That is, McAdoo "thought."


## From the Diary of Thomas W. Brahany

Monday, March 26, 1917

The President, Mrs. Wilson and Dr. Grayson played golf this morning. This afternoon the President, Mr. Vopicka[1] (our Minister to Roumania) and the Postmaster General. About 4 o'clock the President walked to the State, War and Navy Building and made a brief call on the Secretary of the Navy. On Saturday, the 24th, the President and Mrs. Wilson took a walk. On their return they went to the State, War and Navy Buildings. They called on the Secretary of War in whose office they stayed nearly an hour. Afterwards, they made a brief call at the office of the Secretary of the Navy. I think this is the first time in American history that a President's wife has accompanied the President in a purely business call on a Cabinet Officer.

The newspapermen are up in arms. The censorship regulations, made public on Saturday,[2] aim to curb the press effectually. There is general objection to Rule 6 which aims to prohibit discussion of administration policies regarding international affairs unless approved by the Secretary of State. The President is seeing no callers in his office, and nobody except the Cabinet seems to know what his plans are. All important papers from the Secretaries of State, War and Navy are marked "Personal and Confidential," and, by the President's direction, are not opened in the Executive Office. They are sent direct to the White House and opened by the President himself. Ordinarily Executive Orders, after approval by the President, are sent to the Department through the Executive Office so that a proper record of them may be kept. On Saturday the President signed an Executive Order to [increase the navy to] 87,000 strength—we knew nothing about this until we saw it in the newspapers; and the newspapers also gave us our first information regarding the increase of the military departments from four to six. The newspapermen complain bitterly. . . .

Mayes,[3] one of the colored men assigned to the main White House door, cut my hair on Saturday. He is an expert barber, and like most members of his "profession" likes to talk as he works. On Saturday he was even more loquacious than usual. "The President never lets me shave the back of his neck, no siree. All he wants is a fine clippers run up the back of his neck. And he always combs his own hair. The President certainly knows just what he wants. He tells you just what he wants, and he don't care for you to suggest anything else. He has his own ideas. Why do you know when he orders eggs, and he likes them right smart and sometimes asks for them when the table is filled with the finest food, he wants them boiled for thirty minutes, and he times them too, and insists on a full half hour. I don't see how he can eat anything like that." And so Mayes babbled along with his back-stairs gossip. "The President certainly does love his son-in-law, Mr. Sayre. He's sure glad to see him. But I think he's getting tired of Mr. McAdoo. Why a few weeks ago Mr. McAdoo bounded up stairs to the President's room and walked right in— My, but the President was mad. He didn't say anything cross to Mr. McAdoo, but he wasn't very cordial.["] It seems Mr. McAdoo wanted to see him to take up some matter of business. When he left the President said, "Damn it, he makes me tired. He's got too much nerve and presumes on the fact that he's my son-in-law to take up with me in my private apartment matters that a Cabinet Officer ought to take up in my office. I'm getting damn sick of it."

¹ That is, Charles Joseph Vopicka.
² At a conference held at the Navy Department on March 24, Baker, Daniels, Polk, Maj. Douglas MacArthur, U.S.A., Lt. Commander Charles Belknap, Jr., U.S.N., and Leland Harrison agreed with representatives of four press associations upon a set of "regulations relative to censorship." The newspapers of the country were requested to comply with these rules on a voluntary basis pending the enactment of censorship legislation by Congress. The first four "regulations" requested that various sorts of information of possible military value not be published. The fifth stated that "doubtful matter" should be submitted to the appropriate department for clearance. Regulation 6, which was submitted by Polk and which immediately drew sharp criticism from newspapermen not represented at the conference, read as follows: "It is requested that no information, reports, or rumors attributing a policy to the Government in any international situation, not authorized by the President or a member of the Cabinet, be published without first consulting the Department of State." The newspapermen not represented at the conference also strongly objected to not being consulted about the proposed regulations. For the full text of the regulations and a discussion of the conference, see the *New York Times*, March 25, 1917.
³ John Mays.

## Three Letters to Robert Lansing

My dear Mr. Secretary,        The White House. 27 March, 1917.

My own judgment is that any statement along these lines would be a mistake. It would show that criticism was getting under our skin, particularly under *my* skin, which is far from being the fact. It would not stop or soften the criticism.

At each stage of the development of our foreign relations since the war began this sort of criticism has been uttered and in each instance it has been answered, not by words, but by some action which has met with the approval of the major part of the country. The same thing will happen this time. After next week the whole scene and tone will be different.

I am none the less warmly obliged to you for wishing to come to my defense.        Faithfully Yours,   W.W.

WWTLI (RSB Coll., DLC).

My dear Mr. Secretary,        The White House. 27 March, 1917.

I entirely approve. In view of recent despatches from Denmark, would it be possible to complete the transfer before the Congress meets,—I mean, of course, so far as the payment of the

money is concerned and the formal transfer of title? I hope that
this can be arranged.                    Faithfully Yours,   W.W.

WWTLI (SDR, RG 59, 711.5914/219½, DNA).


My dear Mr. Secretary,          The White House. 27 March, 1917.

It is clear to me that the only thing we can prudently do is
to urge both Cuba and Panama to do just what we do.

In case Cuba follows our lead it will be necessary, I take it for
granted, to give her our military protection as fully as we give it
to Porto Rico and St. Thomas. I hope that you will get the
negotiations in course as soon as possible, but that you will first
confer with Baker and Daniels about the practical consequences
and our ability to handle them.

                              Faithfully Yours,   W.W.

WWTLI (SDR, RG 59, 763.72/3759¾, DNA).


## From Robert Lansing, with Enclosure

PERSONAL AND SECRET:

My dear Mr. President:            [Washington] March 27, 1917.

Count Tarnowski called at my house last evening by appointment and discussed his situation here. He asked for the appointment on account of having received a communication from
Count Czernin. After talking the matter over and sympathizing
with him in the embarrassment of his Government and also of
himself in the present situation, I requested him to give me a
transcript of Count Czernin's dispatch which he had read to me.
This he did and I enclose to you a copy. I told him that I would
lay the matter before you and would endeavor to give him an
answer today or tomorrow. Will you please advise me what I
should say to Count Tarnowski?

                         Faithfully yours,   Robert Lansing

CCL (R. Lansing Papers, NjP).

ENCLOSURE

## Count Adam Tarnowski von Tarnow to Robert Lansing

Washington,

My dear Mr. Secretary of State, March 26th 1917

You expressed the wish in the course of the conversation we just had that I should outline for your personal information the substance of my communications to make use of such a written pro-memoria when submitting the matter to the President tomorrow.

I had the honor of informing you of the following:

"Count Czernin has instructed me to draw in a most friendly spirit Your Excellency's attention to the fact that the long delay of my reception by the President renders his position extremely difficult, the public opinion in Austria-Hungary resenting it already, and if this feeling has not until now become evident it is only due to the censure of the press.

My Chief thinks to have shown his desire for the maintenance of the diplomatic relations between the Monarchy and the United States and he believes this desire to be shared by Your Excellency but he must ask not to be placed in a too difficult position.

Besides Mr. Penfield's situation is also growing very difficult as the public opinion begins to lose faith in his good will."

Having been instructed to deliver the above communication orally only, and having written this for Your Excellency's convenience, I need not ask you to consider my letter as strictly confidential.  Very sincerely yours  A Tarnowski

TLS (R. Lansing Papers, NjP).

## To Robert Lansing

My dear Mr. Secretary, The White House. 27 March, 1917.

This is certainly a most delicate and embarrassing situation, but I see only one thing we can do. There is no choice in the circumstances but to say to Count Tarnowski that the explicit acceptance and avowal by his Government of the policy which led to our breach of diplomatic relations with Germany (before the policy had been put into operation) makes it impossible, to our sincere regret, that I should receive him.

This announcement to him (I think it should not until absolutely necessary be made public) can of course be made in the most friendly spirit; and he can be told that we will relieve the embarrassment at Vienna by recalling Mr. Penfield so soon as he (Tarnowski) has heard from his Government and received its instructions.

All of this, I take it for granted, will be at once communicated to Mr. Penfield and he will be told to hold himself in readiness to receive instructions as to himself, pending Vienna's reply to Tarnowski.

In any case Penfield should express again to Count Czernin our deep regret that the Austro-Hungarian Government should have felt itself obliged to join Germany in its sub-marine policy and so interrupt relations which we had hoped might remain friendly in form as well as in fact. In short, he ought to make it plain to Count Czernin that we are acting without feeling in this matter, and merely on principle.

Faithfully Yours,   W.W.

WWTLI (SDR, RG 59, 701.6311/271, DNA).


## To Newton Diehl Baker

My dear Mr. Secretary,        The White House. 27 March, 1917.

This is one of the most extraordinary documents I ever read![1] Thank you for letting me undergo the discipline of temper involved in reading it in silence!

Faithfully Yours,   Woodrow Wilson

WWTLS (N. D. Baker Papers, DLC).
    [1] TR to NDB, March 23, 1917, printed as an Enclosure with NDB to WW, March 26, 1917.


## From Key Pittman

My dear Mr. President:        Washington, D. C. March 27, 1917.

I know that you will understand my purpose in writing this letter and not do me the injustice to imagine even for a moment that I assume to offer my poor opinions in the nature of suggestions.

As a member of the Foreign Relations Committee of the Senate, I am about to be called upon to participate in the initiation of the most momentous events and in the primary determination of policies that must forever affect the existence of our government.

May I say in beginning that my admiration for your judgment, statesmanship and patriotism is beyond expression, and my loyalty to you and the policies you have inaugurated and sustained is, I believe, unquestioned, yet in this most grave situation which now confronts us, while I will endeavor to be guided by the same statesmanship, I realize that in the end I must act in accordance with the dictates of my own judgment and conscience.

Permit me to say that I am happy that I have always found myself in perfect accord with your European policy, and I have no reason to doubt that I will find it just as easy and agreeable to support your future plans and policies without deviation and with the same enthusiasm.

Germany is now carrying on war against our people and our country will soon be at war with Germany. I favored keeping out of war as long as possible, and I now favor terminating it as soon as possible. I believed in the utmost patience, I now believe in the utmost energy. If it is decreed that we must lose thousands of our loved ones and expend billions of dollars in defense of democracy and the lives and the freedom of our people, I would rather that it be done with all humane speed than that it be continued through long years of drawn-out misery.

There is no doubt that preparation for war has frequently prevented war, and at this time, in my opinion, a fearful and astounding preparation may convince our enemies of our power and determination and of the futility of continuing the fight. I believe that a weak demonstration and an attitude of hesitancy at this time would be fatal to our prestige and disasterous to our hopes for an early peace. If the government may be compelled to spend several billions of dollars before the war is over, then let the full amount of such authorization be made at once. Let there be no doubt from the start that the government will be supported with all of the vast resources of the richest country in the world.

I am opposed to giving money to France. I would favor a loan to her without security and without interest. I believe that such course is more in keeping with the dignity of two great nations. I trust that in committee I may have the opportunity to vote for a resolution presented by a member of our party embodying such plans, but I deem it my duty to tell you that I feel inclined to vote for such plans no matter by whom presented or whether in committee or upon the floor of the Senate.

Very sincerely yours, Key Pittman.

TLS (WP, DLC).

## From Charles William Eliot

Dear Mr. President:          Cambridge, Mass., 27 March 1917.

I did not mention in my letter to you of March 22nd[1] some considerations in favor of the Swiss system of universal military training which are highly significant for us. The Swiss Federal Government inspects all Swiss schools to make sure that adequate physical training is received by all pupils. This training is of course just as good in the industries and homes of the country as it is in military service. That is an intervention of the national government in State and municipal affairs which would be very advantageous among us; and the same may be said about instruction in personal and community hygiene, diet, and cooking. These are national interests; because they concern the health and vigor of the entire population. The Swiss Government also fosters rifle-shooting by aiding in regard to the cost of rifles and ammunition,—the cantons providing the needed ranges. This rifle shooting is, however, voluntary; yet nearly all Swiss boys join the rifle clubs, and these clubs have made shooting at a mark a popular sport, stimulated by competitions and fêtes. As a result, the Swiss are the best marksmen in Europe, as has been abundantly proved by their success in the international competitions which before the War took place every year. Now shooting at a mark is first-rate training for both eye and hand, and indeed for the whole body, since the boys learn to shoot in a variety of positions. This training also is just as valuable in the national industries as it is for soldiers; for it is the accurate use of an instrument of precision.

The Swiss legislation is adapted to American use in another way. It will not interfere at all with the education of any boy up to his twentieth year, and after that age it withdraws the young man from his studies or his industrial work only for a period similar to that of the ordinary long vacation in schools and colleges. In the enlisted man's later years, the "repetition course" will not withdraw him from his ordinary occupations more than the fortnight which is allowed as vacation in most industries or employments.

Considered as an educational measure of permanent value, the Swiss law has the advantage that it proceeds not on a discipline of abject obedience but on a discipline which preserves and cultivates the individual's will-power and his personal initiative. The present War has proved that the free-spirited soldier is superior for military uses to one who has been taught that implicit obedience is everything and his own initiative nothing.

Looking to the future, the General Staff Bill or the Chamberlain Bill[2] would provide a kind of army that no democracy ought to maintain, whereas the Swiss legislation would provide a proper democratic army, and also make a permanent contribution to the morale and general efficiency of the country. I am speaking as one educator to another. I hope very much that Secretary Baker will support neither the General Staff Bill nor the Chamberlain Bill; but will use the whole influence of the Government in favor of the Swiss legislation.

Will it be possible for you in your address to the incoming Congress to recognize the fact that the War has proved to be the effective means of advancing democracy in Europe, and is therefore enlisting more and more American 'sympathy and support? The revolution in Russia gives a natural occasion for such an expression on the part of the Government of the United States; but the remark will apply in all the European countries. Would it be possible, too, to recognize our indebtedness to the British fleets for keeping the ocean open to our trade, and, in case of war, for shutting up the German fleet with the exception of submarines? Could you express also the natural sympathy of this country for France, a sympathy which I see is finding rather frequent expression in these latter days? I find the revolution in Russia far the best outcome of the War to date, so far as the future welfare of mankind is concerned; and I have no doubt you do too. It also promises to make the alliance of the United States with the Entente Powers thoroughly congenial and therefore probably abiding.

In New York and New England, there is at this moment much indignation over the transfer of General Wood. People do not know that General Wood is a crippled man. They do not know that a very severe operation on his brain a few years ago, though it prolonged his life and relieved him of some distressing symptoms, did not restore either his bodily or his mental capacity.[3] Is it impossible or inexpedient to publish this sound reason for removing him from a very laborious and responsible position to an easier one? Could it not be done in very considerate terms? Dr. Wood was a graduate of the Harvard Medical School; and I have always been interested in his career, and have a great regard for him; so that I have been very sorry that since his serious sickness he has sometimes shown a lack of the sound judgment which used to characterize him. He has many warm friends and admirers who know nothing about the disabilities under which he has been recently laboring, and therefore attribute his transfer to some unworthy motive in the War Department.

How unfortunate it is that for temporary uses we are obliged to recruit the regular army and the National Guard to their respective maxima! They are both obsolete types.

I am, with great regard,

Sincerely yours    Charles W. Eliot

TLS (WP, DLC).

¹ C. W. Eliot to WW, March 22, 1917, TLS (WP, DLC).

² For the Chamberlain bill, see n. 1 to remarks at a press conference printed at Dec. 18, 1916, Vol. 40. General Hugh L. Scott, on December 12, 1916, had ordered the War College to prepare another plan for universal military training, which Baker presented to Congress on February 23, 1917. It provided for eleven months of training for all able-bodied men nineteen years of age, to be followed by two weeks of training in each of the following two years. The men would then serve in a "first reserve" organization (one which would be fully equipped for rapid mobilization) for four years and one month and in a "second reserve" for seven years. This plan anticipated the training of 500,000 men a year, until ultimately there would be an effective reserve force of 3,000,-000 men. The Sixty-fourth Congress took no action on the proposal before its final adjournment on March 4. See *Universal Military Training*, 65th Cong., 1st sess., Senate Doc. No. 10 (Washington, 1917).

³ Dr. Harvey Williams Cushing had operated on Wood in Baltimore on February 5 and 9, 1910, and had removed a large intracranial tumor during the second operation. In view of Eliot's comment, it should be noted that Cushing, a close friend of Wood, believed that his patient had achieved a remarkably rapid and complete recovery from the operation and had led a perfectly normal and vigorous life, with no signs of recurrence of the disease until 1921. Wood died in 1927 after a third operation. See John F. Fulton, *Harvey Cushing: A Biography* (Springfield, Ill., 1946), pp. 308-12.

## From the Diary of Colonel House

The White House, Washington. March 27, 1917.

I took the 11.08 for Washington. I had a quiet and restful trip. Frank Polk met me at the station and took me to the White House. The President was waiting for me. He had just finished with the Cabinet meeting which he now holds in the afternoon. He was not well and complained of a headache. We went to his study and discussed pending matters particularly his forthcoming message.

The President asked whether I thought he should ask Congress to declare war or whether he should say that a state of war exists, and ask them for the necessary means to carry it on. I advised the latter. I was afraid of an acrimonious debate if he put it up to Congress to declare war. I told him a crisis had come in his administration different from anything he had yet encountered, and I was anxious that he should meet it in a creditable way so that his influence would not be lessened when he came to do the great work which would necessarily follow the war. I said it was not as difficult a situation as many he had already successfully met, but it was one for which he was not well fitted. He admitted this and said he did not believe he was fitted for the Presidency under such conditions. I thought he was too refined, too civilized, too intellectual, too cultivated not to see the incongruity and absurdity of war. It needed a man of courser fiber and one less a philosopher than the President to conduct a brutal, vigorous and successful war. I made him feel, as Mrs. Wilson told me later, that he was not up against so difficult a proposition as he had imagined. In my argument I said that everything he had to meet in this emergency had been thought out time and time and again in other countries, and all we had to do was to take experience as our guide and not worry over the manner of doing it.

I thought it not so difficult as taking a more or less ignorant, disorganized party in Congress and forcing it to pass the Federal Reserve Act, the Tariff Act, the Panama Tolls Act, and such other legislation as he had gotten through. I thought, however, he ought to change Daniels and Baker; that they were good men in peace time but did not fit in with war. That even if they were fit, the country did not believe them to be, and the mistakes that were sure to be made would be laid upon his shoulders because of them. I felt that he had taken a gamble that there would be no war and had lost, and the country would hold it to his discredit unless he prosecuted the war successfully, and he could not do this unless he had better timber than was generally thought to be in the War and Navy Departments. If he did not get rid of Daniels and Baker, then I thought it was imperative that he make changes in the heads of bureaux. He listened with a kindly and sympathetic attention and while he argued with me upon many of the points, he did it dispassionately.

The President, Mrs. Wilson and I dined alone and he and I went to the theater. I could not fail to observe how easy it would be to assassinate him should anyone desire to do so and was willing to sacrifice his own life.

It was a vaudeville performance and a part of it consisted of the film "Patria."[1] I asked the President if it could not be suppressed because it incited ill feeling between this country and Japan, to say nothing of Mexico. He said nothing could be done, although he had thought of writing a letter to the management protesting that it should not be shown in Washington, and having the letter published. I remarked that it was a wonder that mankind got along as it did when there were so many selfish and mischievous people abroad. The President thought that there was more ballast, as he termed it, in the people generally than we gave them credit for, which kept the fools from doing the harm they intended. We returned to the White House and immediately went to bed.

¹ A serial motion picture produced by the International Film Co., an organization controlled by William Randolph Hearst, and first shown in the United States in January 1917. It depicted an invasion of the United States by Japanese and Mexican troops and featured scenes of destruction, pillage, rape, and murder. Wilson later did write a letter to a film distribution executive in which he said that the movie was "extremely unfair to the Japanese" and would stir up much anti-Japanese hostility at a critical time and therefore asked that the showing of the film cease. See WW to J. A. Berst, June 4, 1917, and the other correspondence in regard to *Patria* printed subsequently.


# From the Diary of Josephus Daniels

March Tuesday 27 1917

Cabinet—McAdoo wished German men on interned merchant ships taken off, believing when declaration of state of war was made they would blow them up & might injure docks & do great injury. Thought their action in Charleston & elsewhere¹ justified taking this action. Lansing doubted the authority. Gregory thought the danger was magnified & thought no legal right now to take ships belonging to private citizens. McAdoo thought they were controlled by government of G— Gregory laughingly said "McAdoo wants those ships" I said we criticized Roosevelt for saying we ought to seize those ships. McAdoo said conditions had changed. The President firmly declared we would run any risk—we must be good sports & take our chances, & do nothing questionable & nothing that looking like profit for ourselves.

I brought up proposition for Navy to buy all wireless stations & make wireless a government monopoly.

Burleson: I serve notice that when peace comes it must be under PO Department

President: Is that a threat or a prophecy

Daniels: It is a bluff or a boast.

Resolved to ask Congress for that authority

Redfield: "I think of getting off Council of Natl Defense Talk & talk & do nothing

Baker to Lansing: The talk of Germans going to Mexico is exaggerated

¹ A 2,850-ton German freighter, *Liebenfels*, settled to the bottom in about thirty feet of water near the United States Navy Yard in Charleston on February 1. On March 9, eight officers and crewmen of the vessel were convicted in federal court of having deliberately scuttled the vessel in a navigable stream. *New York Times*, Feb. 2 and March 10 and 11, 1917. Many similar incidents were reported—some later verified, some not—all the way from Boston to Manila in February and March 1917. See *ibid.*, Feb.-March, 1917, *passim*.

## To Key Pittman

My dear Senator,         The White House. 28 March, 1917.

Thank you most sincerely for your frank letter of yesterday. You may be sure that my leadership will be very definite and I hope and believe that it will satisfy you. I should be very sorry if it did not, for I have the warmest personal feeling for you and place the highest value on your generous support.

Cordially and faithfully Yours,   Woodrow Wilson
This letter is hot off my own typewriter   W.W.

WWTLS (K. Pittman Papers, DLC).

## From William Gibbs McAdoo

Dear Mr. President:         [Washington] March 28, 1917.

I am arranging, at the request of the Secretary of State, to pay to the Danish Government $25,000,000 on Saturday, next, the 31st instant, for the Danish West Indian Islands. I understand that you have determined to put the administration of these Islands under the Navy Department. As the Islands are to be transferred on Saturday, next, it is, of course, important that some one be put in charge of the customs administration on that date. The time is so short that it occurred to me that the best plan would be to send the Collector of Customs at San Juan, Porto Rico, temporarily to St. Thomas and have him organize the customs service. I have taken the liberty, therefore, of discussing the matter with the Secretary of the Navy, and I am preparing the necessary Executive Orders to effectuate this plan, if it meets with your approval.

Cordially yours,   W G McAdoo

TLS (Letterpress Books, W. G. McAdoo Papers, DLC).

## To William Gibbs McAdoo

My dear Mac.,         The White House. 28 March, 1917.

This does not seem to me the wise way to handle this. The people of the islands have a particular aversion from being associated in any way with the administration of Porto Rico, and they would not understand.

It does not seem to me that a little delay in handling this particular matter would hurt, and I request that you wait until you can send down a man from here who can be very fully acquainted with that [what] we want done and with the way in which we wish it done. It is my desire and purpose to disturb the conduct of the public buisiness [business] of the islands as little as possible for the present, leave it in the same hands it has been in, and subject it only to our oversight. I am afraid of your idea that we are to send someone down there to "organize the customs service." We must go very slowly in this as in all things else down there until the people get accustomed to us and learn our real spirit.

In haste,                                    Faithfully,   W.W.

WWTLI (W. G. McAdoo Papers, DLC).


## From Newton Diehl Baker

Dear Mr. President:                Washington. March 28, 1917

I am disposed to direct telegrams sent to the commanders of the several departments in accordance with the within copy. The commanders to whom it would be sent are Wood, Bell, Barry[1] and Pershing. Do you deem it wise to soften this instruction in any respect, as, for instance, by directing cooperation with the civil authorities? My own notion is that prompt and decisive action in the first cases occurring, by the Federal military authorities without waiting for any sort of police or legal process will prove a powerful deterrent, while uncertainty of action and confusion of counsel will be bad both for the country and for those who are disposed to make trouble.

Respectfully yours,   Newton D. Baker

TLS (N. D. Baker Papers, DLC).
[1] Maj. Gen. Thomas Henry Barry.


## To Newton Diehl Baker, with Enclosure

My dear Mr. Secretary,        The White House. 28 March, 1917.

I approve this, but suggest that it is important to add that of course it is taken for granted that the several Department commanders will issue such instructions as will safeguard as far as possible the danger of too easily mistaking ordinary offences against the law and against public order, such as the usual police authorities would deal with, for acts committed under the provocation of the present excitement and with seditious or disloyal object.        Faithfully Yours,   Woodrow Wilson

WWTLS (N. D. Baker Papers, DLC).

Washington.
MEMORANDUM for the Chief of Staff:        March 28, 1917.

Please send a telegram in the following form to each of the Department Commanders:

It is thought that individual acts of disloyalty and violence may occur throughout the country in the present situation. The Secretary of War directs that you be instructed that all such overt acts of violence are to be sternly repressed and dealt with. At once upon the occurrence of any such incidents a prompt and vigorous assertion of the Federal power should be made. Evidences of the intention of the government so to act will both prevent a spread of trouble and discourage similar incidents. You will, of course, issue such proper instructions as will safeguard as far as possible the danger of mistaking ordinary offenses against the law for acts committed with seditious or disloyal intent. The former class should be left to the civil authorities.[1]

Baker

T MS (WDR, RG 94, AGO Document File, No. 2560557, DNA).
[1] Baker added the last two sentences to the memorandum after reading Wilson's letter.

## From Harry Augustus Garfield

Dear Mr. President:        [Williamstown, Mass.] March 28, 1917

I earnestly hope that you will be able to stem the tide that presses upon you from this section of our country and maintain, without declaration of war, our status of armed neutrality. New York has gone mad. Most of its influential citizens see red. They entirely fail to appreciate that our traditional sea policy dictates that, as far as possible, we limit hostilities to the sea and to such preparation on sea and land as shall safeguard us from attack. I hope Congress will empower you to take such action as you may deem necessary in the event of a declaration of war against the United States or of actual invasion of our territory or imminent danger of such an invasion. I believe our people will provide all the defence necessary without resort to compulsory military service; at any rate, volunteer service should be tried out. We are ready to vote millions for defence, but not one dollar for aggression, or what our militaristic friends are pleased to call the aggressive-defensive. Incidentally, the present policy of placing the burden of war expenditures upon war profits is sound and should be made a part of our permanent programme.

With great regard and most loyal devotion to you in this try-ing hour, I remain, as always,

Faithfully yours,   [H. A. Garfield]

I tried to make this brief, & fear I have only made it brusque, but I hope it is helpful.

CCL (H. A. Garfield Papers, DLC).

## From Joseph Irwin France[1]

Personally Type-written Memorandum Submitted
in Place of Personal Interview. Confidential.

by Joseph Irwin France. Maryland.

Mr President:                Washington, D. C. March 28, 1917:

I venture to trespass upon your very precious time because it seems to me to be my duty to do so.

I wish to say that I am in sympathy with the motives which have animated you in the formulation of your foreign policy, which policy now seems to me to have been both consistent and constructive.

Your message delivered to the Senate on January 22nd, 1917, I consider to be one of the greatest of American State Papers. I endorse its ideals and purposes and I should be gratified if I could feel that I am to have, in the future, some small part, in co-operation with you, in applying the great principles, therein enunciated, to the solution of the practical and pressing prob-lems of international relationships.

I trust that now we may avoid, in the present emergency, doing anything which might be inconsistent with your past foreign policies and with those ideals and purposes expressed in that message, and particularly, that we may now and "hence-forth avoid entangling alliances which would draw (us) into competitions of power, catch (us) in a net of intrigue and selfish rivalry." May we at this time have enough vision to enable us to perform the service of which you therein speak and use our great power "to lay afresh and upon a new plan the foundations of peace." We should, I believe, add our power and authority to that of other neutral nations "to guarantee peace and justice through out the world."

We seem to be upon the brink of war but I do feel that the next step should not be war but the establishment of a state of armed neutrality which shall at once place back of our words all of our resources, military, naval, commercial and moral, in which armed neutrality we might associate with ourselves other neutral powers.

I feel a deep conviction that such an armed neutrality might, under your leadership, become more than a mere conservative and preservative, a mere negative neutrality to defend our legal rights. Owing to past invasions of our rights we have acquired new and larger rights, particularly the right to demand such restitution as may meet our desires and purposes and it remains for us to determine what form that restitution shall take. I personally feel that we have a right to demand as, restitution the im[m]ediate and full restoration of all of our rights, which can only be accomplished by an immediate peace, since all war curtails the rights of neutrals.

Such a neutrality as I have in mind would be aggres[s]ive and constructive, dedicated to the principles which you have enunciated. It would, with of all of our physical and moral resources, place our Republic in the position of world leadership and enable us to "show mankind the way to liberty." Such a course demands a higher courage on the part of our nation than would be required for a declaration of war.

Should such an armed neutrality fail to accomplish its purpose or prove, after a trial, not to meet the requirements, we still have the last recourse of war for which, by lapse of time, devoted to complete preparation, we would become more nearly prepared. Such a bold course would unite and inspire our people. Our American people are idealists still, in spite of all that has been said to the contrary, and if they are not now resolved upon war, and I believe that they are not, it is because they do not feel that American ideals and truly American principles are at stake. They attribute materialistic motives to those who have been so loudly clamoring for war.

I respectfully submit this to you feeling confident that you will overlook the seeming impropriety of my doing so, an impropriety which, I assure you, would not have been committed but for my confidence in you. I know that you will understand my motives and that you will believe that no other motive animates me than that of a desire to serve and help save this, the only Democracy in the world, this Republic for which you have suffered and which you have served so well.

Most respectfully yours,　Joseph Irwin France

TLS (WP, DLC).
1 Republican senator from Maryland.

## From Matthew Hale

Dear Mr. President:                    Boston March 28, 1917.

Thank you very much for your letter of March 22nd in regard to the Progressive National Convention.[1] Of course I thoroughly understand your position.

Will you forgive me if I bother you with a few of my ideas on the international situation? I fully realize how overwhelmed you probably are with letters from people who think they know exactly how to run the country. My only excuse for writing is that New England is, of course, the hotbed of a strong pro-Ally and militaristic group which is making so much noise at the present time that one might well think that it represented the whole of New England sentiment. Therefore I feel that it might interest you to know that some of us are looking at the matter from a different point of view. In any case a scrap basket can always come to your rescue!

In determining what immediate steps we are to take we must continually bear in mind what our ultimate international goal is, and we must be sure that whatever steps we take now will lead us toward, and not away, from that goal. I feel that your recent peace note and your second Inaugural represent what the great majority of the people of the United States want: the ending of the present war; the establishment of a league to enforce peace; the freedom of the seas; the international reduction of armament; and the protection of the rights of small nations.

From the somewhat chaotic mass of opinions which the newspapers and orators are giving to the public there seem to arise three quite definite plans for immediate action. I am not including in these the pacifists who wish us to relinquish all our rights and simply accept what other countries hand out to us. I do not consider that that point of view is really seriously maintained by any large element of our country.

The first plan for immediate action is the one that we hear of most in this neighborhood. It is that we should definitely throw in our lot with the Allies against the Central Powers. The underlying motive for this is, of course, a desire to have the Allies win and a feeling that our cause is the same as theirs. The people that are advocating this course have been advocating it since the war began. They are now using the latest German outrages against us as an additional argument to force us onto the side of the Allies.

Does this plan lead us toward our goal? It does not. In the

first place, as you have pointed out in many of your public statements, it will make us definitely a partisan in this war and will,
it seems to me, lessen our influence in obtaining a fair settlement and still more in obtaining a league to enforce peace, which
shall include all nations. Secondly, it will create a situation in
the world similar to what has been a source of so much trouble
in Europe,—two groups of allied nations or a world "balance of
power." It will also interfere with the real freedom of the seas,
unless by "freedom" we mean only freedom to ourselves. Finally,
the great mass of the American people are not definitely pro-
Ally and do not feel that the cause of the Allies is our cause
and would not be whole-heartedly behind you in an attempt to
join the Allies. Therefore, it seems to me that this course should
not be pursued in spite of the tremendous clamor that is being
made in favor of it and the tremendous pressure that must now
be exerted upon you to make us adopt this course.

The second definite plan for immediate action is that we
should declare war upon Germany, or (which is practically the
same), declare that a state of war does now exist between us
and Germany, on account of her outrageous acts toward us.
Those who are advocating the first plan are, of course, also back
of this. In addition to them are many people who have what I
consider the old fashioned idea of only being able to wipe out an
insult by the blood of their opponent.

Does this help us reach our ultimate goal? I think not. In
the first place the underlying motive on which it rests is that
of vengeance, and if we go to war acting on such a motive we
have done nothing to advance world ethics; and unless in this
crisis we are able to make the stand of the United States something which will advance world ethics we shall certainly not be
moving toward our ultimate international goal. It is not necessary in order definitely to assert our own rights either as individuals or as a nation to go to war. If a man should tell me that I
have no right to go to my office I should immediately go to my
office and should use such force as might be necessary in order
to get to my office; but it would not be my duty to go into his
house and smash him up generally in order to avenge any injury
that he may have done me. I realize that there are many people
in the country who have an entirely different idea of what our
national honor or our personal honor requires. I think that the
average American citizen feels the way I do on this point. He
feels so partly because he thinks it is the higher ethical standard; and in order to live up to that standard he thinks that the
country should be willing to spend "millions for defence but not

one cent for vengeance." Another reason that makes him feel
this way is a sympathetic understanding of Germany's position.
He feels that we cannot tolerate Germany's actions toward us
and must take active measures to prevent them; yet he can understand why Germany feels bitterly toward us. He understands
that the Germans feel that we are helping the Allies more than
we are helping them; that we have submitted to many of England's arbitrary demands without making a similar resistance;
that we have been shipping ammunition to the Allies; that our
public opinion in so far as it has been expressed in this country
has been more on the side of the Allies than on the side of Germany; and that on the whole our neutrality has been "benev-
olent" toward the Allies. He also understands that the Germans
are in a life and death struggle and that it is natural, though not
justifiable, that they should take violent measures if they think
that by so doing they can save the life of their own country.

He does not in any way, shape or manner justify Germany's
acts, but he does understand the feeling which may have
prompted her to commit them. Therefore I feel that the American people are not now ready to declare war on Germany.

The third plan that has been made is that we should take any
and all steps necessary to maintain our rights upon the seas; in
other words, that we should, if necessary, use our entire naval
force to protect American ships against the German attacks. We
should do this by arming the ships as we have already done and
by the use of just exactly as much force as may be necessary.
For this course I am sure that practically the whole American
people are ready. Of course we all realize that if we do this
and protect our vessels by force, either by arming them or by
the use of our navy, Germany may declare war upon us. If she
does you will then certainly be in a better position so far as our
own people are concerned and you will have back of you a united
nation. It seems to me, therefore, that this third plan is the one
which should be followed and that the other two plans should
not be followed. Of course in the protection of our ships on the
ocean it will probably be necessary and advisable to coöperate
with the navies of the other countries. This would in no way
change the fundamental principle on which you are appealing
to the America people,—namely, that you are simply protecting
our rights on the sea.

Naturally the work of preparedness should go on vigorously
even if you adopt the third plan. We will very likely be driven
into a war with Germany through Germany's declaring war on
us.

This third plan, coupled with a strong appeal for preparedness, would be much more consistent with all your action up
to now in the European war and with your action in regard to
Mexico, than either of the first two plans; it would also establish a much higher code of morals in international affairs; it
would be just as effective in protecting our rights; and finally,
it would be the one course on which practically the entire people
of the United States would get behind you.

Please excuse my setting forth my views in this way. Of course
I realize that you have all the facts and that I have few; that
you have thought about the whole situation far more than I
have; and that you naturally do not need any advice from me.
I have been hesitating for some time in regard to writing you
and I finally decided to do so, because I know that you value suggestions from people, and because I realize that the people who
are clamoring to put us into immediate war are much more
noisy than the rest of us!

Very sincerely yours,   Matthew Hale

TLS (WP, DLC).
  ¹ WW to M. Hale, March 22, 1917, TLS (Letterpress Books, WP, DLC). Wilson
declined an invitation from Hale to attend a convention of the Progressive
party to be held in St. Louis on April 12 on the ground that the crisis in
foreign affairs required his constant presence in Washington.


# From Charles Richard Crane

Dear Mr President                    [New York] March 28 1917

Before going away¹ I want to tell you how content I am that so
much of the world's welfare is in your hands. I was happy to
see you so well and so serene.² The example of the White House
is an immense steadying power that can be felt all over the country.

It now looks as though your hope for a ["]League to Enforce
Peace" was coming into being quite naturally by the rapid extension of democratic governments. With Russia and China
directed by their peoples we shall not have to concern ourselves
so much about the military autocracies of Germany and Japan.
I feel that there is going to be a great and rapid diminution
of these twin menaces. We ought to do everything in our power
to develop and to establish on firm foundations these two peoples
and hold strongly to the principle of direct relations with them.

I do not know about the men at present in control of the
political destinies of China but I do know that the men in the
provisional government of Russia are the best group running
any one of the great powers.

With China we must keep entirely clear of anything that gives Japan the slightest leverage for a claim to suzerainty. The silent and invisible power of Chinese sympathy and solidarity is now with us and it is the greatest force in that country. The Japanese are learning to dread it as expressed in the "boycott."

Affectionate greetings to you and Mrs Wilson and "Good Bye"

Always devotedly   Charles R. Crane

ALS (WP, DLC).
  [1] He was about to leave for Russia.
  [2] The Cranes had lunch with the Wilsons at the White House on March 23 at 12:15; Wilson's next appointment was at 2:15.


## From Walter Hines Page, with Enclosure

Dear Mr. President:                    London. 28 March 1917

I'm in doubt whether I ought to trouble you with a letter, th[r]o' the pouch, from an unofficial person. But for once at least I give this unofficial person the benefit of the doubt, taking the liberty to remark

that she is a lady of more energy than any other one alive; is full of good works; begs (and gets) more money for good purposes than anybody else, somehow makes everybody serve her;

but (to write with self-restraint) she is simply a hopeless liar; she gets everybody into trouble; she "pushes in"; to account for her existence requires a new cosmogony; the better 2/3ds of London has nothing to do with her; and much of the other 1/3 is—in some way or other—at her able command. In a word, she's a dangerous wonder.

Yours sincerely,   Walter H. Page

P.S. I've tried to belong to the 2/3d, but every now and then I wake up to find that I really am, for the time being, in the 1/3d!

ALS (WP, DLC).


## ENCLOSURE

## From Lady Mary Fiske Stevens Paget

Dear Mr. President                    [London] March 20th, 1917

Your letter gave me such very great pleasure,[1] it was so kind of you to spare a moment from your busy life & I must thank you for your nice remembrance.

Please let me express my admiration for the firm unswerving path you have taken—you have always been so right—so just—

your diplomacy is beyond praise & the confidence of all right-thinking Americans is yours.

If America comes in as seems probable, Germany will, I hope, have reason to regret her scorn of our capabilities. She little knows the force of our great country when roused which if "slow to anger" is certainly "of great wrath."

All my thoughts were with you at the time of your election, & my sincere congratulations. I felt that America's interests & honour were safe in your hands & all would be well.

I wish you from the bottom of my heart every success in your new term of office & trust that long ere its conclusion the silver lining of this cruel war cloud may shed its peaceful & softening rays on our overshadowed lives.

Believe me,

Yours always most sincerely   Mary Paget

P.S. Your charming photograph is always before me as it stands on a table in my room, & is a symbol to me of the justice & honour of the leader of my homeland.

ALS (WP, DLC).
¹ WW to Mary F. S. Paget, Jan. 3, 1917, TLS (Letterpress Books, WP, DLC). In response to a telegram (missing) from Lady Mary, Wilson sent New Year's greetings and added the following comment: "I wish with all my heart that I saw how I could be more serviceable than I have been. My heart aches that no way can be found out of the present wilderness of war, but I am sure that you and all like you are striving constantly for the best things."

## From Waldo Lincoln Cook

Springfield, Mass.
My dear Mr. President:                    March 28, 1917.

In acknowledging your very kind and appreciative note of March 22d, I must say at once that the note has given me the greatest possible pleasure. I prize this word from you all the more, because, after the political experiences and conflicts of the past few years, I am conscious of a very real yet peculiar feeling of having summered and wintered with you, in spite of the immeasurable and rather awful distance that separates our respective places in the life and work of our time. Your note, for the moment, suddenly annihilates the distance and brings to me what I recognize as a very human touch.

There is summering and wintering to come,—with more wintering perhaps than we shall enjoy; even so, I shall hope to be of timely service, as opportunity favors me.

I have the honor to be your admirer and friend,

Most sincerely,   Waldo L. Cook.

TLS (WP, DLC).

## From the Diary of Josephus Daniels

1917 Wednesday 28 March

Telegram from Page in London enclosing recommendation from McDougall[1] advising converting ship with armed guard into naval auxiliary—it would then become a naval vessel & its officers & crews if captured would have the honors of war. Otherwise if taken, might be killed—treated as pirates by G— Sent over by Lansing. I went over to see the President who said we had a right to put armed guards on ships & the piracy talk[2] was absurd & if such spirit prevailed the change in character in ship would not avert it. Such change would prevent merchant ships carrying trade & prohibit contraband. Lansing said suggestion was absurd. Pres said Page meddles in things outside his domain. I do not mind this if he gave us his own opinion but he is giving him English opinion

Conf. with Lansing & Baker. President wished us to confer as to protection if Cuba & Panama followed our lead as to Germany. Baker in Panama—Navy in Cuba—could send marines to Cuba. Baker would furnish transport & have soldiers at Galveston to send to Tampico if necessary

6 p.m. Went to Annapolis to present diplomas to graduates. Asked the President to go—said he wished to do so but did not like to go without saying something, and this was not a time to speak. "I would like to talk to the youngsters and incite them to splendid service, but now anything I might say would be subject to being interpreted in a wrong way & I wish to say nothing until I give my message to Congress."

He could not speak unless he said something; therefore I could go as I could speak without saying anything

[1] Capt. William Dugald MacDougall, U.S.N., naval attaché in London.

[2] The German government had threatened to treat the armed guards and crews of armed neutral merchantmen, if captured by German naval forces, as pirates. See J. W. Gerard to RL, Jan. 21, 1917, printed as an Enclosure with RL to WW, Jan. 23, 1917 (first letter of that date), Vol. 40.

## From the Diary of Colonel House

March 28, 1917.

The President, Mrs. Wilson, Dr. Grayson and I lunched together. Grayson left immediately after lunch and we went into executive session. I suggested to the President that he have what I termed, "an executive secretary" in addition to Tumulty. The executive secretary I thought could be used as an aid to inter-departmental communication, and I suggested Vance McCormick for the place. I thought he might be called a "Cabinet officer without portfolio," so as to gild the position somewhat.

The President thought it would create jealousy; that the Secretaries would not like communicating through a second party. He spoke of my having given my services in an unselfish and unofficial way, taking no honors, and yet he said there was a certain note of jealousy he caught every now and then. This did not convince me that my plan was not a good one, but I did not push it further. I am intolerant of petty jealousy and if I were President I would eliminate it or the one guilty of it.

I was surprised to hear him say that Lansing was the most unsatisfactory Secretary in his Cabinet; that he was good for a second place but unfitted for the first. That he had no imagination, no constructive ability, and but little real ability of any kind. He was constantly afraid of him because he often undertook to launch policies himself which he, the President, had on several occasions rather brusquely reversed. On one occasion, he told me, Lansing offered his resignation which he declined to accept.[1] I do not think he does Lansing justice. Any man holding that place naturally comes in conflict with the President, particularly, if he does not hold similar views, which is the case in this instance. Their minds are not sympathetic. The President likes the Baker type, which, indeed, I do myself, but I also respect Lansing's type of mind.

I suggested taking Baker from the War Department and sending him to England in place of Page. He thought Baker would do admirably but said that recently, "in a misguided moment," he had told Page he could continue and he supposed "we would be compelled to have a British-American representing the United States at the Court of St. James." One reason he gave for having told Page was that he could not find a suitable man to take his place.

We talked further of his message. Since last night he had made a memorandum of the subjects he thought proper to incorporate and which I approved, for most of them were suggestions I have made from time to time both verbally and through letters. Unless he changes his mind, he will have a message which could not please me better had I written it myself. He will differentiate between the German people and those who have led them into this disaster. I believe I suggested this to him in letters and cables from England as long ago as the sinking of the Lusitania. I advised the British Government to do this but they never acted upon it, and I hope it is to be done now. My purpose

was, and is, to break down the German Government by "building a fire" back of it within Germany. The President agreed to incorporate the thought that the United States would not be willing
to join a league of peace with an autocracy as a member. That
is the main note I have urged him to strike, that is, this is a war
for democracy and it is a war for the German people as well as
for other nations.

I had a long talk with Mrs. Wilson after the President left
to keep an engagement with Senator Hustings of Wisconsin. I
asked her to try to get the President to be more liberal in his
views regarding republicans, and to influence him to see and
consult with them. I thought it would have a fine effect if he
would send for Root, Hughes and Lodge. I complained that he
was not diplomatic enough. She admitted this and said that she
was even worse than he was; that neither of them could endure
people they did not trust or like. . . .

The President, Mrs. Wilson and I dined alone and after dinner we played games until ten o'clock. This is an in[n]ovation the
President has inaugurated since I was last here. He says he finds
that it diverts him more than reading. We had a thoroughly
delightful evening and I left for New York on the midnight.

Before I left we talked for a half hour reviewing the situation and deciding upon a program. He promised to look over
the War and Navy Departments tomorrow and see what could
be done to strengthen them. Both he and Mrs. Wilson urged me
to return next week to hear him make his address to Congress.

I drove from the White House to Gregory's and picked up
Grayson, who went to the train with me. While I have been at
the White House but thirty-six hours, the President gave me of
his time all that I desired.

¹ The Editors know nothing about this exchange.


## From Gilbert Monell Hitchcock

My dear Mr. President:              [Washington] March 29, 1917

Permit me to put before you in writing the objections to a
declaration of war at this time or to a declaration that a state of
war exists.

First, either declaration would be a change of policy within
four weeks without a change of conditions and a practical con-
fession that your recommendation and our attempt in Congress
to act under it were mistakes. If wrong now armed neutrality
was wrong March 4 when we sought to authorize it. The sink-

ing of a few ships since that time does not constitute a change in conditions.

Second, we have not tried armed neutrality or tested it. We have hardly entered upon it. Germany at this time does not even know officially that the country is united behind you in adopting it. We have not lost an armed merchantman or even finished the work of arming them.

If we give armed neutrality a test there is a possibility that Germany may yet abandon her policy of attacking neutrals or that it may be sufficient to protect our commerce and vindicate our neutral rights. At the worst, if it fails, there will then be opportunity to recognize the inevitable, and those who now oppose war will to a large extent be willing to accept it as the only alternative.

Third, a declaration of war at this time will give an enormous impulse to influences which are increasing the cost of living in this country. The effect upon millions of our people who live upon wages, salaries and small fixed incomes would be distressing and disturbing. We may well anticipate strikes and disorders followed by further increases in the cost of living. Farmers who already find difficulty in getting help will be still further embarrassed and more of the population will be drawn from the country into the cities.

If the war continues two years we will be confronted by a world famine. We did not last year in the United States raise enough wheat for the American people. The Argentine Republic, whose chief export is wheat, has just placed an embargo upon its exportation.

Fourth, public sentiment does not yet call for war or even justify it for the protection of American interests or the vindication of America.

The dominant war sentiment is confined largely to the east where it has been to a large extent inspired by business interests and promoted by organized propaganda. I am aware that there is a strong desire for war among business leaders who lick their chops in eager anticipation of war profits and bond sales. Throughout the rest of the country the real hope is to avoid war as long as possible. The heart of the American people has not been stirred by any recent occurrences. The mass of the people do not believe that America is in danger. They do not believe that American honor can only be vindicated by war, and they do not believe that Germany is trying to make war on us.

If we declare war now it will be due to your influence as the head of the nation and not to a war spirit or war desire among the people. We will be compelled to arouse that spirit afterwards.

Congress is to be in session for some months at least. Why not content ourselves for the present by promptly and unanimously passing a measure commending and approving your action in putting the country in a state of armed neutrality and authorizing whatever may be necessary to prepare on land and sea for a resort to war in case armed neutrality shall prove insufficient? Why not delay the evil of war as far as possible and cling to the last moment to the hope for peace?

Yours very truly,   G M Hitchcock

TLS (WP, DLC).

## From William Gibbs McAdoo

Dear Mr. President:          Washington March 29, 1917.

I have your note of the 28th instant in reply to mine concerning the Danish West Indies Customs Service. The matter can, of course, await your further directions, and I shall take no further steps. What I had in mind was merely to give American direction to the service there until a permanent organization of the Islands is effected, retaining, of course, the native officials and employes in the service. I had assumed that you desired to have this much done.   Cordially yours,   W G McAdoo

TLS (WP, DLC).

## From Newton Diehl Baker

Dear Mr. President:          Washington. March 29, 1917.

I inclose herewith a synopsis of the proposed Army legislation.[1] Where the Act deals with classifications contained in other laws, I have appended the content of those classifications in footnotes for ready reference.

General Crowder tells me that the intention of this draft is to have the selection by lot in each community, as there will be many times more than enough persons available and within the restricted limits of age than will go out in the first contingent. The process, as he has it in mind, is to put the names of all availables in a jury wheel and select them therefrom as jurors are chosen. This is a procedure familiar to every local community in the country, and its fairness will be recognized.

If you think it would be better to try to limit the matter further, by dividing all the persons between 19 and 25 into classes according to their years, and taking them by classes successively from 19 to 25, the change will be very easy to make.

Respectfully yours,   Newton D. Baker

TLS (WP, DLC).
[1] "Summary of the Bill to Increase Temporarily the Military Establishment of the United States," T MS (WP, DLC). The proposed bill provided for the increase of the regular army and the National Guard to full authorized strength and to/draft the National Guard into federal service for the duration of the "emergency." It further authorized the creation of a new "unit" of 500,000 men, and, if deemed necessary by the President, a second unit of the same size. These units were "to be raised and maintained exclusively by selective draft." The draft was to be based upon universal liability to military service of male citizens, and those who had declared their intention of becoming citizens, between the ages of nineteen and twenty-five. Quotas to be raised would be distributed according to population, and individuals would be selected by lot. The bill also provided penalties for persons who failed to register or who resisted registration or the draft. All enlistments were to be for the duration of the emergency. Finally, the bill provided for additional officers for the increased military establishment.

## Two Letters from Edward Mandell House

Dear Governor:                    New York. March 29, 1917.

Hapgood writes that Lloyd George's secretary[1] told him that Lloyd George said—"Great Britain will be fighting for moderate terms at the conference. Some of her allies will be grabbing. We want America in to back up England."

I thought this might interest you.

Affectionately yours,   E. M. House

I had an unusually happy visit with you this time. Please do not forget the Poles.

TLS (WP, DLC).
[1] John Thomas Davies.

Dear Governor:                    New York. March 30, 1917.

Willcox came yesterday to say that he would go to Washington today and try to persuade the republican members of the House to give the democrats control. Willcox also said he was glad you sent "his friend General Wood to Charleston for he talked too much."

And this reminds me of a suggestion that was made to Gordon[1] yesterday by a leading republican regarding Roosevelt's plan to raise a division to go to France. This man said Roosevelt has 54 000 men pledged. I doubt this, but I think he has a great many that are willing to go with him.

The suggestion was that you send three regiments of regulars to France immediately war is declared, thus taking the wind out of Roosevelt's sails. I doubt whether T.R. would go with a second contingent after the first had received all the notoriety and enthusiastic reception from the French.

I am told that the French Attache[2] here said that France would prefer these three regiments at once rather than to have a division with Roosevelt later. In fact, they do not desire any considerable force at this time.

I have read about half of the Tagore books[3] and I do not think at this time you would care to have it dedicated to you, although you would probably agree with most of his conclusions. It is a general indictment of "Nationalism" which he illustrates by the English rule in India. I would suggest that you say that you had not time to read the book and would therefore prefer not to have it dedicated to you because of the critical situation.

Affectionately yours,   E. M. House

TLS (WP, DLC).
[1] Gordon Auchincloss.
[2] Perhaps he meant the French consul-general in New York, Gaston Ernest Liébert.
[3] Rabindranath Tagore, *Nationalism* (New York and London, 1917). Macmillan and Company, Tagore's publisher, had sent page proofs of the book to Wilson (see WW to Macmillan and Co., April 9, 1917), but the letter from the Macmillan Company about Tagore's desire to dedicate the book to Wilson is missing. Sir Rabindranath Tagore (1861-1941) was the son of the "Great Sage" Debendranath Tagore (1817-1905), Hindu philosopher and religious reformer. Rabindranath Tagore was by 1917 a world-famous poet, writer, and musician. He had won the Nobel Prize for Literature in 1913 and had been knighted in 1915.

# From Robert Lansing

PERSONAL AND CONFIDENTIAL:

My dear Mr. President:          Washington March 30, 1917.

In view of certain remarks which you made at the meeting of the Cabinet this afternoon I thought you might find helpful the enclosed memoranda[1] in regard to violations by German officials of the laws of this country and the practice of nations.

Faithfully yours,   Robert Lansing

TLS (WP, DLC).
[1] Four memoranda, all T MS (WP, DLC). "Improper Activities of German Officials in the United States" related selected incidents of espionage, sabotage, counterfeiting of American passports, and encouragement of revolutionary movements in India and Ireland by German diplomats and agents in the United States since the beginning of the war. "Violations of American Rights by Germany since the Suspension of Diplomatic Relations" dealt with the temporary detention and harassment of Ambassador Gerard and his staff, the temporary detention of American citizens and consular officials in Germany, damage to

German ships interned in American ports, the action of German naval authorities who had taken American citizens from the British steamer, *Yarrowdale*, and held them as prisoners of war, and the Zimmermann telegram. The other two memoranda listed "Ships Sunk with Loss of American Lives" since 1915 and "American Ships Damaged or Destroyed by German Submarines" since 1915.

## From David Franklin Houston, with Enclosure

Dear Mr. President:                    Washington March 30, 1917.

I am sending you Alderman's letter. I promised to leave it with you but neglected to do so.

Alderman, as usual, expresses himself very admirably. He says many things that we here think and feel. I think it is strikingly true that the great mass of the American people trust you. They trust you so completely that they have not thought it necessary to advise you. They have assumed that you know the situation and the facts better than they do. I think that the overwhelming sentiment is in favor of going forward and of taking a strong course. The only alternative to a strong forward course is to recede from our former position, to shut ourselves off from international affairs, and to confine ourselves within our own borders. This is impossible. One result would be to run the risk of leaving democracy to the tender mercies of the Central autocracies. I do not believe that we can morally longer throw the responsibility for safeguarding civilization on England and France. The time for debate, as it seems to me, has passed. I believe that the course of action you wish the country to follow should be outlined not in passionate, but yet in very strong and forceful terms. "It is time now, I believe, to sound the tocsin." I know the case is difficult to state and yet I believe it is a very strong one.                    Faithfully yours,    D. F. Houston.

### E N C L O S U R E

## Edwin Anderson Alderman to David Franklin Houston

My dear Houston:                    Charlottesville March 22, 1917.

I quite appreciate your position, and we will simply hope that you can come. With all your burdens, no one should expect much from you.

I do wish I could talk with you about the world situation. I think about it all the time. I believe it to be our duty, as a nation now, as a matter of self interest, as a matter of national honor, as a matter of future world influence and as a matter of keeping quick and vital the national spirit and the national conscience, to go to war with Germany, unless the present control of the German government sees fit to cease its methods of crime and aggression.

Of course, we *are* at war with Germany, or rather they are at war with us. You know my admiration and confidence and affection for the President. In the first place, his knowledge of the real facts goes far beyond anything we outsiders can appreciate; and, in the second place, he has great power of analysis, calmness of judgment, coolness of mind, and a great background of knowledge and understanding. I never permit myself to criticise him, even as a friend, because I have a feeling that in the end it will be shown that he is right. I can understand his aversion to carrying a nation into war that does not want to be carried into war. But he never said a truer thing than when he said that no great war could hereafter occur without our participation. In my judgment, that applies to 1917, as well as to some future date.

The President has been patient; he has been reasonable; he has preserved our dignity and honor; but I do not think it can be done longer without a frank resort to force. Personally, of course, I have never drawn a neutral breath since August 1, 1914. I believe that the victory of the present German system would mean the deadliest blow that democracy has ever received in its splendid progress in human society. I believe our destiny is not to serve the world at this juncture by a soft mediation but by the use of righteous force at the decisive moment to help turn the tide as between the ideals of democratic society and the ideals of autocratic society; and if we do go to war, I pray we shall go at it like practical people, seeing war as war, and using every weapon and forming every alliance, temporary though they may be, and taking every step that can in honor be taken to achieve a victory for democracy and end the present mad condition of affairs in the world. If it means expeditionary force, large numbers of destroyers, participation in the active fighting in the war zone, we should go to it under the best advice our experts can give. If it means credit and food and all sorts of economic aid, then that is the direction to take. Delicacy and dallying do not go down with the Prussian. Force and fear are his controlling motives, and he understands no psychology that is not tied up with these impulses. I confess it is the situation after the war, no matter which way the tide turns, that makes me feel that we should go in for thorough-going reorganization of our life on a basis of defensive preparation. This, of course, is against all of my predilections and traditions, but I have been driven to it by the unfolding of events.

I thought these people might be bluffing, as they are great bluffers, until the sinking of the last three ships. I am in favor of universal service, and I believe the country wants action now. The country trusts the President. They know that he is a patriot with a vision and with heart, but if he should now act simply, directly, forcefully, the heart and pride and spirit of this whole nation will rise to his leadership and to his call in a way that might astound him in its devotion and purpose.

It is time now, I believe, to sound the tocsin, and no man can sound it, if he so wills, so effectively as the President. I wish I could talk with you about this matter. One cannot dictate without consciousness that he is speaking ineffectually about such a great matter.

Give my love to Mrs. Houston[1] and to Charlie Crane, if he is in reach.          Faithfully yours,   E. A. Alderman.

TLS (WP, DLC).
[1] Helen Beall Houston.


## From Newton Diehl Baker

Dear Mr. President:          Washington. March 30, 1917.

I had a long talk with Raymond Fosdick today. He declines to be considered for the Vice-Governorship of the Philippine Islands for two reasons:

First, he is not able to sustain the expense which the place would necessarily entail; and

Second, he feels that it is not a place for which his training has fitted him.

I tried to shake him out of both of these positions, but found it impossible. He asked me to express to you his deep appreciation of your consideration in the matter.

I have just asked him to take charge of some volunteer work affecting recreation and leisure occupation in the Army. He will, at my request, associate with him a representative of the Russell Sage Foundation and one of the trusted lieutenants of Mr. John Mott, in working out a program which will enable us to do something for forces in training to occupy their leisure, so as to prevent as far as possible homesickness and a resort to undesirable recreations. I regard the work as of great importance, supplementing as it will something of the kind already done in the Army by the Army Y.M.C.A.

Respectfully yours,   Newton D. Baker

TLS (WP, DLC).


## From the Diary of Josephus Daniels

1917 Friday 30 March

*Cabinet Meeting.* President, grave, told an anecdote or two, and then spoke of the message to Congress he was writing. He stood up at his end of table & practiced calisthenics, saying he had been sitting at his desk writing all the morning and was stiff. Lane read several telegrams from Cal. saying sentiment was nearly all for war. President discussed the method of his presentation & the changed conditions since he addressed Congress. He wishes to know if in presenting the miasma of German enemies here he could safely trace them to the Embassy— not necessarily to Bernsto[r]ff, but to others in Embassy—Von Papen, Boy Ed & other such[.] L & G & I added that men had been convicted in N.Y. for carrying out crimes against this country & paid for it by G— Consuls.

He wished no argument and no feeling in his message, but wishes to present facts, convincing from evidence, justifying position. McAdoo thought all crimes of G's should be set forth to arouse & stir the people. Redfield told of how 6 chauffeurs had sought places with a woman who talked German & every one said: "And are you, too, true to the Fatherland?" The President recounted some of the absurd stories told of what G's were doing. "There's a German in the cellar" said White House house-keeper referring to inoffensive German employed in White House to tend the fires. "I'd rather the blamed place should be blown up than to persecute inoffensive people"

Should hold places for Gov. employees.

Baker & I: Have efficiency keen in war Be cold blooded.


## From the Diary of Thomas W. Brahany

Friday, March 30, 1917

Soon after I reached the office this morning Hoover telephoned that the President wished the Secretary of the Treasury and the Postmaster General advised that he could not grant them the joint interview which they requested. He wished them informed that he had locked himself in his study to work on his address to the Congress, and did not wish to be disturbed by anyone. I so advised McAdoo and Burleson. Later McAdoo called at the White House and said he had an important matter which should be taken up with the President. Hoover repeated the President's instructions and McAdoo left.

All members of the Cabinet attended the meeting this afternoon. The President has not completed the draft of his address to the Congress.

## To Newton Diehl Baker, with Enclosures

My dear Mr. Secretary:          The White House 31 March, 1917

Here is a matter which I ought long ago to have brought to your attention, because it is of real importance that we should show the utmost consideration and appreciation towards the men who sign the enclosed papers. Among them are some of the most influential Poles in this country. Will you not be kind enough to make the appropriate reply and express the appreciation in which I warmly join?

Always          Faithfully yours,    Woodrow Wilson

TLS (WDR, RG 94, AGO Document File, No. 2638801, DNA).

### ENCLOSURE I

## From Teofil A. Starzynski and Others

Dear Mr. President:          Chicago, Ill., February 19th, 1917.

American citizens of Polish blood, conscious of the solemnity of the occasion, and expectant of events which may affect the future of our country—inspired by the spirit of loyalty, hereby tender to the government of the United States, the services of five hundred officers to be forthwith instructed and trained through their efforts and at their expense.

They are not rich and cannot offer millions, but they give the best they possess, being certain of the unanimous sentiment of their people to follow the American flag, the symbol of liberty and justice, where ever it may lead and against all enemies.

In the hope that the Department of War will give our offer due consideration and will deem it advisable to facilitate the technical necessities, we beg of you, Mr. President, to look upon whatever would seem to be in excess of our civic duty as a token of our affection and gratitude towards you personally.

POLISH FALCONS ALLIANCE OF AMERICA
Dr. T. A. Starzynski          Pres.
POLISH NATIONAL ALLIANCE OF AMERICA
K. Zycktinski          Pres.
POLISH ROMAN CATHOLIC UNION OF AMERICA
Peter Rostenkowski          Pres.
POLISH NATIONAL COUNCIL
Dr. K. Wagner,          Pres.
POLISH NATIONAL DEPARTMENT, P.C.R.C.[1]
John F. Smulski,          Chairman Executive Committee.

TLS (WDR, RG 94, AGO Document File, No. 2638801, DNA).
[1] The Polish Central Relief Committee.


E N C L O S U R E     I I

## From Teofil A. Starzynski

Honorable Sir:          Pittsburgh, Pa. February 27, 1917.

In the name of the Polish Falcons Alliance of America, the organization which initiated the matter of furnishing to the United States in case of need, five hundred trained officers, I hereby apply to you, Mr. President, in order that you may use your influence, if you deem it proper, to help us in obtaining to that end the following means, to wit:

(a)  Proper authority to carry on military exercises in or near Cambridge Springs, Pennsylvania, at or near the Polish Falcons Alliance College grounds, where arrangements have been made to carry on the course of instructions.

(b)  Proper authority for each of the men who creditably finish the course of military instructions to be given, to form voluntary regiments in case of necessity.

(c)  Two or three competent army instructors to conduct said military training, and if possible, such as have some command of the Polish language in order to get the best results.

(d)  Authority to use a properly equipped military camp as near to Cambridge Springs as possible, in order to develop good marksmanship.

(e)  Five hundred modern riffles now in use by the Army of the United States, with a sufficient amount of ammunition and other necessary equipments.

(f)  Four machine guns, ammunition and equipments.

(g)  Necessary aim correctors and reflectors to train and develop accuracy of aiming, etc.

(h)  Targets for proper shooting exercises.

(i)  Five Hundred full equipments, like belts, haver-sacks, tools, utensils, etc.

(j)  Five hundred long military coats.

(k)  Maps, drawings, sketches, etc., for the purpose of proper instructions.

(l)  Field glasses and signal equipments.

(m)  One complete field hospital outfit.

(n)  Tents and field kitchen outfit, sufficient to accommodate five hundred men.

(o)  One complete pioneering outfit.

(p)  A few gas masks and hand grenade waifers or throwers, to instruct in the proper use thereof.

If our request for the enumerated equipments can be favorably considered, we hope to furnish the number of competent young men indicated who no doubt, as well as the whole organization, and through it the people at large, will greatly appreciate the favor, and in case of necessity, gladly render valuable service to the United States in the line of the training received.

Very respectfully,

POLISH FALCONS ALLIANCE OF AMERICA,
By Dr. T. A. Starzynski    President.

TLS (WDR, RG 94, AGO Document File, No. 2638801, DNA).

## To Newton Diehl Baker

My dear Mr. Secretary:       The White House 31 March, 1917

I am heartily sorry about Fosdick, but I dare say he is right in declining a post for which he does not feel his experience has fitted him.

I am very much interested to hear of what you have asked him to do in connection with the work affecting recreation and leisure occupation in the Army. He will undoubtedly be an admirable man for that.

Cordially and sincerely yours,   Woodrow Wilson

TLS (N. D. Baker Papers, DLC).

## To Charles William Eliot

My dear Doctor Eliot:          The White House 31 March, 1917

I need not tell you that I have valued very highly your letter of March twenty-seventh. Your counsel always serves to clear my thinking, and I am warmly obliged to you for it. I wish I could send you a letter worth your reading in return.

Cordially and sincerely yours,   Woodrow Wilson

TLS (C. W. Eliot Papers, MH-Ar).

## To Alexander Mitchell Palmer

My dear Palmer:          The White House 31 March, 1917

McCormick had already spoken to me about appointing Roland Morris to the post in Japan,[1] and I am giving it very serious consideration. It is a suggestion which interests me very much, for I know and admire Morris.

Cordially and sincerely yours,   Woodrow Wilson

TLS (R. S. Morris Papers, DLC).
[1] Palmer's letter, to which Wilson's was a reply, is missing.

## To Gilbert Monell Hitchcock

My dear Senator:          [The White House] 31 March, 1917

I am really warmly obliged to you for your frank letter of March twenty-ninth. I wish I could agree with all its conclusions. My own mind has been forced to the acceptance of a different policy for reasons which I hope I shall be able to state with something like convincing force when I address the Congress. It always disturbs me, I am frank to say, when I find myself differing from those whose judgments I much respect.

Sincerely yours,   [Woodrow Wilson]

CCL (WP, DLC).

## To Joseph Irwin France

My dear Senator:          [The White House] 31 March, 1917

Certainly no apologies were necessary for writing me upon a matter of great public moment, and I want to express to you my appreciation of your very candid letter.

I hope you will feel at liberty to express your opinions to me upon any matter which I have a part in handling.

With much respect,

Sincerely yours,   Woodrow Wilson

TLS (Letterpress Books, WP, DLC).


## From Newton Diehl Baker

Dear Mr. President:          Washington. March 31, 1917.

Would a despatch to Ambassador Francis, phrased as follows, fit the case:

"Would the Russian Government welcome an inspection of the Trans-Siberian Railroad by six American railway experts, with a view to making a report for the use of the Russian Government as to how the efficiency of the railroad can be increased, with possible suggestions as to equipment and expert assistance from America if agreeable to Russian Government?"          Cordially yours,   Newton D. Baker

This seems to me all right.   W.W.

TLS (N. D. Baker Papers, DLC).


## From Newton Diehl Baker, with Enclosure

Dear Mr. President:          Washington. March 31, 1917.

I have just received your note of this morning, and inclose copies of the acknowledgments I have made to Dr. T. Starzynski and his several associates.

I return the letter from Colonel House[1] for your files. I have also sent Colonel House copies of these letters, so that he can transmit them to Mr. Paderewski, if he so desires.

Respectfully yours,   Newton D. Baker

TLS (WP, DLC).
[1] EMH to WW, March 11, 1917.


E N C L O S U R E

## Newton Diehl Baker to Teofil A. Starzynski

My dear Dr. Starzynski:          [Washington] March 31, 1917.

The President has just conferred with me about the patriotic offer to the government, transmitted to him under date of February 19th, and jointly signed by the Presidents of the Polish

Falcons Alliance of America, the Polish National Alliance of America, the Polish Roman Catholic Union of America, the Polish National Council, and the Polish National Department, P.C.R.C., of the services of the officers to be forthwith instructed and trained through their joint efforts and at their expense.

I am directed by the President to express to you, and to the great bodies of American citizens of Polish blood whom you represent, his deep appreciation of the spirit and generosity of this offer and of this recognition of the unity of our country and the common patriotism of our great citizenship, overleaping as it does all questions of ancient nationality or extraction.

The War Department is at present engaged upon legislation which it will recommend to Congress for large additional forces to our national armies. The great need will undoubtedly be for officers who are themselves trained, and therefore able to train others. The offer you make, therefore, is especially serviceable and timely, and as soon as a definite plan is authorized by Congress, this Department will place itself in communication with you, so that it may secure the services of the officers whom you are instructing.

For the War Department and for myself, I beg leave to assure you of our hearty appreciation of this patriotic, useful and generous tender.          Cordially yours,   Newton D. Baker.

CCL (WP, DLC).


## From David Lawrence

My dear Mr. President:                [Washington] March 31, 1917

May I briefly draw to your attention three or four points which seem to me ought to be at least touched upon in your forthcoming message to Congress?

Your message will be looked upon not only by the people of today but by future generations as the exposition of a new foreign policy. The Spanish-American war changed our policy in the sense that it gave us overseas possessions and interests. There is no telling what will be the result of our bigger venture this time. But whatever it may be the Monroe Doctrine will remain the cardinal feature of our foreign policy.

Emphasis might then well be laid upon the circumstances under which we use force. We can now point to our policy in Mexico, our policy of patience and even tolerance under violations to our nationals by weaker nations as having been vindicated by the steady and gratifying growth of Mexico, her restoration of constitutional government and state authority etc. Similarly you could speak of our efforts to redress our own wrongs as in the case of Colombia the treaty with which country it is our profound hope will soon be ratified, thus demonstrating that when we are in the wrong we do not hesitate to acknowledge it and compensate the injured parties. Such a statement by you in your message might go a great distance toward satisfying public opinion in Colombia in view of the fact that expressions of regret are to be eliminated in order to get Republican support for the treaty.

Our right treatment of Mexico and Colombia could be referred to as evidences of our desire to show by Pan-Americanism and the power of example in this hemisphere the relation that ought to prevail between strong nations and weaker neighbors. Similarly it would seem pertinent to emphasize that it is precisely to conserve Pan Americanism, to protect the nations of this hemisphere from the intrigues and schemes that lead to political domination and internal revolution when such revolution suits the sordid purposes of unscrupulous governments, that we now take up arms. This permits reference to the Zimmerman note which reaches into the psychology of the whole situation. With a government in power that does not hesitate to sow the seeds of distrust and friction between ourselves and our neighbors, as has more than once been proved in raids on our own border, which does not scruple to intrigue first with the bandits in the north to stir up trouble with us and then to plan an intrigue with the government in the south; with a government that openly acknowledges that it planned all this in the days prior to January 18th when every relationship of amity existed, who in this hemisphere can feel immune to attack? What nation can feel secure against such a government.

Finally, would it not be proper to make our declaration of the existence of a state of war refer only to the Imperial Government, the Government that authorized submarine warfare, the Government that sent the Zimmerman note which we know by speeches in the Reichstag is deplored by the liberal forces in Germany who, we hope, will some day lead an enlightened nation forward as has been the case with the liberal forces in Russia. By making our war on the Imperial German Government, it seems to me we leave the door open to a resumption of friendly relations at any time *with the German people* of whom so many have come to our shores and become useful and loyal citizens, with the German people who some day will demonstrate by their choice of leaders that they are ready and willing to return to those

ways of honorable dealing and humane action which German
governments have so often in the past manifested in their intercourse with us.                    Sincerely,    David Lawrence

TLS (WP, DLC).

## From William Gibbs McAdoo, with Enclosure

Dear Governor,                         [Washington] Mch 31, '17
    As you have expressed a desire to know all you can of opinion
in the West, the enclosed telegram may be of interest. I have
known Byllesby[1] for 20 years. He is a level-headed, highly successful, unemotional business man.          Affy,    WGM

ALS (WP, DLC).
[1] Henry Marison Byllesby, proprietor of the electrical engineering firm of
H. M. Byllesby & Co. of Chicago.


                E N C L O S U R E

                                    Chicago Ill Mar 31, 17
    I have never presumed upon our past acquaintanceship to
solicit from you any favor and have likewise through the crisis
of the past few years abstained from in any sense endeavoring
to annoy or to offer my advice but now thinking that you will
not misunderstand it, and knowing of my wide intimate connections throughout the middle west and the pacific coast from
the business matters which I have in charge, I say to you in
deep sincerity that the overwhelming mass of the responsible
people men and women of this country are earnestly desiring an
immediate declaration of war against Germany for the purpose
of asserting the dignity of our country and protecting us against
the inevitable punishment which will follow any delay in this
matter. The administration has exhausted every effort to maintain peace. They have been flouted against disrespectfully. The
Country now expects to find in the administration strong vigorous leadership and believe me, Irrespective of party when the
administration does take the step herein so earnestly pleaded for
you will be amazed to find what a magnificent country we have
and how splendidly it will rally to the support of the Administration and the defense of our country, and how absolutely insignificant and how truly worthless will prove in the aggregate the
sum total of pacifists and further desires of Procrastination.
                                    H M Byllesby.

T telegram (WP, DLC).

## From the Diary of Thomas W. Brahany

Saturday, March 31, 1917

The President and Mrs. Wilson played golf this morning. When Hoover came over to the office this afternoon he said, "If the President is writing as he feels Germany is going to get Hell in the address to Congress. I never knew him to be more peevish. He's out of sorts, doesn't feel well, and has a headache. Soon after lunch he went to the study, leaving word that he desired quiet and didn't want to be disturbed. Mrs. Wilson left the house to call on some friends. I thought some noise downstairs might annoy the President, so I sent one of the ushers upstairs to close the study door. 'Who told you to close that door,' asked the President in a sharp tone. 'Mr. Hoover, Sir,' replied the usher. 'Tell Hoover,' said the President, 'that I don't want it closed—all I want is quiet.' He's certainly getting all the quiet he wants now—all of us are walking tiptoe and speaking in whispers."

As usual, the President is sitting before his own little typewriting machine, and slowly but accurately and neatly, typing a message which probably will be his greatest State paper.

Late this afternoon Louis P. Lochner, who with David Starr Jordan, is running the Emergency Peace Foundation, telephoned me that half a dozen special trains would reach Washington on Monday, all of them loaded down with men and women who are opposed to war. These pilgrims are to hold a meeting on Monday in Convention Hall. Lochner wished to know if a committee to be appointed at this meeting might have an appointment with the President. I told him to submit his request in writing and I would bring it to the President's attention. The President has reached a point where he has little patience with the peace at any price propagandists and I don't think he will receive Lochner's committee.

## To Arthur Yager

[The White House] April 1, 1917.

Will you please express to the Porto Ricans at their meeting celebrating the passage of the new organic act my great pleasure that the last legal barrier between Americans and Porto Ricans has been removed. The United States has complied with an obligation of justice. The people of Porto Rico have now the name, privileges and responsibilities of all other citizens of the

United States. We welcome the new citizen, not as a stranger, but as one entering his father's house.

Woodrow Wilson.

T telegram (Letterpress Books, WP, DLC).

## To Robert Lansing

My dear Mr. Secretary,      The White House. 1 April, 1917.

This is the passage in my address which should give form to the Resolution of which we were speaking over the 'phone this evening:

"I advise that the Congress declare the recent course of the Imperial German Government to be in fact nothing less than war against the government and people of the United States; that it formally accept the status of belligerent which has thus been thrust upon it; and that it take immediate steps not only to put the country in a more thorough state of defense but also to exert all its power and employ all its resources to bring the Government of the German Empire to terms and end the war."

I would be very much obliged if you would be kind enough to have the Resolution drawn in the sense of these words.

I am putting this in writing rather than give it to you orally over the 'phone because I know you will wish to have before you just the language I am to use.

Faithfully Yours,    W.W.

WWTLI (SDR, RG 59, 763.72/3761¾, DNA).

## From Richard Heath Dabney

Dear Woodrow:      [Charlottesville, Va.] 1 April, 1917.

Knowing that you wish to be informed as to public opinion on the mighty issues now confronting this nation, I write to assure you that the community in which I live is overwhelmingly for the following things:

1. War on Germany;
2. A fight to a finish, a fight with every weapon, wielded with all the force at our command, till the terroristic Prussian government is crushed to earth;
3. A solemn league with the Allies, including a pledge that we shall stand or fall with them and shall make no peace with the enemy until the terms are satisfactory to all of the Allies;

4. The immediate gift of one billion dollars to France, to serve not simply as a token of our gratitude for past assistance to us and of our admiration for the sublime heroism with which she has defended civilization in this war, but also as the most effective way in which *at the moment* we can defend ourselves;

5. The facilitation of unlimited credit to any of the Allies in need of money;

6. The sending of a small force of regular soldiers (say 5000 men) to the Western front, in order to show the world that we are ready to give not simply our dollars but our lives to the cause of freedom, right & peace;

7. The immediate passage of a law *requiring the military training of every able-bodied young man* in the country.

I wish you could have been present at the mass-meeting of students and faculty on Friday night. I shall look back to it all my life as to one of the most inspiring events in all my experience. There was no hysteria, but the atmosphere was electric with deep, intense, idealistic passion. "Reddy" Echols,[1] making the report of our military committee, was magnificent; and the spirit of our students was superb. Yesterday one of them—a quiet, unexcitable fellow, of brains, character & maturity—said to me that, if Congress failed to declare war, he would be ashamed to live in this country.

You have, my dear friend, a mighty burden upon your shoulders. May you have health and strength to bear it! The University of your native State is back of you, ready to help.

As for myself, if there be any way in which I can assist you or the country, call upon me, and believe me to be, as ever,

Faithfully & affectionately yours,   R. H. Dabney.

ALS (WP, DLC).
[1] William Holding Echols, Jr., Professor of Mathematics at the University of Virginia.


## Franklin Knight Lane to George Whitfield Lane

My dear George,                    Washington, April 1, 1917

I took your letter and your proposed wire as to our going into war and sent them to the President as suggestions for his proposed message which in a couple of days will come out—what it is to be I don't know—excepting in spirit. He is to be for recognizing war and taking hold of the situation in such a fashion as will eventually lead to an Allies' victory over Germany. But he goes unwillingly. The Cabinet is at last a unit. We can stand

Germany's insolence and murderous policy no longer. Burleson, Gregory, Daniels, and Wilson were the last to come over.

The meetings of the Cabinet lately have been nothing less than councils of war. The die is cast—and yet no one has seen the message. The President hasn't shown us a line. He seems to think that in war the Pacific Coast will not be strongly with him. They don't want war to be sure—no one does. But they will not suffer further humiliation. I sent West for some telegrams telling of the local feeling in different States and all said, "Do as the President says." Yet none came back that spoke as if they felt that we had been outraged or that it was necessary for humanity that Germany be brought to a Democracy. There is little pride or sense of national dignity in most of our politicians.

The Council of National Defense is getting ready. I yesterday proposed a resolution, which was adopted, that our contracts for ships, ammunition, and supplies be made upon the basis of a three years' program. We may win in two years. If we had the nerve to raise five million men at once we could end it in six months.

The first thing is to let Russia and France have money. And the second thing, to see that Russia has munitions, of which they are short—depending largely, too largely, upon Japan. I shouldn't be surprised if we would operate the Russian railroads. And ships, ships! How we do need ships, and there are none in the world. Ships to feed England and to make the Russian machine work. Hindenburg is to turn next toward Petrograd— he is only three hundred miles away now. I fear he will succeed. But that does not mean the conquest of Russia! The lovable, kindly Russians are not to be conquered,—and it makes me rejoice that we are to be with them.

All sides need aëroplanes—for the war that is perhaps the greatest of all needs; and there Germany is strongest. Ned will go among the first. He is flying alone now and is enjoying the risk,—the consciousness of his own skill. Anne[1] is very brave about it.

This is the program as far as we have gone: Navy, to make a line across the sea and hunt submarines; Army, one million at once, and as many more as necessary as soon as they can be got ready. Financed by income taxes largely. Men and capital both drafted.

I'm deep in the work. Have just appointed a War-Secretary of my own—an ex-Congressman named Lathrop Brown from New York, who is to see that we get mines, etc., at work. I wish you were here but the weather would be too much for you, I fear. Very hot right now!

Sometime I'll tell you how we stopped the strike. It was a big piece of work that was blanketed by the Supreme Court's decision next day. But we came near to having something akin to Civil War. Much love, my dear boy.          F.K.L.

Printed in Lane and Wall, eds., *The Letters of Franklin K. Lane*, pp. 242-44.
[1] His wife, Anne Wintermute Lane.

## An Address to a Joint Session of Congress

2 April, 1917 8.30 P.M.[1]

Gentlemen of the Congress: I have called the Congress into extraordinary session because there are serious, very serious, choices of policy to be made, and made immediately, which it was neither right nor constitutionally permissible that I should assume the responsibility of making.

On the third of February last I officially laid before you the extraordinary announcement of the Imperial German Government that on and after the first day of February it was its purpose to put aside all restraints of law or of humanity and use its submarines to sink every vessel that sought to approach either the ports of Great Britain and Ireland or the western coasts of Europe or any of the ports controlled by the enemies of Germany within the Mediterranean. That had seemed to be the object of the German submarine warfare earlier in the war, but since April of last year the Imperial Government had somewhat restrained the commanders of its undersea craft in conformity with its promise then given to us that passenger boats should not be sunk and that due warning would be given to all other vessels which its submarines might seek to destroy, when no resistance was offered or escape attempted, and care taken that their crews were given at least a fair chance to save their lives in their open boats. The precautions taken were meagre and haphazard enough, as was proved in distressing instance after instance in the progress of the cruel and unmanly business, but a certain degree of restraint was observed. The new policy has swept every restriction aside. Vessels of every kind, whatever their flag, their character, their cargo, their destination, their errand, have been ruthlessly sent to the bottom without warning and without thought of help or mercy for those on board, the vessels of friendly neutrals along

[1] WWhw.

with those of belligerents. Even hospital ships and ships carrying relief to the sorely bereaved and stricken people of Belgium, though the latter were provided with safe conduct through the proscribed areas by the German Government itself and were distinguished by unmistakable marks of identity, have been sunk with the same reckless lack of compassion or of principle.

I was for a little while unable to believe that such things would in fact be done by any government that had hitherto subscribed to the humane practices of civilized nations. International law had its origin in the attempt to set up some law which would be respected and observed upon the seas, where no nation had right of dominion and where lay the free highways of the world. By painful stage after stage has that law been built up, with meagre enough results, indeed, after all was accomplished that could be accomplished, but always with a clear view, at least, of what the heart and conscience of mankind demanded. This minimum of right the German Government has swept aside under the plea of retaliation and necessity and because it had no weapons which it could use at sea except these which it is impossible to employ as it is employing them without throwing to the winds all scruples of humanity or of respect for the understandings that were supposed to underlie the intercourse of the world. I am not now thinking of the loss of property involved, immense and serious as that is, but only of the wanton and wholesale destruction of the lives of non-combatants, men, women, and children, engaged in pursuits which have always, even in the darkest periods of modern history, been deemed innocent and legitimate. Property can be paid for; the lives of peaceful and innocent people cannot be. The present German submarine warfare against commerce is a warfare against mankind.

It is a war against all nations. American ships have been sunk, American lives taken, in ways which it has stirred us very deeply to learn of, but the ships and people of other neutral and friendly nations have been sunk and overwhelmed in the waters in the same way. There has been no discrimination. The challenge is to all mankind. Each nation must decide for itself how it will meet it. The choice we make for ourselves must be made with a moderation of counsel and a temperateness of judgment befitting our character and our motives as a nation. We must put excited feeling away. Our motive will not be revenge or the victorious assertion of the physical might of the nation, but only the vindication of right, of human right, of which we are only a single champion.

When I addressed the Congress on the twenty-sixth of February last I thought that it would suffice to assert our neutral rights with arms, our right to use the seas against unlawful interference, our right to keep our people safe against unlawful violence. But armed neutrality, it now appears, is impracticable. Because submarines are in effect outlaws when used as the German submarines have been used against merchant shipping, it is impossible to defend ships against their attacks as the law of nations has assumed that merchantmen would defend themselves against privateers or cruisers, visible craft giving chase upon the open sea. It is common prudence in such circumstances, grim necessity, indeed, to endeavour to destroy them before they have shown their own intention. They must be dealt with upon sight, if dealt with at all. The German Government denies the right of neutrals to use arms at all within the areas of the sea which it has proscribed, even in the defense of rights which no modern publicist has ever before questioned their right to defend. The intimation is conveyed that the armed guards which we have placed on our merchant ships will be treated as beyond the pale of law and subject to be dealt with as pirates would be. Armed neutrality is ineffectual enough at best; in such circumstances and in the face of such pretensions it is worse than ineffectual: it is likely only to produce what it was meant to prevent; it is practically certain to draw us into the war without either the rights or the effectiveness of belligerents. There is one choice we cannot make, we are incapable of making: we will not choose the path of submission and suffer the most sacred rights of our nation and our people to be ignored or violated. The wrongs against which we now array ourselves are no common wrongs; they cut to the very roots of human life.

With a profound sense of the solemn and even tragical character of the step I am taking and of the grave responsibilities which it involves, but in unhesitating obedience to what I deem my constitutional duty, I advise that the Congress declare the recent course of the Imperial German Government to be in fact nothing less than war against the government and people of the United States; that it formally accept the status of belligerent which has thus been thrust upon it; and that it take immediate steps not only to put the country in a more thorough state of defense but also to exert all its power and employ all its resources to bring the Government of the German Empire to terms and end the war.

What this will involve is clear. It will involve the utmost practicable cooperation in counsel and action with the governments now at war with Germany, and, as incident to that, the extension to those governments of the most liberal financial credits, in order that our resources may so far as possible be added to theirs. It will involve the organization and mobilization of all the material resources of the country to supply the materials of war and serve the incidental needs of the nation in the most abundant and yet the most economical and efficient way possible. It will involve the immediate full equipment of the navy in all respects but particularly in supplying it with the best means of dealing with the enemy's submarines. It will involve the immediate addition to the armed forces of the United States already provided for by law in case of war at least five hundred thousand men, who should, in my opinion, be chosen upon the principle of universal liability to service, and also the authorization of subsequent additional increments of equal force so soon as they may be needed and can be handled in training. It will involve also, of course, the granting of adequate credits to the Government, sustained, I hope, so far as they can equitably be sustained by the present generation, by well conceived taxation.

I say sustained so far as may be equitable by taxation because it seems to me that it would be most unwise to base the credits which will now be necessary entirely on money borrowed. It is our duty, I most respectfully urge, to protect our people so far as we may against the very serious hardships and evils which would be likely to arise out of the inflation which would be produced by vast loans.

In carrying out the measures by which these things are to be accomplished we should keep constantly in mind the wisdom of interfering as little as possible in our own preparation and in the equipment of our own military forces with the duty,—for it will be a very practical duty,—of supplying the nations already at war with Germany with the materials which they can obtain only from us or by our assistance. They are in the field and we should help them in every way to be effective there.

I shall take the liberty of suggesting, through the several executive departments of the Government, for the consideration of your committees, measures for the accomplishment of the several objects I have mentioned. I hope that it will be your pleasure to deal with them as having been framed after very careful thought by the branch of the Government upon which the responsibility of conducting the war and safeguarding the nation will most directly fall.

While we do these things, these deeply momentous things, let us be very clear, and make very clear to all the world what our motives and our objects are. My own thought has not been driven from its habitual and normal course by the unhappy events of the last two months, and I do not believe that the thought of the nation has been altered or clouded by them. I have exactly the same things in mind now that I had in mind when I addressed the Senate on the twenty-second of January last; the same that I had in mind when I addressed the Congress on the third of February and on the twenty-sixth of February. Our object now, as then, is to vindicate the principles of peace and justice in the life of the world as against selfish and autocratic power and to set up amongst the really free and self-governed peoples of the world such a concert of purpose and of action as will henceforth ensure the observance of those principles. Neutrality is no longer feasible or desirable where the peace of the world is involved and the freedom of its peoples, and the menace to that peace and freedom lies in the existence of autocratic governments backed by organized force which is controlled wholly by their will, not by the will of their people. We have seen the last of neutrality in such circumstances. We are at the beginning of an age in which it will be insisted that the same standards of conduct and of responsibility for wrong done shall be observed among nations and their governments that are observed among the individual citizens of civilized states.

We have no quarrel with the German people. We have no feeling towards them but one of sympathy and friendship. It was not upon their impulse that their government acted in entering this war. It was not with their previous knowledge or approval. It was a war determined upon as wars used to be determined upon in the old, unhappy days when peoples were nowhere consulted by their rulers and wars were provoked and waged in the interest of dynasties or of little groups of ambitious men who were accustomed to use their fellow men as pawns and tools. Self-governed nations do not fill their neighbour states with spies or set the course of intrigue to bring about some critical posture of affairs which will give them an opportunity to strike and make conquest. Such designs can be successfully worked out only under cover and where no one has the right to ask questions. Cunningly contrived plans of deception or aggression, carried, it may be, from generation to generation, can be worked out and kept from the light only within the privacy of courts or behind the carefully guarded confidences of a narrow and privileged class. They are happily impossible where public opinion commands and insists upon full information concerning all the nation's affairs.

A steadfast concert for peace can never be maintained except by a partnership of democratic nations. No autocratic government could be trusted to keep faith within it or observe its covenants. It must be a league of honour, a partnership of opinion. Intrigue would eat its vitals away; the plottings of inner circles who could plan what they would and render account to no one would be a corruption seated at its very heart. Only free peoples can hold their purpose and their honour steady to a common end and prefer the interests of mankind to any narrow interest of their own.

Does not every American feel that assurance has been added to our hope for the future peace of the world by the wonderful and heartening things that have been happening within the last few weeks in Russia? Russia was known by those who knew it best to have been always in fact democratic at heart, in all the vital habits of her thought, in all the intimate relationships of her people that spoke their natural instinct, their habitual attitude towards life. The autocracy that crowned the summit of her political structure, long as it had stood and terrible as was the reality of its power, was not in fact Russian in origin, character, or purpose; and now it has been shaken off and the great, generous Russian people have been added in all their naive majesty and might to the forces that are fighting for freedom in the world, for justice, and for peace. Here is a fit partner for a League of Honour.

One of the things that has served to convince us that the Prussian autocracy was not and could never be our friend is that from the very outset of the present war it has filled our unsuspecting communities and even our offices of government with spies and set criminal intrigues everywhere afoot against our national unity of counsel, our peace within and without, our industries and our commerce. Indeed it is now evident that its spies were here even before the war began; and it is unhappily not a matter of conjecture but a fact proved in our courts of justice that the intrigues which have more than once come perilously near to disturbing the peace and dislocating the industries of the country have been carried on at the instigation, with the support, and even under the personal direction of official agents of the Imperial Government accredited to the Government of the United States. Even in checking these things and trying to extirpate them we have sought to put the most generous interpretation possible upon them because we knew that their source lay, not in any hostile feeling or purpose of the German people towards us (who were, no doubt as ignorant of them as we ourselves were), but only in the selfish designs of a Government that did what it pleased and told its people nothing. But they have played their part in serving to convince us at last that that Government entertains no real friendship for us and means to act against our peace and security at its convenience. That it means to stir up enemies against us at our very doors the intercepted note to the German Minister at Mexico City is eloquent evidence.

We are accepting this challenge of hostile purpose because we know that in such a government, following such methods, we can never have a friend; and that in the presence of its organized power, always lying in wait to accomplish we know not what purpose, there can be no assured security for the democratic governments of the world. We are now about to accept gauge of battle with this natural foe to liberty and shall, if necessary, spend the whole force of the nation to check and nullify its pretensions and its power. We are glad, now that we see the facts with no veil of false pretence about them, to fight thus for the ultimate peace of the world and for the liberation of its peoples, the German peoples included: for the rights of nations great and small and the privilege of men everywhere to choose their way of life and of obedience. The world must be made safe for democracy. Its peace must be planted upon the tested foundations of political liberty. We have no selfish ends to serve. We desire no conquest, no dominion. We seek no indemnities for ourselves, no material compensation for the sacrifices we shall freely make. We are but one of the champions of the rights of mankind. We shall be satisfied when those rights have been made as secure as the faith and the freedom of nations can make them.

Just because we fight without rancour and without selfish object, seeking nothing for ourselves but what we shall wish to share with all free peoples, we shall, I feel confident, conduct our operations as belligerents without passion and ourselves observe with proud punctilio the principles of right and of fair play we profess to be fighting for.

I have said nothing of the governments allied with the Imperial Government of Germany because they have not made war upon us or challenged us to defend our right and our honour. The Austro-Hungarian Government has, indeed, avowed its unqualified endorsement and acceptance of the reckless and lawless submarine warfare adopted now without disguise by the Imperial German Government, and it has therefore not been possible for this Government to receive Count Tarnowski, the Ambassador recently accredited to this Government by the Imperial and Royal Government of Austria-Hungary; but that Government has not actually engaged in warfare against citizens of the United States on the seas, and I take the liberty, for the present at least, of postponing a discussion of our relations with the authorities at Vienna. We enter this war only where we are clearly forced into it because there are no other means of defending our rights.

It will be all the easier for us to conduct ourselves as belligerents in a high spirit of right and fairness because we act without animus, not in enmity towards a people or with the desire to bring any injury or disadvantage upon them, but only in armed opposition to an irresponsible government which has thrown aside all considerations of humanity and of right and is running amuck. We are, let me say again, the sincere friends of the German people, and shall desire nothing so much as the early re-establishment of intimate relations of mutual advantage between us,—however hard it may be for them, for the time being, to believe that this is spoken from our hearts. We have borne with their present government through all these bitter months because of that friendship,—exercising a patience and forbearance which would otherwise have been impossible. We shall, happily, still have an opportunity to prove that friendship in our daily attitude and actions towards the millions of men and women of German birth and native sympathy who live amongst us and share our life, and we shall be proud to prove it towards all who are in fact loyal to their neighbours and to the Government in the hour of test. They are, most of them, as true and loyal Americans as if they had never known any other fealty or allegiance. They will be prompt to stand with us in rebuking and restraining the few who may be of a different mind and purpose. If there should be disloyalty, it will be dealt with with a firm hand of stern repression; but, if it lifts its head at all, it will lift it only here and there and without countenance except from a lawless and malignant few.

It is a distressing and oppressive duty, Gentlemen of the Congress, which I have performed in thus addressing you. There are, it may be, many months of fiery trial and sacrifice ahead of us. It is a fearful thing to lead this great peaceful people into war, into the most terrible and disastrous of all wars, civilization itself seeming to be in the balance. But the right is more precious than peace, and we shall fight for the things which we have always carried nearest our hearts,—for democracy, for the right of those who submit to authority to have a voice in their own governments, for the rights and liberties of small nations, for a universal dominion of right by such a concert of free peoples as shall bring peace and safety to all nations and make the world itself at last free. To such a task we can dedicate our lives and our fortunes, everything that we are and everything that we have, with the pride of those who know that the day has come when America is privileged to spend her blood and her might for the principles that gave her birth and happiness and the peace which she has treasured. God helping her, she can do no other.[2]

Printed reading copy (WP, DLC).
[2] There is an undated WWT outline, an undated WWsh draft, and an undated WWT draft of this address in WP, DLC. Wilson made only a few unimportant changes from the shorthand draft to the draft that he sent to the Public Printer.

## From Newton Diehl Baker

### MR. FOSDICK AND ARMY RECREATION.

Dear Mr. President:                    Washington. April 2, 1917

I have your note of the 31st. My experience with the Mexican mobilization was that our young soldiers had a good deal of time hanging rather heavily on their hands with two unfortunate results. 1. They became homesick. 2. They were easily led aside into unwholesome diversions and recreations, patronizing cheap picture shows, saloons, dance halls and houses of prostitution. I immediately began to consider whether a part of the discipline of the Army ought not to be the regular provision of wholesome recreation, so as pleasantly and, if possible, profitably to occupy the leisure hours of soldiers in camp. The Y.M.C.A. does some of this, but no comprehensive program on the subject has ever been regarded as a part of the regular provision for soldiers in camp. I have discussed the subject a number of times with Mr. Fosdick, and, of course, found him very intelligent in his comprehension of it. I have also discussed the subject with Mr. Mott and with the Director of the Russell Sage Foundation,[1] finding them all sympathetic and anxious to cooperate. I have now asked Fosdick to go to Canada, find out just what they are doing along this line, and coordinate representatives of the Russell Sage Foundation and the Army branch of the Y.M.C.A. in working out a practical plan. Some months ago I asked our military observers in Europe to prepare reports for me on the treatment of this subject in the European armies. So far but one such report has come in, namely, that from Russia, where apparently the only recreation provided is community singing among the soldiers.

I have the feeling that as our young soldiers are substantially men of college age, the experience of our colleges in recreation will go a long way by analogy to aid us. Ultimately I hope to have at West Point a course in recreation, so that young officers will be taught systematically both the importance and the mechanics of group recreation. This idea I have given to Mr. Fosdick, and it may be considered in the work he and his associates are going to do. For the present, however, of course, the immediate task will be to suggest things presently practical for such armies as may be raised in the near future.

Respectfully yours,   Newton D. Baker

TLS (WP, DLC).
1 John Mark Glenn.


## From the Diary of Colonel House

The White House, Washington, D. C. April 2, 1917.

I arrived in time for breakfast. The President and Mrs. Wilson were ready to play golf and I saw him for a moment only. While he was on the links I motored with Frank Polk and we discussed pending matters. He says neither Lansing nor any member of the Cabinet knows what the President will say in his address to Congress today. As far as I know, he has spoken to no one on the subject of this address excepting me. We outlined it together when I was here last week and I have the substance although not the form of it.

I returned to the White House around noon but did not attempt to see anyone other than Polk. My reasons for this were that I did not want the Cabinet members to ask me about the address. I do not wish them to know that the President has discussed it with me, and I do not wish to reveal its contents.

McAdoo telephoned and asked about the address and how I liked it. I evaded a direct answer by saying that from what the President had told me of it I thought it would meet every expectation.

The President read the address to me and I suggested his eliminating a phrase which read something like this: "until the German people have a government we can trust."[1] He was doubtful about this part of the sentence and I had no difficulty in persuading him to eliminate it. It looked too much like inciting revolution. It is needless to say that no address he has yet made pleases me more than this one, for it contains all that I have been urging upon him since the war began. I have tried, time and again, to get the British Government to differentiate between the German Government and the German people, and I suggested this also to the President after the sinking of the Lusitania. I have tried to get the President, as my letters will show, to demand among nations the same code of honor and morals as between individuals. He handles this part superbly.

I suggested, too, a short time ago, that he should state that the United States would not join a league of nations of which an autocracy was a member.

The President was apparently calm during the day, but, as a matter of fact, I could see signs of nervousness. Neither of us did anything except "Kill time" until he was called to the Capitol. In the morning, he told me he was determined not to speak after three o'clock, believing it would make a bad impression—an impression that he was unduly pressing matters. I thought differently and persuaded him that he should hold himself ready to address Congress whenever that body indicated their readiness to hear him. It turned out, that he began to speak at twenty minutes to nine and finished in about thirty-two minutes. I timed him carefully.

I asked him why he had not shown the Cabinet his address. He replied that if he had, every man in it would have had some suggestion to make and it would have been picked to pieces if he had heeded their criticisms. He said he preferred to keep it to himself and take the responsibility. I feel that he does his Cabinet an injustice. He should not humiliate them to such an extent. Not a member knew what he would say until they heard it delivered. I have noticed recently that he holds a tighter rein over his Cabinet and that he is impatient of any initiative on their part.

It would be interesting to know how much of his address the President thinks I suggested. He does not indicate, in any way, that he is conscious that I had any part in it, I think it is quite possible that he forgets from what source he receives ideas and suggestions.

We had early dinner at half past six, for word had come that Congress had been organized and would be ready to receive him at eight o'clock. We talked of everything excepting the matter in hand. There was no one present at dinner other than members of the family who had come to Washington to hear the address, and no one touched upon the coming speech.

When we returned from the Capitol, the President, Mrs. Wilson, Margaret and I foregathered in the oval room and talked it over as families are prone to do after some eventful occasion. I had handed the President a clipping from Current Opinion, giving the foreign estimate of him.[2] He read this aloud, and we discussed the article. I thought the President had taken a position as to policies which no other statesman had yet assumed. He seemed surprised to hear me say this and thought perhaps Webster, Lincoln and Gladstone had announced the same principles. I differed from him. It seemed to me that he did not have a true conception of the path he was blazing. Of the modern statesmen, Mazzini is the one who had a similar outlook, but no other, as far as I know.

I left at 10.30 to take the train for New York. I could see the President was relieved that the tension was over and the die cast. I knew this would happen. Grayson went with me to the station.

1 Wilson did eliminate "so soon as they permit us to deal with a government which we can trust" following "of mutual advantage between us."
2 "Europe's New Estimates of Woodrow Wilson," *Current Opinion*, LXII (April 1917), 243-44. The thrust of the article appeared in its first sentence: "Tardy as they have been in their recognition of Woodrow Wilson in the capacity of man of genius, the European dailies generally more than make amends by the splendor of the gifts they now ascribe to him."

## From the Diary of Josephus Daniels

April Monday 2 1917

Went with committee of editors to see Attorney General about press censorship bill. They feared it was too drastic. Later in the day, with Baker and Polk, had talk with editors about censorship. We wish to censor as little as possible.

Baker called with Mr. Scott,[1] head of Board to secure munitions and supplies more rapidly & with right priority. I named a committee to act with others. It looks to a Commissioner of Munitions & Supplies

President called during meeting of Council—he had heard Navy intended to take over German merchant ships and search them. Message had come to Collector Malone that naval officer said Navy would do this. Members of Cabinet & others had urged this but President had taken the ground that ships belonged to German private citizens and we must save them. Report was error, but I telegraphed to all places where German ships were and instructed not to board them.

8:30 Went up to hear the President's speech on Germany making war on us. Distinguished body, diplomats on the floor, Supreme Court, & galleries filled. Addie[2] up there. Jonathan[3] got in through kindness of Kitchin.[4] President grave and serious but dominated by feelings he was standing for human rights. Said he did not want Capitol guarded by soldiers. But it was done.

1 Frank Augustus Scott, secretary-treasurer of Warner & Swasey Co., manufacturers of machine tools of Cleveland. Baker had just called him to Washington to be chairman of the Munitions Standards Board.
2 His wife, Addie Worth Bagley Daniels.
3 His son, Jonathan Worth Daniels.
4 Claude Kitchin.

# From the Diary of Thomas W. Brahany

Monday, April 2, 1917

Before leaving for golf this morning the President turned over personally to Cornelius Ford, the Public Printer, the completed draft of his address. Up to this time nobody (except possibly Mrs. Wilson) had seen it. The President told Tumulty over the phone that he preferred to address the Congress today instead of tomorrow. This message was conveyed to Representative Kitchin, Democratic floor leader, who expressed doubt if the House could organize in time for the holding of a joint session of the Senate and House today. Shortly after 3 o'clock arrangements were made for a joint session at 8 o'clock tonight. When Forster and I returned to the Executive Office after dinner we were told that it would be after 8 o'clock before the Senate and House Committee called to notify the President officially that the Congress was organized and ready to receive him. The committee came a few minutes after 8 o'clock. It was 8:20 when the President, Mrs. Wilson and Dr. Grayson left for the Capitol. Miss Wilson, Mrs. McAdoo, Miss Bones, Col. House and one or two others left at 8:15. A crowd of several hundred persons gathered at the northeast gate about 7:30. They sang patriotic songs, and cheered when the President's motor speeded by. Many persons were in Pennsylvania Avenue, but the President disappointed them. On the suggestion of Forster and myself, Joe Murphy, in charge of the Secret Service White House force, arranged to have the motors go out New York avenue and enter the Capitol grounds from New Jersey avenue. Forster and I didn't go to the Capitol. The President was back in the White House before 9:30. Apparently his address made a profound impression. A dozen or more men who heard the address called at the office tonight and all of them show[ed] they were profoundly moved. Chief Justice White was one of the cheer leaders. Several of the Secret Service men and one newspaperman told me that Senator La Follette was the only member of Congress who in countenance and demeanor showed disfavor while the President was speaking. Joe Murphy, who was in the President's motor, says the President was visibly nervous and quite pale on the return trip. He was grave but not nervous on the way to the Capitol. Senator Stone met the President tonight for the first time since the President's "group of willful men" statement. Stone extended his hand which the President took, but the President did not speak. Among those who greeted the President warmly after his address was Senator Lodge, who since the last campaign has been a leading member of the President's "in bad" Club. Lodge was warm in his commendation of the address. The President shook his hand and said a word of appreciation. On the President's part there was nothing gushing in this meeting. Lodge is the best informed man on foreign affairs in the Senate and it may well be that the meeting last night will be the first step in bringing him and the President together. Of course they will never be intimate, but with Stone off the reservation, Lodge would be a fine man for the President to consult freely and frequently on international affairs. I said *would be*. In most things Woodrow Wilson is his own counselor.


## Joseph Allen Baker[1] to Arthur James Balfour

Dear Mr. Balfour,                          [London] 2nd April, 1917.

As you kindly requested I have pleasure in handing you the following notes of my interviews with Col. House during my recent visit to America.

The journey was undertaken in connection with urgent business matters, and my stay in the United States was from February 3rd., when I arrived in New York by the s.s. "St. Paul," to March 10th., when I sailed for Liverpool by the s.s. "Carmania." I had numerous opportunities of meeting leading business men in New York, Philadelphia, Washington and other Eastern cities, as also in Detroit and Chicago.

Through a personal friend, (George Foster Peabody of New York), I met Colonel House and found him deeply interested in receiving the latest reports of conditions in England, and anxious to hear how the policy of President Wilson was regarded by our Statesmen. He also seemed anxious to communicate what he knew to be the mind of the President and to explain some of his special difficulties.

My interviews with Col. House took place in New York on Feby. 14th., 23rd., and the last on March 10th. just before sailing. In the intervals he had been in Washington with the President on one or two occasions.

I also saw our Ambassador, Sir Cecil Spring-Rice, in Washington on February 22nd., and on March 4th. Sir Cecil had not seen either the President or Col. House for a considerable time, and wished to know what action, if any, would be taken by the former, and whether it would be of the most effective character to help the cause of the Allies.

On each occasion when I visited Col. House I found him most cordial and communicative. On March 10th. we discussed pre-war experiences in which we had much in common, visits to Germany, interviews with the Kaiser, Bethmann-Hollweg, etc. He had been in Germany, France and England shortly before war broke out with the express object of trying to promote an understanding with these countries and America that would make a conflict such as the present an impossibility. He said he received every encouragement in France and England, but found a changed and harder attitude in Germany than he had experienced on previous visits. He also found the utmost difficulty in getting a private conversation with the Kaiser which he had particularly desired.

He then spoke freely of the present situation, expressing fullest sympathy with the cause of the Allies, and gave interesting particulars of the recent Presidential Election, stating that President Wilson held the same views in regard to a world settlement and a permanent "League of Peace" as he understood were held by Viscount Grey and others of our statesmen. He specially asked that I should see him again after visiting Washington and seeing Sir Cecil Spring-Rice, for whom he expressed the warmest regard. This interview, which lasted about 45 minutes, was most frank; Col. House has an engaging personality, is very responsive and apparently glad to listen as well as to speak. There is no doubt that he enjoys President Wilson's fullest personal friendship and confidence.

On February 22nd. I paid my first visit to Washington, and had a long talk with Sir Cecil Spring-Rice at the Embassy. He seemed to be very anxious as to whether the President was getting to the point of action. Would the President undo the wire and "let the cork out of the bottle," and if they acted would they do what would be of the greatest service to the Allies? This would not be in attempting to mobilize a great land force and withholding supplies for their own use, but rather in continuing to supply us. "No greater service could be rendered to the cause of the Allies than in continuing to supply our requirements in Munitions and Food, and helping us in Finance. We could supply the men and do the fighting if the United States would keep the track across the Ocean clear, and ensure our receiving the full quantity of the necessary supplies. This would be the greatest contribution from the United States. A further advantage would be a thorough exchange of ideas and inventions in Naval matters and coopera-tion in the destruction of the submarine menace."

On the following day, February 23rd., I again saw Col. House, reporting my conversation with Sir Cecil Spring-Rice, and his desire to know when and how the President would be ready to act.

His first remarks were that the President's personal feelings and desires for action were much in advance of anything to which he could give public expression. As a matter of policy he must seem to be pushed into action, as he considered it essential to carry a united people with him. The West and middle West comprise the majority in the United States, and they have been difficult to get into line. He is anxiously waiting to "let the cork out of the bottle," but must have the whole nation at his back. He has been, and is strongly pro-ally, and as expressed by Col. House, is prepared to do all and more than Sir Cecil Spring-Rice suggested. "We want to be your reservoir for everything that America can supply—*Food, Munitions, Money* and *Men*—the latter to volunteer and go over as soon as wanted, or can be carried, and they can be trained on your side if wanted. We are ready also to exchange inventions, naval or otherwise, and to co-operate with our U. S. Navy to rid the seas of submarines."

The above was expressed and elaborated in the most fervent language and most generous terms. One could not but feel that it is the desire of America to co-operate in helping to rid the world of its present common danger. Col. House added, following a suggestion of mine re a joint submarine campaign, "that it must be subdued at all costs or there could be no security for humanity for the future, or the maintenance of any form of International Law or agreement."

The interview was of the most interesting character and all that Sir Cecil Spring-Rice suggested as desired was warmly as-sented to, and much more as well.

Col. House had requested that I should see him again before sailing, when matters would have further developed. I also had the opportunity of again seeing Sir Cecil Spring-Rice, spending Sunday, 4th March, in Washington, and was with him in the Diplomatic Gallery of the Senate on that date, when the historic 64th Congress came to an end.

Sir Cecil told me that he had cabled you the substance of this interview with Col. House.

The action of the seven Senators led by Senator Stone in thwarting the President's Bill for the arming of American mer-chantmen was at first considered a serious setback, and the President was somewhat depressed, but deciding to alter the rules and finding opinion in the country was so unanimously in his favour, and approved of his policy, he determined to take the necessary action.

*On March 10th.* before sailing on the "Carmania" I saw Col. House for the third time and made the following notes:

He recounted the President's feelings over the "hold-up" in Senate on the part of Senator Stone and his allies, saying he felt much discouraged at the result, and the fact that even one man might block the wishes and action of the country. But the resolution to alter the rules that they had wanted to get rid of for a century, and his determination to use the power he was advised he undoubtedly possessed, made him much more buoyant and he determined to forge ahead. Col. House said it had been definitely decided to arm American ships, and have them proceed with their cargoes as soon as possible.

The burden of this interview was Col. House's message to me to carry to Mr. Lloyd George and Mr. Balfour:

"Tell your people to take no steps to hasten matters directly or indirectly, it only hinders instead of helps us. Let us alone and we will go all the faster. The only thing I fear is your trying to push us—the strongest pro-allies resent this."

Col. House then enlarged on the danger of the impression that is conveyed by the string of newspapers in the Eastern States from Boston to Washington, and which are quoted across the Atlantic as the expression of American opinion. The reverse is generally the case; solid American opinion lies West of this, and it is the West that it is absolutely necessary for the President to have behind him. It has been essential for him to secure a united America before taking effective steps.

He then repeated what he told me in our second interview: "Tell them we are with you to the finish of our resources in supplies, money and men. We are prepared to go the 'whole hog.' They have no idea how soon we can raise a big army; many thousands of young men already have the necessary training—cadets in our military schools and State Institutions. Texas alone, where I come from, has 200,000 men who can ride and shoot, and other Western States are in proportion. They are men of the calibre of your Canadians and Australians."

He continued: "Give my warmest regards to my friends over there, Lloyd George, Balfour, Asquith and Grey. Tell them all I am thinking of them all every hour."

There is one fact that is very evident, and that is American

approval and appreciation of the line that has been followed by
our Foreign Office and our Ambassador at Washington in pursuing a policy of discreet silence, and non-interference with American politics and actions. This is spoken of with great satisfaction when compared with the opposite policy of the Germans,
which was hotly resented.

The consummation of Home Rule for Ireland would have
greatly accelerated the decision that the United States have at
last taken.

I am,            Your obedient Servant,   J. Allen Baker

TLS (F/3/2/16, D. Lloyd George Papers, House of Lords Record Office).
   [1] M.P. since 1905; proprietor of an engineering firm in London; promoter
prior to the war of the interchange of visits by members of the Christian
churches of Great Britain and Germany in the interest of international peace
and friendship.


## From John Hessin Clarke

My dear Mr President:            Washington April 3rd, 1917

I listened to your address last night intently and I have read
it carefully this morning. The impression it leaves with me is
best expressed, I think, by what Justice Day[1] (as fine a mind as
I am coming in contact with these days) said as we were returning together from the Capitol.

Speaking after reflection, he said, "I really think there's not another man in America who could have done it so well."

It is a trumpet call to your country and to all genuine lovers
of political liberty in the world.

Be assured constantly, in the trying days before you that your
countrymen, now without respect to political party association,
have every confidence that the hour of national trial finds us
with our most competent national leader in command.

God bless you,            Sincerely   John H. Clarke

ALS (WP, DLC).
   [1] William Rufus Day, Associate Justice of the Supreme Court of the
United States.


## To John Hessin Clarke

                                    The White House
My dear Mr. Justice Clarke:            3 April, 1917

Your letter written after hearing my address to the Congress
last evening has touched and gratified me very deeply. I thank

you for it most warmly. It has brought me just the sort of message of friendship and support I need in the circumstances.

Cordially and sincerely yours,   Woodrow Wilson

TLS (J. H. Clarke Papers, OClW).


## To Newton Diehl Baker

My dear Mr. Secretary:        [The White House] 3 April, 1917

Thank you for your memorandum about Mr. Fosdick and Army recreation. I warmly approve the idea and am delighted that you have secured the cooperation of so admirable a man as Fosdick.

Cordially and faithfully yours,   Woodrow Wilson

TLS (Letterpress Books, WP, DLC).


## To Richard Heath Dabney

My dear Heath:              The White House 3 April, 1917

My address to the Congress last evening is a sort of answer to your letter of April first, though I did not have an opportunity to read that letter until this morning.

I am writing in haste just to say how much I appreciate what you have sent me.

Affectionately yours,   Woodrow Wilson

TLS (Wilson-Dabney Corr., ViU).


## From Walter Lippmann

Dear Mr. President:           New York City April 3, 1917.

I have tried to say a little of what I feel about your address in the following words, which are to appear in The New Republic this week:

"For having seen this (i.e. that this is a war between democracy and autocracy) and said it, for having selected the moment when the issue was so clear, for having done so much through the winter to make the issue clear, our debt and the world's debt to Woodrow Wilson is immeasurable. Any mediocre politician might have gone to war futilely for rights that in themselves cannot be defended by war. Only a statesman who will be called great could have made America's intervention mean so much to the

generous forces of the world, could have lifted the inevitable horror of war into a deed so full of meaning."[1]

I would like to take the liberty of saying a few words to you
about the military service recommendation: It seems to me
absolutely essential to the success of the idea which you have in
mind, that this country be spared the worst features of the war
psychology; and they are raised more than anything else by a
recruiting campaign. I would like therefore to suggest to you the
following plan in order to work out the suggestion which you laid
down:

A register of all men of military age should be made as soon
as possible. That register would of course give information as to
their present occupation and alternate abilities. When that is
done the government could decide which of the men were already employed in essential industries and which ought to be
exempted from military service either because of their physical
condition or because of conscientious objections. Then the government might invite the remainder to volunteer, calling them in
order by classes. The understanding would be that if by this
voluntary method enough troops were not raised compulsion
would be resorted to, but it seems altogether probable that a half
a million men can be raised in this way. I do not know what practical objections can be raised against the plan, but the arguments
in its favor are clearly obvious. It avoids the recruiting campaign;
it avoids helter skelter volunteering and misuse of talent; it re-
tains the volunteer principle for the present; and it lays the
foundations for compulsion if that should become necessary.

I am with very deepest regards,
                    Yours sincerely,   Walter Lippmann

TLS (WP, DLC).
[1] "The Great Decision," *The New Republic*, X (April 7, 1917), 279-80.

## From Walter Hines Page

London April 3, 1917.

5936. Personal to the President.

I venture again to express my deepest conviction that our entry
into the war is the only proper expression of our national character, our ideals and our sympathies and I congratulate you on this
event which is comparable to only two other events in our history
—the achievement of our independence and the preservation of
the Union. Your speech cheers the whole enlightened world and
marks the beginning of a new international era.     Page.

T telegram (SDR, RG 59, 763.72/3642, DNA).

## From William Phillips

Dear Mr. President,                    Washington April 3./17

May I be permitted to take the liberty of adding my deepest congratulations to the many which you are receiving this morning?

Your address was so splendid, so inspiring, so magnificent in every respect that you have already made men better, and made a better country of us.

You have shown us all the true light and every loyal American is proud to follow and serve you in the great struggle that is approaching.

I feel about it so intensely that words seem futile, yet I want you to know of my intense admiration for you in this great service which I feel you have done for the whole world.

With assurances of respect I am, my dear Mr. President,
                    Faithfully yours    William Phillips

ALS (WP, DLC).


## From Cleveland Hoadley Dodge

My dear President                    New York. April 3rd 1917

For the past four years many of my "friends" have looked on me as a sort of a crank and pitied me for the foolish way in which I threw away my money, but today I came to my own, and have had a reflected triumph which has been most gratifying.

Folks are certainly curious creatures. Most of them mean so well, but are so infernally egotistical and stupid. However, in spite of all the solemnity of the hour, I am the happiest man in the country as I realize the masterly way in which you have led on the people to this final result.

Your message reads as if it had been inspired & if it can only reach the people of Austria & Germany & sink into their thick noddles, what an awakening there may be. With the exception of a very few, you at last have the united American people with you. The time is ripe—may God grant that your great declaration may have the effect of bringing the awful war to a speedy end.

With proud thankful heart I offer my hearty congratulations, on what your once friend Mr. Vanderlip said in my hearing today, he considered the greatest state document which had ever been given out in the history of the country

With warm regards to you all
                    Ever devotedly yours    C H Dodge

ALS (WP, DLC).

# From Charles William Eliot

Dear President Wilson:         Cambridge, Mass., 3 April 1917.

Your doctrine of yesterday is sound all over, and to the core. Now come the specific measures which Congress should adopt for carrying your doctrine into effect. On these matters I lately wrote you two letters, one dated March twenty-first, and the other March twenty-second.[1] Yesterday, I received from you a kind acknowledgment of my letter of March twenty-seventh; but in that note you say nothing about the letters of March twenty-first and twenty-second.[2] Those letters state, I believe, some fundamental principles with regard to the re-organization of the military and naval forces of the United States.

Since Germany has created and put in practice a kind of warfare more destructive and abominable than the world has ever known before, I believe that no free government ought to create or maintain a professional army, or any army recruited by voluntary enlistment. I know that the United States is obliged to do that for the moment; but is it not clear that the new army should have no professional character, and that its soldiers should be saved from degradation and brutalization by the consciousness that they are fulfilling a universal obligation to the country, and discharging a duty imposed by their country's laws. The Swiss system accomplishes just that moral result; and the present armies of Great Britain and France are in the main inspired by that patriotic motive. The pay of a private in the Swiss army is sixteen cents a day during either training or active service. The pay of the head of the General Staff is eight dollars a day in active service, and three dollars and forty cents a day in training service. In short, pay is not an object in any grade of the Swiss military service. With this absence of pay goes necessarily the support by the State of the soldier's dependents, if any; and there is no such thing as a military class in Switzerland.

If these moral principles be sound, the principles on which the regular army and the National Guard of the United States are recruited and supported are unsound; and they should be abandoned as soon as possible in order to the wise development of the national character and intelligence.

I am, with highest regard,

                         Sincerely yours    Charles W. Eliot.

TLS (WP, DLC).
    [1] C. W. Eliot to WW, March 21 and 22, 1917, both TLS (WP, DLC).
    [2] As notes attached to Eliot's letter of March 21 reveal, Wilson did not see these letters.

## From William Gibbs McAdoo

Dear "Governor,"                    Washington April 3, 1917

You have done a great thing nobly! I firmly believe that it is God's will that America should do this transcendent service for humanity throughout the world and that you are his chosen instrument.             Affectionately Yours   W G McAdoo

ALS (WP, DLC).

## From Newton Diehl Baker

My dear Mr President:                Washington. April 3, 1917

I have just reread your address to Congress The fact that I am a member of the family I know has not disabled my judgment and I am willing to have future generations judge your administration by that document.

Respectfully yours,   Newton D. Baker

ALS (WP, DLC).

## From the Diary of Josephus Daniels

1917 Tuesday 3 April

Cabinet—Discussed what to do with German ships in American ports. McAdoo wished to take them, 700,000 tons of shipping would help make up for what G— had sunk. Hard to tell which Department had authority & responsibility. Finally decided G— sailors (Reservists) should be removed by Secy. Wilson to Ellis Island. President said it offended him to see people covet these ships. America must set an example of splendid conduct of war. He said it was remarkable what stories people would believe, instancing that many people in Canada do not believe Kitchener was drowned, but that he was taken away because he was a failure.

President said munition makers must give reasonable rates or we would take them over. Give orders at fair prices & invoke the law.

Told me the applause in Capitol grated on him because he felt the gravity & seriousness of the situation & the necessity make applause far from his feeling.[1]

[1] "Think what it was they were applauding," Tumulty remembered Wilson as saying. "My message to-day was a message of death for our young men. How strange it seems to applaud that." Joseph P. Tumulty, *Woodrow Wilson As I Know Him* (Garden City, N. Y., 1921), p. 256.

## To William Phillips

My dear Mr. Phillips:            [The White House] 4 April, 1917

I know I need not tell you that your letter of yesterday has given me deep gratification. I have learned to know your standard so long that I particularly value such accord of sentiment and purpose. It cheers me and makes the way easier.

With warmest gratitude,

Cordially and faithfully yours,   Woodrow Wilson

TLS (Letterpress Books, WP, DLC).

## To William Denman

My dear Mr. Denman:            [The White House] 4 April, 1917

A letter from the Secretary of the Treasury[1] apprises me that you are still waiting for my approval of the plan of building a large number of wooden ships suitable as cargo carriers. I referred the matter, as I said I would, to the Council for National Defense and upon making inquiry about their action upon it found that they had cordially endorsed it, and I understand that their endorsement had been sent to you. I, therefore, had not written you because my own judgment so heartily concurred with theirs. I am sorry if I have in any way delayed the decision and action.

Cordially and sincerely yours,   Woodrow Wilson

TLS (Letterpress Books, WP, DLC).
[1] It is missing.

## To Newton Diehl Baker

My dear Baker:            The White House 4 April, 1917

Your letter of yesterday about the address has sunk very deep in my heart. I thank you for it with a very deep and genuine gratitude.

Cordially and faithfully yours,   Woodrow Wilson

TLS (N. D. Baker Papers, DLC).

## To Cleveland Hoadley Dodge

My dear Cleve:            The White House 4 April, 1917

Your letter is just what my heart desired and I am delighted that you now have the opportunity of pointing out to your friends in New York the truth of what you have all along been telling them, that it was necessary for me by very slow stages indeed and with the most genuine purpose to avoid war to lead the country on to a single way of thinking. I thank God for the evidences that the task has been accomplished. I think I never felt the responsibilities of office more profoundly than I feel them now, and yet there is a certain relief in having the task made concrete and definite.

 With all my heart

Your grateful friend, Woodrow Wilson

TLS (WC, NjP).


## From Herbert Clark Hoover and Others

London April 4, 1917.

The members of the American Commission for Relief in Belgium ask me to transmit to you the expression of our united devotion and of our admiration for the courage and wisdom of your leadership. We wish to tell you that there is no word in your historic statement to congress but finds response in all our hearts. For two and a half years we have been obliged to remain silent witnesses of the character of the forces dominating this war, but we now are at liberty to say that although we break, with great regret, our association with many German individuals who have given sympathetic support to our work, yet, your message enunciates our conviction, born of our intimate experience and contact, that there is no hope for democracy or liberalism and consequently for real peace or the safety of our country unless the system which has brought the world into this unfathomable misery can be stamped out once and for all.

Herbert Hoover, Chairman.

T telegram (WP, DLC).


## From Edward Mandell House

Dear Governor:      New York. April 4, 1917.

Dudley Malone will be at the Shoreham all day tomorrow. I think it important that you have a five minute talk with him.

He has received certain instructions which worry him because he knows they do not tally with your views. He might have made a mistake Sunday as I told you, and through an order which came to the Navy Yard direct from the Navy. The way the German ships and their crews in our ports are handled may make the difference between domestic order and disorder.

I knew your speech would stir the world, but it has done it even more than I had thought.

I enclose a letter from Mezes[1] which is typical of many I am receiving. Sir William Wiseman says that if Shakespeare had written the address it could not have been more perfectly done. I have heard similar comments from many as to the perfection of its English.

Paderewski declares the world has never seen your equal.

Affectionately yours,   E. M. House

TLS (WP, DLC).
[1] Mezes had written that Wilson's address was "the greatest in history." S. E. Mezes to EMH, April 3, 1917, TLS (WP, DLC).

## From Robert Lansing

PERSONAL AND PRIVATE:

My dear Mr. President:                    [Washington] April 5, 1917.

We have not, as you know, congratulated the Russian Government or people upon the establishment of democratic institutions in that country; merely recognizing the Government as the one with which we desired intercourse.

I thought, therefore, that it would be worth while, immediately after the declaration of a state of war, to send a telegram to Francis to be communicated to the Russian Government, going a little further than we did in the telegram of recognition. I submit for your consideration a draft of such a telegram but in doing so I realize that it can be very materially improved in language.

I hope, if you approve of the plan, you will make the corrections which you desire.

Faithfully yours,   Robert Lansing

TLS (Lansing Letterpress Book, SDR, RG 59, DNA).

## From Edward Mandell House, with Enclosure

Dear Governor:                    New York. April 5, 1917.

I am enclosing a cable which has just come from Eric Drummond, Balfour's confidential secretary. Of course it is really Balfour speaking.

Will you not advise me what reply to send. I do not see how you can well refuse this request coming as it does. It might be well to have a Frenchman of equal distinction come at the same time.

Balfour is the most liberal member of the present British Cabinet and it would be of great service to the relations of the two countries to have him here and to talk with him in person.

Affectionately yours, E. M. House

TLS (WP, DLC).

### E N C L O S U R E

May I offer you my warmest congratulations on magnificent speech of the President. We are all deeply moved at its terms and tone. When Congress has responded to the great ideals which he has expressed, we trust consideration will be given to a commission technically expert being sent from here to place at the disposal of the United States Government the experience gained in this country during the war.

It has been suggested that Mr. Arthur Balfour should be the head of such a commission for a short time to coordinate its activity and to discuss wider issues involved.

Would it be possible for you to give me your opinion privately on this? Your telegram would not, of course, be used to forward any proposal which would not meet with the warm approval of the President and your people; especially as the absence of the Minister for Foreign Affairs for even a few weeks has many inconveniences.

T MS (WP, DLC).

## From Newton Diehl Baker, with Enclosure

My dear Mr. President: Washington. April 5, 1917.

I inclose a copy of a despatch just received from General Pershing. The source of this information is not given, but you will observe that General Pershing considers it reliable.

Respectfully yours, Newton D. Baker

TLS (WP, DLC).

### E N C L O S U R E

Ft. Sam Houston, Texas, April 5, 1917.

Number 4926. Following received from source considered reliable that Obregon took precaution to prevent Germans from organizing any movement that Carranza and Obregon both decided Mexico better keep out of trouble and look to United States for future welfare. Informant consider[s] Mexican alliance with Japan as dangerous and believes such does not exist. Informant not confident that Carranza will be able to resist German influence but Obregon will offer determined resistance to such action.

Following from another source in so far as border is concerned there is little German activity. There is considerable activity in Guatemala many have entered on line Pan American Railroad.

Pershing.

T telegram (WP, DLC).


## From John Avery McIlhenny and Others, with Enclosures

The President:                    Washington, D. C. April 5, 1917.

The Commission considers it to be its duty to suggest to you the desirability of an order intended to safeguard the public interest in the present national crisis, by excluding from the Government service any person of whose loyalty to the Government there is reasonable doubt.

Two drafts of the order are submitted; a majority of the Commission favors the adoption of draft marked number one.

We have the honor to be,

Very respectfully,   John A McIlhenny<br>Chas M Galloway[1]<br>H. W. Craven[2]

TLS (WP, DLC).
1 Charles Mills Galloway.
2 Hermon Wilson Craven.


E N C L O S U R E     I

(Draft No. 1).

EXECUTIVE ORDER.

The Civil Service Commission is hereby directed to refuse to examine or certify for appointment in the service of the United States any person whose employment, because of his conduct, sympathies, or utterances, or because of other reasons, may, in its opinion, be inimical to the public welfare.

This order is issued solely because of the present international situation, and will be withdrawn when the emergency is passed.

ENCLOSURE     II

(Draft No. 2)

EXECUTIVE ORDER.

The Civil Service Commission is hereby authorized to refuse to examine an applicant or to certify an eligible when it has a reasonable belief that his appointment to a Government position would be inimical to the public interest owing to his lack of loyalty to or sympathy with the Government in the present war.

This order is issued solely because of the present international situation, and will be withdrawn when the emergency is passed.

CC MSS (WP, DLC).

# From John Avery McIlhenny and Charles Mills Galloway, with Enclosure

The President:                     Washington, D. C. April 5, 1917.

We have the honor to submit herewith a draft of a proposed Executive order which is intended to meet a situation now existing in the executive departments which in our judgment can not be relieved without either the repeal of the existing removal law or the Executive action which we suggest.

We have the honor to be,

Very respectfully,     John A McIlhenny
Chas M Galloway

TLS (WP, DLC).

ENCLOSURE

EXECUTIVE ORDER.

In the exercise of the power vested in the President by the Constitution and the resolution of Congress of April 5, 1917,[1] the following order is issued:

The head of a department or independent office may forthwith remove any employee when he has ground for believing that the retention of such employee would be inimical to the public welfare by reason of his conduct, sympathies or utterances, or because of other reasons growing out of the war. Such removal may be made without other formality than that the reasons shall be made a matter of confidential record, subject, however, to inspection by the Civil Service Commission.

This order is issued solely because of the present international situation, and will be withdrawn when the emergency is passed.

CC MS (WP, DLC).
¹ That is, the war resolution.

## From Melancthon Williams Jacobus

Hartford, Connecticut
My dear President Wilson:                           April 5 1917

The heart of every true American has gone out to you for the magnificent stand you have taken in the leadership of this people through the great ordeal it is facing

I could have said this in a telegram; but I wanted to say it in a letter, for I want to add to it something which, with increasing power, has been pressing upon me in these months.

For the last three hundred years Humanity has been making its quest for political liberty, and it seems as though this was coming now to its full realization

For this century past Humanity has been in search for human solidarity, and there is evidence abundant of how well it has succeeded in its effort.

But unless Humanity is through with its ideals and Civilization has nothing more to adventure, there is one other quest upon which we must enter, and if I do not mistake the signs of the times, it is the quest for authority; for without authority political liberty and human solidarity will disintegrate and disappear

What kind of authority are we to find?

Confronted as we are on the battlefields of Europe with the breakdown of the greatest assertion of human authority the world has ever seen, we are saying to ourselves we must put in its place the authority of the people—human Government—Democracy.

But I do not need to assure you that Democracy is safe only as it is Christian Democracy, and as Christiani[t]y reminded Civilization that there could be no political liberty without religious liberty—and, as a result, we had the Pilgrim Fathers—and again reminded Civilization that there could be no human solidarity without human sympathy—and, as a consequence, we are realizing today the brotherhood of man, so it must say now to Civilization that there can be no authority that will hold together the freedom and the brotherhood we have secured, unless it be an authority caught up into the authority of the justice and the righteousness of God and, as such, taken into human lives and expressed in human Government

That is the quest upon which the peoples of the world have entered. May God bless you in what you are doing to lead them to its realization—The life of America is behind you to the end.

Yours faithfully    Melancthon W Jacobus

ALS (WP, DLC).

## From Francis Bowes Sayre

Dearest Father,        Williamstown, Massachusetts April 5, 1917.

War has just been declared; and I am wondering whether I should leave my work here and where I could help most. The first to fill the army ranks should, I believe, be the unmarried men; but there are other countless ways (perhaps more effective) of helping America. I wonder whether I could utilize the working knowledge of international law obtained through teaching. Could I be of effective service and assistance in the State Department, helping Mr. Lansing or Mr. Polk? I cannot write either of them directly, lest he get the impression that I am seeking an office and be embarrassed to decline. Could you drop me a line as to whether you could use me in the State Department in some worth while way? Or possibly I could assist you personally if you feel the need.

Jessie's and my hearts go out to you in these days, and we know how heavy must be your heart preparing for the terrible business of war. Love and reverence and high pride in all your leadership fill us every day. God bless you!

With deep love from the four of us,

Ever affectionately your son,    Frank

TLS (WP, DLC).

## From the Diary of Thomas W. Brahany

Thursday, April 5, 1917

Thousands of letters and telegrams approving the President's address, offering service and promising support. The President is adhering to his plan not to see callers except on business of highest importance. He has not been in his office, except briefly on Cabinet days, since late in February. There are hundreds of unimportant papers on his desk awaiting signature, among them probably fifty photographs to be autographed. All important papers are sent to the President's study in the White House. Mrs. Wilson helps him with these papers, blotting for him when he

signs, and in many papers filling in the date of approval. She likes
to think she is helping and the President enjoys having her as his
assistant. A big batch of commissions were signed today. Aside
from the newspapermen we've had very few callers this week.
The President and Dr. Grayson went to the theatre tonight. The
House will vote on the war resolution before adjournment. It is
believed that the speech of Representative Kitchin of North Carolina, majority leader against the resolution, will turn a number
of luke-warm or doubtful members. Yesterday it was predicted
there would not be to exceed a dozen votes against the resolution in the House. Today it is predicted there will be more than
forty votes against it. In the President's mail today was the following:

["]23 Wall Street, New York. April 4, 1917. Dear Mr. President: Permit me to congratulate you and the country on your
address to the Congress of April 2nd. It was a superb performance and in every way worthy [of] your country and the great
occasion.

"Allow me also to say for myself and all my partners that we
are most heartily in accord with you as to the necessity of the
United States assisting the allies in the matter of the supplies of
materials and of credits. To those matters we have been devoting
our whole time and thought for the past two years. I write to
assure you again that the knowledge we have gained in those
two years of close association with the allies in these matters
are entirely at the disposal of the United States Government at
any time or in anyway you may wish to use it. With great respect,
I am, Yours faithfully—J. P. Morgan."

The foregoing letter is in Mr. Morgan's own handwriting. I
understand that over $2,000,000,000 has been disbursed by the
allies in this country by the advice and under the guidance of
Morgan and Company since the war began, this being approximately 75% of the amount of the purchases of the allies of munitions and raw materials in America.


## A Statement

*[April 6, 1917]*

The principles embodied in the legislation presented by the
War Department to the Military Committees of the Senate and
House have my entire approval, and its specific recommenda-
tions embody the best judgment of the officers of the War Depart-

ment. It proposes to raise the forces necessary to meet the present emergency by bringing the regular army and the National Guard to war strength and by adding the additional forces which will now be needed, so that the national army will comprise three elements, the regular army, the National Guard, and the so-called additional forces, of which a first 500,000 are to be authorized immediately, and later increments of the same size as they may be needed.

In order that all those forces may compose a single army, the term of enlistment in the three is equalized, and will be for the period of the emergency. The necessary men will be secured for the regular army and the National Guard by volunteering, as at present, until, in the judgment of the President, a resort to a selective draft is desirable. The additional forces, however, are to be raised by selective draft from men ranging in age from 19 to 25 years. The quotas of the several States in all of these forces will be in proportion to their population.

This legislation makes no attempt to solve the question of a permanent military policy for the country, chiefly for the reason that in these anxious and disordered times a clear view cannot be had either of our permanent military necessities or of the best mode of organizing a proper military peace establishment. The hope of the world is that, when the European war is over, arrangements will have been made composing many of the questions which have hitherto seemed to require the arming of the nations, and that in some ordered and just way the peace of the world may be maintained by such cooperations of force among the great nations as may be necessary to maintain peace and freedom throughout the world.

When these arrangements for a permanent peace are made, we can determine our military needs and adapt our course of military preparation to the genius of a world organized for justice and democracy. The present bill, therefore, is adapted to the present situation, but it is drawn upon such lines as will enable us to continue its policy, or so much of it as may be determined to be wise, when the present crisis has passed.

Printed in the *New York Times*, April 7, 1917.

## To Robert Lansing, with Enclosure

My dear Mr. Secretary,        The White House. 6 April, 1917.

I have suggested a verbal change here and there in this message, but of course approve it very heartily.

Faithfully Yours,   W.W.

WWTLI (SDR, RG 59, 763.72/3788½, DNA).


E N C L O S U R E[1]

You are instructed to announce to the Minister of Foreign Affairs that the Congress of the United States on the *sixth* formally declared and the President proclaimed a state of war to exist between the United States and the Imperial German Government.

You may say to Doctor Miliukoff that the United States ín thus arraying itself against the greatest enemy of and menace to democracy in the world does so with a feeling of confidence in the ultimate triumph of those principles of liberty and justice which it has maintained for (over) *nearly* a century and a (quarter) *half* and in devotion to which by all civilized nations lies the hope of universal peace.

You may also say that the Government and people of the United States rejoice that the great Russian people have joined the powerful democracies which are struggling against autocracy and *wish to* express to the Russian Nation their sincere gratification that thus a new bond of friendship is added to those which have so long united the peoples of the two countries. It is the earnest hope and expectation of this Government that a Russia inspired by these great ideals will realize more than ever the duty which it owes to humanity and the necessity of preserving internal (peace) *harmony* in order that as a united and patriotic nation it may overcome the autocratic power which by force and intrigue menaces the democracy which the Russian people have proclaimed.[2]

T MS (SDR, RG 59, 763.72/3788½, DNA).

[1] Words in angle brackets in the following document deleted by Wilson; words in italics added by him.

[2] This was sent as RL to D. R. Francis, April 6, 1917; printed in *FR 1918 Russia*, I, 20-21.

## To Edward Mandell House

My dear House,                    The White House. 6 April, 1917.

Of course there is nothing for it but to reply to Drummond that we shall be glad to receive such a commission and to see Mr. Balfour at the head of it.

The plan has its manifest dangers. I do not think that all of the country will understand or relish. A great many will look upon the mission as an attempt to in some degree take charge of us as an assistant to Great Britain, particularly if the Secretary of State for Foreign Affairs heads the commission. But, on the other hand, it will serve a great many useful purposes and perhaps save a good deal of time in getting together.

In great haste,      Affectionately,   Woodrow Wilson

WWTLS (E. M. House Papers, CtY).


## From Robert Lansing

*Personal and Secret:*

My dear Mr. President:            Washington April 6, 1917.

The more I think over the contents of the enclosed telegram from Mr. Page and the letter from M. Jusserand[1] the more difficult the situation seems to be and the more I am at loss to know just how to treat it.

There is nothing in Mr. Page's telegram to indicate that the British intend to send Mr. Balfour here at the head of an *"expert commission."* He is coming, I should conclude, for the purpose of discussing the whole international situation and arrange in a general rather than detailed way for cooperation involving undoubtedly the Russian situation, the Chino-Japanese relations, the Austro-Hungarian possibilities, the Mexican oil-fields, etc. It would seem, therefore, quite out of place for the Council of National Defense to invite a commission with Mr. Balfour at the head to come here, and even more so to have him head an Anglo-French commission.

There can be no doubt of the very great value it would be to discuss with Mr. Balfour the questions of international politics. I believe much could be accomplished by such discussions. I see no particular reason why we should not say in reply to Mr. Page's telegram that we would be glad to have Mr. Balfour come here, but suggest a month's delay.

The French proposal is more difficult. It is the purpose of that mission to come here to express to you and to the American people the friendship and appreciation of the French Republic. It is apparently not an "expert commission" in any sense of the word; and it would appear to me inappropriate for the Council of National Defense to extend to them an invitation, in view of the membership of the commission and its announced object.

The composition of the two commissions and their different purposes seem also to prevent combining them into one.

I feel very sure that the French, if we should not welcome so distinguished a commission as they propose to send, would be deeply offended and unable to understand our position. You know the sentimental character of the French and how readily they take offense at apparent lack of sympathy and feeling. I do not know how I could ever make M. Jusserand comprehend that just at this time it would be inadvisable for the proposed commission to come here, even if that seemed the wisest course to pursue —and I am not sure that it is.

In the circumstances I believe that it would be expedient to say that you would be glad to receive the commission and were deeply touched by this manifestation of the friendship of the French Government and people. At the same time I would suggest that they should come here *before* the British commission as their mission was of a very different character.

I have studied this problem from various angles and have sought a way to avoid these visits without causing offense, since you so expressed your desire at Cabinet meeting today, but I am afraid there is no way which will not cause ill-feeling and at the present time that must be avoided at all hazards.

In view of the frank statement of purpose in both communications I think that answers should be made without delay for we ought not to give the impression that the proposals are embar-[r]assing, since that might in itself cause offense.

                            Faithfully yours,   Robert Lansing

TLS (SDR, RG 59, 763.72/3669½, DNA).
¹ WHP to RL, April 5, 1917, T telegram (SDR, RG 59, 033.4111/195, DNA), and J. J. Jusserand to RL, April 5, 1917, TLS (SDR, RG 59, 763.72/3669½, DNA).

## From Edward Mandell House

Dear Governor:                          New York. April 6, 1917.

Wiseman has investigated the Tagore matter and advises that you decline to have his book dedicated to you. His reason is that when Tagore was here he got tangled up in some way with the Indian plotters and Wiseman thinks that it might embarrass you if these things should come out publicly about the time the book was issued.

Shall I tell McMillan & Co. your wishes, or will you do so yourself?

In the event you name a censor I would suggest Frederick Palmer, the European war correspondent who is now in this country. He is connected with no newspapers or magazines and yet is favorably known to them all. He has had great experience abroad in this connection and would know how to conduct a censorship with fairness to both the press and the Government.

Mr. Whitehouse is sailing for England the latter part of next week. He wants to go to Washington merely to shake your hand if you will give him that opportunity. Will you not let me know whether you can see him for a moment. He has been useful in the past and can prove more so in the future.

Affectionately yours,   E. M. House

P.S. Mayor Mitchel very much hopes you will give him a favorable reply to the telegram which he is sending today.[1] I know it is hard to comply with so many requests, but it is a time when enthusiasm should be kept at a high pitch.

TLS (WP, DLC).
[1] J. P. Mitchel to WW, April 6, 1917, T telegram (WP, DLC). Mitchel announced the appointment of a committee for New York City to promote recruiting for the army and navy and suggested that April 19, the anniversary of the Battle of Lexington, be proclaimed a "national recruiting day." In reply, Wilson suggested that this campaign be postponed until after the enactment of the appropriate military legislation by Congress. WW to J. P. Mitchel, April 10, 1917, TLS (Letterpress Books, WP, DLC).


## From Josephus Daniels

Dear Mr. President:               Washington. April 6, 1917.
   I closed at .0290. You were right.[1]
Sincerely,   Josephus Daniels

ALS (WP, DLC).
[1] For an explanation of this cryptic note, see the extract from the Daniels Diary printed at this date.


## From Carter Glass

*Personal.*

My dear Mr. President:          Washington, D. C. April 6/17.

My two sons[1] are enlisted for the war; and, having voted in Congress to impose this obligation of service on them, I cannot endure the thought of standing by and doing nothing. It would make me very unhappy: hence I earnestly request that the age limit be waived in my case in order that I may be assigned to active duty somewhere.    Sincerely yours,    Carter Glass.

ALS (WP, DLC).
<sup>1</sup> Powell Glass, age thirty, and Carter Glass, Jr., age twenty-four.

## From William Jennings Bryan

Tallahassee Flo Apl 6 1917

Believing it to be the duty of the citizen to bear his part of the burdens of war and his share of its perils I hereby tender my services to the government. Please enroll me as a private whenever I am needed and assign me to any work that I can do until called to the colors. I shall through the Red Cross contribute to the comfort of soldiers in the hospital and through YMCA aid in safeguarding the morals of the men in camp.

William Jennings Bryan.

T telegram (WP, DLC).

## From the Diary of Josephus Daniels

April Friday 6 1917

Mr. Farrell,<sup>1</sup> president Steel corporation, called by appointment. Had long talk. He finally agreed to reduce from 3.30 to 3<sup>2</sup> if we could settle to-day and he would guarantee all our needs for a year. Other concerns unwilling to come in but his committee could secure help of others or furnish all plates &c. from their own plants. Talked it over in cabinet. McAdoo, Redfield, Lane & others thought 3¢ very good and we ought not to press for lower price. The President felt that we should stand for .0290. After cabinet I saw Farrell again & told him it was .0290 & he agreed & figured it would save $18. mil from current prices.

Burleson proposed excluding papers from the mail papers that criticized. Lansing thought no papers should be printed in German. B— opposed. I said you have made a net that will catch the innocent & most Germans will be loyal. President spoke strongly against action that was more than moderate. Baker & I agreed that there should be no censorship of opinion or comment, only to exclude publication of military news that would aid the enemy.

Wilson reported Germans had been taken off of ships & put in Ellis island.

[1] James Augustine Farrell, president of the United States Steel Corp.

[2] That is, three cents a pound, the proposed price for steel plates and bars for the use of the navy. For a discussion of these negotiations about prices for hundredweights, see Melvin I. Urofsky, *Big Steel and the Wilson Administration: A Study in Business-Government Relations* (Columbus, Ohio, 1969), pp. 192-96.

# From the Diary of Thomas W. Brahany

Friday, April 6, 1917 (Good Friday)

The United States is at war with Germany. The joint resolution (Senate Joint Resolution No. 1) was approved by the President at one-eighteen P.M. today, not at one-thirteen as some of the newspapers reported. The resolution passed the House at 3:14 this morning, 373 ayes to 50 nays. It was attested by the Vice President soon after the Senate met at noon today. Miss Emma C. Clapp, Assistant Clerk of the Committee on Enrolled Bills, brought the resolution to the Executive Office, arriving at 1:10. Rudolph Forster, Executive Clerk, at once took the resolution to the White House. The President, Mrs. Wilson and Miss Helen Bones (the President's cousin) interrupted their luncheon and went to the Usher's room, a small room immediately west of the main White House lobby. Forster handed the resolution to the President, who seating himself at the desk of I. H. Hoover, Chief Usher, signed "Approved 6 April, 1917, Woodrow Wilson."

Forster at once returned to the Executive Office with the resolution. A record of it was made by M. C. Latta,[1] for many years a White House clerk. It was then handed to Joseph Sheehan, a White House messenger, who took it to the State Department. We had many requests this morning from persons who desired to be present when the resolution was signed, and a dozen or more photographers wished permission to photograph the signing. The President was asked by Forster his wishes and he replied that the occasion was too solemn for a ceremony which could serve no purpose other than to gratify curiosity. Besides Mrs. Wilson and Miss Bones the signing was witnessed by Rudolph Forster, I. H. Hoover and Starling,[2] one of the Secret Service operatives detailed to the White House. The President made no comment immediately before or immediately after signing. The fact of the signing was telephoned to the Executive Office at once and Tumulty and I told the newspapermen. Lieut. Byron McCandless, aide to the Secretary of the Navy, was waiting at my desk. He rushed at once to the Executive Avenue entrance to the White House grounds and waived [waved] his hand to an officer in the Navy Department. This was the prearranged signal releasing the wireless and cable messages to see [sea] Navy vessels announcing this country's declaration of war on Germany. . . .

In the President's mail today was the following from James W. Gerard, our Ambassador (recently recalled) to Germany: "Please permit an armor bearer to congratulate you on the perfect speech. There is a lofty idealism about it which puts this war on the plane of a crusade. No more momentous document has ever been written in the history of the world. With devotion, James W. Gerard."

The newspapers are most flattering in praise of the President's address. Commendation letters are coming from all parts of the country. Today A. B. Farquhr[3] of York, Pennsylvania, one of the Directors of the U. S. Chamber of Commerce, called at the office. He said he had heard Lincoln's two inaugural addresses, and was within a few feet of Lincoln when he spoke at Gettysburg. "Mr. Wilson's address on Monday will rank with the Gettysburg speech of Lincoln," he said.

[1] Maurice C. Latta.
[2] Edmund William Starling.
[3] Arthur Briggs Farquhar.

# INDEX

# NOTE ON THE INDEX

THE alphabetically arranged analytical table of contents at the front of the volume eliminates duplication, in both contents and index, of references to certain documents, such as letters. Letters are listed in the contents alphabetically by name, and chronologically within each name by page. The subject matter of all letters is, of course, indexed. The Editorial Notes and Wilson's writings are listed in the contents chronologically by page. In addition, the subject matter of both categories is indexed. The index covers all references to books and articles mentioned in text or notes. Footnotes are indexed. Page references to footnotes which place a comma between the page number and "n" cite both text and footnote, thus: "418, n1." On the other hand, absence of the comma indicates reference to the footnote only, thus: "59n1"–the page number denoting where the footnote appears.

The index supplies the fullest known form of names and, for the Wilson and Axson families, relationships as far down as cousins. Persons referred to by nicknames or shortened forms of names can be identified by reference to entries for these forms of the names.

All entries consisting of page numbers only and which refer to concepts, issues, and opinions (such as democracy, the tariff, the money trust, leadership, and labor problems), are references to Wilson's speeches and writings. Page references that follow the symbol Δ in such entries refer to the opinions and comments of others who are identified.

Two cumulative contents-index volumes are now in print: Volume 13, which covers Volumes 1-12, and Volume 26, which covers Volumes 14-25. Volume 39, covering Volumes 27-38, is in preparation.

# INDEX

Abbott, John Jay, 383,n1

Ackerman, Carl William, 240n2

Adams, John, 302, 303, 307

Adamson, William Charles: and railroad legislation, 13-14,n2, 29-31, 53-54, 54, 66, 156, 157, 258; and water-power legislation, 19-20, 23

Adamson Act (Eight-Hour Act), 352n1, 413, 430n2, 432

Adamson water-power bill, 19-20

Addams, Jane, 302, 303-304,n3

Aehrenthal, Alois, 56n2

African Methodist Episcopal Church, 218n1

Agriculture, Department of, 84-85, 148, 206

Aguilar, Cándido (Mexican Minister for Foreign Affairs), 350-51,n3, 392,-n1

Aguilar, Francisco, 142-43

*Alabama* claims, 303

Alaska general fisheries bill, 179, 207, 209,n1, 230, 236

Alderman, Edwin Anderson, 503-505

Alexander, Joshua Willis: and Alaska general fisheries bill, 209n1, 230, 236

Alexandra Fyódorovna (Empress of Russia), 416

Alfonso XIII (of Spain), 35, 40

*Allemagne et les Problèmes de la Paix* (Scherer and Grunewald, eds.), 49n1

Alsace, 62, 80

Alsace-Lorraine, 26n1, 315n2, 356, 464

Alston, Beilby Francis, 176,n6, 178,n1, 187

America and the Revolution (*Springfield, Mass., Republican*), 451n2

American Fruit Company, 145

American International Corporation, 394

American Line, 187, 189, 364, 436

American Peace Society, 243, 244

American Red Cross, 39, 113n2, 556

American Relief Clearing House, 113n3

American Ships Damaged or Destroyed by German Submarines (memorandum), 502n1

American Society for Judicial Settlement of International Disputes, 250,-n3

American Union Against Militarism, 7-8, 305n1

American University of Beirut, 128n1

America's Threatened Fronts (*Springfield, Mass., Republican*), 451n2

Anderson, Chandler Parsons, 365-67, 385-87

Anderson, Edwin Hatfield, 380,n1

Anglo-American relations: *see* Great Britain and the United States

Annapolis: *see* United States Naval Academy

*Annual Reports of the Navy Department for the Fiscal Year 1917*, 298n1

Apache Indians, 467

appropriation bills, 329

Argentina, 249n1, 499

Armed Merchantmen (Lansing), 71,n1

armed neutrality: *see* World War—maintenance of United States neutrality

armed-ship bill, 279-80,n1, 294,n1, 323, 331; approved by House but debated in Senate, 317-18,n1, 324, 327, 328, 329, 350; and Zimmermann telegram, 324, 325; WW angry at senators who filibustered, 332; WW seeks support of Congress, 367

Armenia, 217, 220n4

Armenian Relief Commission, 113n3

arming of U.S. merchantmen, 4, 66; Lansing on, 71-73, 263-66, 341-44, 360-61, 368-69; and gun sizes, 187-90; Daniels on, 369-72, 387-88, 391, 395-98; WW on, 372

Army (U.S.): *see* United States Army

army appropriations bill, 151, 329

Arnold, Benedict, 455

Asquith, Herbert Henry, 535

Associated Press, 274,n2, 308,n1,2, 323, 324, 432

Association of Railroad Organizations, 54

Atlanta, Ga., 455n1

*At the Eleventh Hour: A Memorandum on the Military Situation* (Masaryk), 56n1

Auchincloss, Gordon, 149, 501,n1

Australia, 213

Austria-Hungary, 39, 40, 149, 211, 217, 464; and Friedjung trial, 56n2; comments on dismemberment of, 75, 76, 81, 159, 357; WW hopes to maintain relations with, 88-89, 95, 129-30,-n1,2, 158-59, 185; food and economic conditions in, 164, 300-301; the Vatican and, 219-20; and peace moves and Britain, 211-14, 260, 262, 267-68, 270-73; and U.S. exchanges on peace prospects, 297-98, 312, 313, 398-99, 421-22; U.S. cannot receive ambassador from, 476, 477, 477-78, 525-26; talk of recalling U.S. ambassador, 477-78

Bacon, Robert, 224,n2

Badell, Mr., 269

Badger, Charles Johnston, 377, 432n1,2

Bailey, Warren Worth, 115

Baker, Bernard Nadal: resigns from Shipping Board, 16, 21, 66